The DIGITAL HAND

JAMES W. CORTADA

The
DIGITAL HAND

How Computers

Changed the Work

of American

Manufacturing,

Transportation,

and Retail Industries

OXFORD
UNIVERSITY PRESS

2004

OXFORD
UNIVERSITY PRESS

Oxford   New York
Auckland   Bangkok   Buenos Aires   Cape Town   Chennai
Dar es Salaam   Delhi   Hong Kong   Istanbul   Karachi   Kolkata
Kuala Lumpur   Madrid   Melbourne   Mexico City   Mumbai   Nairobi
São Paulo   Shanghai   Taipei   Tokyo   Toronto

Copyright © 2004 by Oxford University Press, Inc.

Published by Oxford University Press, Inc.
198 Madison Avenue, New York, New York 10016

www.oup.com

Oxford is a registered trademark of Oxford University Press

Library of Congress Cataloging-in-Publication Data

Cortada, James W.
The digital hand : how computers changed the work of American
manufacturing, transportation, and retail industries / by James W.
Cortada.
p. cm.
Includes bibliographical references and index.
ISBN 0-19-516588-8
1. Automation—Economic aspects—United States.   2. Manufacturing
industries—United States—Automation.   3. Transporation—United
States—Automation.   4. Retail trade—United States—Automation.   I.
Title.
HC110.A9C655 2003
338.0973—dc21   2003012107

9 8 7 6 5 4 3 2 1

Printed in the United States of America
on acid-free paper

To my three mentors, who taught me everything I know that is important about history:

George B. Oliver
Earl R. Beck
Alfred D. Chandler, Jr.

Preface

I learnt to see that utility was the test and measure of all virtues.

—Jeremy Bentham, 1776

Many observers have called the slow growth of the American economy in 2002 and 2003 a "jobless recovery." In other words, as the economy began expanding again, it did so without adding new jobs. Indeed, companies kept laying off people, or simply did not feel a need to hire in order to handle increased volumes of business. The single most frequently cited reason by reporters, economists, and government officials for why new jobs were not added was due to the investments made by companies in computing in the 1990s. These investments in automation reduced the amount of labor content of work, thereby increasing the capacity of existing people, factories, and firms to handle more business. Those remarking on the "jobless recovery" got it all wrong, however. Recovery was due not to investments made in computers in the 1990s but to investments made in computing and telecommunications over a much longer period of time—in fact, over more than a half century. This pattern of investment shows no end in sight, and thus remains one of the most important issues that we need to understand if we are to appreciate how both the U.S. and world economies are transforming, on the one hand and, on the other hand, how businesses and industries are doing so as well. This book begins to tell the story of how computing so profoundly influenced the economy of the United States.

Computers profoundly influenced the structure, activities, success, and failures of most industries. The historical record of the past half century illustrates clearly that this technology affected how industries emerged, operated, and changed. Case studies of the effects of computing on individual processes and companies have long offered dramatic evidence of the profound influence of this technology. But the same can be said of industries and also of the economies in which they resided. The purpose of this book is to describe how that influence occurred over time and still affects industries today. I will do so primarily by documenting how industries came to use computer technology over time.

The title of this book is intended to call attention to its basic theme, the role of computers in the American economy. The metaphor of a hand that is influencing or directing the economic affairs of nations has long been with us, introduced by Adam Smith in *The Wealth of Nations*, published in 1776. One of the points he made greatly affected how generations of economists and historians looked at business, namely, that there is an invisible hand of market forces. That invisible hand generated demand for goods and services from which sprang the whole field of economics and a large body of knowledge about economic behavior. Two hundred years later, the father of business history, Alfred D. Chandler, Jr., extended the metaphor by arguing that modern business enterprises took over the functions of coordinating flows of goods and services in an economy by managing the various processes of production and distribution. He argues that managers and modern corporations were of sufficient strength and quantity to control many of the tasks Adam Smith had assigned to an invisible hand. His perspective led him to call their influence on economic affairs pervasive enough to be *The Visible Hand* (1977) of the economy. Chandler could do that because corporations, organized into industries, profoundly rationalized economic behavior by the early decades of the twentieth century.

On the heels of this development came the arrival of the computer, its rapid deployment across the economy so great that within a half century of its introduction, information technology (IT) was exercising a profound level of influence on management's decisions in ways analogous to Chandler's visible hand and, before him, Adams's invisible hand. As I demonstrate in this book, *The Digital Hand* helps us to realize the extent of the effects of this one class of technology on economic activities. The story of how companies and whole industries came to use computers is by itself a dull tale but when seen in their role as an economic power equal to those described by either Adams or Chandler, they make the subject very important, one that we need to understand because the full effect of that influence has yet to be felt. As most studies of technological trends continue to report, the full development of the technology and the extent to which it can be deployed have yet to reach their apex. In short, we are not yet at the end of the story of the digital hand, rather somewhere, perhaps, in the middle of the experience. Therefore, this book, although clearly intended to be a formal narrative history of the use and deployment of computing, takes the story to modern times.

I recognize that the title may be overstating the influence of computers since they did not replace preexisting mechanisms in the economy, such as management. Indeed, we should acknowledge that in general computing made new means possible for regulating the activities of the economy, much as had the steam engine in the eighteenth century or, to a lesser degree, the telegraph in the late 1800s. Nonetheless, until industry-level studies are done by various historians and the full deployment of computing can be declared completed, we will not fully understand the influence of computing on the economy. To start the process, I am willing to run the risk that the title overstates the role of the digital, although I think the risk quite low.

My contention is that the digital influence and its effects on economic activity are both as pervasive as management's is on the economy and are a natural extension of their role. In other words, without the managerial revolution that Chandler spoke about, we could not have the digital "revolution" that so many speak about today. So that there is no misunderstanding about how I use the word *digital*, I refer not to portions of fingers on a hand but to the type of computer chips in wide use across the world, that is, digital technology. *The Digital Hand* is all about computing and other related technologies and how they, too, became the source of great influences on economic and business behavior.

Business history in the last three decades of the twentieth century has provided both historians and business managers with useful insights into the patterns of managerial practices and appreciation for the functioning of commercial enterprises and economies at large. This is a history book, describing in narrative form what uses of the computer took place selectively in bellwether industries that either were just so large that whatever they did proved enormously influential or were just so innovative that they introduced novel applications to the rest of the economy. A quick example of the former is General Motors and its industry (the Automotive) and of the latter, the Grocery Industry, which developed the ubiquitous bar code. But this is not history just for the sake of history. Understanding historic patterns of adoption of digital technology gives us insight into how specific industries did, and continue to, operate because they are prisoners of existing applications and processes and, in most instances, of long-standing practices and attitudes. In short, modern business history can describe what otherwise would be called contemporary events. Given the contention of so many experts on computing that this is still an emerging technology, we have here, in the use of computers in business, a useful opportunity to study its history to understand the present circumstances of companies and industries.

But why look at the adoption of information technology by industry? Why not by application? Computers do not have lives of their own. They are the tools of companies, organizations, and people. Simply put, managers organized the functions of computers into firms and industries. Computers do not decide to deploy; rather, managers make that call. As Michael E. Porter taught us so many years ago, industries have been a convenient way to cluster companies.[1] Industries acquired distinct personalities, ways of operating, and often novel uses of technologies. They also learned from each other, either by looking over the fence at what another industry did or through industry associations that formalized the transfer of practices and knowledge. One of my contentions in this and in my earlier books has been that investing in infrastructure counts. Often this is done on an industry basis as did the Banking Industry, for example, when it developed with the U.S. government ways of electronically moving money around the economy (before World War II) or later standardized the look and feel of the modern check (1950s). Today's electronic trading networks, already evident in the automotive, utility, pharmaceutical, and defense manufacturing industries, show that this process is still at work. We can conclude that the adoption of digital technology by industries provides relevant insight into how the current U.S. economy came about.

Managers long ago concluded that work practices varied from one industry to another, and therefore it was not enough to keep up with developments in their own. A newly deregulated industry looked for managerial talent in an industry deregulated a decade ago. We saw this pattern at work with the migration of managers of telephone call centers into the Utility Industry in the 1990s. Executives experienced in mergers in one industry moved to another when consolidations began anew. The need for understanding what has happened across the fence has never been greater than today. The Internet is rumbling through industries at a high rate of speed, causing fundamental structural changes for all, although the reasons for existing remain the same, such as manufacturing and selling cars. But new roles were becoming possible too. Bankers became stockbrokers, and insurance firms began to think about becoming bankers. Digital supply chains linked retailers to manufacturers. Digital rivals constantly challenged bricks-and-mortar firms. Everyone, it seemed, was also forming alliances. Most of these recent patterns of change have been directly made possible by the digital.

The historical record has much to say about these trends. It also offers evidence on a far larger set of issues than just the Internet. For example, I demonstrate that those industries that exploited IT in the fullest enjoyed in exchange the greatest economic returns, evidence I routinely apply at the firm level. The historical record also demonstrates that industries profoundly influenced the nature of the digital technology, how it was put together in the form of products and functions, and the pace and rate of technical and economic change. Describing how digital technologies and their uses entered industries also reinforces the notion of some business historians and economists that industries have their own persona, operating almost as living economic entities in which companies are its body parts. By examining what occurred within specific industries, we see that process of operation and change at work.

Most of the literature on the role of a particular technology, such as large computers or the Internet, was contemporary; that is, it described situations as they appeared at the time it was written. Authors often provided very little explanation about how situations surfaced or evolved because they lacked historical perspective. Economic and industry-specific descriptions also had the look and feel of a Polaroid picture of a moment in time. To use a statistical process control phrase, such a perspective was one data point on a chart. What manager wants to exploit a trend line that only has one data point? When American managers embraced quality management practices and process control procedures in the 1970s and 1980s, they continued the long-standing tradition of adopting analysis and fact-based decision making, yet much of the literature on managerial practices failed to provide long-term trends and perspectives. This book—and its intended sequels—begins by addressing that problem by looking at the role of managers and firms in adopting and using one of the most important technologies to come along in the last century. This strategy allows us to move from generalities about today's circumstance to a more substantive view of what is actually occurring.

For historians, however, the value of such a study may really be greater because as they shift their focus to modern business history they will increasingly bump and Americans do not hesitate to invent new uses of computer chips to make a profit. I then conducted my first examination of the effects of the Internet on management and working practices, primarily focusing on the U.S. experience, where this new information infrastructure had affected the economy the most and the earliest. That book, *21st Century Business: Managing and Working in the New Digital Economy*, documented how Americans were experiencing a new round of profound changes brought about by computing and other forms of digital technologies of a magnitude that had not seen since the late 1960s. In that book I began to draw specific lessons from history while also keeping an eye on the evolving nature of digital technologies. Then, I examined the role of all kinds of information across major features of American society, looking at everything from newspapers to the Internet, from radio and books to television and magazines as used in work, leisure, vacations, religion, government practices, and politics. The insights gained there led me to understand the historic appetite this nation has for all kinds of information, not just for what resides in one medium, such as personal computers (PCs). In *Making of the Information Society: Experience, Consequences and Possibilities*, I explained the rationale for this simple lesson: do not limit your view of information only to computer applications. However, since vast quantities of information were being digitized, it was essential to understand the digital features of what occurred in industries. In all three exercises I uncovered new insights and lessons by relying on a combination of historical perspective and an understanding of contemporary events. The book you are holding is another application of the same technique.

Over many years, I have been very sensitive to the fact that when I am writing on business and historical issues about computing my views would be colored by the experiences I had as an IBM employee. Never has that issue been such a difficult one for me to deal with as in this book because the ideas discussed here are central to what I, as an IBM employee, and my company did for decades. That fact that IBM played such a commanding role in the diffusion of information technology over the last half century cannot be denied nor, on balance, can the relatively positive feature of that story. I make no apologies for the fact that I played a small part in that flow of events, beginning in the early 1970s. So, I admit that this book has an IBM-centric view, to what degree I leave it to the reader and future historians to judge.

I have never before ended a preface with an apology to my readers, but I feel compelled to do so in this case because I chose to write on a very broad issue, which means I have had to seem arbitrary, to write chapters that I wish were half their length, and to have to discuss some issues too briefly. I have had to generalize without fully developing explanations. For these sins I ask for understanding. The views I express in this book and the weaknesses exposed are not necessarily those of the people who helped me, of my employer (IBM), or my publisher.

I dedicate this book to three wonderful gentlemen, saints in their profession. George B. Oliver taught me history when I was an undergraduate student at Randolph-Macon College and then handed me off to the late Earl R. Beck at Florida State University, who had to continue the job until I completed my Ph.D. in history. Then in the years following, Alfred D. Chandler, Jr. mentored me as I learned about business history. All three showed great faith in me and devoted many hours to help me to grow intellectually. This book would have been impossible without their investments in me over the past 40 years.

No author writes a book without help from many people. At the IBM Archives, archivists over the past 20 years found thousands of pages of material for me. The current archivist, Paul C. Lasewicz, provided support and supplied many illustrations in this book. No historian of computing can function today without the help of the staff at the Charles Babbage Institute at the University of Minnesota, and I am no exception. The archivist, Beth Kaplan, found illustrations and material for me; the associate director, Jeffrey Yost, hunted down material; and the director, Arthur Norberg, himself a distinguished historian, taught me a great deal, critiqued this book in an earlier version, and gave me both advice and support as I soldiered on. Bill Aspray, at Indiana University, critiqued portions of the book, gave me good advice, and encouraged me at every step. Edward Wakin, of Fordham University, also sought to encourage my lines of research. David Boardwell, at the University of Wisconsin, stimulated my thinking about the nexus of technology and action,, and his influence will be most felt in the sequel.

A number of colleagues at IBM have given particular assistance. Philip Swan, IBM's economist, provided data and kept me honest about my economic statements. Larry Prusak played the role of the classic cheerleader, urging me to complete what was clearly a very large project for a person who had a day job. Michael Albrecht did the same and, in the mid-1990s, made it possible for me to do research and writing on contemporary IT issues that were essential in influencing my views. Several dozen experts on specific industries also provided data, insight, and critiques. Everywhere I turned within the company, I found help, year in and year out.

This is my third project with Oxford University Press, home to a wonderful team of people. My editor, Martha Cooley, demonstrated extraordinary patience and faith in the project. Even a retired Oxford editor, Herbert J. Addison, an icon in business publications, helped me with some of the original notions behind this book. The Production Department at Oxford again did their usual magic. I want to thank Ian Tucker for preparing the index. Once again I want to thank my wife Dora for her constant support as I spent so many days and years working on this book.

James W. Cortada
Madison, Wisconsin

CONTENTS

1. Arrival of Digital Technologies and Their Applications   3

2. Digitizing the American Economy   28

3. Presence and Role of Manufacturing Industries in the American Economy   66

4. Business Patterns and Digital Applications in the Transformation of Manufacturing Industries   89

5. Patterns and Practices in Three Traditional Manufacturing Industries: Automotive, Steel, and Aerospace   128

6. Patterns and Practices in Three Process Industries: Petroleum, Chemical, and Pharmaceuticals   161

7. Manufacturing Practices in Information Technology Industries: Semiconductors, Hard Disk Drives, and Software   193

8. Business Practices and Digital Applications in the Transformation of Transportation Industries: Trains and Trucks   227

9. Presence of Wholesale and Retail Industries in the American Economy   258

10. Business Patterns and Digital Applications in the Transformation of the Wholesale and Retail Industries   283

11. Patterns and Practices in Three Retail Industries: Grocery, Apparel, and E-tailing   317

12. Conclusion: How Computers Changed the American Economy   355

Appendix A: How to Study the Role of Computing by Industry   389

Appendix B: The Universal Product Code (UPC), Optical Character Recognition (OCR), and Point-of-Sale (POS)   395

Notes   397

Bibliographic Essay   465

Index   473

The DIGITAL HAND

1

Arrival of Digital Technologies and Their Applications

When used with insight and ingenuity, computers will permit relief from the most repetitive form of human work. They will make possible more rapid and less wasteful methods of increasing our material well-being.

—John Diebold, 1952

Americans injected digital technology into their national economy in massive quantities during the second half of the twentieth century. The computer became its most widely recognized form. This technology supported and stimulated economic growth and increases in labor productivity. It made possible new products and services and, most important, facilitated fundamental changes in the way work was done in both the private and public sectors, sometimes by design but often as consequences. Put another way, computer chips and the information technologies and products built with them, along with software, contributed profoundly to the changed look and feel of how the economy worked by the start of the twenty-first century. Largely because of the convergence of various technologies and the redesign of work patterns, primarily to take advantage of computers and telecommunications, Americans enjoyed waves of improvements in economic productivity. This series of improvements translated into profits. In turn, these often contributed to sustaining the historic expansion of the American economy, a process that had been underway during the last half of the twentieth century. Many reasons account for the extraordinary prosperity enjoyed by the United States in this period, but one was the successful application of various types of computer-based technologies. The nature of the deployment of technology is also a feature of the modern economy

3

not yet studied extensively by experts on computing; more often they are quick to turn to its consequences.[1] This book illustrates how computer technology (including programs, especially application software) contributed to the overall functioning of the American economy.

This is not a story about digital determinism in which the so-called march of progress is carried along by inevitable improvements in computer technology. Improvements occurred, but they were not inevitable. They came constantly, often in forms that made sense to firms and government agencies to apply in their work. The key point to keep in mind is that in general nobody was forced to use this technology; people chose to embrace it. When companies and agencies found a new way to use a technology, they tried it, learned from their mistakes and experience, reapplied it, and more often than not benefited from the effort. Frequently, users worked with computer suppliers to develop or improve existing technologies as well. Yet, they were also cautious, not always eager to be the first to try something new. The rates of adoption of a technology or of a specific new device, software, or application (including strategies that depended on a specific technology) by users varied across industries over time. This cycle of meeting new innovations, experimenting, applying, and finally relying on them to function was constant, as well as positive. But this cycle was chosen; that is, the story told in this book is about millions of small decisions to use computer-based technologies, choices made because they seemed to hold out the promise of economic advantage.

Managers made these decisions across the entire U.S. economy, in every industry and within most firms. In some industries, that choice was made more frequently than in others. As a result, some enjoyed more or less economic advantages. But every industry participated. Farmers used personal computers; manufacturing firms installed programmable robots; home-based businesses relied on the Internet to go global. The examples are everywhere and endless: computer-based training of first-graders; computer-driven rockets and smart bombs; computerized data collection on factory floors and at supermarket registers; software-based simulation models for economists, astronomers, consultants, political pundits, and all our weather forecasters. For purposes of this book, I illustrate these thousands of decisions, and where possible their results, by looking at a number of sectors and industries within the U.S. economy from 1950 to 2000. I describe the patterns of successful implementation that can be used by managers who are pondering what to do about future rounds of technological innovation or by government officials to guide public policy. They point the way for the historian to conduct further research.

The first two chapters set the table for the rest of the book. Chapter 1 looks at the emergence and the long-term evolution of the core information technologies that made effective use of computers. In chapter 2, I present a brief overview of the U.S. economy as essential context for the discussions about what happened within various industries. This is a crucial exercise because digital technologies were not deployed outside the context of the nation's economic activities. Industries are not isolated elements within any society; they are part of a more complex economic and social ecosystem. That is why I include an extensive discussion about globalization of the economy; it is also part of the story of how technology diffused across industries. When engineers invented new gadgets, and made profound improvements in the capabilities of computers and software, industries adopted them when it made economic sense. To fully appreciate the arrival of the Information Age, therefore, we need to understand the interactions among technologies, industry-specific behaviors, and economic circumstances.

The industries I chose to look at are listed in the table of contents. These are grouped into chapters to reinforce our understanding of shared and contrasting patterns of adoption. These industries account cumulatively for the vast majority of activities within three large sectors of the American economy during the past half century. The three large sectors chosen for study are manufacturing, transportation of goods, and retailing. To know what occurred within these industries is to appreciate the effect of digital technology on large bodies of American work.

I want to answer only a few questions in this book because I recognize that to understand thoroughly the effect of the digital on the American economy as a whole would require more detailed studies of many industries. However, that said, there are some initial questions we should ask. The first, and ultimately the most basic, is how did these industries use digital technology? Second, what were their expectations for them? Third, how did this technology cause the work of businesses and government agencies to change? Fourth, on an industry-by-industry basis, what were the implications for future uses of digital technology? We will ultimately need many specific company case studies to answer that last question at a more detailed level in order to validate or correct the findings in this book. Finally, what were the business and economic results? To a large extent this last question will be answered by looking at the U.S. economy as a whole.

Those Remarkable Little Digital Chips

It is first essential to clarify one very important concept that profoundly influenced both the actions and language of work activities. This concerns the role of the digital. Notice that so far in this chapter the word *computer* has been sparingly used, and the reason is simple. A computer is only one form of digital technology at work. There are many others, such as robots, cell phones, pagers, palm pilots, programmable microwave ovens, smart bombs, carburetors in automobiles, bedroom alarm clocks, digital watches, traffic lights, and electronic toys. All of these are important items in use across the American economy, which have generated revenue and profits for thousands of firms for a very long time. All of these are made possible by the computer chip, what I simply call digital technology. Historians of computers prefer to use such phrases as *computerization* or *embedded processors* to describe the technology in the heart of computers. They also use such terms as *integrated circuits* and *transistors*. But for brevity, I use the slang term *chips* frequently to mean all of the above. I do so because I want our focus to be on the capabilities of the integrated circuit, which does look like a chip or a famous American breakfast cereal, because without it we would not have a fascinating story to tell. The ability to program a computer chip (embedded processor) to do a number of different things, from launching a rocket to making sure that the mixture of air and gas in automobiles is efficient, remains profoundly important. It is that flexibility that made possible the use of so much technology in the American economy.

The second point to keep in mind as we think about the digital chip as the basic building block of many new innovations and tools is the fact that various lines of technological developments merged together as time passed, creating new levels of capabilities, functions, and additional requirements. Some of the major lines of parallel developments include telephony and telecommunications, radio and television, and finally computers. Over time digital technology became the base for all of these other information technologies and devices. Once that occurred, it became possible to merge them together. The most recent example, and certainly stunning by any measure, is the Internet, which blends telephony, telecommunications, television, voice, video, and graphics. Another is the cell phone, which uses computer chips, radio signals, and telephonic technologies. But this is a process that has long been underway. Combining telephone lines and TV-like screens to make possible online computing at work began in the late 1950s and became widespread by the end of the 1960s. Still later, personal computers became the next wave of change. All are illustrations of the process at work. Economists and technologists are currently looking at the convergence of technologies with great interest because the process of blending and mixing together various information and picture- and voice-handling tools and technologies is actually intensifying today.[2] That is made directly and immediately possible by the fact that computer chips and their digital features can be plugged into many devices in different ways. We think of these as intelligent; in fact they are simply able to take instructions on what we want them to do. Those instructions sit inside the integrated circuits (chips), which are little devices with no moving parts other than electrons flowing through them in predefined patterns (the digital I speak of), using software to instruct them.[3]

The analog is another class of computer technology that has long played an important role, too. Unlike a digital computer, which processes discrete pieces of data (such as 2×2 to yield the answer 4), analog devices provide a continuous flow of electrical impulses or answers, such as the constant change in temperature, quantity, or time. Analog computers are rarely used for business applications, the bulk of the work done by computers in the twentieth century; instead, they are employed in continuous flow operations, such as monitoring and controlling operations in a liquid chemical plant or in a petroleum refinery. In these environments, analog computers constantly adjust the flow of activities, such as how much fuel runs through a pipe, based on a variety of variables. Analog computational devices were actually some of the earliest to be applied in a commercial setting. By the end of the 1970s, most had been displaced by the more precise, faster, and ultimately cheaper digital computer.[4] These devices were often used in the 1940s and 1950s in technical, engineering, and scientific applications. They were used, for example, in the design of automobiles and airplanes and in solving nuclear reactor problems.[5]

However, despite the role of the analog, users overwhelmingly relied on the digital computer. So the key notions on technology to watch for in subsequent chapters are the roles of the digital chip and the various permutations (convergence) of that technology. Occasionally we encounter the analog, but not often.

Long-Term Evolution of Digital Technology

Birth of the Integrated Circuit

Understanding the broad outlines of the historic evolution of computer integrated circuits (chips) helps us appreciate their influence on American business practices and economic activity. Chips can be highly specialized, designed to do one thing, such as control the temperature in a building, or they can be used for more generalized purposes, such as serving as the memory in a computer where information is stored and moved around at a user's request. Because of their flexibility, they appear in many products, from airplanes to wristwatches; hence they are also called embedded processors. To a large extent, the business and social history of the computer chip is a tale of deployment in ever smaller forms and in even more machines and devices, as suggested earlier in this chapter. These features endow many devices with a crude form of intelligence and function that they otherwise would not have. Computers replaced mechanical functions, thereby reducing the cost and size of devices that no longer required moving parts, for example, digital variants of mechanical alarm clocks. Over time, the cost of integrated circuits declined while the amount of information they could hold and the speed with which they could perform functions increased. It is why, for example, one could say that if automobiles had increased their productivity at the same rate as computers, a luxury car would cost $5.

We do not need to go through a detailed history of the computer chip, but there are several historic features of these devices important to understand. The granddaddy of computer integrated circuits was the vacuum tube, essentially a device that looked like a large, long light bulb, used to hold information in the earliest computers in the 1940s. Engineers used similar devices to operate radios, TV sets, and many TV-like computer terminals (called cathode ray tubes, or simply CRTs). In 1947, engineers and scientists at Bell Labs invented the father of the computer chip, which they named the transistor. Following years of research on how to reinvigorate an electronic impulse—necessary for long-distance phone calls—engineers had been experimenting with various elements, such as germanium, which possessed the capability of augmenting an electrical impulse. The new technology was licensed by AT&T in the 1950s and 1960s to over 250 companies around the world. The transistor emerged very quickly as the basic building block for computers, while the public was introduced to the new technology in small, portable radios.[6] Throughout the 1950s, additional work to miniaturize transistors yielded more functions and made them more reliable. Then in 1959, engineers at

Figure 1.1
Multiple generations of transistors. Courtesy IBM Archives.

Texas Instruments (TI) and at Fairchild simultaneously developed what we now call the computer chip.[7]

Figure 1.1 is a photograph of multiple generations of chips, beginning with the transistor. However, note the obvious: the technology evolved, becoming smaller and more lightweight. Not so obvious is the fact that it became more reliable and could handle larger volumes of data and more complex instructions. In the 1960s, a variety of suppliers emerged in the United States and, later, around the world. As the devices became more sophisticated, additional uses for them became possible. This is the central point about the evolution of chip technology. The earliest transistors were used in telephone networks and radios. The last of the transistors, before being fully displaced by chips in the 1960s, were used in military and civilian computers and in spacecraft. By the mid-1960s, computer chips began appearing in hearing aids, digital watches, military and space applications, and in general-purpose computers. By the early 1970s, they were also extensively used in automobiles and other forms of transportation and in the earliest microwave ovens. In 1971, Intel introduced the Intel 4004 microprocessor. This chip had multiple transistor-like components and were programmable, a computer on a chip. This chip changed many things, not the least of which was the computer. Computers experienced huge jumps in capacity, horsepower, speed, and complexity of jobs.

The technical history of the chip from then to the present is a story about more capacity, horsepower, reliability, and function.[8]

In the 1970s, American, Japanese, and European manufacturers of small appliances and industrial devices began to use embedded processors in their products. One of the most dramatic uses around the world was found in the personal computer. In fact, without the powerful integrated circuit on chips, the thought of having light, portable computers seems odd. To suggest the extent of their deployment, we can look at their value as products in themselves. In 1971, approximately $2 billion in chips were manufactured in the United States. That volume doubled in 1973 and doubled again to roughly $8 billion in 1979.[9] Demand for these items increased in the 1980s and 1990s. In 1995, for instance, global sales of integrated circuits reached $140 billion, and they nearly doubled again by the turn of the century. About two-thirds of all these chips were used within the American economy. The biggest demand for chips in the 1980s and 1990s, accounting for roughly 40 percent, were personal computers. So one can see how already the computer chip, which originally went into large mainframe computers and still did at the turn of the century, appeared in other devices. By the time the Internet had become widely popular, in the period 1995–1998, all types of computers used only 47.9 percent of all digital chips; the rest went into industrial instruments (10.3 percent), communications (14 percent), consumer electronics (21.9 percent), and automotive processes (4.9 percent); the military and government used the rest. The fastest-growing demand for chips in the 1990s came from consumer electronics, such as televisions, stereos, and home appliances.[10]

At first, improvements in the capacity and power of chips in computers came every several years with the introduction of a new generation of microprocessors or computer systems. By the early 1990s, new products were coming out on a fairly regular schedule each year. The fact that by then roughly 20 firms dominated the global business of manufacturing chips ensured that competitive pressures would lead to new enhancements on a regular basis. By the 1990s, manufacturers had branded some of their chips with names the public came to recognize through advertising, like Intel's Pentium II and, later, Pentium III. Machines with these components, such as laptops, often had little logos on them: "Intel Inside, Pentium III." Over 10,000 different types of chips existed by the start of the new century, most developed for industrial customers, such as automotive or consumer electronics manufacturers. In short, these little workhorses of the Information Age had become highly specialized, making it easier to apply them in an ever-increasing variety of applications.

Birth of the Computer

What about computers, the workhorses for business uses and the focus of much of the rest of this book? The history of the computer has been told many times and is increasingly becoming a familiar story that need not detain us here. However, as with the chip, several trends are important to understand.

A few milestones in the history of computers are linked to waves of expanded use of digital applications. We can think of the 1930s and 1940s as a period of gestation in which prechip technologies were developed or optimized while the experts refined concepts of what a computer should do. They developed early peripheral equipment and built the first computers. Government agencies in Western Europe and in the United States funded them, with the largest number of projects in the United States, the majority at American universities.[11] In the late 1940s and early 1950s, work began on what would become the first U.S. commercial computer, the UNIVAC I. It became the first machine adopted by American business, and 46 were built. This machine received much publicity, both in print and on television, with the result that many managers became aware of the existence of the new technology. In the late 1940s and early 1950s, managers saw computers primarily as government, military, or scientific devices, but the UNIVAC I changed that, suggesting a greater versatility. Those possibilities were not yet clear to most people, particularly to managers, but enough potential interest existed to encourage some firms to start becoming familiar with these new devices. It also led office appliance- and electronic equipment-manufacturing firms to consider moving into the computer business. One of the firms that did was IBM, and after several years of developing computers for the military and later for commercial users, it introduced the 650 in 1953. Designed for commercial customers, it was small and packaged with software and peripherals. It became quite popular, with over 1,800 units ultimately installed in the second half of the 1950s, of which 800 were in use by late 1958.[12]

The IBM 650 system demonstrated to many corporations that commercial uses of computers were possible and made economic sense. Those two realizations occurred during the 1950s. Whereas many historians think of the 1960s as the great decade of acceptance of computers, we now know that the installation of so many 650s across all major industries demonstrated that acceptance came earlier. We also know that nearly a half dozen years had passed before the great surge in installations occurred in the 1960s. Management recognized the potential value of computers earlier than we might otherwise have thought but waited for the massive adoptions of thousands of systems until these were more mature, as ultimately occurred in the mid-1960s. In short, business and government managers knew by the mid-to-late 1950s what to look for in a computer, and they put pressure on the computer industry to respond. Vendors did so with incremental improvements for a number of years but did not introduce dramatically more effective products until after 1964.[13]

Incremental improvements in computers, software, peripheral equipment, and programming techniques continued as the normal pattern during the late 1950s and early 1960s. *Incremental* is the correct adjective to use because improvements were built on previous ones; nonetheless, these innovations were dramatic in scope. During this period, for example, modern computer languages came into their own, along with online processing, two events considered revolutionary and profound by historians of computers.[14] Then in April 1964, IBM introduced 150 products, which included 5 computers, new operating systems, printers, tape drives, disk drives, and various punch-card equipment that fundamentally changed the rate of adoption of computers in the United States. America's most respected business historian, Alfred D. Chandler, Jr., described the effects of this product line in unrestrained language: it made "possible an explosion in the use of computers throughout the world. Few other modern industries ever grew so fast or became such a powerful agent of transformation," a process he argues was jump-started by the System 360.[15] Users in the United States agreed, spending vast sums on this and other products, most often designed to compete against IBM's System 360. In 1963—before the S/360—American organizations spent $1.5 billion on computer hardware. In 1968, at the height of the shipments of S/360s, they spent $4.5 billion.[16]

What made this product line so attractive? For the first time, a company offered a series of products that were compatible; that is, if a company had one computer and needed to get a larger one, programs that operated on the smaller machine could run on a bigger model without rewriting them. This saved users millions of dollars in the costs of converting older software to newer programs, a fundamental problem in the 1950s and an inhibitor to expanded deployment.[17] Compatible systems meant that users could upgrade their systems with minimal interruptions to the computing work of their firms, such as manufacturing products. Customers and all of IBM's competitors embraced this new approach. The computer industry spent the rest of the 1960s growing at nearly 20 percent each year.[18]

Information storage devices called disk drives proved integral to these systems. They looked like very large compact disks (CDs) in stacks in hatboxes. Unlike data on tape, which could only be reached by reading all the data before the piece of information one wanted, with a disk drive one could reach out and grab just the piece of information needed. That ability made access to information very fast. In time it also became very cheap. Disk drives made online systems technically and economically attractive, leading to whole new generations of applications in the 1960s and 1970s.[19]

Standardization across all forms of technology, therefore, became a silent energizer, encouraging adoption of computing. Often overlooked but very important was the role of peripheral equipment during this and later decades. If one had to change the way one fed information into a computer, costs could be high enough to make the justification of a new use impossible. Therefore, all computers could normally handle the array of existing formats and data-input devices in existence. At the same time, new ones appeared that lowered data-input costs as well. Table 1.1 lists many of the basic types of input equipment that appeared over the half century. The number of products offered by vendors in each of these categories proved staggering, as thousands of devices and various models appeared.[20]

The pattern of incremental improvements in computers and their peripheral equipment (most of which was for input and output) already evident in the 1950s continued through the 1960s and 1970s. Online systems and packaged software appeared (e.g., for accounting and manufacturing applications). Companies and government agencies began linking computers to telephone lines to conduct work across the nation.[21] The number of computer systems installed went from about

Table 1.1
Data Entry and Output Devices

Type	Medium	Common Applications
1950s–Mid-1960s		
Punched cards	80-Column Card	Storage, sorting
Tape drives	Magnetic tape	Batch processing Long-term storage
Disk drives	Disk packs	Online, query
Printers	Paper	Reports
Sensors	Components built into machinery	Process control
Image scanners	Machine-printed text	Conversion of data to digital format
1960s–Mid-1980s		
Cathode ray tubes (CRTs)	Terminals	Online, realtime
Key-to-disk	Diskettes	Data entry
PCs	Diskettes, paper	Portable, small file storage, file backup
Mid-1980s–Present		
CD-ROM	CDs	Cheap storage
Laserdisc	DVDs	Entertainment

6,000 in 1960 to tens of thousands by 1980. It was in this period that large computer systems, often called mainframes, became ubiquitous in most medium and in all large U.S. organizations.

The use of these components in different classes of computers proved to be one of the most important developments in the evolution of digital technology. None played a more important role for some early users than the minicomputer. As the name suggests, these were small computers that were used in specialized applications unlike large systems housed in data centers that were primarily used for business applications (e.g., accounting). Initially most popular with engineers, these smaller systems were used for such jobs as online computer-aided design (CAD) of new products, solving engineering and scientific problems, or providing specialized data collection and control on the shop floor of a factory. These were bought directly by engineers and other users, usually not by the data-processing departments, and were operated by users themselves. Also, they were frequently less expensive to acquire and operate: Minicomputers came into their own in the late 1960s and remained an important segment of the computer industry until the 1980s (when personal computers had become powerful enough to displace them),

Data centers were sterile environments in which companies housed their largest computer systems. This one, in New York in 1960, shows an IBM 7000 series system. These systems, expensive and large, were major investments by a company in people, software, and hardware. Courtesy IBM Corporate Archives.

made attractive by their relative smallness, substantial power, and cost advantages. Some of the most widely used minicomputers of the 1970s—the heyday of such systems—included products from the Digital Equipment Corporation (DEC), called the PDP series; Hewlett-Packard (very popular with engineers in manufacturing); and Texas Instruments. Over 100 niche providers of such machines emerged just between 1968 and 1972.[22]

Paul Ceruzzi, a leading historian of modern computing, has made the vital point that the minicomputer "opened up entirely new areas of application. Its growth was a cultural, economic, and technological phenomenon." Specifically, and just as the personal computer in the late 1970s and all through the 1980s did for yet additional groups of people, the "mini" (as it was normally called) "introduced large groups of people—engineers and scientists, later others—to direct interaction with computing machines." For many, it was the first time they directly and personally interacted with a computer by way of a keyboard, the way they would later interact with PCs.[23] By the time high-performance workstations came along in the 1980s and 1990s, displacing minis, a whole generation of users had emerged. When Sun, IBM, and others used digital technology to create powerful desktop machines that did the work of what by the late 1980s looked like large, slow machines (the minis), users were already familiar with the applications that were ported over to the smaller desktop units. Just as minis remained a specialized class of machines, although widely used, so, too, did many high-performance workstations.

Birth of the Personal Computer

In the mid-1970s, the development of the personal computer and its software began, conducted not by the large suppliers of computers but by small entrepreneurs and individuals like Steve Jobs, Steve Wozniak, and Gary Kidall. In the late 1970s, a raft of new machines appeared, sometimes also called microprocessors, initially put together with off-the-shelf components such as the chip. In this period the Apple line of computers came into existence, along with such other early suppliers as Commodore, Altair, and Osborne.[24] In August 1981, IBM, recognizing the emerging market for these small machines, introduced the Personal Computer 1, or simply the PC. That announcement signaled to many managers in corporate and government America that the use of PCs in their organizations made sense. By the end of 1983, Americans were buying over a million machines per year, many within corporations.[25] The rest of the story of the 1980s is largely one of both additional mainframe and online systems implemented in existing and in new enterprises, as well as the penetration of PCs into organizations and into the private lives of hobbyists and workers.[26]

The PC came to play the kind of role with end users that the large mainframe had served for large organizations. It coexisted with large mainframes and was used in business applications throughout the 1980s and 1990s, while at the same time Americans adopted the PC for home entertainment (e.g., playing games, listening to music, and watching videos and movies) and for e-mail and, later, access to the Internet. Minis and high-performance workstations remained the purview of technical communities. Because of the increasing versatility of computers, a user could move an application from one platform to another. For example, by the end of the 1990s, PCs were powerful enough to handle some computer-aided design/computer-aided manufacturing (CAD/CAM) applications, which historically had only been done by using minis, mainframes, and high-performance workstations.

All through the period of the 1950s–1980s, computers grew in capacity to handle larger applications, do more complex work, and handle additional volumes of transactions. The technical history of these systems is one of more capacity, greater reliability, lower cost per transaction, greater variety of software and operating systems, and new online tools. Innovations came constantly, with product announcements literally made on a daily basis by the late 1960s. Only one of many companies, IBM normally had over 3,000 different products and made new product announcements at the rate of several per week. Most of its major competitors did the same. Improvements in an organization's ability to conduct online processing and its linking of telephone lines to computers also occurred, all creating a sense of unrelenting change upon change.[27]

Birth of the Internet

In 1969, the U.S. government launched a network that made it possible for scientists, engineers, military personnel, and weapons vendors to communicate with one another. Thus was born what in time we came to call the Internet. In the 1970s, the number of users expanded. In the 1980s, it became the major network used by academics to communicate with one another—hence the birth of e-mail. By the end of the 1980s, private individuals had gained access to the network by using personal computers. In the early 1990s, a variety of software tools appeared, making it possible for individuals to communicate and use the Internet in a comfortable, nontechnical manner. No development proved more important at that time than the creation of the World Wide Web. After it came on stream in 1993–1994, American use of the Internet expanded rapidly. In 1994, developers of the original web browser, called Mosaic, formed Netscape, announcing its version of the product that September. With an easy-to-use tool now available, interest in the Internet expanded sharply across the American economy first and later around the world. During the second half of the 1990s, it seemed that most corporations had to get a web page up on the "Net." Millions of individual users also began using the Internet.[28]

Companies and government agencies added content (information), as well as applications done over the Internet. Businesses and government agencies began selling and performing work over the Internet, fundamentally changing how work was done within their enterprises.[29] Work done previously on mainframes or only on PCs was now enmeshed into more comprehensive networks of applications, software, and hardware, thereby creating complex infrastructures in which organizations invested collectively several trillion dollars. These became integral parts of how organizations were structured and how they functioned.[30]

As companies and agencies gained experience with IT over the decades, they added new applications onto old ones. They expanded existing uses to new parts of their enterprises and then added capacity to do more. They continuously upgraded old equipment and software to newer models or versions. Whole IT organizations grew up in response to the need to provide this technology and to support it. The IBM Room of the 1940s and 1950s became the EDP (Electronic Data Processing) Department by the end of the 1960s, the DP (Data Processing) Department or Center in the 1970s, and the MIS (Management of Information Systems) Organization in the 1980s. The EDP managers were often engineers and only first-level managers in the 1950s. By the end of the 1970s, some had become vice presidents or senior vice presidents. By the early 1990s, most were being called chief information officers (CIOs) and, in large enterprises, were in command of thousands of employees. These organizations had a vested interest in promoting the use of computers, and they did not hesitate to do so. To a large extent, they all had one mission: to use computers. In the words of IBM president Thomas J. Watson, Jr.: "It became the conventional wisdom that management ran a bigger risk by waiting to computerize than by taking the plunge."[31] All during the past half century, they suggested new uses of IT and worked closely with vendors to design them, influencing the form and functionality of new computer equipment.[32]

Applications, the Reason for Computers

People acquire computers because they want to use them to do something, from playing games to paying bills. As fancy and complicated as they are, computers are simply tools. The same is true of any other device that has computer chips embedded in it. The heart of this book is about the uses of computers and other digitally based devices.

I began this chapter with a quote from John Diebold, one of America's earliest commentators on how advanced technology, and most specifically the computer, could be applied to the operation of any large organization. He wrote this passage at a time (1952) when businesses were just beginning to use computers in commercial operations. Diebold recognized at once the potential benefits of this new technology, as well as the profound change it would bring. At the time, he focused on automation in general. He has been credited with being the first person to use *automation* in a book, although others have argued that engineers at Ford Motor Company invented the term and applied it to manufacturing applications.[33] Regardless of who came up with the word in the first place, in time, users, observers of the computer scene, and technical staffs moved to another term, *applications*. As the number of computers installed in U.S. enterprises and public agencies grew in the 1950s and early 1960s, the notion of *applying* computers to business processes did too. It is a term that today is used across all kinds of technologies and products, making it one of the most visible business terms of modern times.

Throughout this book and as is the custom in the field of computing, I use the word *applications* to refer to the uses to which computers and related devices are put. Let's begin: applications of computers are the least understood part of the whole story of digital technology and computers themselves.

Businesses came to use computers not because they increasingly became less expensive but because they performed functions (applications) deemed beneficial or necessary to the enterprise. Declines in unit costs did not mean that overall expenditures for computers dipped; in fact, the exact opposite occurred because as more systems came online, more programmers and other technical staff were needed to maintain and operate them, and more end users had to be trained and supported as well. Yet, overall, economies of scale always counted as work shifted to computers and thus away from other sources of expense, or created new capabilities that had economic value. In short, computers made it possible for management to perform tasks less expensively than with either earlier information technologies (e.g., adding machines) or manual operations and to do things not practically possible with previous methods (e.g., guiding missiles on their course or analyzing millions of customer records for trends). Machines were now used to improve efficiency, to lower operating costs, to be seen as "modern," and to be competitive in an economy that increasingly relied on more, faster, and ever more precise technologies. The use of computers, particularly in the Western world, followed a long-standing tradition of injecting technology into important processes of life and economic affairs. In summary, machine-based applications proved important, more than a thing of fashion or novelty. To a large extent, technology afforded many applications of sustainable competitive activity in all advanced economies. As with earlier technologies, computers in general enhanced people's ability to expand control and to speed the flow of information and work, materials, and finished goods, while improving the quality and nature of goods and services. Seen within that broader context, computers became the next round of the application of technology.

Since we are discussing computers and their applications, we should also recognize that these machines differed from earlier technologies. First, more than office machines, such as adding and calculating devices or typewriters, computers made it possible to alter the flow of work and the nature of the relationship of employees with one another. Second, they changed the culture and tasks performed in the workplace. The types of workers needed in a workplace with computers were transformed: new levels of education and different skills (analytical and technical) were prized, resulting in the creation of new positions and careers based on knowledge of this new technology and its applications. As with other technologies, changes in skills stimulated fears of job losses and created opportunities for new forms of employment. As historian Amy Sue Bix concluded in her study of the debate on job displacement, "The United States had enshrined the gospel of workplace mechanization as progress, automation as destiny."[34]

No business or government manager normally acquires any technology just because it is cheaper, faster, or better than something else. The hunt for value begins first by looking for a good use for such a system, followed by determination of cost, function, reliability, and practical benefit.[35] Managers' perception of the risk of a faulty decision, and its effects on their careers, was a hidden, additional consideration too.[36] Therefore, to appreciate the history and role of the computer, we have to move from merely understanding how it works to how it is used. When one shifts to that perspective—to users of computers—the focus changes from the nuts and bolts of technology to business issues. Since that is the approach I am taking, this book is more about business history and current management practices than it is a history of computers.

By making that shift, we also arrive at the central issue related to computers—applications. How these machines were used in various industries leads to the inevitable discussion of accounting and decision making, to data collection and analysis, to a variety of command-and-control applications. I use the word *application* frequently in this book because it is the term employed by users of this technology. The word is so widely in use that it hardly requires definition for practitioners. But, so that there is no misunderstanding, I define the term as the use to which computers, telecommunications, and digital (computer) chips are put. I think of such concepts as a payroll application, an accounting application, a data collection application, an airline reservation system application, and so forth. E-mail is also an application. Applications are collections of tasks performed by computers, normally with some human involvement. They lead to predefined, expected outcomes, such as printed payroll checks, information on what a manufacturing plant is making, an airline travel reservation, or an e-mail message. My definition of the word conforms to all prior ones, dating back to the 1940s.[37]

Systems is a second term that is widely used and which appears from time to time in this book, being closely related to applications. A system is normally thought of as the software resident in a computer that does a specific application, for instance, as in a payroll system that collects data on work and then calculates salaries and prints out checks. Often it is also the hardware such software runs on. Some people use the term to mean the human tasks involved in the operation of a piece of software, but normally it refers to specific pieces of software and hardware that work together. Business and scientific communities increasingly came to use the term *systems* as the twentieth century progressed, to the point where the notion of including technology, tasks, and measurements of performance has become routine. The concept of standardizing repeatable activities and technologies became a by-product of this approach.[38] I will have more to say about standards later in this chapter. What is important to realize now is that the development and use of computers and their applications constituted a major example of that process at work. For our purposes, *application* is a broader term that is used to include all the activities involved in, for example, payroll management.[39]

Since the late 1970s in the United States, a third term, *process*, has made its way into business language, primarily as a byproduct of the adoption of quality management practices. This word is used to describe a set of managerial principles governing the operation and control of a collection of tasks that may or may not include the use of computers or other high-tech devices. The process by which one cooks a turkey dinner is a repeatable routine in which certain technologies, like a stove or a digital microwave oven, are used at various stages of the process. One would say that the cook applied (used) the oven to perform the process. Since there was no software involved in the preparation of this meal, computer systems were not used.

How Applications Affected Business Behavior

The three concepts associated with computers—applications, systems, and processes—are important to keep in mind because over time managerial and nonman-agerial employees learned a great deal about how the three interacted and affected the course of business activities. In the 1940s and 1950s, one would have thought about applications. Between the 1960s to the early 1980s, people spoke about installing systems to do specific applications. Subsequently, management looked at groups of activities as processes in which applications of technology were embed-ded. That combination led to the writing (programming) or buying of software and hardware (systems) by technical staff and managers. Over time, the most effective managers increasingly saw applications as part of the larger functions of an enter-prise and thus approached them as components of an environment that needed to be managed holistically. At the dawn of the twenty-first century, this approach, the first behavioral byproduct of applications, had become part of the mantra of modern management practice.[40]

The second byproduct, evident by the late 1980s, was management's realiza-tion that the effective use of computers often required work flows to be designed differently to accommodate the capabilities of computers and software in order to increase their economic benefits. This approach is profoundly important because up to then, that is, from the 1940s to the late 1980s, the more conventional approach was to apply computers to streamline or enhance existing work flows without changing in any fundamental fashion how work was done. Although economists are now documenting the effects of this change in thinking,[41] many managers and consultants believe that it is the shift toward making work more computer-friendly that led to the enormous increases in productivity achieved by the American economy in the 1990s.[42]

This book is an initial attempt to document the historic use of computers, primarily in business but also to a certain extent in government, and so by design is long on narrative. Until we know such basic facts as what applications were used, and how, when, and why they were used, any broad-based conceptual interpretation of applications or computers becomes difficult to create. The elementary task of discerning what applications were in use can be compared to the work of an explorer standing at the edge of a very large jungle with few or no preexisting paths. Like the metaphorical explorer, we have to cut paths through this jungle of applications and industries and, as a result, create some sense and structure (i.e., a path) that makes it possible for others to pass through and understand it. At the end of this exercise we are not left with a full and accurate map of the application jungle, but at least we know more about it than before. Future students of the jungle can straighten out our paths and build four-lane highways through it.

To hack away at this jungle, four basic techniques are required. In combination they cause us to link applications and technology together and to tie the two to the purposes and functions of both an enterprise and an industry to the economy in which they operate. The key is to develop an integrated view of the activities and influences on each of five components—economy, technology, applications, firms, and industries—because nothing operates in isolation. All five also involve interactions among inventions and innovations, especially technology. An improvement in technology causes a firm to alter an application. A new application makes it possible for a company to do something innovative and productive, which had not been economically attractive before. The idea of the holistic is far from new. However, managers and nations constantly relearn the lesson. In looking at the success of the U.S. economy in the 1980s and 1990s, economist Richard K. Lester concluded that a variation of strategies, investments, and capabilities made possible the resurgence: "There has been no standard template for America's industrial renewal." He argues that "the most successful firms understand 'best practice' not as a collection of independent techniques, but rather as a coherent system of mutually reinforcing processes, practices, and strategies."[43] Embedded within them are applications and systems.

Changes in technology affect the mission of a firm or the functioning, even the borders, of an industry. The arrival of disk drives made the direct pinpointing of information possible, leading immediately to online applications in the late 1950s and early 1960s. One leading historian of computing, Paul E. Ceruzzi, argued that development of disk drives "spelled the end of the batch method of processing."[44]

In fact, batch processing has continued to the present day, although Ceruzzi is correct to the extent that batch applications as a percentage of the total amount of processing declined sharply over time.[45] The new technology made all kinds of applications possible. For example, providing online customer service meant that companies could expand mail order businesses or handle queries, as did so many telephone and utility companies. They could also consolidate offices into larger, more efficient customer call centers. In some cases, the Internet is fundamentally redefining the borders of work, industries, and economies. In others, it is melding together pieces of industries to form entirely new ones.[46] Public policies create economic incentives for its citizens to use the Internet more in one country than in another, or they facilitate desired economic behavior, as is evident when one compares practices in the United States with those in Western Europe (for example, Europeans are charged by the minute to use the Internet, whereas Americans pay a flat low fee for unlimited use).[47] In summary, we need to use a holistic approach to understand applications and their history.

Role of Technical Standards and Industry Organizations

"The proliferation of digital devices—each with its own way of representing and communicating information—has heightened the importance of getting these devices to talk to one another, to their applications, and to their users in mutually comprehensible tongues." That is how Martin C. Libicki, a senior fellow at the Institute for National Strategic Studies at the National Defense University in the 1980s and 1990s, summed up the issue of standards and the role they play.[48] Of course, one good quote deserves another, this also by Libicki on what standards do: "Without them, the trillions of bytes on the Net would make little sense, intelligent machines would lose much of their brainpower, one type of equipment could not work with another, and all the data being so busily created would be accessible only to the creators."[49] Technical standards—a little-studied feature of technology and business practices as history—played an important role because in the world of computers they emerged across a wide variety of technologies and functions, enhancing their capabilities. Standards were set for every class of technology in each decade and in every industry. The process continues today with wireless communications, computer integrated manufacturing (CIM), and a broad array of Internet-related technologies and practices.

How machines (and their software) communicated and worked with each other is a standards story, like the IBM System 360 in the 1960s or adoption of Microsoft's operating systems in the 1980s and 1990s. The development of computer languages by technical committees, which then obtained the approval of technical or industry associations and vendors, also played prominently in the computer industry and continued to be a recurring strategy adopted by inventors, vendors, and users each time a major new technology surfaced. They linked together hardware, software, applications, and management practices, and they observed legal requirements. In subsequent chapters, the role of various technical communities within industries demonstrates how crucial they were in the role of computers in changing the way companies did their work.

The fundamental reason that standards are so essential lies in the fact that they long played an important role in facilitating adoption of particular technologies. Examples abound: electricity in the nineteenth century, long-distance phone calls in the early 1900s, low-tech stationery and envelopes in the 1920s, or the very high-tech nuclear reactors in France and the United States in the 1960s and 1970s. In information processing, standards emerged to discipline all types of technology: computers, peripheral equipment, operating systems, programming languages, applications, telecommunications, and even the design and manufacturing practices of computer chips and telephone cables.[50]

Standards also appeared in applications. Standards made it possible for firms to communicate among themselves and to coordinate activities. The Banking Industry is the best example of this process at work. Banks transfer funds through the United States Federal Reserve System, using standards for performing these transactions and electronic transfers first laid down over a half century ago. In the 1950s, today's look and feel of a check—with its numbering system, for example—came into being because the industry agreed on a standard. Automatic teller machines (ATMs) in the late 1980s began communicating with each other as customers began withdrawing cash from an account in one bank by using an ATM of another bank. The ability to do that called for standards. In manufacturing, today's electronic supply chain management processes and protocols are collections of standards set up over many years, beginning with electronic data interchange (EDI) specifications in the early 1970s. The CAD/CAM software from various suppliers has many standard, common features. A reason that some industries adopted enterprise resource planning (ERP) software from Systems Applications Products (SAP) in the 1990s was to have standards. Also, SAP's code is an excellent example of de facto standards set when a particular supplier's product (hardware or software) is so widely adopted that it becomes the standard for a particular application or industry—the idea that everyone is using it.[51] So, too, is Oracle's telecommunications products late in the twentieth century.

Standards are set in essentially five ways. First, technical bodies create them, as in the case of many of the early high-level programming languages that first appeared in the 1950s and 1960s. COBOL, the most widely used programming language by businesses for over 30 years, began in that way.[52] Second, standards are imposed to facilitate sharing of information or functions, a role frequently played by the United States Department of Defense with the information-processing community over the past six decades.[53] Standards came into existence a third way when industry leaders set them, as frequently occurred in the Banking Industry.[54]

The fourth approach, and the one most frequently seen in manufacturing, is the de facto adoption of an application, such as shop floor data collection or computer-based master production scheduling of work in a factory. A variation of that fourth approach is the adoption of a process by which certain activities have occurred, such as accounting practices as set forth by the Federal Accounting Standards Board (FASB), the U.S. ruling body for accounting, or in the use of point-of-sale (POS) terminals by retail firms to capture sales and inventory data.

The fifth occurs when one vendor succeeds in selling so many of its products that the product itself becomes the de facto standard—the majority of the market wants it. Word processors on PCs in the 1980s and 1990s from Microsoft exemplified this process. Another example is IBM's operating system software for large mainframes over the past half century and, most recent, the "open standards" movement within the IT community.

As demonstrated in subsequent chapters, standards facilitated adoption of specific applications, processes, or information technologies. The rate of implementation and the extent of adoption were directly related to the use of standards. The extreme obvious case is that of American checks because they all have the same design for the placement of data (e.g., where one fills in the amounts) and the protocols governing microcoding of numbers. Debit cards share common standards in the data's placement, format, and movement in the banking system.

The use of standards in accounting, manufacturing, and business practices in general has a long history, exercised over the course of at least the past 20 decades in business and even longer in some government agencies (e.g., the postal system).[55] Such a lengthy use of standards conditioned managers to adopt information technologies that facilitated the use of existing practices in more optimized ways. As technologies led to new insights on how best to perform a task, new standards emerged—as they continue to do today. Standards normally were influenced by managerial practices and beliefs, such as the desire evident today to make business processes more computer-friendly. Another effect on the adoption of standards was the perception managers had about the capabilities of a technology, about which I say more in the next chapter. Historians recognized the growing importance of standards in the twentieth century. No less of a distinguished historian of technology than Thomas P. Hughes recently brought together a team of scholars to look at the history of standards around the world, to see what their applications were and, in the process, to partially document the wide extent of the notion of standards.[56]

The account of the arrival of the computer presented in this and the next chapter is admittedly a rosy view of what happened because it glosses over failures and difficulties not always overcome. Nonetheless, the fact remains that the digital arrived and was deployed for rosy reasons—it worked, made economic sense, and eventually became the way in which things were done. We cannot ignore that reality. What also occurred, however, was a complex process of invention and deployment, one filled with controversies, failed initiatives, impaired or destroyed firms, failed vendors of hardware and software (dot.coms are only the latest cases), and often difficult and dynamic economic climates. But to dwell too much on the negative issues would obfuscate the real story, which is positive. The ultimate reality is that a new technology emerged that nearly every government agency and business enterprise in the United States embraced in less than a half century.

Approach to the Study of Applications

The first step in the study of applications is to briefly survey circumstances in the American economy that made the use of computers possible, beginning in the 1950s (chapter 2). A similar, yet smaller, more narrowly based discussion about the economic realities that existed over time has to be included when surveying individual industries. Economic influence always functioned as an important lever. For example, the role of tax policy and depreciation profoundly influenced the timing of when companies acquired large computers, which were capital-intensive investments. The roles of innovation and global competition are also important considerations; today, investments in information technology absorb the lion's share of U.S. capital investments, a share that continues to increase at the dawn of the new millennium.[57] In short, economic and business practices in combination are important to understand if we are to appreciate the use of digitally based applications.

Second, it is important to understand the features and attractions of any application. Why, for instance, is computer-based payroll used? Why does one industry use computers more than another? How is the Internet being used to increase competition or expand market reach? How were applications acquired and justified? In our discussion, it is possible to begin collecting early experiences, simultaneously documenting some of the effects applications have had and continue to impose on organizations and the economy at large. Some applications cut across industries and appear frequently in this book. Accounting applications are ubiquitous; everyone uses them. E-mail now fits into this category as well, primarily because of the Internet, but it, too, existed within enterprises decades ago.

Third, taking an industry view gets one past applications used in all industries, such as accounting and e-mail, to industry-specific uses that often fundamentally changed the nature of the work there and which are not yet appreciated by historians or the public at large. For example, the use of ATMs to conduct banking led in the late 1980s and 1990s to a very sharp decrease in the number of human bank tellers needed to transact business. Moreover, ATMs and computers with telecommunications, it can be argued, facilitated the enormous number of mergers that occurred in that industry in the late 1990s. The banking world looked fundamentally different in the early years of the new century than it did 15 years earlier, and one of the primary reasons is the set of computer-based applications that bankers implemented. So, industry views are essential to any appreciation of the use and effect of applications on management and the economy as a whole. Lester's earlier comment on how industries revived in different ways is in line with the value of an industry-centric view. What little historical research done on computer use reinforces the value of this perspective. For instance, James L. McKenney looked at a small group of applications from different industries and drew the same conclusions reached by Lester. The Bank of America used information technology differently than did American Airlines or United Services Automobile Association (in insurance), for example. Although McKenney found common themes, primarily in management practices, the applications that fundamentally helped a firm were unique to each one and to its industry.[58] The same process is underway in our Internet era, with applications evolving that are also industry-specific and even activity-specific.[59]

Fourth, as the first three steps are taken, it is also important to cross-link patterns from one firm to another and from one industry to another because users learned from each other, regardless of where they worked. Some common patterns emerge, shedding light on how computers were used, why, and for what. These data also makes it possible to begin understanding the extent of deployment in the economy at large. Deployment is an important issue for all concerned. For the historian it leads to answers about how many people used a technology and who they were; the more usage, the more important the technology is and the greater the effect on a nation's history. For the economist, it defines the activities, costs and benefits, and relative value of actions and investments. For the manager, deployment reveals whether the company was ahead, behind, in trouble, had a competitive advantage, or could make more or less profit. What were the costs and benefits to the organization, to an industry, and to the nation, culturally, economically, and from a business perspective? These are all good questions, and all are rooted in deployment. So, everyone has a stake in the issue. Because this kind of study is rooted in an industry-centric approach, appendix A expands on the discussion of the methodology used to develop several critical findings.

Key Findings

Deployment as a point of emphasis departs from the more traditional view of computers and chips in which historians and economists, consultants and managers, focused on how machines and widgets emerged and what they did.[60] One of the findings in this book is that the rate of deployment of computing technologies varied across all industries and within firms in an industry. Some embraced computers sooner rather than later. Understanding why helps to document the profound changes that occurred in the U.S. economy in the second half of the twentieth century and which continue to affect this economy in such a rapid, one might even say, jolting manner.

A related finding is that the rationale for adopting digital technologies varied over time and also differed from one industry to another. Equally important, every industry studied for this book and for the intended two sequels (a total of 46), found economic and operational benefits in using computers. To be sure, there were many common elements in this rationale, such as cost savings, but even that motivation translated into different levels of performance from one firm to another. In other words, all banks and factories were not the same. Social and political policies dictated some of these differences. For example, the U.S. government was one of the earliest users of accounting applications, and soon after, so were commercial suppliers to the government. Aircraft manufacturers were required by the U.S. Air Force in the 1950s to design wings by using mathematically based design applications called computer-aided-design, or simply, CAD software tools.[61] It was only years later that automotive and then other industries did the same thing. I argue that the transfer of experience from one application to another and from one firm or industry to another played an important role in the proliferation of digital technologies throughout the American economy, also accounting in large part for the speed of diffusion.[62] That ability for information and people to move about openly in the American economy was a feature of U.S. society that continuosly made it possible for innovations to find practical homes, a process long recognized by historians.[63]

Closely tied to the notion of openness is my finding that acceptance of an application's viability was a function of who else was seen to adopt it. A dramatic example of this practice involved the personal computer. Until IBM introduced its own PC in August 1981, many companies did not take this new technology very seriously, although it had been available for over a half dozen years and individual employees had used them. But after that, senior and middle management, particularly in computer data centers, could no longer ignore this technology and the applications that so quickly became available to exploit it.[64] Acceptance and growing understanding of a technology or use, in turn, led suppliers of such applications to determine what to develop, build, sell, and support, such that, in turn, acceptance accelerated within business and government circles.

Approach and Sources

Looking at the subject from 1950 to the present makes sense because it was in the early 1950s that computers began moving out of university laboratories and government agencies into commercial enterprises. Computer information technology-based applications had, in general, stabilized after a half century of deployment into widely accepted similar practices. These were overwhelmingly in accounting, distribution (including inventory control and logistics), and shop floor scheduling and tracking. Although that collection of applications provided a base of knowledge that informed early users of computers, the arrival of the newer technology ushered in so many technological changes that once again uses of information technology underwent dramatic changes. As of this writing (2003), it appears that the process of dramatic change is still underway, with no end in sight. It was in roughly 1950–52 that the current round of changes began, providing the reason for selecting that decade as a useful watershed.[65] By the early 1960s, large firms had become the largest number of users of computers and their base digital technologies, such as the integrated circuit (IC), better known as the chip.

Also in the early 1950s, we have the first documented use in the United States of a digital computer in a commercial setting: General Electric installed a UNIVAC I computer system in Lexington, Kentucky, at its appliance-manufacturing plant. It was highly publicized and watched by many companies.[66] Soon after, other firms moved into the fray and began using computers to help manage their operations. From the 1950s to the early 1980s, much of what was applied took the form of highly centralized computer operations in which work was increasingly added to large computers. Not until after the arrival of the microcomputer (the PC) in the business world during the early to mid-1980s did changes occur in the fundamental nature of business applications, where they were used, and by whom. From the 1950s to the present, we have experienced a rush to install and use computer-based technologies at an unrelenting pace that far exceeds the initial round of implementation of information technologies in the period 1875–1930.[67]

The use of computers and their applications is as visible a process as anyone can find in the U.S. economy. The computer industry (as it was known for at least four decades) had always been very public. Early users of computers were so proud of their accomplishments that they frequently rushed into print, bragging about their achievements in thousands of articles and hundreds of books, although most of these appeared in publications of small circulation, read only by members of one's industry. Many other thousands spoke at business conferences about their applications. Computer vendors were equally effusive, publishing application briefs and user guides. The methodical promotion of applications by vendors often dictated what received publicity and what did not. For example, in 1956 the general sales manager at Burroughs, N. L. Mudd, wrote a letter to the entire sales force in the United States and Canada in which he reported that "as part of the Company sales promotion program, the Advertising Division has for some time been preparing and placing installation stories in trade magazines, then reprinting most of the published stories for distribution with material for the monthly sales meetings." He went on to describe how this program was administered for the purpose of producing "free nation-wide publicity of favorable information about our products." He sought stories in all industries so that they could be shared across industries.[68]

In each decade, industry publications from all sectors of the economy also documented the issues dealt with in this book. We can thus study specific cases, trends, quantified measures of deployment, and public policy, including transcripts and reports of very public, noisy law suits—in fact, hundreds of them. Like John Diebold, most people who were observing the business scene sensed almost from the beginning that use of computers would represent a major theme in late twentieth-century America.[69] To be sure, most were also cautious, particularly senior management, who routinely commissioned studies on the potential of computers. Their cautious behavior was more an act of sound prudence than a reluctance to embrace a potentially viable technology.[70]

Despite the existence of a vast body of usable material for the study of applications, historians, economists, and business management experts have only nibbled at the topic in piecemeal fashion. Yet, the large volume of activity alone would guarantee that the issue would be a major one in the field of business management. It is also a subject that nobody has yet integrated fully into the fabric of business historiography or into the lexicon of contemporary management practices.

What few studies we have of European and Asian uses of computers lead me to conclude that applications vary from one country to the next, less because of technological considerations than of either public policy or the way in which firms are run.[71] For that reason, my focus is on the United States, without generalizing on a global basis, although occasionally I make comparisons with other countries. Furthermore, the use of computers in the United States proved far more pervasive in the second half of the twentieth century than anywhere else in the world, and that experience set the pace for other nations.[72]

Two final, basic features of applications should be cited here because as we review one industry after another, these ideas could get lost in the discussion. What the story of computer applications is fundamentally about is, first, the migration of work and other activities from manual and paper-based processes to the digital and from paper pulp to electronic pulses and then, later, to new tasks. Second, as digital technology made possible the convergence of computers and telecommunications by the early 1960s, applications began to be performed in many places, not just in the large, glass-enclosed data centers of old. Although these pristine cathedrals of technology have never gone away, they no longer overwhelmingly dominate the use of computing. Today, we compute in our cars, in airplanes, at home, in our offices, on the beach, and in small and large firms. Often we do not know that we are using computers (e.g., every time we drive an automobile or operate a modern stereo) or massive data centers. These two trends cut across all industries and have emerged at approximately the same time, demonstrating that technology moved across industry borders quickly and simultaneously, like waves across water. Everything happened within the context of American economic realities.

Central to any discussion of the arrival and deployment of applications, both in the private and public sectors (although especially in the former), is the health and characteristics of the American economy across the entire half century. No less of an authority about the American economy than the chairman of the Federal Reserve System, Alan Greenspan, placed IT and the economy in context. In answering a question from a member of the U.S. House Financial Services Committee on July 15, 2003, he noted that all industries were now "high tech" because extensive uses of technology obtained for the economy at large greater economic benefits. Understanding how that economy factored into the story of the computer's diffusion is essential to any appreciation of why certain applications were adopted, to what extent they were deployed, and in which industries. The next chapter discusses these issues, and subsequent chapters review specific examples in a number of industries.

2

Digitizing the American Economy

The number of installed general purpose computers has grown exponentially

from barely 50 systems in 1953 to 175,000 installations in 1976, and the

installed population is projected to nearly double by 1980.

—Charles P. Lecht, 1977

Charles P. Lecht, a computer industry watcher at the midpoint of the first half century of the computer, reflected the optimism evident across much of the American economy about the potential value of these systems. He was also wrong: the number of systems installed by 1980 exceeded his forecast. At the time, many in the business community had initial experiences with computers of a sufficiently positive nature to warrant further investments. Users in the 1950s had struggled with primitive technology both difficult to install and difficult to use; then in the 1960s, they saw important technological developments, in software that made practical applications of computers attractive. By the time Lecht wrote his assessment, almost all major companies with over 250 employees had some experience with computers. Put another way, every major industry and sector of the U.S. economy used computers. This extraordinary adoption of computing took place at a time when the technology's robustness stimulated the necessary investments in computers and made possible appropriate levels of potential opportunities for economic gain to warrant the costs involved. For these reasons no discussion about the acceptance of computers can be restricted to an analysis of the technological evolution of the machine or its base technologies.

In perfect circumstances, I would want the reader to study chapters 1 and 2 simultaneously because technology influenced the economy, and economic circumstances in turn affected the rate of change and adoption of the technology. So which came first, technological innovation or the economy? In fact, the economy existed before the technology, although one cannot understand the effects of the technology on the economy without first having a sense of technical details (which is why chapter 1 focuses primarily on technology). This chapter looks at the broad economic environment in which this technology flourished, identifies patterns in the acceptance and implementation of applications and computers, and then reviews extant evidence on the degree of deployment. This last topic—deployment—will also receive additional attention in each of the industry chapters, as it bridges both economic and business management issues. As each subsequent chapter will illustrate, the two were always interconnected, with the computer (and its applications) serving as the nexus. Thus this chapter begins with an economic orientation and ends with a business manager's perspective.

Evolution of the American Economy

Economists have sliced and diced the modern American economy into several major sectors. Within each sector they have identified specific industries. Within industries there are firms. Within firms there are employees, and outside them, customers and suppliers. When looking at the economy, it is convenient to look at sectors and then industries as indicators. Counting the amount of money that flows through the economy is also an indication of relative size, and understanding in which sectors cash flows occur tells us a great deal about the nature of the economy's activities. Looked at over time, we can generalize with some confidence about major patterns of behavior. Over the last two decades of the twentieth century, historians of technology had increasingly adopted some of the tools and many of the perspectives of the modern economic historian to help understand their own field as well.

The connections between the history of technology and economics are not always so obvious, however. Two influential economists who study technology in historical terms, David C. Mowery and Nathan Rosenberg, have stated that "the realization of the economic impacts of 20th century scientific and technological advances have required significant improvement and refinement of the products in which they are embodied."[1] To be sure, there is always a lag between the evolution of a technology and its adoption and when the economic effects show up in the numbers. They point out that not until the century was more than half gone did economists, for instance, realize "the extent to which economic growth was a consequence of the process of technological change."[2]

To illustrate how one can connect technological innovations and economic realities, we can turn to these same two authors for their interpretation of the adoption of computers in commercial settings:

> The gradual adoption of the mainframe and minicomputer in industrial applications, such as real-time control of chemicals and petroleum refining applications, contributed to declines in the intensity of energy use per unit of output in these industries. Moreover, by supporting more effective modeling and sim-

ulation of new processes, computers made possible the smoother introduction of new manufacturing processes into commercial use.[3]

In short, a direct link existed between technological developments and economics. Put in terms more closely associated with our study, the topic of computer-based applications of technology was at least as much an economic issue as it emerged as a technological one.

During the second half of the twentieth century, the U.S. economy was very large, continued to grow rapidly, and was, in a word, productive. At the end of World War II, the only major economy in the world not in trouble because of wartime destruction was that of the United States. In 1945, it totaled $355.2 billion (in 1958 dollars). In 1970, it totaled $722.5 billion (in 1985 dollars). The economy kept growing during the rest of the century despite short-lived periodic recessions. In each decade it expanded by impressive amounts. Between 1950 and 1960—the period when the first computers began to enter the economy—it expanded by 38 percent. In the next decade—while computers worked their way rapidly into the economy and the Vietnam War went into full swing—the economy expanded another 48 percent. During the decade of the 1970s, when the United States experienced rapid inflation, the oil crisis of 1972–1973, and expanding national debt— it still grew by 38 percent. The Reagan years witnessed another spurt of growth, 22 percent.[4] The final decade of the century—when the Internet came into its own—witnessed double-digit growth, with annual growth rates at the end of the century sometimes over 5 percent per year, considered red hot by economists.[5] In fact, during that decade it was widely acknowledged by economists and knowing business executives that the productivity gains that fueled the expansion of the economy came from the positive impact that investments in technologies (including computers) had delivered. Even the chairman of the Federal Reserve, Alan Greenspan, not known for pointing to one factor as dominant in any of his analyses of the U.S. economy, made this point repeatedly in the last several years of the century. The key observation is that during the era in which computers were infused into American businesses, the economy kept growing, generating the wherewithal to fund development and deployment of the new technology. In turn, the technology influenced the economy, most often at the point at which computers were used—in the use of applications.[6]

Growth of Labor

No discussion of economic activities is ever complete without acknowledging what happens to labor. That old economic maxim is no less true in any review of the role of computers. So what happened to labor in this half century, when supposedly computers were automating work, threatening jobs, and clearly causing changes in the nature of work? The labor force expanded. At the time computers were moving into the economy—say 1954—the civilian work force amounted to 60.1 million people, which was 55.5 percent of the total civilian population. In 1974, employment reached 86.8 million, or 57.8 percent of the total civilian population. Ten years later—when businesses and individuals were rapidly adopting the PC—employment climbed to 105 million, or 58.5 percent of the civilian population. The work force continued to expand in the 1980s and 1990s to the point where unemployment rates dropped from over 7–8 percent in earlier decades to less than 5 percent and in some labor markets to under 1.5 percent. Throughout the entire period, between 18 and 22 percent of employees worked for manufacturing firms. During the whole period under study, the service sector grew faster in the number of workers it employed and over time, in the percentage of gross national product (GNP) than manufacturing, which meant that the percentage of workers outside manufacturing expanded from just over half the work force to over 80 percent by the end of the century. The statistics are fuzzy since economists and government agencies do not always count in the same way, but the trend is unmistakable.[7]

Labor costs in the United States routinely outpaced those in other nations, often because of the relatively larger labor scarcity and an abundance of capital. This pattern is evident in one industry after another. The differences were often so great that management concluded that there was no recourse other than to relentlessly drive out labor content in work—as we shall see, for example, in both the automotive and steel industries. One of my findings is that despite all the discussion about labor, we still have underestimated the role of its cost in encouraging the deployment of various forms of automation in the United States.

The role of unions often presented specific, immediate, and highly emotional problems to management in this period. The existence of highly unionized labor forces, such as those in mature manufacturing industries, frequently led to higher rising costs of labor than in the rest of the world and just as often to unreliable work forces since they (1) did not hesitate to disrupt work by going on strike and (2) negotiated restrictive work rules in their contracts that often made it difficult to change processes with software, particularly in the 1950s and 1960s and, to a greater extent, deep into the 1970s. I do not intend to villainize labor, simply to note that *relative* costs profoundly affected senior management's decisions, particularly in those industries that competed in a global market and where labor content of work began or remained high as, for example, in manufacturing. Where widespread global competition did not exist, as in banking and insurance, labor costs were either high or low relative to domestic considerations, such as what another firm might pay for a worker either in the same industry or elsewhere.[8]

Global consideration is more important for many of the industries discussed in this book after 1970 than before, for various reasons unique to each industry. However, what is very clear is that when one compares labor productivity based on the GDP per employed worker, say, after 1970 through the late 1990s, U.S. productivity increases more than that of other nations as one comes closer to the present. This largely explains why some economists view technology as finally kicking in with positive effects.[9] Simultaneously, productivity tends to converge over time as applications are diffused across other industries and countries, which is essentially the important argument made by economists William Baumol, Sue Anne Blackman, and Edward Wolff.[10] The implication is obvious: to stay ahead requires industries to adopt new applications or processes that continue to enhance even further a firm's productivity. This pattern is evident in all the industries I studied and largely accounts for why work was so much changed by the digital.

Changing Makeup of the Economy

Figure 2.1 documents the percentage of the economy by sector over time. The manufacturing sector in 1947 occupied nearly 27 percent of the economy but by the end of the century claimed only 15.9 percent.[11] But the economy kept growing during the entire period; the number of people working in manufacturing and the dollars generated by that sector actually increased. However, the key trend is that as a percentage of the total, the economy shifted away from manufacturing and toward a variety of service sector industries in the number of employees and, toward the end of the century, in growth. Communications tripled its presence, while utilities doubled theirs, as did banks, insurance, and real estate. Without manufacturing, government, and agriculture (cumulatively about 40 percent of GDP), the rest of the economy (services) almost tripled. Whereas a great deal of concern about the growing presence of government could always be found in the press, the public sector's participation remained fairly constant as a percentage of the total economy. It hovered at just over 12 percent, although it experienced a huge surge in the 1970s, driven largely by the Vietnam War and President Lyndon Johnson's Great Society programs, both of which were expensive and triggered a severe round of inflation. In general, the private sector remained fairly constant during the entire period, accounting for roughly 85 percent of the economy.

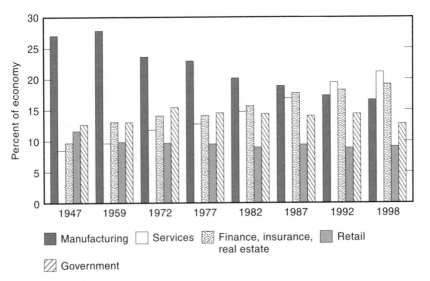

Figure 2.1
U.S. economic sectors, 1947–1998.

Who Acquired Computers?

Manufacturing and government were the largest users of computer technology throughout the entire period. Service sector industries increased their use of computers as a percentage of the total as decades passed. The retail industry did not become a major factor in the computer business until the 1960s and 1970s, and manufacturing and government dominated in the first decade of the new technology. But, as services came to dominate the economy over time, the raw number of computers going into various services industries, such as insurance and banking, climbed significantly.

Although I discuss the amount of computing in one industry versus another in subsequent chapters, a few generalizations here will help create the overall context needed to understand the effect of digital technologies on the American economy. In the 1950s, the percentage of a company's budget that was spent on computing was miniscule. By the 1970s, it was not uncommon for an American manufacturing firm to spend 0.7 to 1.2 percent of its budget on computers. Service sector firms spent less. By the end of the century, manufacturing firms were frequently spending over 3 percent on computers, more if one counts all forms of digital technology. When banks and insurance companies got into the computer game, the percentage of their expenditures rose quickly, from almost nothing in the 1950s to over 3 percent by the early 1970s just for information technology (IT).[12]

In absolute dollars, the amount spent by all sectors on computing hints at the rate of adoption underway. In 1954, American organizations spent $10 million on computers; in 1958, $250 million, clear proof that computers had been "discovered," primarily by industry. In 1963, just before the advent of IBM's S/360 systems and similar products from a half dozen rivals, which stimulated a massive surge in the adoption of computers across the entire economy, expenditures were already at $1.5 billion. By the end of 1973, when the United States was experiencing a recession, expenditures had climbed to $7 billion.[13] Large firms and government agencies were responsible for most of these expenditures, all before the arrival of the personal computer, which in the 1980s led to payouts for computing that made these earlier numbers look tiny.

Sales of personal computers tell the story. In 1978, about $15 million in sales of microcomputers took place; that number doubled in the following year and nearly tripled 1978's number in 1980. In 1983, the year when economists and historians believe that PCs really became popular, volumes climbed toward $500 million, accounting for nearly a million units.[14] In 1999, it was not uncommon for Americans to buy 8 to 10 million PCs per quarter. Globally, expenditures on computer-based technologies had become more than a $1 trillion business, with about half normally flowing through the U.S. economy. Although expenditures were high in all decades, the boom years were the 1960s (when most firms installed their first systems), again in the 1980s (as firms also began acquiring PCs and application software packages in massive quantities), and in the 1990s (when the general public—not just firms and agencies—made the huge investments in PCs cited above, to the point that by the end of the century over a third of all homeowners had access to the Internet).[15]

Economic growth, expansion in the number of jobs and the standard of living, and clear evidence of management's willingness to use technology did not, however, occur quietly. All through the period critics voiced concern about the loss of jobs and the potential negative effects of all types of technology and automation across the economy. Historian Amy Sue Bix has studied this issue from the perspective of the critics and defenders. She observed that despite economic prosperity, there lingered an undercurrent of concern about the potential displacement of workers by the new technology, an anxiety not mitigated by the reality of new jobs being created at the same time or the existence of a strong economy. Business leaders and the publications that supported them heralded the arrival of a new progressive era, thanks to computing, whereas others, not just labor leaders, worried. But even labor leaders accepted the rhetoric of technological progress as a way of improving the quality of life of the working class. Whenever a major displacement of workers occurred, as happened, for instance, with the 53 percent decline in employment that took place among employees in newspaper composing rooms between 1979 and 1983, the volume of expressed concerns rose. In periods of higher unemployment, objections rose, too, whereas the converse occurred when unemployment was low.[16] Bix concluded that "the issue of technological unemployment had never vanished; the post-war gospel of automation only raised the stakes of the debate." Although the debate mimicked many of those that arose as early as the 1920s and 1930s, if there was a difference it came in the requirement that workers had to continuously acquire new skills. At the end of the 1990s, economists did not have a consensus on technologically induced job displacements in the late twentieth century, which made discussion about technological unemployment "a battle of emotions, assumptions, and vested interests."[17] Despite the issues raised by the debate, her conclusion was clear: "The United States had enshrined the gospel of workplace mechanization as progress, automation as destiny."[18] The rhetoric was less a display of empirical evidence than the voice of economic and political agendas.

Despite the concerns, did all these expenditures have any effect on the American economy? It is a good question to ask because within circles of public policymakers, senior executives, and economists, a healthy debate about the business and economic value of computing took place. This debate was less about job displacement and more about economic value. It is important to our study because the debate influenced those who made the actual decisions to adopt all manner of technologies, such as computers, and those who created economic policies that provided such things as tax incentives for those investments. For that reason, we must understand the issue of what has come to be known in economic and policy circles as the productivity paradox.

Productivity Paradox

The answer to the question posed at the start of the last paragraph is difficult to provide because it varies according to one's perch in the economy. Economists worry about national productivity; senior managers about profitability or returns on investments of expenditures for technology, people, factories, and stores; and labor about job displacements. National productivity and expenditures for technology are related to each other, complicating the debate. The nature of their relationship became the heart of the controversy. White-collar workers, like blue-collar labor, also worry about making more money without having to work additional hours. A national government ultimately frets about the economic power of its country versus those of other countries. But all have a stake in the productivity issue. As the number of installed computers in the U.S. economy increased over the last quarter of the twentieth century, discussion turned to the effects this technology had on personal, firm, and national productivity. Economic statistics suggested that national productivity was not growing in proportion to the amount of investments being made in computing, stimulating a debate among economists and some government officials; hence the paradox. In contrast, private sector managers rarely participated in this debate, and for good reason. They were installing computers for specific purposes, and either they got the returns they wanted at sufficiently high rates to warrant additional and continuous investments in these machines or they did not. But when they did invest, they usually showed faith in the intrinsic value of this type of technology, demonstrating the same faith Bix observed among those debating the issue of technologically induced unemployment. This faith, however, was neither blind nor innocent; managers normally analyzed their needs and technical operations sufficiently before spending on IT. Accusations of naiveté or of acquiring computers for reasons of fashion might be true in some cases, but the depth and breadth of deployment proved far too great to think that their interest was ill placed.

A short reminder about some basics in economics is required to appreciate the issue of the productivity paradox. Economists worry about how much work (output) an employee generates because some of the most important measures of an economy's performance are the cost and output of labor. The more output, the greater the opportunity for that individual to enjoy a higher salary and ultimately an expanded standard of living. The two notions are tightly linked, and the terms used to describe them are *labor productivity* and *wage growth*. Often among various measures used are hours of labor and output per hour. Normally, productivity is increased in one of three ways: improving the training and skills of workers, investing more capital in production (e.g., for automation), or enhancing the quality and type of technology to make more products (output) per hour. In general, technology of all kinds—not just computers—produced measurably significant improvements in output (labor productivity) over the previous century and a half.[19]

History of the Issue

The discussion about a paradox began when economists in the 1970s began to notice that the productivity growth of the economy as a whole was slowing at the same time that investments on all kinds of technology—not just computers—were steadily increasing. The questions were these: Why is national productivity declining while we are investing so much in technology? Aren't computers supposed to make the economy more productive? The surge in installations of computers in the 1970s and 1980s was massive, totaling billions of dollars in machines, software, and technical personnel, a trend in expenditures that began to worry some economists. What concerned them was the fact that these investments did not turn up as increases in the traditional productivity measures by which they gauged the performance of the economy. Their knowledge and understanding of economic behavior indicated that something seemed very wrong. Traditional economic data showed that U.S. productivity growth averaged 2.94 percent per year before the middle of 1973 but then dropped to 1.43 percent. Most of the debate took place in the 1980s and very early 1990s. Then, in the mid-1990s, productivity rates climbed again to over 2.7 percent per year, almost three times the rate of the early 1990s.[20] The changed economic picture muted but did not eliminate the discussion about the productivity paradox, just as good times dampened the intensity of debate over technologically induced unemployment but never completely ended it.

Many economists have looked at the question of what role computers played in hurting or helping rates of productivity, and there still is no consensus on what happened. However, by the late 1990s, economists were making a number of empirically based observations. Careful studies of manufacturing firms demonstrated that from 1970 to 1980, U.S. productivity growth lagged behind that of other nations in the manufacturing sector. Then in the 1980s and 1990s, American manufacturing companies exceeded such rivals as Canada, Germany, Italy, Japan, and the United Kingdom. But, as indicated earlier in this chapter, the percentage of the U.S. economy made up of manufacturing had shrunk as a proportion of the total economy. So we have to turn to the services sector for insight. What we see there is that productivity did not match what was occurring in manufacturing.[21] Long before computers were a factor, the service sector's productivity performance remained below that of manufacturing. Between 1946 and 1970, manufacturing's productivity grew at roughly 3 percent per year, while that in the service sector grew by 2.5 percent. Between 1970 and 1980, manufacturing's percentage was 1.4 and that for services 0.7. From 1980 to 1990, manufacturing improved to 3.3 percent, while services came in at 0.8 percent, in other words, with minimal change. Manufacturing invested more in computing in those years (1970–1990) than did the service sector. To put these data in perspective, between 1970 and 1992 manufacturing's share of the total U.S. work force dropped from 26.1 percent to 19.1 percent, while that of services expanded from 62.2 percent to 70 percent.[22]

Although some economists have blamed the computer for not helping to resolve the problem of slow growth,[23] I offer evidence in subsequent chapters that manufacturing firms invested the most in computer technology and ultimately did well in terms of productivity, whereas industries that came late to the computer, or invested lesser amounts in this technology did poorly. Some students of the problem have found it more than a coincidence that rates of investment in technology had a direct effect on productivity. However, reality is not so simple. Two economists who looked at the services sector, Michael van Biema and Bruce Greenwald, concluded that the weak productivity in services was due, first, to a lack of sufficient management attention to the issue and, second, to the inherently complex nature of many services industries. They showed that when management paid attention to productivity in manufacturing it went up, as it did in the service sector also. In other words, there are banks and insurance companies, for example, that have productivity performances equal to or better than the norm in manufacturing and, most important, that have outpaced rivals in their own industry.[24]

Evidence on the effects of substituting IT for other factors of production is accumulating for both manufacturing and service industries to such an extent that we can begin to understand some broad patterns of performance. For example, we know today that by 1994 IT accounted for 15 percent of fixed investments by the private sector in the United States. The ratio of new investments in digital technologies to labor costs approached 5 percent. The ability to exploit IT was thus partially due to the suitability of using IT instead of other factors of production, such as ordinary capital or labor.[25]

The direct contribution of the computer is difficult to quantify because when companies and government agencies were investing substantially in computers, they were also acquiring other types of technology, all in the spirit of leveraging new tools to improve operations. In the case of government agencies, the improvements might not have been for economic reasons but to improve services (e.g., mail-sorting machines) or safety (e.g., the Department of Defense's insistence that military aircraft be designed by using CAD/CAM applications). Even in industries in which one would have expected to see very stable technologies, such as railroads, new locomotives that displaced earlier models in the 1950s–1980s were often more fuel-efficient or had more automated (later computerized) functions. In every industry studied by the U.S. Bureau of Labor Statistics (BLS) over a 20-year period in its attempt to document the role of technology, multiple technologies came into use simultaneously with the computer.[26] Thus, breaking out the specific effects of computers is often difficult to do and, in fact, has not yet been accomplished.

Evidence collected from industry reports and consultants' analyses in the second half of the century suggests that there were sources of productivity evident to managers who were acquiring computers. Citing an example from the 1970s—by which time American companies had been installing computers for some two decades—one report of a survey of managers named four sources of distinct advantages, all related to increased control over operations. The first source of benefits involved a broadened scope of automation made possible by optimizing product quality control in complex operations, all the way to monitoring and controlling various production processes. A second source came from simplifying the design of traditional control systems: "Since these are often electromechanical in nature—such as tape readers in a hard-wired N/C system or relays in a transfer line—system reliability is markedly improved." A third type led to increased flexibility in modifying a system because of software, which, unlike most hardware, could be modified, that is, reprogrammed. The fourth was "a simple computer system controlling a machinery operation can often be used . . . for other general-purpose processing." This study cited, as examples, reports on operations and inventory control.[27]

These four sources of benefits did not sound as exciting and elegant as did discussions about national economic trends and corporate practices, but they were the reality behind a company's, and hence a nation's, rates of productivity in the use of computing. Once again, we see that any understanding of the role of computing had to bring us back (or down) to the level of how this technology was used within a firm. That exercise forces us to consider such traditional managerial concerns as operational efficiencies and speed of execution, twin issues that normally and historically led management to invest in a variety of technologies, not just computing.

The answer to the problem proposed by some, however, was to ignore these realities and instead to admonish management to pay increased attention to the tasks of running companies more effectively. Specifically with regard to technology (one of several areas of focus for them), and drawing on manufacturing's experience, they suggested that management first had to sort the kinds of activities a firm did into either transaction or data-processing orientations. Second, managers should apply appropriate technologies to improve efficiencies of either type since the technical tools for each differ. This is an elegant way of pointing out a lesson of past experience with computers: the most effective uses of computers often came when industry-specific forms of digital technology were used. Examples include ATMs in banking, point-of-sale terminals in retail, CAD/CAM systems in manufacturing, robots in manufacturing floor activities, and modeling software for, say, master production scheduling and shop floor data collection in factories. Proper use of technology makes automation possible, makes distribution of work more effective, and leads to closer links with customers and suppliers. Strategies and specifics have to vary because service sector industries are more diverse than in manufacturing. But the point is that management, not machines, is the issue, even the source, of the problem, a reaffirmation that technological determinism is not (let alone the operative reality). Rather, managerial and business practices and economic circumstances were the imperatives at work.[28]

Recent Developments

During the second half of the 1990s, economists began to look at the returns on investment in information technology across many countries at both the firm and national levels. Several striking facts are now becoming very clear. First, new investments in IT in highly developed and productive economies frequently amounted to 53 percent of the growth in GDP, whereas investments in non-IT capital expenditures were often far lower. Two economists, Sanjeev Dewan and Kenneth L. Kraemer, have made the important observation that in all probability the returns on IT were made possible because those economies had already made investments in other types of capital goods, leaving IT as the next fruitful area of investment. In those countries with the highest investment per employee in IT, Dewan and Kraemer saw the greatest productivity in the late 1990s. The United States led the world. Those countries in which investments in infrastructures (including organizational architectures more suited to highly advanced economies), training, machinery, and then IT were the lowest turned in the poorest performance. Dewan and Kraemer calculated that IT capital growth contributed 1.21 percent out of the total U.S. GDP growth of 2.9 percent per year over the course of 1985–1993, years in which computers supposedly did not help the economy: "IT investment accounted for roughly 41 percent of U.S. GDP growth in the period 1985–1993." Complimenting the findings of Biema and Greenwald, they suggested that further enhancements on return could be derived not just by investing in IT but also in combination with "complementary investments in such factors as infrastructure and human capital, as well as a steady 'informatization' of business models." Those countries that have already developed advanced economies are in the best shape to take advantage of investments in digital technologies. Dewan and Kraemer forecasted that demand for IT would remain strong because of the positive experience with prior investments in this technology.[29] The next nine chapters of this book document what these investments turned out to be, suggesting that we could anticipate additional similar investments in the future. As the economy began its slow recovery in late 2002, once again one could see an increase in investments in IT start again.

Studying applications can help clarify how and when computers helped or hurt productivity. Although it remains unclear to what extent such an exercise will resolve the issue, IT professionals in the 1980s and early 1990s increasingly came to believe that designing applications that optimized computers, as opposed to forcing software to conform to prior manual systems, held the key to gains in productivity. Thomas H. Davenport, the widely read expert in computing and process redesign of the early 1990s, made this point, arguing that changing the nature of work leads to improved productivity. In a study on that design point in 50 companies, he observed that when processes were changed at the same time that computers were integrated into those renovated processes, the opportunity for improved productivity existed and was often realized: "If nothing changes about the way work is done and the role of IT is simply to automate an existing process, economic benefits are likely to be minimal."[30]

Economists have yet to study the effect of IT at the process (work) level in any significant way. A few scattered studies on the manufacturing and insurance industries, for example,[31] produced insufficient quantities of evidence—which is why looking at what people did to change the nature of work, especially when they used computers as part of that effort, offer insights into sources of productivity. It is also why understanding the adoption and use of applications is such a critical exercise. The effort has to be historical in perspective because it took time for any organization or industry to understand how best to optimize a technology. That was the finding of historian JoAnne Yates, for example, in her study of five firms, which adopted a variety of paper-based information-handling tools between the late nineteenth century and the 1920s.[32] Davenport made the same point for computers in the 1950s–1980s. His own taxonomy of the sources for work (process) innovations that leveraged computer technology most effectively is a useful guidepost for testing the motivation and role of applications installed in American corporations in the second half of the twentieth century. Briefly cataloged, they are automation to eliminate human labor in a process, information to capture data for understanding and insight, tracking to monitor the status of work, analysis to improve decision making, sequencing to change the order in which tasks are done or are reorganized for parallel operations, geographic for coordinating work across multiple locations (e.g., countries or states), integration to coordinate the work among multiple processes and work, intellectual for the purpose of sharing intellectual capital (today's knowledge management practices), and disintermediation for eliminating unproductive intermediaries in work.[33]

How Did People Learn About Computers?

"How did people learn about computers?" is a good question, but let us ask it in historical terms: how did business and government managers hear about these new technologies in the first place? It is an important question to answer because it is not just the story of some computer salespeople turning up at a manager's doorstep to sell a machine. Nor is it the impersonal story of economic productivity data. What people believed about computers, firms, and industries made up the reality of how computers affected the U.S. economy. The selection of applications was a very human event, not the cold act of computer chips or impersonal economic or technological imperatives. The process of discovery sheds light on how managers arrived at their decision to use this technology, although listening to salespeople was one way. It is not a story about a technological revolution or an epiphany, but rather of a slow process of realization that a new technology had possibilities.

People found out about computers in essentially three ways. First, they read newspapers, magazines, journals, and books on the new technology. Closely tied to these publications were presentations at conferences, some of which were later published as articles by consultants, engineers, and data-processing personnel. Second, people heard about these machines in their own organizations, usually in dialogue with data-processing "systems men" who had worked with precomputer technologies, such as IBM's punch-card tabulating equipment or with the many accounting machines made by Burroughs. Vendors of this technology were the third source, initially the inventors themselves, such as John Mauchly and J. Presper Eckert, creators of the UNIVAC I, in the late 1940s and early 1950s, and, later, engineers and salespeople from such suppliers as Sperry, Burroughs, GE, and IBM. All three sources—writers or speakers, internal experts, and vendors—were simultaneously active, proved influential, and were in wide evidence first in the United States.

To understand how managers learned about computers, we need to have a sense of what the sources offered to promote the new technology. All three had several features in common. They were boosters of the new technology, touting the features and benefits of computers and often exaggerating their capabilities. All three had a vested interest in the success of this technology. Writers and conference organizers saw these machines as modern, exciting topics. Systems men saw career opportunities, but so, too, did editors and salespeople. Each also believed in the value of this new technology.[34]

American publications, tangible demonstrations of this interest, were the first sources to consult for the earliest commentary on these new "giant brains." Publications and conferences were also the earliest sources of widely available information. As people read about computers in magazines and journals, they also began to hear about them at business conferences. Early users often described their experiences in print and in presentations. Managers at one firm would visit those who had already started to use computers, informally learning from each other. Vendors, of course, also promoted their products through presentations, visits to other installations, and product demonstrations. It was the combination of these activities—publications, presentations, sales activities, and visits to users—that made it possible for managers and their technical staffs (often end users) to learn enough to decide whether or not to install computers. A short review of the first step—publications—suggests how information disseminated and influenced impressions people developed about computing.[35]

Role of Publications

During World War II a shroud of secrecy hung over computer projects in Europe and the United States that kept even the existence of these machines from the public. Within six months after the end of the war, press articles began appearing and new machines were covered as important news stories.[36] In time, the trade and industry press published lengthier reviews, which described what functions computers performed, how they did so, and the costs and benefits involved. During the late 1950s and early 1960s, the number of articles, journals, and books covering the story grew fourfold from the 1950s. Advertisements followed a similar pattern of dissemination.[37] After the arrival of the personal computer—which came to dominate the literature on computing—in the 1980s, the number of articles ran into the tens of thousands. In the 1990s, the Internet dwarfed all other coverage of computing and information handling.[38]

In the period 1950–1965—when mainframe systems were first introduced and widely adopted, particularly by large American corporations—a broad variety of commercial publications carried articles on computing, as did the leading general business press like *Business Week, Dun's Review, Fortune*, and *U.S. News & World Report*. So, too, did more general trade publications, for example, the *New York Times Magazine, New Yorker*, and *Reader's Digest*. By the mid-1950s, business publications routinely exposed their readers to computer technology. These included *American City* (for public officials), *Architectural Record, Bankers Monthly, Best's Insurance News, Business Horizons, Harvard Business Review, Management Science, Office Executive, Publishers Weekly*, and *Science News Letter*. Computer industry journals also emerged, aimed primarily at the new data-processing community, most notably *Datamation*. Book publishers that specialized in business publications did the same: Addison-Wesley, Harper & Brothers, John Wiley & Sons, McGraw-Hill, Prentice-Hall, and Reinhold Publishing Company, to mention a few. Book publishers were the main source for technical literature, for example, on how computers worked and how to program in a specific software language, and they produced hundreds of "how to" guides for the management of systems and applications, although computer vendors published thousands of user manuals. All of this activity occurred during the first 15 years of the commercial life of computers.[39]

In this first period, every major type of application being installed received impressive amounts of coverage, as the notes for the chapters in this book amply demonstrate. Accountants heard about how best to use computers to audit transactions in their journals. Inventory control was a particularly favorite subject across many industries. Bankers heard about computers, and engineers learned about Fortan, the new programming language designed for them. Insurance managers found much to read, as did the military, hospital administrators, public officials, and members of the Retail Industry.

In the second period, from 1966 to roughly 1990, after which PCs and the Internet dominated the literature, almost every widely distributed magazine and journal in the United States published something about computers. In addition to the basic business, engineering, and scientific articles of the first period, which editors kept publishing throughout the second half of the twentieth century, other topics crept into print. Their appearance demonstrated the ongoing diffusion of knowledge about computing in the American economy, covering such themes as movie making, legal issues, art, computer dating, cryptology, decision making, computer aided instruction (CAI), graphics, marketing, process control, personal computing, printing, railroads, space exploration, sports, and transportation. Book publishers continued to bring out technical "how to" literature along with hundreds of management and business books about technology and its use. In this second period, discussions about applications roughly equaled the volume of material appearing on the technology itself.[40]

In the third period—roughly 1990 to the present—the same kinds of literature as before appeared, aimed at management and business and government users of information technology. In fact, this literature appeared in even larger numbers. However, all of it was dwarfed by a new genre of publication: articles and books aimed at the individual user, the layperson, so to speak, first on personal computers and then about the Internet. By the late 1990s, it was not uncommon for a large American bookstore (such as Borders or Barnes and Noble) to have 3 to 4 percent of its in-store inventory devoted to personal computers and the Internet.[41] Much like its predecessors, this new body of material explained how the technology worked, what to use it for, how to do so, and the benefits of such usage. With a third of American homes wired for the Internet, roughly 15 percent of the U.S. population going online daily in 2000, and over 40 percent of all employees doing the same at work, it was understandable why this body of literature would be so huge.[42]

Given the large volume of materials published in the United States, which far exceeded that published on the same topic in Europe and Asia, we can safely conclude that the exposure any literate American received on the subject was massive and continuous. By the late 1970s, many young managers felt compelled to be computer literate, and by the end of the 1980s, most senior executives had grown up in their careers with some exposure to computing.[43] In addition, by the late 1970s, no student in a business administration curriculum escaped some exposure either to the management of computers or to their applications; this was especially the case with graduate students in the hard and social sciences and in business. By the 1990s, even venerable publications like the *Wall Street Journal* and the *New York Times* routinely published technology columns and also had online editions available on the Internet.[44]

Other Sources of Exposure

Radio and TV exposure followed in due course, through the use of computers in live broadcasts of political events, in TV shows presenting answers spit out by computers, and later as props for various comedic and dramatic programming. No event on television proved more revealing and dramatic in publicizing computers to the American public than the presidential elections in 1952. CBS News used a UNIVAC I on election night, November 4, 1952, on live television to predict the outcome of the election. On the basis of early returns from 27 states (3.4 million voters of an expected 60 million) at 8:30 P.M. eastern standard time, the computer "predicted" the outcome correctly to within 4 electoral votes. The impression left with people proved to be extraordinary: smart brains had arrived in American society.[45] The process of exposure in the electronic media has continued unabated to the present day. Thus, for instance, in the 1990s, the resurgence of talk radio provided a natural venue for thousands of discussions over the radio waves about all kinds of topics related to computers.

American moviemakers became interested in computers as the source of stories and themes beginning in the late 1950s. Since then, several such movies appeared each year. Initially, movies did little to inform the public. Rather, they more often reflected themes and concerns already evident in society. The two primary themes were computers as part of crime or computers that were controlling people, workplaces, or the world. *Desk Set* (1957) was the first widely seen American movie involving computers. Starring Spencer Tracy and Katharine Hepburn in a light comedy, it reflected the concerns some Americans had about losing their jobs to computers. In this case, Hepburn, a librarian, was about to be replaced by a computer. The story ends on a happy note, and she does not lose her job because the computer could not perform as well as she in providing answers. A decade later, another widely seen movie, *2001: A Space Odyssey* (1968), had a computer (HAL) that was trying to take over a spaceship. Although computers were used in films almost every year since 1957, movies were more literary and thematic devices than factual sources of information about the technology.[46]

Discussions about potential uses of computers took place within companies and government agencies almost from the first day the press began to cover the subject. A variety of groups within organizations participated on a regular basis and in a similar fashion across many industries. One very large group of technically knowledgable individuals were the systems people, who in the precomputer era either ran large data-processing departments, normally using IBM tabulating equipment, or designed work flows. They often integrated these with machinery from Burroughs, NCR, Remington Rand (later UNIVAC), IBM, and others. Engineers and other technical staffs made up a second group of individuals exposed early on to computers through their own technical journals and societies. This constituency in some cases wanted to invent their own machines and developed much original software.[47] A third, and the one that emerged last, involved line staffs and managers, who by the late 1960s had been sufficiently exposed to computers to understand how they might be deployed. In the earliest years, the leading advocates for using computers in a firm were systems people and engineers. It is not clear yet whether this was also the case in large U.S. and state government agencies. But we do know that in the early 1960s accountants had joined the ranks, and by the end of the decade so had managers from across most functions of an enterprise. This pattern roughly paralleled what occurred with the types of literature of the period. By the early 1990s, one could characterize as ubiquitous across the American work force the availability of some knowledge of computers and applications, as well as skill in using PCs, and argue that they profoundly influenced how organizations were run.[48]

In the early decades of the twentieth century there existed in large companies and government agencies people called systems men. In the decades following World War II, their ranks swelled and they proved highly influential in convincing firms to start using computers. They ran the data-processing operations, using such equipment as punch-card tabulators from IBM and complex billing machinery from Burroughs. They also led the rationalization of work into organized processes. In the early days of the computer, they frequently were asked to do the initial studies to determine whether or not such technology should be used by their enterprise. Often, these technocrats were strong proponents of what they called managerial information, a notion linking reports, information technology, and the flow of data in an enterprise. When the computer came along, they saw this new technology as additional armament in their arsenal of weapons. Although this is not the place to review the history of systems men, it is appropriate to emphasize the fact that they were in place when the computer came along.[49] Because of that fact, systems personnel made it possible for companies to look at computers by deploying a certain amount of technical expertise already on staff. It would be difficult to imagine the adoption of computers in commercial and government agencies for normal accounting and business applications as early as this occurred if these individuals had not been present. Someone had to assess the viability of the new technology and translate what it was into terms that made sense to general management, and these were some of the best equipped people to do so. This role is still played by IT professionals.[50]

The computer also became available at the same time that a new round of interest developed in systematizing work. Richard F. Neuschel's book, *Streamlining Business Procedures* (1950), did for the systems people what John Diebold's volume did for manufacturing executives who were advocating automation. Neuschel's arguments had the additional attraction of calling for systems men to report to chief executives, a suggestion that the systems people endorsed but that was not adopted by senior executives.[51] Almost all large organizations, such as those listed in the Fortune 500, and all cabinet-level departments in the U.S. government, had these kinds of employees. A reflection of the influence of the computer could be seen when the major professional association of systems men, the National Machine Accountants Association (founded in 1951 and which, by the late 1950s, had over 8,000 members), changed its name to the Data Processing Management Association (DPMA). It remained the leading organization for American IT professionals through the rest of the century.[52] Thus DPMA, or more specifically its members, along with a growing cast of consultants and business management professors in the 1960s, made headway in convincing managers that computers could be used for more than just capturing information and lowering costs. They could be deployed to support managerial decision making and to renovate existing work practices. For a while these people even debated the use of computers to create comprehensive information systems, often using the word *total* to describe them.[53]

By the late 1970s, that notion had evolved into management information systems (MIS), a perspective on the role of computing and a phrase that remained in the lexicon for the rest of the century. There were difficulties with the concept and the contribution of the systems men who were now IT professionals because by the 1980s there were many critics of computing. They argued that companies had not yet saved money by implementing IT systems, a position that fed right into the discussion about the productivity paradox. Nonetheless, technically proficient people in American corporations in their various roles provided a great deal of focus on how computers would be used through the second half of the twentieth century. Because they were promoting their own careers and influence at the same time did not change the fact that they served as an important channel for information about IT to flow throughout an organization. Indeed, one could argue, particularly for the 1960s and 1970s and again after the arrival of the Internet, that the IT community constituted the most important channel of information for senior management, increasingly finding their voice as computing became a greater issue for general managers.

Role of Vendors

Of course they were not the only source of insight and expertise available to line management. Computer vendors quickly became another pocket of information whose role evolved over time. In the late 1940s and 1950s, engineers who developed computers personally reached out to government agencies and corporations to explain what their computers could do, a process that continued into the late 1950s. By that time, companies like IBM, Sperry Univac, and Burroughs had begun the process of transferring selling responsibilities to sales forces trained to do this work, relieving engineers of that responsibility and in the process turning that role over to people more capable of "pushing iron." By the end of the 1950s, all major vendors had created sales forces to sell computers, usually having to replace earlier sales teams ill prepared to sell the new technology. Management recruited a new generation of sales and support personnel, largely made up of college graduates who often had technical degrees. By the mid-1960s, the major suppliers had created whole divisions of salespeople, as in the case of IBM with its Data Processing Division (formed in May 1959), which quickly acquired a reputation of being staffed with outstanding salespeople, inheriting the image carefully developed by the firm in its precomputer days. Direct sales forces became the preferred channel of communication by both vendors and customers in the 1960s and 1970s because of the high information and technical content of the required discussions. Their conversations centered on such issues as technical features, cost justification, and application of software tools, particularly packages that began to appear in the second half of the 1960s.[54] In the 1980s, specialized software vendors and business partners (e.g., retail outlets for PCs and other small data-processing products) worked with major suppliers to reach their customers.[55]

The arrival of the personal computer, and the decline in the cost of many software products and peripheral hardware equipment, led to mass commoditization of IT goods and services during the 1980s. This took several forms: PCs, for example, kept dropping in price, selling by the millions with razor-thin profit margins. Over time customers viewed IBM PCs and IBM-compatible PCs as one and the same, acknowledging only minimal differences among brands. The PCs were also sold almost like commodities: in bulk, in retail chains like any other consumer electronics product, and with minimal direct selling by specialized sales forces. This last circumstance was unlike the way in which mainframe computers were sold by specialized sales staffs, calling on potential buyers. Customers still relied on vendors for information about new products and their capabilities, but they could also turn to PC dealers and other small firms for different, similar, and often rival interpretations of information.[56]

In the 1980s, the computer industry fundamentally changed, moving from integrated, vertical providers of "everything" (economists speak of vertically integrated suppliers) to niche players, competing with the traditional mainframe vendors over specific peripherals and software packages and tools. This changed circumstance gave a potential user a growing number of salespeople to meet with and a breathtaking variety of publications about computing to turn to; indeed sources of information expanded exponentially by the early 1990s.[57] That increase of information from so many sources made keeping up with the technology, on the one hand, harder but, on the other hand, simultaneously easier. It became more difficult to absorb available data because an individual now had to look at more information, and it was easier because one could just focus on a narrow, specific issue. By the mid-1990s, the Internet's arrival exacerbated the flood of information while providing yet another channel of data from vendors, associations, and consultants.

Large firms and government agencies almost universally employed dedicated, full-time sales personnel assigned to them by office machine manufacturers from the earliest decades of the twentieth century. When the computer came along, that coverage remained intact because it was practical and affordable; only the personnel changed to reflect the new knowledge required to sell computers. To this day, the largest organizations in the world have dedicated sales and services personnel from all major vendors, such as IBM, EDS, and Hewlett-Packard. Starting essentially in the 1950s, major suppliers of data processing (DP) consulting services, such as Arthur Andersen in the 1950s and IBM in the 1990s, also assigned full-time personnel to their largest accounts.[58] Frequently, very large applications required outside expertise to implement. The first use of computers in a commercial setting, at GE, was made possible by bringing in Arthur Andersen's technical personnel to assist in designing processes, writing software, and getting them launched. By the end of the 1990s, over a third of IBM's revenues came from similar work.[59] No vendor of complex application software could have hoped to install its products by the late 1950s, or really across the entire period to the present, without offering considerable help to a client either as part of the price of the software or as separate billable services. Frequently (many might say normally), when companies attempted to implement completely on their own, they failed or never fully completed the job.[60]

Arrival of Commercial Software

A related trend that first appeared in the mid-1960s, and had become a major practice by the end of the 1970s, was the acquisition of commercially available application software by companies and, later, by government agencies. In the 1950s, for example, if a company wanted a billing package, its own staff had to write it. By the early 1970s, the same firm could buy a prewritten software package that did billing. Installing a software product or system took less time than writing one's own, usually proved easier and frequently cheaper, and typically had all the important functions a normal billing package should have. Firms then modified a package to meet their specific needs, but essentially the move to software products became a widespread practice, one that continues to this day. In the course of that changed approach, major software product firms emerged; Microsoft and SAP are only two of the most visible today. Thousands operated in the U.S. economy, often as small niche players with a few, highly specialized products, normally aimed at specific industries. These products, for example, included routing analyzers for the Trucking Industry and shop floor data collection packages for the Automotive Industry. Notable exceptions were accounting packages, which were sold across multiple industries.[61] Ironically, acquisition of software packages from multiple vendors created a standards problem for MIS organizations called upon to support these products. To gain efficiencies from economies of scale, MIS organizations began imposing standards on end users, stating, for example, which word-processing packages (in the 1970s) or ERP software (in the 1990s) they would support.

Packages had their fashions too, some more attractive in one industry or another at different times. For PCs, by the late 1990s, industry and product watchers ranked packages according to popularity (usually by sales or user feedback on quality), much like movies, music, and best-selling books. In public sector data centers, software packages designed to do something unique created an incentive to standardize across the nation. This was the case, for instance, with software packages that conformed to some federal standard for how reimbursements would be made for Medicare, grants, and so forth. To a lesser yet significant degree, the same occurred in the private sector. A recent example from the 1990s was SAP's ERP software, used by manufacturing companies all over the world. There were other vendors of ERP software, but SAP's products dominated. Packages constantly rose and fell in popularity. In the world of PCs, WordPerfect was the word processor of choice in the early 1980s, but by the early 1990s over 70 percent of all word-processing software came from Microsoft (Word), some 90 percent by the end of the decade.[62] Normally, packages not kept up to date by vendors fell by the wayside. Being up to date means running on the latest computers (and their operating systems) and having new functions comparable to those of competitors in their software.

The pattern of information about computers that came into all organizations is clear. First, a small group of experts talked among themselves in the 1950s, probably no more than 10,000 by the mid-1950s. Published information circulated in large amounts and quickly by the end of the 1950s. Vendors multiplied, as did the number of consultants, DP professionals and associations, and other sources of information. The PC, and later the Internet, caused another explosion in the amount and sources of information available to anyone interested in computing. It was so much the case that one could speak about computing being relatively ubiquitous by the late 1990s, and the average American worker and child were also somewhat informed. That availability of information about computing, which progressed so rapidly through American society in the past half century, was the basic reason that so much had been spent on computing and why Americans relied on this technology.[63]

Put another way, when people did not know about computing technology, they did not adopt it. As they learned about a new product that worked, they did. To be sure, the technology had to evolve, become more affordable, and easier to use, but when information about these changes was not shared, deployment came slower. In those cases in which information (and marketing) about products were poorly disseminated, even though the machines or software were good, they were not widely adopted.[64] Examples also existed in which information was excellent but not the product. Information helped kill those products, often very quickly.[65] In other words, it was not good enough to have a fine product; one needed information about it, too.

Types of Applications Introduced Into the American Economy

With all this activity in adoption of computers and software, were there also discernable patterns in the types of applications acquired over time? It is an important question because one of the findings presented in this book is that companies and agencies borrowed ideas and practices from one another. Historians of business history and business professionals have long understood the concept of learning from other industries. That is why case studies at the Harvard Business School, MIT's Sloan School, Stanford University, and the Haas School at the University of California at Berkeley, as well as "best practices" among consultants and experts, have long been standard fare for management.[66] So, one should expect to see in the acquisition of software and applications the same practice at work. Indeed, in the discussion in chapter 1 about standards, at a technical level that was the case. With applications, a similar pattern played out from one industry to another, with fundamental differences that were often more a question of timing because one industry might embrace an application or technology sooner or later than another. The causes of various rates of adoption are explored in subsequent chapters.

At the risk of overgeneralizing, it is useful to understand some patterns of adoption and, equally, broad types of applications. At the birth of the computer in the 1940s, there were two types of applications: military and scientific. First, the Allied military community had to worry about cracking German military codes and building the atomic bomb, along with designing artillery fire control processes. By the late 1940s and continuing to the present, a long line of applications appeared in every line of scientific inquiry. Astronomers, designers of spacecraft, the medical profession, biologists, geologists, physicists, chemists, and so forth, all created a variety of applications to facilitate study of their disciplines. Typically, these were numerically intense applications that called on computers to perform a great many calculations. That requirement led to the early development of supercomputers and stimulated the continued introduction of larger machines. In time, computers affected how scientific research was done.[67]

A second category of uses, which appeared in the early 1950s, has come to be referred to as business applications (on which most of this book is focused). At first—in the 1950s and early 1960s—preexisting accounting practices were automated, often being moved from tabulating and billing equipment to computers because they could be performed quicker and with less human labor, thereby lowering operating costs. If one were to write a history of accounting applications, the story would be about the ever-increasing migration of accounting to computers, speeding up their turnaround of reports from quarterly or monthly to weekly or daily and from only large companies to the private individual, sitting at the PC. As with computers in scientific research, by the 1970s one could see the technology beginning to affect accounting practices, initially providing increasing amounts and variety of data more frequently and putting stress on long-established accounting practices.[68] Other business-related uses, particularly after about 1965, included online searches for information housed in computers on all kinds of topics—today a major application of the Internet—along with communications within organizations, such as e-mail, presentations, reports (word processing), and online business functions like computerized procurement and order taking. In short, business applications tended to be data-intensive. Scientists needed a great deal of computing (calculating) power. Users of business applications required extensive data storage and access to it.

A third category of applications involved engineering. This class of uses encompassed a wide variety of applications, ranging from the design of products (e.g., using CAD software) to automated manufacturing (using CAM software). Every major industry had engineering-oriented applications specific to that industry. Take the case of manufacturing: by the late 1960s, engineers had developed applications for creating bills of material, doing data collection, and continuously performing material requirements planning and production planning. Shop floor data collection, purchasing, forecasting, and capacity planning were all computerized in the 1960s and had become, by the early 1970s, the way in which one ran a factory. As in accounting, observers noted that the adoption of such applications had become "a quiet revolution"[69]

One can also think of another class of applications, smaller in deployment in the early years of computing but massive in the 1990s, the era of personal computers, in the form of games and entertainment. Historians have barely started to look at these applications, although economists and reporters have been documenting the major events in this class of use because it is one of the fastest-growing. Historians argue that entertainment as an application motivated developers of computer technology to provide additional innovations, which, after their initial use in entertainment, were ported over to such traditional areas as accounting and other business uses.[70] This pattern was especially evident in such tasks as the use of graphics to represent data. Computers create fantastic images of realistically looking dinosaurs and other monsters in movies and enrich the experience of playing electronic games. Games played on computers always existed, such as Baseball and Hangman, using punch cards on IBM computers in the 1950s, Pacman on smaller machines online in the early 1980s, and interactive games on the Internet with PCs today. But not until the 1980s could one speak of games as a class of applications that attracted significant amounts of attention. Today they represent some of the most innovative, leading-edge applications coming to a computer near you.[71]

Another way of looking at applications is by the function a computer performs. For example, one can speak about optical character recognition (OCR), used to read a signature on a check to confirm authenticity.[72] Another is image processing, which is increasingly being used in the medical profession to represent images of the human body in diagnostics, as well as scientific applications, for instance, in presenting representations of atoms.[73] One could refer to just about any type of technology as the lens through which to see applications. The examples cited in this paragraph are also cases of looking at applications from the perspective of the engineer, computer scientist, or technologist. It is, in short, a technocentric view of applications. It is also how the majority of writers who comment on the use of computers have looked at applications.[74]

There are both advantages and disadvantages of looking at applications in this way. The most obvious advantage is the fact that many of the base technologies that made it possible to do such things as scanning (OCR) were usable in many applications and industries, from using checks as data input to speeding up cash register operations in a supermarket. Vendors of hardware and software would take a technology like OCR and apply it to products aimed at specific industries, for example, to banks and supermarkets. Experiences thus gained were then applied to create yet additional uses of the technology. Again, to use OCR, check scanning arrived in the late 1950s, scanners in supermarkets in the early 1970s, and hand-held portable scanners for taking notes from printed text in the late 1990s.[75]

The fundamental disadvantage of this view is that it puts primacy of focus on the technology, not on the application or the reasons for adoption in the first place. This approach also encourages deemphasizing the effects of the application on users and their organizations. It would be as if we focused on the applications of the technology that made an automatic transmission possible in a car. It is a fascinating story, one dating back to the 1920s, but not where the real significance rests. It was not until the automatic transmission became widely available in cars in the 1960s that the really important story became obvious: this application did more to encourage Americans to drive than any other technical automotive innovation in the twentieth century. Few drivers care about how the technology works, only that the car has it and that it is working today. Why people were attracted to this application, how it encouraged them to drive, and the effects of more Americans driving make up the far more important story for historians. Had scholars limited themselves to a description of the application made possible by the technology involved, they would have missed the larger significance. They still needed to understand how the technology underlying automatic transmissions came to be and how it became a feature on cars, but only as an intermediary step to their broader appreciation of the role of automatic transmission first in cars, next in buses, and finally in trucks and other vehicles.

It is time to look at computer applications not just as a series of technological innovations applied in novel ways but also as a series of business and user choices and actions that in turn influenced how people lived and worked. In short, the study of the history of computer applications is far more than a story of technology, science, or engineering; it is the larger story about business practices, the nature of economic activity, and about how people spent vast amounts of their time both at work and in their private lives.[76] To get the nuances of the story right does require, however, a healthy understanding of the interaction of technological underpinnings and their innovations, coupled to their applications. These in turn must be situated into the environment of the users of these applications. Since the majority of computer usage during the twentieth century occurred in work settings, and work settings in turn are in companies within industries, looking at industry-centric applications offers a new and open window into the history of computing, business activities, the nature of work, and effects on the economy, society, and the individual. In short, it is the next logical step in understanding the profound role of the digital on the United States. The extent of the deployment of computing begins to suggest how big a story this has become.

How Extensively Were Computers Used?

Deployment of computing in the American economy became massive. We know this from a large number of data sources. We know how many computers and software tools were sold to companies and individuals over the years. We know the value of these commodities because the U.S. government continuously measured and studied the issue throughout most of the period under study. Computer industry associations and publications constantly counted machines and IT professionals. We know how many people studied computing in colleges and universities and graduated with degrees in computer science. We know how many members there were of various industry associations interested in computer-based applications, such as the American Production and Inventory Control Society (APICS) in manufacturing or the Life Office Management Association (LOMA) in insurance.[77] Lecht's quotation at the start of this chapter illustrates the nose counting Americans have done and continue to do. A month does not go by without some organization or government agency, for example, announcing the extent to which Americans are using PCs, the Internet, or wireless communications. The Organization for Economic Cooperation and Development (OECD) does the same for Western Europe. Americans live in a counting culture; quantification is a central feature of modern information.

Reviewing all these data would easily fill the rest of this book; however, a few general observations are essential (and enough) if we are to understand the magnitude of the use of applications described in subsequent chapters. Although I touched on deployment in chapter 1, bringing that discussion together with the classes of applications just described begins to fill in details in the broad picture that is needed before examining applications within industries.

The value of computer chips is a good place to begin. When first invented, they were primarily put into computers. By 1983, only half went into computers; the rest were used in telecommunications, industrial devices, and test equipment. By the end of the 1980s, they were appearing in significant quantities in consumer goods, from kitchen tools to games and programmable stereos and TV sets. In that same year, automobiles absorbed 6 percent of all chips. In 1983, Americans consumed 38.1 percent of the world's production of computer chips. Then came massive adoption of the PC, which drove demand up even further, as discussed in chapter 1. Manufacturing industries in 1950 bought half of all the accounting equipment available in the U.S. economy. By the end of 1980, they acquired only a third, and by 1991, 21 percent, which tells us that computing had diffused widely across many other industries. The suppliers of computing had gone from annually producing several million dollars' worth of products in the early 1950s to being an industry with sales in excess of a trillion dollars at the dawn of the new century.

Economists have nibbled at the issue of deployment by documenting how much American organizations spent on computing, specifically hardware. Machines are capital goods, and capital investments have long been tracked by U.S. government agencies and by many economists. The data are quite impressive. In 1970, computer hardware accounted for less than 1 percent of total capital investments in the U.S. economy, then rose steadily through the rest of the century. By 1993, just before the wide deployment of the Internet, these investments accounted for 18 percent of such expenditures. The cost of equipment declined throughout the same period by 15.1 percent. What this tells us is that the number of machines in American organizations increased each year by far larger amounts than the percentages just cited would suggest. To be sure, equipment was not static. As a great deal of new equipment came into organizations, so, too, a large amount of "tired iron" was discarded.[78]

Did these investments vary by industry? The distribution of nominal net stock of office equipment from 1950 to 1993 suggests that over 75 percent of the U.S. hardware went into service-producing industries by 1993. Economists define service-producing industries as banking (finance), insurance, and real estate, some of the most extensive investors in this technology by the 1990s. In 1950, their proportion of investments was less than 50 percent. But the extent of the service sector investment should not be a surprise since this part of the U.S. economy grew the largest in the second half of the twentieth century. Already by the end of 1992, for instance, this sector generated over 70 percent of the economy's output and acquired some 70 percent of the nation's nonresidential private capital stock. Those two percentages continued to rise throughout the 1990s. Manufacturing accounted for just over 48 percent of investments in 1950, dropped to 30 percent in 1980, and remained at slightly above 21 percent in the early 1990s. Wholesale trade went from 6.3 percent of the total in 1950 to 11.9 percent in 1993; retail trade, from 3.7 percent to 7.8 percent. The data, in short, are a rough analog of where computers resided in the economy, and hence where the applications did too.

Since the patterns of adoption were created during the first quarter century of use, how computers dispersed across the economy in the early years gives us insight about the basic question of which industries did these systems reside in. Table 2.1 lists Univac systems by industry at the time that most American firms were initially yet aggressively installing their first or second systems. The table presents evidence that computers were most frequently deployed in the earliest years in many industries. Manufacturing firms were extensive early users. As other industries acquired computers, the percentage of total systems in American manufacturing industries declined, even if the total number of computers actually increased. An inventory of installed Burroughs systems for the same period provides additional evidence of broad and early adoption of computing (see table 2.2). As table 2.3 illustrates, diversity of installation continued in the years that followed.

Another observation we can make is that a group of industries adopted the computer later but extensively (retail and wholesale, particularly financial institu-

Table 2.1
Number of Installed UNIVAC 60 and 120
Systems by Industry, Circa 1958

Manufacturing	147
Distribution	48
Government	35
Finance	18
Insurance	15
Utilities	10
Transportation	9
Others	29

Source: "Directory of Computer Users," Part IV-Section E, OAAplications Updating Services (undated, circa 1958): IV-E33–40 (listing firms by name); CBI 55, "Market Reports," Box 70, Folder 4, Archives Charles Babbage Institute, University of Minnesota, Minneapolis.

tions). A collection of service industries provided a surprise in that the number of systems installed was about the same as in all manufacturing industries once the service sector began to use this technology. As one would expect, governments were early users and supporters of computers, and therefore their percentage of the total remained quite high in the early years; over time, as the private sector acquired this technology, the government's percentage not surprisingly, declined.

Transportation remained constant, along with communications, during the first quarter century of use. However, utility industries, while also constant for many years, went through a major round of deployment in the 1970s, driven by such things as the requirement to improve efficiencies in response to sharply rising fuel costs. In aggregate, all the major sectors presented in table 2.3 adopted the computer and, over time, deployment spread out. Thus, for example, in 1959, government and manufacturing combined had over 65 percent of all systems, but 20 years later their combined total had dropped to just over 37 percent. In the 1980s and 1990s, their total percentages continued to decline as other industries progressed in their further deployment of computing technologies.

Just as these systems were deployed across a variety of industries early in the life of digital technology, the variety of applications reflected industry interests. Using the same period as the earlier tables, we can see what kinds of applications were run on both the Burroughs and UNIVAC systems, two major vendors of the period. As tables 2.4 and 2.5 illustrate, many of these firms loaded up their systems first with accounting applications.

What happened to software is also suggestive of patterns of deployment by industry. Sales of software between 1963 and 1974—a period of enormous expansion in the use of mainframe applications—went from nearly nothing to $1 billion.

Table 2.2

Installation of Burroughs 205 Systems by Industry or Function, 1955–1960

Scientific (including operations research)	44
Government	14
Manufacturing	12
Petroleum/chemical	12
Insurance	10
Service bureaus	5
Utilities	4
Distribution	3
Banking	1
Transportation	1

Source: OAApplications Update Service, "Directory of Computer Users" (November 11, 1960); CBI 55, "Market Reports," Box 70, Folder 7, Archives Charles Babbage Institute, University of Minnesota, Minneapolis.

Table 2.3

The Distribution of Computer Systems in Select Industries by Percentage, 1959–1978

Industry	1959	1968	1974	1978
Manufacturing	42.4	33.6	34.7	23.7
Transportation	3.0	3.0	3.1	3.3
Communications	1.1	1.5	1.2	—
Utilities	4.1	1.5	1.4	5.7
Wholesale/retail	1.3	10.5	12.7	7.8
Finance	9.9	15.3	11.8	18.8
Services	14.6	23.1	24.5	25.0
Government	22.9	9.8	8.5	13.6

Source: Montgomery Phister, Jr., *Data Processing Technology and Economics* (Santa Monica, Cal.: Santa Monica Publishing, 1976): 444; and his *Data Processing Technology and Economics: 1975–1978 Supplement* (Santa Monica, Cal.: Santa Monica Publishing, 1979): 652.

Table 2.4
Sample Applications Run on Various Computer Systems, September 1958

Deposit accounting	Payroll
Insurance applications	Petroleum billing and accounting
Inventory control	Production control
Order-invoice writing (billing)	Reservations
Order-sales analysis	Utility billing and accounting

Source: "Summary by Application," Part IV-Section C, OAApplications Updating Service (September 1958): IV-C1–3, CBI 55, "Market Reports," Box 70, Folder 4, Archives Charles Babbage Institute, University of Minnesota, Minneapolis.

Software sales in this period represented only a small proportion of the expenditures on applications because there were other outlays for programming, operating systems, and so forth. Best estimates of the total put the cost to American organizations in 1974 not just at $1 billion but rather closer to $10 billion.[79] Acquisition of packaged software proved extensive. As more software became available as products, one would expect to see rapid growth rates in their sale, and that is exactly what happened. Between 1984 and 1990, before the impact of PC software became so great as to influence profoundly purchase statistics, software sales grew at 13.8 percent per annum. Acquisitions as annual percentage growth rates were actually higher between 1987 and 1990, 14.7 percent to be precise.[80]

By the early 1990s, the PC had made its presence known in the world of software. In 1992, for example, 46.8 percent of all software sales in the United

Table 2.5
Sample Applications Run on Burroughs 205 Systems, 1954–1957

Wind Tunnel Data Reduction (1954)	Operations Research (1956)
Data Reduction (1954)	Petroleum Engineering 91956)
Refinery Simulation (1954)	Pipeline Network Scheduling (1956)
Training (1954)	Service Bureau Applications (1956)
Insurance Premium Calculations (1954)	Inventory Control (1956)
Petroleum Engineering (1955)	Marketing (1956)
Boiler Design (1955)	Reactor Design (1956)
Accounting (1955)	Linear Programming (1956)
Petroleum Equipment Design (1955)	Insurance Accounting (1957)
Nuclear Studies (1956)	Electric Motor Design (1957)
Scientific Calculations (1956)	Engineering Calculations (1957)

Source: "Directory of Computer Users (as of February 1958)," OAApplications Updating Service: IV-E6–8; CBI 55, "Market Reports," Box 70, Folder 4, Archives Charles Babbage Institute, University of Minnesota, Minneapolis.

States was for PC-based products; 42.6 percent of all software sales went to the more traditional markets of the 1960s, 1970s, and 1980s, that is, to data centers with mainframes, supercomputers, and minicomputers. These two sets of percentages accounted for $27.7 billion in purchases. Incidentally, video games—also an application—totaled $3.3 billion in 1992, or roughly 10.6 percent of all purchases of software in the United States. Let us look a little closer at what the owners of PCs were buying that year. Americans in 1992 spent about $5.7 billion on PC software, of which 14.4 percent went for word processors, another 13.8 percent for spreadsheets, and finally another 6.1 percent for database packages. The rest went for various other software packages, such as operating systems. During the boom period for PCs before the wide adoption of the Internet—that is, from 1987 through 1993, after which the Internet became a new factor—purchases of PC application software grew at 20.1 percent per year.[81]

Another way of looking at deployment is to measure the type of technology. One that is very symptomatic of deployment, because it could be used in a variety of applications, is the universal product code (UPC). Before the late 1980s, usage was low, only by some 50,000 enterprises in the United States. By 1994, the number of enterprises applying this technology had more than doubled and nearly doubled again by the end of the century.[82] Banking, like manufacturing, had always been labor-intensive and thus embraced the computer for its potential to lower operating costs. Today no major banking corporation is without ATMs. In fact, the few remaining small banking firms rely on networks of ATMs that are shared across multiple firms and industries, not just by banks.

Some comparative work has begun to document the relative investments in IT in various countries. A couple of brief data points suggests that the American experience was more intense earlier than in other industrialized economies. The value of this observation is simply to suggest that American companies and government agencies experienced the benefits and liabilities of applications sooner and more intensely than those other nations. Thus American managers had access to more information about what worked (or not) sooner than others. This knowledge had effects on competitiveness, innovation, and rates of profitability. The transformation of the U.S. economy into what observers increasingly want to call the Information Age can thus be tied to such issues as the rate of adoption of computing and what computers were used for across the economy. In 1986, spending on information technology in the United States, as a percentage of GDP, was 2; for Japan and Western Europe, each 1.4 percent. In 1990, the United States percentage had climbed to 2.3, Japan had jumped substantially to 2 percent, and Western Europe to 2.3 percent. In 1993, the year before the Internet began to have a profound effect on the statistical evidence, the United States had grown a little, to 2.4 percent of GDP, while Japan had declined to 1.6 percent and Western Europe to 1.8 percent. Even in 1990, when the United States was experiencing a recession, Americans increased their rate of investment in computing. Put in the arcane language of one economist, "On balance, these figures suggest that the United States is somewhat more heavily dedicated to an information-technology strategy than its competitors."[83]

A reminder of an earlier discussion: corporate budgets dedicated to IT rose from almost nothing in the early 1950s to averages of over 1–3 percent by the early 1990s. United States government surveys of the economy now suggest that at the start of the new century, Internet-based business alone accounted for between 10 and 18 percent of business activity.[84] It does not matter which number is right; the fact that there is even that much invested in a technology not generally adopted by the American public a half decade earlier is a harbinger of continued growth in the use of computer-based applications in American society.

Patterns of Diffusion

We now need to tighten up our view of how to measure the extent of diffusion of the digital and its applications. It is a difficult issue to be precise about because data on such matters are uneven in scope and quality, particularly when we try to collect them over time. What we have already seen in the first two chapters is the use of surveys, and we will see others in subsequent chapters conducted by the U.S. Bureau of Labor Statistics, for example, which counted numbers of installations or made qualitative judgments. The number of units of a particular application or machine type represents yet another way of quantifying the extent of diffusion, such as we see with such applications as inventory control and the use of numerically controlled machines. However, on a broader scale this book builds on the methodologies developed by scholars who looked at 10 different processes as implemented in several industrialized countries—Lars Nasbeth and George F. Ray. They favor counting the number of installations by company, as well as the proportion of firms in an industry that apply a particular technology. They have also argued that with this kind of data one can then deal with the larger issue of productivity, or the effect of an application on labor. Given the relatively high cost of labor across the American economy in comparison to such costs in other nations, this seems to make good sense.[85]

Their approach, the one applied already and in the chapters ahead, allows us to test some of the patterns they identified in how diffusion occurs. Briefly stated, the scholars who worked on the project noted several patterns:

- A few firms were willing to be early users of a technology, for whatever reason and despite risks of uncertainty.
- If they were successful in their implementation, other firms were then willing to use the same application because they perceived the risks of doing so to be low enough, thereby influencing rates of diffusion.
- Positive reports on use from those employing the new application carried more weight with other firms than press releases, marketing literature from vendors, and so forth.
- Modifications of early versions of an application broadened their applicability across a firm or an industry.
- Schumpeter may have been right in his belief that adoptions of a new application of technology may then come in bunches. (I prefer to think of them

as waves, often based on the patterns just noted in this list but also as a result of new releases of software, in particular.)

- Cyclical patterns in the replacement of old technologies often influenced adoption. I will show examples of how we can expand this notion to include the idea that as the cost of a particular technology dropped, more adoptions occurred (e.g., in high-performance workstations and CAD).

After a slow beginning in adoption, diffusion picked up speed, at which point several other patterns appeared:

- Managers discovered areas of adoption that were less promising than in earlier circumstances; for example, numerical controlled (N/C) technology was not as productive in an industry with very inexpensive engineers, such as in India.
- Success with an early application encouraged firms to improve current processes, a pattern clearly evident in the Automotive Industry, for example. Motivation for such improvements were typically driven by "fear of being driven out of the industry," or what I refer to from time to time as the "price of admission" to an industry, for example, requiring suppliers of components to large automotive manufacturing firms to use Internet-based purchasing applications.

The findings of these scholars led to this conclusion:

It seems that in the early stages inter-firm diffusion usually predominates, and often it takes this form exclusively for some time after the innovation. In most cases though, firms which have already introduced the new technique will eventually want to build new capacity embodying it; this may be the result of a need for additional capacity to expand production, to replace existing capacity, or to use the proven advantages of the new technique more fully.[86]

Their conclusions were based on factors that influenced diffusion: technical applicability, profitability, available costs and financial resources, size and structure of an organization, other factors such as research and development (R&D), and the attitude of management. In the chapters ahead, we see all of these elements at play in all industries.

Beyond just questions of diffusion, with such large quantities of data to draw on, can we begin to define some patterns of behavior, particularly in business, where the majority of uses always resided?

Patterns, Human Capital, and Implications for Management

Cataloging a combination of activities, in fact, reveals a fairly regular pattern of behavior concerning adoption and use of applications. They were fairly regular because they appeared in each decade in which the digital existed and were reflected in every major application. These can quickly be listed:

- Arrival, transformation, and deployment of digitally based products on a continuous basis, working in both large and small equipment
- Creation and modification of software tools and application programming to leverage and optimize new hardware tools
- Pervasive role of economic preconditions, creating nontechnical business (economic) incentives to use technology
- American proclivity to reach out to a technology to solve problems or improve productivity
- Role of competition and desire to emulate the best within an industry for competitive advantages
- Fast, free flow of information about applications throughout the economy

The list could be expanded, but the point is clear: a combination of factors always influenced events, particularly affecting the activities of end users of applications.

This list stands in sharp contrast to what one normally reads about computers. The most widely used approach to the study of computing is to look at it from the supply-side perspective, that is, from the point of view of the engineers who invented the technology or the vendors marketing it.[87] From that perspective, technological innovation, manufacturing and marketing capabilities, pricing, and market realities play a prominent role in the affairs of enterprises. However important these are for understanding the full story of how computers have and are being deployed, they are only part of the story. The perspective of the user, the acquirer of this technology, makes it possible to expand our understanding about patterns of deployment. That is why these issues, which are relatively pervasive regardless of year, company, or industry, are so important. One can conclude with some confidence that they will continue to be influential in future years, affecting adoption and use of applications.

One profound influence on end users that will not be discussed fully in this chapter but should at least be recognized is, to use an economic term, *human capital*. Economists use this term to mean the availability of the "right" skills and their amount within an economy. Windows's Word is nice, but if one does not know how to use it, that software is useless. The ERP software of SAP is powerful but equally useless if a firm does not have access to people who can install, maintain, and run this application. One limitation of this book is that it does not review the availability of employees in specific industries who are trained and experienced in the use of individual applications and their underlying technologies. The topic is important enough to deserve its own book. The amount of research required of a historian to write it is at least equal to what went into this volume. However, several general comments that inform our study of applications can be made.

There have always been two types of skills required, absence of either preventing the installation or use of application software and hardware. First, one always needed programmers or users skilled in writing, installing, maintaining, and deploying necessary technology (hardware and software). To reduce the extent of that requirement, in particular with regard to PCs, over the past 30 years vendors have attempted to make microcomputers user-friendly. To a lesser extent, the same occurred to large mainframes, applications, and programming. Anyone who has used a PC understands why this remains an ideal, not a reality.[88] This also proved to be the case in the early decades of the 1950s–1970s, and it was the reality that all organizations had to contend with while installing large, enterprise-wide applications at the dawn of the new century. If one could make a technology or tool easier to use, more of it could be sold or bought.

Second, end users—the people using an application—had to understand how the software functioned, what buttons to push, and so forth. Training these people has always been a major function of vendors and IT organizations. There is only limited evidence to suggest that those in particular careers have integrated a deep knowledge of particular computer applications. Engineers come to mind for certain functions (e.g., CAD/CAM), as well as specialists in the medical profession. But in accounting (the earliest and most widely used set of applications), practitioners still learned accounting first, a little about spreadsheets, and even less about application software until they went to work. Groups that did learn included secretaries, clerks, and administrative assistants since in their formal training they were normally taught how to use word processors and spreadsheets, just as secretaries for generations were taught how to type. Most users, however, learned how to use their employer's specific software tools after they were employed. Clerks and customer service personnel always had to be taught how to use an application once they were on the job. Other examples abound: airline personnel who checked in passengers at airports, clerks who operated cash registers (point-of-sale, or POS, terminals) at supermarkets and stores, and operators who worked at large telephone banks such as those used by mail order retailers. Every industry reviewed in this book always faced the requirement to train people on how to use their specific versions of application software and the machines on which they ran, along with the policies and procedures of which this technology was a part.

The exception, of course, existed when an organization hired someone who knew from experience gained at a prior job how to use a specific application. Hiring such an individual was ideal in many ways and became increasingly more possible to do as companies moved away from writing their own application software (which they had to do in the 1950s and 1960s) toward buying standard software products as these became increasingly available (from the 1970s to the present). But new applications, or innovative versions of old ones, still had to be written and were unique to an enterprise. Revamping of supply chains to exploit the Internet is a good example of this process at work, a case about which I will have more to say in the next five chapters.

The United States has been blessed with large numbers of high-quality "human capital," which made it possible to use advanced technologies. Historians and economists have tracked this feature of all industrialized nations for a long time. All their charts place the United States near the top. Their lists include literacy rates, number of engineers and scientists trained; and percentage of the population with high school, college, or advanced degrees and with a specific skill type. At the end of the century, for example, just over 25 percent of adult Americans had graduated from college, still a high figure by world standards. The debates engaged in by historians, economists, and other experts were less about this existing pool and more about how to increase it. For example, F. M. Scherer, an economist at Harvard University, worried "that there are significant limits to expanding the scientific and engineering work force," even though in his study he devoted a whole chapter filled with statistics demonstrating that the United States had many technically trained people.[89]

A recent study sponsored by the Computing Research Association (CRA) demonstrated that the supply of technically trained Americans was impressive but, after looking at the demand for such skills, concluded that there were not enough of them. For example, "universities are still having difficulty recruiting students— especially those who are U.S. citizens—to attend graduate school in IT-related programs." The authors noted that training workers in industry was very expensive but essential: "Companies outside of the IT sector need to recognize that information technology may become a core competency for them."[90] Although these authors concentrated more on technical IT skills, their message was just as relevant for end users, many of whom had to be these IT-skilled individuals. The second quote was the important message. As companies became more reliant on information technology to develop, manufacture, and deliver products and services, their employees needed deeper computer-related skills (application knowledge also) for these enterprises to thrive in an advanced economy. Other experts delivered the same message.[91] What these observations translated into concerned the knowledge of how to use applications.

Linking the issue of what skills were needed to discussions about rates of diffusion of IT in the U.S. economy provides additional insight on the extent of deployment and dependence on computing. The share of the American work force using IT tools rose from 25 percent in 1984 to 51 percent in 1997, according to a credible study of the issue. To be sure, uses varied from one type of worker to another over time, as did the type of applications, but the trend was clear: dependency on computers rose over time as the digital became integrated into routine tasks.[92]

Patterns of IT Value

Finally, before diving into the details of applications, we should understand the basic pattern of adoption and use. The motivating force has primarily been and continues to be leveraging information technology for economic value. Different students of the notion have used various terms, ranging from *cost justification* to *productivity gains*, but the motivation is the same: people want to use computers for economic advantage. Figure 2.2 is an attempt to conceptualize the historic process evident in the American economy during the entire period in which computers existed. It is not intended to be perfect but simply a starting point for observing patterns evident across industries, firms, and government agencies over time.

The figure suggests that IT value was created through the dynamics of three continuously evolving sets of activities. These activities engaged, sped up, or slowed down differently and simultaneously from one organization or industry to another, sometimes in some synchronous fashion (e.g., when a new technology or application was adopted almost simultaneously by many), sometimes not. If we accept the

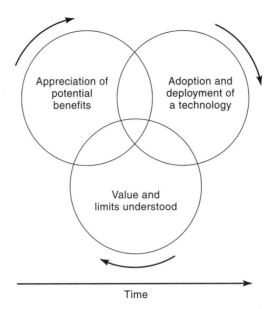

Figure 2.2
Cycle of adoption of IT, 1950–present.

figure as normative, that is, more or less true most of the time, and as an aggregation of the patterns evident in the United States, what we see, are three interrelated activities that were constantly at work. One was the appreciation of the potential benefits of a technology or application by those in a firm who either could influence the decision to adopt or had to decide to do so. Normally, that was a combination of the technical gurus in a firm and line management. The decisions then led to some sort of adoption and, as time passed and knowledge within the firm about the value and limits of a technology or application increased, they were adopted faster or slower. Given the enormous extent of adoption of technology, we can conclude that in general the rates and extent of adoption of applications over time sped up.[93] In turn, that led to more people using an application or technology. That adoption resulted in more people understanding how an application worked, creating opportunities for improvements either implemented by users or requirements made of suppliers of the applications and their underpinning technologies. Richer functionality then came to the attention of decision makers, who had to determine if they should adopt the new version, for example, of Microsoft or SAP products every time it came to market. Adoption occurred only if there was new functionality or there was some other compelling reason to change. Adoption slowed if the new version only fixed problems from earlier ones (e.g., as occurred initially with Windows 2000).[94]

Figure 2.2 implies that there existed a force at work, speed, or velocity, playing a role in the adoption of an application. Indeed, that is exactly the case. As a technology or application became attractive to a potential user, interest increased, and after the experience of using it became known across a firm or industry, usage increased if the story was a positive one, or slowed or stopped if otherwise. All three elements operated at different speeds, and differently in each industry. So, generalizing about how long it takes, for example, for a new application to become known, deployed, and its benefits enjoyed is difficult to do, and would vary by industry. But what is not difficult to state is the fact that all three elements are always at work. In each chapter we will have occasion to discuss velocity or, as many in American industry called it late in the century, cycle time. Being first in originating or deploying an application was not the whole story, merely a first step in a process in which speed of deployment had ultimate economic consequences that incrementally, yet cumulatively, built up a body of knowledge and effects on companies, industries, and the economy at large.

Three environmental influences were also at work in this process, and because of their effects we need chapter 1. First, the nature of commerce changed for a number of reasons, not the least of which was the effect of technology of all types, not just IT. The current changes underway, driven by the Internet, although very obviously profound and extensive, are only the latest. Technology, political realities, and economic conditions constantly affected the nature of commercial activities. These changes and trends provided the context in which management made decisions on whether or not to adopt a technology or application. Thus historical perspective is crucial for any manager who wants to consider the use of a technology, not just for historians. As Michael E. Porter implied nearly a quarter of a century ago, the application of historical views of industry patterns is an essential strategic action for gaining competitive advantages in the marketplace.[95]

Through their work, employees provided the second influence. At the task (work) level, applications became components of what an organization was and did. Applications changed how people did their work, but work also affected which functions applications provided. The decision about what work was done also grew out of the nature of commerce. As commercial priorities and intents evolved, so, too, did the content of work. In short, there existed a symbiotic relationship among work, applications, and the nature of commercial activities.

The realities of industry boundaries further complicated the ecology represented by figure 2.2. Porter made it obvious to business managers that industries existed and were important because they provided markets, sources of resources, rules of the game, identities, and worldviews. Governments tracked, regulated, deregulated, and otherwise taxed and controlled an industry, not just a firm. Porter and others demonstrated that this was also a global phenomenon.[96] Therefore, the patterns of behavior of industries are not just a convenient way to organize groups of applications, such as I have used in this book, but rather a profoundly influencing feature on the strategies, tactics, and work of organizations. Often the evolution of boundaries in an industry influenced behavior, along with the nature or availability of a technology. Mergers and acquisitions are obvious examples, but so, too, are core competencies of an industry.[97] Pharmaceuticals knew, for instance, how to conduct medical R&D and get drugs to market, and they used that knowledge to welcome or exclude allies or rivals. Airlines knew how to manage inventories of seats and thus could use computers to price airfares variously, based on how customers valued specific trips.

The value of IT constantly changed as the sweet spots were shifted and transformed: IT pushed information within organizations in novel ways; new machines and software offered different benefits and costs over time; and science and management practices affected each other. The effects on value were thus holistic and constantly evolving, and it is why the model presented in figure 2.2 should be seen as dynamic and active. When users of applications and their managers complained about the unrelenting changes they kept experiencing, this is what the model is trying to describe.

Conclusions

What we have, then, is a broad, extensive pattern of digital technologies and their applications seeping into almost every corner of the American economy. Nowhere can this be demonstrated more dramatically than by what occurred in manufacturing industries. They were often the first, and certainly the most aggressive, in embracing computer-based applications. Thus the next five chapters are devoted to an overview of manufacturing in the U.S. economy and descriptions of the broad patterns of adoption of the digital in this sector in individual but representative industries.

3

Presence and Role of Manufacturing Industries in the American Economy

We are not only entering a new era in production techniques, with automated

factories and automated warehouses just around the corner, but we are

likewise upon the threshold of new business methods.

—Vincent DePaul Goubeau, 1957

The use of computers fundamentally changed how goods were manufactured and distributed during the second half of the twentieth century. Although there were many other influences on contemporary manufacturing practices, such as globalization and public policies, computers profoundly affected how the work of manufacturing was done and the results achieved. Between the early 1950s and the end of the century, computers had become integral to all facets of manufacturing. Historians of manufacturing practices understated the role of the computer. Economists frequently emphasized other factors—national economic conditions, human resources, capital goods, and national economic policies—and only in recent years, the role of computers. This and the next chapter describe how computers came to play such a dominant role in American manufacturing, complementing rather than displacing these other points of emphasis.

Devoting a chapter to a discussion of the role of manufacturing in the economy, instead of delving right away into a review of manufacturing applications, is made necessary by the fact that to a large extent the debate about the advent of the Information Age has been in response to that about the role of the industrial sector in the American economy. Daniel Bell, with his postindustrial comments published in the 1970s and beyond, attracted a great deal of interest to the question of how the economy was changing.[1] To a large extent, the tone of comments about the economy over the last two decades of the twentieth century proved sympathetic to the notion that something fundamental was happening, typically a transition away from manufacturing and toward a more services-oriented economy. This has led to much discussion about public policy in labor, trade relations, technology, and national research priorities. However, what the next several chapters demonstrate is that manufacturing did not disappear; rather, it changed a great deal of how it did its work. This is an important distinction because Bell's perspective, and that of many commentators on contemporary society, would lead one to believe that the current transformation is away from some industries and toward new ones, often industries that do not make things.

A couple of data points suggest otherwise. First, whereas the percentage of the economy devoted to manufacturing has declined, its absolute volume of work has not.[2] We have manufacturing today that did not exist 50 years ago, such as computers, hard drives, PCs, and software. Second, industries long active in the economy still are, such as automotive and steel. To be sure, global competition exists and has cost some American industries market share, but the majority of industries remain, both in the United States and, in many cases, in an expanded form around the world. More steel is made today than 50 years ago.

What the study of computer applications deployed in manufacturing emphasizes, however, is a series of questions that challenge the assumption that we are overwhelmingly in an Information Age. British sociologist Anthony Giddens has quite rightly pointed out that societies have long had information content in their work.[3] His evidence and logic are too compelling to ignore. On the other hand, Manuel Castells, in a series of books, provides a rich body of evidence that networking societies are changing things through such technologies as telephones and the Internet.[4] However, a close reading of his work, when compared to the topics discussed in this book, should lead to a realization that the changes are more social and cultural. To what extent does the evidence of work being done differently— thanks to computers—alter our image of what kind of economy we are in or are entering? Are we deeply into an information technology–infused economy that does what essentially it has long done? Are we instead entering a postindustrial economy, as some have suggested? These are important questions that are related to public policy, what the nation invests in the economy, and the way people work.

It would be difficult to exaggerate the extent of the computer's influence on the tasks of manufacturing. Go through any American factory and you will see computers embedded in almost every machine on the floor. Discuss the processes and tasks performed in any spot in the building and you will be told about personal computers, hand-held devices with embedded chips, and telecommunications. Even many of the products manufactured themselves incorporate computer chips, such as many of today's toys, kitchen appliances, and all motorized vehicles, from cars to spaceships. In the next several chapters I describe how the application of computers profoundly changed the look and feel of manufacturing, indeed, transformed it, as much as did the introduction of steam power and, later, electricity. The process of transformation has not yet been completed; the introduction of the

Internet and additional improvements in computer-based technologies are continuing to lead manufacturing firms to change their work methods. However, the current transformation of manufacturing can be seen as a longer historical process at work, one that has been underway for over a half century—long enough for us to begin taking a measure of historic changes and draw lessons from the experience.

The quotation at the start of this chapter comes from a vice president at Radio Corporation of America (RCA), one of the great high-tech companies of the mid-twentieth century. By the time Goubeau made his comment, the transistor was already being used in manufacturing. Managers and engineers at RCA understood the potential of the computer; indeed, some were manufacturing components of the new technology (such as computer memories). Addressing participants at a conference of the American Management Association (AMA) in June 1957, he observed that "all these trends reflect the growing complexity of business. We are living in an age when swift, accurate, and automatic regulation of production processes is fast presenting itself as an urgent need."[5] Nearly 40 years later, a team of experts on modern manufacturing techniques made essentially the same point:

> Rapid, relentless, and uncertain change is the most unsettling marketplace reality that companies and people must cope with today. New products, even whole markets, appear, mutate, and disappear within shorter and shorter periods of time. The pace of innovation continues to quicken, and the direction of innovation is often unpredictable.[6]

They made their point before most manufacturing experts had encountered the Internet, which in turn caused another round of changes in how manufacturing companies did their work. Goubeau made the same point in 1957: "Eighty percent of the business we are doing today is in products that did not exist or were not on the market at the time World War II ended. We think that history will repeat itself, and that 80 percent of the products 10 years from now will be different from those on the market today."[7] A comment made when computers were being used for the first time in manufacturing and another made decades later, when such technology had long been applied, suggests two themes that run through the industrial experience of the American economy. First, computers have not yet resolved all the basic economic and managerial issues manufacturing firms have faced over the past half century. If anything, computers have sped up change and increased complexity in these operations. Second, the transformation process resulting from computing is not over.

But why did computing prove so compelling as to change so fundamentally the daily tasks of hundreds of industries and thousands of firms? The heart of the answer can be summarized in one word: *information*. From merely collecting and creating information of use to workers and managers alike, computing evolved into a rich set of tools that could sort and sift data for useful and timely information, quickly presenting information of value. This is as much a story of the hunt for useful content as it is about productivity, profits, and economic transformation. During the last half of the twentieth century, management reached frequently to those tools that promised them the opportunity to leverage information—not just raw data—with which to do their work, create economic value, and sustain competitive performance. In earlier times, workers and their superiors focused most intensely on the search for physical power to move and to bend, that is, to replace human and animal muscle power, more than to rely on information-handling tools. To be sure, information was always an important component of any work scene, but until the arrival of the computer, the ability to use data (and information derived from data) to do work and to work smarter did not really exist to the extent now possible.

To understand how manufacturing changed over time, I first set the industry into the context of the American economy at large and then explain what manufacturers did in the late twentieth century because much of their work was different than that of earlier times. In the next chapter I describe in broad terms the fundamental changes that occurred in the evolution of computer use in manufacturing, both in the office and on the shop floor. I then show the extent of deployment of computing technology over time as evidence of the amount of change manufacturing underwent. There is one caveat, however, to keep in mind: each industry evolved and adopted computers and the digital at different rates and times. This makes generalizations in both chapters essential, on the one hand, to make sense of broad-based patterns but, on the other hand, exposes us to risks of inaccuracies and undue emphasis on influences and trends.

Manufacturing Presence in the American Economy

One would normally think that manufacturing consists of any company that makes things, and indeed one would be correct. Manufacturing firms, however, also design, sell, and service their offerings. That broader mission has not changed much over the past half century. However, two other things have. First, what gets manufactured both changed and stayed the same. American firms still make automobiles and trucks but not TV sets and stereo equipment. Today's vehicles are quite different from those of 1950, and today's entertainment products are programmable and rich in functions not available a half century ago. Printing is a still an industry, and it produces books and magazines, but it also publishes and distributes substantial quantities of materials over the Internet. Not so clearly understood are some industries, such as moviemakers: Are they manufacturers of entertainment or do they just entertain? And then we have new products that are less "things" and more processes and possibly publications. Software is the obvious example, a product that by the late 1990s annually generated over $123 billion in revenue around the world, up from zero in the 1950s and early 1960s.[8] For our purposes, the manufacturing sector of the U.S. economy consists of firms that design, manufacture, sell, and service goods and chemicals and fuels, which is essentially the definition all economists use. The fact that sometimes borders between manufacturing and service firms become fuzzy (because of the trend to form cross-industry alliances or to develop extended supply chains) is insufficient to alter the basic definition. More workers today design and service products than make them compared to the

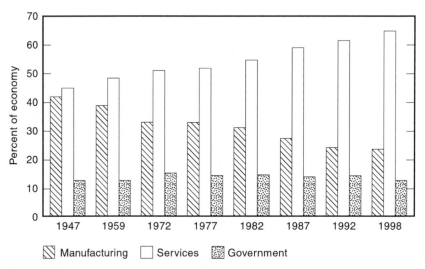

Figure 3.1

Major sectors of the U.S. economy, selected years, 1947–1998. (Source: Table E—
Gross Product by Industry Group, http://www.bea.doc.gov/bea/an/0600gpi/
tablee.htm)

case in 1950. In large part, that shift occurred because of the successful implementation of automation (heavily driven by computers), which displaced workers on
the shop floor. That the percentage of workers making things in a manufacturing
firm has declined over the past half century does not alter our definition.

The American government tracked the economic performance of the manufacturing (often also called industrial) sector for the better part of a century. Figure
3.1 displays data on the relative size of the manufacturing sector in comparison to
two other very large sectors, services and government. The most obvious observation one can make is that as a proportion of the total economy, manufacturing is
smaller. Yet since the economy grew in size by trillions of dollars over the past half
century, the total dollar value of manufacturing actually enlarged.

Whereas manufacturing can range from the single craftsperson (a proprietor-
ship) to a small, privately owned firm (often partnerships), the corporation was the
dominant organizational form in America throughout the entire period under study.
Corporations generated the largest percentage of employment, products, and revenues through the last half of the twentieth century. The largest cluster of American
firms existed in the manufacturing sector, often accounting for over 70 percent of
revenues generated by corporations in any given year. These firms also employed
about 25 percent of the work force in that period. The Fortune 500, a list published
annually since 1954, catalogs the largest firms, most of which were either early
users of various types of computer technologies or the most extensive. They were
also responsible for the bulk of all American exports; only the Agriculture Industry
played a comparatively significant role.

Manufacturing companies accounted for substantial volumes of the U.S. gross domestic product (GDP) during the entire period. Between 1950 and 1994 (the last year before the profound influence of the Internet became observable in economic statistics), the largest 500 industrial firms more than tripled their revenues. They also grew slightly faster than the total GDP of the nation. As a share of the total sales of all corporations in the industrial sector, the largest 500 manufacturing firms garnished relatively large proportions. In 1954 they accounted for 50 percent of the total and, with a slight dip in percentage between 1979 and 1984, continued to win increasing totals, exceeding 60 percent during the 1990s. The turnover rate in the list of the top 500 was 7 percent per year. That began changing after 1981, but the key point to keep in mind is that over most of the period under study, manufacturing was concentrated in ever larger firms; these remained essentially the same over time. Mergers in the 1980s and 1990s accounted for the largest number of changes in the list. Mergers, however, did not normally mean that less manufacturing was done.[9]

There were dramatic exceptions caused by loss of market share gained by Japanese firms, for example, in automobiles and consumer electronics. However, since some of these foreign companies manufactured and, of course, sold and serviced goods in the United States, like Nissan and Honda, their manufacturing activities can be included as part of the story told in this book when they occurred on American soil; involved U.S. capital, employees, and infrastructures; and were sold within the American economy. Their practices profoundly influenced American manufacturing activities, particularly in the 1980s and 1990s, especially in such industries as automotive and steel.[10] As I demonstrate in the case studies on these two industries, such practices affected their competitiveness. Yet, I do not want to discuss the relative competitiveness of the American manufacturing sector in general because that could take up an entire book. It is enough at this point to recognize that manufacturing was big business, that the industrial sector expanded throughout the period, and that it changed profoundly in part because of computing, which made companies either more or less efficient or productive (i.e., competitive), aided the process of mergers, or made it possible to offer new products.

What was the relative position of the American manufacturing industries in this period in comparison to the global economy? It is an important question because almost every commentator on American manufacturing in the twentieth century spoke about the dominance of U.S. industry. The surge in e-commerce in the late 1990s continued to provide evidence of American prowess. Global competition was essentially the preserve of large corporations prior to the arrival of the Internet. Thus, any appreciation of America's role can be gleaned by looking quickly at the number of these firms. Between 1956 and 1969, the percentage of American firms in the largest 50 manufacturing companies around the world always exceeded that of any other nation or region. Then, in the 1970s, as industrialization quickly expanded around the world, U.S. totals shifted. In 1974, when the United States experienced a recession, 24 American firms were part of the top 50; the Europeans had 20, and Japan 6. Ten years later, in 1984, the United States still had 22, Europe 18, and Japan remained with its 6 firms. Then began a sharp decline in the U.S.

total that was not reversed until the 1990s. In 1993, 15 U.S. firms made up part of the top 50; the Europeans stayed with 19, the Japanese 13. As a share of total sales, the Americans were always high. In 1956, 42 of the 50 were U.S. firms, generating 81 percent of all the sales of the top 50. However, American ownership of total sales began declining in the 1960s. In 1959 it was 87 percent; in 1969, 80 percent. Ten years later, in 1979, it hovered at 54 percent; a decade later, 37 percent.[11] These statistics are less a statement of American industrial failures than a reflection of the global expansion that occurred in manufacturing. The data acknowledges, for example, the emergence of Japanese manufacturing on the world stage as a competitive force in the late twentieth century.

Labor, Automation, and the Computer

One of the important changes that resulted from increased use of computers and other forms of automation concerned labor's role and composition. Through the entire period under study, management always looked for ways to improve the productivity of all its assets, often using computers to do the trick. A large portion of any management team's hunt for productivity lay in reducing the amount of human content of any product's cost of production. Machines did not go on strike, could do work repetitively in exactly the same way, did not get sick, and generated costs that could be better controlled. During this entire period, labor content declined as a percentage of the total costs of manufacturing products, while the skills required of employees changed, generally becoming more technical over time. There has been a vast discussion about the effects of computing on labor, and although it would be tempting to delve into this fascinating topic, it would take away attention from the task at hand—to understand how computing technologies were used. However, a few basic patterns enhance our appreciation of the role played by computers in manufacturing.

To a large extent, the discussion about the changing nature of work centered on why people obtained or lost jobs, why some industries acquired workers (e.g., high-tech firms and such new industries as semiconductors and software) while others lost them (e.g., printing, railroads, or steel), and the causes of these shifts. Many sources of change existed throughout the entire period: emerging forms of competition; labor laws and public policies; changing markets; financial restructuring; mergers and acquisitions; stock markets; evolving management incentives; weak union leadership; wars and revolutions; the beginning, expansion, and end of the Cold War; and corporate restructuring. In short, the list is endless.[12] But single-cause arguments simply do not tell the whole story. Arguing, for instance, that computers alone or that the Internet could single-handedly transform an industry is naive. In his seminal study on the role of competition within industries, Michael E. Porter identified over a dozen factors that caused changes. Even technology created its own uncertainties:

> Small production volume and newness usually combine to produce high costs in the emerging industry relative to those the industry can potentially achieve.

Even the technologies for which the learning curve will soon level off, there is usually a very steep learning curve operating. Ideas come rapidly in terms of improved procedures, plant layout, and so on, and employees achieve major gains in productivity as job familiarity increases.[13]

Within the context of multiple forces at work, we have to fit in the role and effects of computing, always bearing in mind that as important as information technology was, its importance was relative to other factors simultaneously at work.

As time passed, it became obvious that manufacturing companies came to rely increasingly on a more technically skilled work force. Of the many factors involved, this was one that always made everyone's short list and, therefore, deserves further comment. To thrive in the workplace, employees increasingly had to have more technical skills than earlier generations. Over time, these technical skills included knowing how to use computers and other devices that contained embedded computer chips or used software. Failure to do so, or to work in an industry that could find or develop new offerings, meant job losses, as occurred in the printing industry in the 1960s and 1970s, culminating in the dramatic case of the automation of printing of daily newspapers in New York. This instance became the poster child for job loss caused by automation (i.e., computers), aggravated as an issue in large part because of the extensive press coverage it received.[14]

Role of Training

Economists, among others, have studied the role of skills, training, and job transformations over time. It became a hot topic among economists, which is why job displacements and human capital appeared as an issue in chapter 2. Discussions ranged from negative accounts of job losses in industry[15] to those about the availability or lack of skilled employees in the field of computing.[16] By examining how computers were used in various industries, economists concluded that in order to perform work, employees in American companies had to become more familiar with the application of computers, whether in the office or on the shop floor. Although historians have yet to do the hard work of documenting by industry how much computer skills were needed and acquired, a quick look at the number of information technology professionals in the American economy hints at the increased amount required. They include programmers, computer operators, designers of applications, and so forth, who provided the IT infrastructure, machines, and software that employees at large used in all industries.

In the early 1950s, there were few of these people. The leading student of this population, Montgomery Phister, Jr., estimated that in the early 1950s there were fewer than 35,000. Data entry clerks—those who often typed information into punch cards—outnumbered the more technical staff by roughly two to one.[17] The number of computer professionals kept growing over the decades, expanding faster than the general work force all through the period, to over 1 million by the late 1970s[18] and to nearly 2.1 million by 1997.[19] There was a similar pattern in demand for data entry clerks deep into the 1980s at which point there were so many online systems into which end users directly entered data or mechanical means to collect information (e.g., scanners) that the need for so many clerks began to slow.

What these statistics did not state, of course, was the percentage of the total American work force that had acquired computer-related skills over the half century. However, we know some things about the training costs incurred by industries. Although a portion of these expenditures went for nontechnical training, such as for personnel practices, teaming, retirement planning, and so forth, a great deal was spent on teaching people how to operate machines and how to do the work of redesigned processes, all of which often included interaction with computers. We lack good historical perspectives on the role training played in modern American history (post-1955). We do know, however, that all vendors of modern technology provided training on their products, including those selling computers and complex industrial equipment. This practice dated back to the origin of precomputer technology and other industrial equipment.[20]

Historically, training existed extensively in such workplaces as the military, manufacturing, and, by the 1980s, among groups of employees empowered to control and change key work processes. Unionized work forces had more job-related training than nonunionized labor. By the early 1990s, over 80 percent of medium to large manufacturing companies had training programs. It was during the 1980s that many of these firms embraced quality management practices, which had as a core principal extensive training of employees. Therefore, we can conclude that the availability of training in the early 1990s grew out of an increase in such offerings all through the 1980s,[21] suggesting that in previous years—that is, from 1950 to the early 1980s—whereas training may have been extensive in manufacturing, it probably occurred at lower rates than in the late 1980s and 1990s. To put that 80 percent in manufacturing in perspective, those academics who arrived at this number reported that in wholesale and retail trade at the time, the percentage of firms involved in training hovered at about 57 percent; financial firms, at 61.5 percent. In the case of all firms, the larger the company, the more likely it was to conduct training. This is important because normally the largest firms in manufacturing were the first or to embrace computers or to have the most extensive use, and thus they could afford to train their employees. Thus 95.5 percent of firms with over 1,000 employees had training programs, as did nearly 92 percent of all firms with over 100 employees. About 18 percent of those who had access to training in the largest firms in the early 1990s actually underwent some education. In manufacturing firms, almost 9 percent of all employees had recently training.[22]

In addition, training in the operation of computers or software and in the management and strategic use of such technologies became increasingly available over time and were often mandatory, especially for white- and upper blue-collar workers in manufacturing companies. The converse was also true, that is, the lowest blue-collar core workers in all industries (not just manufacturing) were the least likely to receive such training. The more technically complex an organization or product line, the more likely these enterprises provided training on the use of computers.[23] It was not uncommon for manufacturing firms in the 1980s and 1990s to spend up to 4 percent of their budgets on training, although more normally it was less. It is not a generalization that would necessarily be as accurate for the 1950s and 1960s, when the actual number of employees deploying computers in manufacturing remained small. What we can be confident of, however, is that those involved did receive training. The hundreds of micro–case studies written over the years bear that out.[24]

As computer technology became easier to use and more commonly available, the nature of training changed as well. In the 1950s, it was not uncommon for engineers to be programmers and systems analysts, designing applications in all industries, including manufacturing. But over time that changed, as did training. Two observers of these changes, Anthony P. Carnavele and Donna Desrochers, made the critical point that "as the occupational structure of the U.S. economy has shifted, so have its skills requirements." Hinting at what training was needed from 1950 to the start of the 1990s, they observed that "the demand for specific vocational skills is giving way to a growing need for general cognitive skills—mathematical and verbal reasoning ability as well as to a new set of general behavioral skills." They attributed this shift to the specific needs of an economy now dominated by the service sector, which had its own requirements.[25] Their own analysis of education and training led them to the same observation made by others, namely, that over the course of the half century under study, formal education on the part of all employees increased. Less than 10 percent of all American employees had postsecondary education in the 1950s; over a third did by the late 1990s. Among factory workers there actually was a decline in postsecondary education between the 1950s and late 1990s, from just under 10 percent to 2–3 percent. Over time, the amount of education and training needed to work in American industry had steadily increased. Staff at the U.S. Bureau of Labor Statistics reported that over 20 percent of manufacturing workers had routinely received formal training of one sort or another, over 34 percent if one added informal training, which in manufacturing was often on-the-job or hands-on training.[26] Clearly, the adoption of computers played a major role in driving up the amount of training that occurred. Put in the arcane, but more precise, language of the economist, a significant correlation existed between investments in computers and the simultaneous rise in expenditures for training.

Makeup of the Manufacturing Sector

Training was emblematic of other changes underway in American industry. The makeup of the manufacturing sector changed over time. In 1950, for example, no semiconductor or software industries existed; by the 1970s, two were well established and, by the 1990s, employed over 2 million Americans. In that decade new industries existed: biotech companies, "building" products based on newly created knowledge about deoxyribonucleic acid, better known simply as DNA, and, of course, the whole wireless world of cell phones and pagers. So understanding the shift in what made up the industrial sector of the American economy is essential to any deep appreciation of how computers were used because applications varied by industry. We need to acknowledge that the mix changed, as happened in other parts of the economy. This is one reason that, for example, economists face constant problems of generalization when reviewing the evolution of the economy or of industries over time. We did not have a computer industry in the 1940s, but we did by the end of the 1950s. We did not have a software industry per se in the 1960s, but it certainly existed in the 1970s. Today it is biotechnology firms that have carved out a recognizable position in the economy, as did wireless communications by the mid-1990s.

The U.S. Census Bureau, which has long been the source of records for the naming and tracking of industries, went from declaring the existence of the half dozen sectors discussed in the first two chapters to 20 by the end of the 1990s. In the 1990s alone, it began to track 79 new manufacturing industries, revised the definition of 186 others, and now recognizes 474 as distinct entities, from personal computer manufacturers to pencil makers. Many of the new industries are obvious: producers of computers, computer peripherals, and communications equipment. Some manufacturing moved to a new sector—information—heralding the arrival of the Information Age. It placed publishing into this new category, for example. This new subsector has 34 industries of its own, 20 of which are new (e.g., paging, cellular and other wireless communications, and satellite telecommunications).[27]

We also need to acknowledge the relative position of one manufacturing industry over another. Since industries copied applications and processes from one another, it is not essential to review the hundreds of industries in the economy at large. However, it is important to appreciate which were the largest since they tended to be the earliest adopters of new technologies or computer-based applications, and their experiences influenced the thinking of managers in other industries. Table 3.1 provides a quick snapshot of the relative size of the largest industries. Large is defined as percentage of dollar sales within the sector generated by a particular industry. What becomes quickly evident is that the relative position of one industry over another changes only slightly over time, once again suggesting that the profound changes taking place in the American economy over the half century occurred more at the operational level than in the grand rise and fall of industries.

What Manufacturing Companies Did

It might seem odd to discuss what manufacturing companies did; after all, they made things. But to understand the role of the digital in modern manufacturing, we must appreciate the various activities of a manufacturing operation because digital applications were modifications of them. For the historian there is the added burden of documenting how manufacturing evolved over time. A manufacturing plant of the early 1800s made things differently than one in the late twentieth century. In addition, its products differed, as did the types of employees. Historians of technology recognize that base technologies influence the nature of how things

Table 3.1

Makeup of the Largest U.S. Manufacturing Industries in the Manufacturing Sector Select Years, 1950–1999 (Expressed as Percentages of Total Manufacturing Sector)

Industry	1950	1960	1970	1980	1990	1999	2000
Metals	12.5	15.2	14.7	15.2	10.8	10.5	10.3
Motor vehicles	11.6	13.2	11.9	9.1	10.4	12.2	11.7
Elec. mach.	6.2	8.1	8.6	9.4	10.1	11.1	11.6
Chemical	6.4	7.4	7.7	8.1	10.6	11.7	12.2
Indus. mach.	8.3	9.3	11.4	13.2	11.4	10.5	10.7
Food	12.7	11.5	10.5	9.0	9.3	8.9	8.7
Textiles Apparel	9.8	6.9	7.0	5.5	4.6	3.3	3.1
Print & publ.	4.7	5.0	5.2	5.6	7.0	6.9	6.7
Instruments	1.5	2.5	2.8	3.4	4.7	3.9	4.1
Paper & Allied	3.7	3.9	3.9	3.9	4.3	3.9	3.8
Rubber/Plastics	1.9	2.4	2.9	2.9	3.3	4.0	3.8
Other mfg.	20.7	14.6	13.4	14.7	13.5	13.1	13.3

Source: Prepared by Dr. Philip Swan, IBM economist, based on U.S. government data.

are made, done, used, and so forth over time. It is a useful notion to use in appreciating the role of computers in manufacturing. Often referred to as *technological styles*, the idea is fairly straightforward. How things are made and the way in which organizations are structured evolve to optimize efficiency and profitability in response to new factors of production. Normally, these factors are cheaper than before (e.g., less expensive raw materials) or are new ways of organizing work. For instance, electricity made it possible for Henry Ford to implement assembly line manufacturing. In turn that made possible factories that were organized differently than before. Changes in the *style* of manufacturing in some industries were close to an innovation later adopted by other industries. In the case of the computer, large airplane-manufacturing companies were often early users of this technology, but decades later all major manufacturing industries had similar digital applications.[28]

The look and feel of how manufacturing changes has been called the adoption of a technological style. One student of the process described it this way:

> As long as the . . . evolution of the relative costs of various types of material inputs, various types of equipment and different skills follows the expected trends, managers and engineers will apply what becomes the "technical common sense" to make incremental improvements along the natural trajectories of the technologies in place, or radical technological changes in those branches of production of goods or services which have not yet achieved the "ideal type" of productive organizations.[29]

Improvements in manufacturing and the products produced tended in this scenario to occur incrementally. Automobiles were incrementally improved over nearly a century. Office appliances (such as tabulating equipment and adding machines) also improved in the same way over the 75-year period before the arrival of the computer. The result over time was a total restructuring of work, including new best practices, different required skills, novel product mixes, new trends in the use of technology, new patterns of location for manufacturing plants and for distribution, and expenditures for different (new) infrastructures. This is exactly what happened to manufacturing in the second half of the twentieth century. The Taylorist-Fordist style of the early decades of the twentieth century evolved into new forms with the introduction of the digital into manufacturing. Today's manufacturing plant, therefore, looks and feels quite different than many from the 1920s and 1930s. One merely has to walk through an Intel semiconductor manufacturing facility or through a Nissan automobile production plant to see the transformation that has occurred.

Over the centuries, several manufacturing styles existed, simultaneously as new ones emerged. First, the water style dominated; in this style, water and steam profoundly influenced how things were made and transported. By the late nineteenth century a second style emerged, often called steel and electricity. Both styles existed in the manufacture of new products in new ways. Then came a third style, usually referred to as the Fordist style, one in which the role of engineers became very important and mass production in very large quantities became the order of the day. Mass production called for large numbers of consumers. This style—the one that preceded the arrival of the digital computer—required a growing level of coordination among three major tasks: the design of goods and processes of production and distribution, the actual manufacture of a product, and finally the management of all the activities of the firm.[30] The highly influential business historian Alfred D. Chandler, Jr., spent the bulk of his career describing the third element, the role of management (the visible hand in the economy), making possible the managerial practices that existed by the time of the computer's introduction into manufacturing.[31]

Fordist Style

Economist Andrew Tylecote has pointed out the strengths and limits of the Fordist style, constraints that made the use of computers attractive in manufacturing. On the one hand, the Fordist approach proved very efficient, making it possible to produce many products cheaply and of good quality for mass consumer markets. Fordism came to dominate the American manufacturing style during the first half of the twentieth century. On the other hand, this approach failed to generate sufficient control over the operation and coordination of the activities of both people and machines. The desire to continue incremental integration of activities in manufacturing, underway for decades, was stymied by the inability of management to use machines, for example, to replace human brains. Machines were already seen as more effective, precise, and reliable than workers. Over time the percentage of workers in manufacturing who actually did not make things (e.g., bolt parts to-gether), but instead coordinated activities, had steadily been rising, faster than any comparable rate of increase in productivity. Batch production often resulted, not always mass production, which was a relatively expensive way to run physical manufacturing operations. In some industries, such as in steel, up to 75 percent of all products were made in little batches by midcentury. The Fordist style also relied extensively on the brute force of machinery, which needed both expensive capital investments and substantial amounts of energy. Tylecote stated that, "what was needed, for control mechanization, was machine intelligence," precisely what the computer made possible.[32]

Tylecote and others have argued that microelectronics ushered in a new style of technology. The change brought about by the digital became as profound as the role played by water, electricity, and steel in earlier manufacturing styles and, in the United States in the nineteenth century, the American system of manufactur-ing.[33] In the language of the economist, computer chips became a key factor of production if not *the* key factor of modern manufacturing. The logic goes this way: if you need coordination—and all Fordist approaches to manufacturing needed massive, increasing amounts of coordination—then you require more information (gathering and manipulating it, presenting results, and transmitting them to man-agers and workers). Using machines to do this sort of work—that is, computers—is effective, fast, and attractive from the point of view of cost. Mainframe computers were first used in the 1950s, coupled to minicomputers in the 1960s and 1970s, and further integrated into large networks of desktop machines in the 1970s (PCs and high-performance workstations), all with the intent of creating and using in-formation for incrementally improved forms of coordination and control. This im-pulse also goes far to explain why computer chips made their way into the machines on the shop floor and in other departments with manufacturing. From the design systems (CAD) of the 1950s to computerized lathes and other machine tools of the 1960s to the use of handheld units to track parts and completed products in the 1970s and 1980s, companies continuously enhanced their control and coordination of activities, so by the end of the century, many firms could mass-produce or manufacture one-of-a-kind (called mass customization) products and do either one cost effectively.[34]

It is easy to move from discussions about Fordist styles to one dominated by computers; however, a transition phase from one to the other, which continued in parallel to the post-Fordist approach, involved automation. It does not yet have its own history; rather, it has been subsumed into the story of computing—and I am as guilty as any individual in doing so with this book—because so much about automation increasingly involved the use of the integrated circuit and computing in general. However, one does not have to use a computer to automate activities. Electrical devices, levers, and even the use of tabulating equipment to rearrange information on cards in the precomputer era were forms of automation. By the end of the 1940s, just before the arrival of the commercial computer, many industries like steel and automotive, were deeply involved in automation. One could argue just as convincingly that the same was underway in process industries, such as

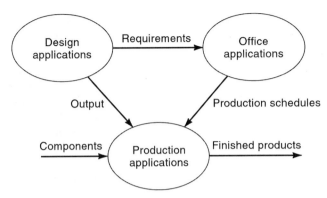

Figure 3.2
Information flows and applications in a factory at the dawn of the
computer. (This is a variation of R. Kaplinksy's Fordist organization
of a factory production chart, Automation: The Technology and
Society *[London: Longmans, 1984]: 24.)*

chemical and petroleum. So, because the emphasis of this book is on the role of
computers, the story of shop floor automation, as distinct from computerization of
production planning and other processes, is yet to be told.[35]

Since the Fordist style of manufacturing dominated when computers first were
used in production, we should take one final view of what a Fordist production
organization looked like. Figure 3.2, taken from the work of economists in the
1980s who were looking back to the precomputer era, illustrates the three features
of manufacturing: design, information coordination, and manufacture. What is particularly interesting is the emphasis on coordination and the flow of information
(by paper, too). In short, manufacturing had already come to be a great deal more
than simply the physical act of making a product—bending metal, hammering nails
into wood, or painting finished goods.

Digital Style

Data collected by IBM to help explain to its employees the activities of a manufacturing plant in the early 1980s (see figure 3.3) shows that manufacturing is still a
key activity. By now, however, firms had over a quarter of a century of experience
with computers, making it possible to create lists that placed greater emphasis on
the coordination of work through computers and office systems. In the accompanying text, the IBM publication stated that "a major goal is to achieve integration
of all applicable systems. These systems include the production, marketing, distribution, finance, administration, engineering, research, and management functions."[36] This had emerged as the holy grail of information processing in general by
the 1960s—called total systems—and remains largely as an aspiration embedded
in the information technology community to the present day.[37]

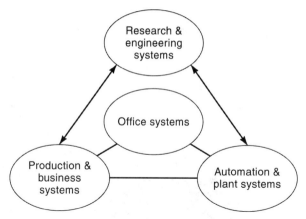

Figure 3.3
IBM's view of manufacturing integrated systems, circa 1985. IBM
employees in the 1980s used the term systems *more frequently*
than the word applications *to emphasize their focus on the role*
of software. Users thought in terms of applications with software
a component of these. Chart is a modification of a representation
in IBM, Applications and Abstracts 1985 *(White Plains, N.Y.:*
IBM Corporation, 1985): 13–1.

The same IBM publication described many of the areas in manufacturing that lent themselves to various levels of computerization, reflecting as much a view from the 1960s and 1970s as the specifics of the early 1980s. Figure 3.4 looks crowded because by the 1970s there were so many processes in what was rapidly emerging as the post-Fordist plant, one littered with a growing variety of computer-based applications. The software and hardware required to work in each of these processes existed either as products from both software and hardware companies (e.g., IBM) or had been written by users. All large American manufacturing firms had software from all three sources. These varied in modernity from old systems written and installed in the 1950s to others that leveraged state-of-the-art hardware and such software tools as database management packages in the 1970s and 1980s. Later, PCs were often integrated into existing mainframe-based applications. In short, as one would expect from the technology style of the development of post-Fordist production, these applications and the software underpinning them were adopted in phases. They also came into companies and industries at different speeds. In one firm, production planning was an earlier priority than, say, engineering or research. In another company, the reverse might be true, as, for example, for producers of high-tech products (e.g., computers). Finally, rates of adoption varied from industry to industry and even from one division to another within a company.[38]

A careful reading of figure 3.4 shows the increased importance of information as an integral part of production. Under production planning and control, master production planning (MRP) had become one of the most important functions in

• INDICATES AVAILABILITY OF IBM APPLICATION OFFERING(S)

Figure 3.4
Industrial sector manufacturing/process.

manufacturing. It could not be done without software tools in factories that had
several hundred or more employees. By the late 1960s, MRP was essential. Oliver
Wight, a leading authority at the time on manufacturing processes, observed that
"the vast majority of the manufacturing companies of any size and complexity in
the United States are tuned in to MRP."[39] In the mid-1970s, the *Harvard Business
Review* reported that interest in MRP was growing because the cost of computers
needed for it was declining at the same time that the need for "tighter operational
control and more rapid and flexible response to change" was expanding.[40] A similar
tale could be told about the penetration of computing into such other areas as plant
operations planning (especially inventory control, which is discussed later in this
chapter) and feedback from production operations which by the 1980s was almost

entirely automated in some fashion or another. By the 1970s, software tools were also commercially available for each of the major functions in engineering and research and for about half of the practices in plant operations. In short, within a quarter century, software and computer hardware had become central to the operations of a medium to large manufacturing organization.[41]

By the late 1980s, computing had become such a major feature of manufacturing that the leading training organization in the industrial sector in the United States, the American Production and Inventory Control Society (APICS), had organized six training and certification programs all essentially computer-based applications: master planning, MRP, inventory management, capacity management, production activity control, and just-in-time practices.[42] By the late 1990s, APICS, along with most large manufacturing enterprises, were expanding core applications to integrate with suppliers, distributors, and customers using the Internet. Some of the language changed, such as the fashionable use of the term *process flow scheduling* (PFS) at the start of the twenty-first century rather than just MRP,[43] but the functions retained much in the style of the microprocessor and the digital, which had become such a central part of American manufacturing.

If one wanted to redirect the discussion about applications into a more simplistic model, it probably would move in the direction of office and manufacturing applications. Long before computers came into existence, manufacturing plants had used adding machines, calculators, and paper reports to track activities.[44] After the computer's arrival, many of the software tools used in other industries were also applied in office applications in manufacturing, such as the use of Microsoft Word in all industries. But that set of applications is not what fundamentally changed manufacturing into what it became by the late 1900s; rather, it was the collection of manufacturing planning and production processes and use of software. Furthermore, by changing how manufacturing was done through the use of computers, engineers and managers learned enough about computing to change even the products they made. It is that combination of changes in production and in what products were made that contributed so much in creating what commentators like to call the Information Age.[45] For that reason, most of my focus in the chapters to come will lean more toward discussions about nonoffice applications.

Therefore, before digging into details about applications, let us consider briefly the functions of a post-Fordist industrial enterprise. In the world of manufacturing that was evolving out of a pure Fordist model of operations, what were the basic tasks that industrial firms performed, regardless of the role of computers? The list provided in table 3.2 dates from the middle period in our story, was intended for those who knew little about computing in manufacturing (let alone about production in general), and is devoid of a computer-centric emphasis, with the exception of one line item—data processing. That list could have been published in the late 1950s or even in the late 1990s, but it would not have reflected the realities of manufacturing before the creation of the modern corporation between 1870 and 1930. It would have represented the majority of the functions emerging as crucial elements of manufacturing in Fordist-style companies in the years roughly before 1960–1965, at which time manufacturing was changing so much that the old mass

Table 3.2
Typical Manufacturing Functions, Circa 1950s–1970s

Research and development	Finance
Design engineering	Industrial Engineering
Manufacturing engineering	Quality control
Marketing	Strategic planning
Market research	Production operations
Sales	Data processing
Advertising	Distribution
Personnel management	Purchasing
Legal	Accounting

Source: Thomas G. Gunn, *Computer Applications in Manufacturing* (New York: Industrial Press, 1981): 1–2.

production systems of the past half century were becoming unfamiliar to newer generations of workers and managers. Table 3.3 lists application areas recognized by IBM experts in 1960, illustrating many of the same topics, although with some additional ones as well. It is worth noting that by 1960, the concept of integrating applications had been sufficiently thought through to be able to propose comprehensive strategies.

Computer-based applications in manufacturing were profoundly influenced by the nature of the work done. Therefore, it is important to recognize that there were fundamentally two types of manufacturing—continuous flow and discrete flow—and even a hybrid of the two. The first involved manufacturing in a nonstop fashion, such as in a chemical plant. The second—discrete—was more what one thought of in manufacturing: the production of individual (hence the use of the word *discrete*) products, such as a pencil or an automobile. It was also the type of manufacturing referred to as durable goods. Discrete manufacturers represented the larger of the two types of industrial firms in the United States. By the early 1970s, for example, there were over 28,000 discrete manufacturing plants in the United States as opposed to several thousand of the other type. Most of the discrete manufacturers

Table 3.3
Manufacturing Applications Portfolio, Circa 1960

Forecasting	Scheduling
Materials planning	Dispatching
Inventory management	Operations evaluation

Source: IBM, *IBM Management Operating System for Manufacturing Industries* (White Plains, N.Y.: IBM Corp., 1960); copy in DP Applications Briefs/Box B-116-3, IBM Archives, Somers, N.Y.

Table 3.4
Differences in Types of Manufacturing, Circa Early 1970s

Characteristic	Discrete Parts	Semicontinuous	Continuous
Diversity of products per plant	Generally large	Moderate	Relatively small
Alternative flow & paths	Very many	Medium	Relatively few
Unit operation automation (production)	Relatively simple	Moderately complex	Highly complex
Achievability of hierarchical control	Relatively difficult	Moderately difficult	Relatively straightforward
Need for materials, flow handling, & automation	Necessary for plant-wide control	Necessary for raw materials processing	Highly necessary
Importance of online automatic test & inspection	Important	Very important	Extremely important
Degree of inhouse automation expertise	Relatively low	Moderately high	Highest

Source: Modified from a table in "The Factory Automation Market" (New York: Frost & Sullivan, 1972): 32; report in "Market Research" CBI 55, Box 3, Folder 35, Archives of the Charles Babbage Institute, University of Minnesota, Minneapolis.

ran small plants (with fewer than 100 employees); only 10 percent had more than 500 employees.[46]

The continuous flow manufacturers were the earliest to apply computers widely to monitor activities in the 1950s. In the 1960s discrete manufacturers came into their own in exploiting digital technologies. As one consulting firm reported at the start of the 1970s, looking backward, "It is not surprising that automation took hold initially in the continuous processing industries, where it was most necessary. As processes became more complicated and throughput capacity increased, automation found its way into the semi-continuous processing and, then, into the discrete-parts industries as well."[47]

Table 3.4 points out the differences among various types of manufacturing. The continuous flow plants could exploit primitive computing most quickly in the 1950s, but the other two types evolved to similar levels in the use of the digital over time. For example, hierarchical control over processes in discrete manufacturing was always a dream in the 1950s and 1960s, an objective that management achieved incrementally by linking together various machines and processes. It was a process still underway at the dawn of the twenty-first century. Because ways of making things varied even within a plant, discrete manufacturers had to wait until the 1960s and 1970s before digital technologies had progressed sufficiently to make them attractive to exploit aggressively. It was much easier to do so earlier in a chemical or petroleum plant, where the variety of production processes were relatively fewer.

The use of digital computers became possible in discrete manufacturing not only because the technology evolved sufficiently to allow effective levels of performance but also because management recognized that there were essentially four reasons to use this technology:

- To broaden the scope of what could be automated
- To simplify the design and control of large collections of shop floor equipment
- To increase flexibility since software could be modified less expensively than hardware
- To increase the number of applications that could be performed with such equipment

Experiences in one sector of the manufacturing world were shared with others. One report from the 1970s stated that "many of the problems that otherwise would have confronted discrete-parts manufacturers have already been solved—often painfully—by the processing industries and control equipment suppliers."[48]

The style in evidence toward the end of the century proved sufficiently different from Fordism to be a fundamentally new, what I recognize as the digital style. It had two important features: a pervasive use of computing in all operations of a plant and manufacturing company and a high degree of integration of discrete activities across a process, plant, firm, and industries, all made possible by IT. This way of doing business could only be dreamed about in the Fordist era. The digital style had emerged rapidly in full form across many manufacturing industries by the end of the 1980s and is the dominant one today. Each of the case studies of those industries in existence before the arrival of the computer provides clear evidence of both the transition away from a Fordist structure to the digital style and how this transformation was accomplished. The cases illustrate both patterns and practices, all of which changed more profoundly than one might otherwise have suspected. Among the established large industries of 1950, I found no exceptions to the transition away from Fordism. In fact, if the transition occurred too slowly, firms that moved too lethargically were punished by competitors who were quicker to change styles. The two most obvious cases are the steel and automotive industries, but the others were not immune from change.

Stages, Patterns, and Practices in the Adoption of Computer Applications

Although companies went through various stages in their transformation out of a pure Fordist style to one more dominated by computerized operations, we can generalize about their phases of evolution. These phases exist because of two conditions that always influenced adoption of new applications. First, a particular software or hardware technology had to have reached a level of operational effectiveness to make it viable before a plant manager considered using it. When such a new technology or software tool appeared, all managers knew about it at roughly the same time because of the energetic marketing of data-processing vendors or because of publications and conference proceedings. Highly experimental applications were exceptions and, when generalizing about patterns of adoption, exceptions are just that, deviations from normal practice.

The second consideration is the practice, evident in many industries, that mimics schools of fish; that is, early adopters implemented a new use of computers and then bragged about it, either out of professional pride or as a marketing ploy to show customers how modern or innovative they were. In short order, other firms adopted the new application because it made operations cheaper or better to perform or in response to competitive threats, quickly shifting in the direction toward which early adopters swam. The rate of adoption was frequently constrained by the early adopters, companies that ultimately were the ones discussed by the press or scholars. Managers were constrained either by a limited view of what to do or because of some overt initiative put up by a rival to block others from doing the same. Managers were often slow to embrace change, slower than we were led to believe.[49] Regardless of the reason, however, patterns of adoption were evident in many industries. The code language for adoption hides the "me too" feature of this practice, describing the rationale as *modern* (the word used in the 1950s) or as *best practices* (a term widely used in the 1980s and 1990s). But the point is that adoption took place in waves, first within one industry and then across others, albeit in modified form, transforming to meet the specific requirements of one industry over another.

Another pattern was a variant of the school-of-fish phenomenon, involving individual companies. Normally, before a whole industry adopted an application from another industry, the first industry had to be an extensive user of the application in question. To achieve that extent of deployment, early adopters had to demonstrate success with a particular technology and its applications, which then caused other members of the same industry to embrace them, thus learning from one another. In subsequent chapters I describe dozens of examples of early adopters in one industry that are serving as role models for other firms, just as industries served as instructive pioneers for other industries.

Did industries adopt applications from firms in other industries that deployed an application not yet in wide use within that company's industry? In general, the answer is no, they did not. Cross-industry adoptions normally occurred when firms within the adopting industry perceived that many companies within the host industry had embraced them.

I demonstrate in the chapters ahead that as a group managers in all industries were very cautious in making decisions about adoption and use of new technologies. Studies about the nature of decision making by managers regarding adoption of IT are few, often narrowly based case studies, with limited empirical basis. However, at the risk of being accused of Whigist historical practices, it is possible to take what we know about management decision making later in the century and assume that many of the same personal and professional conditions were operative in earlier decades, in the late Fordist era.

Neil Rackham, trained as a psychologist turned management consultant, conducted a study about sales behavior in the 1980s, basing his fieldwork on how high-tech firms sold their products. In the process, he collected a great deal of data on how managers bought these products. Rackham discovered that decisions about technology were either big or small. Small decisions concerned such matters as what PC or typewriter to buy. An error in judgment in such matters was relatively inconsequential to a manager. Decisions about major items, however, proved to be another matter. All of the applications described in the chapters that follow were, in each decade, clearly major decisions. The perceived value of adoption had to increase, as did the risk of making the wrong decision. Mitigating risk became an essential element in a manager's decision to adopt a new technology or application. Rackham stated that "larger decisions are more public and a bad choice is much more visible" than a small bad decision.[50] Regarding value, a manager would perceive that an application had sufficient relevance (i.e., value) if the seriousness of the problem to be solved by adoption or the economic gains made possible outweigh the cost and risk of the technology.[51] An earlier study of managerial decision making done in the early 1960s also focused on management practices as applied in high-tech firms like IBM, GE, Kodak, and Xerox, among others. Risk played an equally important role in decisions about complex issues, such as those involving adoption of new technologies.[52]

Three distinct periods of historic significance have emerged, providing definition of the large number of events over the past half century in manufacturing's evolution, described in the next chapter. The definition of these periods may seem arbitrary, and they certainly varied chronologically from one industry to another. That variation is problematic because it lacks the clean cut of a dramatic and obvious historical break, such as those provided by such dramatic events as December 7, 1941, or September 11, 2001. Therefore, one should consider the characterization of the three periods as tentative, an early attempt to carve out a path in the jungle of the Information Age, introduced in the preface. With that framework in mind, it will be possible to examine briefly a number of industries to provide further specificity to our understanding of the role computing technology played in the transformation of manufacturing industries.

4

Business Patterns and Digital Applications in the Transformation of Manufacturing Industries

Economic efficiency consists of making things that are worth more than they cost.

—John Maurice Clark, 1923

If we describe the adoption of manufacturing applications over time by grouping them into periods, we can see more clearly the evolutionary nature of how industries embraced the digital. We can also begin to understand what precipitated an industry's evolution from one period to another. What immediately becomes evident is that several conditions stimulated the move from one phase to another. The most important were these:

- Growth of knowledge and experience with earlier applications and technologies, which led to incremental improvements or further integration of processes and equipment
- Improvements in the performance, ease of use, flexibility, and value of digital technologies, leading to faster, more productive, and lower costs of production
- Emergence of industry-specific digital tools (hardware and software) that performed specific manufacturing tasks, which made the transition from earlier practices easier to achieve, often with less risk of disrupting operations in an economically dangerous way

The periods in the evolution of manufacturing presented in this chapter are intended not so much to be definitive as to be suggestive. They offer a perspective to facilitate a better understanding of the phases this sector went through during the last half century. It provides a mechanism for collecting more precise descriptions of how computers were adopted and used across the industrial landscape. The discussion below is limited to the American experience, where many of the applications were first adopted. Applications were used later in other countries by American firms operating elsewhere or by foreign manufacturing firms learning about these applications as Americans did, from vendors, publications, or conferences or by hiring those experienced in their use. This was especially the pattern until the late 1970s, by which time Europe and Asia had their own sources of knowledge, experience, and technologies upon which to draw. American leadership was particularly evident in the first two phases, less so late in the second and early third, when Japanese managerial innovations became fashionable.

The history of American manufacturing applications can be divided conveniently into three periods: late Fordism and the dawn of computer-driven automation (1940s–early 1960s), start of integrated computer-aided manufacturing (1960s–1980s), and the years of transition from mass production to flexible manufacturing (1980s–1990s), into the era of the digital style. For each I describe key bellwether applications and the digital technological innovations that made them possible. Because the events described are so close to our time, the periods are admittedly somewhat arbitrary since the borders between one era and others remain fuzzy. That imprecision is also created by the fact that companies and industries lived concurrently in one period or another; for example, one industry could be focused in one decade on applications that had already been adopted in an earlier decade (e.g., CAD in aerospace in the 1950s and 1960s, but by retailers designing stores in the 1980s or manufacturers of toys in the 1990s).

First Period: Late Fordism and the Dawn of Automation, 1940s–Early 1960s

American industry came out of World War II intact, avoiding the ravages of war faced by all other industrial states across the entire planet. However, expectations of the economy and of what Americans wanted in the way of personal lifestyles were high for ex-soldiers and their relatives: they wanted to share in the anticipated prosperity. Demand for consumer goods was also great, thanks to pent-up demand for consumer goods unavailable during the war. Factories, however, were old, often in need of modernization. By the late 1940s, engineers were beginning to learn about computers, although these devices were still seen as scientific instruments or as tools for the military. But changes were coming. In 1947, for example, the Ford Motor Company created an organization called the Automation Department. Watched by many other manufacturing companies, it had responsibility for finding new ways of implementing electromechanical, hydraulic, and pneumatic technologies to improve manufacturing operations. That mission meant reducing the labor

Hall-Mark Electronics, in Dallas, Texas, used a computer to manage an inventory of 75,000 different types of electronic components with 500 million parts. This picture, taken in 1978, shows computing equipment physically located in the warehouse itself. Burroughs Papers, courtesy Archives of the Charles Babbage Institute, University of Minnesota, Minneapolis.

content of work and connecting stand-alone processes and tasks into more integrated forms. In 1950 Ford opened its first "automated" plant to much public attention. Although it did not initially use computers, the company's action stimulated interest in automating operations.[1]

At about the same time, the U.S. Air Force began to insist that providers of complex aircraft needed more precise techniques for designing and building airplanes. It turned to an emerging technology it was funding at the time, numerical control (NC) of machine tools. It became available in the early 1950s to ensure, among other things, that wings were designed so they would not fall off at high speeds, as well as to improve the overall quality of design and machining. Early NC equipment (circa early to mid–1950s) was developed to meet military needs but, by the end of the 1950s, began to make its way into other commercial applications.[2] This technology also became the basis for using machine data (the output of NC design or computer aided design, CAD) to instruct new machine tools to cut and bend metal to the exact specifications of the CAD application, leading to what then became known as computer aided manufacturing, or CAM. By the late 1960s, the two were frequently combined into an extended process, often called CAD/CAM. Thus, by the end of the first period, large manufacturing firms understood how to design and start manufacturing by using CAD/CAM tools. Of the two, CAD was the most advanced in the 1950s; CAM's effective and wide adoption began in the early 1970s. Manufacturing managers were not certain how best to deploy these tools and thus mixed and matched technologies with functions to figure out what made sense. One commentator in 1969 noted, "Today it is still the wild exception rather than the rule for centralized numerical control operations coordinated across the board."[3]

These applications epitomized an evolutionary move away from the Fordist emphasis on using equipment and technology to perform transfer tasks. In the period after World War II, as illustrated by Ford's automation department, such uses led manufacturing companies to innovate with continued applications of machines to achieve and improve control over routine operations.[4] Despite much hype about the revolutionary aspects of automation, often the result of hyperbolic press reports, decision makers in manufacturing were a cautious lot. One manufacturing expert in the mid-1950s explained that "in most manufacturing plants automation comes gradually, being adapted to certain machines and processes and not to others." An emphasis on eliminating manual tasks pervaded much of the thinking about how to use any type of technology, not just computers. Arthur C. Ansley, just quoted above, was president of a small manufacturing firm; he explained the approach this way: "Basically, automation is an outgrowth of the concept known as 'feedback,' which means that information about the result of a process is used to control the process itself." What that allowed manufacturing managers and supervisors on the floor to do was to adjust to changes in production: "An automatic gaging device can measure the critical dimensions on the pieces that have been machined or are being machined, and when these start to run too large or too small, the information can be relayed to an automatic device that adjusts the cutting tools to correct the condition."[5] Ansley noted that automation worked best (as of the 1950s) where there were continuous processes, such as in oil refineries and in chemical plants, but that was also true of large manufacturing firms, such as automobile factories and mass producers of consumer goods (e.g., GE). The majority placed emphasis on controlling processes.[6]

By the late 1950s, one could begin to see a set of trends developing in the kinds of applications computers and other machines were being used for, which for all intents and purposes both enhanced control and capped or reduced the work force. One trend included mechanization of the feed to and removal of work from a variety of manufacturing machines.[7] These kinds of tasks lowered labor costs and improved machine utilization.[8] In one survey of this generalized application, it was not uncommon to see more than a 60 percent increase in utilization because machines were being better optimized than before. A second trend involved mechanization of materials handling (also called inventory control and, later, logistics) for a wide range of functions, for example, moving raw materials and parts from trucks to warehouses and then to the factory floor or from completed production to warehouses and then to stores and customers. This was always a labor-intensive activity.[9]

A third trend involved mechanization of the production process, most notably in such industries as radio and television manufacturing (e.g., at GE and RCA) but also in bottling and production of toiletries and automobiles. Labor costs per unit produced dropped while uniformity of the manufactured product increased. Turning, twisting, bolting, screwing, cutting, painting, and moving parts and products were increasingly mechanized—often using robotic devices—and over time acquired computing capability. That additional functionality made it possible for workers to tell machines what to do and when and. They could also instruct those same devices to report what they had accomplished and when and to report variations or problems. Automotive manufacturers were often pioneers, but incremental changes appeared in most manufacturing industries as computer (digital) intelligence was slowly added to industry-specific machines. Paper-making machines were typical. Over time they were interconnected so that pulp flowed in one end of the factory and boxed paper products flowed out the other end, were packed, and were loaded on trucks and trains.

A fourth trend concerned mechanization of distribution, which usually involved sorting goods, assembling and dissembling loads and packets, and loading and unloading, all to the specifications of customers or factory users of the materials. Some plants also attempted to mechanize testing, a labor-intensive activity in complex products, such as electrical equipment, and even in computers themselves at an IBM or Burroughs factory, for instance. Finally, mechanizing packaging became an early application of technologies of all types, involving putting boxes together, stuffing them with products, and labeling them for delivery. The Trane Company of La Crosse, Wisconsin, a leading manufacturer of air conditioners, for example, became an early user of this application, and in the process reduced the costs of its packing materials by 50 percent.[10]

I was careful not to mention computers in the paragraph above because what so many manufacturing firms did was to link a variety of devices together, including old equipment, new manufacturing units, and later, by the late 1950s, either computers or peripheral devices attached to computers (such as magnetic tape, used in very primitive CAD/CAM applications). That is how firms began the process of integrating existing and new devices together. Often data from or about a step in a procedure (such as the arrival of parts in a warehouse) would be fed into a computer, which then transmitted the information to the factory floor, along with a production schedule calculated by computer, that told a work team, "We now have the parts you need; therefore, use them at a particular time in such-and-such machines." Those kinds of marriages between computing and existing technology made possible the early development of feedback control, particularly in production and production scheduling. Optimizing set-up and tear-down times became a very important process that computers began to help with, although more effective in later decades. Every time a new task had to be performed that was slightly different than before (e.g., drill a different size hole in metal) one had to stop, adjust the equipment and then run it again. This was time not spent manufacturing, thus, wasted. Scheduling similar tasks to increase the number of exact repetitions made good use of equipment and reduced setup and tear-down times. By the end of the 1950s, computers were beginning to help with this task.[11]

Several applications suggested how the work in manufacturing began to change profoundly, if in an evolutionary manner, in the 1950s: inventory control, business applications, and numerical control. The first became the most widely adopted new application in the 1950s; the second, the most widely used existing blend of old and new technologies; and the last, the newest, more radical use of computers, as

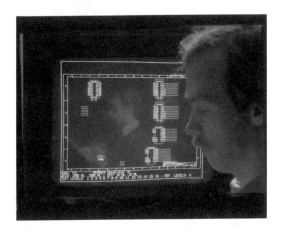

This is what an engineer in 1981 would see on a CAD/CAM terminal. In this instance, the engineer would do all his drawing directly on the screen with a light pen. Burroughs Papers, courtesy Archives of the Charles Babbage Institute, University of Minnesota, Minneapolis.

well as the least deployed until improvements in software and hardware came in the 1960s. By looking briefly at these three major groups of applications, we can get a good sense of how manufacturing firms began to insert computers into existing operations. To avoid fragmenting the discussion of change, I include comments on each of the second applications later in this chapter.

Inventory Control Applications

The history of inventory control can be divided into two phases: the first involves installation of software to manage the ordering, receiving, tracking, and disposition of inventory; the second, optimization of just-in-time inventory control. The first phase characterizes how computers were used in the 1950s through the 1970s and, to a large extent, to the present. The second approach came in full force in the 1980s and has existed concurrently with the first set of applications to the present day. Inventory control applications exist in all industries, from retail operators who buy goods to sell to manufacturers who need parts and raw materials to turn into goods.[12] Even service sector companies have to manage inventories of office supplies, food for cafeterias, and furniture. Airlines think of their seats on airplanes as inventory and manage their utilization of these much like goods and materials.[13] Hotels and hospitals think of the management of their beds as potential inventory control-like applications. However, the pioneering work in the use of digital technology in the management of inventory began and continues to come from manufacturing industries, which is why this application is discussed here.[14]

Various terms have been used in manufacturing circles to describe this class of application: *inventory control, materials handling, materials requirements handling,* to mention just a few. The scope of inventory control historically involved a series of steps that began with determining what materials, parts, or goods were needed; were on hand, or needed to be acquired by a certain date. It is a collection of activities that focuses on the acquisition and movement of inventory. Typical activities involve forecasting demand, ordering, receiving, sorting, storing, moving, picking, checking, packing, shipping, and reporting activities, results, and costs. Over the entire half century, automation of these activities, along with using computing to help optimize them and thus drive down costs, have been in evidence across all companies and industries, not just in manufacturing. The reason management always cared about inventory control, and thus why it was normally willing to invest substantially in computers to support this application, lies in the enormous costs of carrying and using inventory. Inventory carrying costs have normally run between 10 to over 30 percent of the value of goods produced in any industry in any decade in the past half century. If one could reduce inventory carrying costs by just several percentages—a goal frequently achieved in the earliest days of computing—a substantial reduction in the costs of manufacturing could be realized. The sloppier the manufacturing firm was in managing inventory, the greater the opportunity existed to lower costs.[15]

Computers could be used to collect data on what was needed and what was on hand. The objective was to key in data accurately at the source, where inventory existed in various forms (e.g., parts, Work-in-process [WIP], finished goods); do it quickly; and give that information to those attempting to ensure that the right amount of inventory was available or to those working to drive down the costs of inventory. Vendors like IBM developed equipment specifically for this purpose (e.g., the IBM 357 Data Collection System), using keypunches, cards, and later tape and disk. Burroughs thought the application so important that it trained salespeople in the specifics of how it worked, even showing them process flowcharts and how to create such applications.[16] That data could then be used to generate various types of order status reports.[17] By the mid-1960s, such reports could tell shop floor management where discrepancies existed between planned and actual inventories, what were sources of cost overruns, and when parts and goods had to be ordered. The savings could be impressive.[18]

The Foster Wheeler Corporation, using an IBM 1401 computer system in its factory in the early 1960s, cut its cost for inventory on hand by 50 percent. It was a job shop company, which meant that it constantly needed more or different inventory than it had. Accounting controls were of paramount importance. By categorizing inventory into different types, the firm could decide what buying and usage policies it should implement and see the results of these decisions reflected on the bottom line (what should be subject to predetermined minimum economic order practices, how much should be acquired to leverage quantity discount terms, etc.). In this example, the firm generated a series of reports: Weekly Late Material Report, Due Material Report, Vendor Analysis Report, Quarterly Usage Report, and the Weekly Balance on Hand Report.[19]

These applications helped companies operate with smaller on-hand inventories. One industry expert from the 1960s, Justin A. Periman, stated that "decreased inventory results from the ability to 'work' a small inventory harder under computer directions or computer control."[20] Optimization of labor and inventory could be modeled by using software. At Western Electric, for example, optimization "was particularly acute on contracts where the company had committed itself to the purchase of specific quantities during the life of the contract." Too little inventory drove up costs of production; too much wasted funds, especially for inventory that might perish (e.g., rust).[21] Notifying production departments about the receipt of parts or distribution or availability of finished goods became essential in quickly improving operations across the entire factory. For example, IBM installed receiving systems at its Rochester, Minnesota, and Raleigh, North Carolina, plants in the mid-1960s to establish immediate control: "When the order is unloaded from the truck, the vendor's packing list is matched with a card file consisting of one card for each part number on order." Employees could compare what came with what was on order, determine what delivery they accepted (or rejected), update accounting records immediately, and report the "now available inventory" by telephone to the plant. The company's own description of the application used the words "immediate," "control," and concern over the "length of time to process stock" to describe priorities and issues. These were typical concerns of all manufacturing operations.[22]

One feature of all these data collection and analysis systems was the increased frequency of reporting, which made it possible for managers to react earlier to deviations from plans for inventory or production. Before the computer, the one basic tool management used was the annual physical inventory count, which always proved to differ from the reports. Thus a one-time write-off would be taken, which came right out of profits. One manager reported that "everyone deplores this situation and says we ought to do something about it." By moving to monthly reports in the 1960s and, by the end of the 1970s, routinely to weekly reports, management could react to discrepancies earlier, while they were smaller and when there was time to recover from errors or imbalances. Over time, managers learned to link inventory reports to specific shop floor production tasks so that they could isolate a specific step in the production process where problems existed or reoccurred, indicating where decision makers should focus their attention.[23]

The process of using computers for inventory control came slowly, and changes to an installed set of programs were adopted incrementally. For example, one automotive firm (Chrysler), installed its first inventory control application in 1955, using an IBM 702 to capture and report on inventory status. Analytical reports on forecasts, history, and so forth came next. Forecasting alone took several years to put on the computer, beginning in 1958. By 1961, a manager of systems and process at Chrysler could report that "decisions are made, transactions within the Division are completed, paper work is executed, reports are prepared—all within the confines of the computer."[24]

By the early 1970s, inventory management through computers had become a mainstream topic of discussion. Even the *Harvard Business Review* discussed the nature and benefits of computer-driven inventory management practices, declaring that "specialists on inventory and scheduling and also line managers have succumbed to the lure of statistical tools in managing parts inventories." One writer in the review noted, however, that firms were increasingly learning to link together various inventory control applications, just as in other manufacturing applications. Linking requirements planning and inventory control more closely generated more savings and other economic benefits than did two separate applications.[25] But management had been warned as far back as the mid-1960s that such approaches required the same skills as other integrative applications in manufacturing. George W. Plossl and Oliver W. Wight, two highly regarded experts on manufacturing applications in the 1950s and 1960s, observed in 1967 that there already existed a requirement to understand manufacturing control systems, even by "top managers of the future." In fact, that occurred through the 1970s and 1980s.[26] By the 1990s, Japanese inventory control practices had also led to an expansion in knowledge about supply chain management, which I discuss in chapters 6 and 7.

Beginning in the 1970s, Japanese manufacturers, and more specifically automobile firms like Toyota, began building assembly lines that were different from traditional American approaches and which, in time, became better known as the Toyota System. The new lines could produce multiple models of vehicles on the same assembly line. The process for changing dies (the molds that bend sheets of metal into body parts) also was altered, and workers were given more responsibility in controlling the rate of production, even the authority to stop a production line. Workers were organized into teams to improve throughput efficiencies. Toyota and, later, others firms also made their suppliers part of the production process by giving them manufacturing schedules and materials requirements files, making them bring to a factory only those parts needed for that day's production (e.g., tires needed for specific quantities of individual models). That change alone increasingly shifted inventory control responsibilities away from the production center and put it more on the shoulders of the parts suppliers. It also called for a larger sharing of inventory and production planning data with other companies and other plants. In turn, that meant new software applications were needed to replace more traditional inventory control systems such as those described in earlier paragraphs. During the 1980s, all kinds of new technologies were embedded in this approach, such as scanners to read United Parcel Service (UPS) labels, personal computers, and a variety of sensors.[27]

By the late 1980s, this approach was being implemented in all American manufacturing industries, especially in the Automotive Industry, where joint partnerships and partial ownership of Japanese firms were created to share expertise. I will have more to say about these new processes in the next chapter.

Business Applications

There was a class of accounting and financial activities in the beginning of the 1950s that relied exclusively either on manual processes or on the use of office appliances, such as adding machines, billing machines, calculators, or IBM's tabulating punchcard systems.[28] Manufacturing firms extensively used all sorts of these devices. During the 1950s, the firms began slowly to move some of their accounting and financial applications to computers because they could be done faster or less expensively. These applications included accounting, order processing, billing, payroll, and inventory control.[29] All were perfect candidates for use with the relatively new, and not fully understood, computer because business applications were very well understood. Moreover, they were often well documented, which made it easier to program portions of their activities. These functions were sequential and routine, which meant that they could be scheduled to run at certain times (e.g., payroll on Thursday night for all employees), with one paycheck following another. In large factories, such applications were already run on tabulating equipment, and so the data were already captured on punch cards. Every manufacturer of computer equipment in the 1950s and 1960s offered the capability of using punch cards as data entry into their systems, which meant that much of the information needed to feed a computer was already in a form that such technology could use, saving the cost of a major change.[30] Two observers of such business applications noted that "these early computer systems processed data in batches, that is, they executed one program at a time and handled transactions (say, an accounting entry, such as payment of a bill) one at a time from a predefined sequence of transactions (such as all payments in a batch presorted by account number)." Although computers were often unreliable and slow, they ultimately proved less expensive and faster than people, and usually more accurate.[31]

Early on companies emphasized long-established directions—doing normal accounting work, reducing labor content and, improving accuracy—yet they also struggled with the problem of how best to install and run computers, which were anything but easy to use.[32] Accountants expressed anxiety about how to use computers and worried about what effect the machines would have on their work and careers.[33] At the same time they were bragging about how the successful installation of computers had become, in a word, fashionable by the late 1950s. Managers bragged in many industries. Often electronic data processing (EDP) managers were the ones who touted the benefits of computers in accounting.[34] Thus, accountants did not buy fully into the new fashion and were also nervous about their ability to audit transactions processed by a computer. Accountants discussed how to audit computer-based applications, flagged issues of concern, and informed one another.[35] Both accountants and data-processing professionals also learned that adopting computers posed the usual problems of learning new skills (e.g., programming) and of dealing with the unknown, even if often with improved technology. But their concern represented a long-standing one about the use of accounting equipment in general, one still with us at the dawn of the new century. The flurry of new electromechanical accounting that appeared after World War II, but before the arrival of the computer as a viable technology for the private sector, had set off another round of discussions about auditing practices that continued through the 1950s and 1960s. One could argue, however, that accountants had the greatest preparation for using computers because of their more than half century involvement in the use of other accounting equipment. Their experience included tabulating gear, which, by the 1940s, had already become systematized; that is, one fed cards with data into one machine that was linked with other devices that performed calculations and printed reports, providing answers at the other end. All of that activity had to be documented, processed, managed, and audited.[36]

Early Numerical Control Applications

Numerical control (NC) enjoys the luxury of having its own historian, David E. Noble, who used it as a way of demonstrating how development and adoption of a specific technology was less a story about scientific and engineering absolutes than one about politics and social history. He pointed the way for many other historians who were attempting to understand how technologies emerged and evolved. But Noble downplayed the potential business role of NC applications. As war-related products, such as aircraft, became more complicated, so did their design. Constituents for such complex products, in this case the U.S. Air Force, influenced the role of designing and manufacturing to meet its own ends. By the early 1960s, the U.S. Air Force underwrote a good 90 percent of all research and development (R&D) underway in the American aircraft industry. But that developmental work, funded by the U.S. government, led to NC tools that were later used across American industry. The Cold War forced on the American military the necessity to drive development of new weapons and processes for making them, providing an early stimulus for the development of NC tools in the late 1940s and all through the 1950s and 1960s.[37]

Students of the machine tool industry have noted the enormous advances made in NC in the 1950s and early 1960s in the United States, loss of American leadership in the development and sale of such technologies in the 1970s and 1980s, and global deployment of these tools across all types of manufacturing industries during the last two decades of the twentieth century.[38] These events should be seen within the context of a variety of tools developed in the late twentieth century for the purpose of cutting or forming metal and, later, other products, all relying on instructions from computers. The Servomechanism Laboratory at MIT developed the first NC tools in 1952, following some three years of work on this project. These tools and all others that followed were based on two concepts:

- That numerical information stored in a computer could be the basis for both the design of a product or component
- That this information could instruct cutting and molding tools to replicate the product as exactly designed

However, one important technical problem had to be solved in the 1950s, namely, getting one technical standard that lent itself to compatibility across many tools. There were four essential systems; by the end of the 1950s one had been selected, and it influenced the technical configuration of NC systems for years afterward.[39]

The aerospace manufacturers were the first companies to embrace this technology because the U.S. Air Force mandated that these tools be used if a firm wanted to bid on military orders. Their industry was a virtual prisoner of its largest customer, the U.S. government, in the 1950s. In time, these federal mandates benefited commercial contracts, but that was an event still in the future. Other industries also tinkered with the same technology. Many adaptations to other, often less exacting applications, such as the design of power plants and vehicles, were made over the years. But in the 1950s, the equipment and application were cumbersome, did not always work well, and proved to be very expensive. Nonetheless, these adaptations exposed some manufacturing firms to a new class of machining tools, technologies that had the potential of being extraordinarily valuable for their accuracy and ability to control production. The most extensive number of adopters of NC during the 1960s came from metal fabrication plants because NC worked better than, for example, templates and cams. They could be linked to existing machine-tooling technologies, and they virtually eliminated human error while driving down the costs of scrap and inventory. The time needed to manufacture a product shrank.[40] The big breakthrough in the efficiency of such tools came after the development of the microprocessor in the early 1970s. Costs of NC tools and software came down; they began performing better and became easier to use.

But long before those developments, manufacturing companies had experimented with NC tools. As with other applications of computers, those knowledgeable about NC were not shy about writing and speaking about it. Many engineers responsible for knowing about emerging technologies in machine tools were exposed initially and primarily to NC through their trade publications. Others became familiar with this technology through actual hands-on experience (e.g., in the Aerospace Industry). As early as 1956, for example, *Tool Engineering* carried an article introducing the technology, but it also argued that such tools were best used in very large production environments, such as in airplane manufacturing.[41] In trying out these new tools, managers had come to realize that the tools required fundamental changes in production processes, something they were generally reluctant to implement in the 1950s and, for that matter, in the 1960s, until the technology made the effort worth it. Very few industries had the need to produce such precision-dependent components as did aerospace, defense, or producers of complex electronics, like computers.

Numerical control applications were always complicated but never more so than during the 1950s–1970s, when the technology and its applications were emerging for the first time. Effective use required extensive planning to make sure there was a steady flow of work to equipment. Managers found NC equipment very expensive, so maintenance had to be outstanding to avoid the high costs of down time. The NC users needed programmers who could program this specific type of technology. Managers found this kind of technology was best used when they needed to make low-volume, complicated parts. These characteristics also led to the need for more status reports, information that had to be gathered where none had been collected before.[42]

Numerical control is a technology, while today ubiquitous in manufacturing, that experienced a very slow start, in contrast to the use of computers in inventory control and office applications, where proof of benefits already existed. Users in the 1950s and early 1960s were disappointed at the costs and complexity of NC technology.[43] The NC applications, therefore, were not of any great importance in American industry during those years. One international study of the diffusion of NC reported that less than 5 percent of all manufacturing machines were controlled through NC techniques in 1964; this use grew to 15 percent by 1969, twice as much as in factories in Germany, which led Europe in the early use of NC. Large firms tended to be first users, and American firms made up the largest percentage.[44] This is an example of an application that did not work well until the technology had sufficient quality and low-enough cost to make its adoption practical and economically advantageous. Not until that occurred did wide adoption occur. When those conditions were met, NC took off because American industrial managers, although slow to adopt a new technology until proven effective, were always quick to seize on it once it was demonstrated to be viable. In the case of NC, that occurred in the second half of the 1960s.

Since NC tools substituted for human labor, one would expect that in countries where labor costs were high, such applications would prove to be attractive. In fact, that happened in the early years of this technology. The greatest user nation was the one with the highest labor costs, the United States by far. In countries with the least labor costs, diffusion occurred in the 1960s at far lower rates, for example, in Italy and Austria.[45] Of course, the role played by the U.S. government and, more specifically, the air force in stimulating risk-free research on NC proved decisive as well. The British government attempted to do the same thing, but its efforts were far less effective in stimulating deployment of the new technology.[46] In the United States, the largest numbers of these tools were deployed in mechanical engineering applications, cutting metal per CAD instructions. By type of industry, Aerospace had the largest number, 12 times as many as did the Automotive Industry.[47]

The introduction of computers into commercial settings and away from their original purpose, performing scientific or military applications, stimulated changes not always anticipated. Already by the late 1950s it was becoming evident that computers caused changes in how organizations operated. Contemporary observers began noticing the effect of the computer: "Rarely are the functions of an organization such that they remain unchanged in a computerization program. Even what is ostensibly the same operation may change substantially in the overall results."[48] What occurred with NC is a good example; so, too, are general production processes. Not so clear, however, was the extent of the changes. Initially, changes occurred in processes and later, in the 1970s and 1980s, also in corporate culture, business practices, and the organization of manufacturing operations. There were problems, however, in the earlier era in issues related to accurate, fast, and cost-effective input of data into computers and understanding existing and proposed changes to processes, as well as knowing how best to audit and manage data processing. Then there were the twin issues of having people knowledgeable about the use of computers and training a continuous new supply of users.[49] A problem still faced at the dawn of the twenty-first century by those pondering the acquisition of yet other new digital devices is an age-old one, very alive in the 1950s, and involves exuberance for new technology. Richard G. Canning, a leading authority on computers in the 1950s, described it well: "Experience has already shown that the old problem of over-optimism is just as prevalent in this field as it has been in others . . ." but as now, "whether the path is easy or thorny, this new tool deserves the serious consideration of management."[50] Heightened enthusiasm was a problem if one expected too much from a technology. Yet such exuberance also made it possible to implement new tools.

The arrival of the microprocessor made use of NC equipment in the 1970s and beyond much easier and helped drive down costs. But even in the pre-microprocessor years, and despite Noble's criticisms of the technology or the complexity of it, American firms became users, although few in number. The best data available suggest that in about 1971–1972, out of the 3 million installed industrial machine tools in the United States, NC technology controlled some 20,000, in other words, less than 1 percent.[51] By the late 1980s, the technology was ubiquitous across American manufacturing industries.

Second Period: The Start of Integrated Computer-Aided Manufacturing, 1960s–1980s

The second period of the deployment of computers proved to be one in which almost all of the manufacturing applications associated with a computerized *style* of operation came into being. This period began after 1965–1966, when general-purpose digital computer systems that were compatible with other models reached the market (making upgrades and expansion of applications less painful than in the 1950s).[52] These systems also continued to become cheaper than other options, such as older, precomputer technologies or unionized labor, whose cost kept rising relative to work forces in many less-developed economies. These were the years when computing came packaged in smaller systems (minicomputers), which often could then be dedicated to one or a few applications. In this period, the personal computer came into existence and use and engineers began to embed computing capability in manufacturing equipment itself. When we think of the adoption of computers by manufacturing industries, this era was a Golden Age.

Solving manufacturing problems and increasing productivity drove many of the decisions about the application of computers. The need to integrate various activities became increasingly important as separate work functions (e.g., inventory control) began to overlap with other processes, also often with overlapping data collection and other software applications. One observer at the time, Gideon Halevi, explained it this way:

> Inventory transactions could be used both as receiving feedback data for purchasing and as shipping feedback data for customer orders, while job recording could not only be used for computation or wages, but also as feedback to production planning and as basic data for labor costing. The interest in data from one application to another was mutual. The application user could save time and effort by not having to write down input forms for the computer, while data processing saved keypunching work.[53]

But these problems were rooted in business issues. The increased interest shown by senior management in manufacturing industries all across America at the start of the 1970s, in particular, could be laid at the doorstep of basic business considerations. One DP industry publication of the period summarized the problems executives were addressing with computers: "Major pressure for automation continues to come from rising wage rates and the need for higher labor productivity." Although this theme of labor cost permeates the discussion about motives all through the half century, we cannot ignore the periodic effect of the cost of money on capital goods, such as computers: "The high cost of capital is forcing automation aimed at boosting the productivity of existing equipment."[54] By 1981, interest rates in the United States were double digit.

The need for increased integration of standalone applications grew and, for some firms, became critical. Most of these applications emerged out of different departments within manufacturing companies or plant sites, each with its own data and software.

Several problems needed to be addressed by most manufacturing companies to speed up integration of operations. The first concerned how data would be updated and how frequently reported to other departments that depended on them to do their work (e.g., updated inventory information so that the purchasing department could update its own order status records). A second problem, and one that most companies continued to face deep into the 1990s, involved various departmental views of the data. Most departments viewed their data differently than others. There were problems with format, which meant that data in one software application might not port over to another without rekeying. There was the related issue of capturing information needed by one department but not another. For example, the purchasing department might collect purchase order (PO) numbers and a vendor's name, but the inventory control department would not need these data. For accounting, the inventory control people would have to preserve the purchase order data and vendor name on their control documents. For years holy wars were fought within companies over these issues, including what might in hindsight be pedantic—the length and format of a part or product number. Yet such issues had to be resolved to facilitate transportation of information from one system to another to make the integration of applications possible. Often data-processing personnel acted as negotiators among departments, much like the U.S. State Department acted as mediator between the Arab states and Israel.

The final problem involved consequences of sharing. Most departments were willing to share information, but often that, too, created problems: more data had to be collected, their applications had to do or not do certain things, and so forth. Thus, while the adoption of applications went forward, the hunt for integration became both essential and difficult. Behind all the descriptions of the applications in the chapters ahead were these problems and tensions, which remained a feature of the period.

By the late 1960s, engineers and other manufacturing personnel began to advocate distributed data processing, that is, the use of minis to support independent applications that did not have to be integrated (e.g., CAD/CAM). Engineers, in particular, found this approach attractive because the majority of them suspected that their DP departments were prisoners of the accounting departments (into which most DP personnel reported in a company's organization) and would thus treat manufacturing applications as secondary, thereby slowing the work of engineers and shop floor personnel. Such end users saw distributed processing as a quick fix. Another approach, the one general management tended to favor more, involved the use of databases and integrated applications. Databases required standard formats for information that could be used by a number of applications, the key to integration.[55] By the end of the second period, most companies wound up with a combination of both standalone (distributed processing) and the use of various databases. The Holy Grail of integration was rarely found, although always sought after. Often people would brag that they had achieved it. Several presenters at the annual convention of the DPMA in 1966, reporting on their work at the Micro Switch Division at Honeywell, were typical:

> It may be said without reservation that, since the introduction of an integrated data processing and control system, MICRO SWITCH is processing more sales, delivering a greater proportion of orders on schedule, and decreasing the amount of inventory required to support a given volume of sales, decreasing variances, and expending a smaller percentage of its income on clerical expenses.[56]

Nirvana indeed; however, more normal, incremental integration occurred all through the period, even in the earlier years (circa 1960s).[57]

One of the most effective points of integration concerned sales and inventory control applications. As early as the mid-1960s, some firms were able to share information within these two parts of their organizations. Specifically, the ability to share information and do planning increased with financial sales data, finished goods inventory, some manufacturing planning, and production facilities simulation. To do so normally required some common sets of shared data on production, customers, vendors, inventory, and employees. By having some commonly agreed-on sets of data, as one manager of the period put it, "these files eliminate duplication of effort and inconsistencies of data, and make possible the minimizing of variable input data."[58] With the cost of data input always high in this period, minimizing redundancy and errors remained a critical goal.

The availability of better database software tools in the 1970s made possible further integration of applications and control of work.[59] Online data entry had come into its own as well, with data entered through CRTs in combination with batches of cards and, by the early 1980s, scanning of documents as data input. Most of these data went into databases that fed multiple applications. For example, the Allen-Bradley Company, a leading manufacturer of electrical equipment in the 1970s, implemented six applications that exploited data entry capabilities of the period and shared files: Sales Order Entry System, Shipping Order System (to track customer order status), Shop Floor Order System (to track orders in various stages of production by customer), Production/Materials Control System (in this case, inventory control, purchasing, etc.), Shop Floor Control System (to track work on parts, not flow of materials), and a financial system. The company reported that it saved on the costs of doing business with such a system, largely "directly from eliminating paperwork and duplicated paper handling facilities." Fifty manual files disappeared, replaced with online integrated files. Inventory could be found more quickly than before, and labor errors declined. As good as this sounded, one DP manager at the company admitted that "the implementation was not inexpensive. The firm assigned 30 persons to systems development for the five and a half years it took to come online."[60]

A debate over the pros and cons of centralized versus decentralized computing took place in this period, one that raged across all industries but, because of the large presence of applications in manufacturing, seemed most intense there.[61] In general, by the mid-1980s, advocates of centralization tended to win more often than not, although decentralized applications continued to be deployed to the present day. We need to acknowledge, if only briefly, the ever present management concern about control. Larry D. Woods, data-processing manager at Deere and Company, bluntly expressed the anxiety of "glass house" managers: "Much of the computing is leaving our data processing departments. It is leaving in an uncontrolled, uncoordinated manner."[62] He argued that this trend posed the threat "for much of our corporate data also to [sic] leaving the computing." At his company, management chose to use database software as the vehicle for regaining control over information and operations:

> The philosophy was to standardize on the data being used within the company. If this data was the responsibility of a unit, and used only by a unit, then that data became part of a unit data base. If the data was of corporate-wide interest, regardless of who had maintenance responsibility for it, then that data was considered part of a corporate data base.[63]

Woods reported considerable resistance to this strategy both within his company and across the industry. In the end, a compromise proved necessary with a hybrid of centralized and decentralized applications. "Distributed computing is for real. It is here," proclaimed Woods. Most data-processing professionals in the 1970s would have agreed with his declaration.[64]

Beginning in the late 1970s and continuing through the early 1980s, American manufacturing industries felt the sting of global competition, especially automotive manufacturing firms.[65] More than a discussion about the productivity paradox, senior and middle management concluded that combined increases in productivity, quality of products, and flexibility in manufacturing were needed. They engaged in considerable debate about the role of computers and, in the process, continued to invest in them. Double-digit growth rates in expenditures for new applications became quite common by the early years of the 1980s. The major applications were CAD/CAM for product design, engineering, and production applications; manufacturing information systems for overall planning, control, and coordination (essentially an extension of what had been started in the 1950s) but more integrated; industrial control applications, which were routinely dedicated to the control and monitoring of shop floor activities, using programmable controllers, NC tools, and process control; and flexible production systems (which really came into their own in the third period). The dominant applications of the early to mid-1980s were CAD/CAM and manufacturing information systems (engineering, planning, and control). A brief review of these developments, along with the emerging role of robotics, illustrates how this group of applications transformed American manufacturing between the late 1960s–early 1980s.

CAD/CAM Applications

Starting in the late 1960s, but more dramatically after the injection of microprocessors into CAD tools (beginning in the 1970s), CAD applications appeared across wide swaths of American industry. Additional memory capacity in computers, when coupled to ever faster microprocessors, made it possible to exploit dramatic increases in the speed, accuracy, and repeatability of such systems in the design of new products. Large databases also made it possible to reuse, say, previous designs for components. By the mid-1980s, one could begin to display fully designed products on a screen in three-dimensional (3-D) formats. In the 1970s, CAD-based designs could feed machining tools that were also equipped with microprocessors to perform computer-aided manufacturing (CAM).[66] Designs in the 1970s were two-dimensional (2-D), but in the 1980s, with the availability of more computing power, CAD began to produce the 3-D designs, which led to more precise modeling applications by the mid-1980s.

Early users of CAD/CAM software concentrated on modeling individual items, such as components of an automobile or airplane. This allowed prototypes to be designed and inaccuracies in their conception to be worked out before actual manufacture. In time, designs could be linked to those of other components that had to work together, all before manufacturing began. Once done, the output consisted of a collection of data that could then feed instructions to NC machines. Engineers in the early 1960s used teletype machines and some CRTs to get the job done, all very slow and awkward. By the early 1980s, that had changed because large CRTs could display blueprints and other design data, using highly interactive systems. As one user of the late 1970s noted, "The cost of such displays has become sufficiently low that computer graphics can now bring economic benefits to design in a wide range of industries." The technology had to evolve to a point where engineers found it effective, but the economic case had to be compelling, too: "The combined effects of escalating material, energy, and numerous other general costs which are adversely affecting industry have brought about a much greater emphasis on design."[67] Slide rules and blueprints were rapidly becoming relics of the past.

Companies typically began using CAD applications first, then, through use of NC-based tools, integrating CAD with CAM. By the late 1970s, and certainly in most industries by the early 1980s, one could see CAD/CAM applications linked together in three areas of manufacturing activity. First, design and drafting, the initial applications of CAD, dated back to the air force's original requirements in the 1950s, but they were now online and relatively fast. Engineers beginning their professional careers in the early 1980s rarely had memories of a pre-CAD era. Second, planning and scheduling applications began to appear in the late1970s. This second set of applications focused on the integration of NC/CAD with CAM. A third set of applications involved fabrication and machining of components and products by NC-driven tools. Through the 1980s, manufacturers increasingly integrated these three sets of functions.

This integration fundamentally changed how manufacturing was done in the age of the computer and represented a clear break from the Fordist style. A British engineering professor of the period, C. B. Besant, made the point well: "CAD/CAM systems tend to blur and erase the company structures that usually separate the marketing, engineering and production departments. This change can occur without rearranging office walls or the layout of the factory." He was already anticipating "the sharing of essential information with others departments."[68] In addition, productivity increased. In manufacturing sites without CAD/CAM, one could expect a part of work-in-process inventory (WIP) to be worked on only in 5 percent of the time that those components were in the possession of the factory; 95 percent of the time, the components sat there, waiting to be worked on. With CAD/CAM systems, setup and breakdown times on machines were shortened, and hence optimized, leading to this 95 percent wait time to drop sharply. With proper planning, for instance, setup time for NC machines could be reduced by 70 percent.[69]

The modeling capabilities of CAD made it possible by the early 1980s to design even small products by computer, such as shoes and artificial limbs, not just airplanes, cars, and bulldozers. In less than a quarter of a century these systems had moved from primitive plotting pens to online graphics to 3-D. An observer in 1984 described the full range of CAD's capabilities: "Today's CAD units include an expanding array of software that permits such functions as geometric modeling, simulation, engineering analysis, testing, and interfacing with manufacturing, as well as automated drafting. These new capabilities are revolutionizing mechanical design."[70] However, this same observer noted that fully integrated CAD/CAM systems were only in actual use in "a handful of manufacturers."

At the same time that CAD/CAM applications expanded in American industries another set of uses for computers began, often called computer-aided engineering (CAE). Closely linked to CAD/CAM, CAE is a convenient term for describing a collection of engineering applications involving computers from a broad range of engineering functions, such as civil, mechanical, and electrical. An engineer might design something with CAD, which then would have to be analyzed to see if it would work, could handle the stresses it experienced, and so forth. The software used to do that analysis is CAE. Thus, we can think of CAE as sitting somewhere between CAD and final CAM. Typical CAE applications in the 1980s included finite element analysis (FEA), behavior of mechanical systems in motion (e.g., car parts or airplane brakes), and by the mid-1980s rapid prototyping, which made it possible to produce one perfect physical copy for experiment and analysis (see table 4.1). Civil engineers, designing piping for a process plant, began using CAE in the 1980s, but not as extensively as did mechanical engineers (see table 4.2). A new collection of software tools was developed in the 1970s and has evolved today to satisfy the specific needs of electrical engineers who wanted to use CAE applications to design computer chip circuits, computer memories, and other digital devices.[71] By about 1980, a third of the CAE applications existed in the Aerospace Industry, another 25 percent in automotive companies, an equal percentage in electrical and

Table 4.1
Sample Computer-Aided Engineering (CAE) Applications, 1980s–1990s

Finite element analysis (FEA)	Piping
Volume properties	Mapping
Mechanism analysis	Circuit design
Rapid prototyping	Simulation
Surveying	E-CAD databases

Source: John MacKrell and Bertram Herzog, "Computer-Aided Engineering (CAE)," in Anthony Ralston, Edwin D. Reilly, and David Hemmendinger (eds.), *Encyclopedia of Computer Science*, 4th ed. (London: Nature Publishing Group, 2000): 274–278.

electronics firms, and the rest scattered across other industries, such as mechanical products and architectural and construction firms.[72]

Engineers and manufacturing managers expressed growing interest in integrating CAD/CAM in the early 1970s. One survey of 331 firms found that almost all of these companies had installed CAD/CAM applications.[73] A second study, done at the start of the 1980s, provided additional evidence of expanded use of CAD/CAM.[74] A large variety of firms and manufacturing experts began to report increases in speed of design, lowered costs of production, and improved quality with such systems after they had begun using microprocessors in the early to mid-1970s.[75]

Table 4.2
Engineering Functions Affected by CAE, Circa 1980

Function	CAE Applications
Product planning	Product simulation, mission analysis, financial modeling
Design & analysis	Conceptual design, surface definition, detailed layout, finite element analysis, thermal analysis, tolerance buildup checking, interference analysis
Drafting, part programming	Production of drawings, NC tapes; cutter location verification
Manufacturing engineering	Redesign for manufaturability, routing, tool & fixture design, process planning, group technology application
Industrial engineering	Labor & machine time standards, machine utilization analysis
Facilities engineering	Plant & equipment layout, equipment design
Reliability engineering	Quality control, coordinate measuring, machine programming, failure analysis

Source: "The Impact of Automation on Engineering/Manufacturing Productivity," *Impact* (November 1980): 15; Arthur D. Little internal newsletter, "Market Research," CBI 55, Box 8, Folder 19, Archives of the Charles Babbage Institute, University of Minnesota, Minneapolis.

No industry was untouched; the campaign to integrate all or most aspects of man-ufacturing was now in full swing.

Before leaving CAD/CAM deployment, we should recognize one other set of related manufacturing applications: shop floor data collection. Collecting infor-mation on manufacturing processes became an essential building block for all other manufacturing applications designed to link multiple functions together. These dated back to the dawn of the twentieth century. Data collection had been an important application since before Fordist manufacturing, if for no other reason than that managers needed to know who to pay and how much (since workers were paid either on a piece work basis or by the hour) and how to manage the availability of parts. Special machines were developed for this purpose by such firms as IBM and Burroughs, and beginning in the 1950s, so were machines that facilitated the collection of data and that could feed them to a computer. By the late 1960s, CRT terminals were coming into use, and by the end of the 1970s feedback functions had been embedded in many types of industrial equipment. In the beginning, applications were relatively independent of one another, such as the collection of data about payroll, raw materials, WIP and finished goods inventories, cost accounting, engineering, where-used files, and requirements planning.

The Barnes Drill Company, showcased by IBM in the early 1960s for using its 357 Data Collection System, reported typical benefits of such early systems: rapid timekeeping for payroll, speed and increased accuracy over manual systems for reporting inventory data, ability to expedite orders and materials on the shop floor, keypunching expenses reduced by 75 percent, and accumulated cost-accounting data collected in almost real-time fashion.[76] At the same time a manufacturing employee at RCA reported similar benefits in his company.[77] By the mid-1960s, plants began to receive daily production status reports, along with more traditional inventory control data.[78] Many of these early data collection systems relied on tub files of 80-column cards, a holdover from the precomputer era of tabulating equip-ment. These were used all through the 1960s, but a transition was underway to more online systems with CRTs and digital files (initially on tape but quickly on disk).[79]

Lest one conclude that all factories rushed forward to embrace new data col-lection systems, we are reminded by a reporter at *Dun's Review*, who was assessing the situation in the mid-1960s, that factories had done a poor job in collecting information:

Factory management has lagged behind other business areas in really coming to grips with the information explosion. Long oriented to producing things, not reports, handling materials, not figures, and balancing machine outputs, not studying balance sheets, factory managers have only recently realized fully the growing impact of information technology.[80]

Shop floor data collection represented the biggest hole in any manufacturing system then and today. Dun's Review reported what happened without good data collec-tion: bad management decisions, lack of the right parts at the right time, inflexibility in production, and lost orders. Examples of sound methods of data collection (e.g., at GE) demonstrated benefits in reducing inventory, speeding up cycle time, and increasing plant capacity.[81] Publishing these kinds of reports in national magazines, such as *Dun's*, publicized the new technologies and applications. By the early 1970s, integrated data collection applications had become widespread, particularly in large factories and, by the end of the decade, in most medium-sized manufacturing facilities.[82] Data collection had become ubiquitous in American manufacturing firms.

Manufacturing Information Systems Applications

By the mid-1970s the introduction of all the major components for highly integrated, computer-driven manufacturing was well underway. Data collection, inventory control, production planning, CAE, and CAD/CAM applications were now the norm. Numerical control tools were the other components that linked planning to actual production of goods. They were widespread by the 1980s and virtually ubiquitous in the 1990s. The important development in this second period (1960s and 1970s) was the injection of computing into machining tools.

As noted before in this chapter, the earliest tools were highly inflexible, but with the introduction of microprocessor-driven tools in the early 1970s, now called computer numerical control (CNC), machines could be quickly instructed to change their operations. That new functionality drove down labor costs, increased flexibility, and shortened the time it took to cut and bend metal, for example. Mass producers could increase the variety of products they made without building new plants. By the end of the 1970s, these tools had sensing capabilities, which meant that they could alter operations in real time, an essential requirement for the effective use, say, of robots. The availability of sensing devices drove up the sale of robotic devices; in 1981 more were sold than in all previous years combined.[83] With such capabilities in NC equipment, manufacturing firms could extend their automation sufficiently to begin creating flexible manufacturing systems (FMS), the basic new innovation evident in the late 1980s and through the 1990s. Computers could be used to design products, develop production schedules, and then instruct machines to make them. Logistics systems could then physically transport finished goods to warehouses or load them on trucks.

As recently as the early 1960s, manufacturing executives complained that NC machining tools were too expensive and cumbersome.[84] The situation was unimpressive. Roy A. Lindberg, a mechanical engineering professor at the University of Wisconsin, minced no words when he criticized the technology: "No manufacturer can produce an item of any consequence without knowing that it may be obsolete tomorrow." Progress in providing enhanced capabilities was slow: "The metalworking industry has been content to take automation in smaller steps."[85] Standalone NC equipment at the time was made to perform screw operations, and provide electric, air, and hydraulic controls, as well as increasing amounts of tape control (which could be driven by computers since tape was a form of output and a source of programming instructions), while multiple-machine automation was in its infancy.[86] One manufacturing expert, as late as 1973 (after the invention of the microprocessor but just before its wide application in NC tools) prognosticated that NC tools would eventually displace older technologies, although not immediately:

> There are large sectors of the industrial world in which NC is basically inappli-
> cable, and other sectors in which NC may be applicable but not economically
> justifiable. As a result, we can expect that NC technology will coexist with
> older technologies for many years to come. In fact, when these older technolo-
> gies are closely examined they turn out to be themselves layered composites of
> still older technologies.[87]

This is exactly what happened. The factory of the early twenty-first century is an impressive collection of computers and robots, but the journey there has been slow and evolutionary.

Numerical control was one of the gating factors for the rate of evolution to more integrated manufacturing. But slowly this new generation of equipment came online during the second half of the 1970s. In addition to being able to send instructions to individual machines, the activities of multiple devices could now be controlled and synchronized. Monitoring functions also became possible by the late 1970s. In 1981, Allen-Bradley had linked these various capabilities together, mak-ing possible updated factory operations plans. With that kind of development, processes for flexible manufacturing could be created. In effect, a majority of pro-duction steps could now be programmed in advance, started, and then controlled by computers. By having computer chips in all major factory equipment, one could communicate with machines and have them transfer data about what they were doing to each other. Two professors, experts on NC equipment and manufacturing, wrote at the start of the 1980s, after the arrival of the new generation of equipment, that "numerical control is one of the most important basic innovation of our century . . . it has gone far beyond the original cutting-machine tools and has revolutionized manufacturing and other areas of human productive activity."[88] Over 100 new types of NC equipment were reaching the market by that time.

Improvements in the ability to program and maintain this equipment in the 1980s increased the variety of uses (and hence demand) for such technology around the world, including in the United States. Traditional concerns on the part of man-ufacturing companies still influenced their decisions on when to acquire NC equip-ment: the need to lower costs of inventory, improve and maintain quality control, and operate with shorter production cycles. Economist Roberto Mazzoleni observed that "during the 1980s, the competitive strategies of U.S., European, and Japanese companies were characterized by an increasing quest for manufacturing flexibility and a movement toward small- and medium-batch production runs," which led to increased demands for this kind of technology.[89] This execution of the strategy caused firms around the world to install applications for jig boring, gear cutting, laser cutting, electrodischarges, and grinding for special purpose jobs; development of systems for rotational and prismatic parts for general purpose work; and creation of special purpose systems to support flexible transfer lines and FMS with special-ized equipment. Machine and turning centers within factories also were equipped.[90]

Flexible manufacturing factories increased from 8 in the United States in 1975 to 28 in 1980. In 1995, there were approximately 90. In that year, Japan claimed to have 166, Western Europe 208. The point is not so much that one nation or another was ahead but rather that manufacturing had changed extensively. Large American factories tended to rely on more inflexible transfer line approaches, but even these became more flexible during the 1980s. One study, comparing the number of product variants processed by FMS factories in different countries, turned up the fact that in the mid-1980s 41 percent of those U.S. factories that claimed to have FMS could handle up to 10 variants, another 22 percent could handle up to 50 variants, and another 13 percent up to 100 variants. This compared very closely to the Japanese production capability, whereas Western European factories had less flexibility.[91]

Robotics Applications

Although robots can be considered part of the discussion about the adoption of NC tools, they are so unique in the minds of the proverbial "average person" that they deserve separate, if brief, comment. Hundreds of movies and novels have portrayed the robot as a humanlike creature with little or no feelings, made of metal, and often evil in purpose. That is fiction; reality was a far more primitive class of devices, called industrial robots (IRs). These are designed to do a few highly specialized activities faster, more accurately, or less expensively then humans. Manufacturing companies deployed the majority of the machines available in the 1970s and 1980s. They often looked like huge arms protruding out of metal boxes; some were on wheels, others on tracks, and a few were bolted to the floor in production settings or suspended from ceilings. In 1959, Joseph Engelberger joined an early robot designer, George Devol, to develop the first commercial robotic products. Their initial prototype, the Unimate, made it possible for them to establish a company that made robots, Unimation, Inc. Over the years various other firms entered the business.[92] After the invention of the microprocessor, one could build programmable robots, equip them with sensors, and effectively command them to perform and change work. They consisted of three components: a mechanical manipulator, doing the tasks requested of it; a power supply; and the computerlike part of the machine, known as the control system.

The IRs were used to move materials, parts, and tools. They performed repetitious tasks, such as the 2,000 to 3,000 spot weldings required to put together an automobile; spray-painted industrial equipment and vehicles; and inspected paint jobs and the physical appearances of many products to ensure uniformity. In the 1970s, a few robots were being installed; by the end of the decade they were programmable. In the 1980s they were generally of eight types: manual manipulators, sequence-control devices, playback robots, NC-controlled machines, "intelligent" robots, sensory-controlled units, adaptive controlled robots, and learning-controlled robots. But they essentially performed applications that required them to "pick and place,"[93] and as so often happened with the emergence of new technologies, American enthusiasm exceeded the capabilities of the machines. For instance, *Business Week* in early 1981 published a detailed survey of IRs, reporting on the exuberance of American manufacturing executives who were looking forward to embracing this new technology: "Just owning a robot is clearly not enough. Now, the story goes, no self-respecting company wants to be caught without its own line of robots."[94]

Robots were initially most popular in the Automotive Industry in the late 1970s and early 1980s, where they could perform highly specialized, repetitive, precision work cost-effectively. In the 1980s, Japanese manufacturers of consumer electronics began to use a whole new generation of robotic technology. Robots, however, have not been as widely disbursed into manufacturing plants as one might have thought because they are expensive and instructing them was complex all through the 1980s and into the 1990s.[95] In the 1970s and again in the 1980s, they were not always as reliable as required.[96] In short, they had not yet reached the level of sophistication needed to become fully integrated with existing NC-based technologies already installed in factories. One expert on IT in the early 1980s described how best to use robots:

> Industrial robots are not stand-alone devices which can be bought off-the-shelf and plugged in immediately to a chosen application. The robot forms only part of an overall system, even in the simplest applications such as die-casting, and the interface consists primarily of interlocks that ensure the different devices mesh together correctly [and] the whole system operates safely.[97]

The same observer noted that despite the complexity of implementation, once installed IRs reduced the variability in their quality of work more than human workers. In a study conducted at the time, such devices out-performed humans in process control and consistency.[98] The number of their installations document the limited use to which robots were put. In 1987—a quarter of a century after the initial introduction of IRs—American factories had installed about 25,000, the Japanese 118,000, and West European firms another 19,000; in short, not so many by any country.[99]

Just to close out the story of robotics (since we will not discuss them further in this book), in the 1990s, smaller industrial robots were developed, largely to replace older, more inefficient machines but also to perform dangerous work (e.g., bomb disposals). They also became toys, with the latest innovations in technology for entertainment. But as with IRs, toys are still very expensive. For example, the Sony Aibo, which looks like a mechanical dog, retailed for $1,500 in 2000; ATR Media Integration and Communications Research Laboratories showed off a small robot that same year that could ask, "Can I have a kiss." It retailed for $109,000.[100]

Third Period: From Mass Production to Flexible Manufacturing, 1980s–1990s

American manufacturing companies were severely challenged by foreign competitors in many industries through the 1980s and 1990s, although various industries made significant comebacks during the same period. The Automotive Industry, attacked by Japanese firms in the 1970s and 1980s, recovered with better quality products and a larger variety of smaller vehicles. The same happened with steel manufacturing and semiconductors. There were permanent casualties as well; the loss of the consumer electronics industry to Japan may be one. Meanwhile, new industries, first created in the 1960s and 1970s, either now dominated the world market or simply did very well in the United States. These included many computer-related manufacturing industries, such as semiconductors, disk drives, and laptops. At the dawn of the twenty-first century, a variety of new industries built primarily on software was also emerging, such as biotechnology, biology, and the rapidly expanding body of knowledge related to DNA.

In the 1980s, the severe competitive pressures felt by American industries did lead to a number of operational reforms, such as the expanded use of just-in-time logistics, adoption of quality management practices, and "lean" manufacturing. Observers commented at the time that "these reforms aim to improve how companies are doing what they are already doing."[101] In short, the process of evolution, rather than revolution, continued building on an existing base of capabilities. This base, in turn, expanded deeper in those industries that had first adopted computers and later in others.

One of these capabilities, made possible because of investments in a variety of computing applications deployed in previous decades, involved the ability to make single or few products at costs comparable to the economies of scale achieved through mass production. Mass customization, as it came to be known in the 1980s, leveraged such technologies as robotics and NC-driven tools (CAD/CAM). B. Joseph Pine II, the leading proponent of mass customization in the 1980s and 1990s put it simply:

> Advances in the speed, capacity, effectiveness, efficiency, and usability of information and telecommunications technologies constantly lower the costs of increasing differentiation in service as well as manufacturing industries. The instant application of information throughout a firm's value chain allows it to respond quickly to changes in demand and design.[102]

Many of the capabilities he cited were the same that manufacturing had been developing for a half century: just-in-time delivery and processing of WIP and finished inventory, reduced time for setup and changeover of equipment, reduced cycle times in all activities, building to order rather than to forecast, and lowered costs of inventory.[103]

While industries were transforming, the digital continued to appear in ever-increasing varieties of consumer goods. Nothing illustrates this trend more sharply than a Christmas season issue of *Parade Magazine*, about as low-tech and noneconomic a publication as one could find in American society. In its November 26, 2000, issue, *Parade* featured that season's new wave of high-tech products, all equipped with computer chips, which had been programmed to perform specific tasks. In addition to presenting such long-available items as PCs and laptops, it described onboard computing in a farmer's tractor, a hand-held scanner that fed notes to a PC, a second generation of digital cameras, password protected hand-held telephones for children, and a digital wallet. Even one of the cartoons in that issue had a boy telling his mother in the kitchen, "Did I tell you that I've set up a Web-cam in the kitchen?"[104]

Applications continued to change. Mass customization on the shop floor trans-lated into flexible manufacturing systems (FMS), making rapid changes in produc-tion possible. Increasingly, a concept called computer-integrated manufacturing (CIM) affected how various activities and machines were more closely integrated by using software to coordinate these initiatives. As one expert described it:

> CIM combines flexible automation (robots, numerically controlled machines, and flexible manufacturing systems), CAD/CAM systems, and management-information systems to build integrated production systems that cover the complete operations of a manufacturing firm, including purchasing, logistics, maintenance, engineering, and business operations. CIM emphasizes horizontal links between different organizational units of a firm and profits the possibility of sharing data and computing resources, making it possible to break the tradi-tional institutional barriers between departments and create flexible functional groups to perform tasks more speedily and efficiently.[105]

Although quite a mouthful of text, and a concept not yet fully implemented by most companies by the end of the century, it harked back to the total systems approach of the 1960s.[106] But because so many activities in a factory in the mid- to late 1980s were already digitized, linking additional pieces together proved un-realistic. One study of the process pointed out that it took many years, often de-cades, to accomplish, although companies collected incremental benefits along the way: reduced engineering design costs of between 15 and 30 percent; shorter lead times of between 30 and 60 percent; increased productivity of production opera-tions, ranging from 40 to 70 percent; and lowered WIP costs of 30 to 60 percent. Other firms expected to enjoy similar gains from CIM.[107]

In the 1980s, the notion of more flexible operations became a reality in smaller companies as well, demonstrating the continued advance in both the ease with which some of these tools could be used and their ongoing improvement in cost performance. The concept of cells began to appear in shop floor operations in both large and small factories. As two contemporary experts described them, "cells are small groups of two or three components placed together to perform defined proc-essing tasks." These can include machining, welding, cleaning, and inspections. "By joining the processes together in a cell, better control and reliability can be achieved in the manufacturing of parts." When cells were combined into FMS operations, improved throughput occurred throughout a factory.[108]

Thus FMS became increasingly possible through the installation of local area networks (LANs) in the 1980s and 1990s. Miniature telecommunications networks in buildings, LANs, make it possible for various types of equipment to communicate with one another, and hence to coordinate activities. Such LANs appeared in many factories across all industries in the last 15 years of the twentieth century. As figure 4.1 illustrates, a hierarchy of machines and communications began to emerge in

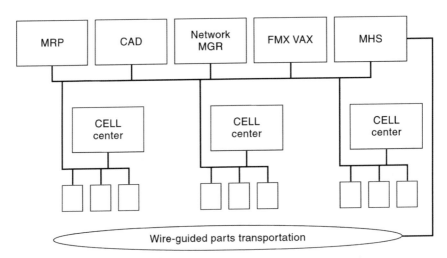

Figure 4.1
Networked FMS approach, circa late 1980s.

the last years of the century in manufacturing plants. Microprocessors and telecommunications were used as lower level controllers to link NC-driven equipment, programmable controllers (usually called PLCs), and other devices into a LAN. Distributed process control could occur while simultaneously operating the overall plant in a centralized fashion. During the same period, databases of plant-wide information were redesigned and reorganized to facilitate this new form of integration, a process still underway in most companies during the early years of the new century.

Lest one think that CIM and FMS were the norm at the dawn of the new century, the truth was that the ideal, fully integrated approach did not exist in any American factory as late as the end of the twentieth century. However, much progress was made in integrating shop floor operations, which included production control, equipment, and processes. This was done by making it possible for data from one task, or application, to pass to another, affecting the latter's activities. The Yankee Group noted that in the early 1980s over 35 companies had implemented some form of FMS and that several hundred were in the process of doing so.[109] Table 4.3 lists some of the American firms that had implemented FMS and CIM approaches.

Successes came slower than desired. New lessons had to be learned about how to connect machines to LANs, for example; experiences that manufacturing firms mastered over time. Management also continued to face the same problem of insufficiently skilled personnel that had limited implementation of new technologies in the 1950s and 1960s. As one student of the problem, John Bessant, put it, there was also "too much faith in the technical fix." The lack of organizational changes to reflect new technical capabilities, or even an overarching strategy in some plants

Table 4.3
Sample FMS Installations in the United States, 1985

Vought Aero Products	Rockwell-International
FMC Corporation	Hughes Aircraft
Cincinnati Milacron	Mack Truck
General Dynamics	Onan
General Electric	Mercury Marine
Caterpillar	Cummins Engine
New York Brake	Sundstrand Aviation
McDonnel Douglas	Boeing Aerospace
J. I. Ce	Buick
Ingersoll Milling	Vickers
Allis-Chalmers	Pratt & Whitney
Deere & Company	Westinghouse

Source: Paul R. Warndorf and M. Eugene Merchant, "Development and Future Trends in Computer-Integrated Manufacturing in the USA," *International Journal of Technology Management* 1, nos. 1–2 (1986): 172.

for implementation, also led to problems. To compound matters, bad change management and managers' reluctance to consider nontechnical options also slowed the optimization of new concepts and technology.[110] Experts in the field warned of the over reliance on technology as the silver bullet. Donald A. Hicks was a typical critic: "Increasingly, observers acknowledged that global competitive deficiencies have too often prompted U.S. industry to look at new technology alone as a panacea." He pointed out that by the late 1980s, leading with innovation, not simply technology, provided a better path to profits. Rather than simply develop new technologies, applying well what already existed was more productive. Training workers and rearranging work flows were as important as implementation of new technologies and applications. Technology was essential, but it was only one of various elements that made a manufacturing company successful.[111]

On the eve of the Internet's expansion across the American economy, manufacturing executives were coming to the conclusion that the holistic approaches they had advocated for decades in the adoption of computer-based tools to integrate operations had to be applied to their own practices. Understanding how organizations operated, changed, and learned became very important. Knowledge management practices grew out of this realization that improvements called for more than just technology. What decisions managers made could be more decisive in many instances than simply what automation they implemented, a key lesson learned from Japanese manufacturing executives in the 1980s.[112] How American manufacturing industries responded to the flowering of the Internet is discussed in the next several chapters.

The Emerging Role of Supply Chain Management

Nowhere did this holistic approach emerge more clearly than in the management of supply chains (SCM). If ever there was a silent, stealth application for computing that made its way through the economy in the 1980s and 1990s, this was it. One reason for its a stealth quality probably was due to the fact that its use did not have a name until the 1990s. Before then, portions of the application had labels, such as MRP or logistics. Particularly in the use of computing in manufacturing, the continuous integration of activities across companies and industries, by using a blend of computing and telecommunications, probably did more to affect how work was done in manufacturing industries in the last 10 to 15 years of the century than any other set of applications. Although historians have yet to study this application, we cannot ignore it. Computers (and more specifically databases and a variety of software tools), EDI, and now the Internet enabled the integration and coordination of the design of products, their manufacture, and physical movement from raw materials and components to products sold and delivered to customers. The whole effort involved the design of applications and processes, careful forecasting, and then scheduling of materials and work. Two students of the process described what changed over the last two decades of the century: "Manufacturing information, as it relates to both the products and the processes that are used to add value through design, production, and support activities, has become highly data intensive."[113] The emergence of SCM practices occurred with fits and starts and over a long period of time, as the case studies in subsequent chapters demonstrate. In manufacturing circles, it represents the largest collection of operational processes in use today, complicated by such factors as the need to customize products; the growing tendency of manufacturing firms to specialize in what they did well within the large value chain operating across the economy, purchasing what they might in earlier times have made themselves (e.g., components); and the arrival of practices such as total quality management (TQM) and conformance to ISO 9000 standards—all of which called for additional documentation and data management. Simultaneously, manufacturing also adopted just-in-time (JIT) practices and concurrent engineering. Historians will later debate the effectiveness of supply chains; it is sufficient for the moment to recognize that this is the most widespread adoption of computerization by the end of the century by American manufacturing industries.

At the heart of today's SCM applications is the age-old process of logistics— the movement of materials and finished products through production and ultimately to customers. In the 1990s, a manufacturing company spent between 10 and 35 percent of its budget on logistics of some sort or another. For petroleum products, the percentage of a product's cost due to logistics was nearly a quarter of the total; for chemicals, about 14 percent; for metal goods, 8 percent. Across the entire U.S. economy, by the middle years of the 1990s, all American firms collectively spent just over 10 percent of U.S. GDP on logistics; however, it is a lower cost than that borne by the nation's economy in 1980, when it was nearly 15 percent.[114] In those chapters ahead that are devoted to trade industries, we see that logistics plays a profound role in such activities as overnight delivery and mail order businesses. Thus, a situation existed in which by the dawn of the new century, logistics applications of computing and telecommunications were present in hundreds of industries across both industrial and service sectors.

We know from the history of supply chain management that, as with so many other applications in manufacturing, islands of automation first appeared as companies improved the productivity of some operation by using computing and telecommunications. Then, over time, these islands were linked together, and eventually one could look back and see what appeared to be an integrated logistics and supply management process of some magnitude. But it was slow to develop, needing many decades. The normal pattern began with improving the transportation of materials and components to manufacturing, their physical movement within factories, and then transport to wholesalers, retailers, and ultimately customers. The sequence of process incorporation and integration into SCM was first transportation, then warehousing, followed in order by finished goods inventory, materials handling, packaging, customer service, and purchasing. The objectives were fairly straightforward—to lower operating costs, improve levels of service, and enhance communications among the various firms involved in the production and sale of a product.[115] Of course, reluctance to share data, which were always guarded as a competitive advantage, slowed the process but was finally overcome with the widespread adoption of JIT practices. In addition, EDI facilitated changes, and the Internet sped up the momentum of enhancing the content and extent of SCM processes.[116]

What little evidence about the role of the Internet that exists indicates that this technology has been used so far for procurement, transportation scheduling, vehicle tracking and enhancing customer service. One study of 181 firms in 1998 indicated that 90.1 percent used the Internet in some fashion in their SCM processes. Management of transportation was the process most widely linked to the Internet, and the least was production scheduling. Ranked in order of use from most to least were, after transportation, order processing, managing vendor relations, purchasing, and customer service. The three business management professors who conducted this study concluded that "the use of the Internet in SCM is rapidly increasing."[117]

A relatively new subprocess that began emerging at the dawn of the new century as part of the SCM process was called a dynamic trading network. These are applications that take existing supply chains from confinement only to suppliers and within firms and use them across the entire range of interactions with all vendors and all customers. Such applications took two forms: first, the creation of wholly owned consortiums to manage the technological links among companies, as was being done, for example, in the automotive and pharmaceutical industries; second, the installation of software packages designed to facilitate the extension of existing SCM processes. Forrester Research, a leading IT industry research organization, surveyed Fortune 1,000 manufacturing firms at the end of the last century, discovering that 51 percent were implementing software tools across various parts of their supply chains, from demand planning to logistics. Packages were limited in capability, online systems did not have the capacity to handle massive increases in volume of data flows, and so forth, all of which were normal problems with new applications. In short, e-commerce, although the subject of much attention as this book was being written (2000–2003), still needed a lot of improvement. Until firms improved dynamic trading networks, which are configurations of companies that come together to satisfy one immediate need with some coordinated response, they were not quite ready to be implemented.[118]

Deployment of Digital Technologies in American Manufacturing Industries

One way to assess the extent of how computer technology—the digital—changed American industry is by documenting the extent to which this new technology was used, not simply focusing on how extensively it was deployed. Throughout the first four chapters, I have discussed deployment in bits and pieces, but now we can begin to pull together a more comprehensive view of the issue as it relates to manufacturing. The end result is not a definitive picture but a collection of data that strongly supports the contention that deployment in manufacturing was massive in the early years and has remained so to the present day. Existing evidence on deployment strongly supports one of the key messages of this book, namely, that computers led to fundament changes in the nature of manufacturing—as it did, by the way, across the entire industrialized world.

Phister's data in table 2.1 (p. 54) show that in general, manufacturing industries were early adopters of computers, spending nearly half of what all American industries did on this technology in the 1950s and, even two decades later, nearly a quarter. That in itself is impressive evidence of deployment. However, by breaking down that data further, as shown in table 4.4, we can see the dynamics with greater clarity. The presence of very large firms comes out in the data for the 1950s for transportation equipment, into which manufacturers embedded technology in

Table 4.4
The Distribution of Computer Systems in Select Manufacturing Industries by Percentage, 1959–1974

Industry	1959	1968	1974
Chemicals	4.0	2.7	2.7
Petroleum refining	5.8	1.1	0.7
Machinery	3.4	5.1	4.8
Electrical machinery	7.0	4.9	4.8
Transportation equipment	11.9	2.2	2.4
Other manufacturing	10.3	17.6	19.3

Source: Montgomery Phister, Jr., *Data Processing Technology and Economics* (Santa Monica, Cal.: Santa Monica Publishing, 1976), 444; and his *Data Processing Technology and Economics: 1975–1978 Supplement* (Santa Monica, Cal.: Santa Monica Publishing, 1979):652.

trucking, automobiles, and of course aerospace—thereby accounting for 25 percent of all investments in the manufacturing sector. However, even in the late 1950s, other manufacturing industries were already spending large sums, even outpacing some industries that later would be thought of as very high-tech, such as communications. A decade later, the "other" category had increased, thereby signaling that a growing variety of manufacturing industries not listed in the table had become extensive users of computers.

What are we to say about the Petroleum Industry, which has always been an extensive user of analog and digital computers? The same question could be asked about chemicals. Although I will have more to say about these two industries in chapter 6, what can be pointed out from Phister's evidence is that only the proportion of their expenditures relative to other industries shrank in the case of Petroleum and stabilized in the Chemical Industry. Absolute expenditures rose through the half century, but these two industries did not expand the number of plant sites as extensively as many other industries. In fact, the last new oil refinery in the United States was built in 1978. Many existing locations upgraded computer systems and added new ones. In many other industries, not only was that going on but also new plants were added, driving up total expenditures.

Usage expanded all through the 1950s and 1960s in response to such stimulants as government support, requirements of the U.S. Department of Defense (DoD), and improved technologies, which made computers attractive tools in driving down costs and expanding production and quality while remaining competitive. However, companies did not run out with wild abandon and acquire this technology. The chairman and chief executive officer of Reliance Electric Company at the start of the 1970s, Hugh D. Luke, strongly promoted technologies that added business value. Yet, when Luke assessed how American manufacturers in general responded to computers, he was not as positive as those who were advocating the digital:

> In spite of the opportunities that are potentially available, one would be quite mistaken to conclude that automation is widely accepted throughout industry. On the contrary, even including the small "islands" or single small applications here and there . . . it is most probable that no more than 10 to 15 percent of our plants can be considered automated with extensive modern facilities.[119]

Luke did, however, salute the extensive deployment he saw in those industries that, in the late 1960s, operated in highly competitive environments: chemical, petroleum, consumer goods, foods, automotive suppliers, consumer electronics, defense, and electronics, to mention a few. His explanation for this rests on the notion that the implementation of computer-based applications requires careful planning, something senior management would not do "for the mere sake of technical accomplishment. Necessity has mothered this technological advance."[120] Luke was not alone in these views.

The U.S. Bureau of Labor Statistics (BLS) has looked at the issue of deployment of many technologies, creating in the process a large body of disparate data about a variety of large and obscure industries. A careful examination of this material fills in many details about the extent of deployment of computers in many industries. Table 4.5 summarizes some of the findings of the BLS. What quickly jumps out as an obvious pattern is that industries that tended to have large manufacturing facilities deployed digital technologies most extensively and at the earliest opportunity. We can also conclude that companies adopted technologies generally as extensively as their rivals within an industry, which is why we could see, for example, that computing was extensively adopted in one industry but not in another in the same period. Thus NC, CAD/CAM, and FMS applications were in the largest manufacturing sites first because these firms could afford the new technology. Those industries that did one-of-a-kind fabrication, such as in aerospace, used mass production, NC-controlled equipment or robotics less, even though they were available and in wide use in such industries as automotive and consumer electronics, where the manufacture of multiple copies of the same product was the norm. Thus the fit of a technology or application became an important gating factor, affecting whether and when some digital use appeared in an industry. Cost effectiveness in comparison to that in preexisting methods and technologies also dictated the rate of adoption.

The converse explanation allows us to understand why an industry might have been slower than another to adopt digital technologies to control and operate the production of goods. For example, in the nonrubber footwear manufacturing industry, like footwear manufacturing industries as a whole, companies were very slow to adopt high-tech approaches to production all through the 1950s to the late 1980s. Limitations of technology were not the gating factors; rather, as economists pointed out, it was "the high cost of the necessary equipment and the small size of most of the firms in the industry." This was also an industry that lacked uniform, industry-wide standards for such issues as grading systems for shoes, necessary to motivate a manufacturer of shoe-fabricating equipment to invent products that could be sold across the industry. Finally, CAD applications came into this industry in the late 1980s, and spread through the 1990s, as a result of declining costs of CAD products. In turn, that deployment led to standards in shoe sizes and so forth. Changes in fashion were frequent, as in clothing, and therefore CAD applications in time came into their own, providing rapid designing capabilities.[121]

A firm's size affected the rate of deployment of computing in manufacturing industries. One study that reflected the circumstances of the late 1980s demonstrated that large companies proved to be the most extensive users of IT; in fact 98 percent reported the use of computing for accounting; 96 percent, for bills of material; 91 percent, for drafting and design work; 87 percent, for managing databases and for performing inventory control, materials requirement planning, and using various NC tools. Medium-sized companies in general used the same applications, but the percentages just cited for deployment occurred in the 1960s and 1970s; for small firms it was not uncommon to see deployments in the 1980s and 1990s, with the exception of accounting, which at that time had reached 74 percent.[122]

In all instances, regardless of whether there was extensive deployment or not of a particular application or technology, with or without the use of computerization, the desire on the part of management to reduce labor costs was an important

Table 4.5
Diffusion of Applications by Select Manufacturing Industries, 1960s–1980s

Industry	Technology/Applications	Years	Diffusion
Tires	Computer control for applying rubber to fabric cords	Late 1960s	1 plant
	Microprocessor-controlled instrumentation	mid-1980s	10–20% of all tires made by using MCIs
	Product testing	mid-1980s	80% of large firms
	Process management	mid-1980s	Modest
	CAD	mid-1980s	75% deployed
Aluminum	Automatic furnace control	1970s	Wide use by large producers
	Computer-controlled cold-rolled products mill	1970s	Limited
	Hall-Heroult reduction technology	Early 1980s	Universal in new plants
	Direct chill casting	Early 1980s	Widespread in new plants
	CAD/CAM in extruding operations	Early 1980s	Limited to building-block adoptions
	Prepress billet shearing & handling	Early 1980s	Limited
Folding paperboard boxes	Offset printing	1970s	Limited
	Cutting & cropping machinery	1970s	Just less than 40% of all plants
	Papermaking machinery	Late 1970s	Limited
	Production control	Late 1970s	Extensive
	Digester	Early 1980s	Extensive
	Materials handling	Late 1970s	Limited
Hosiery	Knitting	Late 1970s	From 36% to 56% of all machines between 1975 and 1980
Motor Vehicles	CAD/CAM	Late 1970s	CAD widespread, CAM moderate
	Plantwide data network	Late 1970s	Extensive
	Spot-welding robots	Late 1970s	1/3 of all U.S. robots are in this industry, 1/2 are used for welding
	Materials-handling robotics	Late 1970s	Second most used application of robots
	Painting robotics	Late 1970s	Extensive
	Programmable machine controls	Late 1970s	Extensive; 40% of all controllers are in this industry
	Transfer line applications	Late 1970s	Extensive

(continued)

Table 4.5 *(continued)*
Diffusion of Applications by Select Manufacturing Industries, 1960s–1980s

Industry	Technology/Applications	Years	Diffusion
Textiles	Continuous computerized finishing	1970s	Extensive
	Production control, dyeing, finishing	Early 1980s	Limited
Steel	Control processes in hot-strip rolling mills and blast furnaces	Early 1980s	Second generation widely adopted
Aerospace	NC applications	Early 1980s	9% of all machine tools in aircraft industry; 8% in missile industry
	CAD/CAM	Early 1980s	Extensive
	Industrial robots	Early 1980s	Limited
	Flexible manufacturing	Early 1980s	2 systems only

Source: BLS, U.S. Department of Labor, *Technological Change and Manpower Trends in Six Industries*, Bulletin 1817 (Washington, D.C.: U.S. Government Printing Office, 1974): 2, 23, 31; BLS, *Techological Change and Its Labor Impact in Four Industries*, Bulletin 2182 (Washington, D.C.: U.S. Government Printing Office, February 1984): 2, 11; BLS, *The Impact of Technology on Labor in Four Industries*, Bulletin 2228 (Washington, D.C.: U.S. Government Printing Office, May 1985): 2, 10, 22, 36; BLS, *Technology and Its Impact on Labor in Four Industries*, Bulletin 2242 (Washington, D.C.: U.S. Government Printing Office, May 1986): 2, 11–12, 25.

factor. If that could be done, management sometimes tried even hardly proven technologies. The slow-adopting nonrubber footwear industry illustrates how some firms focused on lowering labor costs. Even in the early years of computing—the 1950s and 1960s—as others, this industry sought ways to lower labor costs. In other industries, in which computing technologies were more natural, such as in mass production plants in the Automotive Industry (also with large numbers of employees), the motivation to use computers to drive down labor costs proved irresistible. This same theme of lowering labor costs also appeared in other industries, such as banking and retail.

Conclusions

The history of manufacturing in the United States during the past half century is a conundrum because these industries adopted vast quantities of technologies, not just computers, and enjoyed periods of enormous prosperity and growth, although at other times they suffered from effective competition from Japanese and some European industries. The debate over the productivity paradox reflected some of the confusion and concern about what relationship, if any, existed between the deployment of digital technologies and the performance of industries. Yet the puzzle remains, not fully resolved by historians or economists. Some of the issues can be understood better because of the experience industries had with the digital. My research and that of others indicate that the issue is moot because the experience of manufacturing industries in the 1990s demonstrated that IT had a cumulative positive influence on productivity. Furthermore, there was no alternative: manufacturing practices had so evolved beyond Fordist approaches that it was as inconceivable to revert to a precomputer approach to operating as it would have been for firms in the 1930s to revert to approaches that did not include electricity or mass production techniques. A new paradigm now existed for new business models and value propositions, all with the digital embedded either overtly or tacitly in most of what was done.

American manufacturing industries had a propensity to reach out to technology for ways to improve productivity and to expand sales. That propensity is a national characteristic, evident in all American industries and in all periods to one degree or another. We can see that it is a national characteristic by looking at the practices of other nations. The Japanese example is the most instructive and possibly the most extreme contrast. Manufacturing industries in Japan tended to reach out to their employees for innovative work practices rather than just to technology. That propensity led to different strategies for increasing performance, productivity, and quality. Rather than manage ever-growing amounts of inventory, particularly parts and WIP in manufacturing, Japanese manufacturers developed just-in-time strategies and processes. An American automotive or truck manufacturer in the 1970s worried about filling warehouses with parts to make sure the production line never halted because of a shortage.[123] The Japanese, however, were trying to get their parts suppliers to deliver just what was needed for that day's production, thereby reducing the need for all the elegant inventory control approaches developed by the Americans. In time, American firms recognized the benefits of JIT, and adopted it, leading to inventory control applications and processes in the 1980s and 1990s that were fundamentally different from those used in the 1950s and 1960s. Supply chain management became a mantra for the industrial sector by the early 1990s. But, as we saw with manufacturing industries, even these kinds of changes had strong technological underpinnings, which spread even outside of manufacturing. Wal-Mart developed a fundamentally different approach to inventory management, and in the process it nearly revolutionized practices across entire retail and wholesale industries in the United States. This firm accomplished that transformation by applying the inventory control approaches that had first been adopted by manufacturing industries in Japan.

The effective use of computerized applications did not always guarantee economic success. The automotive and steel industries, which are explored in more detail in the next chapter, are examples. Implementation of technologies can freeze into a pattern of behavior difficult to change, but it can also be a way out of a competitive crisis, as both industries demonstrate. The problem, of course, is that it takes a long time. The rates of adoption discussed in this and in the previous chapter demonstrate that it takes years and extensive capital investments to change fundamental practices in a firm, let alone in an industry. Therefore, historians, economists, and managers also need to look at other aspects of business to identify levers of change. Leadership and strategies were most frequently the primary sources of alternative approaches to protecting and increasing growth in a firm.[124] Weakness in both led General Motors in the late twentieth century to fail to perform as well as it had in the mid-1900s. In the same period of GM's recent troubles, Toyota and Honda enjoyed tremendous growth and prosperity. Yet all three firms were extensive users of computers and other digital technologies.

Another observation is that the use of technology had become so pervasive in both the United States and in all other industrialized economies that the digital had become the price of admission to an industry. In other words, it was how things were now done. One could not compete, let alone function, without the digital because processes had been fundamentally changed, as well as how companies worked (e.g., suppliers and distributors) and communicated with one another. Technical standards (e.g., the ability to link to a firm's database or to conform to ISO 9000 guidelines), legal requirements, and consumer tastes all reinforced the requirement that all aspects of how a manufacturing firm functioned would be profoundly affected by digital technologies. In the language of the economist, computing created barriers to entry and opportunities for access and lock-in practices.

Although I have yet to discuss the role of the Internet, that is today's collection of technologies, which—as did the digital computer in the 1950s and 1960s—is transforming how work is done. Did we learn by the late 1990s that it took more than technology to be successful? Downsizing staffs, extensive in the 1980s in many manufacturing industries, continued all through the 1990s, despite massive deployment of Internet-based business applications and processes and a strong period of economic growth in the United States. Loyalty to one's firm declined during the last two decades of the century, and many industries remained weak and uncompetitive in the post-Internet period. Why? Again, technology alone could not guarantee economic success in manufacturing industries. Technology led to productivity and improved quality of production and work in general, but without strong and effective managerial leadership and strategies no firm could thrive. The American propensity to reach out to technology proved most effective when it was coupled simultaneously with strong leadership and sound business strategies. Noel M. Tichy, whose studies on the role of leadership were done in the context of many changes in business and in applied technologies, observed that leadership remained so important fundamentally because "leaders are the people who decide what needs to be done and [are] the ones who make things happen."[125] Computers did not do that. However, to be effective, leaders in industries that were extensive users of technology had to develop and deploy strategies that were also effective in exploiting the digital.

The careful work of Philip Evans and Thomas S. Wurster in describing how the Internet made one's strategies more or less effective clearly demonstrates that the digital was important. They emphasize the specific application of technologies less and the consequences more: the extent to which organizations could or could not reach new markets, deconstruction and reconfiguration of organizations and companies, and the effects of information technologies on skills, work, and leadership. Such an emphasis would not have been possible to support if the existing base of digital technologies already in place, and which was being augmented as a result of the adoption of the Internet, had not been so extensive. In the final analysis, the basics of management still applied in the age of the Internet, as they had in the late stages of Fordism: "We quickly found that many, if not most, of the traditional principles of strategy apply in the 'new' much as they do in the old. Economies of scale, segmentation, and cost position all still work."[126] The lesson for management was clear: manufacturing applications had to serve sound business objectives. For the historian of technology, an equally important lesson emerges: the historical record of computing and its technologies is less a tale of engineering, science, machines, and software and more the story of business history.

To understand better the deployment and effects of digital technology in manufacturing, we will look at the experiences of nine bellwether industries that were large and influential in the American economy. Thus the next three chapters are devoted to specific manufacturing industries, six of which were quietly and profoundly transformed, largely because of computers, and three that did not exist in 1950 but later became substantial in size and influence. With these case studies in hand, we can then conclude with confidence that we have identified the major patterns of behavior in the adoption and use of digital technologies across dozens, if not scores, of manufacturing industries. This is an essential exercise, placing in historical context what occurred before the Internet because we are still in the midst of what appears to be the early stages in its deployment and such related applications as pervasive computing, ubiquitous wireless communication, and construction of new organizational forms and industries. Because we are certainly in transition to some as yet ill-defined, new technological *style*, but one growing out of an earlier way of doing business, the historical record remains the best source of insight about today's trends.

5

Patterns and Practices in Three Traditional Manufacturing Industries: Automotive, Steel, and Aerospace

Industrial change is never harmonious advance with all the elements of the system actually moving, or tending to move, in step. At any given time, some industries move on, others stay behind.

—Joseph A. Schumpeter, 1939

Computer technology became an important, if not the most significant, set of technological innovations in America's largest industries. By looking at how computers were used in these industries, we can move from general cross-industry observations to the precise. Yet we also need to keep in mind that by themselves, computers do not tell the full story because the digital was never the ultimate (or only) source of competitive advantages or the complete arbitrator of an industry's performance. They increased productivity and made for better, more sophisticated products rich in function and safety, but they did not fully protect any industry from traditional competitive pressures or different business models. Technology was part of the defense against rivals and a continuing source of incremental improvements in productivity. In each of the industries reviewed below, senior management reached out to information technologies to improve routine operations and tried to create a competitive edge over rivals, only to learn that the digital, although transformative and a stimulus to efficiency, was not always the silver bullet they sought. In the popular TV series of the 1950s and early 1960s, the Lone Ranger, a self-appointed lawman who went around righting injustices, only fired silver bullets from his six-shooter and always got the bad guys. Communities out West in trouble relied on him for a quick fix. The silver bullets he used always worked to stop outlaws. The analogy resonated well with industry and technology, but unlike the unreality of the TV series, the real world proved more complicated.

These three industry case studies call attention to the fact that the digital initially represented, often for long periods of time, add-on technologies that were adopted to enhance and modify existing core functions of an enterprise. It was only over time that one could begin to observe the digital becoming embedded in the core activities and capabilities of the firm and, by extension, of the industry, thereby unintentionally creating the transformation away from the Fordist style and toward the digital style. Furthermore, as the three cases below illustrate, that transformation was uneven in both scope and results. These are important points to keep in mind because of the danger of putting the cart before the horse. In our Age of Information we are so bombarded by comments from experts, industry observers and representatives, the public relations mills in corporations, and executives touting the wonders of computing that we might forget that companies did not normally use the digital unless there was some reason rooted in business causes and economic expectations. Remembering this reality helps us understand a great deal about why one industry moved faster or slower, as economist Joseph A. Schumpeter suggested was routinely the case.

The three industries reviewed in this chapter represent a collective cautionary tale, because they illustrate the limits of technology, as well as circumstances in which the digital worked effectively. Technological innovations, when installed to improve productivity, normally proved to be successful, although they were not always well implemented. Managers, however, believed that they had to be implemented if for no other reason than just to keep their firms competitive with rivals. Computers and other digital applications reduced the labor content of work, thereby providing management with better control over operations in the face of either poorly managed American unions or relatively unproductive work forces. Industries and their managers worried constantly about issues related to productivity. In the case of labor, which remained consistently a very large component of cost for any product in most manufacturing industries in the twentieth century, the expense of employees declined per unit produced. Productivity could also be improved relative either to automation or to offshore work forces by one of three conditions: stronger work ethics outside the major centers of industry's concentration (e.g., nonunion work forces in the southern United States or in Mexico, as in the textile, automotive components and shoe manufacturing firms), different ways of deploying workers (e.g., teaming practices in Japanese auto manufacturing plants), or effective use of industry-specific technologies (e.g., electric furnaces in steel mills). In short, IT helped lower labor costs, but this occurred in conjunction with other measures.

This demonstrates what Joseph A. Schumpeter, the great Harvard economist of pre–World War II America, had argued. The quotation at the start of this chapter is our reality check, a reminder that transformations were messy at best, and so it

Computers were used to maintain cars once they were sold to customers. In this instance, in 1967, instruments connected to a computer test a car's exhaust emissions, providing information to run diagnostic tests and to tune the motor, brakes, and wheel alignment. Courtesy IBM Corporate Archives.

was with the adoption of computers. Schumpeter was one of the first economists to suggest that we look at the process of technological innovation through the experiences of an industry, the main strategy employed in this book. He argued that "in every span of historic time it is easy to locate the ignition of the process and to associate it with certain industries and, within these industries, with certain firms, from which the disturbances then spread over the system."[1] Schumpeter, the originator of the notion of "creative destruction," has now become the darling of many students of the evolution of technology, and for good reason: technological change is profoundly rooted in principled economic activity. Technology and capitalism, particularly in his view, are closely tied to functions of manufacturing and to industries at large.[2]

Information technology was installed first in the largest manufacturing companies, and even after IT had permeated all sizes of industrial firms they continued to be the greatest users of technologies, particularly the newest forms. Large industries illustrate to what extent Lewis H. Lapham was right when, in 1984, he facetiously said, "No businessman these days dares to embark upon the journey of incorporation without first acquiring a computer so huge and so omniscient as to strike terror into the software of its enemies."[3] On a more serious note, looking at the industries below gives us an opportunity to deal with the role of innovation while discussing simultaneously some of the largest portions of the industrial American landscape. To do so, I examine the Automotive, Steel, and Aerospace Industries.

These industries have a great deal to teach us about large manufacturing, much of it highly concentrated and ultimately subject to global influences. They have some common features. First, these huge industries, with their large and, later, smaller suppliers or rivals, were extensive users of information technology, regardless of what one might think of their rate of adoption or effectiveness of use. Second, they profoundly influenced how other American industries applied computing because they forced their suppliers to conform to technical standards and specific practices. Thereby, these large industries set the pace for best practices or caused specific configurations of technology to drop in cost (e.g., CAD/CAM) because of their economies of scale and the effect those had on technological improvements. Third, all three reflected the strengths and limitations presented by IT, helping to answer the question "To what extent can IT be a silver bullet?"

These three industries also illustrate a subtheme running through American manufacturing industries: that rates of adoption varied. The Automotive Industry served as a technology trend-setter through most of the twentieth century, continuing a tradition that began with Fordism (named after the automotive executive Henry Ford). Later adopters also existed, which is why the Steel Industry is reviewed. There is also another class of users—early adopters—illustrated by the Aviation Industry. Logically, one would expect a discussion of the Aviation Industry first; however, the historically most influential industry was the automotive. Hence we look at that one below, followed by steel since most adopters came later, and leaving to last the smallest community of users—early adopters.

Automotive Industry

The automotive is an endlessly fascinating industry for a number of reasons. First, Americans have the largest number of automobiles per capita in the world. The industry is, therefore, very large. It has long been a major user of all kinds of technology, but it has still enjoyed periods of enormous success and calamities of historic proportions. Several large corporations, each of which operated large manufacturing facilities supplied by thousands of smaller component manufacturers, have historically dominated the industry in the United States. Their collection of plants and companies and the presence of domestic competition made it possible for the industry to adopt early and extensively all types of technologies, more so than some other industries, such as steel. Its companies used computer-based applications extensively, from vast data collection systems to inventory control applications to their more recent adoption of robots. Either of the previous two chapters could have just as easily been entitled "Computing Applications in the Automotive Industry." It is an industry that has relied extensively on computers for strategic purposes, for example, to ensure proper levels of inventory to feed its factories in support of just-in-time manufacturing processes in the 1980s and 1990s. Moreover, this industry has long had to deal with a variety of complex technologies and problems, ranging from fluid dynamics and aerodynamics to the materials sciences, electrons and electronics, and civil engineering. Imposed on top of such complex collections of issues were practical operational realities. As two industry experts reminded their readers at the end of the century, "Its supply chains are broad and deep," while "design costs are large and sunk, driving chronic industry overcapacity and price competition in all but the most fashionable of segments."[4]

The industry's reliance on computer applications, however, represents a cautionary tale about how technology alone cannot protect a company from bad strategies, disruptive international political events, or competitive changes driven by approaches not necessarily based on technology but, nonetheless, are competitively powerful. This observation holds even though the Automotive Industry was truly a trend-setter for the use of computers and other managerial and process practices in the twentieth century. The major conclusion one can reach about the effects of computerization is that despite the fact that the industry was technocentric, it failed to implement managerial innovation as successfully as it did technology. To a large extent, one can point to management's excessive focus on costs of labor—the primary motivation for using computers—as a primary cause of its inability to be as

By 1970, computers were in use in automotive and truck dealerships. The salesperson in this picture is using an IBM 2721 Portable Audio Terminal to query a computer on availability of specific models and colors of trucks that may be at a factory or at another dealership. Courtesy IBM Corporate Archives.

successful as it might have been. The same problem appeared in the Steel Industry, only with more devastating consequences, because labor-management tensions were far more serious.

In 1950, there were seven major automotive manufacturers in the United States, of which three controlled 87 percent of the market: General Motors (GM), Ford, and Chrysler. A fourth, American Motors, owned 4.9 percent of the market, bringing their collective market shares to nearly 92 percent.[5] During the 1950s and 1960s, the Automotive Industry dominated the domestic American market and enjoyed strong sales. These companies had size, required and used large amounts of capital, and had a high degree of product differentiation, enough to satisfy market tastes (e.g., new models every year). By the start of the 1970s, it was said that one out of every seven workers in the United States depended directly or indirectly on this industry for their livelihoods. For purposes of our discussion, *automotive* refers to both automobiles and small truck manufacturing (e.g., pickup trucks). This industry consumed about 20 percent of the nation's production of steel and lead and large proportions of its production of copper, nickel, glass, machine tools, general industrial equipment, and computers.[6] Its companies were also very large. At the start of the 1980s—a period of difficulty and transition for the industry— the four major American manufacturers (GM, Ford, Chrysler, and American Motors) were, respectively, the second-, fourth-, sixteenth-, and one-hundred-and-ninth-largest industrial firms in the United States, the first three accounting for 98 percent of all domestic auto sales.[7] In short, this industry was an important participant in the American economy.

We can divide its modern history into two periods, that before 1974 and that which followed and which remains an era still unfolding, with no clear turning points toward some third epoch yet evident. The first was characterized by dominance in an expanding American economy, with competition shared primarily among the American firms and in the context of continuously expanding demand for its products. In the 1970s, however, the situation began to shift, caused first by sharp increases in the cost of oil (as a result of OPEC's actions), which led to a rapid increase in demand for fuel-efficient vehicles. That demand translated into smaller cars, which had lower profit margins. The change in the market made it possible for Japanese manufacturers, who were already making smaller vehicles, to find a ready market in the United States. Government regulations mandating fuel-efficient vehicles also brought changes to the industry. A dangerous problem also existed in the fact that the Japanese had a very different model for how they manufactured vehicles, which proved far less expensive than the American approach. It allowed firms like Toyota, Nissan, and Honda to compete very effectively in the U.S. market with high-quality, small vehicles, priced below American rivals. Although the American government slowly raised trade barriers (e.g., tariffs) to help its domestic industry, the manufacturing processes of the Japanese were exported to the United States when Japan's firms responded to trade barriers by building manufacturing plants in this country.

To put it bluntly, the American automotive industry responded very poorly to these changes, with the result that in the 15 years between 1974 and 1991 its share of North American sales dropped from about 85 percent to 56 percent. By any industry's measure, this represented a huge change in market share. Hundreds of manufacturing facilities closed, and hundreds of thousands of jobs disappeared. Martin Anderson, an industry expert at MIT, commented that changes in this industry between 1976 and 1982 probably represented "the largest shift in technological, human and capital resources in American history."[8] That process of evolution continued through the rest of the century.

Before the mid-1970s, the operating philosophy in this industry was to mass-produce large volumes of vehicles by using flow methods and dedicated equipment in specialized plants. The idea was to achieve economies of scale and to keep production continuous. In short, it was an industry that constantly drove down costs and maximized output, two appropriate objectives in any period of economic stability. This strategy called for incremental improvements in the technologies embedded in vehicles (e.g., motors), processes (e.g., how cars were built), and tools (e.g., computer applications, such as welding).[9] All through the 1950s, 1960s, and 1970s, there was an endless round of incremental changes as one or another of these three elements influenced the other two. And what did this industry essentially do? It designed vehicles, developed them, built components, assembled them into vehicles, and sold them. It applied the digital wherever technology could improve efficiencies in these functions. In hindsight one might quibble about the pace of adoption, sometimes quick, sometimes slow, but in general fastest after Japanese competition became intense.

Even data centers had to compete with other parts of the firm. For example, at Ford an internal computer service bureau was set up at the start of the 1960s, equipped with an IBM 705, to generate payroll checks, do sales analysis, and carry on inventory control. As one of its managers reported at the time, "Computer Services competes by bid for the work against other data processing units within the company and against outside service bureaus."[10] A fundamental operating principle across all departments, divisions, and companies in the industry of the period was to rely on the lowest bids for goods and services. Application of that philosophy to data processing was typical. So, too, was the emphasis on operating efficiencies. A decade later, GM built a massive integrated parts ordering system to speed up existing applications and newer telecommunications to "reduce total data communications costs."[11]

IT Deployment

Like many manufacturing industries, this one typically deployed its normal collection of technologies of the period: increased use of computers, reliance on NC techniques, improved transfer lines, and automated assembly functions. Drafting work was completely switched to CAD applications by the end of the 1970s, and shop floor activities used NC extensively by the end of the 1970s as well. Transfer lines were automated and universal. Automotive manufacturers focused a great deal of attention on automating assembly because it was always the most labor-intensive. Automated equipment eliminated steps here and there that were previously performed by employees, such as tightening bolts and welding car bodies. These acts of automation (frequently called islands of automation at that time in the industry), often cut in half the labor content of some activities. A robot in the mid-1970s could do the work of 1.25 workers. What management soon realized, however, was that maintenance crews were needed to take care of this equipment, mitigating some of the savings. So while semiskilled workers declined in number, other workers, who had more skills, became necessary. Assessing the impact of computers on this industry from 1960 to 1976, however, U.S. government economist Robert V. Critchlow concluded that productivity gains "exceeded the average for all manufacturing." Employee output increased by 4.1 percent per year between 1960 and 1966. The annual rate shifted to 3.4 percent over the next 10 years. As Critchlow reported, the industry expected productivity to increase between the late 1970s and the end of the 1980s "as new technology brings about further reduction in unit labor requirements in assembly, machining, and other operations." The economic downturn of the industry during 1974–1975 again revealed the need for management to automate further because of the relative high cost of labor. In addition, two-thirds of the employees were covered by union labor contracts that proved inflexible in times of change.[12] However, this thinking and the problem with labor had existed for decades. The industry bragged about its use of computers, as early as the start of the 1960s.[13] All during the 1970s, despite the turndown in the industry's fortunes, what can only be characterized as industrial propaganda continued.[14]

The industry, in the belief that mass production was immutable, focused a great deal of its technological activities on incremental process improvements, taking advantage of new technologies as they came along to enhance existing ways of performing. All of these companies tightened up their inventory management practices, using computers to produce status and volume reports. Ford's IBM 705 at the start of the 1960s, for instance, generated parts reports, purchase requirements, and a variety of exception reports.[15] Chrysler used an IBM 702 system to do similar work.[16]

The development of the microprocessor made it possible to increase cross-plant control of equipment all through the 1970s and beyond, a process still underway. Simultaneously, microprocessors made their way into the products themselves. As one industry observer noted in the late 1970s, "Computers are a key technology in the automobile industry, initially applied to business operations such as payroll and bookkeeping records and subsequently extended to an increasing number of research and production operations." At the time, the industry reportedly had over 400 mainframes, which were used to facilitate auto styling and design, product development, NC of course, and transfer line automation.[17]

Simultaneously, companies improved dies, presses, shop floor machinery, and assembly techniques. Economist Lawrence J. White, writing about this industry at the start of the 1980s, concluded that the incrementalist strategy did not prevent manufacturers from seizing upon a new application when it made sense, even if they were cautious about it: "The automobile industry has usually been fairly prompt in adopting and adapting these processes, but, again, as in automotive technology, the industry has let others take the risks of initial development."[18] Because of their size, the Big Three could conduct experiments in various plants to learn and develop potential prototypes, such as GM did in building the Vega line of cars with the maximum amount of automation possible at the start of the 1970s.[19] Yet, their overall lack of boldness in improving either the quality of their cars or in reducing the retail cost of their products made it possible for the Japanese to leverage their own innovations, if not actually motivating them to develop new and effective ways of running automotive companies in the 1960s and 1970s. The American manufacturers paid a terrible price for Japanese innovations in the late 1970s and beyond in the form of lost sales and market share.

An essential, possibly the most important, element in daily operations was to control the flow of inventory in its various forms, from raw material to work in process to finished goods. As in other manufacturing industries, inventory control was emblematic of management philosophy and priorities. The American approach called for plant managers to ensure onsite availability of a great deal of inventory to feed production processes so that they never stopped. Automotive manufacturers used competitive bidding processes with their suppliers to ensure that costs remained low. Exclusive franchising of dealers made it possible for manufacturers to shift inventory to the selling arm of their industry for distribution into the American economy. The overall approach to inventory control worked well until the various crises of the 1970s.

Although it would be interesting to discuss the industry's failure to respond successfully to these crises, it has already been the subject of much study, so we can quickly summarize the way it reacted. First, companies reduced operating costs by closing plants and laying off workers. Second, they shortened the cycle time for introducing new models from the 5- to 6-year cycles of the pre-1970s to between 2.5 and 3 years, thanks in part to the use of CAD/CAM tools. Third, they began shifting manufacturing from massive lots to smaller lot productions and, in the process, continued expanding automation to drive down costs of manufacture and assembly. Fourth, they modified plants and processes to make them more responsive to changes in models. Each manufacturer varied its strategies, but all of them implemented simultaneously this bewildering array of approaches.[20] They also, but slowly, adopted Japanese manufacturing methods, such as just-in-time inventory control methods. With JIT, fewer suppliers were used, but they were made responsible for supplying the right amounts of inventory needed for any particular day's worth of production. The big manufacturers expanded the use of teaming employees, unlike in the old Fordist model, where they limited the breadth of activities of a worker. American firms in the early 1980s also bought interests in Japanese automotive firms and learned new techniques through these alliances.[21]

The output of vehicles actually improved over time but never to the high levels enjoyed by the Japanese. In the late 1970s, for example, GM plants routinely produced about 45 to 47 cars per hour, whereas Japanese plants exceeded these volumes. Some companies, GM most notably in the late 1990s, continued to falter behind their rivals; GM proved 50 percent less productive than its key Japanese competitors,[22] even though by the late 1980s and early 1990s this American company had climbed to 60 vehicles per hour. But, as observers at the time noted, "it is clear that the strategy of technological transformation became the core component of the United States and Western European industries' restructuring in the 1980s."[23] The Fordist style was finally in retreat.

The industry's historic preoccupation with inventory control could be seen by looking at the turns, that is, the number of times in a year when a stock of inventory would be totally replenished. Higher turns meant inventory was kept for shorter periods of time (a good thing). Turns also illustrated fundamental problems in the industry. An excellent year to look at in the late first period of the Automotive Industry, because it reflected performance at its pinnacle in that era, is 1973. In that year, turns of 5.3 to 5.6 were normal for American automotive firms. But in 1983, Toyota's turns were 88.6, whereas those for American firms hovered in the 11 to 12 range. Toyota continued to improve on the number of its turns, 90 the following year, but even in 1985 American turns were still low, between 11.9 (GM) and 19 (Chrysler). However, as two observers put it, on the issue of JIT the Americans firms "got the message."[24] Although these kinds of improvements are interesting, perhaps even impressive, American manufacturers never regained the market shares they had enjoyed in the 1950s or 1960s. They had lost momentum while the Japanese were able to build on their earlier advantages of smaller, better-quality cars that sold for less.

Observers of management's use of technology were generally critical. For example, Rebecca Morales, who studied the global automotive industry, concluded that U.S. automotive companies frequently implemented technological changes at a faster rate than the organizations themselves could absorb.[25] Others noted that the use of automation came out of a desire to reduce labor content rather than to improve productivity or to increase flexibility.[26]

Yet the industry did become more productive and competitive, partly because of new uses of technology. The major players doubled their investments in R&D for technologies that went either into vehicles (e.g., composite materials to make them lighter) or into retooling manufacturing plants in the 1980s. These expenditures rarely exceeded 5 percent of sales, which were lower than those of high-tech industries, such as computer manufacturers. These funds went into the development of new NC tools, flexible machining, further computerized coordination of manufacturing tasks, and of course CIM. Firms modified their plants to accommodate the changed manufacturing required by the move from rear-wheel drive to front-wheel drive. They increased their speed in changing dies and outsourced many functions, such as design, development of prototypes, and other engineering activities. They further relied on component suppliers. Their fundamental strategy in the 1980s involved shifting to flexible manufacturing, which revolved around the use of CAD, NC-driven machining tools, programmable robots, automated materials and components handling, automated testing, and FMS. In this period, many experiments were launched to test new approaches. Work also went overseas or to Mexico when efficiencies could be gained. Assembly plants in the United States, for example, reduced their labor force by nearly a fourth just in the period from 1978 to 1988, a process they continued well into the 1990s.[27] Morales sums up the results of all of these changes as of the early 1990s:

The U.S. auto industry was beginning to show signs of recovery, despite continued losses, particularly by GM. The global recession was forcing retrenchment in Japan and Europe. U.S. automakers had begun to distinguish themselves by strategy and structure and were responding to the increased competitiveness, market fragmentation, and constant technological change in recognition that these were not permanent features of the market.[28]

Technology contributed to the ability of these firms to outsource component production, various engineering activities, and the development of prototypes, with effective coordination of the work done by the independent vendors that were supplying them. Technology had moved from supporting large, integrated manufacturing processes in a stable environment to one characterized by change, flexible manufacturing approaches, and coordination of multiple organizations.[29]

Complex initiatives always yielded mixed results. In the 1970s and 1980s, these firms fell behind in product development, particularly in the 1970s when compared to their Japanese rivals. The shift to Toyota's approach to JIT inventory control, quality practices, and teaming simply took time to incorporate into the American manufacturing cultures of the period. Perhaps because of its enormous size and hierarchical culture, GM seemed constantly to suffer the greatest number of difficulties in these transitions, a problem that continued to plague the firm to the end of the century.[30] Die change times were also indicators of progress or problems. In one survey of this process, researchers noted that in 1981 a Japanese component affiliate could make a die change in 40 minutes; it took American manufacturers 8 hours. In 1985, the same Japanese firms could do it in 5 minutes, the Americans in 5 hours. The test involved the exact same types of die changes, in this case 15-ton presses used to stamp out transmission housings.[31] When a factory was changing dies, other production workers could not produce products or more inventory was needed to cover for the slow conversion. Productivity declined. (In the first period, it was not uncommon to shut down an entire plant for a month to prepare for the production of new models. In that same period, therefore, one could expect Japanese productivity to be outstanding in comparison to that of the Americans.) In the die study, the U.S. Toyota plant built 80 cars per worker per year, and the GM plant in Fremont only 46. Toyota needed 8 minutes to change a die; GM took 60 hours. Toyota had its JIT well in hand with a 3-hour average delivery time, whereas the GM plant needed two weeks.[32]

The combination of new technologies, quality management practices, and use of teams also had their effect on the overall quality of products. *Consumer Reports*, an American consumer advocacy research organization that tracked the number of problems Americans faced with hundreds of models of cars, noted in 1980 that Toyota experienced on average 24 problems per 100 cars versus 108 at GM. In 1990, GM had improved its performance enormously; it had only 40 problems on average out of every 100 vehicles, but by then Toyota had only 16. Ford in 1980 had 100, and 10 years later, 35. Chrysler had 89, later 31. But the Japanese consistently outperformed the Americans, and the public knew it. In 1980 Honda had 34 problems on average, 14 in 1990; Nissan 47 in 1980 and 15 in 1990, these statistics were based on cars manufactured in Smyrna, Tennessee, employing a 100 percent American work force.[33]

I present these statistics not so much to embarrass GM as to illustrate the huge deficiency in performance that a combination of different strategies and technologies made possible and that the Americans had to overcome. This evidence suggests that just leading with technological innovations did not necessarily generate sufficient competitive advantages. The Automotive Industry had to learn how to combine both sound strategies and effective deployment of technologies before it could make significant improvements in performance. It also had to do it quickly, a goal normally not achieved.

And what about the component suppliers? They were as much a product of the industry as were the large manufacturers. As the Big Three shifted responsibilities for development and delivery of products (components) to their selected suppliers, these smaller firms began to rely on various technologies to manage their operations. They upgraded their manufacturing processes to incorporate NC tools, a process that occurred when the tools were decreasing in cost. Just-in-time practices led to new materials handling processes as well. Observers of these changes in the 1980s noted, that "we are witnessing a period of marked change within the components industry that will ultimately have major implications for its structure and for its global division of labour."[34]

Recent Trends

Several trends and issues were in evidence during the 1990s for both large manufacturers and their suppliers, all involving computers. The first was the continued application of technologies and strategies initially embraced in the 1980s, such as CIM, FMS, and JIT, extending their deployment while simultaneously replacing older hardware and software with newer models particularly high-performance workstations and PCs for design. During this period, the large firms established new alliances with technology companies, first initiated in the early 1980s (e.g., GM's acquisition of EDS) in order to continue importing specialized technology and knowledge for manufacturing firms.

The second trend involved integrating manufacturing and sales of vehicles on a more global basis as the industry became far less insular and more international. Lashing together global initiatives in the design and manufacture of vehicles was first made possible by electronic data interchange (EDI) applications of the 1970s and 1980s and then by the Internet. Over time, it also became increasingly difficult to speak about a domestic Automotive Industry, as global alliances became a reality. On a global basis at the end of the century, the Automotive Industry produced over 56 million vehicles a year, generating over $1.8 trillion in sales. This was now an industry that spent just slightly less than 2 percent of that amount on information technology (both for installation in vehicles and to operate companies). That percentage came out to $26 billion per year at the start of the new century. New joint ventures were often made operationally possible by IT, which allowed the sharing of information and applications, much as was simultaneously occurring in the banking and insurance industries.[35] General Motors and Ford remained the largest producers as measured by the number of vehicles manufactured. DaimlerChrysler merged in 1998, thereby creating the world's fifth-largest automaker, forming a potentially powerful combination of American and European automakers. It was one of 17 such global combination, which experts in the industry anticipated would shrink to about 6. These large firms were also continuing to reduce the number of component suppliers as they shifted design and fabrication to them. Thus the 30,000 suppliers were expected to drop to under 10,000 in the early years of the twenty-first century.[36]

The issues faced at the start of the new century, however, were similar to those of earlier times. One industry analyst, writing for fellow colleagues in IBM in late 2000, noted that the industry faced "immense pressure on margins, excess capacities, and the fact that cars are increasingly perceived as a commodity." Besides globalizing, the industry wanted to continue to apply IT to its core competencies: "A major focus is on design, marketing and branding, which are considered the core competencies of the industry. Manufacturing continues to be outsourced to suppliers or other OEMs."[37] The key applications included more electronics in vehicles in support of function, comfort, safety, security, communication, and entertainment. The industry also used computers to increase margins through sales, in support of boosting overall profit levels. For example, when a salesperson in a dealership could offer financing for the purchase of an automobile through a company's wholly owned financing operation—as GM had with General Motors Acceptance Corporation (GMAC)—the necessary calculations of a loan and credit checking were tied back to the production of an order and to crediting a dealer with commissions for selling financing, and all was made possible and efficient and profitable through the use of computing in the 1980s. Profits on the sale of a car financed by an automotive firm could increase the profit of the transaction by over a third.[38]

The third influence of IT on the industry was, of course, the Internet. The industry reacted to its existence in two ways. First, it witnessed the use of the Internet by customers to seek out information about automobiles and then to start purchasing online. Manufacturers put up web sites to provide information and experimented with selling, although cautiously since such sales would threaten their dealers, who remained the primary channel of distribution. All major firms were reluctant to see that channel disintegrate, although by 2001 roughly 20 percent of American car buyers were routinely going to the Internet for information about pricing and features. The arming of consumers with that kind of data was shifting the balance of power in the negotiations over purchase prices, and consumers increasingly viewed automobiles as commodities. The Internet also made it possible to increase communications between the dealer and manufacturer to levels not practical in the old world of EDI.

The Internet created other opportunities for buying and selling vehicles in the United States. Online dealers began to emerge in the late 1990s, such as AutoNation and CarMax, called mega-dealers, who only sold over the Internet in volume. One economist concluded that this new development would "inject new competitive pressure into the industry."[39]

The Internet, however, was a positive innovation for the Automotive Industry because it built very nicely on the historic reliance these firms had on telecommunications, such as EDI, and in support of the trend of shifting design and production to outsourced firms. The flexibility such technology provided made it possible to begin running a firm on a global basis, balancing manufacturing capacity, coordinating the work of various suppliers, and even offering customers JIT manufacturing of to-order products and services. Core processes began to migrate to the Internet as the technology of choice for transmitting information and further integrating IT into the work of these firms. The processes most evident at the start of the new century included product design and development; manufacturing, including management of the supply chain (often using an ERP application and software, such as the German SAP products); and a variety of marketing applications, such as sales and services, market intelligence, and even emerging in-vehicles services (e.g., Internet access, directions from geopositioning tools, and entertainment).[40] Table 5.1 lists some of the major applications that were emerging at the start of the new century.

The list in table 5.1 in some ways looks very much like one the reader might have seen in the 1980s because, to a large extent, the Internet and globalization were continuations of a historic process of change that began in the mid-1970s. It

Table 5.1
Emerging E-Business Applications in the Automotive Industry

Function	Application Focus	Technology
Virtual product introduction	Design collaboration, digital mockup, product development, prototyping, Computer Aided Engineering (CAE), Knowledge Management (KM)	Computer-Graphics Aided Three-Dimensional Interactive Application (CATIA), Lotus, powerful workstations
Global production	Plant operations, global supply chain management, ERP integration, strategic sourcing, after-market parts, management	Internet, DB tools, e-mail, mainframe computing
Service diagnostics	Application consulting, project management, application development and rollout, call center operations	E-commerce, Internet
Marketing/sales	Customer loyalty, dealer communications, call center optimization, multimedia production, business intelligence, sell service sales	E-commerce, Internet, Domino, Web hosting
In-vehicle IT	Auto client applications, self diagnostics, embedded speech, application hosting	E-commerce, Internet, BI software

Source: IBM Global Services, Industrial Sector, 2000.

is why, for example, the newly created DaimlerChrysler firm had to worry about how best to create an effective global system for manufacturing, diagnostics, and technical support. Or why Ford and GM were interested in global sourcing of parts to drive down unit costs. All were embracing business-to-business (B2B) applications, embedding them into existing applications and processes. In an interview in late 2000, IBM's general manager, responsible for providing consulting services to the industrial sector, pointed out that B2B was emerging as "a company's IT infrastructure: which is moving 'beyond merely taking an order from a customer' to offering 'information on inventory, shipping terms, perhaps even a variety of sales conditions.' "[41] The B2B initiative evident in so many manufacturing industries concerned the leveraging of existing applications and activities by using the Internet and the many software tools that began to appear in support of this new technology. Online trading networks among suppliers and customers were increasingly being created, but again as extensions of earlier efforts to lengthen the classic Michael Porter supply chain from component manufacturer through fabricator to dealers and customers.[42]

Twenty-first Century Challenges

In the early years of the new century, the industry faced a number of challenges and opportunities that would be profoundly influenced by both the effective and ineffective use of computer-based applications. Historically, the industry liked to use IT but sometimes did it too late, too slowly, or out of context with the realities of the marketplace. During the 1990s, it appeared that the industry had learned to avoid some of its earlier mistakes. At a minimum, it now recognized what it had to do. Some of the key issues could be addressed in one fashion or another through the use of computing. These included, first, the impact of e-commerce, which had become customer-driven, that is, not driven by the industry. Customers were now pulling products through the supply chain, if by no other means than by what they ordered and how they configured their on-order vehicle. These orders were fed into various forecasting, purchasing, and production schedules, usually by software. In short, customers did not limit themselves to what vehicles were on the lot for sale. Second, supply chains were profoundly changing to take advantage of the Internet and to increase the use of problem-solving software. Many suppliers, in particular, were not ready technologically to leverage these changes. A third trend involved the increased role of intangible assets, such as the ability to streamline an organization because of the availability of information and integrative applications. However, that capability, in turn, could result in savings for customers in the form of lower costs for vehicles, triggering yet another round of pressures on corporate profit margins, as occurred in the 1970s and 1980s. Because of the impact of the Internet and B2B, both already underway, the industry as a whole had to respond to the emergence of these technologies.

That companies were reacting was evident all over the industry. A few examples illustrate once again that this was an industry that reached out to new technologies in a bewildering variety of ways. General Motors told its employees that they could have Internet services by the first quarter of 2001. Ford announced that it would make it possible for customers to buy cars directly in 2001. General Motors began to offer customers on-board traffic reports as part of its OnStar project and also started testing online ordering in Minnesota. Simultaneously, Ford launched a new generation web site that provided customers with comparison shopping. Delphi Automotive launched an online catalog for the aftermarket, and Info-4cars recruited American dealers. European firms were doing the same: Vauxhall in Britain became one of the earliest, if not the first, manufacturer to offer all its automobiles for sale over the Internet, and Fiat ended the year 2000 by announcing plans to establish a company that offered a variety of noncore business services.

One can safely conclude that as in earlier decades, those who linked these initiatives to a cohesive strategy could expect to leverage technology in a positive way. What is also clear, however, is that the American automotive industry evolved from an insulated domestic one that was focused on efficiencies to one that was now global, engaged in competition and consolidations around the world. It was an industry that was leveraging information technologies faster than in earlier decades as it emerged to both perform traditional core tasks and respond to the increased purchasing power of customers in many industrialized economies.[43] The story is not over, and a happy ending not yet in sight. As two economists summarized the situation at the start of the new century; "A transition of the vast and lumbering automotive manufacturing system and supply chain to a taut and focused one . . . might be difficult to bring about and impossible in any short time frame."[44] But it remained an industry that should have learned that computers were not silver bullets; managerial leadership and its willingness to innovate at appropriate rates to respond to competition was more important than the technology itself.

Steel Industry

The American Steel Industry has provided a generation of economists with a sector of the economy they could criticize and even mock. If ever there was an industry that should have gone out of business because of poor management, bad practices, narrow-minded labor leadership, and ineffective government support, this is it. But it also provided a generation of scholars with a test bed for understanding the dynamics of competitive advantages and disadvantages at an industry level. The only reason one cannot call this the most mismanaged industry in America is because the U.S. Consumer Electronics Industry probably should hold that title since it virtually does not exist today, thanks to superior Japanese competition. The case of the Steel Industry is fascinating because its history over the past century is one of world dominance to near extinction to a partial resurgence at the end of the twentieth century. It is an industry whose slow, very lagging response (or lack of) to technological innovations is a case study of opportunities lost or at least delayed.[45] Lest we blame this situation on the wrong source, it is not the technology but rather management's practices over a long period of time that created an environment in which adoption of technology proved difficult to achieve with the same success evident in the Automotive Industry.

This industry has been studied extensively, primarily by economists but also by various committees of the U.S. Congress almost every time steelworkers went on strike (six times between 1945 and 1962). Almost no student of the industry, however, has commented on the role of information technology in this sector of the American economy. But we should also keep in mind that other factors powerfully influenced the story of technology: managerial practices, management-labor relations, industry cost structures, and physical realities of how steel was made and delivered to customers.

Before I describe the industry's structure, remember that this is an industry that made products as much in batches as in continuous flow operations, although it was a hybrid. Furthermore, skilled labor played a greater role across the entire population of workers in this industry than was evident in many process industries. In other words, each steelworker needed to know more about the art and practice of making steel than did a worker in, for example, the Chemical or Petroleum Industry because, in the latter two, technology had taken over more of the functions of people and thus fewer experts were needed.

The U.S. Steel Industry was intact at the end of World War II because it was never bombed. In the 1950s and 1960s, Europe and Japan had to rebuild their industries. In 1950, the United States had the strongest Steel Industry in the world, producing half the world's supply, and it dominated the American domestic market. By the start of the 1970s, it produced only 22.8 percent of the world's steel, testimony as much to the global expansion of alternative suppliers as to the relative power of the American industry. At the time, Japan, which became a major competitor to the U.S. industry, produced 41.3 percent of the world's supply. In the early 1980s, U.S. output amounted to only 15 percent of the world's production, behind that of the Soviet Union, Western Europe, and Japan.[46] But before I discuss the digital, it is important to understand this industry's structure.

It is often cited as a classic example of an oligopoly, comprising four branches—iron ore mining, pig-iron production, steelmaking, and steel rolling—and dominated by a handful of companies in 1950 that controlled roughly three-fourths of the industry. By the early 1970s, there were 90 firms in the United States, of which 4 produced just over half the nation's tonnage and 8 accounted for 75 percent. The four largest companies were the U.S. Steel Corporation (24.68 percent), Bethlehem Steel (15.54 percent), Republic Steel (7.44 percent), and National Steel (6.46 percent).[47] The percentages of raw steel produced indicate that what U.S. Steel did caused all the others to follow suit during the 1950s and 1960s. In traditional oligopolistic fashion, U.S. Steel set prices, and the others followed accordingly; labor contracts signed by U.S. Steel would then be duplicated by the others; and so forth. During the 1950s and 1960s, some 90 percent of all labor was unionized; labor costs accounted for between 35 and 40 percent of the expense of production, the rest for raw materials and operations. These large companies were called the integrateds: they built up large vertical operations and ran large facilities.

In the 1960s, more modern, smaller firms came into the industry, called minimills. They required less capital, employed more modern technology than the integrated firms, and proved very responsive to changes in the marketplace in terms of products, quality, performance, and customer service. In the 1970s they cut deeply into the market share of the integrated companies.

Through most of the century, the large firms experienced terrible relations with their work forces, marked by mutual mistrust between management and unions and an inability to work for the common good. Every time they were in the process of renegotiating a national contract, lengthy strikes ensued, including the longest in American history. One strike even led President Truman (then becoming involved in the Korean War and thus in need of a steady and increased supply of steel) to threaten to draft all workers and nationalize the industry. In the 1950s, some 40 percent of the nation's inflation originated in price hikes in this industry, increases due primarily to cover the cost of labor contracts with some 500,000 employees. In fact, labor had higher salaries in this industry than in any other in the United States. Higher salaries, cost of capital, and often expensive transportation (because of lengthy distances from customers) made this industry increasingly vulnerable to competition from more efficient and conveniently located minimills and overseas rivals, particularly Japanese in the 1960s and 1970s. By the mid-1960s, foreign steel made up 15 percent of the American market, over 18 percent by 1971—up from 2 percent in 1959. By 1980, there were also 45 minimills in the United States. Clearly the traditional American industry was in trouble.

The large producers also had plant and technical problems. Rather than modernize existing facilities or build new ones (as the Japanese had to because of the destruction of all of their older plants during World War II), the American producers filled in and improved existing facilities, although with incremental improvements in technology. They were constrained in capital and had difficulty driving down labor costs, which forced them to adopt incremental strategies. Industry leaders also expanded plant capacity at times when it was not needed and often installed outdated technology. Often, these plants were not located near their customers. Economist Walter Adams, long an industry watcher, commented in 1982 that "today, the technological lethargy of the U.S. steel industry is hardly a matter of dispute"[48] because "the absence of the sharp wind of aggressive competition made it unnecessary for the integrated companies to apply rigorous standards of evaluation to the many plants they had inherited or acquired."[49] When they did react, with attempts at modernization in the 1960s and 1970s, integrated companies did too little, too late, and too poorly. The industry, characterized by managerial rigidity at the time, made it difficult, if not impossible, for senior executives to reevaluate, let alone change, their strategies and circumstances in either a timely or effective manner. The industry was thus left vulnerable to international competition.

Compounding the Steel Industry's problems were declining demands for its products in the 1970s and 1980s, leaving the large firms with excess capacity and competition from less expensive, alternative materials, such as plastics and composites. In the late 1970s, automotive companies, some of steel's biggest customers, moved to lighter materials in their bid to improve gas mileage and to offer the public smaller cars. Consumer consumption of more electronic products, as opposed to those using steel, also had its effect. Consumption of steel in the United States dropped from 140 million tons to about 123 millions tons in 1985; U.S. production declined from 131 to 95 million tons in the same period.[50] Commenting on the years of the 1970s and 1980s, economist Donald F. Barnett reached a similar conclusion as that of Walter Adams: "The decline of the role of traditional steel making in the United States can be blamed [on] . . . their failure to develop strategic alternatives and to adjust rapidly to market changes."[51] Even one of the most thoughtful analysts of this period, Paul A. Tiffany, blamed everyone: management, labor (particularly its senior executives), and government policymakers.[52] In fact, while I was conducting research on this industry, I could not find an economist with a kind word to say about it until the 1990s.[53]

Management understood what was happening and attempted to fight back with modernization programs (many of which were ill chosen), formed alliances, sought foreign trade restrictions to reduce dumping into the U.S. market at low prices, and reinvested in R&D all through the 1980s. But, of course, there was always a lag time between intent and results. In the 1980s, sales were off by 25 percent and 250,000 employees lost their jobs, not a good environment for fundamental transformation. The one success story that kept building momentum involved minimills, enterprises not saddled with stranded investments from the past. They built plants close to their customers and developed high-quality products tailored to the needs of their buyers, manufacturing products that cost only as much to make as in plants in other parts of the world. Labor input across the entire industry declined in the United States from 7 to 14 labor hours per ton in the early 1980s and to 5 in the early 1990s. Productivity (some of IT-driven) and newer methods for producing steel helped. These changes made it possible to find economists willing to praise the industry: "Today, U.S. integrated producers have the highest profitability per ton of steel produced in the world."[54] The turnaround had been brought about by the industry's success in reducing its operating costs, improving production efficiencies (primarily driven by technological innovations), and increasing sales.

IT Deployment

Nearly all economists who have looked at this industry have focused on issues of grand strategy (e.g., bad choices); the impact of stranded investments in large, old plants; oligopolistic practices; government policies; and the role of technological innovations. Data processing remained an ignored topic, yet throughout the period in question (1950s to the present), all these companies constantly worked on improving operational efficiencies. The huge labor content of the work and the historically terrible relations between labor and management alone would have provided incentive for any manager to acquire data-processing tools to improve control and management of labor productivity. In time, with the introduction of computers and later microprocessors as new equipment was put into plants, the digital's effects would be felt. But admittedly, the use of computers in this industry stood in sharp contrast to that, for example, in the largest manufacturing firms in the Automotive Industry.

The initial use of information technology in this industry reflected patterns evident in other industries: first in accounting and labor tracking, then in inventory control and production planning, and finally in production feedback processes (largely because of the arrival of the microprocessor). Although applications were similar to those in other industries, steel tended to be slower in adopting them. Published cases of implementation, therefore, have to be suspected as the exception, not the norm.

Initial applications were in such traditional accounting areas as payroll, accounts receivable, accounts payable, sales tracking, and inventory control. Many of these applications were first developed by the large, integrated firms in the 1920s and 1930s and operated on the exact same IBM or Burroughs equipment until the 1960s.[55] Vendors such as IBM attempted to get this industry to modernize. Although IBM did not publish one single application brief on any of the integrated firms between the 1950s and the late 1980s, it produced hundreds on all other major American industries and many of the nation's largest firms. Those it published were from niche players, touting applications that had become common in other industries. For example, there was the Carpenter Steel Company, of Reading, Pennsylvania, which produced high-quality specialty steels—a market the integrateds never had—and used IBM unit record equipment in the mid-1960s to process payroll, job order costing, and payables distribution and to perform sales analysis. The firm used an IBM 357 Data Collection System in support of the process. Its labor-reporting application was typical of many of the day, evident in numerous industries: collecting attendance and job information data, data on hours and wages assigned by employee, and records by job.[56]

Plant managers, however, also looked to computers for help in actual production processes, which were technical and often complex and normally required real-time judgment by experienced employees who had, for example, to gauge when to increase temperature or materials or otherwise alter the rate at which production occurred. As more modern electric furnaces came on stream in the 1960s, particularly at smaller new facilities, the opportunity to experiment with computers increased. The Lukens Steel Company, for instance, used an IBM computer in the very early 1960s to help determine the level of heat needed to produce various kinds of specialized steels and to build models of specifications for new grades of steel. An internal IBM memo attached to the description of this application noted that this was the first installation in the United States of a "computerized operator guide control for electric furnace steel making."[57] More typical during the 1950s–1980s, however, were more humble applications, doing such tasks as production forecasting, order entry, inventory management, work scheduling, and manufacturing work order processing, all providing management with a variety and increasing number of reports. These applications became ubiquitous in large facilities by the end of the 1950s and in minimills from their beginning. By the end of the 1960s, the vast majority of these applications had moved to computers, rather than being left on punch-card tabulating systems.

As in the Automotive Industry, managers emphasized the control of inventory. Lunkenheimer, a medium-sized valve manufacturer, installed a computer-based system in the 1960s that allowed it to cut inventory costs in half by more tightly scheduling availability of materials, linking them to production schedules, and then shipping them quickly to customers. Forecasting each activity provided the benefits. One manager at this company noted that "without the computer, this forecasting finesse in the form of detailed projections would be impossible to develop."[58] It was a fundamental improvement in operations for this firm.

Even though significant process control arrived in the 1970s because of the availability of the microprocessor, some attempts were made even earlier to apply the digital to the integration of the multiple complex processes in a factory. In the integrated firms, massive and heavy quantities of steel and other materials needed to be managed, chemical analyses conducted, and temperatures monitored and controlled. Often the digital would be introduced when a firm installed some other new technology, as for example, during the construction of sintering plants, new blast furnaces, basic oxygen steelmaking plants, and electrolytic tinning lines. Management looked to computers for increased amounts of integrated control, from data collection to highly automated control. Two engineers at U.S. Steel reported in the mid-1960s that "recently, computers have been installed on blast furnaces for data logging and alarm monitoring." They also noted, however, that "there are at present no generally used automatic feedback systems on the basic oxygen steel making process itself."[59] Feedback mechanisms were precomputer. Computer-based approaches arrived in the 1970s. The same two engineers were perhaps too candid in their report about trends in computing when they admitted that their industry had very little experience with computers because, in hindsight, their perspective was probably more a comment about U.S. Steel and other integrated firms than about the minimills of the 1960s and 1970s.

All of this discussion raises this question: what was the extent of deployment of computers in the American Steel Industry in the years just before its fundamental transformation in the 1980s? In the 1970s, the industry began to change the basic technologies with which it made steel, improving direct reduction processes; building smaller, newer mills that applied basic oxygen processes (BOP); and later building integrated mills and installing electric-arc furnaces and vacuum-digesting techniques. The U.S. Bureau of Labor Statistics (BLS) reported in the late 1970s that automated, computer-driven production control applications could be found in less than 10 percent of all the plants, the majority in rolling mills. Minicomputers were used to drive these applications, either as dedicated control units or as satellites to larger systems (e.g., for production planning and reporting). Hot strip mills were usually some of the most modern facilities in the industry and thus became early users of minicomputers to control shop floor activities.[60]

A decade later, in the mid-1980s, the BLS looked at the industry again and reported that management still focused on reducing costs of labor, raw materials, and energy but was also concerned about improving product quality. Applications from the era of the 1970s were being installed, although "diffusion of many of these technologies has been slow." Minimills still led the way in the use of computers, even though they had less capital to spend on them than large firms, like U.S. Steel. Most technologies were implemented in incremental fashion as they proved productive elsewhere within the industry; normally, elsewhere meant somewhere in the United States, not necessarily in Japan or in Western Europe. Management normally chose incremental improvements of all kinds of technology, not just the digital, because of the high costs of building new facilities. It proved cheaper in the short term to retrofit many existing facilities. The BLS reported, however, a "dramatic increase" in the use of computers, largely tied to the increased installation of oxygen furnaces and a new generation of strip mills, many of which were initially installed with computers sporadically across the industry in the late 1960s and through the 1970s. Retrofitting old plants with computer-driven applications accounted for between 50 and 85 percent of all digital installations of the late 1970s and early 1980s. Setup times declined because of automation, but labor costs did not because computers simply caused unskilled labor to be replaced with those who could program and maintain complex computer-driven equipment. Energy costs declined, as did prices for scrap materials, while quality yields increased, all offsetting labor expenses. However, management had much to replace in the 1980s. A 1978 report on the industry by McGraw-Hill, based on surveys of steel industry executives, noted that 26 percent of all the plants and equipment were already technologically obsolete and hence too expensive and noncompetitive.[61] Even industry executives admitted publicly that they had a problem. One told a reporter, "We've screwed things up so they'll never get untangled."[62]

Initiatives to modernize and become more competitive in the 1980s paid off in the 1990s. Minimills, in particular, led the way in the renewal of the industry largely because they began as green field operations and expanded over time in number (capacity grew from 4 million tons in 1994 to 14.4 million in 1996). But the integrated firms improved as well, and joint ventures with foreign partners made the domestic industry more global also. Industry complaints about dumping and trade restrictions were indications of increased globalization, despite attempts by members of the U.S. industry to slow its progress.[63]

Before leaving the 1980s, one should recognize that the effort expended was both enormous and positive. Real production costs came down 28 percent, and the productivity of labor rose 60 percent. These improvements meant that a ton of steel produced in 1991 cost $480; had the productivity changes not occurred, this expense would have been $669.[64] Labor productivity, historically awful, improved by nearly 300 percent between the early 1980s and the mid-1990s, suggesting more how terrible it had been earlier than how remarkable the improvement proved to be later.[65] But it was never enough. One economist observed just before the arrival of the Internet that "the integrated U.S. steel industry never achieved a degree of modernization comparable to that of its foreign rivals. Most of the investment effort consisted of an endless 'rounding out' of existing plants."[66]

Recent Trends

The Internet created the largest new source of fresh IT applications in the 1990s, more than did the historic continuing decline in the overall cost of computing and the increase in the capacity of computer technology, software, and telecommunications bandwidth. Ultimately, it may prove to be the most industry-transforming technology since the development of the computer itself. Yet almost predictably, the industry was very slow to wake up to the importance of this technology. One executive noted in 2000, "If you had asked me about e-commerce two years ago, I'm not sure I would have known what you were talking about." But soon after, e-commerce came to steel. Major customers, such as the Automotive Industry, forced steel suppliers to start using the Internet. Suppliers put up web sites with information about products and terms and conditions, which buyers looked at in making their purchasing decisions. In short, customers forced the Steel Industry to merge into their supply chains. The major development in this regard occurred in the late 1990s with the establishment of two electronic trading markets in the metals arena: MetalSite LP and e-Steel. In early 2000, the latter reported that over 50 U.S. steel mills were participating in this virtual B2B market. MetalSite sold between 160,000 and 200,000 tons of steel through its site per month in early 2000, and e-Steel conducted transactions closer to 40,000 to 50,000 tons per month. Both brought buyers and sellers together and expanded their operations at the start of the new century. They functioned, in effect, like online auctions. Industry experts predicted that up to 50 percent of all steel would be sold over the Internet by about 2005. Suppliers were selling their capacity, and buyers were looking for best deals.[67] The president of the Steel Manufacturers Association, Tom Danjczk, sounded positively high-tech in late 1999: "The guy who can fill the order in a day [over the Web] will win the order over the company that can fill it in six weeks. Unless you add value, e-commerce will chop you out."[68] In this quotation, we see tied together the IT opportunity and the market challenge.

By late 2000, deployment seemed well underway. One survey indicated that many purchasers were using the Web to inquire about products and prices, although less than 10 percent had yet bought steel online. Transactions were taking place through third parties, for example, e-Steel, which most mills had signed on with. Expectations were that sales would rise exponentially during the first decade of the new century, fundamentally transforming how selling and purchasing occurred. However, once again the Steel Industry was also being accused of being slow in moving to the Internet and still remaining somewhat less than buyer-friendly, this time in regard to electronic commerce. However, the process was underway. Approximately 90 percent of steel buyers used the Internet to look up prices and products, although deployment beyond that initial phase remained limited. Despite that fact, however, suppliers and buyers were displacing old EDI applications with the Internet. So what was slowing adoption? One industry report in 2000 clearly stated that "taking the Web sites beyond the informational stage to actual buying requires gathering real-time data on production schedules, inventories and prices for all products. This information is already routinely gathered for reports. The challenge is making it readily available at the touch of a button to qualified consumers."[69]

Buyers were driving sellers onto the Internet faster than the other way around. The central event in the world of industrial online purchasing at the start of the new century was the electronic-procurement programs being implemented by GM,

Ford, and DaimlerChrysler. Combined, they represented the largest customers for steel in North America. This automotive-purchasing initiative held out the prospect of affecting many industries, not just steel. General Motors's group vice president for worldwide purchasing said that his company's online application would be "the world's largest virtual marketplace for a wide array of products, raw materials, parts and services."[70] Automakers were implementing systems that would reduce their purchasing cycle times by automating purchase authorization and accounting and contractual processes, all by using a portal.[71] That application alone would fundamentally change the entire scope of how the Steel Industry worked with customers. From a historic perspective, the pattern was the injection of IT into manufacturing in the 1980s and early 1990s to improve efficiencies and competitiveness and then, in the early years of the new century, expansion of IT's use to customers and to a global market.

Structurally, the use of the Internet facilitated patterns of organization evident in other industries: global markets and consolidations. Just as in banking, IT made it possible to merge large enterprises, particularly in the United States, so it could also happen with steel. In 1999, nearly 49 percent of North American steel came from 10 firms. Western Europe's top 10 produced 75 percent of that continent's steel, and in Asia the top 10 accounted for 44 percent.[72] But for many reasons beyond the scope of this chapter, one could expect further consolidations in Asia and Europe before they could occur in North America, resulting in a stiffer competitive environment for the American producers. With global demand the greatest outside of the United States, American alliances with foreign producers became more possible through virtual trading markets, such as those created by e-Steel and MetalSite.

Before moving to another industry, I should acknowledge the enormous transformation this industry underwent and the role the digital played later. In the wrenching restructuring that brought the American industry back to life, it shut down dozens of outmoded mills, slashed capacity by 30 percent in the 1980s and early 1990s, invested some $50 billion in new technology (some of which went to computing, software, programming, and IT operations), raised labor productivity by nearly 300 percent, and reduced its expensive work force by 60 percent.[73] The American industry was the most expensive steel provider in the world by the early 1960s, and yet by the early 2000s it was often competitive. However, problems of foreign dumping into the American economy remained, as did the industry's compulsion to call for trade regulations. These practices signaled that technology and strategy had not yet fully resolved the Steel Industry's problems. On December 29, 2000, LTV, one of the industry's largest firms, filed for bankruptcy protection and called for the government to restrain unfair trade practices by foreign competitors and to provide emergency loans to the firm, arguing that hot-rolled steel prices had dropped to a 20-year low, against which it could not compete. This story about the Steel Industry ends sadly at the time of this writing, with LTV announcing that it would sell off core assets, lay off 18,000 employees, and probably have to stop paying pensions to 70,000 retirees because of the financial paucity of even its pension program.[74]

Aerospace Industry

The Aerospace Industry has long been seen as an early adopter of post–World War II technologies, not the least of which are for information processing. It is also an industry that developed some of the most high-tech products of the century, such as modern aircraft and spaceships. This industry enjoyed a half century of prosperity, largely because of the Cold War, which created an enormous demand for its products over many decades. American military services and the National Aeronautics and Space Administration (NASA) were its largest customers. It operated at the heart of what President Dwight D. Eisenhower termed the "military-industrial complex."[75] The Aerospace Industry, as part of this complex, became the source of many new high-tech innovations in manufacturing, composite materials, and avionics software for aircraft, missiles, and spaceships. Its close relationship with the U.S. military, the needs of the Cold War, and the complexity of its work explain why computer-based applications were started in this industry so early, so rapidly, and ultimately so extensively.

It is a complex industry by any measure. Some 43 percent of the nation's scientists and engineers who were involved in any form of significant R&D worked for or with this industry at one time or another. It was the beneficiary of most of the U.S. government's high-tech R&D dollars from the 1950s through the 1970s. Frederic M. Scherer, an economist who has studied the industry, observed that "what goes on in the industry cannot be called private enterprise in any conven-

An airborne computer was built by Burroughs for the U.S. Air Force to link aircraft to the nation's SAGE defense network, 1960. By the late 1950s, the Aerospace Industry was under great pressure from the military community to miniaturize all its electronic systems. Burroughs Papers, courtesy Archives of the Charles Babbage Institute, University of Minnesota, Minneapolis.

The airborne computer built by Burroughs, shown in the photograph on page 152, was deployed in the early 1960s in the air force's RC121 planes. Burroughs Papers, courtesy Archives of the Charles Babbage Institute, University of Minnesota, Minneapolis.

tional sense; it lies instead in the gray area between private and public enterprise."[76] To give a quick insight into the size and scope of the Aerospace Industry, in 1965 the U.S. government spent about 4 percent of the GNP on aircraft, missiles, and other advanced weapons systems, and during the Vietnam War that percentage rose. All firms in this industry needed computers to design, manufacture, operate, and service their products.

Unlike the Soviet Union, which chose to run state-owned defense factories, the American government opted to funnel the production of weapons and aircraft through the private sector. Companies in this industry were either lead contractors on a project or suppliers, and they played both roles simultaneously. Key suppliers were recognizable household names: Lockheed Aircraft, North American Aviation, McDonnell-Douglas, Boeing, United Aircraft, and Grumman Aircraft. They also brought into the process thousands of smaller firms that made specific components (e.g., jet engines), which are part of the industry, as well as others that manufactured components used in other industries (e.g., Honeywell's thermostats or IBM's computers and software). In short, the industry's composition was not so neat as many others. The BLS did have a formal definition: aircraft and parts (SIC 372) and missiles and space vehicles (SIC 1925).[77] During peacetime, concentration in the hands of a few loyal producers tended to be high, as occurred in the two other industries studied in this chapter. During wars, the construction of aircraft spread out to additional suppliers. In the years following the end of the Cold War, the Aerospace Industry increasingly evolved more extensively as a manufacturer of commercial aircraft and further expanded its role by competing in an international market, primarily against European rivals. When selling to the government, manufacturers frequently followed a pricing policy of cost plus (within reason), whereas

Manufacturers were extensive users of word processing and other office applications, not just CAD/CAM and shop floor systems. Here word processors are being used at Boeing in 1981. Courtesy IBM Corporate Archives.

for the private sector price performance became the more operative practice. Government work was always more profitable than that in the private sector; in the 1950s, the industry had 19 percent after-tax returns on invested capital, versus the 12 percent enjoyed by manufacturing companies in general.[78] Thus, the transition to increased private sector sales in the 1980s put pressure on the industry's historic rates of profits.

IT Deployment

However one defines the Aerospace Industry, it spilled over into so many other industries during the Cold War that it became a major conduit for technology and manufacturing practices to the rest of the American economy. My repeated references to NC technology throughout this book are examples. Often expensive new uses of computing would be developed in this industry, funded largely by the U.S. government, and then later transferred to other industries. A variety of computer-based simulation applications was one example, as was almost every form of advanced vehicle control software (e.g., avionics first in the military, which then later appeared in commercial aircraft, robots, and even in automobiles). It would be difficult to underestimate the importance of this industry in transforming how the digital changed the way in which things were designed and built in the last half century.

These companies performed several fundamental activities. First, they designed new, innovative, high-tech devices and aircraft that had not existed before. *Complex* and *high-tech* are the correct adjectives to use to describe the salient characteristics of their products. For example, a typical American fighter of World War II could be built on the basis of roughly 8,000 blueprints. In 1961, a military plane required between 50,000 and 100,000 drawings.[79] This work required the use of just about every new form of computing that came along, including software tools that the companies developed; thus few off-the-shelf software products were used during most of the period under study. It would not be until the 1980s and 1990s that this situation began to change, when commercially available tools like telecommunications (and especially the Internet) were deployed. Second, this industry manufactured complex equipment, often deploying the very latest high-tech machines and software available to get the work done. But the products it made were not mass-manufactured; this was a job shop industry. One did not produce millions of F-16s or 737s; a firm would build hundreds, with many incremental improvements in later versions of a product retrofitted into earlier-built aircraft. Thus one could walk through a Boeing assembly plant in 2002 and feel that it looked similar to the same facility 30 years earlier, except that now robots were doing welding, computer-driven test and diagnostic censors and PCs were everywhere, and there was a great deal more security. However, one would still see bays with airplanes in various stages of construction.

Because unit costs were so high for any individual product or program, the industry placed a heavy premium on simulating design, stress, performance of materials, and so forth before bending metal, relying extensively on computers such as those built by CDC and Cray. Modeling activities became the transformative path to the digital style. Thus, although the production floor in 2002 might have looked similar to that of the 1950s, many fundamental processes did not. They were often housed, almost unseen, in engineers' offices, where CAD/CAM terminals and large databases replaced old-fashioned Keuffel and Essen Company (K&E) drafting tables, paper-based blueprints and punch-card tub files.

In the 1950s, automated drafting tools—the precursors of CAD—became widespread in this industry and the kinds of accounting tools and packages evident in other large manufacturing industries were continuously updated to provide the highly detailed accounting reports government agencies required. In the late 1950s and early 1960s, much of the innovative conversations about integrated engineering and management information systems first took place within the confines of this industry before spilling out into others.[80] Two important providers of IT goods were IBM and CDC, and often they were subcontractors in the development of specialized software and instrumentation. Hewlett-Packard and, later in the 1960s and 1970s, minicomputer manufacturers, were also. Table 5.2 lists the kinds of applications this industry wanted or used by the mid-1960s, either writing software itself to facilitate some of this work or, later, acquiring software tools to help.

In comparison to many other industries, however, this one had many years of experience with computing. In the early 1960s, many companies moved to their

In the late 1950s and early 1960s, Burroughs developed techniques and equipment for space and missile applications. This is the D210 Magnetic Computer to be used in early missiles; it had nearly the same amount of computing capacity as earlier mainframe computers, circa 1962. Burroughs Papers, courtesy Archives of the Charles Babbage Institute, University of Minnesota, Minneapolis.

Table 5.2

Aerospace Engineering Management Information Systems Applications,
Circa Mid-1960s

Proposal preparation	Production scheduling
Contract negotiations	Task control
Functional engineering and project management	Budget management
Data collection	

Source: IBM, *Engineering Management Information System for the Aerospace Industry* (White Plains, N.Y.: IBM Corp., 1966): 1–45; DP Application Briefs, Box 116-3, IBM Archives, Somers, N.Y.

Table 5.3
IBM 701 Installations in the Aerospace Industry, 1958

Boeing Airplane Company	2 Systems
Douglas Aircraft	5 Systems
North American Aviation	1 System

Source: R. Hunt Brown, "Office Automation Applications Updating Service," Supplement no. 6 (March 1958), attachment, "Directory of Computer Users": IV-E-15; CBI 55, "Market Reports," Box 70, Folder 4, Archives Charles Babbage Institute, University of Minnesota, Minneapolis.

second or third round of computer system upgrades. Furthermore, many of the systems aerospace firms installed were the very largest available at the time. Table 5.3, for example, lists the number of IBM 701 systems installed in this industry in 1958, computers considered very big and advanced in its day.

Before concluding this brief overview of the Aerospace Industry, we need to understand better the impact of NC applications. One member of the industry in the early 1960s captured the significance of its application, calling it, "perhaps the most exciting single development in manufacturing in the last 50 years." Of course, the earliest NC equipment did not use computers but "relied primarily on manually created instructions which were punched into tape and fed into the machine tools."[81] By the late 1950s, products were too complicated for such methods. How complicated NC applications had become with the use of computers became evident by the start of the 1960s:

> In a typical computer-numerical control application, the first step is utilizing the computer to make a series of logical decisions based upon a set of standard conditions. Next these decisions are projected mathematically into the specific axes a machine will have to follow in order to fabricate the part. Finally, these figures are punched into tape or cards which, in turn, are used for direct control of the manufacturing equipment.[82]

The same manager from the period described an emerging era of profound change in how objects were made, all of which came true within a decade: "At this very moment, for example, computers are being used to generate instructions for jobs such as welding, flame cutting, inspection, component insertion and testing, filament winding, glass cutting and paper slicing. And this is just the beginning."[83] By any measure, the act of manufacturing was changing profoundly. Computer-based applications came quickly and, as the data on deployment suggests, were being implemented extensively in this and other bellwether industries by the end of the 1960s. By the end of the century, there were very few workers who could remember a time when NC tools were not widely used.

Like other large industries, this one next embraced PCs in the 1980s and 1990s and used the Internet late in the century to communicate with suppliers of parts

By the 1970s, even airports used computers to communicate with pilots and commercial aircraft to facilitate smooth operations. In this 1970 photograph, the Burroughs Optical Lens Docking System (BOLDS) helps pilots of a 747 park the aircraft at a terminal in the Los Angeles International Airport. Burroughs Papers, courtesy Archives of the Charles Babbage Institute, University of Minnesota, Minneapolis.

and with customers. The pattern of adoption largely mimicked that of the Automotive Industry and thus need not detain us further. The one notable exception was the absence of an e-market for consumers; one simply did not legally buy airplanes and rockets over the Internet. But the Internet became part of the infrastructure of these large firms, helping to block the rise of new rivals.[84] E-market consortia also had their limits in this industry. As one study of the organizational effects of the Internet reported, "In large industries such as automotive and aerospace manufacturing, the emergence of consortia has significantly dampened enthusiasm for start-up e-marketplaces."[85]

Conclusions

The three industries studied in this chapter are emblematic of big American manufacturing industries, with everything that was strong and weak in the powerful industrialized economy of the United States. First, these were bedrock industries that propelled the American economy to greatness through most of the twentieth century, although some ultimately proved to be most vulnerable to international competition. They pioneered most of the uses of computers deployed in manufacturing industries around the world. They moved to embrace computing at different speeds, normally when the case for them proved compelling or circumstances forced reluctant management teams to sharpen their productivity. I devoted very little space to analyzing how effectively these industries used computers because that would require a company-by-company analysis, which is not the focus of this book. However, given the widespread adoption of computers and telecommunications across so many firms and their suppliers, it almost does not matter—except to the historian. The economies of scale and the nature of how work was done had changed so much by the 1980s that the thought of any return to the situation before, say, 1960, proved impossible. Once the influence of all kinds of technology began to affect the overall operations of an industry, it had no choice. We saw, for example, that the emergence of the minimills in the Steel Industry—which in effect, placed the large mills on the economic defensive for the rest of the century—was a disadvantage that the larger mills had yet to overcome at the dawn of the millennium.

Two scholars who have looked at how automation affected all manufacturing, Morris A. Cohen and Uday M. Apte, made this salient point applicable to the three industries studied in this chapter and to those reviewed in the next:

> The impact of new technology on performance in manufacturing environments has been profound. It has redefined expectations for quality, precision, and the overall efficiency of the production process. It has also modified the economics of manufacturing by altering both fixed and variable costs, as well as by increasing capital investment requirements.[86]

These were not two wide-eyed enthusiasts for technology; their study was as much a collection of comments on the limits of computing as it was an analysis of how the digital was used at the end of the century.

A second reality involved the enormous increases in labor productivity evident in these three industries and in so many other corners of the American manufacturing sector. One economist stated that "much of the increase in productivity growth can be attributed to the sustained heavy investments in information technology and the resulting increase in the nation's IT capital stock."[87] That could happen only if management used IT across all the major functions of their companies: design, manufacturing, logistics, sales, and service. The Internet reinforced work in these functional areas but also intensified work and communications links within firms; made possible ties and alliances with other enterprises, especially suppliers; and finally, did the same in markets with customers. Organizational boundaries began blurring, especially in the Automotive Industry, and least in the Steel Industry.[88]

However the role of the employee is evident in all three industries. Firms were run by people, not computers. Managers still determined when and how computers would be used; the most effective managers deployed technology the best, but other managerial teams failed to be as innovative or productive as they might have been. The role of labor in American industries is also crucial to the story. The sad truth is that one of the primary reasons for important increases in the productivity of labor across many industries, the use of the computer, occurred because American management and labor had poor relations, at least far worse than, say, those in Japan. To be sure, the high cost of labor also proved to be an important incentive for adopting computers in a wide variety of transformative processes. Ironically, however, such adoptions also increased the technical skills required of remaining employees, which suggests that perhaps in the years to come fundamental problems in management-labor relations will remain, if somehow not addressed. The lesson of the computer is that unless one could eliminate 100 percent of labor, the digital does not fix management-labor problems.

To what extent did the digital permeate the activities of process industries, which were quite different in the tasks they performed from the kinds reviewed in this chapter? The short answer is, a great deal. Computing had an even more profound effect on process industries than in the three discrete manufacturing cases described above. Yet, process industries received less publicity about their deployment of the digital than did either automotive or aerospace firms, so their stories, although in some ways new, exhibit patterns evident in many manufacturing industries. When viewed in combination with the kinds of industries just examined, it becomes much clearer how pervasive computing had become and to what extent this technology fundamentally altered the way in which work was done. Therefore, the next chapter is devoted to an examination of the Petroleum, Chemical, and Pharmaceutical Industries.

6

Patterns and Practices in Three Process Industries: Petroleum, Chemical, and Pharmaceuticals

A successful control system is a well-organized collection of components, each
with a definite function and designed to interact with the others. This
compares very closely to an army, with its outposts, headquarters, and main
striking forces.

—George O. Manifold, 1964

Process industries have been an important and large segment of the American economy through the twentieth century. Obvious industries include papermaking, chemical, petroleum, petrochemical, and pharmaceuticals. Because of the nature of the products they produce, they have long relied on various forms of instrumentation, process control, automation, and computing. Examining three clusters of these industries—petroleum, chemical, and pharmaceuticals—gives us further insight into the role and effects of the digital in manufacturing. In reality these industries are sets of industries. The Petroleum Industry has several distinct components, whereas the chemical is almost as difficult to define as was the military-industrial complex because of its variety of components, ranging from petrochemical products to plastics, inorganic materials, and fertilizers to drugs and other medicines for animal and human consumption. These industries, especially chemicals, have been made possible by advances in science.

In the previous chapter I examined industries that, in the parlance of business, performed discrete manufacturing, and I provided several examples of patterns of computer adoption. The industries reviewed in this chapter are quite different in the way in which they manufacture and in how raw materials, WIP, and finished products flow continuously (or semicontinuously) from entry into the plant until exit. These plants have long tended to be large, complex facilities and organizations. Whereas in discrete manufacturing many closed-loop processes could operate relatively independently of one another, and did in the first two decades after World War II, in process industries there has always existed a greater sense of urgency to consolidate and integrate closed-loop processes. Both types of manufacturing firms did so, making enormous strides in the 1960s and 1970s. But process industries had started to move from open- to closed-loop systems and processes in the early decades of the past century, often relying on pneumatic tools with which to govern the flow of materials, work, and final products—thereby having a substantial array of technical skills before the arrival of the digital. This trend predated what occurred in discrete manufacturing industries, usually by over a decade and always as measured by the extent of deployment. Much of these various technologies governed the transformation of chemicals into new products and their physical movement. These functions required computers to enhance knowledge about and control of the movement and synchronization of information with production.

With computers, production plants that typically had hundreds of closed-loop systems, each with their own personnel, could be further consolidated to the point where, by the early 1970s, several technicians operated hundreds of them from a centralized control room. In discrete manufacturing, particularly in the 1950s and 1960s and even much later, the fully automated plant remained more of an objective than a reality. *Islands of automation,* although commonly used to describe discrete manufacturing processes, would have been an unfamiliar phrase in any process industry in any decade during the last half century. Discrete manufacturers operated with larger work forces between the 1950s and 1970s than did process plants. Therefore, discrete manufacturers concentrated intently on reducing the labor content of work whereas process industries focused more on process improvements, which in turn led to improved cost performance of both their products and labor.

Process manufacturing has some unique features that affected the way in which computers would be used. Processing normally occurs in closed containers, such as pipes, which means that employees cannot see the status of the work and must, therefore, rely on a vast array of instruments to serve as the eyes and ears of managers and workers alike. Equipment used in processing plants is often large and made to order for that facility, whereas discrete manufacturers could usually buy commercially available manufacturing machines such as painters and drill presses. But the most obvious feature of a process manufacturing facility is that work is continuous.[1] The industry also had semicontinuous processing, such as in papermaking and glass production (even steel fits into this category). Thus, while raw materials are being transformed (as in continuous processing), operations are really batch-oriented, which does make it possible, for example, to visually inspect the status of work and to make adjustments.[2] In semicontinuous processing, commer-

The picture shows IBM salesman Elvin Wolf in 1965 with a seismic report produced by an IBM S/360 system. The individual on the right is a petroleum exploration expert; both are at a drilling site in western Texas. The S/360 was used to analyze data to determine where best to drill for oil. Courtesy IBM Corporate Archives.

cially available manufacturing equipment is also more in use than in continuous processing plants.[3] Table 6.1 summarizes the differences as viewed by experts working in the 1960s and 1970s, the period marked by extensive adoption and experimentation with initial digital applications.

At the plant level, the role of closed and open loops was always central to any discussion about the application of computers. In the Chemical Industry, for example, it was not uncommon for hundreds of closed loops to exist in facilities operating in the 1950s and 1960s. One report in 1972 said that "the location of so many loops at remote locations became unmanageable and led to the concept of a central control room where all process instrumentation could be located." As the ability to deploy the digital increased through the 1960s and 1970s, computer chips and their associated hardware and software appeared in most closed-loop systems, all tied into the control rooms referred to in the above quotation. The same report pointed out that "with the advent of the process computer as the electronic heart of the newer, more complex control systems, electronic instrumentation emerged as the approach" of choice.[4]

In the Chemical Industry, there also emerged over the course of the past century a community of engineers, usually called chemical engineers (but sometimes other titles), whose purpose was to design processes and systems that they could

Table 6.1

Process Versus Discrete Manufacturing Characteristics

Characteristic	Discrete	Semicontinuous	Continuous
Diversity of products per plant	Generally large	Moderate	Relatively small
Alternative flow paths	Very many	Medium number	Relatively few
Unit operation automation (production)	Relatively simple	Moderately complex	Highly complex
Achievability of hierarchical control	Relatively difficult	Moderately difficult	Relatively straightforward (once process operations are controlled)
Need for materials- and flow-handling automation	Necessary for plant-wide control systems	Necessary for raw materials processing	Highly necessary
Importance of online automatic tests and inspections	Important	Very important	Extremely important
Degree of in-house automation expertise	Relatively low	Moderately high	Highest

Source: Adapted from Exhibit 3, Frost & Sullivan, *The Factory Automation Systems Market* (New York: Frost & Sullivan, 1972): 32; CBI 55, "Market Reports," Box 3, Folder 35, Archives of Charles Babbage Institute, University of Minnesota, Minneapolis.

implement to convert any raw material into some product, regardless of what the material was or, more important, what the end product had to be. This very significant feature of process industries facilitated the early adoption of computing because this community of technicians was already conditioned to use electrical instrumentation and to think in terms of systems and processes, and they had the intellect to learn about computing at a level of detail that would allow companies to apply digital technology relevant to process industries.

The consequence of the nature of continuous flow manufacturing, the presence of science-based product development, and the availability of a large chemical engineering community all made it possible for computing to be adopted extensively by all process industries. To be sure, these industries used traditional accounting applications, porting them over to computers at the same time as did other manufacturing industries. Yet, the broad use of computing from the late 1950s onward was unmistakable in accounting and manufacturing operations. Computing also played an increasing role in R&D, most specifically in simulations toward the end of the twentieth century.

Adoption of the digital in process management was not always easy. The first documented case of the use of a computer in process manufacturing occurred in 1957; over the next decade, rapid deployment took place across many of these industries. The journey proved to be a hard one. One report from the period documented the fact that "early experience was mostly negative, mainly because of process software problems as well as noisy inputs and unreliable mainframes and peripherals," problems mostly fixed by the end of the 1960s as better software and hardened equipment became widespread.[5] The firms that proved most successful in deploying computing were the ones that began to install digital technology when their in-house expertise in automation technologies were already strong.

I selected these three process industries because they illustrated very different methods of using computers than did discrete manufacturing. In addition, each displayed a range of end products that varied in sophistication, from raw crude oil and inorganic minerals, which were both bulky and heavy, to the very small, sophisticated products of the Pharmaceutical Industry. Each shared some common patterns of use, such as accounting and logistics, while also illustrating unique applications, from managing networks of pipelines in the Petroleum Industry to computer-based R&D in the Pharmaceutical Industry. We see a large variance in the value-added outputs, from gasoline to some of the most advanced science-based products in the world. Yet like all process industries, these three also had common applications: accounting, transportation, inventory, and links to suppliers and customers.

One of the most interesting, subtle, and even counterintuitive features of these industries is the special role played by R&D, supported by the use of computing.

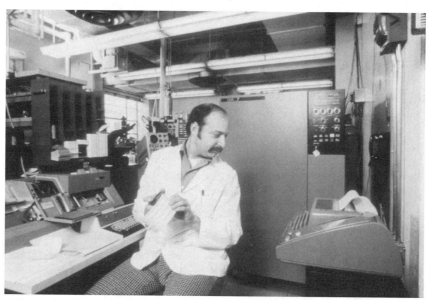

Collecting data from test instruments at a pharmaceutical laboratory in New Jersey could be accomplished with a minicomputer (in this case, an IBM System/7) in 1972, which this chemist used and analyzed. Courtesy IBM Corporate Archives.

In the Petroleum Industry, the extensive investments required to move oil around and to identify sources of crude through geodetic studies led to some very advanced uses of computing throughout the entire period. Some of the most advanced scientific computing was needed to perform shock wave analysis and to avoid the expense of a dry hole. At the other extreme is the computer-dominated research practices needed to participate successfully in the biotechnology and bioinformatics transformation currently underway.

These industries employed fewer people than did discrete manufacturing but, like firms in the industries surveyed in the last chapter management was concerned with labor productivity, particularly in petroleum and chemicals. Unlike automotive and steel, these process industries enjoyed better management-labor relations and achieved productivity improvements with less turmoil. One reason for this, I believe (but which I have not proven in this book), is that several conditions facilitated the use of technology. First, there were fewer workers in these industries who could be threatened by job displacements. Second, the population of workers tended to be more technically trained and skilled, many having scientific and engineering training, and therefore would be expected to gravitate more naturally toward all kinds of technology. Third, work just could not be done without relying on technology. One cannot do research on DNA without using computers; one cannot track millions of gallons of petroleum by looking at glass pipes; chemicals have to be converted into products through complex, scientifically based methods. In short, the work force and the working environments in these process industries were just different, and the industries were so large—particularly the Chemical Industry, which sprawled out into so many others—that they influenced the nature of the American economy.

Petroleum Industry

This is the one industry of the post–World War II period that became the subject of so much attention around the world because it was the source of a series of oil supply and pricing crises; was tied up in various Middle Eastern wars, including most recently the war in Iraq of 2003; and involved questions of national security as American dependence on Arab oil remained high through the second half of the twentieth century and into the present day. However interesting and important all these issues are in understanding the international economics of the recent past, we can safely bypass most of that history because, regardless of political considerations, day in and day out this industry still drilled for oil, refined it, shipped it to customers, and thereby fueled the American economy.[6]

This industry has long had an image of being stodgy, even old fashioned, although nothing could be further from the truth concerning the use of technologies of many types. Of all the long-established manufacturing industries, it has consistently been one of the most high-tech, extensive users of computing technologies all over the world, from the oil fields in the Arab Emirates to its retail gas stations across America. The breadth of its inventory of software applications is impressive by any measure.

To understand the nature and value of these applications, we first need to appreciate how the industry was structured. This industry was essentially made up of four parts over the past half century. The first was production, which involved the location and extraction of natural gas and crude oil from the earth. The second consisted of refineries, which manufactured such finished products as gasoline, jet fuel, kerosene, and other liquid, petroleum-based products. This second cluster was often called the Petrochemical Industry. A third piece of the industry consisted of firms or divisions of companies that marketed and sold products, both wholesale and retail. Gas stations fit into this segment of the industry. The fourth component was transportation, which in the United States usually consisted of all the pipelines that moved oil from wellheads to refineries (as well as ships for foreign oil) and by truck and pipe to retail outlets. Over the past century, the largest firms in the industry have generally attempted to play an active role in each of the four segments. Some smaller firms are also active in one or some of this industry's sectors.

In the decade following World War II, seven vertically integrated firms dominated the industry and were called the Majors or seven sisters. Five were based in the United States, the others in Europe. The American firms were Exxon (Esso initially), Texaco, Gulf, Chevron, and Mobile. British Petroleum (BP) and Royal Dutch/Shell are the two major European firms, although sometimes experts in the industry like to add an eighth, the French Compagnie Française des Petroles (CFP). In 1950 these eight companies controlled 100 percent of the production of crude oil outside of North America and the Communist bloc. In 1970, they still controlled 80 percent. Control always involved an extensive array of alliances, supported by national governments. In short, it was an oligopolistic arrangement, operating on a global basis for much of the twentieth century. In addition to these firms, in the 1950s a series of smaller companies emerged, called the Independents, which found, extracted, and sold oil on the spot market. They caused national governments in producing nations to play an extensive role in determining prices, availability, and other terms and conditions as the century continued.[7]

In 1950 the United States produced most of the oil it needed; by the early 1970s it was importing over a third of its requirements. On a worldwide basis in 1974, the United States produced 15.6 percent of the world's supply, 10.6 percent in 1998. In 1974, the Middle East produced 38.9 percent and, in 1998, 34.8 percent. Newly emerging economies in the intervening years added to the total supply of oil, such as the North Sea fields in the Atlantic Ocean off northern Europe and fields in Latin America. Beginning in the late 1990s, new sources emerged in Asia and in what used to be the Soviet Union.[8]

At the end of the twentieth century, oil companies went through another round of mergers and acquisitions to reduce overall operating costs and to enhance what economists liked to call forward integration, which meant firms participating in more sectors of the four parts of the industry.[9] National governments permitted these changes after several decades of attempting to control industry dynamics. In

August 1998, British Petroleum and Amoco merged; then in December, Exxon and Mobil. Other mergers occurred around the world as well. Members of OPEC (Organization of Petroleum Exporting Countries, established in September 1960) expanded their ownership of assets in the American economy, most notably Saudi Arabia, which acquired half ownership of Texaco's American refining and distribution network in November 1988. The newly merged majors accounted for about 4 percent of the world's crude oil production. One of the reasons such mergers could occur was due to application software, which made it possible to integrate various operating units. This possibility held out the promise of further efficiencies of scale while extending market share, or what economists call scope.

IT Deployment

Because of the widely differing activities of each of the four parts of this industry, a brief survey of computing by sector is desirable. Production is the first area to look at. There are essentially two basic activities involved: determining where to drill for oil and gas, a geological exercise, and drilling holes and extracting the crude oil and natural gas. The earliest applications of computers in production were used to accumulate and present data on various processing conditions, beginning in the 1950s. Linking existing instruments to computers allowed firms to begin presenting information useful to operators in the field. During the 1960s and 1970s, software increasingly directed instruments to change their activities in real time, thereby bringing a profound level of automation to field production work. The same trend appeared in refinery operations.[10] In the 1950s and 1960s, the majors all experimented with centralized computing and data collection from field operations.

With the availability of smaller computer systems (e.g., IBM 1400s) in the 1960s and minicomputers in the 1970s, local computer operations were established in the field and normally linked to some centralized control function, particularly as software increasingly took over functions performed by field personnel. By the late 1960s, one could speak about a computer production and control system that monitored the status of remotely located wells, collected production information, and generated a raft of management reports. Automating these functions proved essential since many wells were small and isolated, and tens of thousands of them were scattered all over the United States. Typical applications included monitoring and scheduling production, conducting automated well testing, controlling secondary recovery, operating alarms for problems with flow and leaks and machine failures, performing data reduction and reporting, executing engineering computations, and managing optimized gas plant controls. These firms were increasing overall production and yields per site, determining when it was best from an economic perspective to abandon a field, reduce production downtime, lower operating costs, utilize field engineers more effectively, and inform management. In the 1950s, much of this work was done by batch processing, but by the end of the 1960s a great deal was done by real-time online computing.[11] By the early 1970s, drilling operations themselves were coming under computer control to monitor drilling activities (such as drill penetration rates), report results in offshore drilling, optimize drill-bit life, and reduce various testing operations. Many locations would have a staff of one to three DP professionals to do this work. However, extensive deployment of computing in drilling operations did not occur until the end of the 1970s.[12]

Determining where to drill for oil has long been a critical activity, requiring extensive knowledge of geology and calling for good judgment because drilling was always an expensive operation. Dry holes normally cost millions of dollars in unproductive expenses. In the 1950s, it was hoped that computers could be used to model geological conditions and perform analysis to help firms determine where to drill. Not until the amount of computing increased sufficiently in the 1960s did this become possible. At that point the first geological and geophysical mapping applications were written, a collection of applications that companies enhanced continuously to the present day. These applications included the study of shock wave reflection patterns and analysis of data from test well drilling. By the end of the 1960s, many firms had developed software applications that helped in well-drilling control, using mathematical models to determine in advance where best to put wells and relying on financial models to figure out what to pay for mineral rights; other applications were used for online testing and then pipeline management systems. By the end of the 1970s, these tools were in wide use, reducing the amount of guessing by highly experienced personnel—their work and decisions now controlled more by computers.[13]

When initial experimentation with computer-based models started at the beginning of the 1960s, it was not clear to management in general, and even to DP professionals, exactly how useful computing could be in the area of simulation. Thus one commentator from the period could casually argue that simulation made it possible "to allow management to 'play around' with supply and distribution schedules, or the design of complex process facilities, without disrupting present operations." But managers quickly learned that software could better handle the "interpretation of tremendous volumes of seismic and geologic data." One of the earliest databases of such information, known at the time as the Permian Basin Well Data system, had become "a huge electronic library of information relating to one particular oil producing area."[14] Today no drilling occurs without extensive computer-based modeling of options. At the same time, all drill sites are overwhelmingly automated, extensively controlled from remote locations.

Refining is as close to pure manufacturing as one gets in this industry, with the critical task being the conversion of raw crude into a variety of products that can be shipped in bulk to other firms (e.g., gas stations), are converted into consumer products (e.g., cans of oil in a Kmart store in the 1990s), or are shipped as raw materials for other industries to use (e.g., plastics). A typical refinery looks like an organized bowl of spaghetti, with many miles of pipes going every which way and attached to large, tall containers that do the transformation of crude to various products. The key notion to keep in mind is that all the work is continuous, placing a premium on uninterrupted operations and absolute understanding of what is happening at every stage of the process. Long before the arrival of the computer, the industry had developed a raft of analog-based instruments to support these objectives. Computers were then used to take control of these instruments, monitor and manage them, and redirect activities as needed to optimize continuous production. Over the entire period we are looking at, firms continuously upgraded instruments, digitizing many of them, and optimized the whole process.

Refineries are large, complex, and expensive installations, providing perfect locations for computing; thus it should be of no surprise that some of the earliest installations in this industry were housed at refineries. By the middle of 1963, nearly 50 refineries in the United States had installed one or more computers to increase production of products, to reduce operating costs, and to improve quality control. Standard of California used its system to control catalytic cracking operations; American Oil in Indiana used a computer to manage 437 tanks controlled by 13 pump houses, and also for more traditional inventory control, production management, and shipments. How things changed from the 1950s to the 1960s can be gleaned from a description of what occurred at American Oil's refinery in Whiting, Indiana:

> There was no scarcity of basic data at the Whiting refinery. During 70 years of operations, such information had been developed each day through the use of gauge sheets, unit morning reports, weekly stock reports, routine staff reports and similar documents. These items of information, however, arrived at different times and were difficult—if not impossible—to assimilate.

Management elected to install a computer system to integrate these data and improve delivery time:

> The system today [1960s] involves a smooth and rapid flow of data from 13 reporting locations to a computer system. Supervisors at the various pumphouses mark sense tank inventory and shipment information onto cards. These cards are collected periodically, automatically translated into standard punched codes and fed into the computer system. Final result: a daily IPS (inventories, production and shipments) report providing all the information needed by management, ready and waiting by 8 A.M.[15]

The same location next upgraded to online systems, feeding data into its applications in real time. Later, all refineries connected their various analog instruments to computers, translating analog readings into digital data. Information on deployment in these early years demonstrates the importance of computers to managers. Refineries had 5 computer systems in the United States in 1959, 10 by early 1961, and 110 by mid-1968.[16] Rapid deployment of computing in process industries was normal in the 1960s and not limited just to refineries. Between 1963— the year in which a significant number of systems was installed across the nation in process industries—and 1968, the installation rate averaged 48 percent per year, and 55 percent around the world.[17] In short, this was the era when computing arrived in volume in all process industries. In the 1970s and 1980s, refineries filled up and upgraded and enhanced their systems, but in the 1960s they had figured out what to use computers for and had begun to invest in them. By the start of the

1970s, about 25 percent of all American refineries, which constituted about two-thirds of the entire industry's production capacity, were using computers.[18]

Process control increasingly involved all refining processes, from crude distillation to online gasoline blending. In the 1960s and 1970s, open-loop processing spread widely across the industry. Data were gathered by instruments, which software turned into reports presented to supervisors, the basis for their decision making. These decisions were then relayed back to the equipment by computers. Increasingly in the 1970s and 1980s, the industry moved to closed-loop applications, in which employees were removed from decision-making steps, delegating them to software, which used decision tables to automatically make many more incremental operational decisions and adjustments. This approach took advantage of the growing experience the industry was acquiring with software and the fact that refineries were becoming increasingly large, and thus more complex to operate. Economists from BLS observed in the 1970s that it was not uncommon for a refinery to have over 1,000 instruments and sensors linked to a computer system. Some of these collected complex data systems, from chromatographs to mass spectrometers and octane analyzers. Computers helped with the complexity, but as in other industries, speed in resolving problems proved an essential benefit of these systems.[19]

The third sector of the industry, wholesale and retail sales, is perhaps the most visible part to any American because its companies sold the bulk of their products either through gas stations or to fuel oil companies that, in turn, delivered gas and heating oil to homes and businesses. Increasingly in the 1980s and extensively during the 1990s, products were also sold through nonindustry-controlled retail outlets, such as oil in quart containers at Kmart, 7-Eleven, and so forth. The most visible application, in a sense novel in the 1950s and 1960s, was the deployment of the gas credit card. It is unique because the Retail Industry embraced the credit card later than the Petroleum Industry, with the two exceptions of restaurants and hotels, which also were early adopters, particularly by large firms in the Hotel Industry. Much of the early experience with credit cards on a massive basis, therefore, came out of the work of such oil companies as Mobile, Esso (later Exxon), Gulf, and so forth. Credit cards were developed in the 1950s,[20] and by the early 1960s, 60 petroleum companies routinely issued gas credit cards; in fact, they had issued 70 million of them. A quarter of all purchases made by the public in the United States via credit cards in the early 1960s came from gas credit cards, involving billions of dollars in small transactions. In the late 1950s, only 10 percent of all Americans had a gas credit card; one third of all adults did by the mid-1960s. It was also not uncommon for Americans to have multiple gas credit cards.[21] In short, credit cards brought about a major change in how petroleum companies interacted with their retail customers in post-World War II America. These cards exposed millions of American adults to credit cards in general, conditioning them for bank-issued cards before the major expansion of the likes of American Express, Mastercard, and Visa in the 1970s and 1980s.

We know a great deal about the early history of this application thanks to an extraordinarily well informed report presented at the 1964 annual meeting of the

Data Processing Management Association (DPMA) by James C. Beardsmore, Sr., at that time employed in the marketing department of the Gulf Oil Company. The reason, he said, that the gas credit card was such a significant application grew out of the fact that the volumes of transactions, and the dollars involved, were so extensive, whereas simultaneously the number of billing centers and personnel involved to process these transactions had grown so very quickly, that his industry faced huge costs and managerial issues. At the same time, management focused intense efforts on providing high levels of customer and dealer services, because of growing competition in the American market. The application was not always computerized, although increasingly so to reduce costs and improve service. One major consideration was getting bills to customers, leading to processes and programs whereby a certain number of bills was created and mailed every day.

Beardsmore characterized Gulf's operations as typical for his industry. The extent of computer technology deployed was impressive. Just before IBM's introduction of the System 360—which Gulf installed—it first used IBM 1401s and then IBM 1460s to support this application, along with early bar code readers and punch-card peripheral equipment. He said the firm borrowed time on the company's 7070 and 7074 systems to do processing. Before 1961, the firm did not use a credit card imprinter and had to develop one with various suppliers because that became the critical data-gathering instrument needed to capture information about an individual sales transaction. His company's credit card accounting system consisted of a customer master record, which triggered the billing and accounts receivable processes. Once data entered the billing system, the application was typical of that which existed in most companies during the 1960s.[22] Gulf and other firms also implemented incremental changes in the application. The most visible for customers arrived in the mid-1990s when they could insert their cards into the gas pump and have it authorize their purchase without requiring a signature. It was fast and paperless, saving gas companies and retail outlets the expense of handling millions of small transaction documents. The use of credit cards by American automobile and truck drivers has remained to the present an essential sales tool of this industry.

The actual form of the credit card—a plastic document just slightly larger than a calling card—illustrated the interaction between applications and technologies. As one group of observers in the 1960s argued, "the optical scanner was one of the factors which made possible the introduction of credit cards."[23] The problem this industry faced with credit card sales prior to the arrival of the plastic card and optical scanning was serious:

> The conditions under which the credit slip is filled are often difficult. The card might be exposed to rain, be covered with grease from the station operator's hand, be bent or mutilated during handling, and so on. The imprinting on the card must be clear and uniform in order to be scanned.[24]

Moving from paper stock to plastic (itself a petroleum-based material) and to pressure-type imprinters resolved the problem. With the card's uniform lettering impressed on slips, a scanner could be used to read these slips, regardless of whether or not they were dirty or otherwise in less than pristine condition. Initially 80 to

92 percent of all documents submitted to scanners were read; later versions of the scanners read higher percentages of these papers. Companies outside the Petroleum Industry also made it possible for customers to use their gas cards to make purchases in stores. That capability forced all card issuers to standardize lettering and design of cards, and the use of both scanners and software applications supporting this billing process.[25]

The fourth area of the Petroleum Industry, and also the one that relied extensively on computing, involved transportation of oil and natural gas. The industry needed to transport crude and natural gas (which could be liquefied for that purpose) to refineries, and then to regional wholesalers and dealers. Local wholesalers used trucks to make deliveries to homes and businesses. Companies delivered natural gas almost universally by pipelines. Most transportation occurred in one of two ways: ever larger tanker ships would move crude oil from overseas sources (e.g., the Middle East) to American refineries or by pipelines from wellheads. Refineries normally shipped their finished products by pipeline around the United States or, for specialized products, by tanker trucks. After World War II, the industry integrated its network of pipelines from all across the North American continent and regularly increased the diameter of the pipes themselves to expand the volume of product it could ship. Software helped by minimizing the expense of running oil and its various derivatives through the system and to ensure their continuous flow to the right refinery or wholesaler. The industry as a whole created whole bodies of practices and policies, as well as interfirm trade agreements to optimize the use of the pipeline network.[26]

For the same reasons that computers appeared in refineries, they did so in transportation, often first by the majors. Although simulation applications were tried in the 1960s, it was not until the 1970s that enough computer capacity existed to make simulation tools sufficiently effective. Yet warehouse location studies were successfully simulated in the 1960s, largely because they required fewer data for analysis than, for example, geological studies.[27] When automation arrived in refineries, companies applied these approaches to the management of pipelines: flow monitoring, notification of emergencies, and so forth.[28] Before the arrival of the computer, the industry had trunk line stations along the entire network, staffed with employees who were keeping track of their section of the pipeline. Instruments increasingly communicated with computers housed in centralized facilities, displacing workers in the field. The key strategy was to run trunk stations as unmanned as possible. By 1958, nearly a third of all trunk stations were controlled remotely, and by the end of 1966, half of them were. That number climbed to over 60 percent by 1970 and, in the 1980s, to nearly 100 percent.[29]

Tied to this deployment was a series of other applications of the digital. Delivery scheduling was an early application that remains central to the entire network. Field process controls were linked to more traditional applications seen in other industries, such as administrative business, accounting, financial, and auditing work. The major changes in the 1970s were the industry's initiatives to computerize scheduling and to link online and central control processing in order to move greater volumes of product through existing pipelines.[30] Economists at BLS reported that "productivity for complex pipeline scheduling is being increased through better computer programs for data base updating, original and revised scheduling, and shipment report preparation." Pipeline engineering design also became more widespread, and firms continuously upgraded pipeline instrumentation through the 1970s and 1980s. The result was that by the end of the decade "for many pipelines, monitoring and regulatory tasks, including the operation of unmanned pumping stations, are performed by headquarters dispatchers using solid state electronic telecommunications equipment and computers."[31] Minicomputers at online stations could be activated to take charge of the operations of a specific section of the pipeline. About 10 percent of all pipeline operators used computers to schedule flows in 1971; that number rose steadily through the decade. The industry learned early on to centralize its computer operations as much as possible and to link applications together, for example, scheduling and inventory control. Management also added pipeline-specific applications, such as computer-controlled leak detection systems that reduced the number of employees' inspections.[32]

It is easy to dismiss accounting applications as being ubiquitous, uniform, and mundane, with little differentiation by industry. However, because these are ubiquitous applications, we must acknowledge them. We should realize that, at least during the late 1950s, many manufacturing firms, including members of the process industry, moved their applications from tabulating and accounting equipment to computers. The Ashland Oil and Refining Company was typical. In October 1956, it installed an IBM 650 computer system, one of over 1,500 firms to do so over the life of this product line. In addition to using the system for scientific and engineering applications, it also ran accounting work through the same computer. Early applications involved billing and payroll, which held out the promise of reduced costs of labor. By 1958, the company had written software that allowed it to run a series of accounting applications on this system: accounts receivable, aging analysis, depletion, depreciation and amortization schedules, daily refinery inventory, and other programs. The programs were batched, and data entry occurred with cards. Many of these programs were essentially sort/merge operations, which accounts for why this system had 10 sorters, 7 collators, and 17 card punches. As in so many companies, management integrated computing into existing accounting applications. The report from which this paragraph was written originated in 1958 and noted that the company "was able to integrate the machine [meaning the 650] into the present machine accounting section with a minimum of change." The technical staff then moved on to the installation of magnetic tape and, later, the IBM 305 Random Access Memory Accounting Machine (RAMAC) storage.[33]

In the late 1950s, others did the same. For example, Standard Oil Company of California also installed an IBM 650 and had an IBM 704 for the purpose, as stated by comptroller W. K. Minor, "of utilizing these machines whenever they will effect savings over the best manual or punched card system or render improved or more timely service."[34] In those days, before a software industry existed, a "system" included a variety of software tools provided by the vendor of the installed computer, in this case IBM. Systems included system control software (also known as operating systems), utilities (such as sort/merge programs), compilers (e.g., for Assembler and Fortran computing languages and, by the early 1960s, for a new generation of compilers, such as COBOL). All application software, however, was written by EDP programmers in a company or by contract programmers from consulting firms. General Petroleum Corporation, located in Los Angeles, installed a Datatron-Cardatron system in November 1956 to run a payroll-accounting system and a production lease profit and loss application. Like other firms, however, it often had to anticipate savings from the installation of computers. One employee stated that "we remain convinced that we will save time and money, and produce for management information not now available. The degree to which success in these areas is finally reached will not honestly be known for perhaps another year."[35]

The applications described above were cataloged by the major functions within the industry. However, a few observations about the sources of these various types of software are in order because they apply to this and other industries. There were essentially three classes of software: the first provided monitoring functions; the second, basic accounting applications; and the third, advanced complex modeling tools. Accounting applications were quick rewrites of tabulating applications of the 1940s and 1950s, enhanced with tools provided by key computer vendors, such as Burroughs and IBM, for sort/merge packages, compilers, file managers and teleprocessing access protocols (e.g., VSAM), and operating systems. By the 1970s, commercial accounting packages were widely available across all industries, including this one, along with such widely used database packages as IMS and DB1 by the early 1980s. Commercially available accounting software has remained the norm to the present day. Reports on business applications were usually homegrown affairs, using COBOL in the 1960s through the 1970s. The distribution of business applications took place either through commercially available products or internally created reports written in RPG, COBOL, and C++, to name a few programming tools and languages.

As for monitoring software, the earliest tools were developed in the years prior to the existence of programming. One of the major providers of such software tools were companies that were predecessors to Texas Instruments (TI). Originally formed in 1930 as the Geophysical Service, later the Geophysical Service, Inc., by J. Clarence Karcher and Eugene McDermott, the firm developed aids to help explore for oil, relying on methods for measuring seismic waves to map conditions under the surface of the earth to determine the possibility of oil deposits. The business became successful, and in a later reiteration during World War II it acquired a substantial amount of expertise in electronics, much as did many other firms like IBM and National Cash Register (NCR). That newly acquired knowledge led the Geophysical Service to concentrate more on electronics after World War II, although it remained committed to geodetic explorations in the industry. In 1953, it acquired Houston Technical Laboratories, which specialized in gravity meters used in geophysical work, selling its services and products to petroleum firms around the world. At the end of the 1950s and extending over the next two decades, TI also manufactured and deployed integrated circuits designed to conduct seismic studies under contract to the industry. Applications and software from TI were initially in, to use a later term, *real time*. Gradually, the use of digital technologies and both batch and online software tools characterized the collection of software packages used by TI and the Petroleum Industry.[36]

Across the entire industry, beginning in the 1950s and extending into the 1960s, batch reports of monitoring applications were written internally within its firms, in such languages as Fortran and Assembler. When online processing became available in the 1960s, a long process of converting monitoring applications to computer-based software began. In the 1980s, specialized software vendors began to offer software products to the industry for various monitoring applications.[37]

A large class of applications consisted of modeling tools. These were the most complicated packages in the industry. The same could be said about modeling software packages in use in aerospace and pharmaceutical companies. These packages came from a variety of sources. Individual companies wrote some of the earliest modeling tools in the late 1950s and through the 1960s, for example CDC and, later, Cray and more specialized software firms, often in conjunction with joint development projects with the largest firms in the industry. In fact, each of the major firms had one project or another with a local university or a computer vendor, a pattern of development that has continued to the present day in this and in many other industries.[38]

Software's Effects on Productivity

Productivity in this sector of the industry increased; in refining, productivity grew all through the half century at rates of between 2.9 and 3.2 percent, despite oil crises, partly because of increased demand. Occupations became far more complex, more technical, and IT-centric through the entire period.[39] Pipeline transportation productivity grew at an annual rate of 10 percent in the years 1958–1967 as demand and pipeline management practices improved dramatically; then it dropped to 1.9 percent between 1967 and 1986, largely because of declines in output in reaction to various international oil crises, which periodically reduced demand. Automation in the earlier period actually caused an annual decline in employment of 3.5 percent, evidence of the effects of automation and, specifically of the increased centralization and complexity of the control systems used to manage the network of pipelines.[40] This sector of the industry, as well as the other three, installed many of the new computer systems that came out in the 1980s and early 1990s, largely because of the increased capacity that was so essential to the centralized applications embraced by all four sectors. Larger systems also made possible simulation applications in all four sectors, especially in pipeline management practices in the 1980s and 1990s. A BLS economist in 1988 concluded that "the petroleum pipeline industry has attained a high degree of automation."[41]

I can quickly summarize the complex history of computers in pipeline management. In the 1950s, traditional accounting applications were the norm, although a wide variety of analog instruments was in wide use. The first use of computers to manage the flow of petroleum occurred in the early 1960s and expanded over the next two decades. Upgrades to all major applications occurred continuously, although most dramatically in the 1980s and 1990s as major improvements in computer capacity and sophistication provided new opportunities to control the cost of operations and improve the overall efficiency and effectiveness of the enterprise. By the end of the 1980s, all firms operating in this sector relied on computers and industry-specific applications to do their daily work. Intelligent terminals and PCs came into wide use by the early 1990s, and programmable control logic units were embedded in many monitoring instruments and machinery by the late 1980s. The hot applications in the 1980s included improved scheduling and dispatching, leak detection systems, power optimization, and shipment documentation. All were infused with extensive upgrades in telecommunications across all four sectors in each decade.[42] As in the other sectors, one labor economist noted that

> because of the increasing use of centralized computer control systems involving the operation of almost all the functions of a major pipeline, there has been a shift away from operators involved in such manual operations as opening and closing valves and switches, checking tank levels, and reading meters. These functions have been almost completely taken over by the computer. Pipeline personnel tend to be skilled in computer operations and programming.[43]

This industry's dependence on telecommunications to support many of its strategies for centralized computing meant it would be an early user of EDI and later the Internet.[44] Common IT systems and industry-wide practices facilitated the spate of mergers that occurred in the 1990s. They were designed to further operationalize efficiencies and expand global reach to sources of crude oil, natural gas, and to markets. IT issues in these mergers were now news items.[45] Standardization, therefore, once again became a high priority within IT organizations in the industry for such applications as telecommunications, ERP packages, and desktop computing.[46] IT was seen as an essential component of what was happening in the industry. The *Oil and Gas Journal*, clearly not an IT publication, acknowledged the role IT played in helping companies to survive the commoditization of energy that occurred in the mid-1980s, a lesson that it reminded readers of the 1990s.[47] At the start of the new century, in the industry, expectations included further global consolidations of what by then many called the energy industry, often facilitated by the kinds of digital applications already installed in the industry. The industry had many very large players who had the resources to continue optimizing computing. In 1990, Royal Dutch/Shell Group and Exxon were on the list of top ten global companies, as measured by market capitalization; in 1998 they were still there. Both had been leaders within the industry in transforming major segments of their businesses in the 1980s and 1990s, despite oil spills and wildly fluctuating prices for crude oil, and increased competition from ever-larger rivals.[48] As they entered the new century, oil company executives again reached out to IT to help support their strategies of consolidating and expanding markets.

Petroleum is an example of an industry in which IT effectively supported corporate strategies, but only in collaboration with industry-wide coordination of such activities as prospecting and transportation. As one observer in September 2000 wrote, "IT and the information it drives are making it possible for energy companies to expand their reach into remote pockets of the world, to understand the consumers that buy their products, and to align their supply chains and procurement efforts with partners."[49]

The Internet became the next enhancement to the variety of telecommunications tools already in use. It was especially useful to retailers in expanding communications and disseminating information, ordering products, and communicating levels of supplies in their tanks. Purchasing practices changed, much along the lines evident in the steel, automotive, and aerospace industries and for the same reasons. Communications with tankers expanded, making it possible to send information back and forth in graphical, audio, and textual formats.[50] In this industry, as in so many others, the Internet emerged as a basic component of the infrastructure of the supply chain management process.

Chemical Industry

The discussion of process industries logically moves from petroleum to chemical because they are interconnected. Many products produced after World War II were based on petroleum—hence the often-heard term *petrochemical industry*. Many of the processes for the production of chemicals were similar if not exactly the same as in petroleum, so that one could correctly assume that the application of the digital in the Chemical Industry paralleled that in the Petroleum Industry. To be sure, there were also differences.

The biggest initial difference is how to define the Chemical Industry. In the mid-1990s, this industry (or industries) accounted for over 10 percent of all manufacturing in the United States and for 1.9 percent of the U.S. GDP—so it was large and also complex. Essentially, the industry was made up of three subsets, defined by the products they made. The first involved the production of basic chemicals, such as acids, alkalis, and salts (inorganic) and petroleum-based products (organic). A second subset focused on intermediate chemical products, including plastics, synthetic fibers, pigments, and colors. A third component was populated with manufacturers of consumer chemicals, such as those used in drugs and medicines; others manufactured cosmetics and soaps, and still others specialized in the production of paint, fertilizers, and even explosives. After World War II, all three groups expanded enormously, particularly those whose products relied on organic materials, such as petroleum-based intermediary substances. Organic products were so closely related to each other, because of their shared base in hydrocarbons, that chemical engineers have been able to develop manufacturing processes that could be used in a similar manner with a wide variety of products. They also constituted the high-tech end of most of the Chemical Industry.[51]

Whereas the U.S. industry dominated and led the world in production and market share in 1950, by the late 1960s European and Japanese firms were expanding their global presence, partly because of the transfer of knowledge from the United States to their national industries. Excess capacity, particularly in the petrochemical side of the industry, led to the restructuring of plants in the years immediately following the oil shocks of the 1970s, and pharmaceutical firms continued to introduce new products.[52] Most restructuring in chemicals occurred, however, in petrochemicals. Many of the key players in the industry are familiar companies: Dow Chemical, DuPont, Exxon, Montsano, Mobil, Union Carbide, Occidental Petroleum, and Eastman Chemical, to mention some of the best-known firms.

These firms are part of an industry in which R&D is the source of new products. It has long been recognized that the Chemical Industry was the first science-based industry. Historian Alfred D. Chandler, Jr., explained what that meant for the industry in the post–World War II period, when raw materials, like oil were abundant: "The huge growth of markets and the availability of cheap, low-cost raw materials intensified the need for technological innovation to increase minimum-efficient scale of chemical plants."[53]

Members of this industry relied on two strategies: first, chemical engineers developed manufacturing processes that were efficient and cost-effective; second, the industry invested vast sums of money to develop new products. However, chemical engineers made up the one group most responsible for the application of computers in the industry, except for the more traditional accounting and financial departments. Early in the twentieth century, and initially at the Massachusetts Institute of Technology, engineers were trained in what came to be known as unit processes, which means that they learned about processes and practices that could be applied to the manufacture of many chemicals. By mixing and matching various operations, companies could manufacture a wide variety of end products. Over time that capability led to the development of a variety of best practices, including how best to design and operate chemical plants. By midcentury, chemical engineers knew how to build large plants that were capable of continuous production along the lines used in the Petroleum Industry. By focusing on large facilities, these engineers also had to develop ways to improve economies of scale. As new chemicals came on stream, such as polymers and plastics, they adjusted production processes. Many chemical engineers worked for specialized firms that concentrated on the application of production methods for hire, making up a subsector of the industry called specialized process design and engineering contractors, or SEFs.[54] To a large extent, their greatest contributions were in the production of petrochemical products, but they became increasingly active across most segments of the Chemical Industry as the key agents for the diffusion of expertise about all kinds of technologies, including IT, both within the United States and around the world.

Research and development in such areas as synthetic materials, highly effective fertilizers for farming, and the enormously increased variety of medicines were all made possible by the innovation of new products during the last half century. In pharmaceuticals, for example, it was not uncommon for a firm to spend annually 9 to 12 percent of its revenues on R&D, which exceeds the 5 to 6 percent found in high-tech companies in general or the 2 to 5 percent evident in manufacturing industries. Through the entire period under study, more new products came from the American Pharmaceutical Industry than from any other branch of the industry.[55] However, other sectors of the Chemical Industry used R&D as a way to remain competitive and find new sources of revenue. David A. Hounshell and John Kenly

Smith, Jr., demonstrated this point very clearly in their massive study of R&D at DuPont during the course of the entire twentieth century. What makes their study so fascinating is their account of how R&D was an iterative process, operating with fits and spurts, evolving, failing and succeeding, but increasingly drawing the attention of the most senior managers of the firm.[56]

The combination of R&D and the development and refinement of production processes all through the post–World War II period often led firms to ponder differing business issues. For example, with the wide diffusion of polymer science (the source of much of the common processes in the industry), the situation a manager faced was that "the crucial problem in innovation shifted from *how* to produce different products to *what* to produce."[57] The SEFs had thus reduced, paradoxically, the strategic importance of process technology and processes by the 1980s.

IT Deployment

For an understanding of computerized plant operations, we must turn to the 1950s and 1960s. Two specialists on the industry noted that "the plant design and engineering tools in use today have not changed much from those of chemical engineering in the 1960s. A more systematic use of computerized software engineering tools in the design and operation of plants is in its early stages."[58] Modularized construction of plants and, more specifically, of equipment within plants became increasingly the norm as the decades passed. The evolution of the integrated control room was a direct result of this process of continued transformation and the injection of the digital across all kinds of operations. It is the evolutionary introduction of computing over time that, in hindsight, proved to be extensive, although one might have thought that little new was done after the 1960s. But as occurred in petrochemical plants in the Petroleum Industry, there had been much activity over time.[59]

As in so many other industries, accounting applications were often some of the earliest to be installed. All the leaders in the various sectors of this industry were large enterprises with many decades of experience in using punch-card tabulating equipment and the kinds of accounting machines sold by Burroughs, NCR, and Felt & Tarrant. They upgraded to computer-based batch accounting systems in the 1950s and later moved to online systems, many in the 1960s. For accounting and increasingly for process management, chemical firms began to install computers in the late 1950s. The BLS inventoried the growth: 5 systems installed by the end of 1960, 31 by the fall of 1963, 90 by the fall of 1966, and 156 by mid-1968.[60]

Interest quickly turned to the use of computers for managing operations. One of the earliest such applications was installed at the small Luling Company for controlling the manufacturing process.[61] Acceptance of the value of computing had to be demonstrated, as in other industries, before widespread deployment occurred. The direct use of computers to control instruments emerged as the initial area of application to catch the attention of engineers.[62] Modeling operations became an early application as well, one that by the end of the 1960s had become very important. Problems addressed with software were basic: "Plant operations is largely a problem of determining when a batch has finished processing at a given stage and finding a unit in the next stage in which to put it. [But] processing time for a given product at a given stage . . . is not constant, so again it is necessary to report to distribution functions."[63] Running a seven-step production process through a simulation tool on an IBM 650 computer required 800 commands; it took time to write the programs but helped engineers define how the flow of activities should occur.

By the late 1960s, numerous plants had started to link shop floor instruments together by way of the digital, leading to the emergence of a highly computerized control room approach. By the mid-1960s, engineers had also worked out the cost justification practices needed to rationalize requirements for computing. Mathematical models for deciding how best to optimize plant operations were also now increasingly used.[64] The 1970s and 1980s were marked by further deployment, upgrades to hardware and software, and implementation of distributed computing, first in the form of minis in plants and later of microprocessors embedded in instrumentation and production machinery.[65]

Computers seeped into R&D operations, although it is not clear at this time if this occurred at the same rate as in other industries. However, given the enormous emphasis on R&D in the Chemical Industry, extant evidence suggests that engineers used computers extensively. Case studies of usage exist, suggesting that in the 1960s major adoptions occurred and were added to over time.[66] The earliest applications involved linking instruments together and then modeling activities.[67] Research and development involved both the development of new products and refinements of existing manufacturing processes, each subject to the increased use of modeling and monitoring applications through the 1980s and 1990s. In fact, by the 1990s, methods for doing both had evolved into a growing body of best practices across many parts of the industry.[68]

Before reviewing the period after the arrival of the Internet, we need to resolve the question of what effects computers had on this industry. As in all manufacturing industries, the hunt for productivity proved relentless, and nowhere more so than in lowering the cost of labor. Chemical companies, like refineries, were very successful in reducing the labor content of work through extensive automation. Although R&D remained a labor-intensive, high-skilled set of operations, computers significantly helped to drive down costs in production, as well as across the entire industry as a whole. The industry at large expanded all through the half century, but its work force declined in number. In the critical period 1959–1964, one would have expected to see a dramatic improvement in productivity as the initial introduction of digital computing took place. In fact, between those years the work force dropped from 112,500 to 81,900. One observer cited the role of the digital computer:

> Companies like Monsanto and Goodrich turned their operations over to digital computer control. The dramatic changes in production practices brought about by computerization and continuous-process operations became apparent to the Oil, Atomic and Chemical Workers Union when their members struck oil-

refining facilities in the early 1960s. Walkouts failed to significantly slow production at the new automated factories. The plants virtually ran themselves.[69]

All through the 1980s and 1990s, the number of workers kept declining. Historian Harry Braverman observed that "the work of the chemical operator is generally clean," involving "reading instruments" and "keeping charts."[70]

Recent Trends

Finally, we need to look at the effect on this industry of recent developments, particularly the Internet. Several patterns that mimic what was simultaneously occurring in other manufacturing industries are already discernable. For example, before the Internet, chemical companies used EDI to link to their suppliers, and after the arrival of the Internet they began to port that application to the new telecommunications infrastructure. As in other industries, using telecommunications to facilitate buying, selling, and tracking of raw materials and nearly finished products lowered operating expenses. Outsourcing some of the logistical functions of the firm increased in the early 1990s, made attractive by the fact that as much as 60 to 80 percent of a chemical company's manufacturing cost structure went to supply chain operations. Transportation costs in this industry alone could be reduced by over a third through effective management of supply chain operations.[71]

The integration of software applications extended from the telecommunications infrastructure into the firms themselves, much as occurred, for example, in the Automotive Industry in the 1980s. Chemical firms formed alliances with software providers to enhance internal knowledge about IT and to build applications that made individual companies more competitive. The extent of these activities is not fully clear, but it appears that all the major firms had various projects underway.[72] For example, DuPont signed an agreement with Computer Sciences Corporation in 1996 to run the firm's IT infrastructure and provide software services. Simultaneously, Dupont hired consultants to upgrade applications in manufacturing, marketing, distribution, and customer service. Simulation software from Aspen Technology, for example, appeared all over the industry, and other vendors sold to companies that were modeling application software packages for molecular design. Still other firms had started to sell PC-based research and development tools in the mid-1990s, particularly for the pharmaceutical segment of the chemical industry.[73] Part of the reason for what appeared to be a series of major overhauls in the portfolio of IT applications and telecommunications infrastructures was, of course, management's concern over Y2K, the fear that systems would not operate after January 1, 2000. It is one reason that SAP AG, for example, a German software firm that was selling enterprise resource-planning software (ERP), did so well in this industry; its software was Y2K compliant.[74]

At the same time, firms in this industry were again modernizing existing applications. Key areas of emphasis in the late 1990s involved further enterprise integrative applications (e.g., supply chains), outsourcing of IT infrastructure, collaboration (especially among drug manufacturers), and more effective exploitation of knowledge management principals.[75] Vice president and CIO at Dupont at the time, Robert Ridout was typical of his colleagues in the industry. He publicly stated his company's strategy: "We're reorganizing the company into a more fully integrated chemical operative with more discrete business units that operate more independently." He outsourced a great deal of the internal IT infrastructure; his staff wrote new software and acquired application packages, all in response to global competition, enormous market volatility, and a new wave of product innovations.[76] However, his was not a unique strategy because in the late 1990s many in this industry used technology to weather another round of increased competition and cyclical changes in products, all to lower overall operating expenses.

Increasingly throughout the decade, chemical companies focused primarily on managing their supply chains. In a survey of manufacturing firms conducted in 1999, of which the Chemical Industry accounted for 22 percent of the respondents, 87 percent reported that spending on IT would remain the same in the face of another round of cost-cutting measures, precisely to support modernization of supply chain management systems.[77] Even mergers and acquisitions were sublimated to supply chain initiatives as an important way of leveraging economies of scale. For example, when Dow announced its plan to acquire Union Carbide in August 1999, its ability to execute the merger was, in part, made possible by IT. As in other industries, ERP was a key application, which is partly why SAP did so much of its business in this industry. At the same time, customers were demanding faster and more accurate delivery of competitive products. But, as in the Steel Industry, knowledge of the Internet came slowly. DuPont's CIO (Ridout) was blunt on the matter in late 1999: "I'll bet that at this time last year, no one [in the Chemical Industry] had heard of E-commerce. . . . E-commerce is starting to emerge in the chemical industry, and it's bringing new opportunities and new threats."[78]

A survey of IT conducted in 1999 pointed out that on average a chemical firm spent 2.5 percent of its revenues on IT and that 20 percent of the company's revenues came from e-business, dramatic proof of the use of the Internet and older telecommunications applications (e.g., EDI). The proportion of suppliers linked electronically to chemical firms hovered at 23 percent, and 19 percent of customers were connected. These same firms reported that 6 percent of their IT budgets were being invested in e-business and the Internet and that 11 percent overall paid for application developments. Half the firms reported that they were selling over the Internet.[79]

The statistical evidence of the increased use of the Internet, which started in 1998–1999, was reinforced by reports of future plans. The big shift in the early 1990s, a period characterized by concern over supply chain management, involved moving from merely improving internal supply chain applications to extending them externally to customers and suppliers. By the end of the century, that shift caused a surge in interest in the Internet. As one report in *Chemical Week* noted in early 2000, "The chemical industry is being drawn into a frenzied drive to initiate Internet-enabled sales, service, and management strategies—or 'e-business.' " As we saw in other industries, e-infrastructures firms appeared: e-Chemicals, Chemde, CheMatch, and ChemConnect, all third-party firms that were providing Internet sales and distribution services to the industry and to the industry's customers.[80] The best evidence suggests that by 2001, all chemical companies in the industry were using the Internet in one fashion or another as part of their supply chains and that nearly half had even appointed e-business leaders to leverage the technology.[81] Yet the industry average of volume of business generated through the Internet remained at about 20 percent, which was probably several percentage points more than in most manufacturing industries but up sharply from nearly zero a mere two or three years earlier. Surveys at the end of 2000 indicated that all the major players in the industry expected to see sharp increases in e-business transactions, much in line with what was happening in the other manufacturing industries discussed in this book.[82]

While chemical companies spent a great deal of time and resources in the 1990s to drive down operating costs through implementation of updated IT applications, new supply chains, and the Internet, more traditional uses of the digital continued apace. Nowhere was this more the case than in the secretive, yet strategically important, area of R&D. Modeling of chemical processes, for example, leveraged expanded computing capabilities and more advanced software through the 1990s, especially in pharmaceutical firms. The use of genetic algorithms underlined some of the more advanced uses of computing. Innovations in measurement technologies and software also facilitated expanded use of computers in R&D. To a large extent, R&D had always relied on mathematical modeling, which in turn was advanced as better IT came along. What the industry asked of computer scientists in the late 1900s was for new breeds of computer-based modeling tools that could either partially or totally automate creative modeling processes. It wanted other tools to increase the speed of R&D and to help in improving the quality of R&D in the face of growing complexity. As members of the R&D community explained, what they needed from computers was the ability to generate models of highly structured processes to reduce the time it took to do the work without having to code all the constitutive and balance equations. By the end of the century, new tools were appearing from a combination of industry-academic initiatives and software vendors to do just that.[83]

Pharmaceutical Industry

In the last several years of the twentieth century, the Pharmaceutical Industry captured the attention of the American public as computers had in the 1960s and 1970s and the Internet had in the mid- to late 1990s. One could hardly read a national magazine that did not discuss the possibility that the twenty-first century would be an age of biotechnology. In the 1990s, over a dozen state governors announced initiatives to create bio–Silicon Valleys. *Time* magazine dedicated an issue in January 2001 to the development of a whole generation of drugs based on DNA. Although how this sector of the Chemical Industry used computers has been discussed throughout this chapter, and its use paralleled the applications and dates of implementation evident in other chemical firms, there are sufficient differences to require a separate discussion. This is also a very high-tech, high-profile process industry, one that captured the imagination of many Americans. It is also an industry in which profound changes have occurred in the last several years of the twentieth century that may, in hindsight, be seen as radical as any in any other century because of the initial mapping of the human genome, completed in 2000. The Pharmaceutical Industry has been successful in developing a remarkable collection of drugs, which in concert with advances in medical practices have led to fundamental and positive changes in medicine around the world and, in the process, have enriched the firms involved. In short, the industry is an American success story: "Its products dominate the world market. It leads in the development of new technology and for decades has achieved a rapid pace of innovation."[84] Finally, it is also an industry that relies extensively on computers to do its most important work: R&D and the manufacture of drugs.

This industry spent 12 percent of its revenues on R&D in 1980; by the late 1990s, its rate of spending had increased to over 20 percent.[85] In one aspect of manufacturing, it created chemical reactions or developed products from biological processes (e.g., antibiotics). The second aspect of manufacturing is the actual preparation of final products, for example, pills, patches, or liquids that can be ingested orally or administered by other means. Purifying, mixing, and packaging were always key steps. Like other process industries, pharmaceuticals automated the continuous flow of these activities and, by the 1970s, used computers to monitor instrumentation and to control the flow of manufacturing events.

Gary P. Pisano, a leading expert on the industry, reminds us that the transformation it is undergoing is not a simple one: "The molecular biology revolution . . . cannot be understood as a single technology." Instead, one needs to appreciate the fact that it resulted from "a constellation of several distinct, but related, trajectories of scientific advance." These included new and old sciences, genomics (new) and chemistry (old). He viewed the profound changes as "the overlaying of successive waves of scientific knowledge building upon one another in a complex technological landscape."[86] Thus this industry, although an extensive user of computers, had a broader range of IT applications than one might have expected in an earlier period.

The years from 1950 to 1990, as in the case of so many American industries, were good for the Pharmaceutical Industry. Key firms were profitable; they brought to market many useful, indeed wonderful drugs and enjoyed enormous growth and profitability. Between 1954 and 1978, returns on new drugs averaged 20.9 percent, as compared to 10.7 for manufacturing firms in general. Between 1982 and 1992, although profits dropped, they nonetheless came in at 18 percent, again outstripping manufacturing industries as a whole. Unmet needs, extensive public funding for R&D, and patent protection all helped fuel decades of prosperity, also making possible enormous economies of scale.[87]

IT Deployment

Research and Development is still the exciting story of transformation. Computers played an important role in facilitating the biorevolution, and it is continuing to do so in the early years of the new century. In 1950, a pharmaceutical laboratory looked very much like labs in secondary schools or in universities decades ago: lots of test tubes, microscopes, notebooks, and so on. By the end of the century, electron microscopes, robotics, and a large array of simulation software and computers occupied the same space. The most important changes in the industry in the past half century occurred in R&D, not in manufacturing.[88] The results were impressive: over 1,200 new entities (types of products) introduced between 1946 and 1991. After that period, the introduction of new products based on biotechnology ushered in yet another revolution (a quite correct term) in medicines. Research on new medications that was conducted by doctors and biologists also occurred in universities and at U.S. government laboratories. In the end, converting scientific and medical findings into medicines that could be approved by government regulators around the world became the primary core competence and value added by this industry.[89] In other words, the industry did R but excelled in D.[90]

Part of the reason for the various consolidations that occurred in this industry could be attributed to the growing cost of R&D, which grew as a management issue over time. By the early 1990s, all the major firms had sales in the United States in the range of $1 to $3 billion and, on a global basis, $4.5 to over $8 billion. The key players were Merck, Bristol-Myers Squibb, Glaxo, American Home Products, Elli Lilly, Johnson & Johnson, Pfizer, SmithKline Beecham, Marion Merrell Dow, and Upjohn. Beginning in the 1980s, new firms specializing in biotechnology emerged, a few of which remained independent while others were subsumed into existing firms. In the United States, R&D was made possible by the large number of qualified researchers available inside the industry and American universities. The local market was also massive: 27 percent on average of all sales took place in the United States.[91]

Increasingly in the 1980s and 1990s, the discovery of DNA, first made in the early 1950s, finally led to a body of knowledge sufficiently developed for pharmaceutical firms to begin to develop products based on this insight.[92] During the 1990s, momentum built as firms learned to work with genetic materials. At the risk of great simplification, I will state that what researchers wanted to do was to understand the genetic basis of a disease, which would allow them to determine how to predict what protein would be produced by it, and then they could try to develop a means to block it. Companies like Biogen, Genzyme, Genetics Institute, and Millennium Pharmaceuticals made up part of a new wave of many firms in the 1990s that applied high-tech tools to develop DNA-based cures. All the major historic firms in the industry did so also. The use of mathematics and computing, particularly in the search and screening phases of research, proved essential all through the 1970s to the present day. The promise of reward was enormous and kept growing over time. At the start of the twenty-first century, most drugs tackled symptoms of diseases and, more specifically, some 500 different proteins, although the human body has over 30,000. The DNA-based cures, however, seemed to provide the potential of cures to all diseases at their genetic roots, not just treatments of symptoms or a few illnesses. Thus the potential market opportunity was vast.[93]

Taken in 1963, this photograph illustrates the kind of large systems used by ethical drug manufacturers in the United States to handle inventory and production control and payroll and sales statistics in support of 50,000 pharmacies. This a Burroughs B280 system coupled with a B220 (in background). Burroughs Papers, courtesy Archives of the Charles Babbage Institute, University of Minnesota, Minneapolis.

By the end of the 1990s, researchers were routinely cataloging code sequences from genes in computer databases. In fact, the output of the mapping completed in 2000 was a database of information (public genome database). The next step was to narrow the possible proteins involved in the creation of a disease through the use of both software simulation packages and robotics. Robots, for example, used probes to pick up droplets of liquid DNA, deposit them on sheets of nylon, and then repeat the process, depositing some 1,000 droplets on a sheet and thereby creating a microarray. Several dozen microarrays were then collected and doused with radioactive dye and genetic material from a variety of human tissue types (e.g., from various organs, healthy and unhealthy). The responses were cataloged and began to reveal to scientists what worked together or did not. The process was highly automated, from the databases of information and results to the physical movement and mixtures of materials.[94]

In fact, a highly computerized subfield of R&D is now recognized as bioinformatics. Here, the challenge for scientists and other laboratory workers is to run through many millions of combinations of materials that could possibly cure an illness; this is called screening. The field of bioinformatics emerged to speed up the process of identifying what works.[95] Firms are applying a rapidly growing collection of algorithms to predict how various proteins function by comparing new proteins with existing ones. Often the output is a videolike, graphical representation of how a protein moves and reacts when doused with a drug. One can visibly see if a potential curative drug disables a bad (disease-causing) protein. Through this high-speed iterative process, which at the same time collects data on what does not work, scientists improve the use of algorithms to increase the odds of finding the right combination of drugs to disable a diseased protein. Once discovered, the next step is to develop doses that can be fed to animals and humans. As one expert on the industry described the process, "High throughput screening (HTS) is an automated, robotics-based technology for testing vast numbers of new compounds against a large number of ways."[96] Computer images and potential drugs are displayed on a screen and can be altered one atom at a time to obtain positive results.

The industry has long been involved in tracking the results of its research because it has had to keep meticulous records of its experiments, for example, as part of the routine process of gaining regulatory approval to launch new products. Traditional computing applications were used, from general-purpose computers to spreadsheets, word processing, and industry-specific software packages.[97] Often called laboratory information management systems (LIMS), these software tools dropped in cost all through the 1990s, making it possible for both small and large firms to use IT. The U.S. Food and Drug Administration (FDA) found the use of such tools so widespread that it issued guidelines on electronic record keeping, called ruling 21 CFR part 11, documenting practices used in electronic signatures and records.[98]

As important as the role of computers was in the R&D process and in the management of those activities, one should not forget that pharmaceutical firms were also businesses, looking to the digital to help deal with commercial and managerial issues. Although the industry had a reputation of being slow to adopt IT for business applications, it nonetheless spent 2 percent of its revenues on this technology in the early 1990s, and that percentage rose during the decade.[99] The surge underway in pharmaceuticals, stimulated by the move to DNA-based products, occurred at the same time that firms had too much manufacturing capacity, and thus competition increased. And, of course, there was the Internet. Outsourcing occurred, facilitated by the use of computers and telecommunications, for example, in the performance of preclinical and clinical testing by niche players. Product development and packaging often mimicked what occurred in the Automotive Industry, for example, when a tire supplier was asked to develop a product for a new vehicle and then to ensure that sufficient supply was delivered daily for the number of vehicles to be built that day.[100] Traditional production databases kept evolving to take into account extended supply chains and, for the same reasons found in other industries, to lower costs, increase quality, and reduce capital expenditures.[101] Simultaneously, marketing software that linked customers to pharmaceutical firms continued to be installed across the entire industry.[102] Business applications in the 1980s and 1990s, as in other industries, were often designed to speed up the introduction of products to the market. In the Pharmaceutical Industry, where regulatory practices slowed the introduction of new drugs, steps were taken to speed up R&D, production, and review cycles—all by using computing. Although rigorous studies of the effects of computers have not been done for this industry, the collective opinion is that this technology helped.[103]

Recent Trends

Finally, we must ask, What role did the Internet play in this sector of the broader Chemical Industry? When compared to the other industries in this book, this one came late to the Internet. George H. Lofberg, a senior executive at Merck & Company, admitted in late 2000 that "we are only at the very beginning of understanding and capitalizing on [the Internet's] potential to transform many long-established processes in the pharmaceutical industry and the healthcare field as a whole."[104] Normally the first phase of a company's or industry's use of the Internet involved posting information about its products and services to newly minted web sites, then creating the capability of conducting e-commerce. The Pharmaceutical Industry in 1999–2000 was still essentially stuck in this first phase of Internet use, having posted brochure-type material to their sites. Consultants and analysts complained that the industry would be severely damaged by providers of drugs from other sources and that customers would become irritated if it did not move more aggressively to exploit the Internet.[105] By the end of the century, Internet-based drug-stores were beginning to appear; even Amazon.com sold medicines online. One study of the industry's reaction to the Internet politely stated the problem as an inability of the pharmaceuticals to quickly adopt its technology, let alone measure the value of its use. To be sure, there were exceptions, but observers consistently commented on how slow this industry had been to use the Internet.[106] One report noted that "pharmaceutical execs are content to form business-to-business (B2B) task forces and e-commerce committees to study possible opportunities." The report slammed the industry for always being slow to adopt new forms of information technology.[107]

Yet, the industry did put up web sites to give doctors access to information about their products (called detailing). Early experiments with e-commerce were often problematic, in many cases because the primary customers for such information, doctors, had themselves been slow to use the Internet.[108] Pharmacies, however, were moving online much quicker, and the cost of drugs began to fall in some instances by 2000. For example, Viagra (sildenafil) sold for $9.03 at a "bricks-and-mortar" drug store but could be bought over the Internet from an online pharmacy for $8.34 (which included cost of shipping). Patients, customers of medicines, used the Internet extensively to learn more about drugs and medical issues. In the last quarter of 1999, for example, the U.S. government estimated that 14 percent of all visits to the Web were to health sites. The same study noted that 28 percent of all adults have visited such a site. In short, patients were doing what they did at work in other industries: they began to use the Internet. Online pharmacies and medical information sites were more aggressive in getting online than pharmaceutical manufacturing firms in 1999–2001. Yet, studies done on the economic value of moving supply chain activities to the Internet had already indicated as early as 1996 that this industry could cut its costs for sales, marketing, and distribution nearly in half, which is why a number of "infomediaries" came into the industry, sandwiched between the old firms and their customers.[109]

The business climate for the industry had been excellent in the last several years of the century. In 1999, for example, the world market for its products grew by 11.9 percent, driven by the introduction of new products, aging populations, better diagnostics, and so forth. The American market grew by 16.9 percent. With demand for its goods so great, one can understand the reluctance of firms to risk fundamental changes to their business model when it appeared in the short term not to be necessary.[110] Thus, just posting promotional materials on web sites probably seemed to make sense. Although disease management, virtual detailing for doctors, and other applications were slowly appearing at the end of the century, none of them had caused fundamental changes to the business structure of the industry.[111] The sale of pharmaceutical products, normally done by retail firms (not the manufacturers), went ahead at the end of the century. In 2000, the FDA had identified over 320 web sites that sold pharmaceutical products. Some pharmaceutical firms, however, were beginning to sell over the Internet, such as Glaxo, using what, at the start of the new century, appeared to be the industry's most advanced set of Internet applications: communications with customers, online dialogue with research and product developers, and e-marketing.[112] Thus, we can conclude that, although slow to adopt the Internet, when the industry began to do so, it did so in ways similar to the earlier experiences of other industries.

Conclusions

These three industries teach us a great deal about the use of information technologies in the American economy. In all three, firms found positive uses of computing in its ever-changing forms over the decades, primarily for extraction (R&D and product development) and manufacturing. They tended to use technology less for sales and marketing, as in the case of the pharmaceuticals. All three exploited the ability of large digital computers to perform a variety of simulation studies. The Petroleum Industry modeled geological conditions and weighed them against the economic risks of drilling. Chemical firms conducted simulation studies to develop new products. The pharmaceuticals used computing to study the features of DNA, dramatically translating that newfound knowledge into a new generation of medications.

The evidence from these three industries demonstrates, first, that deployment of similar types of applications in the manufacture and distribution of raw materials and finished products was extensive, even ubiquitous. Second, deployment occurred at roughly the same time across each of the industries. On the other hand, each had very different experiences in applying computers to sales and marketing. Third, all three were slow to use the Internet, but customers often provided the push needed to get process manufacturing firms to move more aggressively to adopt it. This pattern stands in mild contrast to that which occurred in the Automotive

Industry, for example, where the large firms were more aggressive in forcing their component suppliers to use the Internet (and EDI) as part of the industry's widening and nearly ubiquitous supply chain management practices.

After examining these industries in the context of other manufacturing sectors, we can clearly see that their reputation for using technology did not match reality. Oil companies were considered slow to adopt computers, although in fact the opposite was the case because digital technologies were very suitable in supporting the fundamental activities of these companies. A similar observation could be made about chemical firms; however, since these were science-based, one always assumed that they were probably extensive users of computers. In fact, they were for manufacturing and, later, for R&D, but their accounting applications were similar to those used across the entire American economy. Then, there are the pharmaceuticals, which always had a stodgy reputation but, because of the industry's dramatic, visible, and rapid move into DNA-based products, were forced by the realities of the required science to become extensive users of computing applications in R&D. Although DNA gave the industry great press coverage, it did not obviate the reality that its use of computing across all lines of business was not particularly dramatic and, in fact, lagged in some cases behind that of other process industries (e.g., in using the Internet).

In all three, adoption of applications took place as extensions of ongoing practices. There is little or no evidence that the intent was to change radically any existing process or business model. The firms bolted IT onto existing functions, judging the value of the digital within the context of traditional patterns of cost justification. Thus one could observe rapid adoption of computing in order to monitor and manage instruments in factories but saw senior executives in the Pharmaceutical Industry wondering why they should move business functions to the Internet in the absence of a compelling business case.[113] That compelling case, it so happened, began to emerge by 2000 when customers of their products (e.g., pharmacies) pressured the industry to provide Internet-based services. Thus, we see in this industry evolutionary adoptions of computing, although in hindsight, looking back over many decades, we see that the collective effect of so many adoptions did fundamentally change many of the ways in which tasks were performed.

To what extent did computing change the strategies of the three industries? Did the Internet or any other class of IT fundamentally change the success or failure of a firm? In all three industries, computing helped the most in two areas: in driving down operating costs and in supporting complex, science-based R&D and intensive computing-based operational support (e.g., as in the geological studies done in the Petroleum Industry). So far no single use of IT has profoundly changed the structure or dynamics of companies in all three industries. Given the fact that the Internet began to change the fundamental structure of other industries—such as the Trucking Industry, the financial sector, and some discrete manufacturing industries— one could expect that over time the same would occur in these process industries. Hospitals and pharmaceutical firms could, and probably will, force pharmaceuticals to participate in their supply chains, which today are increasingly Internet-based in function and management. There is some evidence that in the Petroleum Industry computing was used with some effect in expanding market reach to global proportions by using virtual markets, but even here the historical record notes that this was a global industry long before the arrival of the computer.

When computing resulted in fundamental changes in strategies, it happened exactly where it had always played the most dramatic role: in the development of new products. Many sectors of the Chemical Industry, especially the pharmaceuticals, were able to create whole new lines of products over the past half century—such as fertilizers for agriculture,[114] synthetics (e.g., plastics and other composites), and now DNA-based medications—because of discoveries based on science. The use of computing in R&D has consistently aided in the creation of new products, which in turn have fundamentally contributed to the creation of new markets, divisions within firms, and differing levels of profits and revenues. Increasingly, the dependence on computers for analyzing scientific data and performing modeling applications became more important, to the point where today it is impossible to conduct meaningful R&D without their use. That was not the case in 1950, when test tubes, microscopes, and an array of analog instruments were the only tools available to these industries.

By examining these three industries, we have entered a corner of the American economy that relied extensively on advanced uses of science and all kinds of technologies. One of the fundamental characteristics of the American economy in the second half of the twentieth century was the creation and successful operation of industries based on advanced uses of science and technology. The most obvious examples of this process at work are the rise of such industries as computer manufacturing, biotechs, and software. High-tech industries had more than a high profile by the dawn of the new century; they had a tangible and still growing presence in the economy. By examining several of these new high-tech manufacturing industries, we can round out our analysis of the role of computing in the large manufacturing sector of modern America. For that reason, chapter 7 looks at how several of these industries used information technology.

7

Manufacturing Practices in Information Technology Industries: Semiconductors, Hard Disk Drives, and Software

Killer applications help technological advances change from curiosities into moneymaking essentials.

—Bill Gates, 1995

After World War II, whole new industries emerged that did not exist before. The Software Industry is a good example; it did not surface as a recognizable economic entity until the late 1960s. Many other industries emerged in response to the increased use of computers across the entire economy. Most were in the manufacturing sector, producing tools for the Information Age, but others provided services, like consulting and managed operations (e.g., of networks and data centers on behalf of clients). Examining the use of computers in new IT-centered industries allows us to fill in many details about the deployment of digital applications across the economy. These are industries that did not have a stock of precomputer-based processes and applications; they began with a clean sheet, so to speak, such as the Semiconductor Industry. This circumstance poses some interesting questions, useful in expanding our understanding of how the American economy was evolving at the dawn of what possibly could be the Information Age. To what extent did these industries deploy the digital in the same way as long-established industries? How did their high-tech products and knowledge of computing affect their ability to leverage the technology for operating efficiencies and effectiveness and in their performance in the marketplace? A related question, to which we can contribute a partial answer, concerns the position these industries had in the American economy.

The essential task of this book is to compare how work was done in 1950 and at the start of the twenty-first century, tracing the often silent transformations that occurred along the way. Part of the transformation of work in the American economy took place within large, new industries created after 1950. The three chosen for this chapter are visible, substantial in size, and important components of the contemporary economy. Others could have been added, such as the Computer Industry itself (although its scope remains unclear), but these three are sufficient to shed light on patterns of behavior in emerging sectors of the American economy. The implication I make is that the IT sector is a bellwether of things to come—hence the value of the cases in this chapter—but that kind of assertion may be premature. What can be said is that the industries reviewed here are new, did not exist in 1950, and reflect new elements of the American economy. In short, they cannot be ignored. Moreover, they were businesses that had to invent, build, ship, sell, and service products and thus were subject to many of the same economic influences that affected other manufacturing industries.

Before examining them, therefore, we need to situate these new IT-centric industries into the broader context of the American economy. Sociologists and economists have argued for decades about the complexion of the New Economy, as have U.S. government agencies charged with tracking its evolution.[1] At the start of the new century, no consensus existed on many of the details, in part because some of these industries were just emerging (e.g., biotechnology), some became very IT-intense in the products they offered (e.g., machine tools), and still others were subsets of existing industries that had yet to break out into their own (e.g., electronic games or even those toy manufacturers specializing in high-tech products). The explosion in the number of dot.com firms in the 1990s, with their initial positive impact on the economy in the latter part of the decade and their negative impact on the stockmarkets at the start of the new century, simply made it obvious that new elements at work in the economy were far different from those at the halfway point of the twentieth century.

Neither space nor time permits us to explore fully the broad issue of what made up the economy of the Information Age in America. But looking at the issues related to identifying new industries and measuring their performance, as faced by the Department of Commerce, gives us a quick view of some of the fundamental changes underway in the economy at large. In 1950, the U.S. government still used metrics (developed during the period from roughly World War I to the start of World War II), which defined industries in an age before the use of computers in commercial settings had become widespread. Those definitions of industries and their associated Standard Industrial Classification (SIC) codes remained essentially unchanged until the 1990s, although the volumes of revenues within them were periodically recalculated to account for inflation and the changing value of the dollar over time. However, such agencies as the U.S. Bureau of the Census and the U.S. Bureau of Economic Analysis began to identify new industries in the 1970s; their economists were already aware that new enterprises and industries were emerging

Table 7.1
Selected New U.S. Industries, 1990s

Semiconductor machinery manufacturing	Paging
Fiber optic cable manufacturing	Cellular and other wireless communications
Reproduction of computer software	Telecommunications resellers
Manufacture of compact disks	Credit card issuing
Cable networks	Telemarketing bureaus
Satellite communications	Industrial design services

Source: U.S. Census Bureau, "New Industries in NAICS," update of March 30, 1998, http://www.census.gov/epcd/www/naicsind.htm.

and raised questions about their identities and how they should be cataloged and measured. In the late 1990s, the U.S. Census Bureau began implementing a major change in its traditional topology of the economy, moving from the traditional SIC (division, major group, and industry group) system to a new one called the North American Industry Classification System (NAICS).[2]

With NAICS the government recognized as separate industries some 350 new clusters of companies. A press release stated, "A few of these industries reflect 'high tech' developments such as fiber optic cable manufacturing, satellite communications, and the reproduction of computer software."[3] Many low-tech industries were also identified, such as bed and breakfast inns, environmental consulting, warehouse clubs, and pet supply stores. However, as table 7.1 illustrates, many new high-tech industries were operating in the American economy, many of which arose in the 1960s and 1970s or later and which were now as important as numerous precomputer industries had been in the past. Many of the new industries were also in what economists traditionally referred to as the service sector, such as environmental consulting. The service sector grew enormously through the second half of the century, indicating that change to NAICS made sense, but note all the new manufacturing industries also recognized.

One of the activities that all the affected agencies undertook involved the restatement of revenues for these newly identified industries, going back as many years as possible. Thus, new data on size and scope have begun to appear from such agencies as the Census Bureau, the Bureau of Economic Affairs, and the Bureau of Labor Statistics. It is important to realize that this process is still underway because for years to come there will be many disagreements about the size of many of these industries, as Martin Campbell-Kelly pointed out when he explained his research problems while writing a history of the software industry.[4] The problem of definition is a global one for governments in Europe and East Asia as well. The U.S. government agencies, however, were taking important steps to explain their methodologies for cataloging the new industries.[5]

Before I discuss some of these manufacturing industries, a quick look at proportions helps put the new firms into context. In 1997, the government reported

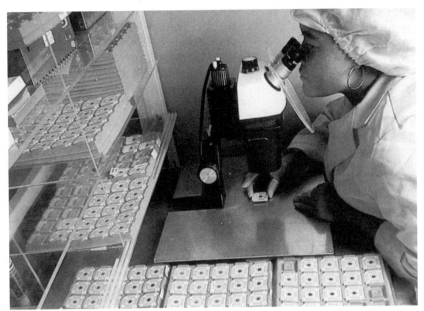

Like many computer manufacturers, Burroughs also made microcircuitry. This photograph was taken in 1983 at the company's plant at Rancho Bernardo in southern California, and it illustrates the high-tech nature of the work. The employee is working in a "clean room" environment, which is far more sanitary than even many hospital operating rooms. Burroughs Papers, courtesy Archives of the Charles Babbage Institute, University of Minnesota, Minneapolis.

that there were 377,776 manufacturing establishments in the United States, employing 17,557,008 workers, or about 17 percent of the total work force. Chemical companies totaled 12,371 firms, petroleum and coal another 2,147, and rubber and plastics an additional 16,892. Industrial equipment, fabricated metal products, and electronic and other electrical equipment totaled over 110,00 more enterprises. Printing and publishing—by the 1980s very extensive users of computing—consisted of over 62,000 firms, textiles over 23,000, and lumber and wood products nearly 37,000. These were the kinds of industries that were now being recataloged into new components, such as those listed in table 7.1.[6]

So many industries of a high-tech nature were discarded as candidates for this chapter that I should explain why. The Computer Industry is as about as ill defined today as is the Chemical Industry. Does it consist of just the manufacture of computers, or does it also include peripheral equipment and software? What about the role of services, which has become such an important component of a computer company's revenues since the early to mid-1990s? In short, there are far too many methodological problems involved in exploring this industry that would detract from my objective. The other obvious candidate for inclusion is consumer electronics. The problem here is the sad reality that the U.S. economy no longer has an indigenous Consumer Electronics Industry.[7] I chose to discuss only industries that existed at the end of the century. Historians are just beginning to kick the carcass of this dead American industry, but this book is about lessons taught by history to industries that still exist. Finally, case studies of other high-tech industries either are the subjects of future volumes in this series on the digital hand or are just not big or significant enough to add to our understanding of the broad patterns of computer use in the American economy.

Semiconductor Industry

"This industry constructs complex electronic systems performing functions that were science fiction only a few decades ago."[8] Even economists, who are not noted for being exuberant about the industries they describe in normally cold, dispassionate language, could not help getting excited about the Semiconductor Industry. Richard N. Langlois and W. Edward Steinmueller saw it as part of a much larger transformation in which the American economy was increasingly acquiring a broad array of computer-based segments. As in computer chips (see chapter 1), it was the adoption of the products of this industry by many other industries that made it so essential to understand. When economists traced the evolution of the Semiconductor Industry, with all their rankings of size, competition, and volume of chips distributed, they provided a surrogate measure of the expanded use of computer-based applications across the entire American economy. Sometimes called the "crude oil of the information age," economists have long recognized the role this industry has played in manufacturing: "the basic building blocks of many electronics industries."[9] Over the past half century, the combination of improved capacity and reliability of these devices, on the one hand, and the dramatic decline in the cost of individual products, on the other hand, made it possible for this technology to be adopted in ever-increasing ways. As noted in chapter 1, this industry was born out of the invention of the transistor in the late 1940s, emerged as a group of firms that were producing products in the 1950s, and then was recognized as a new industry in the 1960s. By the end of the 1970s, it was global, giving American companies substantial competition in the 1980s, particularly from Japanese firms, and was transitioned through the 1990s with the reemergence of the American industry.

This industry grew rapidly. By the early 1960s, American firms were shipping over $300 million in semiconductors annually, and annual growth rates ranging from 8 to 12 percent were fairly normal at the time. Many firms came into being in the early to mid-1950s, and then a second wave of new companies entered the industry in the years between 1959—when the integrated chip was developed—and 1965–1966. Table 7.2 lists firms functioning in the proto-industry; note that producers ranged from traditional electronics firms (e.g., RCA) to those that were totally new (e.g., Fairchild). The global industry grew to $19 billion in 1980 and

Table 7.2
Selected American Semiconductor Manufacturers,
1955–1975

Electronics Firms*	Semiconductor Firms
Hughes	Fairchild
Philco	Texas Instruments
GE	National
RCA	Intel
Westinghouse	Motorola
Sylvania	American Microsystems
Raytheon	

*Most firms operated in multiple markets; therefore, to a certain extent, which column a company is listed in has to be considered partially arbitrary.

Source: Data from table 2.6, Richard N. Langlois and W. Edward Steinmueller, "The Evolution of Competitive Advantage in the Worldwide Semiconductor Industry, 1947–1996," in David C. Mowery and Richard R. Nelson (eds.), *Sources of Industrial Leadership: Studies of Seven Industries* (Cambridge: Cambridge University Press, 1999): 33.

to $137 billion in 1997, an impressive annual growth rate of over 12 percent. The U.S. economy was the beneficiary of over half of all the dollars spent in the past half century on semiconductors.[10]

Early customers for this technology were American military agencies, because of the Cold War, and then American agencies and companies that were supporting the space program. Commercial demand for these products began in the late 1950s, primarily for computers, although it was often depicted as coming much later; however, industry statistics clearly demonstrate that as early as 1963 the U.S. government acquired only 47 percent of all semiconductors, whereas industrial users—typically the industries studied in this book—picked up almost another 37 percent. The rest went into consumer products, such as car radios, hearing aids, televisions, and musical instruments (primarily organs). To be sure, early industrial users concentrated on computers, communications, test and measuring instrumentation, and controls. Military applications involved space, aircraft, missiles, communications, and surface systems, among others.[11]

This was an industry whose products were adopted by the government, giving the industry the critical mass and scope necessary to support the commercial markets that had emerged by the early 1960s. Combined with continued product evolution and declining costs, this industry was able to expand all through the last four decades of the twentieth century. As it went global, various national industries specialized in various types of integrated circuits. The Japanese, for example, specialized in computer memory chips in the 1980s and drove down costs so much that these kinds of devices (often called DRAMS) became the centerpiece of Japan's semiconductor industry. On the other hand, more advanced types of devices became essential elements of the American industry in the 1990s. Through the last decade of the century, American producers excelled in the development and sale of logic devices, digital signal processors (DSPs), and mixed-signal chips (essential for networking technologies), such as those that went into the hardware infrastructure of the Internet.

Complex devices of this type were often referred to as design-intensive components, commanding higher prices but also requiring very sophisticated design and manufacturing applications. This was always the case with every generation of semiconductors, beginning with transistors and continuing through the integrated circuits of the 1960s and the "computer on a chip" products of the 1970s. This is an industry that has relied on computer-based applications from its earliest days. Without using computers it would not have been able to design or manufacture new generations of products. The confluence of evolving products and their complexity, cost, and world demand in the 1990s brought the industry to a point where it had coalesced around categories of products. The largest segment, now virtually made up of commodity products sold cheaply, was the manufacturing and marketing of computer memories. The second consisted of logic units, chips designed for specific customers. The microcomponent market made up a third segment, composed of a variety of products like microprocessors, microcontrollers, and a subgroup of microcontrollers.[12]

Before reviewing how computers were applied in this industry, we need to understand the price performance of computing over time because one of the motivating factors behind the continued, unrelenting design of new products and innovative ways of manufacturing them was the need to lower the price of production while increasing sales. In 1962, the average price per integrated circuit hovered at roughly $50. In 1964—just two years later—the average price had declined by more than half, to $18.50. Imagine the effect on the Automotive Industry if in two years the cost of its products had dropped by more than half. No industry surveyed in this book had that kind of fundamental shift in the price of a product, with the exception of the Hard Drive Industry, reviewed later in this chapter. Moreover, by 1965 the cost had dropped to $8.33, and by 1968 to $2.33.[13] That rate of decline has continued to the present day.

When we look at the numbers from within the industry itself, that is, at the production costs for these components, we see a countertrend. While prices for products sold dropped, the cost of building factories to make them rose, making the Semiconductor Industry one of the world's most capital-intensive by the 1980s. In the early 1970s, one could build a semiconductor manufacturing facility for about $20 million. Within a decade, the cost had risen to $100 million; then tripled by the early 1990s. By the end of the 1990s, costs had reached $1.2 billion, leading industry watchers to expect prices to keep on rising during the early years of the new century. Simultaneously, products had become so complicated and had to be changed so frequently in the face of global competition that companies in the 1990s were compelled to form collaborative alliances or specialize in specific types of

A major producer of computer components in the late twentieth century, IBM, through its automated production line (circa 1962), assembled transistors at the rate of one per second. These transistors were installed in IBM's computers through the 1960s. Courtesy IBM Corporate Archives.

products (e.g., DRAMS, produced in Asia) and very advanced logic units in what is called in the industry "fabs" and "foundaries." These very expensive factories were increasingly being asked to produce components that had more features and functionality, often replacing older product lines after a few months or as long as after a few years of production. To manufacture a new semiconductor often required new manufacturing equipment, greater automation, and new processes.[14]

To help understand the digital applications, the majority of which are for the design and manufacture of chips (normal accounting applications are a given), it might be helpful to know what a chip or integrated circuit is. It is not essential to have a detailed technical appreciation of what they are or how they are made to understand the functioning of this industry. A chip consists of a semiconductor material, such as germanium or silicon, which is purified and thereby made ready for use. It is placed on some platform, is chemically coated, and is etched to create paths for electrons to pass through the semiconductor material. Multiple units are simultaneously treated in this way and then are packaged together. Over the years, these devices became increasingly smaller, to the point where no human could see the etched paths without using an electron microscope. Computer modeling thus became a widespread tool across the industry. Through a microscope, the chips look faintly similar to what one sees when looking out of a window of an airplane as it flies several hundred feet over a city—little square and oblong structures are rising from the ground, and the streets are surrogates for the etched paths. Or if using simulation software, one could discern the slightly blurred images of a sunken ship as seen through a videocamera.

From a few to thousands of these units are packaged together into products that can be held in one's hands. Because of the transformation that occurs to the semiconductors and to the other chemicals that are used, these units are also transformed. Let me use a nontechnical phrase: they are baked. Think of a multilayer cake, where each layer is a different type (chocolate, followed by angel food, then by a light pastry), each covered with a different frosting. Then imagine thousands of baked cakes that are exactly alike, right down to the number of flakes of flour used, and one begins to understand what a computer chip is (electronic layer cakes) and sense the complexity of the manufacturing processes. Add one more requirement: that customers will only buy these cakes if they are exactly alike; all made to their specifications. This puts the manufacturer in the position of having to worry about precision, on the one hand, and, on the other hand, increasing the number of cakes that come out of the oven just right. "Just right" in this industry refers to yield; the more chips that are functioning as designed, the greater the number sold. Higher yields lead to greater profits.[15] Table 7.3 lists the key production steps required to bake a chip.

These clearly were not products that were going to be manufactured like automobiles, steel, or TV sets. From the very beginning, manufacturing developed quickly into a frightfully complex process, one that mixed together science, engineering, technology, project management, precision manufacturing, automation, and computing, all against a backdrop of constantly changing products and price structures. This was an industry that knew from experience that its products underwent a reduction in cost per function roughly 100 times every 10 years. One could very easily argue that of all the products manufactured in the twentieth century, this was one of the most complex.

Table 7.3
Basic Steps in the Manufacture of Semiconductors

Oxidation: a wafer's surface is coated with a silicon dioxide film.
Photolithography: a circuit pattern is printed.
Etch: a circuit pattern is etched in the wafer.
Ion implant: electrical properties are adjusted repeatedly to form a complete circuit.
Thin films: this is a process for wiring the devices and adding a protective layer.
Electrical test: this is a process for testing that the chips perform as intended.
Packaging: wafers are diced and chips are placed in packages.

IT Deployment

When companies first manufactured transistors, engineers used precisely structured processes to design them. They were built by hand by highly skilled workers, soldering components together, for example, and building prototypes to test them. The process was expensive and slow. It also required workers so skilled that they were difficult to find in sufficient quantity. Therefore, during the 1950s, manufacturers found various ways of automating some of the basic steps. The first comprehensive leap forward in automation occurred in the late 1950s when IBM's manufacturing organization designed a mechanized system for assembling transistors. Assembly, fusing, and welding functions were automated, along with etching, cleaning, and packaging. A transistor could be manufactured in just three hours (instead of several days), producing 3,600 units per hour: "The conventional manual assembly line . . . depended upon the dexterity of experienced operators often working with microscopes. Only three people were now required to monitor the status of the entire system and to direct corrective action as required."[16] The quality of the transistors produced in this way also quickly improved over the manual processes of the past.

I should point out that this industry did not use computers to design and build transistors in the early 1950s; it took the kinds of automation that, for example, IBM introduced at the end of the decade to stimulate the use of computers in the 1960s in the manufacturing process. The approach of IBM made it possible to manufacture transistors in batches, with hundreds of devices in one wafer, and many wafers could be fabricated simultaneously. The key lesson, first for IBM and later for the industry at large, was the need to have those who designed semiconductor products work closely with those who manufactured them. Historians are uncovering evidence that this lesson may actually have been learned a few years before IBM's innovation, but it was the link to automated approaches there that appears to have spread the insight across the industry.[17] This increasingly became a requirement for the successful production of many high-tech products across numerous industries as the century progressed. We are now seeing that lesson applied, for instance, in the Pharmaceutical Industry. In the case of IBM, by the early 1960s manufacturing managers and their engineers pushed for the design of transistors into wafers, reduced chemical processing, and standardized packaging. Thus, was born the concept of packaged electronics, which made possible the use of computers to manage parts of the production process. The concept was called solid logic technology (SLT), and it quickly became an industry standard.[18]

That approach led IBM to combine product development and manufacturing engineering into one organization so that it could better coordinate activities. Materials handling and production processes became more complex through the 1960s as engineers at IBM designed increasingly sophisticated chips and learned what information needed to flow through the production process, some of it using computers. The data collected included information on yields, maintenance, work in process (WIP), quality control, and test results. Engineers found that in order to collect and use these kinds of information, they needed "a series of computerized information systems for production control and yield management." Production lines were compartmentalized and structured to facilitate data collection and control.[19]

The testing of finished products became a major application in the early 1960s. The reason is not hard to find: because employees could not manually test millions of chips per day; the process had to be automated. One engineer stated that "every diode or transistor for a particular module had to be individually predetermined to meet its specification with assurance greater than 99%, so that the fraction of assemblies requiring rework would be accessibly small." Computer-driven testing techniques made it possible to test 36,000 devices per hour.[20] By 1967, SLT had reached its maximum efficiency. Modules manufactured in 1964 had a failure rate of 0.003 percent per 1,000 hours of operation, and two years later, because of the learning curves achieved in combination with improved testing, performance had improved threefold. By 1967, this meant, for example, that performance was "comparable to a machine with 3000 circuits, such as the CPU of a System/360 Model 30, having only one module fail every five years."[21]

The arrival of monolithic integrated circuits—normally called *chips*, as opposed to the earlier term, *transistors*—forced the entire industry to develop new tools, processes, and software for the design, manufacture, packaging, and testing of most semiconductor products. By the late 1960s, new applications had been developed for growing crystals, for aligning masks to wafers, and for integrating mechanized wafer-handling procedures. Increasingly through the 1970s, more tasks were automated, driven by computers, especially those required to speed up or improve the quality of testing and debugging of design and production problems. The arrival of very large-scale integration (VLSI) products in the 1970s, and used through the 1980s, continued this process of automation and redesign of manufacturing processes. Because of the density of chips, lithography and yield management became increasingly important in the 1970s and 1980s.

To illustrate the issues faced by engineers, which increasingly drove them to use computers to manage design and production, we can compare two semiconductor logic technologies, one from 1964 and the other from 1980. In 1964, production required 16 basic steps; in 1980, 38 steps. Steps in lithography rose from 5 to 14, and the number of terminals per chip rose from 3 to 122. The number of circuits per wafer rose from 300 to 273,000. At the same time, engineers had to increase their yields, that is, the number of chips manufactured that worked as required by design specifications, in order to maintain profitability. By the end of the 1970s, yield management practices had become highly computerized. Looking back, one IBM engineer commented that, "during the sixties and seventies semiconductor products were key to the economics of computers. Now the computer itself is indispensable to the fabrication of semiconductors. The rates of advancement have now become mutually dependent."[22]

In the 1970s, CAD/CAM and CIM applications became the norm for every chip manufacturer in the world. With every new generation of products, the old applications and processes were found wanting and were replaced. By the early 1990s, software for the design, manufacture, and testing of chips became more object-oriented, that is, were written in modules that could be constantly changed. Databases were extensively used to organize information. Typical CIM applications by the late 1980s included factory management, planning, scheduling, simulation, machine control, process control, and specification management, all supported by individual software application tools. Like software application packages in many industries and functions, these included communications infrastructure, e-mail, databases, virtual bulletin boards, logging, data collection, and reporting capabilities.[23] Open CIM architectures also became increasingly the norm as engineers sought ways to change applications rapidly in response to the requirements for developing made-to-order chips or for ongoing transformations in the production processes.

Whereas processes for the design and manufacture of transistors had to be invented in the early 1950s, by the end of the century even this very complex production process had become substantially stabilized. One study of the industry's practices concluded that "today's principal VLSI products . . . are manufactured worldwide using very similar manufacturing equipment and processes," although the performance of various manufacturers varied widely.[24] Several circumstances caused variation, such as what kinds of chips were being made, the quality of the staffs of a manufacturing firm (e.g., small fabs tended to have inferior labor and equipment performance), and various levels of investment in modern or older equipment and software. Historians who looked at several of the earliest entrants into this industry suggested that the engineering or business biases of the founders often profoundly influenced what products were made and even how they were made. The historians also noted how critical it was in this industry to integrate or at least link R&D to both product development and manufacturing processes.[25]

By the late 1990s, experts in the industry had concluded that "a fab must have computer systems providing strong process control, excellent data collection and excellent data analysis capabilities." In addition, a fab had to be organized in such a way that it could optimize problem recognition and resolution while maintaining technical skills. In the 1980s most firms had embraced a number of additional approaches to the management of production that were not technical. The most important was the massive increase in the use of statistical process control (SPC). These tools and techniques were part of the broader Total Quality Management (TQM) practices that swept across most manufacturing industries, beginning in the 1950s in Japan and in the United States by the early 1980s.[26] These kinds of data provided automated systems with early warning of out-of-control situations. By the end of the century, all fabs had engineering databases, bar codes, magnetic cards, and sensors to track inventories. They had very effective software to provide in-line yield analysis by deploying digital image-processing and laser-scanning machines to inspect chips and wafers in various stages of fabrication. Design and manufacturing instructions were routinely simulated before production. Engineers (and later computers) used the data generated to instruct manufacturing processes and equipment.

With the use of SPC, TQM, and their experiences, this industry had acquired significant change management expertise, cutting across organizational structures, technologies, product development, and employee management, thereby satisfying a key requirement—to have a culture and a set of processes for continuous improvement. Reducing cycle times, improving yields, responding to the continuous decline in the costs of chips, all in the face of rising capital expenditures, dictated that this industry would have such skills or not thrive. One study concluded that "the ability of the firms to coordinate R&D and production was perhaps the most important determinant of their success over time."[27] It was a clear statement about the need for continuous change and improvement.

Recent Trends

The use of computers over such a long period of time in the Semiconductor Industry also affected the fundamental strategies of its firms. Specialization, for example, became increasingly widespread. The Japanese, for example, majored on the production of inexpensive memory chips, the Americans on higher end, more leading-edge products. Design work became highly automated and a specialty within the industry (done by "fabless" companies).[28] Other companies specialized in manufacturing (done by "foundries"). The ability of one type of firm to access the capabilities of the other, particularly for the fabs to work with foundries when coupled to the relative standardization of manufacturing processes and technologies, made it easier to implement strategies that depended on specialization. This was particularly the case in the United States, where out of the world's total of some 500 fabless firms in 1998, 300 were situated in North America. The majority of the most modern foundries, however, were in Asia. Fabs specialized in design and R&D, outsourcing fabrication, whereas foundries increasingly learned how to make short production runs a profitable business. Fabless companies supplied services to customer firms in fast-changing industries, such as PC manufacturers and those in telecommunications. In the 1990s alone, fabless companies enjoyed growths in revenue in the range of 32 percent per year.[29] Collaboration among firms also became particularly evident in the American economy, less driven by the use of computers and more by two others factors: enormous capital requirements and support for collaboration by government policymakers.

One can sense the nature of the technical skills required to design and manufacture leading-edge semiconductor products by looking at the kind of employees in such an enterprise. In a presentation IBM managers used to describe the activities of their Microelectronics Division in the late 1990s, which manufactured integrated circuits (chips), they reported that 33 percent of their employees had technical and professional skills, 31 percent were production employees, 25.6 percent were devoted to sundry technical operations, and the roughly 10 percent remaining were managers and administrative personnel. In this division of IBM, 2.4 percent had doctorates, 11.5 percent had master's degrees, and 24.4 percent had bachelor's degrees. Of the total population, 20.2 percent had associate degrees. Roughly a fourth had graduated from high school, over 6 percent had some college education, and an additional 10 percent had other types of education. Professional and technical skills were held by nearly 60 percent of the employees, and another 31 percent were skilled in production processes. Formal education, from associate to doctorate degrees, were in electrical engineering, mechanical engineering, materials science, chemical engineering, chemistry, physics, and metallurgical engineering.[30] In other words, this was a world of scientists, engineers, and technical manufacturing personnel.

Another characteristic of this industry was the requirement that senior management be technically familiar with a wide variety of processes and content, ranging from R&D done to how chips were manufactured and tested. The evidence gathered so far by students of the industry clearly indicates that the level of technical knowledge possessed by senior management profoundly influenced the strategic direction of the firm.[31] Since senior management had a basic responsibility to coordinate the various functions of the firm, to do so in a very high-tech industry required technical knowhow, not just managerial knowledge.[32]

The establishment of SEMATECH in 1987 by 14 American semiconductor firms showed that increased collaboration also had to reach outside the firm. Established initially to help all members improve their manufacturing processes, it transformed its mission to improving the technological capabilities of American firms that built equipment used by semiconductor manufacturers to make chips. Today SEMATECH has the look and feel of an industry association.[33]

When this industry was formed in the 1950s and 1960s in the United States, it had virtually no competition. As knowhow of designing and manufacturing semiconductors diffused around the world, American firms faced competition in the 1970s and 1980s, but they rebounded in the 1990s. Economists attributed the rebounding that occurred to three circumstances. First, U.S. firms stopped manufacturing chips that did not lend themselves to substantial product innovations. Second, they improved their overall manufacturing productivity. Third, they increased the quality of their products.[34] The second and third causes grew directly out of enhanced uses of computing. This American industry did well when there were opportunities for substantial product innovations, created by results of R&D that were both scientific and technological.[35]

The Semiconductor Industry underwent a great deal of scrutiny in the mid-1990s by government policymakers concerned about U.S. security and economic development if the industry faltered and by economists and others worried about remedies when sales of semiconductor products seemed to stall. Yet, by the late 1990s, its products were being acquired by ever-increasing numbers of industries, from computer manufacturers to those specializing in toys and dolls. One industry analyst identified the increased demand for an enormously varied set of products as coming from expanded global communications, e-commerce, increased use of digital products in the home, and "unfettered personal mobility." He predicted double-digit growth rates for this industry in the early years of the new century. The capability of American firms to design and manufacture new products made such growth possible.[36]

I have mentioned the injection of chips into consumer products in earlier chapters. However, it bears mentioning here within the context of this industry's ability to develop specialized products. Automobiles are an excellent example of what drove demand for semiconductors. Late in the century, vehicles were becoming more computerized with the introduction of the Internet; there arose a new generation of braking systems, computer-controlled air bag and steering systems, and a wide variety of on-board plug-and-play entertainment systems. In 1998, the electronic systems in a car cost a manufacturer on average $894. That expense rose in 1999–2000 to over $1,000. While auto manufacturers around the world were increasing their revenues at the end of the century at roughly 1 percent per year (and actually down in 2000 and 2001 in the United States), sales in the automotive component market, where a large number of chips were used, grew annually at 9 percent. Global positioning systems, advanced braking, air bags, higher voltage batteries, a new generation of dashboard instrumentation, and climate-control systems drove this demand. Vehicle manufacturers continued their historic trend of the previous 20 years of replacing mechanical systems with digital electronic ones. In 1999, the worldwide auto semiconductor market stood at $10 billion and increased to $11.8 billion the following year. As this chapter was being written (mid-2003), forecasts from the Semiconductor Industry for what automotive customers were buying suggested that in 2003 sales would exceed $15 billion. The Semiconductor Industry was now part of the automotive supply chain, serving as a key provider of components. Dan Wecker, vice president of a components-manufacturing firm, commented that "things like antilock brakes, air bags, and electronic sensors used to be a differentiator in the industry" but that "now, most of those things are standard. Having the whole wiring infrastructure completed before the car is sold will allow drivers to load up software and get additional features they're looking for. That will be the new differentiator."[37]

Packaged industrial computers became an increasingly important market for the products of the Semiconductor Industry. These were PC-based industrial computers embedded in or part of control applications and machinery of many industries and systems for industrial controls. The PCs in this environment did not necessarily look like the devices one used in an office (screen or keyboard) but could be specialized computer chips collected together on different platforms. Applications included those requiring complex algorithmic or mathematical calculations (e.g., in materials handling) or simultaneous uses of operator interfaces, sequencing of controls and motions (particularly important in manufacturing and transportation), or data processing. Customers designed some of these chips (e.g., automotive engineers), usually with widely available software design tools. In addition to the Automotive Industry, the Semiconductor Industry was also an extensive user of specialized chips for its own purposes (e.g., in operating manufacturing equipment). But many other industries were increasing their use of specialized chips. Process industries, for example, continuously enhanced their monitoring of such variables as temperature and pressure and had an appetite for graphical user interfaces. Manufacturers continued to integrate various production processes with computing, using semiconductor products embedded in equipment made to perform specific processes.[38]

Hard Disk Drive Industry

The Hard Disk Drive (HDD) Industry is an excellent example of one of the new industries to emerge almost invisibly in the post–World War II economy. Even many people working in IT do not yet recognize it as a fully developed industry, replete with firms, associations, customers, best practices, and business running into the tens of billions of dollars each year. Part of its near anonymity can be attributed to the fact that most of its customers are manufacturers of mainframe computers and PCs. Even IBM, which over many years was not recognized outside the industry as a large manufacturer of disk drives, produced a high percentage of the industry's output and was recognized within this community for introducing the majority of the technical innovations to come from this sector. Like other industries that built the "plumbing" of the Internet, the HDD industry was crucial to the digitization of the American economy.

What Is a Disk Drive?

Before we examine this nearly stealth industry, we should understand its basic product, the disk drive, because most people have never seen one. Yet everyone in the world who has used a computer since the 1960s has relied on this industry's products.

A hard disk drive is a machine that stores data in digital form, making it possible for an individual to go directly to a specific piece of information. In contrast, magnetic tape, although it, too, stores information in digital form, does not permit direct access to a specific piece of data but rather requires someone to read all the files before the one they want. Disk drives and disks have come in many shapes over the years, but to understand how they work, think of them as old phonograph players and records or encased CDs. One could go directly to that portion of the surface where a favorite song had been etched and retrieve it through some device that reads the data (e.g. a phonograph needle riding on the surface of the record), bringing these data into a stereo system, where they could be translated into sound one could hear. Essentially that is what occurs with a hard drive. It is that part of a computer system where information is stored until it is brought into the computer to be read, used, and changed and then restored back on a disk drive. In a large computer system, such as a company might have, the disk drive might be the size of a refrigerator, with rows of them holding trillions of pieces of data. On a more humble scale, a floppy diskette or a CD in a personal computer is part of a disk drive system. The disk drive system consists of the storage medium (e.g., CD), a self-contained disk drive that reads and writes to the medium, and the software embedded in these devices that communicates back and forth with the computer. The entire package makes it possible for software applications and people to retrieve, use, and store data.[39]

Perhaps the most important feature of a disk drive is its ability to allow one to access directly a piece of information because that capability is what makes online applications possible. Batch applications are normally done today by disk drives instead of tape (the latter being the case in the 1950s and halfway through the 1960s) because the ability of a person to "talk" to a computer, interacting with it in real time, was not possible before the invention of disk storage in the mid-1950s. Initially more expensive and more limited in capacity than magnetic tape, over the years the cost of this medium has declined steadily to the point where storage costs are now so low that vast quantities of data reside on disk drives, offering the possibility that in several years they will store more information than is printed on paper.[40] Table 7.4 catalogs technical milestones to illustrate the churn and progress over the years, making it possible to say that today the most data in digital form are stored in disks.[41]

The first commercially available disk drive was invented by IBM, which often led the industry in additional innovations over the next several decades: "IBM displayed engineering brilliance in overcoming critical technical constraints."[42] Looking briefly at IBM's disk drives illustrates the emergence of this new sector of the IT world. In 1956, IBM shipped the first commercially available product, called the RAMAC, or IBM 350, the first movable-head disk drive. The disks rotated at about 1,200 rpm and were roughly 2 feet in diameter. In time, new products came out that were smaller and faster. In 1963, the IBM 1311 had a recording density 10 times that of the RAMAC, although its speed had increased only to 1,500 rpm. Seek time for data dropped from 600 ms on the RAMAC to 150 ms on the 1311. Costs dropped during the 1960s and reliability improved, as did capacity and speed of operation. Microprogramming in the 1960s and 1970s made it possible to manage ever larger amounts of data. Between 1967 and 1980, the cost per megabyte (Mb) of disk storage dropped by a factor in excess of 20, making it the least expensive form of active storage available to computer users. In the 1970s, the widely used IBM 3330 disk drive had a recording density of 4,040 bpi, and its average seek time had dropped to 30 ms. The arrival of the Winchester technology in the form of the IBM 3340 in 1973 continued the rapid pace of innovation. For the first time, regular maintenance of a disk drive was no longer needed. To give a sense of how costs had changed, in 1957 for $1 a computer center could store 6.8 thousand bytes of information; in 1981, the same (by then a highly inflated dollar) rented space for 1.19 million bytes.[43]

Rapid innovations continued in the 1980s, with capacity improving annually at a routine rate of 60 percent. Between 1980 and 1995, the price per megabyte also dropped to an annual rate of 40 percent. Recording surfaces became denser, making these devices smaller, an essential requirement if they were to be used in PCs, for example. A disk drive's size, called form factor, dropped from 14 inches to 5.25 and ended the decade of the 1980s at a now standard 3.5 inches. The inability of a manufacturer to move from one form factor to another was often the cause for that firm to drop out of the business of developing, fabricating, and selling disk drives.

This technology is often judged by the ability of a disk drive to improve the performance of its head and media. Known as areal density, this is the amount of

Table 7.4
Selected Major Product Innovations in the Hard Disk Drive Industry, 1956–2000

1956	IBM 350 RAMAC—first commercial disk drive
1963	IBM 1311—first removable disk pack
1966	IBM 2314—first drive with ferrite core heads
1971	IBM 3330—first track-following servo system
1973	IBM 23FD—Sets industry standard for 8-inch diskettes
1973	IBM 3340 "Winchester"—first drive with low mass heads, lubricated disks, and sealed assembly
1976	IBM 43FD—first drive with two-sided recording
1976	Shugart Associates SA400—first 5.25-inch flexible disk drive
1979	IBM 3370—first thin film head disk drive
1980	Seagate—first 5.25 rigid disk drive
1981	Sony—first 3.5-inch flexible disk drive
1982	Control data—first 9-inch rigid disk drive
1985	Quantum—first drive mounted on a card
1988	Conner peripherals—first 1-inch-high 3.5-inch disk drive
1991	Integral peripherals—introduces first 1.8-inch disk drive
1992	Hewlett-Packard—first 1.3-inch disk drive
1993	Seagate—first 7,200-rpm disk drive
1995	Iomega zip—first embedded servo flexible disk drive
1997	Seagate—First 10,000-rpm disk drive
1998	Hitachi—first 12,000-rpm disk drive
1999	IBM Microdrive—first 1-inch disk drive
2000	Seagate—first 15,000-rpm disk drive

Source: Adapted from a much larger list by Disk/Trend, "Five Decades of Disk Drive Industry Firsts" (undated, circa February 2001), http://www.distrend.com/5decades2.htm.

data that can be put on a square inch of the surface of a disk drive and that can then be read by one arm. This, too, improved over the years by many factors. By 1997, one could buy a disk drive that could store 2,638 megabytes per inch. During the 1990s alone, areal densities increased by 60 percent per year. Thus by 1997, to put it in some perspective, in 1 square inch one could store as much data as exist in a 40-volume encyclopedia.

This industry shared with semiconductors a fixation on yields. The more stable the manufacturing process, the greater the yields that were possible. Learning how to improve manufacturing and design were just as important to both industries, which is why knowledge management, use of simulation software, expert systems, and computer-driven manufacturing have proven to be so critical. But before we can fully understand the dynamics of yield and CIM practices in this industry, we need to ask, How are disk drives made?[44]

IT Deployment

In general, and in most decades, one began by manufacturing the important components, such as heads, media disks, and semiconductors, and then packaging them into final products. Over time, most components became increasingly available as standard products from other vendors, and their manufacture was always very sensitive to yield analysis. Components were assembled to form a disk drive through a series of multiple steps, using machine and human steps and processes, and finally tested primarily through automated means. These various steps were also yield-sensitive. Failure to perform as designed at any step forced products or components to be scrapped or reworked. New production processes and products inevitably began with low knowledge levels about their performance, requiring constant yield analysis, just as in the Semiconductor Industry. Machine downtime, as in such traditional manufacturing industries as automotive and appliance firms, also negatively affected yields. Companies sought yields in the range of 80 to 90 percent for finished products, up to 98 percent for components.

By the 1980s, the HDD Industry was using software to simulate production processes and to understand some elements of yields. Applying yield-loss modeling programs, other software for in-line product inspection, and statistical tools became essential in this industry.[45] Expert systems in the 1980s began to provide estimates on batch qualities. Many of the lessons learned in using simulation software came from the Semiconductor Industry. In both industries, as products became more complex, testing increased, and over time that function became increasingly automated. Even production often looked similar. For example, fabricating read-write heads was a similar process to that used by the Semiconductor Industry to build simple integrated circuits, although the labor content in HDD was higher because of some additional steps. Engineers optimized testing in both processes by using software, as well as experience. Testing before a major or irreversible operation, for example, proved to be very effective in improving yields. Doing testing when a modular assembly had been completed was also an effective approach. In-line assessments at the end of a process step provided useful feedback by making it possible to alter subsequent process steps to avoid errors and lower yields.

Engineers in this industry learned that as a general rule automation (hence computer-driven production processes) did improve yields, particularly as components shrank in size, one generation of product after another. To the degree that computing helped improve the effectiveness of initial production, this experience demonstrates that yields were more sensitive to the influences of computerization and the insights gained through automated testing, as well as to the improving skills of engineers. As production stabilized and a product became mature, with automated processes and computerized activities also stabilizing, yields tended to be more affected by the cost of labor than by the expense of a process.[46]

For the entire history of this industry, American firms never lost market leadership, often dominating market share at rates of between 75 and 85 percent. Its dominance was made possible by a combination of organizational skills—the ability to manage R&D, production, and distribution. Leveraging a combination of technical processes in the United States with manufacturing in East Asia became the winning strategy. Balancing knowledge and economies of scale while continuously changing products, firms always operated in a highly competitive market. Over 250 companies entered the industry over the course of the past 40 years, but fewer than 30 survived at the end of the century. Twenty-eight firms dominated 98 percent of the world market in 1995, shipping over $26 billion in products.[47] The major firms in this industry were different from those manufacturing semiconductors. Leaders included IBM, Seagate, and Quantum.[48] Because so few dominated, one could reasonably look for oligopolistic behavior, although one would not find it because of the technical and market dynamics that kept competition at an intense level through most of the last half century.

This industry had to invent manufacturing processes and determine acceptable economies of scale to remain profitable and competitive. Let's deal with economies of scale first. Costs were driven very high by the expense of "clean room" fabrication facilities, pricey test equipment, and R&D. Additional charges were incurred for precision tools, molds, dies, and other equipment. Every time firms developed a new generation of products, most of the production and testing tools and procedures had to be modified or replaced, especially between the 1960s and the end of the 1980s. The need was slightly less in the 1990s because by then some standard components could be used, such as fabrication equipment and housing (packaging) for drives. In 1989 a factory that manufactured between 900,000 and a million units was said to enjoy profitable economies of scale. By the mid-1990s, that same factory would have had to produce roughly 4 million units per year to remain profitable. Increases in capacity requirements always strained manufacturing.[49] In short, the Chandlerian requirement of sufficient investment in manufacturing infrastructure appeared once again, this time right in the middle of the IT sector of the economy.

Expensive engineering knowledge included the ability to produce miniature motors, operating some of the most complex manufacturing processes in any industry—primarily to coat disks with thin films of magnetic materials and even manufacture specialized chips—whereas final fabrication of surface-mount technologies was a fully automated process late in the century. Product life cycles ran 1 to 3 years in the 1960s and shrunk to between 9 and 12 months in the late 1990s, although some products emerging at the end of the century were closer to 6 months. Speed to market and economies of scale came to dominate the concerns of this industry.

Dieter Ernst, an expert on the economics of HHD, has suggested that the best way to understand how companies designed, manufactured, and sold disk drives was by viewing how firms managed their supply chains: "The HDD industry is probably the most demanding sector in the electronics industry."[50] Fast R&D, rapid increases in production, and equally prompt acquisition of components put a premium on being able to operate a smooth supply chain, all in concert with the timings required of its key customers—historically, the Computer Industry—which also was constantly introducing new products and functioned in a competitive environment that became even more intense and volatile during the last two decades of the century. Because of the high capital costs and the intense body of specialized knowledge required, it was no surprise that the number of firms in the industry shrank over the decades. Ernst observed that complexity led surviving firms to establish complex supplier networks, operating on a global basis. The top six producers, although all American-based firms, over time exported production to East Asia, keeping most R&D in the United States. Thus, unlike in many other industries, where R&D and manufacturing were actually situated literally at the same geographic locations, the HDD Industry had to learn to combine the two, with many time zones and distances between them, and not lose time or incur additional expenses.[51]

Mastery of the supply chain made it possible for American companies to dominate even in what were always weak sections of a market for many other U.S. industries, that is, low-margin, high-volume segments. This is an industry that shifted work to lower labor costs earlier than most American industries, while keeping R&D in the United States. In the early 1980s, for example, Seagate, Computer Memories, Ampex, and Tandem pioneered the movement of fabrication to East Asia. At the time, over 70 percent of worldwide production resided in the United States, another 12 percent in Japan, and the rest in Europe. By 1990, Singapore had become the largest center for the manufacture of disk drives, producing 55 percent of the world's supply. Almost 75 percent of the components needed could also be bought in East Asia. Using automation, computer-based management and simulation, and comparatively inexpensive labor, American firms found fabrication in East Asia profitable.[52] By the end of the century, over two-thirds of all hard drives were produced in the region. By the late 1990s, the availability of local sources of materials and components had become a major economic consideration in favor of continued production in East Asia. As a result of so many years of production in that area, local knowledge about fabrication and component providers grew. Those capabilities made it possible to transfer new designs from the United States to East Asian facilities. By the start of the twenty-first century, even some R&D was being done in the region.

But the transfer strategy had started earlier, when IBM initiated cross-national expansion of the supply chain with production in Europe in the 1960s and then extended its initiative to Asia to lower labor costs.[53] Manufacturing was easier at that time, a pure fabrication of components. Other firms, however, proved more aggressive over time in transferring additional elements of their manufacturing processes to Asia. In the 1970s, for example, both Motorola and National Semiconductor tested offshore chip manufacturing, which began to come to the attention of disk suppliers. Tandem established the first manufacturing site in Singapore in the 1970s, although Hewlett-Packard had worked with local component supplies since 1970.[54]

Seagate's initiative in moving to East Asia had a profound effect on the company's strategies and is an example of how the use of computing in R&D and manufacturing was of strategic importance. Seagate's production network was made up of final assembly and testing of disk drives, subassembly and manufacture of components, sourcing of components and subassemblies from various providers, and development and prototyping of components and final products. Included in this last piece of the production network was process engineering, which defined how things should be made. During the 1980s and 1990s, first Seagate and then others began to transfer various parts of their supply chain to East Asia. By the late 1990s, Seagate had developed volume production processes and test software in Singapore. Volume manufacturing took place in Bangkok. Facilities in the United States (Minnesota and Oklahoma) did some final assembly work and testing, primarily focusing on high-end products for mainframe computer manufacturers. Seagate even manufactured 3.5-inch disk drives in Ireland. In other words, high-end work continued to remain in the United States, and high-volume, low-margin production was sent overseas.[55]

Continued improvements in telecommunications technologies over the course of the last quarter of the twentieth century made it possible to move information across various geographies and to facilitate the conversations that inevitably had to take place between development engineers and manufacturing personnel. Without excellent telecommunications infrastructures, deployment of an extended supply chain would not have been possible. More than just cheap long-distance phone calls, there was the use of EDI and, increasingly in the late 1990s, the Internet: "With the help of computer-based information networks and management systems, electronic firms can now synchronize product development, marketing, production, and procurements across national boundaries and continents."[56]

This capability came online, along with computer-based control of manufacturing, at the same time that changes occurred in design methodologies. For example, beginning in the mid-1980s, engineers began to use plastic instead of metal more frequently, which reduced the need for mechanical engineering. Increased use of standard ICs and other printed circuits also lowered the number of components in a disk drive. More standard and fewer components made it possible to automate fabrication even further. Such assembly automation processes as surface-mount technologies (SMT) reduced the number of steps in a production regimen, including testing, which in turn led to further simplification of what seemingly remained frightfully complicated R&D and manufacturing processes.

What effects did proximity have on the whole process of design and manufacture? As knowledge increased about production and standardization of automation tools and components, ever-increasing elements of the production chain emerged in Asia, demonstrating that proximity still mattered, despite EDI and the Internet and a variety of information technologies. Yet colocation was possible in many parts of the world, providing there were good transportation and communications. For all intents and purposes, prototyping remained in the United States through the last half century, although expanded use of CAD systems in the 1990s and reliance on the Internet and EDI for backbone networks made it possible to share work across borders. Engineers were reluctant to transfer as much prototyping to Asia as they did manufacturing.

Recent Trends

One interesting consequence of the deployment of technology, computing, and process design outside the United States has been the transfer of technical knowledge, a process also evident in some of the industries studied earlier in this book. When manufacturing first began in Asia, it was done to lower labor costs because much of the fabrication work between the early 1960s and the end of the 1970s remained labor-intensive. Components had to be manufactured and then assembled into disk drives. The R&D and other engineering capabilities remained in the United States. As automation took hold in the 1970s, and certainly by the start of the 1980s across the entire industry, expertise began to take root in Asia, often under American management or contract. Local skilled workers could contribute to the development of manufacturing processes. Savings in labor costs and time played a role because the amount spent on R&D and process design remained very high. Nevertheless, at the start of the new century, the bulk of R&D resided in the United States.[57]

Related to the use of computing today in the design,[58] manufacture, and testing of products is the growing application of commoditization of components, processes, and reusable algorithms. First, engineers in this industry, and by extension their firms, knew a great deal more about manufacturing HDDs at the end of the century than two decades earlier. Second, as evident in many other high- and low-tech industries, they tried to use common commodities across multiple products to the extent possible. Western Digital, a highly respected firm in the industry, strived by the end of the century to have 70 to 80 percent of its commodities used across product lines.[59] Project and process modeling and skills also made it possible to shorten ramp-up times for new products across the industry. In fact, cycle times declined all through the 1990s in Asia, as local knowledge and standard approaches became increasingly operational. By the end of the century, new products could go from zero production to millions of units in less than three months. One observer considered that capability "routinized, and American firms excel at it."[60]

The ability to move production overseas long before many other industries did so taught HDD firms a great deal about how to coordinate technology, management, and organization in complex global environments. To a large extent, the use of computing facilitated the process, making it increasingly possible to design and fabricate either where labor was less expensive than elsewhere or where skilled employees were available. Over time, support functions developed for the manufacture of components, training of employees, and implementation of government policies in support of the industry. David McKendrick, an economist, has argued that complexity of products and the successful deployment of multiple sites for R&D and fabrication has had the result of making it possible for the American HDD Industry to excel at manufacturing. It was also an industry that did not benefit from either government or extensive university R&D. Innovations occurred quietly within the industry with little publicity, "achieved through heroic mechanical and materials engineering efforts in firms, especially in IBM, rather than through publicly funded research."[61]

This industry never showed signs of becoming more stable, despite the fact that some components in the products did so, and thus some rules of the road had emerged in manufacturing. At the dawn of the new millennium, innovations continued to be fed into the industry from semiconductor manufacturers, customers (most often equally technically competent engineers at computer firms), and a growing number of university R&D programs funded by this industry. Telecommunications, manufacturing automation, computer-based testing, and extensive expert systems and simulation software were such integral features of this industry that, as with the Semiconductor Industry, one could safely argue that it was almost always impossible to make products or innovate without extensive use of computing. It was one of those industries that, if we could allow it to serve as a harbinger of future economic sectors, could only have come into existence if computer science and the application of computing elsewhere in the economy had reached substantial levels of volume. In other words, a post–Fordist Style of manufacturing had to exist.

The model of competition this industry presented stands in sharp contrast to that which occurred in such long-established industries as automotive, steel, or even consumer electronics. Technological innovations have played a profound role in stimulating and sustaining competition, indeed far more so than government regulations, the fear of antitrust litigation, or the prior existence of firms like computer or other electronic companies. To be sure, firms that had existed before the arrival of disk drives came and went in this industry; IBM was the most obvious example, and yet it was clearly the longest-running provider of innovations in the HDD Industry. There were three prices of admission to this industry: technical prowess, substantial amounts of capital, and the agility to keep up. Played out across a global landscape, although primarily in the United States, East Asia, and parts of Western Europe, the ability to leverage all three elements proved to be crucial. But ultimately, the development, use, and sale of technology set the rules for this industry. Whereas other industries bolted IT onto existing organizations, applications, and processes, the HHD Industry made computing an integral part of its operations in highly symbiotic ways. We cannot speak about the Internet, for example, being bolted on to this industry in the way I describe its arrival in most of the industries in this book. The same could be said about the role of software and hardware in this industry as compared to so many others. In short, the HDD Industry might be giving us a preview of what other industries will look like later in the twenty-first century.

Software Industry

Along with computers, software is the most obvious building block of the Information Age. All digital devices require software to run. The digital thermostat in one's house, the electric clock on the nightstand, computers in huge data centers, others directing the flight of airplanes, and of course the operation of PCs, would be impossible without software. With over half of the U.S. population in late 2000 having used the Internet, according to a Pew survey, and with over 75 percent of the American work force having interacted with computers at one time or another, one can safely conclude that more Americans have interacted with software than with most elements of the American economy.[62] Americans have worked more only with cars, other telecommunications tools (e.g., televisions, radios, and telephones), and eating utensils, yet most have never seen software. Although one of the most ubiquitous features of modern life, it is also one of the most obscure and little understood. So, too, is the industry that produced it.

In fact, software is so obscure that invariably when authors discuss it, they must go through the obligatory explanation of what it is and the kinds that exist,[63] although some technical histories of software are available.[64] Software, of course, are the instructions fed to a computer that make it do our bidding. Software can be application programs—the subject of this book—but it can also be instructions that allow a computer to do its nonapplication chores, such as bringing data from a hard drive into a mainframe, or that makes it possible for a PC user to print a page from a Word document. Software programs are tools to do certain tasks faster in a computer, such as organize files more efficiently, or to permit navigation through the Internet with English-like commands. Software also consists of commands collected together to offer people a language for communicating with computers, such as Basic, Fortran, and C++. Software comes embedded in computational equipment, such as the instructions in a computer chip to balance the consumption of gasoline and air in a car. They also come as programs on CD ROMs, which people purchase at a store and load into their computers, such as an applications package. The physical object began as a deck of 80-column cards in the 1950s, appeared on the doorsteps of many data centers in the 1960s in the form of 2,400-foot lengths of magnetic tape, then as diskettes in the 1970s and 1980s, and, finally in the last decade of the century, on CDs. Invisible, first, within large mainframes and, later, even with PCs, software could also be sent over telephone lines to computers, and today that approach is widespread.[65] In short, software came in many forms.

So, too, did the Software Industry. Government agencies and observers of IT so far have not been able to define clearly what makes up the Software Industry. Part of the problem is that it evolved over time. For example, in the 1950s, users or hardware vendors wrote software. In the 1960s, companies appeared that sold software products, but people still continued to write their own, over half of all programs, in fact. In the 1990s, vendors issued software products like books, that is, "publishing" programs.[66] Who wrote software remained somewhat unclear all through the 1950s and 1960s; not until the 1970s did U.S. government economists even begin to observe their activities. In fact, regular tracking, much as we saw for other industries, did not begin until the 1980s. Ever since, however, definitions of the industry's components continued to shift or to be a subject of debate.[67]

To a certain extent, however, we can generalize about the industry. Through the last half century, manufacturers of computers and other hardware often provided for free, or for a fee, a number of software programs, such as operating systems, programming languages, and even application packages (e.g., for accounting). These were normally provided in order to sell or lease hardware, where most of the companies' focus and profit lay, particularly in the early decades. For example, IBM did not charge for software in the 1950s and 1960s.[68] Between the 1950s and the present, individuals and organizations wrote hundreds of billions of lines of software, often exceeding the total output of those vendors who came into the industry before the arrival of the Internet, to sell commercial software packages.[69] Beginning in the mid-1960s, firms that sold software products emerged, selling first to users of large mainframe systems, then to those who needed specialized applications that ran on minicomputers (e.g., engineers), and finally, after the arrival of the PC in the late 1970s, to individuals (e.g., some of the early spreadsheet and word-processing products).

Since we are taking an industry-centric view of applications, we will have to put aside that large community that constantly wrote its own software applications and briefly review the scope of the commercial software market. This approach gives us yet another view of how pervasive computing had become in the American economy in the twentieth century. By the 1960s, there were at least 50 software providers operating in the United States. The largest, Computer Sciences Corporation (CSC), sold packages for accounting, ticketing, income tax preparation, and banking, and in 1965 it generated $17.8 million in revenue. By the end of the decade there were over 2,800 organizations that wrote contract software for a client or marketed their own products, establishing for all intents and purposes what we would today call the Software Industry. Estimates of how much American corporations and agencies spent on software (their own creations and those of suppliers) rose from about $3 to $4 billion in 1965 to annual levels in the region of $8 billion by 1970.[70] This was about 28 percent of their total expenditures on computing, a statistic that held for most of the entire half century. In the 1970s, the software market continued to expand in response to the growing need for software applications, normally designed for specific types of computers (e.g., mainframes or minis). In that decade, sales of software expanded rapidly by a factor of 5.5.

In the 1980s, in addition to already existing markets, the PC created new opportunities, leading many software providers to shift from a relatively craft-oriented production of programs for thousands of customers to mass (published) software that was marketed like books, in some cases bought by millions of users. New names became widely recognized in this period: Lotus, Microsoft, Ashton-Tate, and WordPerfect. In the first half of the decade, 15 firms controlled 72 percent of the market, with Microsoft, Lotus, and Ashton-Tate dominating.

The Software Industry enjoyed a remarkable period of growth, reflecting the rapid adoption of computing across the United States. From a few hundred millions of dollars in sales in the mid-1960s, it reached its first billion dollar year in 1974. Average annual growth rates in the 1980s and 1990s remained consistently above 10 percent, generated by over 20,000 firms, most of them small.[71] By 1992, just over 46 percent of all sales of software were to Microsoft customers; another 42 percent to mainframe, mini, and supercomputer users; and nearly 11 percent to consumers of video games. The PC software market grew rapidly, at 20 percent per annum between 1987 and 1993, faster than the overall software market, which expanded in the same period by 12 percent. Thus, the expanding role of the PC

Table 7.5
U.S. Software Investments in Billions of Dollars, Selected Years

Type*	1960	1970	1980	1990	1995	1998
Prepackaged	n/a	0.2	1.4	15.3	29.3	40.7
Custom	0.0	1.1	5.7	21.9	35.7	64.1
Own account	0.1	1.8	7.5	29.1	43.0	54.2

*These data represent a major—yet only an initial—initiative by the U.S. government to identify the key sources of investments in software.

Source: Bureau of Economic Analysis, "Recognition of Business and Government Expenditures for Software as Investment: Methodology and Quantitative Impacts, 1959–98" (undated, circa 2000): 32–35. For access to the economists who did the study, go to Robert Parker, robert.parker@bea.doc.gov, or to Bruce Grimm, bruce.grimm@bea.doc.gov.

once again became evident, this time in the sales for software.[72] By the end of the decade, one could speak of an American industry that sold tens of billions of dollars of software each year. As two economists concluded, after tabulating data on this industry's size and scope, "Without computer software, much of American industry could not function; without current software technology, much of American industry could not compete in the world market."[73] Table 7.5 lists investments made in software since 1960 by type (packages, custom software written to order, and in-house written programs—called own-account software), to suggest how realistic this observation was about today's economy.

IT Deployment

How did the Software Industry use software itself? To answer that question, we should recognize some obvious facts. To write software, one must use computing and other software tools, such as programming languages, their compilers, other utilities, and hardware. So we can begin by saying that 100 percent of this industry used computing from its earliest days. Contract programmers who wrote packages for users did, too. This industry, along with data centers in companies, created a large pool of technically skilled workers capable of designing and writing software. Despite cries from time to time about the lack of sufficient numbers of programmers,[74] this population rose from several hundred at the start of the 1950s to over 560,000 by the end of the 1980s and exceeded 620,000 by the end of 1996.[75] This is a constrained view of how many people could program because these statistics reflect only individuals employed as programmers. In addition, hundreds of thousands of systems analysts, computer scientists, consultants, engineers, and students also wrote software, which raised the number to at least 2 million or more. That population expanded even further after the arrival of the PC, which made it possible for millions of people to dabble in programming by either writing software or modifying existing packages through their selection of parameters and options. So, although the absolute number of residents of North America who programmed may never be known, it would be reasonable to conclude that they ran to several million people by the end of the century.[76]

How people wrote software, however, changed over time, as did the way in which both employees of software vendors and data centers used computers. Through the entire half century, programming remained a craft, both labor intensive and reliant on extensive technical skills. To be sure, many attempts were made to improve programming productivity and the cost efficiency and functional effectiveness of software.[77] These initiatives essentially involved four strategies:

- Use of higher level programming languages to make it possible for a programmer to write software faster, more accurately, and with less skill than before[78]
- Development and use of modules of prewritten software, often called reusable code, to reduce the amount of new software that one had to write[79]
- Application design techniques to streamline production of software, add new functionality, and balance all the resources required to run it, such as hardware systems, other software, and people[80]
- Formalizing into processes various steps in the design and creation of software to reduce errors and improve the quality of programs[81]

Yet all these steps led two generations of commentators to argue that programmers and the industries in which they worked had not improved the quality or efficiency of their essentially craft-oriented work to the extent that, for example, computer hardware had developed. For many of these observers, the lack of effective innovations in software development, maintenance, and use had held back the arrival of the Information Age, and this circumstance continued to constrain the use of automation techniques and the digital at the start of the new century. The few economic studies conducted on the relative cost of software over time suggest that productivity increases in price performance averaged about 5 percent between the 1970s and mid-1990s. Unlike computer hardware, in which major breakthroughs in semiconductors drove down costs, no comparable technological price driver emerged in the world of programming and software. Declines in the prices for PC software ranged closer to 6 percent and in some instances as much as 15 percent, but these price improvements were largely accounted for by the fact that more copies of a package were sold, making possible price declines in a highly competitive segment of the software market.[82] Relative development costs per line of code (the master copy) remained high. Technical innovations were incremental and iterative over time.

In the 1950s, a programmer would draw a flowchart on paper, showing the various steps a program had to take, and then type out each line of software on 80-column punch cards. The cards would then be run in a computer, recoded as operations errors appeared, and again rerun. This iterative process eventually led to programs that did their jobs. By the early 1960s, some programmers were beginning to design their programs online and to write their software, using a data collection terminal (such as at an IBM 3740 data collection system). During the 1970s, programming became increasingly structured, that is, driven by formal processes and project management techniques.[83] In the 1980s, notions of reusable code (pieces of software) came into vogue, along with tools and techniques to facilitate this approach (often called Computer-Aided Software Engineering (CASE) tools).[84]

Whereas in the late 1970s and early 1980s the industry made a large number of incremental strides in improving productivity, it was still labor-intensive. At the time about half the employees in the industry were directly involved with computers. We know very little about the distribution of work in the Software Industry. However, one case study of software companies in California suggested that programmers made up about 16 percent of the work force, and the systems analysts who designed software made up another 11 percent. That the industry was still labor-intensive, however, is made evident by the fact that nearly 16 percent of all employees were keypunch operators, people who entered data (software) into computers. How did these statistics compare to manufacturing firms in general in California at the time (1978)? As expected, the number of programmers was high, far more than half the percentage needed for manufacturing. These software providers also had far more managers than needed in manufacturing, which employed many more workers for production and maintenance.[85]

Recent Developments

In the 1990s, tools to enhance productivity became very widespread—along with operating systems that had first made their appearance in the 1960s and that made possible a wider use of various programming languages—as well as more modular software tools and utilities.[86] The need for productivity had simply grown. By 1996, with over 2 million people programming just in the United States, programming tools were in great demand. The population of programmers kept growing into the new century, particularly in East Asia and in Western Europe. Partly because of the wide adoption of PCs and partly because of increased reliance on software across the American economy, growth in the deployment of programs had, between 1987 and 1994, expanded by 9.6 percent each year around the world. In short, software and programming had become big business.[87]

From the 1950s to the present, enormous strides were made in developing technical software standards in an attempt to systematize its development.[88] But, as Frederick P. Brooks, Jr., one of the most influential commentators on software, concluded in the early 1980s, "The tar pit of software engineering will continue to be sticky for a long time to come. One can expect the human race to continue attempting systems just within or just beyond our reach; and software systems are perhaps the most intricate and complex of man's handiworks."[89] Simulation tools created to facilitate design and development began to make their appearance in the 1960s. Many hoped that they would address the kinds of problems Brooks had been speaking about since the early 1960s. For example, at Michigan Bell's data center, DP personnel modeled some applications to determine the right mix of hardware and software in the mid-1960s. By the late 1970s, IBM was touting a variety of methodologies and simulation tools to help estimate the effort required to write software.[90] Ironically, on the one hand, the Software Industry fueled the economy with digital tools but, on the other hand, remained a craft-based industry. However, where it was able to automate and computerize functions, it did so.

Over the course of the half century, software products became increasingly more complicated, lines of code growing from hundreds to hundreds of thousands (as is typical today for a Microsoft product). Highly stable, disciplined production processes of the 1960s and 1970s gave way to more iterative approaches in the 1980s and 1990s. By the mid-1990s, a typical set of production tools used by programmers included attachment to local area networks (LANs), linked to servers used just for programming or shared with computer systems that ran actual applications. Online design tools became common, along with computer-based testing tools that were used to constantly test new software for performance and errors during the course of the day. Today, analytical tools can track the number of keystrokes required to write a line of code, the time required to build modules, and so forth. In short, many computer-based tools had come to the industry[91] in a variety of approaches and digital artifacts.

Nowhere was this more obvious than in the use of various computer media for the delivery of software to customers. In the 1960s, when software was first sold widely as a product, vendors delivered to customers either boxes of 80-column cards or 2,400-foot reels of magnetic tape. These media were also accompanied by publications, called user manuals, describing the software, how to install and debug them, and how best to use them. This documentation alone often proved massive— tens of thousands of pages, for example, to describe a mainframe operating system with all its various software tools or thousands of pages for major financial application packages.[92] These could be run off from a software vendor's mainframe on demand as products were sold. The use of cards declined in the 1970s, becoming fully displaced by magnetic tape and, for small software products, diskettes by the end of the decade. Both users of mainframes and minis essentially received their software in this manner in the same way for the rest of the century. Disk packs were rarely used because of the potential variety of disk formats and the cost of the packs themselves.

A major break with this pattern, however, occurred with the arrival of the PC. Instead of selling and shipping hundreds or a few thousand copies of a software package, suppliers like Microsoft and Lotus had to deal quickly with millions. To accomplish this feat, they began to look at software in the same way as a book publisher did, adopting many of the production techniques found in both the music business and in publishing. First, they published software on diskettes and, by the late 1990s, routinely on CDs, just like music. User manuals were published in book form, on CDs, or embedded in software as part of the programs themselves, for example, the Help icons in Word or Excel. Embedding reference materials into software made it possible by the late 1990s for a user to have a dialogue with programs. (For example, in Word 2000—used to write this chapter—when I made a grammatical error the software would inform me of that fact, often displaying an animated paperclip with eyes and commenting on the problem and how to fix it.) Along with manuals, CDs were published and shipped to dealers (often also to bookstores) and made available through the same channels of distribution, such as Amazon.Com or Barnes & Noble.

In addition—first with large mainframes and today increasingly with Intranet users—other automated, computer-driven methods were employed to increase the efficiency of software delivery. In the 1980s, IBM began to dial its customers' mainframe computers, often at night, to deliver over telephone lines corrections or changes to software and microcode already installed in these systems. These were corrections to errors or updates to allow computers to work with newly installed peripheral equipment or to improve system reliability. By the end of the decade, the delivery of new releases of application packages also took place electronically. During the 1990s, when the Internet became more available, the industry began to show more interest in electronic delivery mechanisms. In fact, Steve Jobs, one of the founders of Apple Computers, argued frequently in favor of this approach, as opposed to the widespread use of cardboard boxes that contained a software diskette (or CD) and a user manual.[93] But at the end of the century, most PC users still received their software in little cardboard boxes.

Increasingly, however, software vendors began to make available to their customers updates to software products online, allowing them to download new releases, such as a variety of Microsoft products and Norton antivirus tools. Corporate networks—called Intranets—only delivered software tools to their users in this way. For example, at IBM, where all 300,000+ employees had access to the company's internal network, they could enter a menu of products that the firm had corporate licenses to use and download either the whole software product or updates, all at will.[94] From the Software Industry's perspective, then, a vendor only had to deliver one copy of a software package to IBM, which it then loaded into the company's server, feeding the internal network. When and where an employee wanted a specific package was of no concern either to the vendor or to the operators of an IBM data center. Downloads took place around the clock seven days a week, worldwide.[95] Distribution costs for both dropped to almost nothing.

The Software Industry gained enormous visibility in the public's eye after the arrival of the PC. No event so demonstrated that fact than the announcement of Windows 95, covered as a major news story in the United States for months prior to the initial shipment of the code. News programs on television, for example, discussed its new features, and industry magazines, as well as general-interest and widely distributed magazines, compared the new release to earlier ones. This was software, not a new novel or automobile.[96] It should come as no surprise that this would have occurred, however, given the fact that at the time nearly a third of American homes had a PC and nearly half the work force had access to PCs or some other form of computing at work. The market for such news and marketing hype ran into the tens of millions of people in the United States and similarly around the world. The PC, in short, had made the Software Industry highly visible. Software stores in shopping malls simply reinforced the fact that a whole new category of products was now a major component of the American economy, sitting alongside automobiles, clothing, furniture, books, music, and groceries. During the second half of the 1990s, even advertisements sent to people's homes came in the form of CDs, especially the free offers for a certain number of hours of airtime on the Internet if someone would simply sign up with AOL or some other provider.[97]

Conclusions

The industries discussed in this chapter range from the now highly visible Software Industry to the nearly invisible Hard Disk Drive Industry. Even the Software Industry remained a stealth industry until the early 1970s, operating without much identity for over a decade; firms that produced disk drives only began emerging from their anonymity at the dawn of the new century. Because of the high-profile coverage computer chips received, literally almost from the day they were invented, firms that manufactured them were always seen as a protoindustry and, by the end of the 1980s, as a full-fledged one. Why should we be concerned about these industries' exposure and recognition?

When a collection of companies is recognized as constituting an industry, a number of events occur. First, the firms more openly and overtly either learn from one another or try to protect trade secrets. The point to remember is that recognition affects marketing and R&D behavior.[98] Although I have not reviewed in detail the histories of these three industries, those who have done so have noted the altered behavior.[99] Second, over time, practices emerge in the industry that improve its operations or are byproducts of the economic realities it faces. Pricing practices and product marketing frequently affected hardware vendors and, even more dramatically, developments in technology, as in the Semiconductor Industry. Given the increased role of IT in the American economy, these new economic realities tell us more about what was happening at the levels of applications, processes, or firms than do generalized studies of an economy's performance at a national level that were done before the industry-level analysis was performed.[100]

Third, once industries are recognized, they attract government and academic economists, business experts, and others who study their behavior, giving additional insight on how to leverage effectively a new class of technology or business practices, for example, by observing what books are sold on management practices. When an industry is "hot," managers write books on how they function. In the Software Industry, for example, members of such firms as Microsoft and Lotus have written on business practices.[101] The combination hardware and software firm, Apple Computers, has spawned its own authors as well.[102] Intel's founder and CEO, Andy Grove, was considered a management wizard, out-publishing many business professors.[103] In short, these emerging industries of the late twentieth century offered the rest of the economy lessons about business and managerial practices.

As the IT content of work, products, and structure of non-IT industries increased over time, these were the industries that made up the economy in tandem with software and hardware industries. Just as manufacturing industries became the bulk of what constituted the American economy in the early decades of the twentieth century, so, too, these new industries began incrementally to define the complexion of the economy of the twenty-first century. That reality was recognized, for example, by various U.S. government agencies—which is why in large part NAICS came into being—listing among other things many new information-based industries. But, unlike the early twentieth century, when the proverbial buggy whip industry gave way to the Automotive Industry, these new industries emerged alongside more traditional ones, such as automotive and steel. The real news is that the IT industries redefined many activities, products, and practices of existing industries through the implementation of computer-based uses of IT. Thus, for example, the Toy Industry was not simply manufacturing baseballs and dolls but also producing products with embedded computer chips. French fries and hamburgers were cooked in the Fast-Food Industry with increased use of computer controls. Automobiles became mobile data centers with thousands of lines of software tucked under their hoods or behind digitally equipped dashboards. Old Economy companies transformed themselves into New Economy firms, as, for example, GE did with many of its manufacturing divisions, which used IT to add information-based services to their offerings.[104] The list of firms that changed profoundly in this way is nearly endless.

There was a corresponding approach to the use of computers in these new IT industries that paralleled the patterns of application usage in more traditional manufacturing firms. At their birth, these newly emerging IT industries tended to have manual production processes, which over time became increasingly automated, made possible by computing. These industries also adopted the same tools used in others, for example, CAD/CAM and CIM manufacturing processes. Like the others, however, they also developed applications unique to their own requirements, such as software and testing equipment to help manage quality and yields in the manufacture of semiconductors.

The move toward greater reliance on automation and IT was driven by the same factors that influenced previously established industries: cost performance, reliability, and functionality. Just as they experienced increased pressures for change or heightened competition because of some new technological innovation, as in pharmaceuticals, for instance, the same imperatives operated within the newly emerging IT industries. In short, they were not immune to the laws of economics. This was a point recently made by Carl Shapiro and Hal R. Varian in their highly influential study of the Internet, *Information Rules* (1999), in which they demonstrated a basic rule of economics known since at least the time of Adam Smith: "Technology changes. Economic laws do not."[105] Furthermore, as numerous studies have indicated about many industries, the concentration of new industries in specific geographies speeds up the creation of industry identity, synergies in skills and knowledge (as in the Semiconductor Industry), and national competitive positions.[106]

So, what are we to conclude from the study of these three high-tech industries? The evidence suggests that Shapiro and Varian were right: industries behave like industries. Adoption of computer applications followed a pattern evident in many industries, with only the specifics and speed of adoption really subject to great variation. These two observations tell us that there is value in looking over the fence to see what one can learn from other industries. It means that technologies and practices were portable across firms and industries, and nations as well.

We will next exercise these two premises by glancing over the fence at industries considered radically different from manufacturing, those concerned with the distribution and trade of goods. The next several chapters are not so different from the first seven because, increasingly over the last half-century, the activities of trade and manufacturing industries have merged more closely together because information technology made it possible to more tightly couple supply chains, from manufacturing to retail. Over time, manufacturers extended their supply chains (e.g., automotive), and some retailers performed the same function by extending their supply chains back into manufacturing (e.g., Wal-Mart). The injection of computing into supply chains increased the interdependencies and integration of industries to such an extent that we can begin to understand why some observers think traditional industries are disintermediating. In fact, what has been happening slowly for many decades, and at increasing speeds during the 1990s, has not been so much the disintermediation of industries as the further integration of their processes across industries to improve speed to market, price performance, and the ever-continuing initiatives to constrain rivals and increase market shares. In the process, they created a certain amount of confusion about industry boundaries.[107]

8

Business Practices and Digital Applications in the Transformation of Transportation Industries: Trains and Trucks

Today's sophisticated carriers are equipping their vehicles with onboard
computers and communications systems that keep the drivers in constant
contact with their dispatchers and clients.

—Anonymous Transportation Industry consultant, 1997

Goods moved physically through the economy from manufacturing, in the form of parts and subassemblies, and then from production to customers, to retail outlets where they were sold, and to the ultimate consumer. This pattern has not changed for at least 2,500 years; and indeed it is the ultimate description of what occurs in any economy: making, selling, and buying. In modern times, most goods were distributed to the ultimate consumer through a complex network of wholesale and retail outlets. Transportation provided the physical link between manufacturing and distribution to consumers. Through the second half of the twentieth century, the most fundamental trend in transportation involved its continuous integration backward into manufacturing and forward into retailing processes. That historic trend enabled the closer ties between manufacturing and distribution industries noted throughout this book, largely because of their ability to share and integrate

227

their collective use of information with which they ran individual firms and industries.

That historic process of integration occurred in a variety of ways and resulted in one of the most efficient supply systems in existence in any modern national economy. It included the design and use of vehicles that worked well in transportation and in factories, warehouses, and stores. Standard sizes of containers, labels (including bar codes), and compatible equipment for loading and moving parts and goods emerged constantly through the period. The ability to take a trailer from a large freight-hauling 18-wheeler and put it on a railcar or ship, both designed for that purpose, is an example of the combined processes of integration and deployment of common standards. When historian Thomas P. Hughes studied the role of systems, he recognized the rising tides of holistic, integrated processes and approaches that had come into full force by the 1960s in the United States.[1] In this chapter and across all the other chapters, I contend that the process of standardization and integration of both processes and technical systems that Hughes was wise enough to discover proved far more extensive than he might have imagined. In fact, one can argue that these trends fundamentally changed how the economy worked at the street level, with important influences on the makeup of industries and their surprising integration or desegregation. Nowhere do all of these activities appear so conveniently evident than in the Transportation Industry.

A fundamental driving force that made it possible for these historic processes to occur has been the deployment of digital technology across all transportation industries, following many of the patterns evident in both manufacturing and retailing industries. In other words, if the transportation industries had not used computer and telecommunications technologies as other industries did, the efficiencies noted in previous chapters could not have occurred, nor could the raft of changes in the relationships between retailers and manufacturers that had developed by the end of the twentieth century. In short, the glue that held compatibility and integration together from one sector of the economy to another was the collection of information systems deployed in so many industries. Almost every one of them, if not all, involved the use of computers, telecommunications, and embedded digital processors (chips) in a wide variety of machines and other objects. The ability of information systems to transmit data among themselves and with employees became just as much a revolutionary transformation in transportation as in manufacturing and retailing.

In the second half of the twentieth century there were essentially four ways to move goods through the economy: by trains, trucks, airplanes and ships and barges. All participated actively in the profound changes that occurred in transportation. Roughly 80 percent of all goods moved across the global landscape of advanced economies by trains and trucks, especially in North America. Ships continued to be used for transport outside the United States and on major rivers, and deployment of aircraft increased, especially for small package deliveries. But because of the importance of trains and trucks, examining their use of the digital illustrates how all forms of transportation applied computing in the development of new, more

A railroad yardmaster used computer-generated reports to make up trains of freight cars. This is an example from the late 1950s, by which time computers were in wide use to help manage freight car inventory. Courtesy IBM Corporate Archives.

efficient distribution and logistical processes. Thus, for example, when one looks at the use of satellites to track moving trucks, be assured that the same application was being used to monitor ship traffic. Following Vilfredo Pareto's 80/20 rule, and looking at the experience of trains and trucks, we can illustrate the interconnections between manufacturing and retailing and the informational exchanges that made it possible, for example, to deploy JIT processes across the entire American economy. In such an analysis one sees further evidence of holistic changes fundamental to the activities of many business enterprises.

The story that follows is more than a tale of trains and trucks and adopting technologies to improve their efficiencies and competitiveness. It is also an account of how technologies made it easier for certain types of goods to move more efficiently, as well as more and more by truck instead of by train. What is not discussed is the story of the rise of air transport as an increasingly attractive way to move goods, mainly because at the end of the twentieth century it still represented only a small portion of the total picture. However, we should recognize that air transport has become increasingly integrated with ground transportation, particularly for the movement of small packages. We have only to remind ourselves of UPS and Federal Express, both of which use a combination of trucks, aircraft, and computers to integrate transportation and logistical processes in order to provide highly reliable, cost-effective, fast, and novel services (e.g., next-day delivery).[2] The other glaring omission in this chapter is the use of light trucks, vans, and automobiles by consumers to carry home their purchases. This last leg of the transportation process lies outside the scope of my study since the use of the digital by consumers is already accounted for in my discussion about innovations in modern automobiles and in the review of how consumers bought over the Internet, a topic explored more fully in subsequent chapters on retailing practices.

Railroad Industry

No historian of nineteenth-century American history could ignore the reality that railroads were the ultimate high-tech industry of the day. Steam technologies, trains, tracks, the telegraph, the modern corporation, even the emergence of the job of manager, all derived from the development and expansion of railroads. Every major new information technology developed in the nineteenth and twentieth century found extensive users in this industry. Although it is usual in the late twentieth century to think of railroads as old-fashioned, along with the telegraph business and the Morse code, at one time they led the way in creating modern commercial enterprises. Alfred D. Chandler, Jr., the universally acknowledged dean of business history, stated that "railroads were the most numerous, their activities the most complex, and their influence the most pervasive."[3] Railroads made it possible for the emergence of both mass production and merchandising because this form of transportation could deliver goods all over the nation in sufficient quantity and at affordable prices. They facilitated the development and growth of the industries discussed throughout this book during the last decades of the nineteenth century and through the first half of the twentieth. In fact, Chandler, who is normally circumspect in his use of adjectives, spoke of the changes wrought by the railroads as a "revolution," not so different in scope as might now be occurring with the deployment of the digital.[4] Thus, it should come as no surprise that in 1950 railroads were ubiquitous and served as the most complex and integrated transportation system in the nation, linked to manufacturers and retailers across the continent of North America and even into portions of Central America.

The volume of freight hauled in the 1950s and 1960s remained consistent and high, declining after trucking became a more widespread alternative mode for transporting goods. However, all through the second half of the twentieth century, manufacturers and wholesalers still transported their heaviest cargoes by train. These included agricultural products (e.g., grain and corn), livestock, ores (e.g., coal and iron), chemicals (both liquid and powder), forest products, and manufactured goods (e.g., trucks and military armament). In the first 15 years of the computer era, railroad revenues from freight traffic ranged between $8.1 and $8.5 billion. For purposes of comparison, passenger traffic in those years declined from a high of $213 million in 1955 to less than $95 million in the mid-1960s, by which time automobiles and airplanes had cut deeply into the railroad's passenger market.[5] At the end of the 1960s, however, railroading was still big business; one out of every four employees in transportation worked in this industry. At the start of the 1950s, railroads hauled over 60 percent of the nation's freight, and at the end of the 1960s, still over 40 percent. In subsequent years its percentage of share declined, although

Table 8.1

Relative Size of Various U.S. Transportation Industries, 1970–1996 (Number of Vehicles in Millions)*

Mode	1970	1980	1990	1996
Single-unit trucks	0.90	1.41	1.70	1.74
Class 1 rail freight cars	1.42	1.17	0.66	0.57
Other rail freight cars	0.36	0.54	0.55	0.67

*Data rounded.

Source: Modified from table 2 in Bureau of Transportation Statistics, *Pocket Guide to Transportation* (Washington, D.C.: U.S. Department of Transportation, 1998): 4.

revenues expanded through the 1970s and 1980s at an annual rate of 0.4 percent, whereas worker productivity grew by 4.7 percent. These data clearly reflect the use of a variety of new technologies to improve performance, such as the deployment of diesel locomotives to haul longer trains, using larger cars, as well as computing to manage the logistical network.[6]

All during the second half of the twentieth century, this industry experienced intense and growing competition for freight and passenger business, which compelled it to adopt a broad range of technological innovations, which in hindsight proved effective in lowering operating costs while improving productivity. The industry also underwent a continual, multidecade process of consolidation into fewer, larger firms, a process that extended to the end of the 1990s. This consolidation promoted the further use of common standards, practices, and technologies, reflecting a pattern of constant integration and coordination that had been underway for over a century. By the end of the 1960s, computers were beginning to play an important role in the historic process of coordination and, increasingly, centralized control, and they contributed to improved productivity of workers and rolling stocks.

Table 8.1 provides a brief picture of the relative size of various transportation industries, as measured by the number of vehicles in use in commercially moving goods. These data reaffirm the continued importance of railroads at the end of the twentieth century. Table 8.2 catalogs employment populations, again demonstrating the large number of workers in transportation. But note how employment in the Railroad Industry declined substantially over time, evidence of productivity gains within the industry, on the one hand, and, on the other hand, the results of effective competition at work from the Trucking Industry.

IT Deployment

Railroads had a long history of using various forms of telecommunications and data processing. Besides the telegraph, they used every other form of communications that came along: telephony, radio, EDI, cell phones, and satellites. It was one of the first industries in the private sector to use punch-card equipment, and it became

Table 8.2
Employment in U.S. Transportation Industries, 1970–1996 (Number in Millions) *

Industry	1970	1980	1990	1996
Railroad	0.63	0.53	0.28	0.23
Trucking and warehousing	1.13	1.28	1.63	1.64
Air	0.35	0.45	0.75	1.12
Transportation services	0.12	0.20	0.36	0.42
Water	0.21	0.21	0.18	0.17

*Data rounded.

Source: Modified from table 14 in Bureau of Transportation Statistics, *Pocket Guide to Transportation* (Washington, D.C.: U.S. Department of Transportation, 1998): 22.

a major customer for almost every type of adding and calculating machine available in the twentieth century. Applications of these technologies reflected practices evident in other industries: accounting, finance, rolling stock inventory control, tracking train inventories, maintenance records, logistics, payroll, and so forth. In the 1950s, railroad companies were some of the largest enterprises that could afford to use computers. For example, IBM targeted this industry for its early systems, such as the IBM 705, to generate and track waybills, to track requisitions for parts and supplies used in repair and maintenance, and to monitor movement of trains. As in other industries, the IBM 650 computer system of the mid- to late 1950s proved to be a popular technology. The New York Central Railroad, for example, installed five of them, then a RAMAC, and later a 705. This railroad began to use a 650 in 1955, primarily for car accounting, payroll, and collecting statistics. Data on the movement and status of locomotives, cars, and trains were added over the next two years. As in manufacturing firms, one reason the 650 appeared in this industry was because of its ability to process more data more quickly than previous information-handling systems, performing essentially the same applications as before.[7]

Because of the huge stock of railroad cars, locomotives, and other equipment that moved constantly across the nation, routinely shared by various railroads, processes for accounting and tracking had long been a mainstay of data processing in the industry. Computers were quickly installed to handle these same applications. Punch cards which had been used to track a car's identity, destination, contents, and so forth before the arrival of the computer were now used with mainframes in the 1960s and 1970s, and afterward mainframes (and key-to-disk devices were the key data-transfer medium. This application made it possible for railroads to increase the timeliness of information about the location of cars and freight, both for the line (mainly for tracking and planning purposes) and for customers eager to learn the status of their deliveries.

Keeping track of cars—by using waybills describing their origins, destination, and content—proved central to any improved efficiency. Without good records, a car with freight could sit in a railyard for days while employees figured out whose merchandise was on board or how best to deploy an empty car. By the mid-1960s, having information online, instead of in batch cards and reports, improved the accuracy and timeliness of the process. Online systems also improved worker productivity since now one individual could handle three to four times as many queries as before. The use of CRTs illustrated how a new technology changed the way in which employees worked. A description of the change, written in 1965, is worth quoting:

> This was not only due to the electronic as opposed to the mechanical speed of the device, but in large part due to the fact that each CRT display unit had its own buffer memory so that all the operators can key in requests at the same time. In addition, characters are brought out in less than a second and it is therefore possible to tell the operator the whole story on a car rather than just the last movement. The advantage of this is that the operator can often see from the supplementary material displayed, the reason for a car's delay or something peculiar in the nature of the shipment and so inform the customer.[8]

The application continued to evolve, even acquiring an industry-wide name, Automatic Car Identification System (ACI), one that railroads continued to enhance with new media, software, and applications for the rest of the century.

In the 1960s and continuing to the present, railroads used computers to improve the efficiencies and effectiveness of dispatching and scheduling, enhancing these applications at the same time that they were changing their inventory control processes. By the early 1970s, scheduling and dispatching had become a whole set of processes that relied extensively on computers and software tools known as centralized traffic control (CTC). These applications had a similar look and feel to the central pipeline management control systems deployed by the Petroleum Industry at the same time. The adoption of computers between the 1950s and the mid-1970s, however, proved to be a gradual process, focusing primarily on cost reductions, particularly in labor, and in increasing the loads that rolling stocks could handle. At the same time, computers provided improved services, including more current information to customers about the status of their shipments. The lion's share of improvements in technology—as measured in terms of capital expended—occurred in improved locomotives and cars and in the introduction of piggyback (truck trailers) cars and unit trains (which carry only one type of freight, like coal or chemicals).

Computers came into their own between 1957 and 1967. Digital and analog tools were adopted to control car speeds and to aid in switching, first in large yards, later in smaller ones. In 1957, 20 yards used such tools; by the end of 1967 that number had increased to over 50, with 3 small classifications yards[9] using computers. Further automation of yard traffic added another dozen or so in the early 1970s. The first use of digital computers occurred in 1955, and 192 digital computers were installed across this industry by the end of 1967, by the end of 1969, that population had grown to 252 systems. In the early 1970s, all large railroad companies (Class I companies) used computers. However, most firms were new to computing.[10] One study of the period indicated that in early 1965, of all the railroads that had adopted computers, only 4 percent had had them for seven or more years, which was about the same percentage in most manufacturing industries. Yet, unlike in manufacturing, deployment came slower in railroads. The same study indicated, for example, that 91 percent of all railroads had adopted computers for the first time only in the 1960s.[11]

Using CTC applications to control the movement of trains over 50 to 100 miles of track became a major application in the 1960s.[12] To deploy such an automated system, railroads had to install analog sensors on tracks and to centralize data collection and command-and-control processes. In 1957, only 32,000 miles of track out of a total inventory of 269,000 miles of lines were managed with CTC applications; by the end of 1967, deployment had extended to 49,000 miles out of 254,000 miles of track. The ACI applications were standardized in the early 1970s, which in combination with detectors, sensors, microwaves, and other systems made it possible to enhance automated tracking of trains. Tracking went electronic and paper records declined sharply, along with the confusions and delays inherent in older approaches. Simulating alternative routing became widespread by the 1970s, as it would be in trucking in the 1980s.[13]

Before discussing the developments of the 1970s and 1980s, I should note that railroad companies had also become enamored in the 1960s with the same kinds of ideas about total, comprehensive systems that automated vast amounts of work in manufacturing companies and in the Trucking Industry. Recall that the concept, normally called Total Systems or some variant of the term, but always with the word *total* in the title, called for extensive use of computers in highly integrated applications, cutting across many functional areas. Advocates in the Railroad Industry argued for integration of systems and applications and real-time data collection and transmission, all worthy in a complex industry that was critical to the economic and military welfare of the nation. Its advocates confidently declared its advantages:

> The benefits of the total information system may be broadly stated in three groups: 1) the reduction in operating expenses through better management control, 2) an improvement in net profit by providing better management tools for the better utilization of resources, and 3) the reduction of clerical personnel through better data handling.[14]

Although the language was all too familiar to anyone buying IT products in any decade during the second half of the twentieth century, it was the basis for most justifications of digital applications.

Then, as now, it remained more of a wish than a reality, although each industry attempted to move in that direction. Thus at the dawn of the twenty-first century, much work was already integrated electronically—but not in the 1960s and 1970s. The pioneer in the Railroad Industry was the Southern Pacific Company, working in tandem with IBM. This railroad's version was called TOPS, or Total Operations Processing System. Beginning in the 1960s and through the 1970s, the line continued to add to it. An early adopter of computing applications, the Southern Pacific could attempt to create TOPS because it had already put in place many of the key applications (with the concommitment requirement of having DP expertise in house) and an effective telecommunications system. Southern Pacific's infrastructure in the 1950s included IBM 650s and an IBM 704, and in 1961 it installed an IBM 1401. These systems did waybill revenue accounting, handled centralized payroll, did car equipment and disbursement accounting, processed freight claims, managed materials control, and generated a variety of reports on traffic. When IBM introduced the System 360 family of computers in the mid-1960s, Southern Pacific acquired one also, a Model 30 for accounting applications.

Management became interested in pursuing TOPS for two reasons: first, to reduce the cost and burden of clerical work in yards, agencies, and general accounting departments and, second, to provide management at all levels with accurate, timely information on such issues as utilization of cars, locomotives, and terminal facilities. By the late 1960s, the company had installed 420 terminals at 300 locations and collected data on some 100 events. A raft of reports on these activities were then produced and disseminated across the company.[15] Table 8.3 lists the kinds of activities about which the railroad company collected data. I cite this list because all other railroads in one manner or another did the same, either manually or, in time, by using software and sensors. The company's telecommunications network was used to transmit data to collection centers and then to send reports throughout the enterprise. The network in the late 1960s consisted of nearly 3,400 miles of microwave, and it continued the use of teletype systems. In short, this was a primitive EDI-like network, with data rather than voice moving information across the company and at the time considered state of the art.[16]

Despite the implementation of various digital and analog applications in the 1950s and 1960s, it was not until the following decade that massive deployment occurred across the industry, involving a variety of uses that went past traditional accounting and financial applications. However, the introduction of computers into

Table 8.3
Types of Activities Tracked by Computers by Southern Pacific Railroad, Circa 1969

Cars interchanged	Manifests and passings from other roads
Cars to and from industry tracks	Train accounting
Cars loaded or emptied	Train arrivals and departures
Waybill data on every loaded car	Work performed
Cars bad ordered	Locomotives assignments/status
Cars to and from cleaning tracks	Locomotive maintenance
Service requests	Caboose ssignments/status
Hold and diversion requests	Crew assignments
Car orders	Waybill revenue data and collections
Car distribution orders	

Source: Adopted from data in IBM, *Total Operations Processing System for the Southern Pacific Company* (White Plains, N.Y.: IBM Corp., 1969): 4, "DP Application Briefs," Box B-116-3, IBM Archives, Somers, N.Y.

the industry in the 1950s and 1960s had a sufficiently positive effect on railroads that they were encouraged to embrace computing more aggressively in the following decade. A combination of factors led to this positive experience. One analyst summed up the confluence of applications and effects at the end of the 1960s:

> A good many railroads adopted centralized data processing fairly early in the life of the first generation computer. Together the decline in passenger traffic, the substitution of Centralized Train Control for telegraph and train order, and the increased use of other business machines and labor-saving forms, greatly reduced the number of clerical workers required.[17]

When the same commentator noted that the number of clerical workers in the Railroad Industry had declined, the combined population of clerical employees and professional and general workers dropped from 234,387 in 1946 to 138,273 in 1966. As in other industries, shrinking one's work force remained an important objective for senior management at all railroad companies. Computers, operating in tandem with other technologies (e.g., bigger trains) and in the context of market realities (e.g., decline in passenger business), reflected patterns of interest and adoption that were seen in other industries. Of course, part of the decline in the number of workers could be accounted for by the loss of market share to trucking firms. Nonetheless, the role of computing in this area should not be discounted.

A BLS study from the late 1970s identified over 80 yards that had automated classification functions for cars and locomotives, making it possible to reduce the number of yard supervisors and yard crews. Switching applications became relatively widespread, reducing the number of clerks needed. The BLS reported that by the mid-1970s, all Class I companies used digital computers and that over 20 percent of tracks were under the control of CTC applications.[18]

By the mid-1980s, the portfolio of applications then in use by American railroads included an array of deployments for maintenance and engineering, marketing, office systems, and more enhanced rail operations. In the last group, computers were routinely used for freight data entry and waybill management, car movement control reporting, crew management, terminal management, transportation planning, car scheduling, and intermodal terminal management—all applications that had now become ubiquitous in the industry. By this period, railroad-centric accounting applications had evolved through at least two generations of data-processing technologies and applications, as IT moved from primitive batch to online systems, from standalone files to databases. Mature applications in accounting included freight revenue accounting, car accounting, demurrage accounting, computer assisted rating, and freight filling.[19]

The digital had become embedded in technological innovations that in earlier decades would not have been combined in any assessment of computer usage. For example, microcomputers had now been embedded in locomotives to help in collecting performance information to assist in maintaining these new machines. They performed diagnostics on problems and provided information in support of preventive maintenance activities. In the 1980s, such systems were part and parcel of modern locomotives; by the 1990s, many older locomotives had been retrofitted with some of these tools. In addition, CTC continued to expand, covering 30 percent of all track miles, up from roughly 22 percent in 1972. Virtually all classification yards had become extensive users of computers to track cars and to monitor and determine their deployment. But CTC was the major application of the period because the movement of rolling stocks remained a major opportunity for improved performance and cost cutting. As one report from the mid-1980s explained:

> Advantages of CTC include the capability of routing trains to minimize delays; decreasing fuel and track requirements, including maintenance and capital costs; eliminating written train orders; improving communications between dispatchers and train crews; and lowering labor costs for train crews, dispatchers, signal operators, and track maintenance crews.[20]

Computer-aided dispatching (CAD) was the major innovation of the early to mid-1980s, considered in the industry as a further enhancement of CTC in support of the overall objective of deploying computing to improve operations across an entire railroad. Thus CAD used software to notify dispatchers what routes they had to work with, considerations to keep in mind, and routes to assign. Dispatchers could accept these recommendations or override them. Routine traffic was increasingly directed by such digital applications, making it possible for dispatchers to expand the number of miles of rail lines that any individual could manage.[21]

Implementation of computerized tools and applications improved productivity while the industry was simultaneously shrinking, helping to make it possible for many lines to remain profitable, primarily by driving down the cost of labor and improving the utilization of rolling stock. The number of employees dropped from a high of 590,000 in 1970 to 300,400 in 1986,[22] and remaining employees had to acquire more technical skills to survive. Employment continued to decline to the end of the century, while technical skills increased generally across most professions as computer-based tools became the norm, from the humble word processor in the office to the complex CAD/CTC systems.[23]

Recent Trends

The industry enhanced its telecommunications linkages to its digital applications through the 1980s and 1990s, going through new rounds of integration as railroad companies merged. The Internet and EDI were subsumed into existing infrastructures. To a large extent, these actions were extensions of long-standing patterns of usage. For example, railroads had been some of the earliest adopters of EDI, dating back to the early 1960s, and for the same reasons they had been early users of the telegraph. In fact, EDI in transportation appeared first in railroads, then spread to other industries like trucking and airlines. The ability of railroads to refurbish and update their communications infrastructures was made possible by the continued resurgence in business, particularly in the 1990s. Between 1990 and 1997, railroad traffic increased by nearly 48 percent, and the industry had, since 1985, enjoyed annual growth in revenues of 4.1 percent. By the late 1990s, there were some 40 regional railroads and 7 Class I systems, making all of these companies complex, with large rolling stocks all over the nation, and capable of investing in IT.[24] With the resurgence of business came additional pressures from customers to streamline the flow of data, reduce paperwork, and provide more real-time information. Customers forced B2B exchange of data on the railroads, and in turn, rail management saw these uses of computing as a way of enhancing their competitive position. Bills of lading, for example, became more detailed and went online.[25]

However, railroads continued to adopt new applications and technologies slowly. This became obvious whenever a railroad company had to link its IT applications to those in other industries. This problem had ebbed and flowed over the years, notably with trucking firms and shipping lines, most dramatically with the former. Trailers pulled by trucks had also been transported by trains for several decades—known as intermodal transportation—and as reliance on combined truck-train transportation grew, so did pressure for tighter integration. Pressure from trucking firms started in the 1980s, and extended through the 1990s because the volume of trailers hauled by railroads had continued to increase at the rate of between 3 and 5 percent each year. Railroads had moved 3.1 million trailers in 1980 and 8.8 million in 1998, and now these trailers accounted for 17 percent of all rail revenue. Only coal transportation proved to be a larger market segment (23 percent). So the pressure to integrate data and to coordinate the movement of trailers simply grew. Greg Stefflre, a lawyer in the transportation industry, described the important state of affairs at the end of the century: "There's poor communication among the parties and not much use of modern technology to speed the interchange process."[26] Leaders in the Trucking Industry complained that railroads were simply too focused on mergers and acquisitions.

But consolidations had their effects on the use of computing. At the end of the century, five North American railroads began to experiment with virtual marketplace applications. Called Railmarketplace.com and introduced in early 2001, it coordinated activities of the Burlington Northern Santa Fe, Canadian National, Canadian Pacific Railway, Norfolk Southern, and the Union Pacific. This network provided the necessary flows of information for buying and selling and streamlining purchases, as well as expanding trading communities. The B2B applications were brought on stream, some through that site, others using iRail.com, which already existed to support the passenger transit portion of the industry. Railmarketplace.com focused on automating requisition and purchase order applications and was linked to manufacturers of railroad cars and supplies. As seen in so many other industries, the intent was less to help customers directly as to reduce operating costs. In comparison to manufacturing industries, railroads came late to online B2B applications but, when they did, borrowed from the experiences of manufacturing companies. Thus, the kind of collaboration between suppliers and customers, to information on needs and forecasts, was new to this industry at the end of the century.[27]

I want to end this short overview of the Railroad Industry with an account of one transformation that epitomized the important changes that occurred: the end of the caboose. These were the colorful cars that were attached to the ends of trains for over a century. Only the locomotive had as much charisma (if it is possible to say that machines can have this characteristic). Cabooses were a base of operations for conductors and brake operators. Many movies showed the interior to be fitted with a stove and a pot of hot coffee. But they were also offices in which the conductor could fill out his paperwork—he was responsible for all the documentation associated with the operation of his train. Brake operators monitored from this car the functioning of the brake system, overheating axles, and gears. Blame the computer for the demise of the caboose because with the arrival of centralized traffic control, digitized record keeping, and radio communications between dispatchers and conductors, the old requirement for onboard paper handling by the conductor disappeared in the late 1970s and through the 1980s. When work rules changed, and crews no longer had to spend their nights on trains, even the dormlike mission of the caboose also disappeared. Electronic sensors on brakes, axles, and other parts eliminated the need for an onboard crew to stand watch. Electronic monitors mounted on the last car of a train also provided continuous feedback on air brake pressure to the engineer in the locomotive.

By the mid-1980s, it was not uncommon to see trains without cabooses. In fact, in 1985, nearly 1,000 trains were cabooseless. The demise of the caboose was a good thing for the railroads. A typical caboose weighed 30 tons, and now fuel did not have to be expended in hauling it around. In addition, no longer did a railroad have to spend annually, on average $36,000 (in 1985) to maintain each caboose or replace older ones, from time to time, at an average cost of $80,000 apiece. The decline in the number of employees riding on a train also drove down operating costs, and the use of sensors and other technologies improved the quality of planned and unplanned maintenance.[28] Like the last scene in what may have been one of the greatest western movies ever filmed, *The Man Who Shot Liberty Valence* (1962), staring Jimmy Stewart and John Wayne, the caboose traveled off into the distant horizon of the nation's history. Only the locomotive looked essentially the same; however, it had changed into a far more powerful machine, loaded with analog sensors and digitally based applications that monitored everything, from oil pressure to how fast the train should go, and communicated with dispatchers through satellites, GPS, and other digital systems.

Trucking Industry

Countless American movies and novels have portrayed truck drivers and their industry as something less than sophisticated or high-tech. Scandals and bad press for decades have characterized its trade union (Teamsters) as a barrier to improved productivity. Yet the historical record presents a far different picture of this industry. The most obvious point to make is that the Trucking Industry embraced computing and other technological innovations when they made economic sense in support of improved productivity or because manufacturers and retailers forced the industry to integrate into their own systems, such as JIT processes. Whereas the application of the digital varied over time and across the industry, the world of trucking also changed profoundly between 1950 and the end of the century. Part of the change can be attributed to IT but even more to a variety of other factors, such as the construction of faster, safer national highways all over the United States; the use of larger trucks and detachable container vehicles; and most important, pressure from the industry's customers to integrate the Trucking Industry's own operations with those of other sectors of the economy.

This last point cannot be emphasized enough because, unlike trains—which handled primarily raw materials and freight far too heavy, bulky, or voluminous for trucks to carry for practical or economic reasons—the Trucking Industry interacted with all sizes of companies in every industry and, because they were not restricted to travel on rails, could go to every building on almost every road in North America. Trains ran on tracks, and their customer sets were far more limited. For instance, trains did not deliver consumer goods to stores—at best, they delivered to some very large wholesalers and even then, only to some—but rather to factories and to other large, specialized businesses, such as book, magazine, and newspaper printing plants. Trucks moved more hours per day than trains (e.g., 16 to 18, in the 1950s versus 2 to 6 for trains), whereas trains spent vast quantities of time each day in classification yards and terminals (hence the reason for so much interest in using computers to optimize car management and utilization).[29] In short, the Trucking Industry was so aligned with the Retail Industry that it could be considered an extension of it. As providers of components to manufacturing, trucking had indeed become an integral part, even an extension, of many industrial industries. Whereas the Railroad Industry could adopt technology largely at its own pace to satisfy its own agenda until at least the early to mid-1980s, the Trucking Industry could not; it was too closely linked to the activities of its customers.

In fact, in many cases, truckers were part of their customers' enterprises because some manufacturers and retailers operated their own fleets of trucks. Even the U.S. Postal Service (not even called the post office anymore)—for many decades the largest employer of civilians in the United States—had its own fleets of trucks, and at the end of the century, so did Wal-Mart, then the largest retailer in the world and now also one of the largest employers in the United States. Commercial truckers thus faced pressure to improve operations from within their own ranks. The press for productivity and improved services extended beyond the normal competition that one would expect among commercial trucking firms. These competitive influences manifested themselves most extensively as the effects of government deregulation of the industry unfolded in the early 1980s, at the same time that manufacturing and retailing industries were extending their supply chains forward and backward, respectively. As one result, trucking enterprises became far more high tech than one might have predicted in 1950. At the risk of putting too fine a point on the observation, truck drivers—more than an iconoclastic image of the fiercely independent American, almost the alternative cowboy of the twentieth century—were major players in the digitization of work in modern America.

Even if we leave aside the fact that this industry was highly integrated into the manufacturing, wholesale, and retail industries, it was a large industry on its own as measured by traditional economic metrics. The Trucking Industry in the United States in 1996 (to use a recent data point just as the Internet was becoming important), it made up 3.1 percent of the GDP, or 65 percent of all transportation services.[30]

This industry, much like the Railroad Industry, was not normally on the minds of those who commented on the Information Age, the digital economy, and the age of the computer. Even surveys of the American economy of the late twentieth century either ignored both industries or gave them short shrift, often lumping trucks, trains, planes, and ships into the ambiguous term *transportation*.[31] Yet because of its pivotal position in the economy, trucking could not be ignored in any assessment of how work and industries changed because of the digital. Its importance is made even more evident when we consider that the proportion of all goods and materials that moved across this nation by truck increased steadily over the past half century, taking market share away from railroads and all kinds of waterborne craft. It continued to move far more tons than airlines, despite some inroads by the latter into the transportation market very late in the century.

As measured by ton-miles (one ton of freight hauled one mile), in 1950 truckers hauled 15.8 percent of the nation's total; railroads carried 57.4 percent. Ten years later (1960), truckers transported 22.2 percent of the total, railroads 44.3 percent, demonstrating that the shift to trucks was underway. This process of growth continued slowly over the next few decades.[32] By the late 1990s, truckers hauled 60 percent of the nation's freight; of course, the total volume of freight hauled by all types of transporters had grown substantially over the past half century too.[33] This industry collected 81 percent of the total revenues expended for freight in the mid-1990s; annual growth rates of 2 to 2.8 percent were typical.[34]

After deregulation in 1980, the industry constantly experienced intense competition and low margins and was often affected by the relative ease of entry into the business by individuals or small firms. Capacity grew; by the late 1990s, over 3,000 carriers per year entered the market. This highly fragmented industry ended the century with over 500,000 interstate carriers, of which some 30,000 were for-hire carriers; the rest were private fleets.[35] Many of the largest trucking enterprises and their emerging rivals leveraged technological innovations to improve their relative performance, which in turn made them more attractive than railroads as freight haulers.

The Trucking Industry is normally characterized by the size of the loads carried: truckload, less than truckload, and package express. The first category involves truckers who haul full loads long distances. In the second smaller loads, from several customers, are consolidated to gain economies of scale. The third haul small loads, such as the packages delivered to houses and offices by Federal Express or UPS. A new category of firms began to emerge in the 1990s in response to customers' interest in having truckers handle more of the logistical tasks previously done by wholesalers and retailers. The heart of logistics is the management of information to get goods to the right place at the right time and, of course, at a competitive price. The largest firms in the industry moved rapidly to provide logistical services to remain competitive. Companies found these services useful, a crucial element in their attempts to lower the costs of inventory and reduce cycle time. Whereas the process of integrating truckers into that effort began in the 1980s, it reached full stride in the 1990s. If a trucker could perform logistical services better or faster than a manufacturer, wholesaler, or retailer, especially if they could be provided at lower cost, truckers often won the business.

Before we explore the industry's situation in the late twentieth century, in which it led with IT to be competitive and to grow, the historical experience of earlier years has to be accounted for because prior activities influenced the industry's ability to leverage information, communications, and computers in the late 1900s.

IT Deployment

Trucking firms always had several problems that lent themselves to the use of communications and computing technologies. Like trains and airplanes, they roamed all over the large landmass of the United States and Canada. Managers had to track their vehicles and the freight they carried, and they had to optimize the use of trucks to drive down costs, optimize profits, and provide competitive, timely services. Almost every form of communication that came along found a home in this industry: shortwave radio, onboard PCs to communicate with satellites, and cell phones. The industry was heavily regulated by government agencies, even after deregulation began in 1980, and customers wanted careful record keeping, too, which generated a great deal of paperwork for this industry. Changes in the flow of freight from one locale to another, from one trucker to another, from truck to train, or from train to truck, all added to the complexity of keeping up with the flow of data. Data were necessary to bill, to make corrections and adjustments, and so forth, much as in the Railroad Industry. So just as computers were brought into the Railroad Industry, they were brought into the Trucking Industry, although a few years later. The delay was primarily due to the fact that firms were smaller and thus did not have the same economic wherewithal to embrace the new technology as rail lines did.[36] Larger trucking firms had used punch-card technologies before the arrival of the computer for such applications as accounting and freight inventory control, many beginning in the 1930s and 1940s. Eliminating paperwork was the most pervasive justification for moving to such technologies and, later, to computers because of the complexity of data handling and the associated high cost of labor. The central piece of data needed to run the business was the freight bill. To put this class of documents in perspective, in the early 1960s, over 221 million were in use by Class I motor carriers (470 firms), each costing a trucking firm on average $16.69 to generate and use. One trucking executive in the mid-1960s explained the problem his industry faced: "A single piece of freight shipped on our line only, between two points such as Chicago-Memphis, creates a clerical handling requirement involving 15 different people and over 40 different handlings of the bill not including data processing coding and punching steps."[37] Computers made it possible to combine data from freight bills with other information, such as maintenance labor, tractor and trailer utilization, and other operations, to improve management's control over the efficiency and cost of doing business.

The need to drive down costs in the early 1960s—when the industry first embraced the computer—was intense. For every dollar of revenue billed, a firm could expect to make only 5 cents; therefore, if a rival lowered its charges by only 5 percent, a trucker's profit could be wiped out. This industry also had some of the highest costs for clerks in American industry, driven up over the years by the fact that they were members of the Teamsters Union, which had negotiated some of the highest salaries in the American economy. So the hunt for productivity had started early in this industry, and the computer was brought into play once it became cost-competitive with earlier data-processing technologies to help control these expenses. But cutting clerical costs in a service-intense industry was never enough since the ratio of labor to revenue for large truckers hovered at 60 percent, whereas clerical labor was 6 percent. So firms also had to use computing in all kinds of operations to drive down costs—hence their interest in comparing multiple types of data to find ways to improve operational efficiencies.

At one firm, Gordons Transport, a Univac system went online in 1959, and by 1964, as one executive at the firm reported, "We have programmed just about every conceivable batch operation that we have felt would be economical on this equipment"; it was now contemplating a move to online systems, "which would give us the information we need to control costs in every department" because of the currency of data and the ability to compare multiple types of information.[38] Computer technology held out the promise of eliminating the repetitive handling of paper, retyping information from forms, and reprocessing punch cards and other documents through older data-processing equipment. Many other firms in the 1950s and early 1960s still manually processed freight bills, but by using computers were able to compare data, understand what kinds of profits were made by type of freight hauled, and so forth. The industry rarely used computers in the 1950s.[39]

There were some cases of early adopters. For example, one firm that installed an IBM 1140 system (and two 1311 disk drives) in 1964 eliminated many manual steps; for those steps that had involved punched cards, going online also reduced the number of paper files. Comparing data in a timely fashion made it possible to contain costs by allowing employees to determine the fastest, most economical method of shipping each item.[40]

By mid-decade, many of the bread-and-butter applications that had run on earlier forms of data processing or that were in wide use in other industries within the economy's transportation sector were being implemented in the Trucking Industry. In addition to freight bill applications, rafts of other reports were now being produced by computers: daily revenue edits, daily freight registers, cash receipts, decentralized cash applications, aged trial balances, centralized statements, bills, interline payables, commodity reports, accounts payable, payroll, and the usual general ledger functions of old. Profitability statements became an important new addition to the information pool available to management, including traffic line profit and loss analysis, terminal profit and loss reports, and customer profit and loss. Revenue and tonnage reports mimicked those in the Railroad Industry.[41] Increasingly during the decade, firms added more information-handling applications to their computers, involving maintenance control systems, terminal performance reporting, dispatch performance analysis, and claims management.[42] Such applications spread across the industry during the 1960s and 1970s and were adopted immediately by new firms that were entering the market in subsequent decades.

The industry in the 1970s was buffeted with large increases in the cost of fuel, which stimulated use of more diesel engines, twin trailers, and more efficient vehicles. The same oil embargo of 1973 that drove up the cost of fuel also caused federal and state governments to change speed limits, truck sizes, and weights. Labor costs represented about 60 percent of the total expenses of trucking companies during this decade, we and they also went up as the nation experienced double-digit inflation rates by the dawn of the 1980s. Interfirm freight consolidations increased, putting additional pressure on companies to track information on what they moved and how. Many of the computer applications they adopted in the 1970s thus extended what they had worked out in the 1960s. Nearly all Class I carriers routinely used computers in the 1970s, and Class II companies (smaller than Class I) rapidly adopted smaller, less expensive minicomputers to perform similar, if more limited, work. Rates, billing, and scheduling remained at the heart of how management deployed the digital. Using computers to control vehicles, drivers, and shipments played a lesser role but, by the end of the 1970s, expanded as the earlier wave of applications had been installed and used for years.[43]

One BLS survey at the dawn of the 1980s pointed out that computers had been installed in over 900 intercity trucking firms. But only about 40 percent of these companies had yet used computers to control equipment, such as monitoring maintenance or driver behavior. Load planning and communications had increased, and 40 percent were already applying the digital to these functions. Load planning made it easier for a company to deploy an empty or partially empty vehicle sooner, thereby generating more revenue than before while minimizing empty backhauls (a truck going back empty to its point of origin). Dispatching, using a combination of computer-based tracking of movements and telecommunications (including radio), also proved effective in controlling costs.[44] What is crucial to understand is that in the 1970s, as in the 1950s and 1960s, the Trucking Industry focused its use of computers on controlling costs and responding to regulatory requirements, all within a competitive environment. It would not be until the 1980s and 1990s that, these firms also had to respond to growing demands for logistical services by their customers.

Yet, as early as the dawn of the 1970s—before the oil embargo of 1973 had started to affect the industry—computers had already initiated the historic process of altering daily routine. Trade magazines, presenters at conferences, and observers of the industry were already documenting the change. Rather than fill the next several pages with a litany of testimonials, let one suffice. Treasurers of any company are notorious for controlling purse strings with a firm hand; the chief financial officer at Hollander Storage and Moving Company, Richard A. Hollander, proved to be no exception. Having a personal, as well as professional, stake in the success of this company gave him added incentives to make sure expenditures paid off; yet he commented less on cost savings and instead focused on the way IT had changed operations:

> Use of the Data Processing System has given my company the following bene-fits: Substantial reduction of time spent in securing van line revenue figures; handling of accounting procedures by less experienced employees. Since no figuring of percentages is needed, the computer is almost free of error. At all times, the company has a detailed report on what monies the van lines owes the company or vice versa.[45]

Hollander also noted that "the drivers' trip analysis—all are much improved over the difficult to compile types previously handled." But adoption remained anything but a simple process because of the complexity of the technology and, as could be heard in every industry, "newest computer discoveries are not always applicable to the moving and storage industry because of its very special nature."[46] Like others surveyed in this book, firms in the Trucking Industry had to learn how best to apply computer technology, matching operational needs to technical functions in ways that made sense.

The federal government took significant steps to deregulate many aspects of all transportation industries, including trucking, at the start of the 1980s, and this is a story that need not divert our attention. However, we have to recognize that deregulation stimulated more intense interest in improving operational efficiencies, thereby enhancing one's competitive position, and resulted in the growth of ever larger regional and national trucking firms. As enterprises grew in size, they needed better ways to manage larger quantities of assets and volumes of business across larger geographic areas, all prime targets for computer applications. By the mid-1980s, the industry had access to a variety of applications, home-grown software tools, and commercially available software packages. Table 8.4 lists some of the more widely adopted applications of the decade. Many of the items in this table were functions that had been performed before the arrival of the computer. Some had even been partially automated through the use of earlier data-processing tech-nologies (e.g., adding machines for accounting applications), but the important point is that by the mid-1980s all of these functions were also being performed by large enterprises that were using computers. One IBM study completed in 1988 documented the fact that there were commercially available software and installa-tion services from a variety of vendors (not just IBM) for each of the items cataloged in table 8.4. Some of these tools were also being installed by maritime and railroad firms as well, demonstrating once again the cross-industry movement of new ap-plications and software tools.[47] The market for such tools was large. In 1988, for example, there were over 39,000 Class I, II, and III trucking firms operating in the United States and an additional 100,000 to 150,000 owner-operators. However, Class I and II companies were the primary users of computers in this industry, operating millions of trucks. The entire industry also accounted for 4.9 percent of the nation's GNP, generated by hauling some 40 percent of the total intercity ton-

Table 8.4
Typical Computer Applications in the Trucking Industry, Mid-1980s

Motor Freight Accounting	Production Operations	Business Professional
Revenue accounting	Terminal/shipment control	Motor freight accounting
Freight claims accounting	Load monitoring	Performance analysis
Equipment accounting	Pickup/delivery	Terminal shipment control
Freight bill transmission	Shipment routing	Route/load optimization
Freight bill processing	Dock operations	Dock operations planning
Equipment inventory & control rating	Routing	
Terminal shipment control		
Load monitoring		
Pickup/delivery		
Shipment routing		

Source: IBM, *Applications and Abstracts* (White Plains, N.Y.: IBM Corp., 1985): 21-4–21-11.

nage carried that year by all forms of commercial transportation.[48] The industry was becoming more efficient and larger as the decade progressed.

Customers now began to influence more directly patterns of computer usage in the Trucking Industry. In the decades of the 1960s to mid-1980s, truckers deployed computing to improve internal operational efficiencies, but the emphasis then shifted to competitively attractive performance in the eyes of manufacturing, wholesaling, and retailing customers. This changed emphasis was at least as profound as had been deregulation at the start of the 1980s. I have already discussed the role of manufacturing in its relations with transportation, and I will have more to say about those interactions with retailers in subsequent chapters. However, a few summary comments are necessary, even at the risk of repetition, because of profound changes in the industry's reach. As the national highway system was built, beginning in the 1950s but essentially completed in the 1970s, truckers could reach vast new areas of the nation within hours or a day or two. Whole new communities sprang up, with new factories and shopping outlets scattered across the nation. Anyone driving through the United States in the last three decades of the twentieth century could not help but notice how the countryside was filling up or how cities in certain parts of the nation were growing rapidly, Atlanta and Nashville in the South, for example, or Phoenix in Arizona. These communities filled with people, manufacturers, wholesalers, and retailers.

Truckers proved to be the most flexible, cost-effective transporters to these centers, and thus were brought into supply chain management processes. First, they were required to track more precisely the flow of freight in transit; they did so increasingly in the 1980s through electronic and digital means. Second, beginning with manufacturers and then with retailers, they had to access their customers' databases to get shipping orders, perform updates, and submit bills. Large retailers, such as Wal-Mart, J. C. Penny, and Sears, along with manufacturers, sought to eliminate paper invoices, and in fact most were successful in achieving this goal by the end of the century. National retail chains became integrated into warehousing and even into transportation, or forced their trucking vendors to do so, through telecommunications and the digital. As concentration in various retailing industries soared in the 1980s and 1990s, the power to make truckers conform to such integrated supply chains increased.

Recent Trends

Trucking firms, working with warehousing and manufacturers, had to increase the number of replenishing runs to provide retailers with JIT services, often forcing truckers to supply their customers with partial loads. This practice drove up their expenses, motivating them to find other ways to contain costs of operations. Lean retailing practices dramatically increased the number of short loads. For example, the percentage of total dollar volumes shipped to retail establishments on a daily or weekly basis quadrupled between 1988 and 1992, from 8.7 percent to 33.9 percent.[49] This is a very significant shift in such a short period of time. Trucking firms had to become proficient with technologies being introduced into their customers' operations, such as the use of bar codes, which their clients wanted applied to cartons, not just to merchandise, and which could be scanned by everyone participating in the supply chain, from manufacturers to truckers to customers. In the small-package delivery business, bar codes were in wide use by the late 1990s as a way of feeding data to a database on the status of delivery that customers could check by themselves by accessing the trucker's web site. These applications were a far cry from those implemented in the industry 10 to 15 years earlier. Now, in addition to using innovations in all kinds of technology to improve the bottom line, they also had to use them in support of their own customers' balance sheets.

   The initiative to make these kinds of changes in the use of the digital in trucking, which came from outside the industry that's, from customers, had become a virtual ground swell, surging from all sides. The way members of this industry could make sense of all the demands made upon it was to create or adopt—as did the other industries—rational systems characterized by commonality of shared technologies and applications and deployed in a highly consistent manner across industries. It was often an ad hoc approach because the Trucking Industry did not organize its IT activities to the extent evident in manufacturing, retailing, or banking. But truckers arrived at standard approaches that made it possible for companies across the economic landscape to integrate operations as loosely or tightly as they saw fit.[50] As several observers of the Trucking Industry noted, the implementation of such time-sensitive applications from outside the industry "have drastically altered the role of the trucking service provider in the economy by altering the size, distance, and frequency of shipments and by increasing the importance of transportation reliability, timeliness, and speed."[51] Large truckers did better in this kind of environment, then smaller firms because they could more easily justify the enormous investments in information technology, software applications, and telecommunications required to sustain these kinds of services on a national basis.

To achieve the integration of each of these features into the routine of daily service, many truckers were forced to, first, invest massively in new applications of the digital and telecommunications and second, go into the business of logistics. Logistics now included the use of information with which to move freight to the right place, at the right time, and at the right cost. Increasingly, customers shifted responsibility for doing all three to the Trucking Industry or to firms that specialized in managing logistics.[52] That transfer of work made it possible for customers to have on hand less inventory and smaller or fewer warehouses and to reduce cycle time from order to payment. Outsourcing logistics became a major way of reducing expenses in manufacturing and retailing, particularly in the 1990s. Management's assumption was that those who specialized in a specific function as their core competence should be able to do it less expensively than a firm whose expertise lay elsewhere. Furthermore, by shifting functions out of the firm (or the industry), one could improve the quality of a balance sheet. All of this outsourcing was made possible by the slow development and implementation of a variety of software tools in the 1970s and 1980s, that which when brought together into well-integrated systems made the new lean retailing and JIT strategies of the 1990s possible to implement. Specifically, the key applications were related to software that tracked and communicated information on fleets, individual vehicles, specific shipments and components within shipments, schedules, and planning. Firms injected IT and telecommunications all over the logistical system, from automated radio-tracking systems to onboard PCs in trucks to cell phones on the road to national distribution centers and centralized dispatching services. By the mid-1990s, one estimate held that 60 percent of all manufacturers in the United States had outsourced logistics, and a great deal of that business went to well-established, technologically fitted trucking firms. Truckers, when necessary, formed alliances with logistics companies or created their own. For example, Schneider, one of the largest trucking firms in the nation, created a new subsidiary, Schneider Logistics. Its primary competitor, J. B. Hunt, established Hunt Logistics to do the same thing.[53]

By the late 1980s, EDI proved crucial to the Trucking Industry. Both manufacturers and retailers required its use, and small-package delivery firms used it essentially to take away a large part of the package delivery business from the U.S. Postal System, beginning in the 1980s and dominating in the 1990s. Carriers used EDI to report on status and results and to bill and collect for services rendered. As truckers became part of their customers' operations, they were forced to lower prices in order to keep their contracts. In large part, that required more efficient use of all assets, such as loading trucks most effectively. The Trucking Industry, therefore, went through another round of upgrading the systems used by dispatchers in the late 1980s and throughout the 1990s, mimicking what had occurred earlier in the Petroleum Industry. Many routine parts of their work were now taken over by computers, such as scheduling truck maintenance, determining schedules and travel routes, and modeling costs. By the end of the century, it had become fairly routine to track freight in real time. Truck drivers had become familiar with the use of PCs to monitor the performance of their vehicles, to communicate with dispatchers, and to respond to changing schedules.[54]

In short, by the end of the century, national trucking firms all had applications in the following areas: telecommunications, computerized scheduling and freight tracking, navigation and positioning systems to know where vehicles and packages were at all times, and even sensing and tagging. Telecommunications involved the use of satellite services, cellular phones, and optic technologies. With the arrival of the Internet, they were linked through that new form of communications, about which I have more to say later. As the cost of computing dropped, its diffusion into the truck became cost-effective, especially by the early 1990s. Trip-recording applications about all kinds of truck activities could be installed either in PCs or as computer chips embedded in various parts of a truck. By the end of the century, one out of every six trucks on American highways were fitted out with these kinds of applications. In short, and without hyperbole, the Trucking Industry had become an Information Industry.[55]

Perhaps the one application that came closest in appearance to a Star War use of computing grew out of Cold War systems. The need to have near real-time tracking of trucks and their contents led the industry to adopt what came to be called automatic vehicle location (AVL) systems: GPS technology, sensors on trucks, and computerized maps and driving instructions were integrated together to give dispatchers a way to direct vehicles and to know where they were at any time and to give drivers the instructions they needed to make the most efficient trip. Satellites and GPS technology were the Cold War components, coming directly from U.S. military services and made available to civilians by the mid-1990s. Firms bolted onto such systems a variety of tagging technologies to identify trucks, drivers, parts of trucks, and of course data about the loads they carried. In the small-package business, UPS and Federal Express extended these systems by adding real-time Internet package tracking, using the Web. By the end of the century, all the major small-package delivery services used this application: Airborne Express, DHL Worldwide, Emery Worldwide, Roadway Express, and of course UPS and Federal Express.[56]

The use of all these new technologies and applications in combination fundamentally changed or added to the portfolio of daily operations in this industry. Supply chain management and next-day delivery were the two most obvious examples. Package and load tracking at the single unit level was new; indeed, it would have been new even as late as 1980. However, EDI had become relatively pervasive, as was the use of joint customer-trucker process teams to integrate functions and information across the various supply chains. Companies began to supplant EDI with the less expensive, easier-to-use and manage Internet as their backbone communications system by the end of the century. However, AVL, EDI, and other innovations demonstrated that the Trucking Industry had greatly changed its look-and-feel, beginning before the arrival of the Internet as a public tool. In fact, the Trucking Industry illustrates once again the historic reality that changes in the way industries operated extended far beyond the mere adoption of any one specific technology. Several observers of the industry noted, I think correctly, that, "the

Table 8.5

Fleet Management Technologies in Use by U.S. Trucking Industry, Circa 1997

Routing and dispatching systems

Onboard computers

Mobile communications

Automatic vehicle location/global positioning systems

Source: U.S. Federal Highway Administration, *Commercial Vehicle Fleet Management and Information Systems* (Washington, D.C.: U.S. Department of Transportation/Federal Highway Administration, October 1997): 10, 13.

management of information is becoming as important as the management of freight for the trucking industry."[57] The historical record indeed suggests that this statement reflected reality by roughly 1992–1995.

To what extent did all of these applications exist across the industry? All the major carriers used various forms, but to understand the scope, it helps to review some reliable statistics. By 1997, 3.6 million trucks were operating in the industry. Of that number, 3.2 million were large vehicles, such as those operated by national trucking firms. Across the entire nation there were 44.6 million registered trucks, including privately owned vehicles (such as pickup trucks and minivans) and delivery vehicles, which might be used by a small retailer within a city. Of the 3.2 million vehicles—the ones of interest to us—approximately 80 percent were in private fleets, such as those of retailers and manufacturers. That number dropped in subsequent years as a result of the surge in outsourcing logistics then underway.[58] Many of these truckers, of course, were early users of the supply chain management applications discussed in the last several pages. That left over 600,000 vehicles operating on a for-hire basis, still a very large number. Both private and public fleets used the applications previously described. Table 8.5 lists the major fleet management technologies new to the industry in the 1980s and 1990s that had been widely deployed. These systems allowed either total automation or significant participation of the digital in decisions involving basic functions of the industry (see table 8.6. The) reason for presenting this material in tabular form is to highlight the complexity, breadth, and basic nature of the role computers were now playing in the industry. One study, the source for the data in these two tables, concluded that "motor carriers appear to have a clear understanding of currently available ITS, including the limitations of particular systems." It also noted that "carriers are investing in ITS cautiously and selectively. Those carriers that already have adopted one or more ITS have invested only up to the level of their current needs."[59] As in the past, the best equipped were the largest firms.[60]

The last few years of the twentieth century saw no letup in the rejuvenation of the Trucking Industry, which technology has essentially stimulated as part of the industry's broader adoption of new processes, from manufacturing through retailing, starting in the 1980s. Schneider Logistics, Inc. (SLI) illustrates how technology and business strategy provided new opportunities for truckers. It took advantage

Table 8.6
Commercial Vehicle Fleet Management Decisions, 1990s

Maximizing revenue per mile	Driver home time
Maximizing revenue per trip	Importance of particular accounts
Minimizing unladen mileage	Shipment origins and destinations
Equipment availability	HAZMAT routing considerations
Maximizing equipment utilization	Inventory management
Minimizing fleet operating costs	Pickup and delivery times/dates
Driver availability	Size of shipments
Backhaul opportunities	Road and weather conditions
Drivers' hours-of-service limits	

Source: Adapted from U.S. Federal Highway Administration, *Commercial Vehicle Fleet Management and Information Systems* (Washington, D.C.: U.S. Department of Transportation/Federal Highway Administration, October 1997): 15.

of the outsourcing underway in manufacturing, wholesaling, and retailing in the 1990s to enlarge its business, passing on trucking assignments to Schneider Trucking or to other business partners. It collected marketing and logistical information, which SLI shared with its partners and customers. The parent firm—Schneider National, Inc.—had steadily grown over the years into one of the nation's largest truckers. It continued to expand in the 1980s and 1990s, in spite of deregulation, increased competition, and the arrival of JIT and lean retailing. By 1998, it was a global firm with over 20,000 employees, who increased revenues in the middle years of the 1990s at annual rates of approximately 18 percent. Key customers were innovators in supply chain management: GM, Chrysler, Nabisco Foods, and PPG, for example. The logistics arm operated as a relatively independent part of the firm, often sending up to 95 percent of its business to carriers other than to Schenider National. The ability of SLI to operate efficiently and to grow rested largely on its information-handling operations, which could provide services to customers and link a variety of carriers together.[61]

The industry began to use the Internet in the late 1990s, primarily as a ready-made communications backbone to which individual companies added their own web sites. The American Trucking Association (ATA) and IBM—earlier than in other industries—established an Internet service (1996–1997) for such uses as e-mail and the creation of web pages, demonstrating once again that communications was still one of the most important classes of technologies in this industry. The number of onboard mobile communications expanded; Qualcomm alone claimed to have 185,000 truckers as customers in 1997. In fact, all during the 1990s, the industry led many others in the deployment of advanced wireless communications applications, including wireless dispatching and tracking, and even expensive, satellite-based uses. A variety of IT and telecommunications firms introduced to this industry new wireless communications services during the last several years of the century. Highly visible firms, like UPS aggressively exploited the Internet to enhance business services to customers. The company averaged 21 million visits to its web site each day in 1999 from people inquiring about services or the status of a delivery. It channeled every inquiry and transaction it possibly could with customers through this web site. Tracking packages became one of the most used applications, with 2 million customers each day logging on to the site. The company also began to provide replenishment services to retailers. When an individual paid for a product at a POS terminal, that POS system told UPS to deliver a replacement to that store. In 2000 FedEx launched a service to help small customers sell goods over the Internet, using FedEx services, of course.[62]

Because the Internet has already played an important role in all transportation industries, we can use this industry to show how many industries at the end of the century were linked more closely together than the traditional economic descriptors of manufacturing, transportation, and retailing sectors might indicate. In fact, to put a fine point on the issue, the Internet has made it more difficult to think of these sectors as independent units, the historic view of them for nearly a century. Rather, we may wonder how much longer we can think of them as separate building blocks in the economy, a topic I will discuss more thoroughly in the final chapter.

In the case of the Trucking Industry, extant data, based on surveys, show that 51 percent of all carriers used the Internet in some fashion by the end of 1998, an increase from 11 percent in 1996. By the end of 1999, and certainly not past the first quarter of 2002, that number had climbed to 75 percent and possibly to over 95 percent by the end of the year.[63] These are very high levels of deployment. Why? A team of economists recently set out to answer that question:

> The key reason that the Internet is affecting the industry stems from the availability of more detailed information to customers and competitors about goods and services, prices, and timing. Firms are changing the way they gather, process, and disseminate information. The changes in information result in both potential for greater efficiency in traditional transportation activities and in the creation of demand for new types of transportation activities.[64]

The consequences are predictable: greater pressure on prices, increased demand for new services, and improved productivity for competitive reasons. As did manufacturers, retailers pressured their suppliers to become more intimately engaged in their internal operations—and their transportation providers to do the same. To improve operations, the industry also acquired its collection of information handlers, such as Transplace.com and Freighquote.com. These information brokers have become a crucial cog in the industry, helping truckers to aggregate loads and negotiate prices. The same economists observed in 2002 that "many incumbents in the trucking industry are restructuring to offer integrated transportation solutions by including logistics and other transportation options to their corporate portfolios of asset-based transportation management services."[65]

Thus, the Trucking Industry entered the new century with an installed set of uses for the Internet that were transformative, not only for the firms in the industry but also for their customers. The economists, whose surveys are the basis of the previous discussion, discovered that over 70 percent of the firms they contacted used the Internet to attract new customers and market their services. Over half also used it for a myriad of communications. Nearly a third already used the Internet for such functions as managing online shipment of orders from existing customers, providing online pricing, handling freight pickup requests, recruiting drivers and other personnel, providing real-time shipment tracking, and making available a variety of forms, permits, and even bills of lading and proof of delivery documentation. Newly emerging applications with about 10 percent participation by trucking firms included special discounting programs, real-time trailer tracking, and posting of drivers' schedules. They also discovered that the incremental expense of performing a transaction over the Internet was nearly 15 times less than by traditional paper means.[66] It is also one of the earliest industries that was able to derive explicit economic advantage by using the Internet to reach out to new customers. In manufacturing firms, the greatest economic benefits were initially in the reduction of operating costs. In fact, nearly two-thirds of all the changes in the acquisition of new customers could be attributed in one fashion or another, but directly, to the use of the Internet.

Whereas adoption of the Internet varied in degree and type of application from one firm to another—as we see in all industries reviewed in this book—the Trucking Industry's use of this technology correlated positively with the growth of assets, market share, revenue, miles operated, volume of shipments, and number of transactions by its firms. Service costs, which have remained the same, were affected by other computer-based applications more than by the Internet. The economists who conducted the most comprehensive study of the industry's use of the Internet concluded, "Web usage is facilitating growth of individual trucking firms—and the industry as a whole—by allowing firms to offer more services to their existing customers and to offer services to new customers."[67] The contribution of the industry to the GDP of the United States, however, has not yet changed dramatically. In the early 1990s, it was about 3.1 percent, and at the end of the century remained at about 3.2 percent, with the industry growing annually in that decade at about 5 percent, roughly the same as the GDP as a whole. The greater story that may emerge in the years to come is the economic impact of the Trucking Industry on manufacturing and retail industries because a critical part of the infrastructure of the "new economy," with its e-business and e-commerce, is having a highly efficient, very reliable transportation network. Some economists have attempted to quantify the multiplier effects, and of course that work has to be seen as speculative, especially in the context of a history of the industry. However, with that caveat in mind, one credible study suggested that the Trucking Industry's multiplier effect could soon add an additional 0.1 percent growth to the U.S. GDP. In monetary terms, that positive effect could run close to $200 billion of additional GDP.[68]

To sum up, the Trucking Industry enjoyed sound growth and profits in the last years of the twentieth century, when the whole U.S. economy did well. Consolidations strengthened large carriers, weakened smaller ones, and thereby, along with implementation of various technologies, made entry into the industry increasingly more difficult. This industry also faced a chronic shortage of drivers and, in

2000, rising fuel costs. Yet sales volumes increased. For example, the top 100 for-hire carriers increased their revenues by 12.7 percent in 1999 from 1998, while the U.S. economy (GDP) grew 4.1 percent. In 1999 the industry enjoyed profit margins on average of 3.49 percent, the best since 1986.[69] However, at the dawn of the new century, common services and similar information technologies made it possible for other transportation industries to compete with truckers. For example, United Airlines and American Airlines began to provide same-day freight delivery; railroads also offered guaranteed delivery service. Truckers crossed industry lines, too, providing overnight shipping services, for example. The ability of one firm (or industry) to intrude into another's market was made possible by the wide deployment (and hence already existing) inventory control and supply chain management tools and processes, many accessible through the Internet.[70]

Conclusions

What do these industries teach us about deployment of information technologies and their effects on patterns and content of work? To what extent do these industries mimic or depart from practices evident in manufacturing? These questions are important because of the argument I present that transportation industries were the physical link between industries that produced products and those who sold and used them. To emphasize a basic theme, in a thousand different ways, in hundreds of industries, and involving tens of thousands of individual firms and departments within companies, a process unfolded of further integration of activities and information to drive the daily work of the economy. This took place in the second half of the twentieth century in a relatively simultaneous fashion across the economy, although specific types of activities occurred more in one decade or another, and some sooner or later, from one industry or firm to another. The overall effect was the act of filling in pieces of what can reasonably be called an overarching national, now increasingly international, integrated supply chain. This statement reflects a conclusion based on what we know occurred in manufacturing and transportation, and it is further supported by the evidence presented in the next chapters on wholesale and retail industries.

In the case of the two transportation industries studied here, the evidence shows that in the beginning, that is, around 1950, the thought of becoming tightly synchronized with other industries was not on anyone's mind. Rather, a second basic theme, evident in every industry studied in this book, was the desire to drive down costs of operation, specifically, the expense of labor. So cost reduction provided the initial impulse for the adoption of computers, not a desire to integrate into some other industry's basic processes. Subsequent adoptions were then influenced by the industry's response to increased competition and to the opportunities presented by technology to improve one's market share. This newfound strength emerged from the ability of firms to offer new services (scope), leverage national reach (scale), and still drive down operating costs. As in manufacturing and retailing, cost containment remained the determinative influence in transportation, on what digital applications were embraced through the 1950s and 1960s. As the costs of IT dropped over time, computing provided a cumulative positive shift in the expense of digital applications when compared to the cost of labor and earlier methods of operation. That shift in relative costs made adoption of the digital easier to accept. Adoption also became more attractive as the technologies themselves improved in functional performance, reliability, speed, and capacity during the 1960s–1980s. The convergence of telecommunications and computing, which had been going on during the entire period, picked up momentum in both technological improvements, costs, and performance in the 1980s and extending to the end of the century, with the stunning result that information could be gathered and exchanged cost-effectively across any geography, at any time, and often without human intervention. Those results made it possible to adopt new applications of the digital that were at best pipe dreams to the advocates of total systems in the 1960s. These patterns of adoption were as much in evidence in the Transportation Industry as in manufacturing and retailing.

How are we to account for the timing of adoption of various applications in the Transportation Industry? I have already suggested that cost-effective technological innovations provided one gating factor, allowing forward movement or constraining the adoption. The influence of suppliers and customers on each other emerged as a second element, however. For example:

- A manufacturing company that decides to implement a JIT production process requires a trucker to deliver tires at certain times of the day, driving the truck right into the building.
- A trucking firm figures out that it can gain a competitive advantage over rivals by serving as a miniature warehouse on wheels for customers trying to offload the cost of storing inventory, both agreeing to JIT strategies.

The list is endless, but the point is simple enough: industries shared their computing experiences with each other and sought out or demanded that technology be used to integrate the fundamental transactions of the market. So, availability of individual technologies and software tools, on the one hand, and encouragement of suppliers and customers, on the other hand, influenced the time at which any industry moved to some new application. Comments about how slow one industry or another was in adopting an application can thus be seen as evidence not so much of incompetence or Luddite behavior but rather of a new business strategy, new operational tactics, or the realization that a firm was dependent on the way another industry performed its work.

The results proved to be similar, however: all industries, at different speeds, adopted many commonly shared applications and in the process bent these technologies to their own industry's peculiarities and purposes. In manufacturing, CAD/CAM is an example already discussed, and we will see bar codes in retailing as another. But every industry had these kinds of cases.[71] The integration of various forms of communications and the ability to track moving objects—train cars, trucks, and freight in transit—were the operative examples of the process at work in the Transportation Industry. Railroads and truckers functioned like schools of fish (as we saw in manufacturing), resulting in adoptions that occurred more or less in the same time frame across the world of transportation. The extent to which "more or less" played out as "sooner rather than later" was a function of the extent to which standardization had become as essential to the functioning of any individual firm within an industry. Railroads, for example, absolutely needed consistent practices for monitoring rolling stock, ways to share that stock among different lines, and processes for accounting and billing. Truckers felt less of this kind of pressure, but they needed to pace their adoptions of technologies and applications to remain competitive with retailers. That meant adopting whatever software and telecommunications tools and standards retailers and manufacturers required. Thus, whereas almost all industries began the 1950s by operating relatively independently of other industries, when making decisions about adoption of specific technologies, it had become evident by the mid-1980s that transportation, like the others, could no longer make such decisions without the influence of other industries.

I contend that this shift, which was both subtle and probably more obvious to us in hindsight than to the decision makers at the time, had two consequences that can only be described as an oxymoron. The shift first led to industry-wide realizations that individual members should immediately adopt certain applications. An industry's major magazines and journals provide the evidence for that conclusion because of all the studies they conducted on who was doing what and why, along with cajoling articles on why their industry should adopt a particular application. That press, in turn, contributed to a greater sense of industry community than had existed before the 1950s, sharpening the definition of who was in a specific industry. To be sure, other processes contributed to this growing sense of identity, such as government reports and regulations, industry associations and national meetings, and the cross-hiring of members of one firm by other enterprises in the same industry. But contemporary articles also lead one to suspect that there was unstated peer pressure to conform in the area of digital applications; railroads and truckers felt it, just as did manufacturers and retailers.

A second trend made the shift an oxymoron: at the same time, companies linked parts of their operations in some more intimate fashion to those of other enterprises in different industries, giving one the sense that their industry was desegregating. The process of desegregation became a prominant example of the change occurring in the digital or the information economy by the early 1990s.[72] In fact, however, desegregation was not really taking place; the borders between industries were simply becoming fuzzier and harder to identify because of the linkages created among suppliers, transporters, and vendors. General Motors never went away, nor did the Southern Pacific Railroad; they just performed their work in some different ways. The digital can be identified as the direct, overt, and most obvious instrument for the establishment of the linkages, while simultaneously confusing commentators and participants about where one industry ended and another began. Add into the mix some of the new business models developed by the end of the century, such as virtual trading markets, and one can understand why there was confusion about industry boundaries.

Finally, there is the information itself, the data that moved through computers, telecommunication networks, companies, industries, and ultimately people. The sharing of data between customers of trucking and railroads clearly increased dramatically during the half century. It sped up decisions, improved utilization rates of all assets involved, improved productivity of assets and people, and reduced the time it took for events to occur.[73] The Transportation Industry today performs in many ways that are profoundly different from those in 1950, even though the basic act of moving freight remains the same. Technologies were always in support of that fundamental raison d'etre for this sector of the economy, just as IT changed much in manufacturing but not the fact that manufacturers were still in the business of making products. As in the manufacturing industry, in the transportation industries we have seen a shift of knowledge, cognitive behavior, and responsibility away from workers to computers. In manufacturing, robots perform certain tasks, and mathematical algorithms in software do the calculations for CAD; both are examples of the process at work in other industries. In the transportation industries (including the Process Industry), decisions on optimized routes through which to move freight increasingly shifted to computers, to the point where, by the end of the century, human participation in some processes is to override normal procedures on an exceptional basis and relinquish routine tasks to computers, such as approving repetitive or standard operational decisions.[74]

Information presented and used in novel ways over the decades, when combined with computer technology (and its expanding variety and reliability of functionality), made it possible for manufacturing and transportation industries to conform to patterns of IT usage that stimulated change for competitive advantages. Whereas efficiencies were enjoyed more often in manufacturing than in transportation, nonetheless they existed here, too. By the end of the century, members of the Transportation Industry could, in the words of a team of economists, allow "people and firms to do things that they could not do otherwise, rather than being more efficient in their traditional activities."[75] However, as seen by the experiences of both the manufacturing and retailing industries, both efficiencies and novel applications were deployed across the economy.

We now move to a discussion of what occurred further down the supply chain, in warehousing and retailing. These later industries demonstrate the extent to which linkages to suppliers and manufacturers have been profoundly integrated, thanks to the digital. To illustrate the patterns involved, we now turn to a series of illustrative case studies.

9

Presence of Wholesale and Retail Industries in the American Economy

They came, they saw, they handled, and they bought—usually more than they intended purchasing when they entered the store.

—Edwin Merton McBrier

It would be safe to say that every adult in the United States has bought something in a store. Stores—the most visible element of all retail industries—are, after money, the most familiar component of the American economy. Although not everyone has been in a factory or in a government building, he or she has been in grocery stores, department stores, hardware stores, and shoe stores; everyone has shopped at Wal-Mart, possibly at Kmart, at J.C. Penny's, or in small specialty stores for everything from antiques to clothes and from fine wines to spring plants. In short, this is the most ubiquitous industry in America, and it has been for over a century.

Yet, people know less about how this industry operates than they intuitively understand manufacturing. Retailing is a complex body of business activities that culminates in what a shopper sees and buys. It is a large segment of the American economy today, roughly 9 percent, and over 15 percent if we include wholesalers. It also has long used information technologies. No segment of the American economy has changed so much because of information technology than retail, with the possible exception of the Trucking Industry. In earlier chapters we saw how manufacturing industries were transformed partly because of their use of IT, but as I demonstrate in the next three chapters, greater changes occurred in retailing than even in the industrial sector. Although computing came to retailing in aggregate later than to manufacturing, once it did, the industry was greatly changed. Computers were rare in retailing in the 1950s, but other forms of information-handling equipment were not, such as electronic cash registers and adding machines. By the end of the twentieth century, one would have been hard pressed not to find the digital present in almost every store in the United States. Every chain store used computing, a large percentage of products were tagged with digital markings, and retail firms had become integral parts of the largest application in American computing history—supply chain management.

With the analysis of how retailers used computing, we complete the story of the emergence of the modern supply chain management process. What happened in retailing adds further evidence to Chandler's thesis about the visible hand and how investments in industries continued to take place. Successful firms in retailing invested substantially to update and upgrade technologies and processes to remain competitive.

At the start of our story (1950s), manufacturers had moved goods to retailers, who then did the same to consumers. Then an unanticipated, fundamental change began slowly to occur in the 1980s. The flow of market power reversed, with consumers now indicating through their purchases what they wanted retailers to sell. In turn, retailers used various information technologies to dictate to manufacturers what merchandize to make and how and when to ship it, thereby changing a nearly century-old pattern of comparatively loose relationships between stores and factories. The reversal appears to have occurred in two phases, both stimulated by IT. The first involved the collection of data from point-of-sale (POS) transactions by retailers, which made it possible for them to tell manufacturers what to make and when to deliver the goods. This phase started in the mid-1980s and has continued to the present. The second wave of change came with more effective data mining of POS information on consumer behavior and online shopping over the Internet. Improvements in data mining began in the early 1990s, but the Internet's vast quantity of information and the growing willingness of American consumers to buy there appear to be affecting the flow of the supply chain from consumers to manufacturers. This increased influence of consumers did not become apparent until the end of the 1990s.[1]

The trade sector of the economy had been innovative for over a century. This chapter began with a quotation from an early partner of Frank W. Woolworth, the founder, in the 1880s, of the first major variety store in the United States. By putting goods on tables instead of on shelves behind counters, shoppers could, essentially for the first time, handle merchandise they contemplated buying. As McBrier described the experience decades later, "People were not accustomed to being invited to handle and see for themselves,"[2] Although they adapted well to this innovation and bought more than they wanted. Ultimately, it has always been the intention of a store owner to have customers buy more than they intended. Retail firms used computers to attract and monitor customers, to keep operating costs down, and to remain price-competitive, profitable, and innovative.

Before I describe the role of computing in this sector of the economy, I should explain its makeup because, as with manufacturing, it is complex and diverse. Even what it is called remains confusing: is it retail, trade, distribution, wholesale, mail order, catalog, or e-tailing? Within the industry there are subcategories of descriptions: grocery, specialty, chains, and so forth. The industry is present on every main street in America, in every town, city, county, and state. Some large retail corporations also manufacture; others operate around the world. The industry's business practices and points of emphasis differ from those of manufacturing; government agencies, banks, insurance firms, and other components of the American economy. Without understanding the role the digital has played, it would be difficult to appreciate how computing became such an important element in modern economic activities.

The combination of all wholesale and retail sales in the U.S. economy over the past half century typically accounted for about 16 to 17 percent of the GNP. I refine those statistics later in this chapter, but this quick snapshot tells us something about the scope of the industry. Manufacturing, contributed roughly 30 percent of the GNP in 1950 and, by the end of the century, around 21 percent, and manufacturing, transportation, and retail combined contributed between roughly half of the GNP in 1950 and nearly 40 percent at the dawn of the new century.[3] To understand how either manufacturing or retailing performed in this half century, one has to look at the two together because they were so linked, and this bond became ever tighter as the century progressed. If one had to pick a single cause for this historic interdependency, one would choose computing and the flow of information that this technology made possible. By looking at the combination of these two sectors, which are such a large portion of the economy, it becomes possible to appreciate even further how computing fundamentally influenced the business activities of this nation.

Now and Then in the World of Retailing

Walk through an early twenty-first century department store or grocery and you will see why it would be difficult to exaggerate the presence of computing. First, an electronic eye opens the door for the customer, and a count is automatically made of the number of people going in and out of the store. Merchandise is tagged with machine-readable clips or, more frequently, bar codes (about which I have a great deal to say in the next chapter). Digital kiosks are appearing in many stores to provide customers with more information about products and access to online catalogs. Computer-printed prices are posted on the shelves. At the checkout counter, purchases are scanned, immediately updating the store's inventory records and sending a buy order to the manufacturer or wholesaler to replenish the sold item. The replacement probably comes to the store within 48 to 72 hours, already tagged and ready to sell. More advanced tagging now embeds chips inside clothing, boxes, and even books, as both a security measure and a way of tracking inventory. The cash register of old has been replaced with a POS terminal, which can check a shopper's credit, determine if he or she has bounced checks, verify the correct price, update the store's accounting records, and collect information about one's buying habits by individual—all of which are then used immediately to change the mix of goods offered or to quickly replenish them. Many stores also have a web site on the Internet, with information on products and store hours; the most advanced have the capability of taking orders online, thereby combining bricks and mortar and electronic channels of distribution. As we saw in chapter 8, trucks delivering merchandise to stores are virtual warehouses on wheels, equipped with PCs and geopositioning technology; they are scheduled to arrive at stores in a highly choreographed manner, just as at manufacturing sites.[4]

Now picture that same department store or grocery in 1950. One would see the cash register, probably an electric one, but not a computerized POS terminal. What would surprise our shopper is how extensively large department stores used accounting equipment to track inventory, place orders, and monitor cash flows. Burroughs and NCR became two of America's most prestigious and successful corporations because of their ability to provide information-processing technologies to the Retail Industry, beginning in the late nineteenth century. Small stores had little information technology, although a desktop Burroughs adding machine in the backroom was not all that uncommon, even as early as the 1920s.[5] For the entire twentieth century, the two fundamental applications of information technologies were used for inventory control and to improve labor productivity. As new technologies came into existence, the largest retail and wholesale enterprises adopted them first in their industries. As the cost of technologies dropped and their value became widely evident, smaller enterprises also acquired them.[6] This pattern of deployment paralleled that in manufacturing industries, where the largest firms were usually the early adopters. Just as manufacturers often used computing more than one might have thought, so, too, did retailers. One usually thinks that until the development of the universal product code (UPC) and POS scanning in the 1970s, stores did not use computers; that adoption occurred massively in the 1980s.[7] However, as I illustrate in the pages that follow, computing existed in this industry even in the 1950s and 1960s to a greater extent than historians have previously acknowledged.[8] One textbook written in the early 1970s acknowledges in unambiguous terms the existence of computing long before the Internet and at the dawn of the digital cash register:

> The single largest impact on internal retail operations has come from the computer. A device that can handle information at tremendous speeds, the computer is being used by retailers to solve their information-handling problems: the time lags that occur between an event—a request for credit, a payment, a stock depletion, or an order, for example—and a reaction.

In fact, the authors complaine that computers presented problems for retailers in that "the advances are coming so quickly it is difficult to select a system and keep it up to date."[9]

Near the end of the twentieth century, most discussions about the use of the Internet concerned shopping.[10] Amazon.com, a firm in the Retail Industry, has been the subject of a growing body of literature on the New Economy.[11] The U.S. government's studies of the digital and the Internet focus largely on Internet-based commerce.[12] There is now an extensive literature on how to exploit the Internet for economic advantage, and a great deal of that discussion concentrates on retail, with *e-commerce* and *e-tailing* the fashionable terms to use.[13] The most widely distributed college textbook on retailing at the dawn of the new century, written by Michael Levy and Barton A. Weitz, gives EDI and the Internet extensive coverage, with almost every chapter including some reference to them and whole chapters devoted to IT. In fact, the first sentence in the first chapter declares, "Retailing is evolving into a global, high tech business." Two sentences later, they state, "Retailers are using sophisticated communication and information systems to manage their business."[14] But as we see below, many of manager's concerns have not changed over the decades, and almost as important, they have long experimented with IT. In short, it is no accident that they have embraced UPC, POS technologies, and EDI and are now adopting the Internet. As in manufacturing, experiences with IT slowly, but ultimately extensively, influenced how retailers and wholesalers operated. Understanding that experience suggests, as it does with manufacturing, how retailers use current IT and how they will perhaps deploy, it in the future. Shared objectives changed less than the technologies used to achieve them.

Although the use of IT is far more extensive today than in the 1950s, a quick look at a textbook from the earlier decade would seem familiar to a retailer today:

> The minimum of records which the small store should keep are sales records and cash records.
>
> Large stores have need for a more complex system of records and professional accountants are required to install and operate these systems,
>
> which now often include the use of electronic punched-card equipment.[15]

Both textbooks have chapters on similar topics: store operations, purchasing, inventory control, customers, merchandising, pricing, and so forth. In both instances, over half the texts are devoted to the management of information. To be sure, the earlier one focuses on the data and not on the artifacts used to handle this information (e.g., books, paper, and adding machines), whereas the newer volume is replete with references to hardware and telecommunications. It also contains many illustrations that show IT technology, such as POS terminals, "dumb"[16] CRTs, and people using kiosks and the Internet. Much as manufacturing texts from the 1960s showcased computers to make the industrial sector look modern and high tech, so, too, do publications on retailing today.[17]

Before leaving the general topic of the role of trade, we should keep in mind the fundamental functions of this portion of the economy because computing was used to support them, just as the digital was used to facilitate operations in manufacturing. Table 9.1 lists major areas of activities found in all retailing (and to similar extent in wholesaling) through the entire half century. Table 9.2 provides a similar list of operations in retailing circa 2000. What stands out is the consistency of how this sector operated and its way of generating revenues and profits. The applications of computing and telecommunications were implemented in support of these functions. Over time this technology changed profoundly and, in turn, influenced how work took place.

Table 9.1
Typical Retailing Functions, Circa 1950s–1970s

Store operations	Sales
Advertising	Merchandising
Accounting	Finance
Inventory management	Pricing
Personnel	Purchasing
Consumer behavior	Store layout and design

Source: Committee on Retailing, *Principles of Retailing* (New York: Pitman, 1955): xi–xvi; Don L. James, Bruce J. Walker, and Michael J. Etzel, *Retailing Today: An Introduction* (New York: Harcourt Brace Jovanovich, 1974): vii–xvi.

Table 9.2
Typical Retailing Functions Circa 1980s–2000s

Planning	Human resource management
Supply chain management	Merchandising
Purchasing	Pricing
Communications mix	Store operations
Customer service	Accounting
Consumer behavior	Store layout and design

Source: Michael Levy and Barton A. Weitz, *Retailing Management* (Burr Ridge, Ill.: McGraw-Hill Irwin, 2001): xvii–xxvi.

The Wholesaling and Retailing Presence in the American Economy

Role of Wholesalers

Wholesalers are firms that buy products from manufacturers or producers, or they are extensions of manufacturers and sell their goods and produce to retailers. Each industry had them. Often serving many retailers, they provided a variety of goods from many manufacturers or specialized in narrow lines of products. Their value lay in their ability to buy in bulk—hence cheaper than a retail outlet—and to warehouse the merchandise, aggregate various goods, and deliver merchandise to stores. They were always more prominent in some retail industries than in others. For example, the Grocery Industry relied on wholesalers most, needing them to aggregate manufactured foods, meats, vegetables, fruits, and thousands of household products. These goods accounted for about 18 percent of all products sold through wholesalers in the second half of the twentieth century. Machinery, equipment, and their supplies represented the second largest category of products distributed through wholesalers.[18]

In the 1950s, over half the wholesalers in the United States operated in large cities, many concentrated in a few urban centers. For example, the Apparel Industry's leading wholesalers were literally clustered in one neighborhood in lower Manhattan, nicknamed the "Garment District." Others, such as the Furniture Industry, settled in midwestern cities, for example, in Chicago.[19] During the last several decades of the century, the physical distribution of wholesalers spread across the nation as the interstate highway system expanded, making it possible to distribute goods easily, inexpensively, and quickly across the country. Where major new highways intersected, manufacturing, distribution centers, and wholesalers established local operations. Thus new centers appeared, for example, in such southern cities as Nashville and Memphis. The development of a high-quality national highway system cannot be overemphasized as a profound influence on the Wholesale Industry. As one U.S. government report from the mid-1970s described the effect of these new roadways, wholesalers could do "more efficient scheduling of pickup trucks for intracity shipments and of intercity trucking," reducing "the number of miles of transportation required" and thereby improving the efficiency of the physical distribution of goods. By the end of the century, the United States had the most productive, widespread wholesale network in the world.[20]

Between 1960 and 1973—when large portions of the national highway system were built and when the U.S. economy expanded rapidly—wholesale revenues in the United States (GNP) grew at an annual rate of 5.3 percent. Productivity within the industry also improved, despite the fact that between 1960 and 1973 the number of people employed expanded by 36 percent, to 4.4 million workers.[21] In the 1970s and 1980s, largely in response to competition and the introduction of various technologies, the tasks performed by this industry increased in scope to include managing inventory for their customers, extending credit, physical assorting of goods, and even pricing them. In the 1970s and 1980s, the industry grew at a slower rate than in the previous two decades, closer to 3 percent. The recessions of 1974 and 1980 were part of the reason for the slower growth rate, but it was also partially caused by new relationships that emerged in the 1980s between large retailers and manufacturers (described in more detail in subsequent chapters). Large retailers were often the originators of innovative users of IT, which so profoundly influenced cross-sector relationships. Productivity increases in this industry in the 1970s and 1980s mirrored those of the economy as a whole, about 1 percent per year, although in some years they actually declined (e.g., 1974, 1976, 1979, and 1980), primarily because of the condition of the U.S. economy.[22] Between 1950 and 1985 (using 1986 dollars) the industry expanded from a base of $500 billion to $1.1 trillion. By the end of the century, the wholesale Distribution Industry had generated $2.5 trillion in the American economy.[23]

The statistics on wholesaling show that despite recent initiatives by the Retail Industry to link directly to manufacturers (largely through EDI, UPC, and POS data), and advances in the delivery of products, wholesaling in America remained a strong segment through the entire period. In other words, although often de-

One of the features of computing technology in the 1970s was its ability to be used in multiple industries. In this 1975 photograph, we see a device to transfer funds electronically and to perform other monetary transactions and data movement. Burroughs designed this equipment (TT602) for banks, other financial institutions, retail and wholesale locations, supermarkets, hotels, hospitals, and manufacturing companies. Burroughs Papers, courtesy Archives of the Charles Babbage Institute, University of Minnesota, Minneapolis.

scribed as mature, the Wholesale Industry continued to play a vital role in the emerging, information-intensive supply chain management practices that emerged during the last two decades of the century. Much of the literature on retailing focuses on explaining the role of retail firms—those that have stores—and about their relationships with manufacturers, often deemphasizing or ignoring the critical role played by wholesalers through the entire period.[24]

Role of Retailers

Part of the reason for this lack of emphasis could be due to the very large size of the retail end of the supply chain. People see stores every day; very few see wholesale operations or their warehouses. Furthermore, the retail industries collectively represent a large physical asset spread all over America.

In 1950, retail trade industries employed roughly 7 million workers and expanded steadily during the boom years of the 1950s and 1960s, with a payroll of some 10 million in 1965.[25] At the height of the Korean War (1953), retail industries enjoyed sales of $170 billion. Two decades later (1973), revenues reached $514 billion and in 1980 climbed to over $700 billion.[26] In the mid-1970s, there were nearly 1.7 million retail firms in the United States; nearly half were very small, with less than $50,000 per year in revenue. In part because of what computing made possible in the last two decades of the century, the number of large enterprises grew rapidly, fundamentally changing the character and level of concentration in the industry but by no means eliminating the ongoing surge in the number of small enterprises that continued through the 1990s.

It was also a labor-intensive industry through the entire period. Just before the major introduction of various new IT tools in the early 1970s, it employed some 12 million people. Even in 1997, after the wide availability of the Internet, it remained a labor-intensive industry, employing over 21 million people, or roughly 18 percent of the U.S. work force. It was also an industry that kept growing to the end of the century. Retail sales in 1997, for instance, reached $2.566 trillion, a figure that is considered by some experts to be an understatement of the true size of the industry.[27] In 1992, just several years before the wide availability of the Internet for retail purposes, there were 1.1 million retail firms in the United States, of which 6.3 percent had more than one store; only 7.4 percent of all stores had annual sales of over $2.5 million.[28] There were, in short, many small enterprises among the growing number of supply chains.

Because of the physical presence of retail establishments across America in such large numbers, technologies had to overcome the problem of their wide dispersion. In 1950, every main street in America had stores, and many crossroads in rural communities had country stores, which also served as gas stations, post offices, and community meeting places. Industry experts have long noted the decline in the number of retail establishments in large cities and the construction of malls in the suburbs, which simply reinforces the fact that this industry was physically everywhere. Shopping malls, which first arose in the late 1950s, are an almost unique American phenomenon, now seen around the world. In the 1970s and 1980s, malls of various types and sizes were built in the United States at rates faster than the growth in the overall population.

The amount of selling space devoted to retail also expanded. As measured by the amount of retail space per customer, in 1964 there were some 5.3 square feet per person. By 1974, roughly when the Grocery Industry was experimenting with early POS systems, square footage per person had increased to 9. In 1988, by which time POS, EDI, and other forms of IT were in wide use, particularly among large retail corporations, square footage had risen to 16 per person, and it continued to expand to 19 square feet in 1996.[29] Today, the number of malls runs in the tens of thousands. Although there was much discussion about the overbuilding of stores and malls in the United States by the end of the century,[30] and at a time when e-tailing and the Internet had captured the attention of economists, business leaders, and members of the retail industries, retail trade still had many of the same physical features as it had for decades. There were stores, shelves, and tables loaded with merchandise; never enough well-informed clerks to help; and, of course, ubiquitous checkout lines.

Before I delve into discussions about the makeup of the wholesale and retail industries, a final comparison of their relative size at the end of the twentieth century helps put into perspective the proportions of the economy each occupied. The NAICS data for 1997 indicate that there were over a half million firms in the Wholesale Industry and to 1.5 million in retail. Wholesaling that year employed 6.5 million people versus 21.2 million in retailing. Wholesale trade generated sales of $4.2 trillion, retailing $2.5 trillion. Wholesale had higher revenue numbers because it sold to firms and government agencies, not just to retailers.[31]

Makeup of the Wholesale Industry

This Wholesale Industry experienced considerable changes over the past half century, driven by such factors as direct links between large retailers and manufacturers, consolidations among wholesalers, wholesalers that elected to own retail outlets (e.g., as occurred frequently in the Grocery Industry), the prosperous American economy, and normal competitive forces. However, because so many retail firms were small, the need for a middleman supplier, who could buy in bulk and sell in small quantities, remained a requirement through the half-century. Various technologies improved the operational efficiencies of wholesalers, such as computers for inventory control; larger, more efficient trucks, running on a national network of highways; and so forth. Technology, however, did not eliminate the need for this service in the national supply chain. As one group of commentators argued in the 1970s, the need for wholesalers existed because "the small retailer could not obtain such small quantities directly from manufacturers. Many smaller hardware, grocery, office supply, automotive supply stores, beauty shops, and gift shops rely largely on full-service wholesalers."[32] Their statement characterized circumstances in 1950, as well as in the early years of the new century. At the time that computers first came into commercial use (1950s), wholesalers were performing many of the same functions that they had performed a half century later: anticipating the requirements of their retail customers, providing some credit toward purchases, providing various guarantees and adjustments concerning the quality and types of products sold, and resolving complaints from stores. One survey of wholesalers in 1950 suggested that they provided as few services as possible to retailers, although store managers wanted more, for example, pricing and placement of goods on shelves.[33] As new forms of IT became available after 1975, wholesalers were pushed into providing additional services, which became easier to accomplish through computing.

There are many descriptions of how the wholesale portion of the economy was structured, but they essentially fall into two types—one based on their function, the other on those sectors of the retail industries they served. The most widely used descriptions of their functions are drawn from various U.S. government agencies that tracked their economic performance. Government economists generally characterized the industry in three ways:

1. Merchant wholesalers, who sold and transported goods from producers and manufacturers to retailers or to other companies. By the early 1980s, they

Table 9.3
Sources of Revenue in the U.S. Wholesale Industry, 1973

Retail Sector Served	Percent of Total Sales
Groceries	18.7
Machinery, equipment, supplies	11.5
Motor vehicles and equipment	8.5
Electrical goods	6.2
Lumber and other construction materials	5.2
Beer, wines, and spirits	4.3
Hardware and plumbing equipment	4.3
Dry goods and apparel	3.8
Paper and paper products	2.6
Drugs and proprietaries	2.0
Furniture and furnishings	1.9
Miscellaneous	31.0

Source: BLS, *Technological Change and Manpower Trends in Five Industries*, Bulletin 1856 (Washington, D.C.: U.S. Government Printing Office, 1975): 52.

accounted for some 80 percent of all wholesale revenues, indicative that through the second half of the century that was the case also because the industry did not change its structure as rapidly or dramatically as did others.
2. Manufacturers' sales branches and offices. They accounted for less than 10 percent of all wholesale business.
3. Agents, brokers, and commission merchants, who had as much market share as the second group. This was also the segment that changed the most, but only after the arrival of the Internet, which made agentlike activities economically attractive in the direct consumer market.[34]

Table 9.3 lists the major retail segments served by American wholesalers in the middle period of this study. Note the large variety of products sold by wholesalers, from small to large items and from few to many. Keep this variety in mind as we look at the key uses of IT in this segment of the market: inventory management, logistics, and pricing, to mention just a few.

Economists usually describe this industry as being divided into three categories: those that sell durable goods (items with a normal life expectancy of three years or more, like refrigerators), nondurable goods (items that should last less than three years, like pencils), and food goods or perishables (products that need to be sold and used quickly, like fresh meat, vegetables, and fruit). Sales of durable goods were slightly higher than of nondurable goods through the period, and durable goods wholesalers tended to employ nearly a third more workers than nondurable suppliers. Late in the twentieth century, of the more than half million wholesale establishments in existence, nearly 340,000 sold durable goods; the other 184,000 focused on nondurable goods.[35]

From the 1950s through the 1990s, disposable income rose in the United States, as did the work of wholesalers in providing goods to retailers for Americans to buy. In this period, wholesalers had to deal with a great variety of existing products (e.g., automotive parts), whole new classes of products (e.g., personal computers and other electronics), new technologies (e.g., equipment to physically pick and move products in warehouses and computers to track inventory), and novel ways of doing business (e.g., placing bar codes on products and managing forecasts drawn from POS data). All the major studies of wholesaling in this half century focused on continuous changes in how work was done. In the 1960s, many of the fundamental changes brought about by computing and logistics made their initial impact on various parts of the Wholesale Industry.[36] The number of initiatives to improve productivity and speed of execution increased through the 1970s and 1980s.[37] Competitive pressure to keep prices in check also haunted this maturing industry through the same period.

One can quickly summarize the broad business patterns affecting the industry and against this backdrop, later describe how and why it adopted the technologies that it did. The first decade after World War II proved to be a period in which the American economy expanded rapidly, which in turn translated into high demand for new goods. There were many new businesses both in retail and in wholesale. In the second decade after the war (1955–1965), the industry achieved full stride, and all kinds of products were distributed across the nation through a well-developed logistical infrastructure. The next 10 years (1965–1975) continued as a period of growth in sales, and the industry enjoyed very high profits in comparison to previous or subsequent years. But it was also a time in which the industry and the economies in which they worked experienced accelerated inflation, both in the United States and around the world. The next decade (1975–1985) ushered in a long era of transition, one still underway. Economic recession, followed by rapid inflation and escalating interest rates, played havoc with the balance sheets of many wholesalers. Imports into the United States created enormous pressure on retailers and wholesalers to control or drive down costs, improve efficiencies, and speed their responses to changing market conditions. These three changes came at a time when inflation and competition forced many wholesalers to shrink in size. In the decade following (1985–1995), wholesalers made significant improvements in their operations through the use of computer technology. It became their golden age of computing.

The gross domestic product (GDP) of the Wholesale Industry for the period in which massive investments were made in IT, that is, between roughly 1977 to the end of the century, was strong. Thus IT expenditures occurred when the whole industry prospered, in other words, when it could afford such expenditures. Between 1977 and 1998, this industry increased its GDP by 5.5 percent, whereas the Retail Industry increased by 3.7 percent. To put both sets of numbers in context, the Manufacturing Industry expanded by 2.9 percent, and the national GDP grew by 3.1 percent. So, wholesalers did very well in comparison to other industries. Their two greatest periods of growth came in the 1980s and 1990s. In fact, in the latter decade, the industry's GDP reached 6.9 percent; retail had a GDP of 5.7 percent, and manufacturing as a whole, 4.9 percent. In every decade from the 1970s onward, wholesale outperformed other industries.[38]

In the years following 1995, when the Internet became widely available, the industry continued to focus on reducing operational costs. It also developed marketing alliances and adopted a new generation of supply chain management techniques. These changes often called for new services and closer links to customers. In this last period, the focus in the industry also began to shift beyond suppliers to end customers, much as occurred in some manufacturing firms. That shift translated into the creation of virtual organizations, participation in global markets, introduction of mass customized and postsale services, and formation of new partnerships and alliances. E-business also altered relationships between retailers and wholesalers in the years after 1995.

The industry, however, remained fairly consistent in some of its basic concerns through the half century. Wholesalers were fixated on reducing costs by improving operational efficiencies. Improvements involved streamlining processes, reducing or eliminating redundancies, and increasingly toward the end of the century, speeding up their ability to respond to more and smaller orders from retail customers. They adopted all the major managerial fads of the half century, from managing by objectives (MBO) in the 1950s and 1960s to Total Quality Management (TQM) in the 1980s and 1990s, as a way of improving the quality of shipped orders, especially in the 1980s and beyond.[39]

Makeup of the Retail Industry

The Retail Industry has always been a highly fragmented collection of big and small stores, very large chains, and many specialized categories of retail outlets. An effective way to describe this industry is to begin with its current composition, because that is what we are most familiar with, and then to work back to what it looked like in 1950. Table 9.4 provides a snapshot of the industry in the late 1990s from the perspective of U.S. government economists. The data include restaurants and bars—establishments I have chosen not to review in this book, although they are, quite correctly, forms of retail outlets. They did not lead in the innovation and deployment of IT applications but rather adopted those that were developed elsewhere in the industry. For individual restaurants and bars, electronic cash registers and accounting applications ran on PCs or were widely outsourced to accountants; chains adopted some of the applications that were implemented by individual department stores. The other major segments of the Retail Industry in the table are obvious, and the proportions occupied by any of its components have been relatively stable for a number of decades. However, because several were important innovators of IT, I provide case studies of them later in this book. The table lists under "Miscellaneous" many important segments of the industry, such as drug-

Table 9.4
Components of the U.S. Retail Industry, 1997

Component*	Number of Establishments	Sales in Billions	Number of Paid Employees
Automotive dealers & gasoline service stations	202,237	788,232,182	2,283,756
Food stores	171,057	416,047,374	3,109,336
Miscellaneous retail	367,639	365,915,784	2,795,472
Building materials, hardware, Garden supply, mobile home dealers	67,469	146,210,993	830,357
Furniture, furnishings, & equipment	115,124	136,092,998	861,605
Apparel & accessories	126,863	116,613,976	1,116,140
Eating & drinking places	475,907	—	100,000+
General merchandise stores	34,899	—	100,000+
Retail trade totals	1,561,195	2,545,881,473	21,165,862

*The rankings from top to bottom are by sales revenues.

Source: Adapted from U.S. Census Bureau, "1997 Economic Census: Bridge Between SIC and NAICS SIC: Menu of SIC Divisions" (November 11, 2000): 3, http://www.census.gov/epcd/ec97bridg/INDXSIC2.HTM.

stores, liquor stores, used merchandise stores, fuel dealers, and an assortment of nonstore retailers, of which the most obvious are catalog houses (major players in Internet retailing), vending machines, and direct selling.

A common discription of the Retail Industry includes six segments: food services, food retail, pharmacy/drug, specialty, direct marketing, and general merchandise. A seventh is beginning to emerge, called category killers. Food services are restaurants, and there are many chains that have aggressively adopted IT applications, such as McDonalds and Burger King. Food retail comprises grocery stores, the segment that pioneered development of the UPC and the POS. Pharmacy/drug firms, increasingly in large national chains, were early users of POS and built online drug profiles of customers. Major U.S. chains included Walgreens, Eckerd, and Revco. Specialty stores were the fastest-growing segment at the end of the century, specializing in narrow groups of products like coffee, apparel, and books. Key American retailers included Starbucks, Victoria's Secret, Eddie Bauer, and the Gap. Direct marketing included the catalog outlets, TV shopping networks, and over-the-phone sales. High-profile participants included Home Shopping Network and QVC channel, as well as direct retail channels such as J.C. Penny's, L.L. Bean, Starbucks, and even the Metropolitan Museum of Art. General merchandise retailers, which sold a large variety of products, were increasingly parts of large, global chains. They included Wal-Mart, Sears, Kmart, J.C. Penny, and Target. Category killers specialized in one broad type of product, such as toys (Toys 'R Us), elec-

Table 9.5
Fifteen Largest U.S. Retailers, 1998

Wal-Mart Stores	Home Depot	Albertsons
Sears Roebuck	Kroger	Federated Department Stores
Kmart	Safeway	Walgreens
Dayton Hudson	Costco	CVS
J.C. Penney	American Stores	Fred Meyer

Source: Adapted from Michael Levy and Barton A. Weitz, *Retailing Management* (Burr Ridge, Ill.: McGraw-Hill Irwin, 2001): 14.

tronics (Best Buy), or even books (Barnes & Noble), and computers (CompUSA). Table 9.5 lists the 15 largest American retailers, ranked by volumes of sales from the top down. They were all household names, leaders in the industry during the last two decades of the twentieth century.

As we move back in time toward 1950, this industry's landscape changes. For one thing, there were few national chains. Wal-Mart—the largest chain—did not come into existence until the 1970s, but when it did, its management used IT to alter inventory and supply chain management, almost single-handedly changing the way in which retailers conducted business by the early 1990s. Grocery chains were few (discussed in more detail in the next two chapters) and had not yet developed UPC or installed POS applications. There were no such things as killer categories, taking market share away from large chains, but there were many specialty stores, selling everything from books to meat.

The modern history of retailing in America is a complicated story, and we need to understand some of its major features because, after the middle of the 1980s, how the industry evolved resulted directly from its adoption of UPC, EDI, POS, and other B2B and supply chain applications. Other factors also played a part—such as globalization and national economic conditions, to mention two obvious ones—but other than in banking, one would be hard-pressed to find an industry influenced so profoundly by one family of technologies.

Wholesaling and retailing have fascinating histories, and it is tempting to delve into their past. However, I can summarize the early history by saying that in the late nineteenth century the emergence of a national rail system made it possible to move goods around the country in quantity and cost-effectively. That development played a large role in the emergence of large wholesalers (sometimes also called jobbers) and mail order businesses. The growth in both the size and number of cities made possible the emergence of mass retailing after 1880. The business model of the mass retailer—sell in high volumes, turn over inventories frequently, offer lower prices than specialty stores, take cash payments to avoid credit and debts, and rely on the pivotal role of the store buyer—remained essentially intact until the mid-1980s.[40] In the mid-1980s, the injection of IT into the supply chain process led to fundamental changes, such as the decline in the power of the store buyer and a great reliance on POS data to tell manufacturers what to produce and stores what to sell.

Grocery stores in the format of a supermarket began to appear around World War I. By the end of the 1920s, small chains of grocery stores had emerged around the nation, just as chains of department stores had started a generation earlier. Chains expanded into the suburbs after World War II and increased in numbers, and new entrants joined the industry. The one example so frequently cited at the end of the twentieth century was Wal-Mart, established by Sam Walton in the early 1970s, which had become the largest retailer in America in the 1990s. Its revenues at the end of the century equaled the combined sales of Kmart, Sears Roebuck, and Kroger's. Wal-Mart was to retailing what GM was to automobiles or IBM to computing; it was large and influential, often setting the pace for the use of computing and other business practices by rivals, suppliers, and customers.

One of the driving forces in the operations of a store, particularly a chain, and which led to great interest in IT through the last century,[41] was inventory management. Each type of merchandise has a product number, called stockkeeping units (SKUs), which have been used for decades to track inventory. Over time, the number of SKUs that retailers had to manage increased, thereby complicating the data-processing aspects of inventory management. It is not uncommon today, for example, for a discount club like Sam's or Stop & Shop to have 10,000 distinct SKUs, and a grocery story could have between 25,000 and 40,000, some even as many as 60,000. A category killer, such as Home Depot, frequently manages 80,000 SKUs. A mass merchandiser, like Wal-Mart or Kmart, routinely deal with 100,000 to 150,000 SKUs. A department store like Dillard's or Federated can have between 800,000 and 2 million SKUs. That is a massive amount of data to track, and the variety of products that each SKU represents increased in number all through the century.

Before the early 1980s, when POS, EDI, and other uses of IT came into wide use, retailers ordered products they thought they needed long in advance, such as next fall's women's clothing, hoping they guessed right. Orders were large and infrequent (e.g., a few times a year), with the exception of groceries, which had to have more and smaller orders because of the perishable nature of their merchandise. In the pre-1980s business model, successful retailers had to manage inventory levels and merchandise for what they had. By the 1980s, the long lead times between ordering and selling had increased the risk of being stuck with inventory that could not be sold (e.g., unpopular clothing styles) at a time when inflation increased the cost of doing business. Risks also grew because of two other long-term trends: proliferation of products and the increased amount of total selling space per capita, which ushered in a period of heightened competition and price pressures. More SKUs meant increased uncertainty about what would or would not sell, with the attendant risk that a retailer could run out of popular products and not be able to replenish stock in time. Between 1988 and 1992, it was not uncommon for retailers to have doubled the number of SKUs. Coupled with the rapid expansion in the number of strip malls, stores, and large shopping centers, which outpaced the growth in population during the last three decades of the century, retailers had to find ways to drive down costs and reach new customers. The effects on profits were predictable. As several students of the process discovered, overall margins "declined between 1977 and 1987," resulting in an assortment of bankruptcies, mergers, and acquisitions by more successful firms.[42]

The period of the 1970s and 1980s is crucial to our story because this is the time when new forms of computing were widely adopted across the industry. Department stores, which were large enough to be early adopters, were particularly hard hit during these years because they were unable to adapt quickly enough to changing consumer tastes at a time when category killers—specialty stores—expanded, some into national chains. Old stalwarts like Macy's, Gimbels, Saks Fifth Avenue, Federated, and Wanamaker had to file for bankruptcy protection in the late 1980s and early 1990s.

Too much inventory and too many stores chasing too few customers highlighted the inefficiencies of the old wholesaling and retailing supply chain. Markdowns in the price of unsold inventories became increasingly necessary. Lost sales due to stock-outs also increased in the 1970s and 1980s. The cost of holding inventory grew when inflation drove up the cost of capital, sometimes to double-digit interest levels. The Apparel Industry, for example, experienced $25 billion in losses in 1985 alone, with slightly more than half the figure caused by markdowns. Because of the leadership shown by retailers in developing modern supply chain processes that addressed the problem of wrong inventory at the wrong time or in insufficient quantities at the right time, the next two chapters describe how specific industries adopted IT practices. In fact, both grocery and apparel retailers, along with such mass merchandisers as Wal-Mart, were highly successful in introducing new computing applications in the last quarter of the century. The industry's use of the Internet is also discussed in the next two chapters.

Technical Styles and Changes in Wholesaling and Retailing

Chapter 3 ended with a brief discussion about patterns of adoption of information technologies by manufacturing firms. Did the practices evident in the world of wholesaling and retailing mimic those in force in manufacturing industries? Did they differ? In addition to these obvious IT considerations, there are two others: the role of Tylecote's notion of technical styles and fordism in distribution industries. Recall that historian Andrew Tylecote observed that different industries over time developed different working styles. A factory in 1870 was operated differently than one in 1970. They made different products in different ways, using different materials and components. Did the same apply to wholesaling and retailing? How did computing affect their styles? Historians have labeled a style of manufacturing Fordism (mass production), but there have been fewer attempts to characterize retailing in various forms and phases. I describe in the pages ahead how computing clearly influenced the look and feel of both wholesaling and retailing during the last two decades of the twentieth century.

Wholesaling—that is, the use of middlemen between manufacturers and producers, on the one hand, and retailers, on the other hand, as channels of distribution to markets (i.e., stores)—had a style, a way of doing business, that was structured through its own business practices in the United States by the end of the 1880s. Advances in transportation (more trains and then greater use of trucks), communications (telephones and later telecommunications), and accounting and banking practices (checks, cost accounting, and electronic funds transfers) did not fundamentally change the basic role of wholesalers for a century. As Chandler demonstrated, businesses in general filled in the cracks in their business models and roles all through the years from the 1870s through the 1920s. Wholesalers followed that pattern, constantly adopting information technologies to buttress their basic functions until the 1980s.[43]

Did some form of Fordism exist in retailing? The question is intriguing yet complicated to answer because of the enormous variety of retail outlets in the United States. However, I can identify essentially three types, or perhaps styles (using Tylecote's notion), of retailing that in time were profoundly affected by IT. All three coexisted for much of our period of study.

The first was the single store, in the language of the economist, usually a specialty store (e.g., only sold hats or shoes), but it could also be a country store in rural America. These stores dominated retailing until the last years of the nineteenth century, both in sheer number and in the percentage of retail sales they garnished. They still outnumber other retail formats, although they do not collect the lion's share of the industry's revenues. Small, close to their customers, and with a great deal of personal service, their IT tools were simple. The most common for decades were paper files that kept track of credit accounts for customers. By the 1920s, small adding machines such as those sold by Burroughs became relatively common, especially in country stores, where part of the cost of such a device would have been assumed by the U.S. Post Office, which appointed the store owner the local postmaster. Change boxes slowly gave way to cash registers, such as those sold by NCR, in the four decades before World War II. This information infrastructure of account cards, adding machines, and cash registers remained essentially intact until the late 1980s, when inexpensive cash registers appeared that could also track inventory. But in all decades, the small store normally either determined what inventory to acquire or allowed distributors to routinely replace sold merchandise (e.g., local distributors replacing standard food products in similar volumes, such as milk, eggs, and potato chips). That practice of assigning shelf space to a distributor carried over even to the largest retailers of the late twentieth century, with the just-in-time replenishment processes designed by Wal-Mart and others.[44]

The second type of store, larger in physical size and carrying more variety of merchandise, was the department store, such as Gimbels or Marshall Fields. Initially in the late 1800s these were multifloor, urban firms, which in many cases evolved into multistore chains that slowly spread across the nation during the twentieth century, such as Sears and Marshall Fields. These stores carried out the same functions as the single store, but because of their larger size they had far more complex information requirements. By the end of the nineteenth century, they had acquired a style of operation and an IT infrastructure that remained relatively intact until late in the next century. Because they had departments, individual sets of accounting records were kept to track performance, cash collection, and inventory. With many employees working various shifts, accounting, payroll, and personnel records became essential for day-to-day operations. Complex credit and billing systems emerged. Marshall Fields, for example, became the first major user of punch-card equipment in the industry, acquiring this technology at the dawn of the twentieth century from the firm that eventually became known as IBM.[45] The large variety of accounting products available from Burroughs and others went into these firms, too, such as billing and accounting machines, cash registers, tabulators, calculators, adding machines, pneumatic tubes (to move paper from one floor to another), and a myriad of paper-based information processes.[46] They used all these IT systems concurrently.

Buyers were the kings and queens in this style of operation. They selected what merchandise to acquire, often placing orders months in advance, and were held accountable for having the right mix of goods. The signs of their failure were the markdowns that filled the "bargain basements" of Gimbels and other retailers. Their reign did not end until the late 1980s, when part of their responsibilities were subsumed into new IT processes. These new methods included the collection of customer purchase data by POS terminals; the use of UPC labels to track the physical flow and sale of merchandise, down to the SKU level; and the use of EDI to signal to wholesalers what to deliver to specific stores and when and, by inference, to tell manufacturers what to manufacture. Thus, the style Tylecote refers to remained intact until these new IT systems could be lashed together in the 1980s. Following Chandler's notion that firms that survived and thrived were those that invested sufficiently in, among other things, distribution and marketing, we can observe that this pattern existed in the Retail Industry between the 1870s and the present. Toward the end of the twentieth century, the industry's investments in IT were significant, resulting in substantial changes in marketing, merchandising, accounting, and inventory practices.

A third type, or style, is a variant of the second, and it involved the emergence of the very large chains in the last three decades of the twentieth century. Wal-Mart is the most obvious example. These were stores that depended heavily on a complex web of IT applications, telecommunications, direct links to suppliers (not just wholesalers but also manufacturers), and highly integrated supply chains where manufacturers saw the retailer's forecasts and buying preferences and shared in POS data to determine what to make and ship.[47] This third model is currently receiving the greatest amount of attention by those commenting about the convergence of the Internet and e-business with bricks-and-mortar retailers.[48] These firms are global and often have hundreds of store fronts and growing numbers of SKUs. They normally have their own regional distribution centers that dwarf in size the warehouses of major wholesalers several decades earlier. These facilities are tightly linked to stores and suppliers. It is not uncommon, for example, in a warehouse owned by Wal-Mart, to see trucks arrive with goods in the morning that are shipped out of the building in the afternoon. These warehouses operate 24 hours a day, 365 days a year, and are larger than a square city block. This style of retailing is different from the gentle inner-city department store of the 1950s, which had a tearoom on the fourth floor where mothers took their daughters to lunch.

In the last decade of the twentieth century, a new style of retailer emerged that in time we might refer to as a fourth model, possibly a new Fordism, and it came in two forms. The first was the totally online e-tailer, epitomized by Amazon.com and eBay (which some would argue is an auction house, not a traditional retailer). They had warehouses to store some merchandise but essentially used telecommunications to link to suppliers who delivered directly to customers, allowing the e-tailer to track the transactions and take a portion of the revenue as its fee. Customers used the Internet to reach these e-tailers to inquire about products or to conduct transactions.[49] Many of the processes used in this kind of retailing emerged out of catalog-retailing practices more than one century old.[50] A second emerging variant was the combination Internet-based operation and traditional physical store, such as Barnes & Noble, which sold many books and CDs over the Internet but also had walk-in stores where one could exchange merchandise or buy additional products. In the middle years of the 1990s, the two models were distinct; one was either an e-tailer or a bricks-and-mortar retailer. Later, major chains operated in both channels but treated them as distinctly separate lines of business. Not until the early years of the twenty-first century did a merged model begin to appear, made possible by the linking of preexisting IT applications so that customers had multiple, yet integrated, channels for transacting business. That integration of applications also occurred between a retailer that was supporting both stores and Internet sales through its supply chain to manufacturers and producers.[51] Without extensive application of the digital in computing and communications, this new style of retailing would not have been possible.

Thus, what we see first, in retailing in particular, as well as in wholesaling, is that (as in manufacturing) the largest firms were the first to need and use the constantly emerging new forms of IT. Second, they adopted new applications of computing in an evolutionary manner until the development of the UPC and more advanced forms of telecommunications (EDI and the Internet). At that point there was a spurt forward in the adoption of new uses at a speed that exceeded previous developments. That extensive adoption began to cause changes in fundamental tasks, as in manufacturing in the 1970s and 1980s, with the wide adoption of CAD/CAM. As in manufacturing, historic roles of retail firms remained the same: to promote products, to sell them, and to get them into the hands of their customers. As with manufacturers, the use of information technologies came into the industry early, long before the arrival of the Internet that has so captured the attention of commentators on modern work practices. What we can say, therefore, is that a new style of retailing was emerging during the last two decades of the twentieth century, made possible by the extensive use of computing.

Information Flows in Retailing

Before I discuss the adoption of specific applications and technologies in the next chapter, a brief overview of information flows in retailing provides the context for the use of IT in retailing (just as I identified the context for manufacturing applications in manufacturing practices in Chapter 3). This discussion is essential because both industries had a symbiotic relationship; each knew what the other was doing in adopting technologies for the physical movement of inventory, automated accounting practices, IT in products, data mining for customer interests, IT-driven inventory management practices, and ultimately the merger into tighter formats of supply chains among manufacturers and retailers.

How did information flow in the 1950s, at the dawn of the computer's arrival in commercial settings? Figure 9.1 illustrates in general terms the developments in chains and large individual stores. Essentially four sets of information flowed back and forth through a retail enterprise (store or firm) and across the formal or ad hoc supply chain to and through wholesalers and finally back into manufacturing. Different representations of the flow of information are possible, but the key point of this figure is that there were interactions among the acquisition of goods, the physical movement and disposal of them, and the collection and management of cash, people, and stores. In a chain store of the 1960s, various forms of IT would have been used in support of each cluster of data.

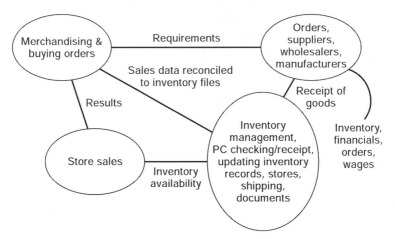

Figure 9.1

Information flows in a department store, circa 1960. IBM employees in the 1980s used the term systems *more frequently than the word* applications *to emphasize their focus on the role of software. Users thought in terms of applications with software a component of these. Chart is a modification of a representation in IBM,* Applications and Abstracts 1985 *(White Plains, N.Y.: IBM Corporation, 1985): 13–1.*

• **INDICATES AVAILABILITY OF IBM APPLICATION OFFERING(S)**

Figure 9.2
Distribution (wholesale). Courtesy IBM Corporate Archives.

Now examine figures 9.2 and 9.3 which illustrate the kinds of specific applications a wholesaler and retailer would have used in the mid-1980s. Note the enormous complexity in figure 9.3, which illustrates applications common to many sectors of retailing and those unique to only one. In both figures we see (note dots outside the circles) that at least one computer vendor of the time (IBM) had products in support of these applications. If we added software tools from other vendors, the number of IT products available in support of these two collections of applications would actually be greater.[52] The document from IBM, from which these figures came, was written to instruct field personnel about customers' uses in var-

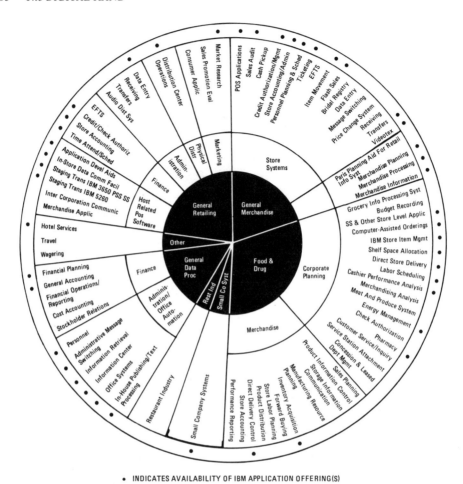

• INDICATES AVAILABILITY OF IBM APPLICATION OFFERING(S)

Figure 9.3
Retail/point of sale. Courtesy IBM Corporate Archives.

ious industries in the mid-1980s. In an instruction manual from the period, we learn that, as in manufacturing, some basic accounting applications remained central to the operation of a retailer:

- Customer service includes the billing, accounts receivable, sales analysis, and credit management application areas.
- Financial applications include general ledger, accounts payable, and payroll application areas.
- The inventory management and inventory acquisition applications include demand forecasting, forward buying, inventory control (accounting), and purchasing.[53]

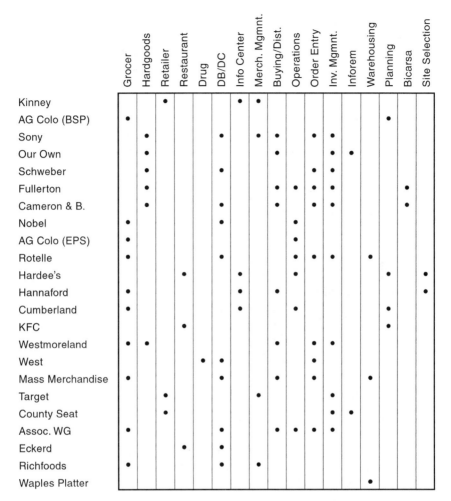

Figure 9.4
Application brief summary. Courtesy IBM Corporate Archives.

This document was written when IBM was on the verge of dominating U.S. sales of POS equipment (late 1980s), taking market share away from its archrival in the Retail Industry, NCR. In fact, by the end of 1987, IBM had become the leading provider of POS equipment in the world and thus familiar with the practices of many retailers in the United States and elsewhere, especially those of the largest firms in the industry like Wal-Mart, Sears, and J.C. Penney. For that reason, it is worth looking again at this company's application wheel (figure 9.3). What is particularly stunning is the variety of information-handling applications that were emerging from this technology, in effect, a store-level system of applications. Variations of these products and applications were used in large and small enterprises, including the EDI software and tools available at the time. Figure 9.4 told IBM employees which applications the firm had documents for (application briefs), describing the deployment of all types of retail applications (including POS) that could be used for marketing. However, for our purposes, the chart is more useful as an indicator of the kinds of applications operating successfully in the mid-1980s and the specific retailers using them.[54]

As with manufacturing industries, software was used in retailing and wholesaling mostly to improve efficiencies and speed and to integrate applications so that information from one could flow to and affect other collections of data and applications. Linking data processing made possible the integration of disparate functions. As in manufacturing, to a large extent the story of digital applications was similar: the creation of new software tools, investments in IT as its costs kept coming down, deployment across many industry segments, and finally integration of applications across departments, stores, companies, and industries. As in manufacturing, the management of various aspects of inventory, from acquisition to sale, proved essential and was the primary focus of retailers through the half century. The ability to use POS data by the end of the 1980s provided a second focus: understanding customers and improving a retailer's ability to sell additional merchandise. That second focus—the customer—went far toward making possible the "killer apps" that stimulated the profound changes currently underway in the industry. More than the adoption of the Internet for e-commerce, it was the ability to collect, analyze, and alter business practices in response to market conditions, beginning in the 1980s, that made possible so many changes. A similar transformation in the management of inventory in the 1970s had had an equally similar effect on the industry, as shown by the emergence of Wal-Mart and other retailers of the same ilk.

So, as was evident in manufacturing industries, retailing industries were transformed simultaneously from earlier business models by the adoption of a variety of computer applications that were integrated, cross-functional, and linked to telecommunications. The confluence of when changes came to an industry and when it installed IT was more than a coincidence. For that reason, the next chapter is devoted to an overview of the adoption of computer-based applications in all wholesale and retail industries.

10

Business Patterns and Digital Applications in the Transformation of the Wholesale and Retail Industries

The two most important things we can do are manage inventory and lower expenses.

—David Glass, 1999

The use of information-processing tools by wholesalers and retailers changed over time in response to the arrival of new technologies, but the reasons for their use remained relatively constant. Inventory and labor costs were high on the list of concerns through most of the twentieth century in all firms; that clearly was the message conveyed by David Glass, Wal-Mart's CEO, following two decades of remarkable growth by his company. Information-handling technologies came into their own when their costs declined enough to offset the costs of managing inventory and labor with previous methods. During the last decade of the twentieth century and in the early years of the next millennium, competition over quality, pricing, global economics, and growing consumer demand for more and varied products made the use of computing essential, thereby continuing to reinforce the ubiquitous position of IT. Just as there were phases in the evolution and adoption of technology in manufacturing, so, too, did wholesalers and retailers experience waves of deployment. To be sure, technologies had to become increasingly reliable and cost-effective, as in manufacturing. Retailers and wholesalers also worried about the cost of labor and inventory. The third similarity with manufacturing was the emergence of industry-specific digital tools, such as UPC and POS (in the case of retail), which made possible automation of tasks unique to these industries.

The new reasons for adopting a digital technology, however, did not always mirror precisely the circumstances that were motivating manufacturing. There were also significant differences. First, although there were many precomputer IT tools in all distribution industries, computers did not begin to appear in this sector of the economy until nearly the end of the 1950s, unlike in manufacturing, where these information engines were first installed at the start of the decade. To a large extent, the reason for the later arrival can be attributed to the absence of fewer large enterprises than in manufacturing, in combination with the lack of available alternative technologies that could displace calculators, adding machines, and tabulators.

A second difference lay in the initiative retailers took in developing and deploying unique technologies: credit card sales and, especially, the universal product code (UPC). Although I can characterize the deployment of computers in manufacturing as widespread by the end of the 1960s, retailers and wholesalers did not fundamentally arrive at their new style of technology until the end of the 1980s. Thus the eras differ from those in manufacturing. But, as in the industrial sector, chronological periods in the adoption of the digital provides a useful mechanism for cataloging events and their consequences. The middle years of the century were quiet (concerning the arrival of the digital in retailing and wholesaling), but by the end of the 1980s one could describe the industry as noisy and busy, adopting all kinds of computing and changing business practices in fundamental ways. By the end of the 1990s, that adoption made links between and among wholesalers, retailers, and manufacturers so close and interdependent that one could begin to speak about the entire economy as moving to its own new post-Fordist style. The look and feel of the American economy and the rhythm of the wholesale and retail business had changed sufficiently by 2000 that patterns of behavior from 1950 seemed antiquated because, indeed, they had been transformed.

Before discussing applications of computing, I should note that impressions and realities varied in retail industries as they did in manufacturing. Just as the Petroleum Industry was viewed by many observers as a late adopter of computing—although in reality it had been an early and effective user of computers—so, too, a similar process could be seen at work in retailing, and even more so in wholesaling. One industry watcher in the mid-1950s acknowledged retail's backward reputation: "Much has been written criticizing the retailing industry for being lax in investigating and employing office automation equipment." However, this observer also noted, "In turn, retailers have complained that the equipment manufacturers have not produced machines suitable for application to the retailing field." An internal report by an expert on the Wholesale Industry at IBM in 2000 leveled a similar charge against wholesalers, suggesting that they were not keeping up with both the business realities of modern retailing and its IT tools.[1]

Retailers proved reluctant to invest in technologies that did not immediately result in lower operating costs because they faced intense competition, far in excess of that seen by many manufacturing industries in that period. Yet, they had not hesitated to use other information technologies in the decades before the arrival of the computer.[2] In the 1950s, their need for gains in productivity was sufficient, however, to "rouse the reluctant retailing dragon."[3] As occurred in the Petroleum Industry, there is much evidence of experimenting with new accounting and IT systems in retail in the 1950s.

The history of retailing (and most of wholesaling) applications can be divided into three periods, about which the rest of this chapter is organized. The first, covering the arrival of the digital and early applications of computing, occurred in the 1950s through the early 1970s—a relatively long period of gestation—as they tried to find ways to exploit the emerging technologies. They discovered that general-purpose computers by themselves did not provide economically compelling, industry-altering applications. However, in the second period, the years from the early to mid-1970s through the 1980s and even into the early 1990s, circumstances changed radically. New technologies that were industry-specific (e.g., POS and UPC) and those, that proved to be cost-effective and functionally attractive (e.g., EDI) spread throughout these industries. The third period, encompassing the years when the Internet came into its own in a commercial setting (post-1994), brought fundamental changes to the way in which retailers and wholesalers did business, building on the momentum started with POS, UPC, and EDI applications in earlier years. Both industries entered the twenty-first century by undergoing basic

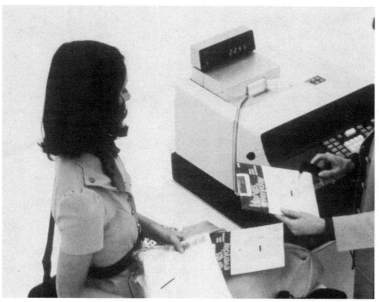

This is a very early use of a point-of-sale terminal by an American retailer in 1973. The sales clerk passes a wand over a piece of magnetically encoded merchandise to collect price and inventory information, calculate change, and print a receipt. Courtesy IBM Corporate Archives.

changes in how they performed their work and communicated and interacted with customers, suppliers, and rivals. It was a period still unfolding as this book went to press.

First Period: The Arrival of the Digital to Warehouses and Stores, 1950s–Mid-1970s

Americans came out of World War II with money to spend and a massive pent-up demand for consumer goods caused by their scarcity during the war. Companies needed to replenish everything, it seemed, from office supplies and furniture to whole buildings. Manufacturing industries converted back to peacetime production of goods, and retailers expanded their sales and the number of stores around the country. They did this during a period when many new households were being created and while homeowners were creating the biggest baby boom in American history, as well as the modern middle class. Between 1945 and 1954, retail sales more than doubled. Variety and department store sales increased by 60 percent; and small stores did much better. After 1954, variety stores picked up momentum, too.[4] Variety stores had the resources necessary to adopt computers and other expensive IT, and they included such household names as Sears Roebuck, Montgomery Ward, and J.C. Penney, all icons of American retailing.

During the national economic boom, however, average gross margins, expenses, and profit percentages did not balance proportionately with the growth in sales. Profits trended downward among chain stores and probably in other retail sectors with intensifying competition. Pretax net gains for national chains in 1950, for example, had been 10 percent, but they declined over the next four years, drifting down to 7 percent. Regional chains turned in a poorer performance, moving from 8.9 percent down to 6.7 percent.[5] At the time, payroll proved to be the largest expense, 17.4 percent of sales for national chains (in 1950), 18.8 percent for regional chains. In 1954, the cost of labor to national chains amounted to 18.7 percent of sales, for the regional chains (usually called regionals) 19.8 percent. One contemporary report on the industry noted that "payroll as the largest single expense category, and one which has been advancing steadily, offers a natural point of attack."[6]

Executives concluded that they had to increase the productivity of their staffs. The collective choice made by management in the 1950s was not to rush to computers, as we saw in manufacturing at the same time, but rather to a nontechnical option, self-service and checkout. Many stores in the 1950s spent their innovative energies on increasing the already occurring trend of open shelves and counters which the Grocery Industry had developed in earlier decades. Customers could wander around the store, look at merchandise, and bring it to a checkout stand at the front of the establishment for purchase. This format reduced the number of clerks required, eliminated many departmental checkout stands, and increased productivity at the checkout counters. A byproduct of this change in layout was the increased importance placed by management on next improving productivity at the cash register, creating the historic preconditions needed for the development of digitized, point-of-sale terminals in the 1970s and 1980s.

Attacking the Inventory Problem

This discussion about employees' productivity does not discount the significance of inventory management. Inventory was another giant expense for all stores, and the need to drive down its cost, while increasing inventory turns, was always a compelling business issue. Most studies of the industry emphasized concerns over inventory management, instead of balancing those with personnel costs. In reality, both have to be considered in any analysis of the adoption of technologies in these early years. When personnel productivity increased in later decades—in part because of the reformatting of stores—inventory management became an issue of greater importance.[7] However, it was the combination of personnel practices and inventory management that together provided much of the justification for industry-specific applications for computing until the late 1960s.

We should not minimize the importance of sound inventory management. A computer veteran of the period, Walter M. Carlson, recalled that "the retail industry faced daunting problems in tracking inventory, following buyers' trends in making purchases, and increasing customer services to gain customer loyalty."[8] A study of variety chains in 1951 reported that "inventories piled up substantially, especially for the national chains, and fewer stock turns were realized."[9] A report published six years later continued to reiterate similar inventory problems: "Inventories at the end of the year were higher than at the beginning of the year." To put the costs in perspective, in 1957 inventory expenses amounted to about 11 to 12 percent of a store's sales, while payroll ended the year at just over 19 percent of costs.[10]

But how could computing technologies or other forms of record keeping help with inventory expenses? Was this not just a problem of acquiring merchandise that was bought in the wrong quantities or that customers did not want to buy? These were problems that always dogged a retailer and went far in providing the business justification for data mining of customer purchase data in the 1980s and 1990s, which became a standard application in all substantial retailing operations by the end of the twentieth century. In fact, online retailers, such as Amazon.com, were valued not because of their profits (often negative) and cash flows (which often were poor) but because of the data they had collected about consumer behavior. Both poor and effective inventory managers have the same problem: record keeping and the challenge of understanding what that information says about consumer behavior.

An application brief written in July 1956 to tout the virtues of the Dennison Print-Punch System for ticket inventory control and sales analysis described the operational problem. After explaining the requirement in those days of having to put tags on all merchandise to track inventory and to perform sales analysis, the report bemoaned how the problem increased with the volume and variety of inventory:

By the mid-1970s, terminals were nearly ubiquitous in all work settings, not just in offices or factories. In this example from 1976, an automobile salesperson could query a nationwide network of 700 dealers to find a specific car for a customer. This application was used by both new and secondhand auto dealers in the United States. Courtesy IBM Corporate Archives.

> Perhaps nowhere are the difficulties of such record-keeping so burdensome— ordinarily—as in the ladies ready-to-wear section of almost any large department store. Thus, the principles of any office system that will simplify the task in a department store are likely to have broad possibilities of usefulness, allowing for minor revisions, in almost any kind of establishment where there's a wide diversity of items and in large quantities.[11]

In this instance, management opted for a small, four-part identification ticket, which could provide data that were mechanically processed as part of tracking inventory, using an accounting machine. The cards were machine-readable, providing data on additions and deletions from inventory. An official at Kobacker Stores in Toledo, Ohio, used this system, reporting that without mechanization this useful information would have been too expensive to collect. The data captured through this approach provided information that, "tells us continuously whether our total inventory is at acceptable standards" and "tells us accurately and quickly which styles are most popular and whether—item by item—we have them in adequate supply or on order." It also allowed the store to measure how effective its advertising campaigns were. Reflecting the spirit of confidence in IT that existed at the same time in manufacturing, managers noted that "we get all those benefits by a procedure that is relatively low in cost and that is practically fool-proof."[12]

Other clothing stores, primarily large chains, adopted this kind of system in the 1950s. Bloomingdale's, for instance, installed a similar system in 40 selling departments within its main store in downtown New York and in several dozen other departments in other stores. In the early 1950s, Macy's in New York had also started to mechanize its ready-to-wear inventory so that it could provide its buyers with accurate daily and weekly reports on inventory.[13]

Predigital POS Initiatives

When discussing the history of retailing, it is normal to date the industry's interest in POS technologies to the 1970s; however, some chains began to address problems with productivity and data collection at the point of sale with computing as early as the mid-1950s. The W.T. Grant Company in New York launched the major initiative of the period. In 1957, this company generated $400 million in sales, up nearly $50 million over the previous two years. In the mid-1950s, it had 574 stores, and by the end of 1957, 691 stores in 41 states, making it a large retail operation. The manager of standard methods, Glen P. Charpie, began to look for new ways to improve point-of-sale accounting systems in 1952. The problem he worked on involved "cash register expense," the accumulation of operating costs and capital investments; existing technologies were not up to the task. He convinced the Monroe Calculating Machine Company to build a prototype of a workable point-of-sale system, the first in the nation. During the summer of 1957 a prototype was installed in the company's store in Pompton Lakes, New Jersey, code-named Elly (short for electronic computer). In January 1958, management decided to expand the system to more than 20 stores. The Grant Distributape system collected an analysis of a store's retail sales by department and produced a series of reports by store. A combination of cash registers and adding machines were used to record data on paper tape; these devices collected results at the rate of 1,000 transactions per minute. Various store and inventory reports were then produced, along with statistical analysis of merchandising data; physical inventory counts were made, and open-to-buy positions reported. The system also collected payroll-reporting information. In short, it was a rudimentary in-store accounting system.[14]

A more sophisticated project took place under the sponsorship of the Associated Merchandising Corporation, which acquired an RCA Bizmac computer to implement POS applications in the mid-1950s. Burdine's Department Store installed a Royal Precision LGP-30 computer system in its Miami, Florida, store in 1958 to collect and analyze over 3,000 daily transactions. Reports from this system included one on errors and one on cash; others were generated on sales by type, salesperson, department, and class of merchandise. The new system proved less expensive than the 24 employees required before its installation to process and audit sales information.[15]

During the late 1950s, other department stores experimented with computers for various applications. One of the larger projects of the time involved the use of a UNIVAC 60 system by J.J. Haggarty Stores, a women's specialty shop, making possible charge account services for large numbers of customers. The company had experimented with charge accounts since the 1930s and, in the years immediately after World War II, with tabulating equipment. The standard credit-accounting process that eventually became available across the industry was moved to the computer; a process for opening an account, performing a sales transaction, authorizing extended credit, doing daily closeouts, and generating cash payment reporting were part of the system. Data resided on punch cards. This system calculated and printed billing and collection notices. Haggarty's was the first company to adopt 90-day charge accounts and the first to mechanize its billing in retail. By using a computer it reduced the cost of generating bills, produced reports rapidly and daily, and kept customer records current within the month; clerks added new accounts at almost no cost, and billing statements were only generated for active accounts.[16]

Big Chains and Big Computers

Inventory control applications, of course, were always the subject of much attention on the part of large chains. Montgomery Ward used an IBM RAMAC 305 system—the first computer system to have disk drives—to store and access data. Its engineers had concluded that they needed data-handling functions more than raw computing, so they used the system in the company's distribution organization to feed inventory to 80 retail stores and 37 catalog centers.[17] Inventory billing had long proved especially onerous because it was slow, subject to errors, and labor-intensive. A pharmaceutical firm experienced in using IBM punch-card equipment since 1920, the Norwich Pharmaceutical Company also installed an IBM RAMAC 305 for the same reason as Montgomery Ward: it could handle 50,000 records and process information in random sequence. This system, which made it possible to quickly prebill in ever larger volumes, was started in October 1958. The effects on workflows mimicked what occurred at other retail firms:

> Under the previous system, seven separate handlings were required to prepare a sales analysis report. Now, under the new procedure, only three are required. Sales reports and cost of sales are now prepared the day following the close of a month for shipments from Norwich. Preparation of financial statements have been reduced by one week. Timely reporting and direct inquiry of sales and inventory information have enabled operating personnel to closely follow inventory and sales trends.[18]

By the late 1950s, computer vendors had already identified a market for specialized equipment in support of these applications. For example, IBM touted a merchandise control system for retail chains in 1959, using its 1401 computer system.[19]

Wholesalers were also busy in this first decade of commercial computing. Bergen Drug used an IBM RAMAC 305, beginning in July 1959, to conduct online accounting and inventory control, making it the first drug wholesaler in America to use a computer for this purpose. Inventory control was its central application, tracking products and a growing matrix of discounts, and using prepunched cards for stock picking. The computer produced reports on inventory, purchasing and receiving, accounts receivable, and returns to manufacturer.[20] Super Valu Stores, a food wholesaler, used a UNIVAC File-Computer to do the same job—process orders and provide inventory control.[21] The Henry B. Gilpin Company, a wholesale drug firm, revamped its warehousing and inventory control operations with the use of a UNIVAC 60 system, making it possible to handle 500 orders each day, shipping some of them within an hour of receipt, while maintaining current records. Like other systems of the day, these were based on the use of punch cards as the paper trail for merchandise and picking orders, and they used online data or information on tape for the batch processing of reports and invoices and for ad hoc inquiries. The effects on Gilpin were the same as observed elsewhere: order-processing time was cut in half; completed invoices were shipped with products; expedited orders were accurately reported; "there was almost complete elimination of overtime," as well as faster, more accurate reports and a greater sense of "tighter management control" over daily operations.[22]

Although the variety and extent of computing in retailing and wholesaling industries in the 1950s paled in comparison to that in manufacturing industries, firms were clearly beginning to install applications in support of central activities of the industry. These applications were overwhelmingly used for accounting and information. In the 1960s, however, deployment of computing for these applications, and many others, began to have wider influences on the nature of work. The industry was settling into a now recognizable pattern in its adoption of digital applications. Tracking sales and providing information about inventory (on hand, on order, and stock-outs), through the use of computers increased, although results in the form of better inventory control only improved as the decade progressed.[23] A second important trend involved the continued deployment by large retailers of ticket systems on merchandise to track inventory, such as the Kimball system mentioned above. By the early 1960s these systems were beginning to feed data to digital systems for analysis; the IBM 1282, could read documents produced at the point of sale, like punch-card sales checks, many of which included a customer's account number. Early optical scanners also came into use at this time, such as the IBM 1418, which read merchandise price tags.[24] A similar pattern of adoption took place at Giant Target in Cleveland, Ohio. The company used optical scanning to collect data to generate reports on daily, weekly, and monthly sales and inventory.[25] Silently, almost invisibly, merchants, (like manufacturing firms) installed computer-based accounting systems that leveraged the speed and power of the digital.[26]

Hard data on the deployment and consequences of computing for the period of the late 1950s and early 1960s remain sparse; only impressionistic information is available. For example, C. Robert McBrier, the vice president of finance at Woodward & Lothrop, an upscale department store in Washington, D.C., gave a speech in 1963 to a group of data processing professionals, summarizing the current situation:

> Some department stores have installed medium-sized computers, primarily for the processing of accounts receivable and for billing, but only a few are devel-

oping sophistication in their merchandise data systems. In contrast, we find that the national chain stores specializing in "ready-to-wear" are practically all now employing computers, and their merchandising decisions are based on facts available from the electronic processing system.[27]

He was blunt and frank, however, in his assessment of achievements: "There are very few real success stories to date, and I know of no executives who are representing that they have received great benefits from new systems."[28] Echoing a point of view held in manufacturing industries at the same time—that is, before the arrival of the IBM S/360 and other similarly designed computers of the mid-1960s—McBrier complained that systems were too expensive and that their "up time" was less than that of mechanical devices, speculating that until both of these problems were fixed the prospects for extensive deployment of computers in retailing would remain limited.[29]

The U.S. government's own nose count of computer users suggested that McBrier might have understated the extent of deployment of this digital technology. By roughly 1965, some 500 computers were in use in 300 of the larger retail firms in the United States. The difference between his observation and the government's count can be largely explained by the fact that some of the more aggressive, early users of computers were wholesalers, whose inventory was in the 500 systems counted by government researchers. Applications on these 500 systems started with accounting and, by the early 1960s, included more efficient inventory control, sales forecasting, scheduling of work, and rudimentary software tools for measuring merchandising and promotion results. Wholesalers focused considerable attention on using these machines to improve the efficiency of warehouse management (especially space), physical movement of goods, and inventory management.[30]

The perception that retailers were more laggards in the use of computers, than manufacturing firms triggered the kind of debate in the mid-1960s that McBrier's comments revealed. One professor of management, Donald H. Sanders, even went so far as to conduct a study of 100 small southwestern firms to understand the reluctance of retailers to use computers, concluding that the technology was not yet cost-justified or tailored to the needs of the industry. Sanders also pointed out, however, that employees also resisted adoption of computer-based procedures because of their "fear of a reduction in security and in social need satisfactions." The most experienced employees consistently fought adoption, despite the fact that computing created new positions; loss of status proved to be an essential influence in the rate of adoption.[31] Samuel B. Harvey, a corporate systems manager in the mid-1960s, acknowledged that retailers were perfectly prepared to spend money on computing, but the technology did not fit as neatly into their industry as in manufacturing. The lack of a technical heritage that could facilitate the transition to computers posed a bigger problem. Manufacturing firms had long worked with punch-card technology, so tabulators became a technical bridge to computers. Harvey noted that "in the retail industry punched cards had at best been of marginal value and at the worst had been involved in some disastrous fiascos. The bridge to computers from punched cards was not present." Therefore, the kinds of insights about the industry that computer manufacturers had in the industrial sector were simply not there. He cited the example of lack of product development in POS technology and the inability of computers to handle the large volumes of sales that would have to be captured on computers (e.g., 50,000 sales per day in a large department store).[32]

Yet, as the 1960s continued, larger firms did implement computer-based stock control, sales management processes, and inventory management applications. Clerical functions that were automated worked reasonably well, as they did in manufacturing industries. Merchandise control applications still did not measure up, although inventory management systems did provide some improved performance. Users continued to complain in the late 1960s that the cost of computing remained too high relative to other options.[33] An important study conducted near the end of the decade suggested that there was more to the story than simply expensive hardware not designed for retailers. David McConaughy, a professor of marketing at the University of Southern California, after conducting his own survey, concluded that there was "a close correlation between the current use of automatic data processing in department store inventory management and the method of inventory management." A store that maintained perpetual inventory records tended to deploy computing most successfully because in such an approach the requirement was to process large amounts of data in short periods of time, a good use of computers. The firms most happy with computers reported that they had improved control of branch stocks, identified movement of goods, and made planning inventory needs more effective "due to faster reporting of information, improved breakdown of information, and the availability of additional information possible with computer-based systems."[34] In other words, as in manufacturing and process industries, *fit* proved important as a source of benefits. In addition, as smaller computers became available in the late 1960s, with their lower costs, new users adopted this technology, making it easier to justify automation.[35]

The various retail industries entered the 1970s, collectively frustrated with the level of technological innovations underway. Inventory control software tools remained elusive, largely because of the intense amount of work needed to label and track so many stock items. Large stores, for example, carried over 100,000 items, and as one report from the period noted, such a large number required millions of workers' hours to count and order inventory. The consequences were frustrating:

> The time required to count and order also placed a limit on the extent to which turnover could be improved by ordering more often in smaller quantities. Furthermore, the great number of ordering decisions that had to be made limited the department manager to a cursory consideration of most items so that the quality of the decisions suffered. Poor ordering decisions led to stockouts, overstock, and low turnover.[36]

Large chains continued to lead the way in putting punch-card tags on products and collecting them at cash registers for subsequent updating of inventory records. That information then made it possible for chains to establish automated forecasting and reordering rules that could be programmed, and other computer-driven guidelines could be created for maintaining safety stocks and setting order quantities based on patterns of sales.

When the results of such approaches were reported within the industry, the news was relatively good, providing one was willing to invest in the development of these complex, expensive computing applications, some of which took years of incremental programming and trial and error to implement. The benefits typically fell into three categories. First, sales rose when inventory management applications went online because there were fewer stock-outs. Second, when customers learned that a particular store tended to have what they wanted; they were more likely to return. Third, these systems also shifted away from store personnel a substantial amount of the burden of counting stock, maintaining inventory and sales records, reordering of merchandise, and so forth. Therefore it was possible either for store personnel to spend more time with customers, and improve sales and promotions, or (as occurred later in the century) for chains to reduce the number of clerks on the floor.[37]

POS Just Before the Birth of the Digital Cash Register

Point-of-sale applications—the second leg in any family of computerized applications of the period—were still very expensive and primitive during the early years of the 1970s. Because there would be an enormous change in that situation by the end of the decade, understanding the reality at the store level at the dawn of that change is essential if we are to appreciate the magnitude of the transformation that was about to occur. There were anticipation and nervous concerns around the industry that change was in the air. One reporter for *Datamation* began an article in 1971 with the comment that "the retail industry is on the threshold of a conversion to electronic point-of-sale terminals from mechanical cash registers."[38] A manager at Dayton's, a Minneapolis-based department store chain, however, reminded everyone that "although there are some personnel cost savings which can be estimated" from using new technologies, "added equipment rentals are projected to more than offset these savings."[39]

Retailing was (and continues to be) an intense transaction-oriented business; thus, digital application had to be able to handle a large volume of data very quickly. At the start of the 1970s, some affordable applications were coming on-stream to collect the thousands of pieces of information necessary to make any system attractive, both in terms of how a sales transaction was conducted with a customer and, from the broader perspective, of how inventory and labor were managed. By the early 1970s, retailers had adopted the concept of stockkeeping units (SKUs) and were beginning to develop software tools to track them. This was most evident in the Apparel Industry where, for example, an item of clothing had to be stocked in a half-dozen different sizes, each in several colors. As explained in the next chapter, apparel retailers led the process of developing new technologies and applications to exploit SKUs. Credit checking was a second issue at the time; stores had developed several ways to check credit balances of their customers and to determine if a check should be honored. Credit authorization had evolved so much that several national services existed, along with a company's own credit depart-ment. A clerk, however, had to call in a credit check by telephone. Automating that process, by integrating a POS system, did not occur until late in the century, al-though attempts were made to use CRTs that were connected online to records in a limited number of instances by the dawn of the 1970s.

At the time (early 1970s), most cash registers were mechanical, often equipped with punched paper-tape outputs that could be read with optical scanners. Yet, most stores still read these tapes at the end of the day to understand what sales had occurred. There were more advanced electromechanical tools (e.g., the Uni-Tote terminal since 1965) but these were in such limited use that they can be considered exceptions. Finally, there was no automated system for recording the product sold at the point of sale. The printed punch ticket attached to a product had to be removed and, subsequent to the sale, "read" to understand what was sold. As a reporter for *Datamation* observed, "The most common method in use for collection of this data is to remove the ticket physically from the goods, collect it at the point of sale, and process it at the close of business in batch mode. Currently there are some limited installations of special-purpose readers located at the point of sale which can read these tickets and record the information on tape as the transaction occurs."[40] But this was the exception and still experimental.

Despite limitations of the technology, management's focus on the point of sale had clearly shifted from merely collecting cash to accumulating data. As one mem-ber of the industry described the situation:

> Today, the point-of-sale system for data capture of many retailers consists of a variety of punch tickets, punch cards, punch paper tape, and optical cash reg-ister journal tapes with some keyboard data entry on conventional cash register keyboards. Point-of-receipt or order processing marking systems are generally not computer based, but rather are in a manual mode.[41]

This observer sounded very much like his manufacturing counterparts in the 1950s, who complained that their shop floors were cluttered with unconnected systems and hardware of various ages and sophistication. Indeed, his observations were exactly the same:

- Inaccurate records because of input errors
- Undeveloped data because not all departments were using the same software tools
- Inadequate speed or content of reporting
- Lack of performance measurements
- Limited flexibility to provide relevant, timely information[42]

Much as a manufacturing counterpart in the mid-1950s would have written, "The retailing industry has only superficially tapped the full operating and reporting power of the computer."[43]

As stores began to install electronic cash registers and data-processing terminals in the early 1970s, they began to understand what an expanded future for POS might be. Already, managers could see a substantial decline of manual entry of data

By the late 1970s, Quaker Oats had an inventory of over 2,000 application programs running on a national distributed processing network for administrative functions, inventory control, and order handling at sales offices and plants. This photograph from 1978, shows the ubiquitous, large-format computer reports in wide use for nearly a half century. Burroughs Papers, courtesy Archives of the Charles Babbage Institute, University of Minnesota, Minneapolis.

by clerks. The amount of labor required per unit of sales of stock clerks and book-keepers declined too, whereas the work of data-processing professionals (such as programmers) increased slightly. Data enry at a POS terminal was beginning to occur, with information stored either in the store's own computer or at a remote headquarters. During the night, batch processing of these data updated inventory records, generated cash reports, and triggered orders for additional merchandise. Statistics on sales gave new tools to buyers, resulting in substantial increases in the rise in stock turnovers from the late 1960s through the early 1970s.[44] Then came the revolution.

Second Period: An Age of Growth and the UPC Revolution, Mid-1970s–1980s

The most important digital developments of the twentieth century that affected the ability of industries to use computers were, undoubtedly, the invention of the computer chip, the ability to transmit digital data over telephone lines, probably the birth of the Internet, and most certainly the creation of the universal product code. It would be difficult to exaggerate the importance of the development of this last item for both the industry and for the economy at large. Originally developed in response to the needs of the Grocery Industry in the 1970s, by the end of the century it was in use in all retail, wholesale, and manufacturing industries; it also appeared in many other industries, like package delivery services, on magazine covers, and even in libraries. In retail industries it swept aside the old product punch tickets like a tidal wave, linked stores to warehouses in ways that were clearly cost-effective, changed buying relationships between retailers and suppliers, shifted the economic balance of power away from manufacturing to retailing, and in the process made retailing one of the most computer-intensive industries by the end of the century. In short, the UPC met the basic requirements scholars demand of any change before they endow it with the adjective *revolution*.[45]

So the history of the development of the UPC is important in its own right, as well as because it demonstrates once again a pattern evident in a number of industries with multiple members that come together to create technical standards and compel IT vendors to develop industry-specific tools. Manufacturers did this with CAD/CAM and EDI, for instance, and the Banking Industry did it with electronic funds transfer (EFT); general credit cards (e.g., Visa, Mastercard, and American Express), which had become so critical to retailing by the 1980s; and even in the design and processing of checks (1950s). The development of the UPC contributed greatly to the computerization of POS activities, to the creation of in-store processing systems in the 1980s and 1990s, and to the distribution of IT applications across enterprises, both big and small, as the cost of computing continued to drop. This process of deployment is the subject of two of the industry case studies presented in the next chapter (grocery and apparel). A measure of its success and historical importance can be gauged by the extent of its adoption. The UPC came into existence at the dawn of the 1970s; by 1994 there were over 110,000 manufacturer-specific identifying numbers; 177,000 just three years later. Almost every physical product manufactured by a company in the United States in the early years of the twenty-first century either had a UPC or some of their components did; it was almost ubiquitous.[46]

Origins of the UPC Initiative

Figure 10.1 is an illustration of a UPC label. Appendix B provides a description of this remarkable innovation and its related technologies. Stephen A. Brown, who

Figure 10.1
*Barcode for Alfred D. Chandler, Jr.
and James W. Cortada (eds.), A
Nation Transformed by
Information (New York: Oxford
University Press, 2000).*

has written on the history of the bar code (as the UPC is frequently called), concluded that the UPC became "the most significant productivity improvement in the (grocery) industry since the introduction of the supermarket."[47] Why and how did the UPC emerge out of the Grocery Industry? At the dawn of the 1970s, it was one of the largest industries in the United States, with sales of in excess of $100 billion and employing over 1.5 million people. Members of the Grocery Industry had concluded in the 1960s that if a standard way could be arrived at for identifying products, they could improve overall productivity, especially if products could be identified through machine-readable symbols. Information-handling industries at the time, although they saw the wisdom of such a logic, did not conclude that an extensive initiative was justified to create a new technology in support of standardized, machine-readable labeling; existing products were good enough. Retailers, on the other hand, soon focused on improving productivity at the checkout counter, as noted earlier in this chapter. Increasingly in the 1960s and through the 1970s, the belief grew that increased productivity could be achieved by speeding up the checkout process, thereby reducing the amount of labor required for this activity, and by automating the reordering of inventory.[48] Individually, stores could do little; collectively, they might attempt some initiatives. So, working through the National Association of Food Chains (NAFC), beginning in January 1970, individual members launched an inquiry that led to the creation of the Ad Hoc Committee on a Universal Grocery Product Identification Code.[49]

The history of the UPC can be told quickly, but it is an important story that has much to teach other industries about how to develop and deploy new technologies. Six grocery trade associations established the Ad Hoc Committee, populated by senior executives (usually CEOs) from Heinz, General Mills, Bristol Myers, General Foods, Kroger, A&P Tea Company, Wegman's, First National Stores, and Super Valu Stores. The committee took four years to get its work done. The first UPC scanned at a supermarket checkout counter was on a package of Wrigley's gum at Marsh's Supermarket in Troy, Ohio, in June 1974. Soon after, use of this symbol spread rapidly; by April 1976, typically 75 percent of the products in a supermarket bore the label. The earliest, most intense users were in the Grocery Industry, which I discuss in the next chapter. However, just for the record, by late 1975, over 64 percent of all registrants of the UPC label were in the food and beverage industries. By 1994, they accounted for only 28.4 percent because a host of other retail and manufacturing industries had by then become extensive users.[50] As Appendix B describes, codes were issued to companies and other organizations (e.g., government agencies and even book publishers), and thus one could track in the economy, by name of enterprise, where interest in the UPC existed. Major users in the early 1970s included health and beauty aids manufacturers; chemicals, housewares, and building and home supply retailers; and even alcohol vendors. By the 1990s, retailers that were using the code also included those selling lawn and garden products, sports equipment, books, fashion apparel, computers, automobiles (and their parts and supplies), and office equipment and supplies.

The committee faced the possibility of various incompatible systems if it could not settle on a standard; that was key. It commissioned studies and asked vendors of POS technologies to propose symbols in the early 1970s. The committee developed criteria for using scanners, taking advantage of two emerging technical realities: the availability of ever cheaper computer chips and a mature understanding of how lasers could be used to read (scan) data, transferring information to machine-readable forms. National Cash Register, IBM, and other potential vendors designed labels that could be used under difficult conditions (as was essential with oil company credit cards). Tests were conducted, and then, on March 30, 1973, the committee voted in favor of what is now the all-familiar UPC symbol. What this committee had done was to pick the Uniform Grocery Product Identification Code (UGPIC). Next came a second industry-wide committee to determine how best to administer the code since it was clear that a registry process would be needed. Such a registry system was created in the mid-1970s. The early installations and test beds lay in the Grocery Industry, where all the major players quickly embraced the standards. The extent to which manufacturers of dry grocery products put these symbols on their goods in 1976 was estimated to be 92 percent and 65 to 80 percent of the entire mix of products in a supermarket.[51]

With such extensive deployment, it became possible to shake out problems and improve the performance of the technology and its accompanying software applications to the point that other manufacturing and retail industries began to take notice of this new tool. Technical committees and registrars tracked the technology, made recommendations for improvement, and worked with government agencies and consumer protection groups to ensure effective deployment.[52] In 1981, standards for shipping containers were adopted; these facilitated the extension of the UPC into the emerging supply chain processes then appearing in both manufacturing and retailing industries. One of the reasons that the UPC had to spread grew out of the fact that not all goods sold in grocery stores were food; they included health and beauty aids, household cleaners, and so forth, which came from other industries. To take full advantage of the technology, the Grocery Industry wanted others to adopt the symbol as well. During the 1980s and 1990s, that was what happened.

At the dawn of the 1990s, the largest U.S. government purchaser of goods— the Department of Defense—adopted the UPC as a requirement of its suppliers so that it, too, could manage its inventories. The ad hoc committee and its successors had initially avoided working with government standards organizations, such as the American National Standards Institute (ANSI), for fear that the effort to establish and deploy standards would simply take too long. The UPC, unlike CAD/CAM, expanded initially not through government support but by way of private sector endorsement and adoption. The committees were careful to protect the adopted standards so that usage would spread across products and industries. Ultimately the UPC became a de facto standard for such systems around the world.[53] Over the years changes were made to the standards to accommodate other industries and products, but the basic concept remained the same.

Mass merchandizers like Wal-Mart, Kmart, Sears, and others, experienced in handling large volumes of broad categories of products, embraced the new symbol. Deployment occurred in waves across industries. For example, apparel firms in the late 1980s had labeled only about 22 percent of their products with UPC, but by 1992 that figure had jumped to 60 percent. Equally important by the 1990s, the actual labeling was being done primarily by manufacturers, often as a condition for doing business with large retail firms or because that had become the practice in a retail industry.

What exactly then is the application that developed so fast? Two students of its history explain its use:

> When a consumer purchases an item . . . the bar code scanner at the checkout register reads the U.P.C. symbol on the item. The point-of-sale register uses the Code to look up the item's current price from a database in an on-site or central computer. At nearly the same time, the information that the shirt [e.g.] has been sold is relayed to Federated's buyers. There, the information is used in two ways. First, it provides Federated with immediate and precise knowledge of what is selling and what is not. Buyers can use this knowledge to adjust their purchases from vendors. Second, it triggers a process of replenishing the stock of a particular fabric, size, color, and style of shirt at the store.[54]

Information is often sent automatically through EDI to a warehouse or manufacturer for replenishment. The UPC labels on boxes and items make it possible to quickly load trucks with the right merchandise or to pick the correct items in a warehouse. The whole process of collecting data is fast and cheap. So, what started out as a quick way to scan sales to reduce the cost of processing a customer's purchase became very rapidly (and unintentionally) the basis for fundamental changes in how retailers determined what to stock and how to get merchandise.[55]

The second leg of the new application in this industry—EDI—became critical to the success of UPC once the Grocery Industry and others had concluded that being able to communicate inventory information to warehouses and manufacturers was technically feasible and economically advantageous. Computer-to-computer ordering became a major initiative, at first within the Grocery Industry, beginning in the mid-1970s, but then across many retail segments by the early 1980s. The UPC standards committees established criteria for the universal use of EDI applications. Unlike in manufacturing, which began to use EDI as private networks that were established by a major manufacturer linked to its suppliers, the Retail Industry gravitated early to universal EDI standards, which in time spilled over into manufacturing. The notion of standards in EDI communications, regardless of industry spread through many industries. These were linked to UPC standards and eventually were folded into ANSI.[56] Integrating UPC, EDI, and ANSI took place between 1988 and 1992, just before the arrival of the Internet as a publicly available network.[57]

With the spread of two key technologies—UPC and EDI—retailers improved their management of proliferating products, that is, keeping track of growing varieties of goods. In turn, they could choose to offer more variety to their customers. A supermarket in 1960 might have had 6,000 different products and 9,000 in 1974. By 1994, such stores routinely managed between 40,000 and 61,000 different products, generating sales that year of between $200 and $400 thousand per week.[58] The ability to handle more products led to the kind of expansion of floor space per customer discussed in the previous chapter. Expansion was not limited to groceries; it also occurred in both the Apparel Industry and among general merchandisers.

One ramification discussed earlier but bears repeating here is the change in the balance of bargaining power created by the UPC. The balance of power shifted because now retailers had more of the best information about sales trends. Before the existence of UPC and POS software tools, manufacturers had the best data. Manufacturers had received daily information on sales from many firms and industries; retailers, typically at the end of the month. Now retailers got that information in real time, or at least daily, *before* the manufacturers: "An agile retailer can, for instance, stock up on a popular item before its manufacturer realizes that it is in high demand," resulting in "unanticipated, yet profound" consequences (e.g., buying products more cheaply).[59]

The process of adoption was never as easy as my narrative suggests. In its first years, it was difficult for a supermarket to adopt the UPC (with the real expense in POS terminals displacing old cash registers) if no one else did, such as suppliers of a supermarket's groceries. Having some merchandise scanned and others keyed was awkward and expensive; it was better to convert all products to the labels so that everything could be scanned, an ideal that never reached 100 percent, even today.[60] Manufacturers hesitated at first to agree to stamp their goods with the code unless stores were willing to use it because adding UPC labels increased the cost of manufacturing. To make the new system work, everyone had to agree to adopt UPC— hence the enormous significance of retailers coming together through empowered standards committees supported by the CEOs of major firms. That led to the creation of sufficient critical mass quickly enough to make the whole initiative possible. The situation was, in short, a classic example of the effects of economic network externalities at work, except in this case not involving telecommunications. No U.S. government assistance was required, desired, or accepted in the 1970s and early 1980s. Retailers worried about the costs of adoption, but during the 1970s and 1980s the expense of computing continued to steadily decline while the functionality of computers and software improved, making systems of UPC, POS, and EDI cost-effective and technically possible.

But it was technically still a complicated process. Electronic (digital) POS systems and in-store computers first became available in the early 1970s, and thus had to go through their own period of shakedown. Worst of all, software applications had yet to be written that could handle inventory control, cash management, accounts payable, and data collection from UPC. As late as 1980, experts had to explain the features of the integrated and separate applications relating to UPC and POS. Outside of the Grocery Industry, early adopters were large firms, just as in manufacturing; in both industries they had the most to gain and could afford the initial investments in development and pilot projects.[61]

Patterns of IT Adoption

Because the Retail Industry has many forms, generalizing on the rates of adoption of various technologies and applications in any decade remains problematic. The

BLS data for the 1970s and 1980s, however, are helpful in providing a useful perspective. In 1977, the BLS noted that vendor-marked merchandise tickets remained primarily an application used by large department, apparel, and discount stores. Credit authorizations via computer were also the purview of large department store chains. However, some grocery stores became linked to bank computers early on in this decade. Government researchers concluded on the basis of a massive survey that 1 out of every 300 retail units used computers in 1974, up from 1 out of every 400 in 1968. In mid-1975, 50 supermarkets used the UPC and reported that they would expand their adoption of it once the quality of the scanners improved, along with the percentage of total inventories covered by it.[62]

The same government agency reexamined the Retail Industry at the end of the 1980s and observed that "several major innovations are having an impact on productivity and employment. Computerized point-of-sale terminals are becoming widespread in retail establishments such as supermarkets, department stores, discount stores, and specialty stores that sell a wide diversity of items." Warehouses now routinely used microprocessors to control conveyer systems and automatically guided vehicles.[63] This time, the BLS reported that the use of POS terminals was "widespread in large firms," that 80 percent of all retail firms now used these systems, and of those systems, computers managed 43 percent. Scanning devices were installed in over 70 percent of all supermarkets and drug stores. Video merchandising reached over 50 percent of all American households. Microprocessor-controlled conveyer systems in warehouses remained limited, used by the very largest wholesalers and retail firms.[64] During the 1980s, the cost benefits of these new technologies had become evident and were publicized. They improved productivity of workers, increased sales, and single-handedly changed the purchasing balance of power in favor of retailers. These systems had been so enhanced that customers, for example, could now pay for their goods with credit cards, which were machine-readable and thus added to the base of information available to retailers and manufacturers about buying habits and product demands.[65]

Computers in Wholesaling

Use of computing in warehouses—both by wholesalers and large retailing firms—changed in this period, too, although diffusion of technologies proved slower in the 1980s than in the 1990s. Like manufacturers, warehouse managers lashed together a range of technologies, from pure electronic systems to complex state-of-the-art digital devices and everything in between. Retail firms focused more on automating stores and inventory files than their warehouses.[66] However, those that did so found microprocessor-managed conveyor systems attractive because they facilitated the receipt, movement, and storage of merchandise. These systems could physically move goods but, ultimately more important, could generate data, monitor activities, and record and report results. They were very expensive and thus most appealing to large, high-volume warehouses. However, the future role of warehousing IT in the emerging national supply chain was already evident. The BLS commented that "in advanced conveyor networks, synchronization of data with the merchandise that it moved reduces unit labor requirements at least 25 percent and affects the skills required in several occupations."[67] The BLS economists still focused on labor savings—the same concern retailers had in the 1970s—but that interest, as we saw earlier in this chapter, had shifted because benefits derived from having the right amount of inventory at the right place at the right cost began to appear larger and strategically more significant.

Wholesale distributors were responsible for more than merely running warehouses, so one would expect these firms to be interested in a wider array of digital applications. In fact, they were adopters of a variety of applications. As early as the mid-1970s, one could detect a wave of adoptions not evident in the 1950s or 1960s. The major applications of the early to mid-1970s, which continued to be installed through the rest of the decade, were in support of expediting shipments, streamlining preparation of a variety of documents (e.g., bills of lading and invoices), and improving inventory turnover rates. The use of bar codes improved warehousing operations, and conveyer systems were becoming more effective because of the use of microprocessors to determine what to pick and move and when. Distribution centers appeared at new sites near major highways. A variety of new materials-handling equipment, stacker hardware, and automated stacker-retriever systems came into their own. Increasingly through the decade, wholesalers relied on computers to provide additional services to their customers—retailers—in such areas as primitive JIT order replenishment, packing, tagging, and so forth. Over 40 percent of all wholesalers in 1972 used computers for accounting and inventory control; that percentage grew each year through the decade.[68]

By the mid-1980s, it was obvious that computers were the source of the largest number and type of changes in affecting how wholesalers did their work. The BLS made the same observation at that time: "These developments are largely associated with the availability of computer-based information and technology systems which make possible geographic expansion, better management controls, and enlarged wholesale distribution functions."[69] Intensified competition compelled wholesalers to improve productivity and drive down their costs of goods and labor. They achieved successes, increasing labor productivity roughly 10 percent per annum during the 1980s. Nearly 40 percent of all wholesalers had installed computer inventory control systems by about 1984, reducing substantially the amount of labor required to track goods and place orders.[70]

During this decade, wholesalers increasingly used computers to establish delivery schedules and perform automated vehicle load planning. This was, and continues to be, an important function because so much of a wholesaler's deliveries consisted of many low-volume, wide-variety orders. By the end of the 1980s, the frequency of delivery of such orders was quickly rising as retailers implemented JIT processes for taking delivery of inventory. Computerized route scheduling and vehicle load planning proved more efficient and quicker to use than that done by employees (as had been the case in earlier decades). Nearly half the industry used these kinds of applications by the end of the decade, and by the early years of the 1990s, almost all did.[71]

But if one wanted to compare the physical look and feel of a warehouse of the 1980s with, say, one from the 1950s to sense what changes in style had occurred, one should pass by the computers in the main office and go into the storage area itself. There microprocessor-controlled conveyor systems, initially installed for the first time in the 1970s, had come into their own, making it possible to operate more efficiently larger distribution centers. Such technology made it possible not only to move goods around the floor with robotic machines but also to put them on various shelves (some as high as 100 feet off the ground), posting goods in warehouses in locations that optimized their retrieval according to distance, frequency of delivery, and patterns of demand. Typically, there was a pattern to the adoption of this kind of technology. First, a large wholesaler would install computer-driven conveyors that sorted goods and used code scanners to identify inventories and move them quickly. The next generation of technology increasingly integrated software and equipment that could monitor the time needed to select items for shipment or to compare shipments picked with original purchase orders. In the 1980s, the two applications operated independently; by the early 1990s, wholesalers were merging all of their shop floor applications into integrated systems. These systems typically reduced by 25 percent the labor required for a unit of work while increasing the technical skills of those remaining in such areas as computer-based equipment maintenance, software and IT management, and accounting. Part of the reason for the decline in labor also came from the use of automatic guided vehicles (AGVs) on the floor. These are battery-operated vehicles without human drivers, run instead by microprocessors capable of selecting and moving goods within the building.[72] Some portions of warehouses were so automated that management saved energy costs by keeping few or no lights on.[73]

The whole world of retailing and wholesaling, however, was not fully aware of the broader implications of the new applications at the time of their deployment. Operational considerations, such as immediate returns on investment and labor productivity, remained central for most managers in the 1980s. However, a few industry watchers had already identified emerging shifts. Dale D. Achabal and Shelby H. McIntyre, both professors at Santa Clara University, explained in the *Journal of Retailing* in 1987 that "advances in information systems and communications technologies are significantly enhancing the prospects for retail productivity improvements, and promise to change the face of retailing."[74] They, too, indicated the importance of the UPC, heralding a computer-driven set of applications originating at POS stations. They pointed out the rapid expansion of standard EDI systems, as opposed to the proprietary systems in earlier years of manufacturing firms and network providers (e.g., GE, McDonnell-Douglas, and IBM). They also acknowledged the then emerging use of store-based electronic retailing (e.g., allowing consumers to order from a store's warehouse) and the installation of wide-area-networks (WANs) in large stores.[75]

The importance of POS to the industry could not be overstated. One survey pointed out that 69 percent of the capital investments made by a group of chain store retailers went into POS systems in 1989. This same group of stores also reported that half had already been extensive users of scanning technology; 42 percent used EDI, clear evidence that the linking of POS and EDI was well underway. Overall across the entire Retail Industry, POS expenditures amounted to 46 percent of all capital spent; 66 percent used scanning, 35 percent EDI.[76] What was the situation with supermarkets, the merchants who started the whole move to POS in the first place? The same survey indicated that POS accounted for only 2 percent of capital investments; the majority had already installed this equipment during the 1970s and 1980s. Ninety-four percent scanned at POS terminals—the highest percentage in the Retail Industry—and 75 percent had not yet used EDI, although 71 percent reported that they intended to do so soon.[77] The initiative to use EDI had come primarily from such dry goods sectors of the industry as apparel (the subject of an industry case study in the next chapter).

Third Period: The Networked Age: The Arrival of the Internet, 1990s and Beyond

Many patterns evident in the 1980s in the deployment of software and hardware remained the case in the early 1990s as the process of filling in key applications of earlier years continued: use of POS and EDI, automated physical movement of goods, closer integration and information sharing among distributors and their client retailers, and so forth. But as in manufacturing, the ground also kept shifting beneath the feet of the major players in these industries, the ones that felt the earliest need to change or add more uses of computers. Nothing made that more obvious than the intervention of the Internet in the American economy. However, as in manufacturing, the reactions of business managers to the Internet were conditioned by their company's technical experiences (e.g., prior use of EDI), demands of the market (e.g., to prepare shipments for direct placement on the retailer's shop floor), and economic realities (e.g., globalization and Internet-based supply chain management). Many IT initiatives were larger than just the Internet, such as the continued revamping of supply chains from the "push" strategies of earlier decades (moving goods from factory to retail) to "pull" approaches (in which customers, through their buying habits, and retailers pull products to them). These larger trends created the initial momentum for management to consider the role of the Internet as part of those broader initiatives. Only after the Internet had become a visible element in the industry did that new networking technology begin to influence the work of retailers.

Looking at the industry trade press's coverage of IT issues in the 1990s could lead one to be confused about applications because of the injection of the Internet into the picture, the continued filling out of supply chain management, the ongoing installation of enhanced POS systems, the data mining of customer information, the emergence of online shopping, and the expanded use of credit cards. All of these events occurred in the context of increased competition and overcapacity in retail brick-and-mortar facilities. What remained constant, however, were the primary roles and missions of retailers: to manage inventory costs and availability, to understand and sell to customers, and to operate day-to-day operations that have long characterized the industry (e.g., purchasing and merchandising).

From the 1970s through the 1990s, one IT overall pattern existed: the collection and use of some five basic types of information. All applications of computing used these data in one fashion or another. There were, and are, data about products, vendors, customers, finance (and accounting), and employees. Supply chain management applications and POS focused on products, customers, finance, and vendors. Traditional accounting and financial applications used data about vendors, employees and products. Customer relations management (CRM) applications used data about customers and finance (sales). Enterprise management planning (ERP) software tools, which appeared first in manufacturing industries in the 1980s and then in retail during the 1990s, used data about employees and accounting. Internet-based applications used all five types of data, which partially explains why this new form of networking is so versatile and increasingly popular with customers, vendors, wholesalers, and retailers.

These five categories of data appeared in all major functional areas of an enterprise, going far to explain why computing and its attendant applications had been deployed across entire enterprises. Distribution centers used product information to learn what to order and what was on order and to forecast delivery. Accounting for costs and financial implications was always part of the equation for distribution center managers and remained so at the dawn of the twenty-first century. Departments responsible for finance and accounting used software tools to track gross margins and operating costs of products and stores. Customer data helped support financial forecasts and other predictions about sales and budget requirements. In short, these were applications designed to track performance in support of controlling expenses. Merchandise management departments relied on product and sales information to determine what to buy, when, and how much. They used supply chain performance data to select vendors, customer data to create marketing and merchandising strategies, and financial and accounting data to figure out what was selling quickly, slowly, or not at all. Their concerns also included tracking inventory turns, sales, and gross margins—all compared to business plans.

Store operations have been the subject of much of this chapter, and nowhere so much as with POS applications. Stores worried about sales—by product, by department, and by store. They tracked labor costs and requirements by hours needed, by person, and by cost. Sales forecasts linked to personnel requirements made it possible to determine how many employees were needed, their cost in salaries and benefits, and so forth.

Thus IT departments increased in importance over the decades because they served as the gearboxes for the collection, movement, and presentation of these five classes of data. The IT applications were historically developed in support of operational improvements. The Internet, however, also made it possible to create new channels for distributing information and products to and from wholesalers and manufacturers and to and from customers. By the end of the twentieth century, IT

Table 10.1
Key IT Application Areas in the Retail Industry, Circa 1995–2001

Electronic shelf labels	Store management
Scanning	Customer service
Electronic fund transfer	Data mining
Supply chain management	In-store kiosks
Sales-based ordering	EDI
Internet (electronic) sales	

departments were contributing to the marketing strategy of a retailer, not merely serving as a provider of backroom support.

A cursory view of the industry's literature of the 1990s makes it clear that a cluster of applications, some new (e.g., e-tailing) and others more traditional (shelf labels), remained high in the retail industry's use of IT. Table 10.1 lists some of the applications that received extensive coverage in the industry's publications during the second half of the 1990s. One might argue that with the exception of e-business, the list could have come from the 1970s or 1980s, and that is the key point. As new technologies became available, such as the Internet, cheaper computers, and more sophisticated software tools, they were adopted in support of the business functions of a firm and across its industry, just as in manufacturing, banking, insurance, and other sectors of the American economy. To be sure, how tasks were performed did change, but applications and technologies served a business master. The reason for stating what might otherwise be an obvious point is that since roughly 1997 to the present, the discussions about the Internet in the press, radio, and television have been so extensive that it is easy to lose sight of what retailers actually deployed in the way of digital applications in the late twentieth century. With an understanding of this broader picture in mind, we can begin to make sense of how these various applications fit into the broader scheme of operations.

Changing Role of Consumers

One area of business operations that received increased attention in the 1990s concerned customers. Nearly a quarter century of data gathering from POS systems had conditioned the Retail Industry to study consumer buying patterns; it is how, for example, the industry was able to shift the supply chain from a push to a pull style of performance. During the 1990s, more sophisticated uses of data-mining tools came into wide use, and the notion that a company could build a data warehouse became popular. In support of merchandise managers, these data warehouses (really just large collections of digital files) could be mined for insights on what products were selling and why and to forecast possible changes in consumer patterns. Every major retailer in the United States had data mining and based many of its purchasing and marketing decisions on the results of these applications.[78] Data mining of customer information was not limited to retailing; one major survey across many industries suggested that nearly 52 percent of all Fortune 1000 companies were active users of this application at the turn of the century, up from 18 percent as recently as 1999.[79]

In effect, customers that used the Internet practiced a reverse version of data mining by going to web sites of stores and manufacturers for information on products. By early 1998, major retailers either had information-laden web sites for customers or had plans to implement them.[80] This use of the Internet by customers is not the same as online purchasing, which I discuss below. Rather, consumers were reluctant to buy online during the first couple of years of its availability; they preferred to hunt for information online and then to make their purchases in a store or through a mail order catalog. Not until the last four years of the century did they begin to buy over the Internet because, on the one hand, retailers made it possible for them to do so and, on the other hand, consumers became more comfortable in using this new shopping channel. By then, millions of Americans had access to the Internet, thanks to their PCs at home and at work. Both practices—surfing and then buying on the Net—increased the attention retailers paid to using computing to enhance their relations with consumers. Customer relationship management (CRM) practices before the arrival of the Internet focused largely on understanding consumers' wants and needs, often not doing it well.[81] The basic post-1995 concept of CRM, however, called for customers to be able to get to a retailer through multiple channels: in a store, through a catalog, or online. Using databases, customer-centric processes, and online tools (such as the Internet), firms began a historic shift from being merchandise-oriented to being customer-centric. It was a process still emerging but already very evident, and it was profoundly different than in the 1970s or 1980s. Data warehousing had evolved into one of the building blocks of modern CRM processes.[82] The transformation was slow and painful. Mark Poole, a consultant on CRM at the end of the century, observed that "retailers are good at collecting pieces of data, but typically they have no idea what each individual customer represents to their enterprises because they haven't implemented the technology they need to tie the data together."[83] The whole process of doing so proved complicated and expensive.

Eight-Hundred-Pound Gorillas and the Internet: Changing Patterns of Retailing

Wal-Mart was the proverbial 800-pound gorilla in the Retail Industry through the 1990s, so whatever it did caught the attention of all its rivals. It was an extensive user of data mining and data warehouses. Specific, quantitative evidence of its use of IT has always been hard to get; however, in August 1999, some information on the firm made its way into the trade press. It had been rumored that only the U.S. government had more data online than Wal-Mart in the late 1990s. The company had about 101 terabytes of data, which it made available to its 7,000 vendors. One terabyte can store 250 million pages of text, so 101 terabytes of data amounts to over 25 billion pages of information. As an NCR public relations director described this quantity of information, it was like having a stack 1,600 miles high of paper.

To put that volume in a business perspective, in 1990 Wal-Mart estimated that its first data warehouse had only 300 gigabytes of data. One gigabyte of data is roughly equal to a pickup truckload of paper; 300 gigabytes of information, to three floors in a university library crammed with journals. These comparisons are fun to make, but the key point is that Wal-Mart massively increased the volume of computerized data it needed to run its business in less than a decade. The increase was steep because, in the mid-1990s, the firm had "only" 44 terabytes of sales data. With the more enhanced data warehouse, over 10 million customer transactions were being collected daily; over 120,000 complex data-mining questions were sent to the data warehouse each week.[84] All these data made it possible to blur (integrate) more than before the lines between supply chain management activities and merchandising.

What was happening with POS systems, the primary source of data input from customers? This is a different question than asking about the second-most important source of data input from customers, the Internet (from hits on retail sites for inquiries and purchases), which did not become important until the end of the century. Kiosks represented a new variant of in-store communications with customers, which allowed them to select goods not available in the store at the moment they were there. Kmart, for example, installed kiosks in over half its physical stores by the spring of 2001. They were also connected to Kmart's Internet site, Bluelight.com, and to the company's main databases, so that sales could also be tracked from the store in which they took place. At the same time, Kmart intended to outfit all of its more than 2,000 stores with kiosks.[85] Touch-screen technologies also were going into these stores to make it easier for consumers to interact with Kmart's computers. Roughly 55 percent of specialty retailers in the United States were implementing web-enabled POS systems at the same time. The fundamental trend could be summarized in one word: *integration*. Retailers were integrating their online and offline POS and other CRM applications and processes at the end of the century. Although difficult to do, especially colleting data in a timely fashion so that they could be used in real time, this did not deter the large chains from starting the process of integration.[86]

Supply chains were enriched with additional functions, but the biggest change came with the Internet. Using the Internet was less expensive than establishing private networks, as was normally done with EDI networks in earlier years. That made it possible to establish multiple telecommunications among buyers, sellers, retailers, customers, vendors, manufacturers, and other interested parties. In addition, small stores could also participate in the world of supply chain management applications that depended extensively on the use of telecommunications and IT-based applications.[87] As POS installations within a chain expanded, for example, POS terminals and in-store computer systems were integrated directly into supply chains. The press was full of such stories. Wal-Mart, Revco, Kmart, and so forth all refurbished their supply chains in the 1990s. Renovations focused on tighter integration of otherwise disparate applications, improved efficiencies, and increased speed of performance, much as manufacturers had done in integrating their various islands of automation in the 1980s and early 1990s.

To illustrate, Revco, a large chain, renovated its supply chain management applications to improve management of vendors, marketing and buying, movement and replenishment of inventory, distribution, transportation, and the processes for receiving and stocking products. James Mastrian, Revco's executive vice president for marketing in the mid-1990s, said that the new applications were designed to meet a basic business requirement: "We had to collapse our total [product] cycle time—from the time of the sale off the [store] shelf until the product returns to the shelf." Furthermore, it had to support closer ties to customers: "We wanted to transition ourselves into collaborative trading partner relationships, where the marketing and buying decisions are customer- and demand-driven. And we wanted our inventory replenishment to be computer-generated, not just computer-assisted."[88] Paper-based, computer-generated reports were replaced with software that made decisions, or provided online recommendations. All data was "warehoused" for common access and further integration.

As should be evident, even beyond any discussion of online, Internet-based sales, a large family of digital applications existed before the arrival of the Internet and online shopping. What should also be clear is that retailers integrated many applications over time, beginning decades earlier, and then added Internet-based applications to their collections of digital uses toward the end of the century. Without those other applications in place, it would be difficult to understand how e-commerce could have occurred. By itself, the Internet proved to be insufficient to make such applications possible. The degree to which customers embraced the Internet is normally described as a question of easy use of a new technology or some unique economic or cultural factors that encouraged its employment.[89] However, the use of the Internet is too new an element in American business for historians to cast judgments on practices and motives. What we can conclude is that without the confluence of a variety of applications that are sufficiently developed to lend themselves to integration, online inquiries and purchases would have undoubtedly been impossible. This does not minimize the historic importance of such technological innovations as the introduction of the World Wide Web or, earlier, of PCs, which made it possible for Americans to learn how to interact with computers online. But technology alone did not carry the day, nor did an isolated application here or there within a firm or industry. Rather it was the total collection and continuous integration of data files, computing, industry-specific software and applications, cheap computer memory, and reliable and cost-effective telecommunications (i.e., telephony and the Internet) that made e-commerce possible. Future historians will be able to explain more fully the rate of adoption of e-commerce when they precisely document the evolution of these various elements.

Early Patterns of E-Commerce

In the meantime, we can identify early patterns of e-commerce (also called e-tailing by merchants) and their effect on the Retail Industry. There are two types to consider: bricks-and-mortar retailers, such as J.C. Penney and Wal-Mart, and pure online vendors like Amazon.com. I deal with the "pure plays" (as online merchants were called at the dawn of the new century) in the next chapter because at that time they represented less than 20 percent of all retail sales in the United States.

Between 1994–1995 and roughly 2001, large retailers established a presence on the Internet, usually at first with web sites that merely provided information about the firm and its products. Over time, these web sites were redesigned and enhanced two or three times, often giving customers the capability to order products directly off a company's site, paying with a credit card. These channels were not integrated with physical stores, a change that began in 1999 as retailers realized that all channels of distribution had to be integrated.

There was enormous hype in 1995–1997 about online shopping as the coming new wave.[90] But, as often happened with the arrival of a new form of IT, reality proved quite different, and adoption of the new was slower than anticipated. Part of the problem, of course, was figuring out what people would buy online, an important insight that did not begin to manifest itself until 1997. One survey of e-commerce concluded, "Despite the fact that online retailing hit $3.7 billion in sales by 1997, a majority of the items sold were products consumers need not try on, such as computers, CDs, books, and music."[91] Over time, the goods people were willing to buy online slowly grew. By mid-1999, major retailers had taken the plunge in the belief that if they were not active on the Internet, they ultimately would lose market share. As one industry watcher commented, "It's on everyone's radar screen."[92] Drug chains believed that their products had similar characteristics to CDs and books because they were small, easy to ship to consumers, and did not need to be tried on. Roughly 40 percent of the drug chains with web sites also had online pharmacies, making this sector of the Retail Industry relatively more aggressive than others in establishing a presence on the Internet.[93] But as a whole, the entire industry took its time, trying to figure out how to leverage the technology with customers. They were individually reaching the conclusion that the objective was not so much to make a revolution in retailing as to "extend the physical-store brand, leveraging name equity, and acquire expertise however they can to reach customers in their homes with compelling, unique selling propositions."[94] An assessment done for the industry in late 1999 concluded that "e-commerce players have largely managed to capture the public fancy and Wall Street ardor," predicting that e-tailing would expand rapidly.[95]

From the perspective of IT applications—in addition to the fact that e-tailing was a brave new world for retailers in general—there were other issues, not the least of which was the lack of software applications to handle the transactions. One observer noted that "the lack of software applications keeps today's [2000] e-Marketplaces in commerce kindergarten. A new applications architecture—and a revamped vendor community—that supports the full trading life cycle is needed."[96] Yet, when software tools were implemented for both business-to-business (B2B) and business-to-consumer (B2C) transactions, the early emergence of new business models could be seen. The Internet provided low-cost access for

Table 10.2
Highly Effective Users of IT in the Retail Industry

Company	Why
Wal-Mart	Pioneered most of the IT applications used widely in the industry: EDI, POS, JIT delivery; has largest data warehouse; spends $500 million annually on IT.
Gap	IT key to firm's 20% annual growth rate; 70% of its IT applications were created in the 1990s (e.g., custom-design store replenishment system, reducing inventory costs). Installed software that allows stores to receive inventory directly from manufacturers, bypassing distribution centers.
Home Depot	Thriftiest chain, spending .05% of revenues on IT, which it uses to cut delivery lead times by half. Sales personnel use 5,600 Telxon pen computers to access inventory data and place orders, placing special orders through a wireless link to EDI. Has very high transaction rates.

Source: Adapted from "America's Best Technology Users," *Forbes ASAP* (August 24,1998): 80, 82.

vendors and customers to each other, generating roughly $8 billion in sales in 1998 and another $18 billion in 1999.[97]

By late 1998, retailers were beginning to be recognized for their ability to apply the digital to their basic business functions. Table 10.2 lists some of the leaders, as identified by *Forbes ASAP* in August 1998. The list is short (as it was for other industries, too) but suggests what kinds of applications engendered star quality. The same article attacked J.C. Penney for being "way behind the technology curve," blaming the company for its flat market share over the previous four years. The article took the position that J.C. Penney failed to invest in inventory and distribution systems comparable to its competitors and that only in 1998 did it finally begin to leverage customer information, in the process providing mounting evidence that using the Internet had become a critical competitive factor in retailing.[98] Note that the leaders all had various but integrated applications.

The pace of e-tailing picked up between 1998 and the end of 2001, with mail-order firms best positioned to exploit the Internet since they had the backroom applications needed to fulfill orders, maintain online customer records, and mine them for information on consumers' behavior and preferences. They essentially used the same software tools deployed before the arrival of the Internet.[99]

A summary of a retail chain's digital applications at the dawn of the twenty-first century illustrates what the new look and feel of retailing was, compared to that in 1950. Table 10.3 lists the basic applications drawn from a standard textbook on the industry published in 2000. Note how they encompassed the breadth of retailers' activities. This short list provides clear evidence that the Retail Industry had found or developed industry-specific applications and technologies, which made it possible for participants to justify and leverage IT for economic advantages.

Table 10.3
Widely Deployed Groups of Digital Applications in the U.S. Retail Industry,
Circa 2000

POS systems	Online inventory control and replenishment
EDI systems	Logistics and supply chain management
Data warehousing	Ticketing and marking
Customer loyalty programs	Quick response (QR) delivery systems
Internet web sites and ordering	E-retailing

Source: Michael Levy and Barton A. Weitz, *Retailing Management* (New York: McGraw-Hill Irwin, 2000): 327–343.

By the end of the century, the Retail Industry, working with many manufacturers, had collectively adopted the UCCnet (Uniform Code Council), a standards body responsible for providing a registry of information about products to retailers and wholesalers. Although the adoption of these standards to facilitate the exchange of information about products proved to be a slow and arduous process, it made it possible for small retailers to use the Internet with other participants in the national supply chain, right along with the large retailers.[100]

What happened to wholesalers in the late 1990s? Did they, too, enter the new century with a portfolio of relevant applications, or did the Internet make it too easy for retailers to bypass them and go straight to manufacturers? As late as the early 1990s, supply chains were linear sets of activities, with products going from manufacturers to wholesalers, then to retailers, and finally to customers. By the end of the twentieth century, networking had made possible the evolution of supply chains into networks in which at any point in the chain one could make electronic contact with any other point. A retailer could bypass a wholesaler and order and take delivery from a manufacturer. A customer could communicate with or order from a retailer, wholesaler, or manufacturer. A manufacturer no longer had to distribute products through its own private channels or just to wholesalers. Industry watchers recognized that manufacturers, customers, and retailers had been more alert to these changing circumstances than wholesalers, especially as e-business and e-commerce expanded sharply in 1997–2000. To survive, wholesalers became participants in other firms' supply chains, providing labeling and fulfillment services and relying extensively on digital applications, and consolidated into larger, merged corporations to achieve the scale and scope needed to survive.[101]

The major families of digital applications of interest to wholesale firms at the end of the century were similar to those in the Retail Industry. They included e-business, use of the Internet, supply chain management, inventory control, sales force automation, data warehousing, and B2B and B2C applications (primarily the former). The automation of warehouse and distribution centers remained, of course, of intense concern to the Wholesale Industry.

Conclusions

The central event in the history of IT in retailing and wholesaling of the past half century was the development of POS technologies and software, especially the UPC, which spawned a series of new applications and changes in how these industries did their work. The single most important consequence of that development was the repositioning of many retailers and wholesalers within the emerging national supply chain. As one leading observer of the industry, Roger D. Blackwell, put it, "Rather than being the least important entity, it's now the *most* significant."[102] I think he placed the right degree of emphasis on this point. In 1950, manufacturers dominated the national supply chain. Of course, nobody thought of the process of distribution as a supply chain, although manufacturers, wholesalers, and retailers understood their relative positions vis-à-vis one another: manufacturers supplying wholesalers, who in turn dealt with retailers at the opposite end of the chain, next to the customer. A half century later, all three industries used the formal concept of a supply chain, and their positions had changed. Instead of information and initiative starting with the manufacturer and flowing all the way to the customer, the traffic reversed in enough sectors of retailing and manufacturing to allow us to characterize it as a profound trend. Retail customers increasingly triggered economic activity, stimulating demand for products and support services, and pushed data and responses back to manufacturers.

This change was specifically made possible by IT technology, along with a healthy dose of leadership from several industries that stimulated exploitation of the digital. The Grocery Industry led the way at the point of sale; the Apparel Industry, at the use of EDI and other JIT techniques that so relied on IT; and the Internet-based retailers, at the new communications technology. But retail's transformation also occurred as a result of a string of unintended consequences that was merely exploited but still required leadership. In writing their account of the Internet-based company eBay, David Bunnell and Richard Luecke gave us an example of that process at work: "With no road map to follow, eBay executives and employees have had to invent this business on the fly—in 'Internet time.' As a result, its evolution has been a consequence of strategic intention, reaction, and opportunistic response to unfolding events."[103] Their observation of an Internet-based firm could almost as easily have described the way in which many retailers felt their way through POS and EDI applications in the 1970s and 1980s and the linked version of the two in the 1990s.

The largest enterprises in both wholesale and retail led in the use of technologies in innovative ways, deploying them across their many retail outlets. In time, as technologies dropped in cost, became easier to use, and were linked to manufacturers and wholesalers, they spread to small chains and, by the end of the century, to most store fronts. The mechanical cash register was ubiquitous in 1950; a half century later we saw them in museums. The spread of IT applications through the largest enterprises followed the same pattern as in manufacturing, with the largest firms normally leading the way—with the exception, of course, of the Steel

Industry, which was very slow to embrace different technology-based formats for running a business.

Technology caused profound changes in the structure of retailing, perhaps in some sectors more so than in manufacturing, although it is too early to say with certainty because we are still seeing the transformation unfold. But three basic changes have already been caused directly by the use of IT. The first, already mentioned, was the shift of the relative position of retailing in the national supply chain. The second was the decline in the central role of wholesalers. By no means am I suggesting their demise, far from it. Rather, they no longer acted as the exclusive gatekeepers between retailers and manufacturers; they represented one of several access points to merchandise and customers that any of the four parties to retailing—manufacturers, wholesalers, retailers, and customers—could reach. The economic power of each either declined or increased. Clearly, the economic power of retailers rose, and sharply, especially in the 1980s and 1990s. Customers gained economic flexibility, too, particularly after online shopping became a reality at the end of the twentieth century. Both manufacturers and retailers had their economic sales trimmed, but not folded. They remained vital to the economic order in the world of retailing.

The third fundamental shift was the ability of new niche players to enter retailing on a massive basis, that is, with all the accouterments of powerful retailers: national brands, large chains, and scale and scope. The examples were everywhere: Toys 'R Us, Borders, Office Max, and Victoria's Secret, to mention a few. New general-merchandise retailers also emerged, often exploiting IT very effectively—Wal-Mart being the operative case par excellence. However, not everyone benefited from this development.

General department stores—the giants at the midpoint in the last century—suffered the most by the arrival of niche players with national reach, which were able to take away portions of their business. Such old-line chains as Lord & Taylor, J.C. Penney, Macy's, and Dillards, to mention a few, came under serious attack beginning in the 1980s and continuing to the present day. During the 1990s, they lost market share to the likes of Wal-Mart, Target, Circuit City, and others, which gutted portions of their business. The conventional interpretation accuses the management of old-line firms of not understanding how new rivals were eating away at their core businesses, and it is probably a fair charge to make. Members of the industry acknowledged as much. The retired chair of Neiman Marcus, Stanley Marcus, was blunt on the matter in an interview in early 2001: "When the Gaps started eating off the plates of department stores, management wasn't aware of what was happening until it was too late."[104] A similar problem existed in manufacturing industries from time to time that had less to do with the adoption of IT than with understanding the changing nature of competition. Periodically, all industries suffer from the problem, and continuously some unit an industry is afflicted with it.

The overexpansion of retail space by existing and emerging chains and niche players exacerbated the problems of competition, raised the stakes of scale and scope, and resulted in many new retail chains that did not exist in 1950. By the end of the century, the old-line department stores were struggling not to be a thing of the past. They had closed down departments that had been mainstays for decades (e.g., books, sporting goods, toys, and cards). Customers realized that corners were being cut, which simply led them to adopt new shopping habits, such as buying their electronics at Circuit City and their Christmas cards at Hallmark.

It should be obvious that IT facilitated the transformation: those who survived helped kill off those who did not. Inventory management—indeed, access to inventory—proved to be critical, and EDI, among other things, helped. The POS-generated data aided those retailers that were light on their feet and swift enough to increase their market share at the expense of the slower. In fact, when the history of retailing in the 1980s and 1990s is authoritatively written, I suspect we will read that the most pervasive single cause of change may well have been the exploitation of POS-generated merchandising data in ways that were far more efficient, effective, and timely than in the previous eight decades of the century.

Although much had changed in retailing, a great deal did not. Retailers never forgot that their primary mission was to sell merchandise to customers who were walking in the door of a store. Mail order and Internet-based businesses never dominated the industry; retail store sales always did. Thus technologies had to support inventory management, control personnel costs, and provide the right merchandise at the right time for the right customer. When they did so, retailers adopted them; when they did not, retailers languished. That is, retailers applied technology in support of core business processes. A recent example, post-1999, involved the merger of in-store retailing with online channels, so that a customer could access a retailer through a store or the Internet for information, to make a purchase, or to return a product. The process provided to customers multiple points of entry into the firm. E-tailers did the same in reverse, investing, for example, in warehouses so that they could buy in bulk to be price-competitive. It is, for instance, a large part of Amazon.com's story after 1999. These kinds of integrative, flexible applications of IT could only grow out of experience with multiple channels of distribution, building on a large base of preexisting systems.[105]

As I did with manufacturing industries, I look at specific parts of the retailing world to get a closer look at how information technology worked its influence within companies and across the American economy. For that reason, the next chapter is devoted to two industries and the emerging Internet-centric format (e-tailers). The first two provided leadership across all retail industries with their actions and influence; the third case study teaches us about contemporary realities with the Internet. The three instances help round out the survey of how IT so profoundly influenced the making, selling, and buying of goods in the modern American economy.

11

Patterns and Practices in Three Retail Industries: Grocery, Apparel, and E-tailing

Pile the goods high and sell them cheap. Let the buyer do the work. Maintain
a market day atmosphere all the time.

—Joe Weingarten, 1918

The familiar is not always so obvious. The POS terminals in supermarkets, an
average of over a half dozen credit cards in our wallets, electronic tags on our
clothes, and detectors at store exits are so widespread that we think nothing of
them. They are just there, as if they had always been there. However, as the previous
chapter demonstrates, retail industries have been incrementally adding digitally
based applications for decades, one on top of another. In addition, they have continuously replaced older software and hardware with newer tools. The POS systems
have gone through three or four major generations (depending on which vendor's
products one counts). Tags on in-store merchandise have evolved through at least
three generations of technology, all within a quarter of a century. Just as in manufacturing industries, the history of digital applications in retailing is not merely
the story of initial use or of the extent of deployment across an industry but also a
tale of replacement and upgrades and most important, fundamental changes both
in how people did their work and in the transformation of companies and industries. As in other decades, Americans have adopted a variety of information tools
of multiple technological generations so that their world has become cluttered with

them. No set of industries did more to make information tools and artifacts so obvious or so present in American life as did retailers.[1]

No set of retailers played as important a role in creating this clutter of informational artifacts and uses than did the three examined in this chapter. The Grocery and Apparel Industries invented new tools and deployed them everywhere, so they are obvious candidates for study in more detail. Sales over the Internet (e-tailing) were a new way of selling and buying that promised to expand quickly over the next few years, and thus they, too, warrant further examination. Combined, the three were involved in two experiences of American consumers. First, almost everyone has, many times, been helped by computers in buying food and clothing, both knowingly and not knowingly. Increasingly, many people make their first purchase over the Internet. Therefore, these cases reflect a large and important slice of American retail life. Second, because some of the firms in these three case studies were so large, smaller enterprises adopted their business practices and their influence spread simultaneously across the entire retail sector. Much as General Motors influenced the IT practices of thousands of both small and large suppliers to its factories, so, too, large retail enterprises affected other players in their industry by fiat and example.

Large general-merchandise retail firms are not included specifically in this chapter. To a great extent, I have described their role in the previous chapter, which, along with the three cases described here, gives us a reasonable picture of the patterns of adoption and consequences as they evolved across the entire American Retail Industry. This picture makes it possible to complete our description of the use of the digital in the physical manufacture, movement, and sale of goods in America over the past half century.

Grocery Industry

The Grocery Industry is the largest component of the entire Retail Industry. In the late 1950s, approximately one out of every six dollars spent by a consumer in the United States was spent in a grocery store. Similar statistics could be cited for expenditures at the dawn of the twenty-first century.[2] To put these data in relative perspective, in the early 1950s, of the total of some 1.7 million retail establishments in the United States, over 384,000 were food stores; the next largest categories of retail operations were restaurants and bars (319,600 establishments) and apparel shops (119,700). We can also reasonably postulate that a very high percentage of teenagers who worked in the second half of the century did so in the Retail Industry, primarily in grocery stores, supermarkets, and restaurants. By themselves, grocery stores were one of the largest economic sectors of the economy.[3] As the nation's population expanded and its residents spread out into suburbs and new communities, the Grocery Industry followed, occupying space in many of the new shopping malls built over the past half century.

The industry's structure also changed in significant ways. I have touched on this point in the two previous chapters, but it bears revisiting here because of the

A department store salesperson is recording inventory on hand that could be scanned into a computer, circa 1966, with an IBM 1287 Optical Reader, which fed data into a S/360 computer. By the end of the 1960s, this had become a widely deployed application in large department store chains. Courtesy IBM Corporate Archives.

implications these transformations had for the use of IT in the industry. After World War II, there were essentially three types of food stores. First, there were niche players, specializing in one type of product line, such as butcher shops and bakeries. The small, family-owned general food store was a second category. Sometimes they were part of a little chain of two to four stores, all typically located in the same community or in nearby towns. The third format (to use a grocery term) was the supermarket, an enterprise usually larger than the family-owned stores and often part of a regional or national chain. Although all three formats never went away, the number of niche players declined sharply over time, as did the small "mom and pop" enterprises, displaced by both regional and national chains. By the 1980s, these were replaced in turn, primarily by fewer but very large regional chains, while national chains continued to expand across the nation. The most remarkable format was the supermarket, which began to appear early in the twentieth century and which became the place where most people bought their groceries by the end of the 1960s.[4] At that time, these larger stores captured approximately 70 percent of all food sales.[5] Over time, supermarkets also grew in size, managing two to three times as many SKUs as they had at midcentury.

The chains, in combination with the large supermarket, introduced the majority of new developments in this industry. Their ability to offer an increasing variety of products in each store and the economies of scale and scope they achieved were made possible not only by a wide variety of technologies but also by the influences of these technologies, as we saw with the development and deployment of the UPC. However, this symbiotic relationship extended far beyond computing. As two students of the industry concluded, "Improvements in communication, refrigeration, and transportation made possible the physical existence of modern supermarkets, influencing not only distribution functions but also customer shopping habits."[6] The process of conversion to supermarkets had started long before the arrival of the computer. Joe Weingarten, quoted at the beginning of this chapter, is often credited with opening one of the first such stores. He can also claim to have invented the first shopping cart.[7] In 1932 there were 300 supermarkets in the United States, over 8,500 by the end of World War II, in excess of 14,000 in 1950, and double that number by the start of the Kennedy administration.[8] The number of chains also declined in the 1950s, from 866 chains that were operating 4 or more stores in 1953 to 790 in 1958. More important was the trend among chains to operate 10 or more stores; their number declined from 279 to 247 in 1958, demonstrating that the process of concentration of market share into fewer hands had already begun.[9]

Economists and professors of business management have extensively studied this industry, all counting the number of stores, cataloging sales over time, and measuring productivity. So we have a great deal of data on how this industry evolved. We know, for example, that the trend of supermarkets to expand under the banner of regional and national chains kept going after the 1960s. In fact, they tripled by 1965 over 1945's number, as did the variety of products each store offered (9,000 in the late 1960s from 3,000 in 1945).[10] By the late 1970s, supermarkets generated 76 percent of all grocery store sales, even though they made up only 19 percent of all stores of all formats. Corporate chains operated two-thirds of all supermarkets by the late 1970s.[11]

Of the 30,000 supermarkets extant in the late 1970s, about 1,000 had deployed scanning systems.[12] Smaller stores were only just then beginning to consider POS and scanning, constrained, as noted in the previous chapter, by such factors as cost and the extent to which food producers were putting UPC labels on their products. In short, chains and supermarkets led the way. But a combination of other technologies continued to make expanded use of the supermarket format attractive to both merchants and customers. Writing at the end of the 1970s, James L. Brock, a well-known industry watcher, observed that "the development and growing use of technology such as the automobile, growth in commercial and home refrigeration facilities, and new food manufacturing and processing techniques including frozen food, 'instant' cake mixes, and extensive prepackaging, also created favorable conditions for supermarket growth."[13]

Fierce competition has long been a major feature of this industry, and with the expanded use of chains and supermarkets, pressure on profits escalated. A great deal of the rivalry turned on the issue of who could provide the lowest prices for goods, even though chains and individual stores constantly sought ways to offer services that would justify charging more, such as for deli items and, later, prepared

The Apparel Industry was an aggressive user of all kinds of computing. In this 1977 photograph, a POS system is being used in a Utah clothing store. The price tag has a bar code, but note that in this instance the clerk elected to key in sales data. Courtesy IBM Corporate Archives.

meals. In short, this industry epitomized competition over price. Its members addressed the challenge by improving efficiencies, as with the UPC and scanning.

The severity of the assault on profits cannot be underestimated. In 1956, for instance, profits averaged 1.97 percent; by the end of 1971, they had declined to 0.92 percent, nearly in half. Put another way, return on net worth dropped from 14.40 percent to 8.88 percent.[14] The problem of declining profits, which could be correctly attributed to increased competition, always originated from the actual expenses of operation rather than from prices one could charge for products. Over the Entire period, the three most important sources of increased cost (and hence what a grocer attempted to control at the store level) were labor, advertising, and real estate. Large stores, chains, and wholesalers also worried about inventory turns, just as did any other retailer.[15] Chains could leverage their size to negotiate lower wholesale prices for inventory, a strategy of growing importance as the century progressed. In combination with competition, margins remained thin, and pressure to improve efficiencies and expand market share continued all through the 1980s and 1990s. In the 1980s, the industry also suffered from the sharp growth in competition from a new quarters—fast-food restaurants—a problem that has continued as the nation's consumers found less time to prepare meals at home. The industry responded slowly but, eventually, extensively, with ready-to-eat meals that could be purchased in supermarkets, but restaurants are still a threat.[16] Wal-Mart's partial entry into the food business, and, more important, its overall effect on retailing at large, also forced food chains to lower their prices. Wal-Mart's "everyday-low-price" (EDLP) approach made it the leader in distribution efficiency, but it also showed grocers how they, too, had to operate.[17]

Two industry experts, Jay Coggins and Ben Senauer, have argued that innovations in the industry were in response to continued competitive pressures from the 1970s to the present and that part of this industry's reaction was to deploy various technologies, such as UPC and EDI. However, they also point out that the cost of labor was a major force on balance sheets. These observations reflect the same kinds of concerns evident in manufacturing industries through the second half of the twentieth century. Salaries were part of the problem for grocers, even though they tended to be some of the lowest in the American economy. A larger concern was simply finding enough qualified help in what historically had been a labor-intensive business; turnover in some stores exceeded 100 percent a year, and 60 to 70 percent was fairly common. Coggins and Senauer, therefore, note that, supermarkets have an incentive to find labor-saving capital that can substitute for workers."[18] Computer-printed labels on shelves, for example, reduced the amount of labor needed to mark goods, as did experiments underway at the dawn of the new century with self-checkout systems.

The industry was not immune to the influences of the Internet either, as some firms learned how to exploit the technology. In the end, most chose to use it as part of their EDI and supply chain management processes. A few attempted to sell over the Internet. "Pure play" online vendors, who took orders over the Internet, represented a new but small segment of the market. Traditional brick-and-mortar stores put up web sites to advertise and communicate, and at the end of the century even began to take orders online for customers to pick up. At the time, the leading Internet grocer in the United States was Peapod.Inc, which in 1998 had the nation's fifth largest e-commerce site. A decade earlier, before the arrival of the Internet as an e-business channel, Peapod came into being to sell software for stand-alone, dial-up, computer-based shopping with Safeway. In 1998, it had sales of $69 million and had caught the attention of the entire industry, which feared it might be the wave of the future, as experts in the Grocery Industry began to predict. For example, Deborah Lowe, at San Francisco State University, forecasted that by 2001, 20 percent of all grocery sales would go through the Internet; she proved to be overly optimistic. Bill Gates, CEO of Microsoft, predicted that one-third of all food sales would be handled electronically by 2005. There were online players active in the market: ShopLink, Streamline, and HomeRun on the East Coast, and on the West Coast HomeGrocer and Webvan. Even Priceline.com began to offer groceries online, beginning in November 1999. Prices for goods purchased online were reportedly 20 to 50 percent below store costs, but it was not clear if that level of discounting could be sustained. Price proved once again to be the primary consumer test of the attractiveness of a grocery store's offerings; that factor had not changed over the past half century. The point is, however as in other industries, grocers experimented with new formats.[19]

If we look at the overall economic performance of this industry, before diving into a discussion of its use of IT, what do we see? First, the share of consumer's income spent on food fell from 13.9 percent in 1970 to 10.9 percent in 1996. Expenditures on food eaten at home also fell, from 10.3 percent in 1970 to 6.8 percent in 1996. Both trends reflected the growing affluence of the American consumer in the world's most prosperous economy. The industry, however, managed to preserve profit margins, despite the fact that its levels of profit were historically lower than in many other industries. Median weekly sales per square foot dropped from $11.71 in 1960 to $6.34 in 1996, but then store sizes kept increasing also. Weekly sales per labor hour rose all through the 1960s and 1970s and then began a long-term decline, largely attributable to the increase in labor-intensive in-store services, such as expanded deli departments in the 1990s. Two economists concluded from this mixture of data that the industry operated under intense competitive pressures but, at the same time, had "provided a healthy return to its investors" because it had found innovative ways to operate, and some of the necessary changes involved the use of IT.[20]

The concentration that occurred in the face of competition and various new forms of rivalry in the 1980s and 1990s was in response to the need to achieve higher levels of what Alfred D. Chandler, Jr., characterized as "scale and scope." This pattern can be illustrated by several statistics. In 1989, 50 percent of all retail grocery sales came from chain supermarkets and only 23.4 percent from independent supermarkets. Small stores generated an additional 18.9 percent, convenience stores 7.7 percent. Ten years later, in 1999, chain supermarkets had increased their market share to 61.8 percent, a dramatic lift in a short period of time. Independent supermarkets lost share, shrinking to 15.5 percent of the market; convenience stores also lost share, dropping to 6.2 percent. There are data for 1999 on wholesale club stores (but not for 1989), which had 4.8 percent of share. At the same time, the volume of sales actually increased, so everyone earned more. In 1989 all grocery stores combined brought in $351 billion in sales revenue; in the late 1990s, $472 billion.[21] All stores had increased sales over the decade by an average of 34.7 percent; however, supermarkets did better, growing by 41.8 percent. Payroll continued to be a major expense item (11.41 percent in 1989; 11.2 percent in 1999). Total employment costs remained relatively constant, 14.95 percent to 14.01 percent, despite heroic efforts at reducing them.[22]

At the dawn of the new century, the Grocery Industry was robust but saddled with continuing competition from niche chains, other retailers (e.g., Wal-Mart), restaurants, and even the Internet. Yet it continued to be a major participant in the economy. It employed 3.5 million workers, operated 127,000 stores, and generated sales totaling over $800 billion, of which $365 billion came from supermarkets. The industry's net profit after taxes sat at 1.18 percent. Labor represented 52.3 percent of total operating expenses (not to be confused with the percentage of total costs cited above, which of course would be smaller because the cost of inventory is included). The consumer had a rich variety of goods to choose from, on average over 49,000 in a typical supermarket, and spent 6.4 percent of his or her disposal income on food bought at all stores. Consumers were making an average of 2.3 trips to their grocery stores each week, and they were also spending 4.2 percent of their income eating out. To put all these data into a partial global perspective, consumers in Canada spent 9.2 percent and in Japan 12 percent on store-bought food.[23]

Major chains—all of whom were extensive users of computing—included Safeway, Vons, Bruno's, Kroger, American Stores, Albertson's, Winn-Dixie, Publix, Food Lion, Super Discount Markets, Cub Foods, A&P, Stop & Shop, Giant, and Tops, to mention a few. Like their predecessors in earlier decades, they worried about slow growth (expansion came from taking market share, not necessarily from selling more food per capita) and increasing population, changing consumer tastes, lack of food price inflation, and intense competition.

The ability of this industry to consolidate into ever larger chains over the past half century was made possible in part by the use of information technology in support of operations. Expansion into new markets always had to be done within the context of maintaining operating costs low enough to make wholesalers and retailers price-competitive at the retail end of the supply chain. As chains learned how to apply various types of technology, not just IT, they could grow through acquisitions and the construction of new stores to attack existing rivals. The UPC became an important component of the IT infrastructure, but it was not the first nor did it function in isolation from other applications and technologies. To a large extent, our understanding of how this industry deployed IT could be seen through the actions of the chains because they were the first to use computers and were, of course, over time the ones that most deployed computing, if for no other reason than that they owned most of the grocery stores. Smaller stores also later used computing as the cost of computing dropped or because circumstances forced them to do so.

IT Deployment

The story of computing in the 1950s and 1960s mimics that of other industries because it centered on accounting and inventory control applications, with large chains the first to embrace the computer. The focus of early IT uses concentrated on improving back office and warehouse operations. Not until the mid-1970s did the industry as a whole begin to implement digital applications in the shopping areas in stores and not until the 1980s that grocers began in earnest to integrate their various applications into cross-functional processes and systems. This is not to say that attempts to put computing into stores had not been discussed earlier. As two observers as far back as 1965 had noted, "Studies of American female consumers indicate a desire for contact with store personnel in supermarkets, and the introduction of a system where punched cards, automatic totaling, and mechanical bagging might further reduce now limited contact, could affect consumer reactions adversely." Systems could also be so restrictive as to reduce the ability of a customer to make impulse purchases.[24] The most widely adopted form of in-store automation in the 1950s and 1960s was not digital but rather mechanical—vending machines for cigarettes, candy, and soft drinks. Electronic cash registers were as close to high tech as grocers were willing to get inside the store itself.

Instead, computers, were installed in the headquarters of grocery chains to do accounting for both retail and wholesale operations. One early computer used for this purpose was the IBM 1140 Data Processing System. Relatively inexpensive in the early 1960s, it proved useful for inventory control and billing, accounts receivable, sales analysis, purchase order writing, inventory reports, and order book writing. The system used disk drives, so major files could be kept on separate disk packs for convenience, security, and backup. The system promised a systematic approach in managing the flow of data (i.e., paperwork), from receipt to shipment of orders, with integrated production of invoices, updating of accounting files, and so forth. As an IBM publication of the day touted, "Business growth is easily absorbed because of the system's storage potential, its high speed processor and its flexible printer."[25] Food Marketing Corporation, a wholesaler in the mid-1960s, used an IBM 1401/1311 system primarily to handle warehousing applications and accounting, using the computers to help stabilize and control the cost of goods, spot sources of profits, and improve customer service through faster order processing. Identifying opportunities to lower costs, primarily through better management of stock, led to substantially lower accounting costs. As in other industries with warehousing functions, the central collection of applications focused on ordering, receiving, shipping, and billing inventory as quickly as possible so that the minimum amount of inventory remained in stock, yet always with the right mix of products.[26] Another wholesaler (Florida Retail Owned Grocers) used an IBM 1440 system for similar purposes, which resulted in reduced paperwork, overtime, and stock-outs. In this case, the organization had moved from tabulating equipment, which had consumed 450,000 punch cards every month, to a system that needed only 50,000 cards because EDP stored the data on disk packs.[27]

In general, these kinds of applications were implemented successfully because there was sufficient knowledge on the part of vendors and users of earlier systems (e.g., IBM 305s and Burroughs and NCR accounting equipment) to make them work. But, in part because of the expense of the technology, users worried about unused computer capacity, and thus they constantly tried to find additional ways to add applications once they had a system in-house. One report from the early 1960s noted that "the computer and its auxiliaries have had a great impact on chain and large store offices," in which systems were loaded up with applications in accounting, inventory control, reordering, credit evaluation, credit card calculation, billing procedures, sales prediction, pilferage evaluation, and error control. As in manufacturing, savings in inventory were only part of the exchange for the expense of these systems. Firms reported declines in clerical personnel costs, especially in preparing payrolls, because of the large number of employees all grocery stores had. Pilferage was another area in which computer-based applications helped reduce expenses. Pilferage alone could destroy the margins of any warehouse or store in this industry; using computer-printed tags and cards on merchandise proved more efficient than earlier techniques in helping grocers track their goods.

But the big savings came in inventory. Kroger in 1963 reported that its systems made it possible to cut cash requirements by $5 million, or 2 percent of daily sales. Safeway and Stop and Shop did the same. Reports of lowered inventory stock levels in stores—by having the right merchandise at the right time—ranged from 5 to 10 percent to over 18 percent.[28] Companies kept reporting these kinds of benefits for years, thereby encouraging each other to deploy such systems to impose discipline and structure on inventory management and use of personnel. One final example is Allied Supermarkets, Inc., in Detroit, which, ran 240 grocery stores. It installed a CDC 3300 computer system (complete with dual processors) in 1967 to handle the flow of data needed to manage such a large collection of stores and associated warehousing functions. To put things in context, its stores each normally carried about 8,000 different types of products and generated $1 billion in sales. Digital applications made it possible to have shorter lead times in replenishing inventory, which meant quicker turns and higher probability of earnings by having more of the right kinds of products in the stores. Constant restocking of warehouses and stores and concurrent receiving and shipping became easier to perform and track. To manage the whole process, the system generated 60 various reports on volumes, types of goods sold, and so forth. Thus, handling large quantities of data in a timelier manner improved inventory turns to such an extent that the firm's data processing vice president, R. Lee Paulson, said proudly that his system had "enabled management to increase inventory turnover to among the highest in the industry while making a substantial reduction in out-of-stock conditions."[29] For the rest of the century, these kinds of applications were universally installed, with constant upgrading to newer generations of computer and telecommunications technologies.

The biggest story in computing in this industry was scanning, of course. By adding UPC and POS data gathering to their existing base of applications in the 1970s and 1980s, large chains were able to further automate, streamline, and control both the management of inventory and cost of personnel in the 1970s and 1980s. But not until the 1990s did one finally see the effective use of customer purchase data at the individual consumer level.

In hindsight it would seem easy to portray the grocery industry as rushing forward to embrace the UPC, but as noted in the previous chapter, this was not so simple. In the mid-1970s, *Progressive Grocer*, the leading industry publication, reported that grocers were slow to adopt the new technology. In 1975, fewer than 40 supermarkets were scanning UPCs. Economic benefits of scanning were not yet proven, although executives polled by the magazine were in agreement that scanning was going to become a permanent part of the grocery business. Resistance from unions, fearing loss of jobs, and consumer groups concerned that they would not know what prices grocers charged them also momentarily slowed the rate of adoption.[30] Government economists, however, observed a slow adoption of scanning across the industry in the mid-1970s in spite of these two sources of resistance.[31] Table 11.1 documents the pace of adoptions in the middle years of the

Table 11.1
Deployment of Scanning in U.S.
Grocery Stores, 1974–1978

1974	6
1975	42
1976	102
1977	206
1978	520
1979	1,200

Source: *Progressive Grocer* (December 1978): 38; J. Barry Mason and Morris L. Mayer, "Retail Merchandise Information Systems for the 1980's," *Journal of Retailing* 56, no. 1 (1980): 68.

1970s. Adoption of scanning is, as the data suggest, a post-1978 story, even though the technology came online earlier in that decade. Not until the mid-1980s had this application sufficiently expanded to make a real difference in how the industry did its work.

There always seems to be confusion about when a technology (or application in this case) is invented and when it is adopted. For the historian, both are important. The development of an innovation later makes adoption significant. On the other hand, without understanding the innovation, its adoption cannot be fully appreciated. Confusing the two is easy. The headlines are about the development of scanning, for example, so one can understand why a book on the subject would tell the exciting story of its creation. Studies by academics on innovations tend to focus on the invention of a technology, not necessarily on the less glamorous, slower process of deployment. Such was the case with UPC. Nonetheless, in the face of inflation and higher costs, this industry invested time and money in new technological innovations in the 1970s.[32] Despite false starts and technological difficulties, POS systems began to appear.

Gating factors at the time ranged from understanding the economic benefits to the chicken-and-egg problem of simultaneous adoption by food producers and stores. But there were less glamorous issues to deal with, too, not the least of which were technical. Software to run POS applications and then to link them into existing installed inventory control systems came slowly to the market and proved to be equally lethargic in performing reliably. However, the number of installations picked up to a remarkable degree at the end of the 1970s, suggesting that many of these earlier concerns were beginning to wane. Sales of POS cash registers suggest that conclusion. Through the first half of the 1970s, shipments of POS terminals grew slowly, from 19,300 in 1972 to 42,300 in 1974 to 51,100 in 1976. In 1977, however, shipments jumped to 73,700. How did this pattern compare to the shipment of electromechanical cash registers, which were the mainstay of all retailers? In 1972 retailers took delivery on 182,000 units, 96,100 in 1974, 19,800 in 1976, and 10,300 in 1977. Looked at in another way, the percentage of any type of electronic cash register installed in a store grew from 9.9 percent of all units in 1972 to 96.5 percent in 1977.[33] What these data tell us is that the shift was fundamentally to electronic units, of which POS terminals were simply part of the product mix. Nonfood merchandisers in general led the way in the broad adoption of all types of units, but the grocery chains led in the earliest uses of POS technology. It was a change in basic cash register technology of historic proportions.

By the end of the decade, the evidence was in on what kinds of benefits a retailer could expect with this technology. Faster checkouts and more efficient scheduling of labor had been demonstrated, along with savings from not having to price every item. Giant Foods reported a 29 percent reduction in the time necessary to check out customers, with almost no checker errors, and payroll cost reductions. Many benefits that in later years would be considered hard benefits were at the time positioned as soft savings. These included collecting information that could be used to allocate shelf space, automated reordering, determination of price elasticity, measures of the effects of special sales promotions, and merchandising mixes.[34] Whereas the industry paid attention to consumer concerns, grocers increasingly set these aside as the operational benefits of the technology became evident. Consumers would either have to live with the changes or be conditioned to accept them as beneficial.[35]

In the 1980s and through most of the 1990s, grocers implemented a wide variety of computer-based applications, built primarily on those installed earlier. First, earlier applications were more fully deployed, such as scanning at POS stations, and were enhanced. A second emerging pattern involved the initial use of POS data collected about inventory and customer preferences, most notably during the 1990s. A third practice concerned the use of a myriad of other digital tools, such as portable hand-held terminals to change prices on shelf labels, to order inventory, and so forth, as well as tools widely deployed in other industries, such as CAD software to design stores or reformat their layout.[36] As chains grew in size and number, and because they were the primary and most extensive users of IT, they continued the process started in the 1950s of deploying ever-increasing amounts of computing apparatus, software, and applications across the industry. Exploiting scanned data collected at the front of the store at the checkout counter continued to grow in importance. It is easy to see how fast the technology spread. In the early 1980s, over 7,500 supermarkets used this technology, and by mid-decade over 50 percent of all sales were scanned.[37] By the end of the 1980s, over 90 percent of the supermarkets in the United States were doing some form of scanning at POS. One survey of 18 companies suggested that almost all also used various hand-held terminals to order, track, and price (or verify pricing) of inventory.[38] Store operations had changed profoundly as a result of such broad deployment. One review of the industry's practices (1983) provided a very early description of these changes:

With hand-held micro computers in the aisle, minis in the office, scanning at the front end, electronic ordering and invoicing in the warehouse, sophisticated analysis of item movement, computerized assistance on promotional decisions, and the availability of sensitive programs to fine tune shelf space allocation, the stage is set for extraordinary advances in operating and merchandising precision.[39]

In short, a digital platform on which to build additional applications soon existed across most of the industry.

One of the earliest byproducts of the buildup in digital information from POS involved managing the receipt of inventory in a new way, known as direct store delivery (DSD). This involved taking delivery of merchandise directly from a manufacturer into the store without using a warehouse. Products were priced by vendors or truckers, scanned at the back door of the store, and then put right on the shelves. Retailers avoided the cost of warehousing, insurance, and shipping; DSD was easy to justify from their perspective because it increased unit profits. At the dawn of the 1980s, however, it was also labor-intensive since it meant that many smaller deliveries were constantly being made, and standard DSD practices were not yet common across stores in a chain. Therefore, cross-store ordering and inventory management were initially difficult to execute and often resulted in a great deal of additional paperwork to track receipts and invoices. Yet as early as 1976, 25 percent of a supermarket store's sales came via DSD processes, and 27 percent of a store's products were delivered in that way. For managers, automating pricing and receipt of inventory, as well as getting correct data, became a major objective and challenge, especially since stores were beginning to move away from pricing individual products. One report in 1980 noted that "retailers and manufacturing are attempting to clear the thicket of paper work surrounding DSD," stimulating further automation and use of scanners to receive merchandise and digitally update price tables used by POS terminals.[40] The industry as a whole moved quickly in the early 1980s to establish industry-wide standards for receiving documentation, which went far toward reducing the paper trail that had previously accompanied the use of DSD. As a process, DSD had been around since the early 1970s, but until data tracking by computer became cost-effective and efficient, it waned. By the early 1990s, computer-based DSD was in wide use across the industry.

Another byproduct involved selling scanned data about products and customers to manufacturers. This was a relatively new application in the 1980s, and so there was much discussion about how to do it and why. Initially, information about products was sold or shared with suppliers and manufacturers. By the early 1990s, stores were beginning to use individual customer-buying data to help make merchandising decisions. While the debate went on about how to make money by selling data, stores still worried about the cost of scanning equipment, but as the deployment data above indicate, they continued to install the infrastructure that made possible the collection and use of market intelligence. One report described the strategy in clear terms:

Central to the process is a way to link customers—such as via a check cashing card—with their scanned purchases. Data is then analyzed for recency and frequency of purchase, and by amount spent either in total dollars, by department or by SKU. Retailers are clearly sold on the idea, if not yet on the needed software and hardware.[41]

But it was a slow process of adoption as they felt their way along this new application.[42]

Tied to POS scanning and this new use of data was a variety of other applications, such as automation of the issuance and use of coupons, electronic funds transfers by customers to pay for groceries, credit checks, installation of in-store ATMs, and use of credit cards. Each was an individual digital application, all were in various stages of limited development and deployment in the 1980s and 1990s, and all were the subject of much discussion within the industry. By the end of the 1990s, they were also widely deployed but not yet ubiquitous.[43]

Despite complaints about the lack of software—a false criticism because retailers other than groceries were extensive users of such tools—the Grocery Industry struggled with how best to extract useful insights from what was rapidly becoming a vast collection of data, most of it from POS systems and, increasingly through the 1980s and early 1990s, from frequent shopper programs. In this application, a shopper was issued a card, which when presented at the checkout counter entitled the consumer to discounts or other benefits, that made possible the move from paper coupons to electronic credits. The application enabled stores to collect information about the specific shopping practices and tastes of its consumers. By the end of 1993, however, roughly only 18 percent of chains and 14 percent of independent grocers used frequent shopper programs. Furthermore, those who had collected substantial amounts of data did not yet fully exploit it. Industry publications continued to publish tutorials and defenses of the concept of database marketing programs as late as the end of the century, long after other retailers had become comfortable with the application. Steve Weinstein, writing for the *Progressive Grocer* in June 1999, blasted the industry, saying that grocers "are not all making good use of the data generated." The Food Marketing Institute reported at the same time that 41 percent of a group of surveyed grocers had no intention of even having frequent shopper programs, let alone collecting such data, because they were not convinced that such programs generated more sales or profits.[44]

One of the original justifications for POS and scanning had been the promise of saving labor costs by posting price labels on shelves instead of on each product. Stores quickly began to produce such labels, despite initial customer concerns. This was a fundamental departure from earlier procedures. In the late 1980s, a further refinement appeared with the limited use of electronic shelf labels. However, this is a good example of a digital application whose time had not yet come but was a logical extension of an earlier, paper-based one. The idea was to have a tiny liquid crystal display (LCD) price label on the shelf, changed either with some hand-held unit or by transmission via wire from the in-store computer. That would mean less labor (no paper notices on the shelves) and could permit a store to change prices during the course of the day to encourage, for example, more shopping on a Monday, as opposed to a busy Saturday, or in the early afternoon during the week. All during the 1980s and 1990s, however, adoption occurred slowly as grocers determined what effects this new application would have on sales and costs.[45]

As in other industries and in the Grocery Industry in the 1960s and 1970s, interest in reducing labor costs was paramount on the minds of all grocers, a concern that continued through the 1980s and 1990s. They constantly weighed the benefits of digitized methods against the potential for less labor content in work. In addition to the normal concerns about work elimination and use of automation that tracking systems and POS data provided, grocers paid considerable attention to using in-store computers for labor tracking, much along the lines in manufacturing firms. The most important use of computing for labor management concerned time and attendance and scheduling. In the 1980s, anywhere from 2.5 to 3 percent of all store sales paid workers assigned to checkout stands. These percentages did not include the cost of labor for warehousing, inventory management, or stocking shelves. The front end of the store was always the most customer-sensitive as well. If a store cut back on checkout clerks, the lines got too long, irritating customers. However, having too many clerks was a waste of money. Balancing supply and demand, using software tools to suggest work schedules, held out the promise of better utilization of labor. Proper balancing made it possible to control overtime expenses and compliance with union contracts. By the late 1980s, *Progressive Grocer*, the leading industry publication, began to report cases in which computerized labor tracking generated economic benefits.[46] This became an increasingly important application in the 1990s, with over 20 percent of all grocery chains using such software tools by 1993. By then, quantifiable results were being reported—for example, minutes, instead of a day, to schedule labor in a store, an 11.3 percent increase in customers served per hour, and a 10.44 percent decrease in the number of minutes it took to check out a customer in Kroger's stores.[47]

One final issue made its initial appearance in these years that would loom much greater in importance in the 1990s: the integration of various warehousing, backroom, and in-store systems. It appeared first in the sales arguments made by IBM, NCR, and others when promoting their in-store computer systems, but the notion spread slowly among grocers for many of the same reasons as in manufacturing, distribution, and process industries. But the case in favor of integration became more compelling as the amount of installed computing increased. As Suart Denrich, manager of information systems at Valu Food argued in 1987, "It is an absolute necessity that all systems be integrated because of the multitude of systems at [the] store level. We have eight different data systems just within our small company, and it takes a lot of man-hours to cross-reference those systems."[48] Ronald Tanner, a reporter for *Progressive Grocer*, reported that "the buzzword is integration," predicting that as standards expanded, such as the Uniform Communication Standard (UCS) across the industry, along with deployment of minicomputers in stores, retail outlets could handle multiple applications that before could only be done with, for example, PCs.[49] Popular in-store systems that made such integration possible included both the NCR Tower and the IBM S/36 computer systems. How-

Table 11.2
Supermarket Computer Applications, Circa 1986

Accounting	Liquor inventory/ordering
Authorized check file	Markdowns
Automated pricing	Meat-cutting tests
Bakery recipe costing/pricing	Meat/produce tonnage
Cashier price lists	Order guide/price book
Cash management	Payroll
Checker productivity analysis	Pharmacy systems
Credit authorization	POS/scanning
Customer data base	Price changes to wholesaler
Deli recipe costing/pricing	Product mix/profit analysis
Departmental operating statements	Projected gross profit reporting
Depreciation	Returned-check system
Direct store delivery	Shelf allocation analysis/assignment
Energy management	Shelf tagging
Forms generation	Standard orders
Graphics	Statistical analysis
Inventory management	Time and attendance
Loan amortization	Unit pricing
Labor analysis	Warehouse systems
Labor scheduling	Word processing
Last-in-first-out (LIFO) inventory management	

Source: Modified from Robert E. O'Neill, "Supermarkets Will Spend Big in '86," *Progressive Grocer* (May 1986): 118.

ever, store managers were not rushing toward some integrated computerized future, as shown in 1987 by the comments of Dennet Withington, the vice president of management information systems at Price Chopper, a 60-store chain: "There is a lot of gold out there that people are not gathering because they are too deeply rooted in the past. To realize the potential of computerization, we will have to wait for an entire generation of mangers to die."[50] However, the list of applications now going into the Grocery Industry was not short. All of the applications in table 11.2 were in various stages of deployment, and all lent themselves to both in-store and intrastore processing.

By the middle years of the 1980s, the industry at large was upgrading systems used to manage warehousing, filling in the gaps in its supply chain processes, and slowly moving to the use of EDI and other networks to link stores, warehouses, and suppliers. In addition to the traditional advantages of such systems, implications of new ways of doing business emerged, such as automatic order replenishment, which, as one grocer put it, is "a leap of faith to let a computer write your order."[51] Called in those years computer-aided order (CAO) systems, 20 percent of the large chains used them in the early 1990s, but they were increasingly deployed all through the decade. Such tools were also part of a larger implementation of an emerging industry-coordinated strategy called efficient consumer response (ECR), a collection of processes (with software tools) designed to make grocers competitive with mass merchants, which were increasingly becoming their rivals. With ECR, grocers and manufacturers deployed the kind of close replenishment practices seen in manufacturing. They mostly focused on improving operations in warehouses, that is, replenishment from vendor to warehouse, less from warehouse to store. Leaders in the use of IT in the industry, such as Giant Foods and Lions Food, often led the way in extending linkages to stores, thereby encouraging the industry at large. In 1994, however, one industry observer noted that "CAO is still a fledgling program in the grocery industry."[52]

Recent Trends

The POS systems continued to drive the industry's use of technology during the 1980s and 1990s, but at various speeds of deployment. Warehouses embraced bar codes slowly, in fact, behind grocery chains. The latter were almost all using bar codes and scanning but, as late as 1998, one industry survey suggested that only 7 percent of all grocery warehouses did so.[53] Cross-docking did make inroads in warehouse practices, accelerating the need for greater use of bar codes. Network connections to suppliers spread, with many chains reporting that they were linked electronically to their suppliers (an estimated 25 percent) and that electronic invoices and receipts were spreading rapidly through the industry as a way of reducing administrative and labor costs. By the mid-1990s, DSD, ECR, and EDI were increasingly integrated. Once again, Giant Foods became the poster child of advanced uses of IT. Nonetheless, wholesalers still resisted ECR because they did not see more economic benefits for them; rather, the technology proved more beneficial to stores that enhanced their economic purchasing power. Chains that owned both warehouses and stores, such as Food Lion and Giant Foods, pushed ahead with integration of these two pieces of their businesses.[54]

As a result, by the mid-1990s, for essentially the first time, grocers were using IT as a strategic tool instead of as a means for reducing operating expenses. Industry leaders started to deploy technology to reach consumers, for example, by using IT to get accurate prices to consumers or, as wholesaler Fleming declared, using computing as "a strategic enabler to grow the business." What made Fleming's initiatives crucial was the fact that it was the largest wholesaler in the nation, second only to Kroger as a distributor in the food industry in the mid-1990s.[55] By the end of the century, many in the industry also saw the new applications as the implementation of the final elements of their supply chains, even using the term *supply chain management* to describe their initiatives.[56]

While traditional concerns regarding labor, effective use of POS systems, efficiency in warehouses, customer service, and price competition conditioned the adoption of IT in the 1990s, the Internet made its appearance and, as was the case in most industries, stimulated a great deal of debate and concern and, by the dawn of the new millennium, resulted in the start of some fundamental changes. Early reports about the Internet spelled danger. One observer thought that "as the world becomes increasingly wired, traditional food retailers risk losing upscale, high-margin customers to electronic-commerce marketers." Wars between two e-commerce grocers—Peapod and Streamline—were viewed as ill harbingers of the future. *Progressive Grocer* asked, "Will stores survive?" and called Internet selling "this wild frontier." One report said, "As a retailer you don't need to lose a lot of share before the economies of your store start to change."[57] That was in 1997—the first big year for the Internet in the Grocery Industry. During the next two years, the industry's leaders tried to understand the Internet and how it might affect their business. A few began to set up web sites to provide information about sales promotions, but as a whole the industry took a watch-and-wait position. How customers were reacting to the possibility of shopping online proved to be at the heart of their initial concerns, followed by its costs and benefits.[58]

By 2000, grocers had seen evidence to the effect that only 10 percent of all Internet shoppers had purchased groceries online, often buying health and beauty aids, vitamins, herbal remedies, cleaning products, and pet supplies. Of "real food," dry goods were the primary types of products that shoppers acquired. In one study, over 50 percent of the consumers questioned about online shopping said that local grocery stores did not offer it.[59] Some, like Giant Food, Food Lion, and A&P, however, became early proponents of integrating the Internet into existing IT strategies and infrastructures, particularly for improving supply chain efficiencies, developing new merchandizing offerings, and engaging in e-commerce with suppliers. Nick Ioli, Jr., A&P's senior vice president and CIO, was quoted in January 2001 on how Wal-Mart's aggressive use of the Internet was posing a threat to grocers: "Companies in the food-retail industry that don't step up right now are not going to be in good shape for the future from an industry perspective." Thus A&P, for one, had started to redesign its processes around a customer-centric business model, moving away, as were others in the Retail Industry, from the old models of manufacturing to customer, push-driven approaches.[60]

The industry experienced a jolt when in 2000 a number of Internet-based companies in their industry suffered as dot.coms all over the nation collapsed. ShopLinc.com and Streamline.com Inc—two major pure players in this industry—collapsed. Priceline.com, which had announced it would start selling groceries online, terminated this line of business. Peapod.com survived but experienced financial turbulence all year, and HomeRuns.com (owned by the Hannaford Brothers supermarket chain) was sold off to the Cypress Group LLC, an equity firm, and then shut down in July 2001. NetGrocer's aggressive expansion program shriveled in the face of budget cuts. These reverses for online groceries signaled to the industry that the period of wild growth was over, that more traditional uses of IT made more sense. However, the industry's own surveys also suggested that customers were more eager to embrace the Internet as a shopping channel than was the Grocery Industry.[61] They were buying online books, medicines, and just about anything other than groceries. In other words, online sales were occurring more frequently in other segments of the Retail Industry, where retailers made progress in developing online loyalty programs, web sites, marketing, and home-shopping applications.

Grocers were extensive users of other forms of telecommunications, such as EDI with suppliers and warehouses and dial-up telephone systems for credit verification and use of debit cards. Large grocery chains, however, came to a similar conclusion at the same time as other retailers about the need to blend the Internet with existing brick-and-mortar facilities, most settling on this strategy in late 2000. Internet-based grocers were up for sale and became attractive candidates for acquisition if they could be fitted into existing physical stores. Traditional chains led the way. Royal Ahold and Safeway, for instance, bought majority interests in Peapod.com and GroceryWorks.com, respectively. Kroger, Albertson's, Publix, and Supervalu all began building proprietary Internet sites to extend their existing channels to customers.[62]

If one were to judge the amount of activity related to computers just from the volume of trade publications that appeared in the 1990s, one would have to conclude that the Golden Age of computing in the Grocery Industry existed in the last decade of the century. In the 1980s, for example, *Progressive Grocer* published nearly 30 articles in the 120 issues it released in that decade. The number grew nearly fourfold in the 1990s, replete with a technology department that was preparing material for every issue of the journal by mid-decade. The number published in the 1980s was nearly a 50 percent increase over that in the 1970s; in short, the publishing record suggests that computing had become big business later in this industry than in others. However, the reality proved to be somewhat different. The diffusion of applications first installed in the 1970s and 1980s accelerated in the 1990s, along with upgrades of earlier uses. Then, at nearly the end of the century, the Internet was introduced. But because the Internet looms so large today, I should note that grocers were still installing and using applications that had been cost-justified long before their access to the Internet.[63] Grocers integrated the new technology very slowly into existing operations, and only if cost-justified. In short, the innovative period really dated to the decade of the 1980s, when for many firms computer usage was new and changed how businesses functioned.

Members of the industry might not reach the same conclusions as I have. For example, *Progressive Grocer* ran an article in mid-1998 asking if retailers were already too high-tech. Computing had become "pervasive . . . affecting everything from front-end to backdoor applications."[64] But the real question grocers asked was whether they were buying the right applications. In the late 1990s, all grocers increased their annual expenditures on IT by double-digit percentages, including capital investments in computing. Integrating applications for effectiveness and to drive down costs of IT (and operations) had been a growing priority across the industry in the 1990s, and at the end of the century the Grocery Industry still had a reputation of not effectively exploiting the vast quantity of data that their systems collected.[65] One student of the industry assessed the situation at the start of the new millennium in this way:

Compared with other retail segments, supermarkets have long displayed a hearty appetite for technology, and many grocery retailers continue to innovate as they enter the 21st century. But experts also see a troubling pattern of delayed implementations and missed opportunities that suggests the industry is lagging behind its retail peers in taking advantage of the latest in digital capabilities.[66]

The dilemma grocers faced was how to digest IT in sensible ways in a "low-margin, high-volume, intensely competitive businesses." Being early adopters of bar codes was old news, and they were beginning to use data to build customer loyalty programs but not enough to develop effective marketing programs by sharing information with upstream buyers and category managers. Susan Reda, the author and a senior editor at *Stores*, noted that "management remains leery of sharing this mother lode of data with consumer product goods manufacturers and ultimately, of stepping too far outside the current paradigm."[67] Struggling with the issue of long-term return on investment (ROI) for most IT hardware and software, versus investing elsewhere for shorter term returns, was the same problem the industry had faced a half century earlier. Despite criticisms from and impatience within the industry, grocers had changed much in the way they operated and what tools they used over the past 50 years. Cautious and nervous, they demonstrated bold leadership when called for, as in the development of bar codes and scanning, and timidity over the unknown, as with the arrival of the Internet.

Apparel Industry

The Apparel Industry is a highly instructive case because it illustrates clearly how retailers in many lines of businesses changed the way in which they performed some of their crucial tasks by using computers. The role of computing also illustrates how this industry, like others, fundamentally altered its relationships with manufacturers and other suppliers. The importance of this industry as a lens on altered work patterns in the United States is reinforced by the fact that its stores ran the gamut in size and scope, from small dress shops and shoe stores to category killers like national electronics, clothing, and department store chains. Category killers, like the Gap or Limited, emerged as retail powerhouses in the late twentieth century, competing against traditional department stores whose clothing departments in 1950 often made up a large share of their offerings, such as J.C. Penney and, for many decades, Sears. Like the Grocery Industry, this one is also everywhere: no shopping center is without its collection of assorted clothing and shoe stores; almost every main street in America also has these kinds of shops, and fashionable avenues in the largest cities in the United States are dotted with them.

This is an industry, however, that needs some definition because of their integral relations with a variety of manufacturers and suppliers. Traditionally, when one speaks about the Apparel Industry, it is not uncommon to include textile and clothing manufacturers, two industries that have different ways of creating raw material and converting them into products suitable for human use. In fact, most accounts of the Apparel Industry concentrate on the manufacturing portion.[68] It is nearly impossible to discuss one sector of the Apparel Industry without at least mentioning the other two components. For our purposes, I limit the discussion to the retail arm because it is this part of the economy that so dramatically illustrates how computing changed so much within the world of retailing at large. As with other retailing sectors, chains normally led the way. Much that was said about retailing and computing in chapters 9 and 10 apply directly here since a large proportion of the firms discussed were merchants that were selling clothing. Like the Grocery Industry, however, it is also an industry that most residents of North America have dealt with directly, even though the dollar value of their purchases is less than, for example, that at either an automotive retailer or furniture store.

When economists study the Apparel Industry, they normally discuss how changes in retailing and global competition fundamentally transformed its manufacturing processes. The challenge manufacturers faced at midcentury was their highly inflexible production process, called the progressive bundle system (PBS), in which parts of an item of clothing were precut and progressively put together, using workers who specialized in specific tasks much as on a production line and ultimately leading to a completed garment. Although it might take less than 30 minutes to sew a pair of pants together, such a process takes 40 days to complete because it has to move from one sewing station to another. Because of the soft nature of cloth, automating or speeding up this labor-intensive production was nearly impossible, despite heroic efforts to use CAD/CAM, other high-tech tools, and even nontechnical alternative manufacturing processes. So long as styles did not fundamentally change, such as men's suits, underwear, or socks, manufacturers could maintain larger than desired buffer inventories to meet the needs of retailers. Although that never fully held true, it was more the case in 1950 than at the end of the century, when Americans acquired on average 27 pieces of clothing each year, making the Apparel Industry big business, as well as also one in which fashion changes were far more frequent than at midcentury.[69]

Increasingly as the century progressed and the number of apparel stores grew, so, too, did the power of regional and national chains. In the 1950s, only a tiny percentage of all clothing stores were owned by chains. By 1972, chains accounted for 6.4 percent of all stores and 17.9 percent by 1992.[70] From the early 1970s to the middle of the 1990s, size, economic purchasing power, and computing converged to trigger fundamental changes in all sectors in the Apparel Industry, not just retailing. Power to make decisions about what products to manufacture and sell shifted from manufacturers to retailers. In the 1980s, retailers (primarily chains) used POS data to lower their cost of inventories by dictating what products they wanted and insisting on shorter lead times. Thus, instead of ordering fall fashions only in the previous spring, they also wanted to be able to replenish fall fashions in the fall. The use of suppliers around the world, whose labor costs were lower than those of American manufacturers, put stress on North American producers to improve their productivity. The whole cycle of events also extended the apparel supply chain worldwide, and the product mix became far more complicated. For instance, the number of SKUs increased all through the 1980s because the variety of fashions did, too. The number of selling seasons went from 2.8 on average (1950s–1970s) to 3.2 for basic fashion products by the early 1990s and, for highly volatile sectors with fashion clothing, to as high as 3.7. That increase reduced the number of weeks in a selling season, leading to additional turnover of goods and the need for faster replenishment. That series of circumstances led to the lean retailing that became so pervasive across the industry. A central component of the new approach was the increasing demand by retailers for just-in-time delivery.[71]

IT Deployment

To make JIT happen, retailers—again, primarily chains in the beginning—started to share with manufacturers sales data collected at POS checkout counters, and far more willingly than did the Grocery Industry. Their strategy of leading with information in changing how manufacturers responded to them called for a far more extensive use of EDI than in the Grocery Industry. Bar coding became an important element, the lingua franca necessary to integrate POS data, automated replenishment orders, and EDI-based communications. Bar coding arrived in retailing in the 1980s; between 1988 and 1992 in particular, its use increased 2.75 times, and in the same period the use of EDI expanded sevenfold. The results were dramatic; in that same short period of time, sales volumes driven by these systems rose from 13 percent to 32 percent.[72] In those same four years, the percentage of domestic shipments to chains rose by 64 percent and to mass merchants by 12 percent, suggesting the growing power of larger enterprises in dictating the move to lean retailing. In turn, these changes also forced manufacturers to improve their productivity in order to remain competitive; reducing, for example, work-in-process inventory by a third and shifting replenishment from an average of three to two weeks.[73] Even the Grocery Industry, which invented bar coding, did not experience so rapid a shift in such a short period of time. For apparel merchants, the economics of the new approach were just too attractive to ignore.

A major study of the Apparel Industry concluded that "companies that have adopted new information systems and management practices, participating in a well-integrated channel, are the ones with the strongest performance today."[74] Increasingly through the 1980s and 1990s, merchants focused on optimizing the quality of their data, inventory costs, replenishment practices and processes, and "time to market" rather than just labor and costs of goods, such as occurred in the Grocery Industry. In apparel, as in general merchandising, having the right product at the right time and at competitive costs began to make more sense. In fact, it became more essential because of increased competition and more possible because of computers and telecommunications. The industry achieved its two objectives by the early 1990s by participating in IT-intensive supply chains that were global and efficient. Mass merchants led the way, Wal-Mart being the most important. Other clothing sellers followed at various rates; by 1993 J.C. Penney used EDI to process 97 percent of its purchase orders and 85 percent of its invoices. Similar stories about the extensive shift to automated processes could be told about Dillard's and

Federated, two major department store chains of the 1980s and 1990s. Smaller firms followed this kind of commitment, although at a slower pace because of the relative cost of the technology to them.[75]

The basic building blocks of lean retailing in the Apparel Industry did not exist in any extent before the 1980s. Some POS data were captured for marketing purposes in the late 1970s and early 1980s. Computing was limited before that period to general accounting applications, most of which were batch and had no fundamental effect on the overall strategic performance of the industry. But all that had changed by the early 1990s when the major building blocks were in use by all major chains:

- Bar codes and the uniform product code (UPC)
- EDI and information processing
- Technical and operation standards across firms
- State-of-the-art distribution centers

Bar codes proved attractive to apparel merchants as a way of precisely identifying products and managing inventory; 60 percent of all goods were marked with bar codes at the SKU level. In the process of deploying this technology, firms shed a large body of tracking paperwork, which had now been converted to digital files. Also, EDI continued to improve in cost performance and technical reliability through the 1980s, thereby creating economic incentives to rely increasingly on this form of communication with suppliers. The industry collectively developed technical standards to make it easier for multiple firms to communicate, and that also made it possible to link POS-generated data directly to EDI systems. Modern warehousing meant electronic tracking of receipts and shipments, electronic payment for goods, and accurate replenishment processes, all highly automated and digitized. Continuous replenishment and cross-docking procedures became increasingly cost-effective and practical as management digitized the amount of control over routine activities. Cross-docking in the 1990s soared, and although definitive data on the extent of deployment is not yet available, it was not uncommon for large chains to have 60 to 70 percent of their products delivered in that way. Standards spread across the industry, essential for retail price tags or stickers, prices for various types of goods, pricing data, use of the UPC bar code, EDI transmission formats, and so forth.[76]

Studies of those chains that had adopted such digital and communications applications indicate that they outperformed their rivals, as measured by profits and growth in market share.[76] Space does not permit us to go through the data, and in any case, another consequence is more important to understand. Because of the high cost of implementing these various applications, smaller firms were driven out of the market, leading to a further consolidation of the industry into the hands of ever larger firms. Small, family-owned chains were pushed out because category killers and large chains could sell a greater variety of products for less. Between 1977—when the earliest forms of lean retailing began to appear—and 1992, almost every segment of the industry became more concentrated. Sales generated by the 50 largest apparel and accessory stores rose from 27.8 percent to 52.4 percent. Sales in the four largest firms rose from 9.1 percent to 17.9 percent, a huge growth in share in such a short period of time. Men's and boys' clothing sales reflected similar patterns, with the top 50 firms doubling their sales and the top four rising from 8.5 percent to 20 percent. Family clothing stores saw a similar pattern: the top 50 rose from 46 percent of sales to over 76 percent, and the top four rose from 23 to 35 percent. So even the sector within the industry that was already highly concentrated continued to consolidate. How did this general pattern of consolidation compare to grocers? The top 50 grocery stores in 1977 claimed 43.5 percent of all sales; by the end of 1992 this had grown to 49.9 percent, not a dramatic increase. The four largest firms actually lost share, dropping from 17.4 to 16.1 percent. General merchandise stores, which had been the most concentrated before the massive adoption of computer-based lean retailing, grew for the top 50 from 77.3 percent of sales to 81.8 percent, with the largest four rising from 37.7 to 47.3 percent. Of all the various segments of retailing (building materials, general merchandising, clothes, shoes, etc.), apparel firms consolidated the fastest in this period. The largest chains dominated their industry as became a force the Internet.[78]

At the firm level, and more specifically at the store level, these four collections of applications fundamentally changed inventory management, demand forecasting, and stocking decisions. Ideally, a retailer wants just the right amount of the right kind of inventory to optimize sales and investment in the cost of goods. The key is to understand the demand for goods and their availability and to have the capability to order and receive in good time the additional products demanded by customers. All of these steps require timely information and, as time passed, receiving it in real time. The POS systems provided sales data, not demand data, so the industry had to merge traditional forecasting and merchandising initiatives and practices with POS, EDI, and so forth, which was a new process in the 1980s and 1990s and was still under development at the turn of the century. Automated replenishment ordering, often called vendor-managed inventory (VMI) works very well, for example, in the Automotive Industry, which has high volumes of consistently managed inventory, making B2B uses of VMI attractive. But such approaches work less effectively when they have to take into account the whims of consumer tastes, especially in regard to women's fashions and the interests of teenage shoppers (one of the fastest growing retail segments at the end of the century). Thus VMI has worked well in the Grocery Industry, where inventory turns increased by 100 percent in the 1980s and early 1990s (a positive development for controlling costs of inventory), but it is not yet clear how effective it will be in apparel retailing, other than for basic products that do not change quickly in style or volume (e.g., men's underwear and socks). The industry as a whole has learned how to collect and analyze POS data to update demand forecasts and to integrate that information back into its VMI processes and applications.[79]

The one major study of the industry's practices, covering 1988–1992, pointed out that success went to those firms that used all four building blocks, that adopting one or two did not provide as many benefits as the combination of all four. This was a lesson learned over time because the process of implementing these applications took years to work through. Implementing both EDI and bar codes at the same time was fairly uncommon in the late 1980s (about 25 percent of those surveyed had done so). Four years later, 75 percent had adopted the two applications, leaving less than 10 percent not yet implementing these processes.[80] Bar codes went in first; next merchants implemented automated replenishment processes. As standard bar codes were used, it became possible for merchants to relay data to suppliers via EDI. With those two technologies in use, one could also build other applications, such as logistics systems, and exploit digitally intense warehouse management practices.

As in other industries, basic IT infrastructures were needed and had to be implemented holistically both within a firm and across the industry, as well as its supply chain, before one could see improvements in economic performance. The consensus among industry watchers was that both the manufacturing and retail sides of the Apparel Industry sharply improved their overall economic performance during the 1990s, a process that took nearly two decades to accomplish.[81] Increasingly, ever larger retailers came to dominate the market, and because they found it easier to work with larger apparel manufacturing firms, they stimulated the emergence of bigger producers of clothing. What had started out in 1950 as an industry with many small manufacturers and retailers scattered around the world had moved substantially to fewer, larger firms, to enterprises that could afford to invest and leverage digital technologies.

Recent Trends

But what effect did the Internet have on this historic trend? Would the availability of relatively cheap, ubiquitous communications change that dynamic of concentration? What role would online shoppers have on small and large apparel retailers? These questions are difficult to answer because the Internet is still new, but they are significant because already its effects were felt by consumers and retailers alike in the Apparel Industry. As in the rest of the Retail Industry, apparel merchants met the Internet in 1994–1996, tried to sort through the technology for their operations, and in time created web pages with information about their firms (1996 forward). Then, near the end of the century, they provided customers with the ability to buy from them on the Internet, and either to pick up or to return merchandise at brick-and-mortar stores.

Consumers found buying clothes over the Internet a far more comfortable experience than acquiring food online. In 1999—the first year for which we have very good data—roughly 2 percent of all apparel sales were done over the Internet, so the process of e-tailing was underway.[82] Customers preferred to buy from well-established catalogers with whom they had had positive experiences, such as L.L. Bean and Lands' End.

As retailers went online, they learned quickly that they needed to introduce liberal return policies, to build entry points through which consumers could communicate with them, and to write a variety of data-mining applications to track the interests of customers. We should recognize that catalog vendors surged quickly into this channel and that the chains followed soon after. Firms like Eddie Bauer, in existence as a brick-and-mortar chain since the early years of the twentieth century, with 550 stores, went online in 1996, following the practices of catalogers. What made the selection of digital applications and fulfillment processes effective at this firm was precisely its catalog heritage. Sally McKenzie, merchandising director, admitted as much: "Our catalog experience prepared us well for our venture online" because "the whole distribution and fulfillment operation was already built in." Its web site was typical of turn-of-the-century Internet locales: one could view merchandise, place orders, communicate back and forth with the company, and authorize the firm to send e-ads and comments about special deals. But not all succeeded. Levi Strauss, also a long-established apparel firm, launched two sites in November 1998 (levi.com and dockers.com) but failed to make the transition, shutting both down in 2000.[83] Most American catalog firms got on the Internet, using this technology as a major channel—in fact, encouraging customers to use it over traditional call centers. At the turn of the millennium, brick-and-mortar stores were also broadly represented online. Table 11.3 is a sampling of American firms on the Internet in 2000. Note the presence of so many category killers, some of the newest retailers in the Apparel Industry. Table 11.4 lists some general merchandisers known as major apparel retailers who also had a presence online.

Table 11.3
Apparel and Footwear Internet Sites in the United States, 2000

www.abercrombie.com	www.esprit.com	www.onehanesplace.com
www.shoes.com	www.fanwear.com	www.pacsun.com
www.ae-outfitters.com	www.fila.com	www.partysmart.com
www.bananarepublic.com	www.gap.com	www.patagonia.com
www.bluefly.com	www.guess.com	www.payless.com
www.boo.com	www.harrods.com	www.queensboro.com
www.brooksbrothers.com	www.hatworld.com	www.reebok.com
www.bugleboy.com	www.intmale.com	www.silhouettes.com
www.coat.com/bcfdirect	www.iuniforms.com	www.skechers.com
www.champssports.com	www.jcrew.com	www.spiegel.com
www.cintas-corp.com	www.kennethcole.com	www.styleclick.com
www.coldwater-creek.com	www.landsend.com	www.sydandsam.com
www.prowebwear.com	www.legwear.com	www.todaysman.com
www.delias.com	www.llbean.com	www.undergear.com
www.dockers.com	www.neimanmarcus.com	www.victoriassecret.com
www.eastbay.com	www.nhl.com	www.footlocker.com
www.eddiebauer.com	www.nicolemiller.com	
www.ezegna.com	www.norfstromshoes.com	

Source: Ernst & Young, "Global Online Retailing," *Stores* (January 2000), sec. 2, "Who's Selling on the Web," unpaginated, http://www.stores.org.

Table 11.4
General Merchandise Internet Sites in the United States, 2000

www.bloomingdales.com	www.macys.com
www.dillards.com	www.nordstrom.com
www.fashionmall.com	www.shopko.com
www.jcpenney.com	www.wal-mart.com
www.kmart.com	

Source: Ernst & Young, "Global Online Retailing," *Stores* (January 2000), sect. 2, "Who's Selling on the Web," unpaginated, http://www.stores.org.

One key advantage the catalog merchants had over many other retailers was their databases on customers, built long before going online. For example, Lands' End already had a mailing list of some 9 million people, 45 percent of whom had purchased from the company within the previous three years. In 1999, it mailed out 150 million catalogs. The firm began to post its website address in its catalogs to encourage visits to its site and to begin funneling orders through that channel. However, years before, as well as after, the arrival of the Internet, telephone order takers quickly accessed a customer's file, showing prior business, orders, and shipping information. Approximately 90 percent of phone orders were shipped within 24 hours. Quick delivery was possible because the firm had other digital systems that sent pick orders to the warehouse, along with shipping labels, and another system charged the customer's credit card for the cost of the merchandise. Yet another digital application calculated the postage fee, based on predetermined weights for merchandise, saving Lands' End the effort and cost of weighing each package.[84]

E-tailers on the Internet

A new form of retailing became possible with the fusion of computers and telecommunications—the virtual or strictly Internet-based retailer. While existing companies with buildings dominated B2B sales over the Internet, as did retailers serving consumers, a new model for retailers arose because of the Internet. Although there are few data to define precisely what portion of online sales are conducted by e-tailers, that is, retailers without store fronts or catalogs, we know this new type of merchant had a growing presence. The data are imprecise because available statistics merge online sales information about e-tailers with those of existing brick-and-mortar firms. For example, at the start of the millennium, a highly influential study of the Internet's effect on the American economy, conducted by researchers at the University of Texas, clustered together all types of online sales. In addition, the researchers also combined all dot.coms, not just retail dot coms. In defining the American Internet economy, these researchers created a useful four-layer model, made up of infrastructure providers (Internet service providers, backbone carriers, and telecommunications companies), application providers (those who created and sold software and services needed to perform Internet-based transactions), and a third group called Internet intermediaries (those who generated revenues by facilitating e-activities, such as Yahoo, ZDNet, and Charles Schwab). They put all the B2B and B2C firms, including the pure plays, into a fourth category. Included in this fourth grouping were such brick-and-mortar participants as Target and J. C. Penney, as well as Amazon.com and E-bay). During the last few years of the twentieth century, most of the growth in Internet economic activity came from the first three layers, that is, from those building the infrastructure of the Internet. That should be of no surprise since the Internet as a vehicle for commerce and communication was still being built, expanding and growing much like a young child.[85]

We have the situation, therefore, in which all kinds of businesses operating on the Internet were mixed together to create a generalized, impressionistic view of its economic role. The Retail Industry was not immune from this impression; in fact, when many commentators waxed eloquently about the new economy, more often than not they cited online sales as its emblem. The subject has been the topic of hundreds of books and tens of thousands of articles over the last several years. Many commentators, it seems, liked to generalize and to be euphoric. For a typical example of this rhetoric, self-styled Internet business strategist David Siegel declared the following in 1999:

> Over the next ten years, the Internet will drive changes in consumer behavior that will lay waste to all the corporate re-engineering and cost-reduction programs that have kept so many MBAs and programmers burning the midnight oil. These changes will be so profound that companies will have to realign themselves with an ever sharper focus on the customers than they have now.[86]

The researchers at the University of Texas proclaimed in 2001 that the Internet was transforming the economy "to an extent few people would have imagined just a few years ago."[87] Some economists, however, felt more comfortable with e-business ranges closer to 10 percent or less by the early 2000s. Thousands of positive quotes could be offered, but only time will tell whether these forecasts will come true. What they do, however, is create a sense of expectation that the Internet is radically changing the nature of retailing, and doing it quickly.

The problem is lack of precision. To be sure, as demonstrated in this and in the previous two chapters, the Internet is playing a growing role in the world of retailing and wholesaling. But it is doing so largely through existing firms and industries, extending traditional capabilities in new directions, much as in the manufacturing industries. To summarize where we are, as of this writing, approximately 10 percent of all consumers bought over the Internet, and their total sales, as of the end of 2000, amounted to less than 1 percent of the total U.S. economy. To be sure, reaching even these rates of activity required double-digit growth in the value of transactions over the last three years of the twentieth century.[88] At the same time that online sales were increasing (17 percent more in 2000 than in 1999), e-tailers were going out of business. In fact, in 2000, Forrester Research, a leading industry analyst, reported that over 200 e-tailers had folded.[89] This all suggests that the number of pure-play Internet retailers was smaller than the hype would lead us to believe. Although they offered a new business model and were the extreme users of computing, they did not yet represent mainstream activity in the Retail Industry.

What is happening is very consistent with the historical experiences of many industries that are using various forms of computing technology: major players in an industry learn to incorporate the technology in quiet ways to improve operations and generate new sales opportunities. The same Forrester report, while documenting the demise of major e-tailers, concluded that the reason online sales were growing is because "traditional brick-and-mortar retailers, such as Sears, are figuring out how to harness the peculiarities of electronic selling." The same analysts also reported that "surviving 'pure-play' companies born on the Internet, such as Amazon.com, were learning that sound business practices would outlast lavish infusions of speculative capital."[90] Vice president for public relations at the National Retail Federation, Pamela Rucker, was more blunt: "People who had wacky business models on the Web are falling victim to market forces. When they were left to their own devices, they either had to turn a profit or die."[91]

At the dawn of the new millennium, the vast majority of observers of the American scene were highly optimistic and enthusiastic about the future of online commerce. The historical evidence suggests that they were right to be positive, but only to the extent that existing industries and their companies would dominate the new cyberspace. The pure plays were at least for the moment a tiny fraction of the economy and within retailing. But these new firms were the ones that received so much attention. Why include them in this chapter if we do not know how many there were (are) and if their total contribution to the Retail Industry was small during the 1990s and early 2000s? First, people's fascination with them alone would justify their inclusion here. Amazon.com, for example, was perhaps the most important new brand in America in the 1990s, and it was originally a pure play.[92] Online auctioneer E-bay comes in at a close second because it, too, is an Internet-based firm.

A second, more important reason draws our attention. Because they are the subject of so much focus by the press, business school professors, and consultants, these firms have become the source of much new trial-and-error experimentation with online retailing by the industry at large. When Sears or Target, Wal-Mart or Kmart, adds Internet-based retail channels, it has kept in mind the best and worst practices of the pure plays. Knowledge about computing and its applications has flowed freely and quickly across all industries within the U.S. economy for decades. The public performance of the dot.coms has not been an exception to that rule; if anything, these firms have served as the ultimate example of that process at work. They are why, for example, distinguished economists such as Carl Shapiro and Hal R. Varian could write a best-selling book, reminding all business leaders that "technology changes. Economic laws do not." That is, basic universal practices known to make companies successful were not abrogated by pure plays. In other words, one still needed capital to expand, to offer goods and services consumers would buy, and to turn a profit.[93]

My lengthy, sober discussion of the pure plays is not intended to discourage enthusiasm about the Internet when conventional wisdom holds that if we discount it we put ourselves in economic peril. Rather, I wish to reinforce a key theme in this book—that the historical record shows that computing technologies were adopted and integrated into the fabric of businesses slowly at first and then aggressively when they were fully understood and justified economically. As extreme adopters, pure plays are a class of fascinating businesses that succeeded when they followed the historic practice of existing firms and failed when they did not. Also, any discussion about e-tailing takes place in what clearly is a very early stage in the use of the Internet for selling. In other words, more than 95 percent of all buying and selling, although they often involved computing (B2B, POS cash registers, and computer-intensive logistics and warehousing), was not done through e-tailers as of 2001, or possibly 2002. The big story, routinely ignored, is that incrementally, over time, portions of the selling and buying of goods and services have acquired elements of computing. This is the fundamental change that makes plausible any claim that the U.S. economy has become high tech during the past half century.

With all of these caveats and considerations in mind, e-tailers are a worthy subject for a brief examination since so many lessons are being spun off from their experiences and because so many retailers are interested in what is happening to pure players.

Nature of E-tailing

What makes a pure-play retailer an e-tailer is the fact that it conducts all sales online. It will have brick-and-mortar offices, often even warehouses (such as Amazon.com), and it may even do some paper-based marketing with catalogs and flyers sent through the U.S. Post Office, but its market is virtual. Most important, such firms do not have stores. What makes them the most high tech of all retailers is the fact that, of any segment of the market, they most rely on computers and telecommunications to exist. If ever there was a radically new business model to enter the American economy in the past 75 years, this is it. All of its functions are either fully or heavily automated as a collection of computerized applications, linked to those of an array of business partners and allies. All are accessed through either EDI (e.g., to suppliers) or the Internet (the channel to customers and suppliers). The normal business model for an e-tailer is an Internet site at which products are presented and to which customers come to view and place orders. The e-tailer may also use the site to advertise its, or (for a fee, of course) someone else's products and services and it processes orders by taking payment with a credit card and placing a pick or ship request for the product to its own warehouse or to the manufacturer or wholesale supplier for shipment directly to a customer. Traffic through the site is monitored as an application in order to perform traditional marketing and merchandising duties and to justify the fees other firms are charged for advertising. Rarely does an e-tailer take ownership of inventory, but it must ensure that it has timely access to goods demanded by the market. It must also

Table 11.5
Critical E-tailing Applications, Circa 2000

Vendor Management	Customer Care
Procurement	Customer database management
Sourcing	Customer services
Mediation and collaboration	Partner management
Bidding and communications	Sales
Marketing	Sales and marketing support
Marketing and advertising	Supply Chain Management
Online catalogs	Collaborative forecasting
Online community trading	Collaborating planning
Trading	Scheduling
	Logistics

Source: Modified from Peter Fingar, Harsha Kumar, and Tarum Sharma, *Enterprise E-commerce* (Tampa, Fla.: Meghan-Kiffer Press, 1999): 50–54.

ensure that it has either a highly reliable delivery partner (e.g., UPS, Federal Express, and U.S. Postal Service) or its own vehicles (e.g., Peapod.Inc.).

Essentially four groups of computer-based applications are used by e-tailers: vendor management, extended value and supply chain, marketing, and customer care. Table 11.5 is a catalog of the key elements of each as they existed at the turn of the century.[94] E-tailers normally did not go through the more traditional phases of using the Internet as did existing firms. That is, they did not start by publishing interactive brochures, followed by procurement or catalog-style sales. Rather, to be in business, an e-tailer had to launch all four classes of applications, continuously improve and enhance them, and rush to scale up enough to have a meaningful impact in the market.[95] With these applications in place, an e-tailer was liberated from the physical constraints of a store and could sell around the world because access to it was a telephone line.

Internet-based retailing came to life after 1994 with the availability of browsers. An early example was actually an online auction firm, eBay, which began operations in 1995 and became a corporation the following year. Unlike the mythology that it began as a way for founder Pierre Omidyar to sell collectable Pez containers, he had been thinking about creating an online trading firm and, in fact, did, called AuctionWeb. The case of eBay is of enormous interest because it went from being a small site, where people could offer products and possessions for sale and have other people bid on them, to one that listed 129.1 million items worth $2.8 billion by the end of 1999, making it the largest online auction house in the world and creating billionaires out of its founders and first CEO.[96] Another online firm, Priceline.com, proved almost as successful by doing the exact opposite, called reverse auctioneering. In this case, customers offered to buy a product or service (such as an airplane ticket) at a certain price, and vendors responded with what they are willing to offer.

Thus traditional retailing began to take on novel forms on the Internet. Many began in the 1990s by selling computers, software, and books. Amazon.com, which has already been discussed in earlier chapters, became the poster child for e-tailing.[97] Many of these firms failed to turn a profit in their early years but were tolerated by investors in the belief that eventually they would, particularly if they came to dominate a sector of the market, such as eBay did with auctions and Amazon.com was attempting to do with books and music. The volumes of transactions some of these firms handled, through computing, in which customers did their own browsing, ordering, and order checking, proved startling even if the total sales over the Internet of all firms was still a small portion of the nation's retail scene. For example, Amazon.com conducted automated transactions with some 12 million shoppers in 1999. This same group of shoppers ordered nearly $2 billion in products from this one site.[98] The thought of so many people coming to a site captured the attention of entrepreneurs, venture capitalists, and the press at large, and in many cases, the numbers were tremendous. Amazon.com and Toys 'R Us were visited 123 million times during the holiday season in 2000; customers visited eToys over 21 million times. Even brick-and-mortar firms had huge volumes of shoppers at their Web sites: Barnes & Noble had 20.5 million visitors, Wal-Mart 18 million, J.C. Penney 14.4 million, and Best Buy 12.4 million.[99] Of course, a visit to a web site did not necessarily result in a sale; in fact, only a tiny minority of such visits did. Nonetheless, they gave a firm the opportunity to advertise and to attempt a sale.

Equally sensational were the failures, reminding the Retail Industry of some basic economics. Firms typically failed for two reasons. The first, and most pervasive, was the inability of some enterprises to generate either sufficient cash flow or profits to cover the volume of expenditures (known as the burn rate) they were incurring. Amazon.com was notorious for consistently losing money for years as it expanded; on the other hand, eBay made huge profits almost from the beginning. The crisis of the dot.coms was building in 1999 and culminated in 2000 as e-tailers expanded too fast but could not quickly turn a profit, for example, eToys, which finally shut its digital doors in mid-2001. The economic realities in these early years of e-tailing were sufficiently different to affect the reach for profit. In the late 1990s, for example, e-tailers spent about 119 percent of revenues on marketing-related activities, whereas brick-and-mortar companies spent 36 percent. To acquire a customer cost an e-tailer on average about $82, as compared to $12 for a traditional retailer. Price sensitivity, a crowded Internet market, and competition from stores all drove up marketing costs at a time when most customers did not know much about individual e-tailers, which thus had to invest in creating an identity. The extent of the investment required was unanticipated and constrained the opportunity of e-tailers to be profitable.[100]

Another reason that e-tailers ran into problems was the inability of many firms to manage effectively the development and operation of the four major collections of processes listed in table 11.5, the most important of which involved logistics.

Most online shoppers turned to e-tailers for their Christmas shopping in 1999 and 2000, often in the two- to three-week period immediately before Christmas. The inability of some e-tailers to obtain the appropriate supplies of toys and get them to customers before Christmas, in particular, proved to be deadly. Pure plays and mixed Internet and brick-and-mortar retailers were caught short. Toys 'R Us became the poster child after 1999 for how not to sell on the Internet. It simply could not handle the volume of orders. Like others, it learned that to be successful it had to have (1) enough computing to handle the volume of transactions, (2) access to enough supply to meet demand, and (3) a scalable supply chain process that could ensure delivery in a timely manner.[101]

Because events in 2000 were so dramatic for e-tailers, a brief summary of both the positive and negative activities in that year provides a more balanced view of the occurrences that might affect subsequent trends. On the positive side, e-tailers experienced a surge in holiday sales that exceeded by 50 percent of their sales in 1999, generating over $10 billion in revenues. Industry estimates suggest that over 35 million customers made online purchases, from both brick-and-mortar Internet channels and e-tailers. About 80 percent of all Internet users bought online in 2000, up from nearly 70 percent the previous year. Customers were generally happy with the experience, which suggests that they would continue to buy online in future years. The best evidence we have also suggests that online purchasing extended to increasingly diverse income groups, not just to the wealthy or technologically adept.

But pure players also had problems. Approximately two-thirds of all deliveries were inaccurate, that is, not as ordered. One survey suggested that 12 percent of e-tail orders requested for delivery before Christmas did not arrive, so the problem did not rest solely with eToys; it was a bigger issue that cut across the entire industry. Whereas customers were generally happy with online purchasing, their satisfaction with the performance of their e-tailers declined. Their satisfaction also dropped because they were charged additional fees for rush delivery before Christmas. Even trying to get into an e-tailer's web site during the holiday season was challenging—16 million failed to do so, which is comparable to saying that 16 million people could not physically get into a store to even attempt to make a purchase. The shakeouts in 2000 and 2001 occurred partly because of the problems just cited but also because of more long-term causes, discussed before, such as the failure to make profits or to have sound business plans properly executed. The cumulative results proved lethal for MobShop.com, Mercata.com, eToys, Petopia. com, Pets.com, Furniture.com, Streamline.com, and Boo.com, to mention just a few.[102]

Those operating as e-tailers became historically significant at the very end of the century when their volume of transactions and their public visibility made them influential as trendsetters. Both the business and Retail Industry publications of the day paid a great deal of attention to them. A critical activity of many of these e-tailers was creating alliances with suppliers and shippers, thereby making headlines.[103] Failures, of course, were covered in detail, such as eToys.[104] Keeping score on the growth of Internet-based sales and publishing forecasts of future sales also called attention to this small sector of the retail community.[105]

The pure plays were very much a nascient development within the broader Retail Industry, with many of the same startup problems others had faced. What constituted appropriate and profitable business models also plagued other industries at different times in their early days. The Computer Industry of the 1950s comes quickly to mind; it took almost a decade for suppliers to shake out and for executives to determine what it would take to be successful. Many firms then began to leave the industry, and new ones emerged to replace them. The same thing happened again when PCs rapidly evolved into consumer commodities in the 1980s and early 1990s. Selling on the Internet was new, and most retailers were cautious about jumping into this channel (as we saw in the Grocery Industry). As in the early Computer Industry, retailers experimented. Amazon.com bought warehouses, and at the end of the century other firms exchanged their early "grow at any cost" strategies for others that were intended to generate profits, and still other firms became parts of bricks-and-mortar enterprises. The story of pure plays is thus complicated by the fact that as of this writing online selling over the Internet to consumers is less than a decade old. Moreover, it is a new way of doing business, which despite the hype has so far only carved out for itself a very small percentage of the retail market. At best, its future is before it, with all the lessons for management to master also to come.

Conclusions

The industries reviewed in this chapter were both ubiquitous in American society and emblematic of patterns of behavior across the Retail Industry. Their approaches to the adoption of computers, as well as the purposes to which these systems were put, provide a window into the larger issue of how computers were applied across the entire economy over the half century since the start of the Korean War. What is striking is the extent to which the story of computers in retail and wholesale industries parallels the experiences of manufacturing industries. Accounting applications—followed by leveraging IT to control labor and inventory costs and then adding a raft of uses to tighten up the unseen, yet very real national supply chain—were the heart of that experience. From time to time, one industry or another would intervene to create technical standards or to prod computer vendors into developing new forms of machines and software, such as we saw with the development of bar codes and the scanning of POS data. Another clear pattern is the extent to which industries in retail, wholesale, and manufacturing were porous, that is, how quickly experiences in one leaked quickly into others, as in the deployment of EDI across many industries.

Once again, these three case studies, along with the industries reviewed earlier in this book, show that retail industries had their own personalities, issues, and rates of adopting digital and telecommunication-based applications. As seen in other industries, machines and software tools configured specifically for the use of an industry tended to make deployment of computing occur faster than might otherwise have been the case. To be sure, the Grocery Industry, and to a slightly lesser extent both the Apparel Industry and the Internet pure plays, were extreme examples of this process at work. Whereas grocers were continuously thought to be slow adopters, the historical record shows otherwise. Members of the Apparel Industry were considered to be low users of computers, but the consolidation of that industry into large chains belied that perception. In all retail industries, consolidation into chains was a common pattern across the entire half century. In turn, chains were the earliest and most extensive users of computers, creating the applications and their justifications, forcing vendors of IT to build devices and write relevant software, and changing the way work was done. Two of the industries studied in this chapter—grocery and apparel—fundamentally changed since 1950; the third, e-tailers, did not exist before the 1990s.

Circumstances and implications do not end with today, of course; the technology of the Internet is stimulating whole industries to revamp old processes and applications and to implement new ones. We are beginning to see the emergence of the hybrid Internet retailer, a category that began as a physical channel and that is now finding the Internet to be a complementary one; that is, customers shop online but then go to the store to examine a product or try it on. Examples include the Gap, J. C. Penney, and Wal-Mart. One could expect this emerging combination to ultimately, dominate the retailer sector. What is very clear from the historical record of these three case studies is that management has folded and continues to fold the Internet into the fundamental fabric of their businesses. Not all e-tailers will disappear; some brick-and-mortar firms may evolve into pure plays, and already some pure plays are acquiring brick-and-mortar features. Several major waves of technologies have swept over the entire Retail Industry, ranging from computers to bar codes, and now it is the Internet.

Because of the intense interest businesses have in the Internet, we should ask, what insights about adoption and applications can one glean from the historical record? It is a fair question for managers to ask; it is also one historians avoid because their experience suggests that unintended, unpredictable circumstances always alter well-intentioned forecasts. However, as the last three chapters have demonstrated, the future has already arrived in some partial manner in various parts of the industry and has yet to make its appearance elsewhere. That ragged reality gives us license to suggest some implications.

One can expect that brick-and-mortar retailers that sell products most suitable for sale online either must do so or face severe, even lethal competition, most likely from other brick-and-mortar firms or e-tailers. In this category are merchants that sell consumer electronics, some types of clothing (especially men's), and department stores in general. On the other hand, other types of retailers seem immune from such a threat, such as convenience stores, where consumers pick up milk, bread, or soda; the Grocery Industry is the operative example because people still like to squeeze their fruits and vegetables; and in bars and restaurants, people still have to physically do the drinking and eating. Companies that can drive down costs by leveraging the Internet were normally the first to find useful applications of the technology and will probably continue to do so as the costs of running a business and using the Internet slide up and down over time. The same pattern was evident over the past half century as costs of computers changed right along with the expenses of running various departments and functions in all enterprises. Therefore, in terms of competitive positioning, the Internet was thrown into the caldron with all other forms of digital and telecommunications technologies.

The historic mega-application that weaves its way across the half century and throughout every industry described in this book is, of course, the national supply chain, which led retailers to become part and parcel of the application, the process itself. Along the way, retailers, grocers, and general merchandisers, for example, reversed the flow of economic power through their use of information. Instead of manufacturers telling them what to sell, retailers told manufacturers what to make (and still store in inventory). That event was completely unanticipated, but when it became evident, retailers seized on it. To be sure, Wal-Mart was an early leader in that reversal, but it would be incorrect to assume that it was the only one. In fact, the reversal appeared quickly in many parts of the Retail Industry. The continued application of the digital to the ongoing improvement in the efficiency, effectiveness, and speed of operation of the national supply chain remained the historic process. In short, history tells us that retailers will continue to improve this process through the extensive use of IT in all industries, and not just limit it to the Internet. They will want better trucks, well-built highways, GPS, pervasive computing (anytime, anywhere IT), not just the Internet.

The three retail case studies suggest that consumers were more eager to embrace the Internet than were the merchants. However, this observation should be viewed with some circumscription because the Internet is still in an early stage. We simply have insufficient data on consumer behavior to be firm in any conclusions. Discontinuities between the views of consumers and the actions of retailers is not a new phenomenon, of course; recall the differences of opinion over the wisdom of adopting bar codes, shelf labels, and scanning at the checkout counter. But perhaps here the consumers were slightly ahead of the merchants because, when they used the Internet effectively, they gained economic power by comparison shopping and switching retailers if the retailers did not satisfy them. Retailers have a track record of focusing first on lowering operating costs, then on pricing competitively, and then on consumer interests. The change in economic power in favor of the consumer has already motivated retailers to pay more attention to shoppers—hence the enormous increase in the use of digital applications to improve marketing, merchandising, and customer care processes that emerged in the second half of the 1990s.

All segments of the Retail Industry have been at different stages of adopting various IT-based applications over the past half century. That continues to be the case today. In fact, that is so much the case that IBM's experts on the retail and wholesale industries catalog companies into groups according to the extent to which they have deployed the Internet and other current uses of the digital. They speak of hesitant explorers, innovators, pioneers, and laggards, and they have even created mental models of where in various stages firms operated. Such models are useful in consulting, of course, to help advise clients on what to do next and why, and for the historian they suggest typologies with which to view rates of adoption, types

Table 11.6
Major Areas of Automation and Other Uses of IT, Circa 2000–2002

Competitive positioning	Exchanges
Supplier relations	Category management
Alliance relations	Inventory management
Competitive strategies	Merchandising
Consumer relations	Product and service management
Business scenarios	Brand management
Supply chain management	Channel management
Transportation	Consumer acquisition
Distribution center operations	Consumer retention
Marketing/advertising/promotion	

of applications, and how knowledgeable people thought about the Internet at the dawn of the new century. Industry observers have created such frameworks for decades, and business archives preserve examples from all major industries, not just from the retail community.[106]

The Internet and other digital technologies already play important roles in most aspects of retailing. Put in more formal business terms, retailing management is in the process of continuing its use of the digital in a large variety of functions (listed in table 11.6). The list is endless, but in one way or another each industry was doing something with every item in the table in 2002. Most have been applying the digital to various degrees to almost every item for decades; the adoption of the Internet was thus another step on a long journey.

As suggested in chapter 9, retailers picked their next applications more from their focus on cost, and in some cases in response to competition, than out of any sense of long-term strategic considerations. On the other hand, we saw that manufacturing industries, although also focused on costs (e.g., of labor), proved more willing to invest in IT for strategic reasons at the expense of gaining an immediate ROI. Failing to use IT as a competitive weapon made it possible for killer categories to emerge, for Wal-Mart to become the largest retailer in the world (and the second-largest employer in the United States, after the national government), and for e-tailers to come into being. There is little evidence to suggest that retailers were enthusiastically deploying IT for competitive advantages; they did so as an effective response to competition, not normally as a proactive initiative. On the other hand, the history of this sector of the economy shows that the industry was more than capable of launching initiatives and providing excellent leadership for the proactive deployment of new technologies when they could be demonstrated to lower operating costs. In the 1990s, most American industries across the entire economy spent on average about 4 percent of their revenues on IT. Retailers did the same, as did manufacturers. On the other hand, specialty retailers spent nearly 7 percent, as much as the Insurance Industry and nearly as much as banks (8.5 percent).[107]

Putting the role of the industries featured in this chapter into the broader context of how the nation changed the way in which it manufactured, transported, and sold and bought goods is essential to get a fuller understanding of how computers fundamentally changed the nature of work and how industries functioned. For that reason, the next chapter provides an integrated view of how all these industries were linked together over time and the implications of these historic trends.

12

Conclusion: How Computers Changed the American Economy

Finally, it must be remembered that the technological changes upon which

productivity gains rest are bound to have a more or less disruptive influence

on individuals and institutions.

—John W. Kendrick, 1961

Computers profoundly changed the way in which work was done in the American economy during the second half of the twentieth century. The nation's experience with this technology reinforced the argument offered by economist John W. Kendrick, quoted above. He conducted one of the first major studies on productivity in the United States, which caused him to face the issue of what effect technologies had on the nation's economy.[1] Today we know that the digital hand transformed many activities in the economy but not its purpose.

Computing reinforced the primacy of the corporation as the single most widely used form of business organization, while changing how tasks were performed within it. Computers also affected industries in the same way. The work of a generation of economists, looking at firm and national levels of economic patterns of behavior, and of business historians, examining firm-level activities, created a great body of knowledge about American economic activity. Yet, as Michael E. Porter stated nearly a quarter of a century ago, it was important to look at economic and business behavior through the lens of industry-level performance to understand more fully the activities of an economy. This book, about what happened to a group of American industries, focuses on one major feature of their activities—their use of digital technologies in the form of computer-based applications—and how these processes influenced their actions and, as a byproduct, increased our knowledge about the nature of modern economic and business activities. The role of computers was so significant that by the end of the century one could think that the human hands of managers, guiding many routine operational business activities, were being assisted by the evolving digital hands of computing.

The use of computers clearly represented a major change in the affairs of thousands of companies and hundreds of industries, but it was only one facet in the activities of modern American businesses and the economy in which they functioned. However, as demonstrated in over a dozen industry case studies, computing played an important role in defining the work of contemporary business enterprises, serving as a useful lens through which to view the modern business landscape. Setting our sights on the industry level proved as useful as selecting one of the other two logical options normally available to any observer: the firm and the national economy. Besides attempting to fill a gap in our understanding of business activities (by looking at issues at the industry level), this study affirmed the continued importance of industries as economic coalitions. Indeed, widely deployed applications of the digital helped sustain industries as modern institutional communities of practice that shared similar values and concerns, while either learning from or collaborating within the confines of individual industries. Rather than forcing industries to disappear or shrink in importance, computers reinforced their highly influential position in the economy, at least for manufacturing, transportation, and retailing in the United States.

What these case studies collectively teach us about the economy and the role of computing can be summarized quickly. Computers were widely used across all these industries and were in many other industries dependent on them. Computing came early and quickly, and it permeated all aspects of business activities across the entire economy within a half century. Management assigned to this technology a great deal of work previously done either by employees or earlier information-handling technologies. This shift in responsibility to computers was not limited to handling information but also included performing tasks and making judgments. What developed in the Process Industry and in inventory reordering in the Retailing Industry are dramatic examples of this pattern at work, one evident in all industries. Management's desire to lower operating costs was the greatest motivation for the adoption of the digital. Improved market performance, such as providing better customer service was second. We can consider growth as a given motivator, a ubiquitous managerial mantra seen through the entire period. As technology improved, the opportunity to expand a firm's or industry's reach and performance did too. However, management never waned in its simultaneous desire to drive down operating costs by shifting work away from preexisting technologies and people to computers. The result of the dual interest in driving down costs—particularly labor and inventory—and the aspiration to make and sell more goods led to the most pervasive killer app of the second half of the twentieth century, to what managers many decades later to called supply chain management. In hindsight, filling in the gaps in traditional business transactions through the use of digital technologies was the most fundamental application of computing in the twentieth century in manufacturing, transportation, and retailing.

As dramatic and profound as is the story of the deployment of the digital to the history of modern business and the American economy, its implications are yet to be fully appreciated because they are still unfolding before us. But some patterns of behavior are already identifiable.

The great tension in this book centers around the question of whether or not the digital hand represented a substantial shift in the way manufacturing, distribution, and sales took place. The deployment of computers in the supply chain processes of the nation provides the greatest body of evidence to suggest that, in fact, a digital hand was at work; computers did alter how work was done, in some cases even the role of managers, and caused management to reconfigure organizational structures, resulting in more openly blurring the traditional borders of industries. The greatest evidence of these consequences at work was the increase in interfirm and interindustry cooperation that occurred as the century aged. Specific areas of work also changed more than others, for example, in research and development, where computers became profoundly important (e.g., in aviation, semiconductors, and pharmaceuticals).

The use of computers by increasingly expert employees distributed decision making throughout an enterprise and shifted power, control, and the course of events away from some groups of managers to teams and experts. We saw these trends in the work of engineers in automotive firms, scientists in pharmaceuticals, and software writers everywhere. By the end of the century, one consequence of the digital hand at work was that managers had more highly skilled workers to manage (as a percentage of the total work population in a firm) than they did a half century earlier. As every experienced manager knows, a highly trained, well-educated, confident worker has to be "managed" far differently than a less skilled, poorly educated laborer. The short answer to the question, did a digital hand exist, is yes; furthermore, the metaphor of the digital hand is useful in helping to partially frame many of the business transformations of the last half century. In the final analysis, the important activities in an economy are the mundane because they involve the largest number of people, occur most frequently, and are themselves the course of events. Computers were best used in the daily chores of a firm, but they spun off consequences that were profoundly important to entire companies, industries, and the economy at large. So, we can answer basic questions about the influence of computers on the American economy by looking at its uses and, in the process, stimulate further research, which in turn provides management with some basic insights from the previous experience of this nation's physical economy. Findings can also give management a greater sense of how to use computers and an awareness of the types of potential consequences of their deployment.

It is not my intent to forecast the future, but the historical record does give us a rich context that should not be ignored by managers and policymakers. To bring all our work to closure with a sense of the context involved in deploying computers, this chapter will explore the influence of computing on the economy, implications for the economy at large, the lessons and implications for managers, and political behavior.

Did Computers Take Over the American Economy?

Common patterns of adoption existed in manufacturing, transportation, and retailing industries. The historical record demonstrates several features of this adoption, which were all present, functioned concurrently, and built momentum over time. In each instance, curious, early adopters took steps to learn about the technology and often experimented with it on a limited basis. In every industry studied, these were very large firms—no surprise there. However, a second wave of early adopters made up of small firms demonstrated boldness in adopting these technologies. They were not well known and almost none became major players in their industries,[2] although some were eventually folded into other companies that became important or large. The point is that each industry had its early adopters. They demonstrated willingness to learn about how best to deploy a technology, then shared their experiences through industry conferences, became centers for marketing pilgrimages sponsored by computer vendors, and published articles about their applications.

An equally facilitative process, one that became evident after an industry had collectively gained some experience with computing, involved industry-wide initiatives. The timing varied from one industry to another, and it is not fully clear why that was the case. However, just by relying on the industries studied for this book, we can draw some conclusions. The industry-wide initiatives undertaken by the Grocery Industry and the Apparel Industry, for example, occurred after it had become obvious to individual firms that there was an opportunity to leverage more effectively technologies that had yet to be packaged into usable forms. In both industries, that opportunity occurred in the 1970s. But the Banking Industry had led the way in the 1950s when it standardized a variety of cash management practices, including the design of checks. Did that industry's initiative, which was well known by the 1960s, cause other industries to consider doing the same? We just do not know; however, since information and practices seeped into one industry from another, we can speculate with confidence that such was the case. By the time of the Internet's arrival, that practice was definitely widespread; thus, when one industry, for instance, the Pharmaceutical Industry, organized virtual trading consortiums on the Internet, other industries, such as the Steel Industry and the Chemical Industry, were doing the same, and just as telling, simultaneously. Such timing was not an act of coincidental clairvoyance. When an industry as a whole embraced a specific technology, like POS and scanning, that action encouraged firms in an industry to adopt the technology sooner rather than later. The reasons were straightforward: the technology was designed to meet the specific needs of the industry, and vendors priced it at a level affordable by its members. Political and other economic forces worked their influence on managers, as did peer pressures within the industry.

All industries and their firms had varying business models, thresholds of expenses, profits, and revenues. No two firms or industries generated the same volumes of sales or had similar cost structures. What proved too expensive in one industry or firm may not have necessarily been the case in another. As the cost of performing a computerized transaction declined over time—normally at rates near 20 percent a year for most of the half century—some companies and industries found computers and telecommunications at some point to be cost-justifiable when compared to preexisting costs of doing work. The historical record indicates very clearly that establishing the cost-justification of technologies of any type always remained on the minds of decision makers. Large traditional manufacturing firms, such as those in the Automotive Industry or in the Aerospace Industry, could afford the heavy price of early computing. Affordability included being able to bear the cost of leasing hardware, writing software, supporting staffs to maintain the technology, training end users, and ultimately of altering fundamental business practices. Managers in other industries had to wait for further improvements in the technology or in its cost-benefit performance, as we saw in both the Grocery and Trucking Industries.

Two circumstances stimulated the adoption of computing by dramatic amounts over time. First, technology evolved from one-of-a-kind types in the 1950s to highly standardized forms in the 1960s and 1970s, which made it easier and less expensive to deploy the digital. Second, the wide availability of commercial software products that appeared across many industries by the end of the 1970s also contributed new functions and made it easier to implement additional uses of computing technology. Standard technologies in hardware, software, and telecommunications reduced the risk of not being able to use them or to find trained staff to operate them. Once, for example, the proverbial "everyone" was using COBOL to write business applications, the pool of qualified programmers who could write in this programming language expanded. That meant staffs experienced with one type of technology (e.g., COBOL), wanted to adopt more of the same, in this instance, additional applications written in COBOL. Also, IT products could be sold to more organizations because the necessary expertise needed to understand their value and know how to use them now existed. In this instance, it was easier for a vendor to sell a software package written in COBOL to a company that already used other software written in the same programming language; learning how to use the package was minimized, and a DP manager might not have had to hire additional staff to run it. Conversely, lack of prior knowledge of a particular type of technology slowed the rate of its adoption. The Trucking Industry in the 1950s demonstrated that circumstance with mainframe computer systems and again with the Internet in the 1990s. The Steel Industry clearly suffered from this problem several times during the last half century.

Another historical process at work can best be described as the snowballing effect. If a person forms a small snowball, then rolls it down a snow-covered hill, the snowball becomes larger as snow on the ground adheres to the rolling ball. As the weight of the snowball increases, it gains momentum, unless something slows its progress, such as a protruding rock or tree or moderation in the angle of the hill. A similar process can occur with technology. These industries demonstrated that such a process occurred from time to time with digital applications. As one after another embraced a specific application, others who were more cautious took the time or gathered up the courage to consider similar adoptions. As personnel turned over from one firm to another, those with experience in computing encouraged their new employers to adopt familiar technologies. The opposite also occurred; when one firm wanted to install a particular technology or application, it often recruited employees of other firms who had some direct experience. Often vendors enabled the process by suggesting the names of individuals who could be hired by other companies. The IT vendors also facilitated adoption by training customers on the installation and use of specific applications, software, and hardware. In fact, for some vendors, training was one of the two or three major methods of selling their products.[3] These various activities built the key momentum that made it possible to use the phrase *digital hand* to describe the fundamental effect of computing on the economy.

This momentum also created its own technological moments of fashion for specific applications. Our case studies were littered with them: inventory management in the 1950s; POS adoptions in the late 1970s and early 1980s; ERP packages in manufacturing in the mid-1990s; virtual trading networks at the end of the 1990s; even business management practices, such as MBO in the 1950s, TQM in the 1980s, and KM in the 1990s. Historians of technology and economists tell us that moving from batch to online processing in the 1960s and 1970s resulted more from the nature of the hardware and software than just from economic imperatives. The causes reviewed in this book suggest that in addition to these incentives, industries collectively talked themselves into adopting an application at a particular time. Read the trade literature for any industry over several decades, and this pattern becomes very obvious. Leaders and voices in an industry attempted to persuade other firms to adopt by reporting on rates of adoption and accrued benefits and then admonishing laggards. As firms crossed the finish line with a community-approved application, their achievements were celebrated in trade publications, sometimes in the national press, and always at industry conferences. Free publicity and self-aggrandizement were powerful forces at work. Only when a technology's time was not ripe did negative reports and outright discouragement of adoption appear. This typically proved to be the case early in the life of a technology, as for example, when database management software tools first appeared in the 1960s; they really did not function well and required far too much effort to convert existing software programs in order to use them. The same occurred in the Insurance Industry as vendors tried to tout the "paperless office" in the 1980s; costs and functions were not yet attractive, and so the industry spoke with one voice, criticizing the technology in its early stages. However, once cost issues and technical problems were resolved, this industry embraced scanning of documents as a major initiative.[4] The same process occurred in the dozen or so industries discussed in this book.

Each industry eventually crossed some fine line, where its ability to conduct normal business was not possible without the extensive use of computers and specific applications. Several circumstances made this the case. First, participants had to be users of specific applications, hardware, and software in order to gain business. The U.S. Air Force insisted that the Aerospace Industry use CAD tools in the 1950s; the Automotive Industry required its suppliers to use specific EDI tools and shared databases and be able to build and bill with prescribed software packages by the mid-1980s; suppliers and transporters of consumer goods had to adopt the Grocery Industry's UPC standards in the 1980s and 1990s; and so forth. Second, as adoptions increased, the nature of work done by companies (and industries) were transformed, often reducing the cost of performing a task to such an extent that one could no longer be competitive doing it in the old way. That is, the skill to do a task in a precomputerized manner no longer existed, was too expensive, or was too slow to do in any other way. In short, a new *style* of performance dictated what got done, how, and at what speed and cost. The process by which industries underwent this transformation proved subtle and incremental and varied in speed and intensity by application, company, and industry. But their effects were cumulative. Beginning roughly by the end of the 1960s, results became evident from one industry to another. A physical tour through a factory or an office stocked with terminals was surely a sign that things had changed in some fundamental manner. Timing and rates of change varied, of course, but the process was evident in every industry I looked at. Thus, one could speak about a new *style* in evidence at the end of the twentieth century that did not exist in the early 1950s.

Computers, of course, did not take over the economy; management in thousands of companies individually made decisions of economic advantage to them and to their firms. The technology did not have a determinist agenda of its own; it was merely a powerful tool that attracted firms when it seemed advantageous to use them. In that sense computers were no different than any other tool that people adopted and improved since they started using stones and sticks to augment their personal effectiveness. This is an important point to remember because the way in which computers became crucial in the American economy has much to teach those who want to understand how other artifacts of human activity came to be adopted.[5] Ultimately, computing became a pervasive feature of the American economy, certainly by the late 1980s if not earlier.

But, before moving to a more detailed assessment of how enterprises and industries operated, let us circle back to the role of managers because ultimately the discussion of "hands" by Adam Smith in the 1770s, by Alfred Chandler, Jr., in the 1970s, and by me in this book focuses a great deal on the role of people—managers and leaders—and thus this question remains: did computers change their purpose? The short answer is that computers did not change their role, their purpose for being. One can look at descriptions of the mission of a manager published in the 1950s and find that it squares nicely with what managers do today. They hire, fire, and train employees; attempt to deploy them in economically productive tasks; allocate resources; create and implement strategy and tactics; spend and make money; worry about profits, stockholders, and government regulators; and lose sleep at night worrying about competitors. Computers did not eliminate those fundamental demands on management.

What computers did, however, was to change the way in which each of these tasks was accomplished. Along the way, computing made it possible to alter the scale and scope of activities at the firm level, blurred industry borders, and changed tasks as it became possible to perform activities less expensively, more precisely, quicker, and with more predictable and higher levels of quality. So, one more time, I want to emphasize that the digital hand did not take control of firms and industries away from managers, at least so far; human management teams still did all the tasks so well documented by Alfred D. Chandler, Jr., Peter F. Drucker; Michael E. Porter; and so many others. Yet we must not lose sight of the fact that computing did change many things.

What Changed in the Way Enterprises and Industries Operated?

The question of what changed in the operation of enterprises and industries can be answered in two ways. First, we should look at the changes that directly affected managers. Second, we should view the changes at a more analytical, theoretical level. Both provide insight into the role of computing through the prisms of applications and industries. Because the activities of managers are the building blocks of how an organization is structured and run, we can see the digital in action in six explicit ways, thereby influencing the work of management.

First, there is computing's effect on supply chain management. As we saw from one industry to another, particularly in manufacturing and retailing, managers incrementally tightened the linkages along all points in the supply chain—from extracting crude oil to making home deliveries of groceries ordered over the Internet. The motivations were to reduce costs, improve speed, and thwart competitors. Routes to market, although often the topic of much discussion in the business press, were less of a consideration. Over the past half century, millions of managers reduced costs and minimized labor. They did not consciously look at the entire supply chain for grand strategies in support of these twin objectives until at least the 1980s; but they did focus on specific areas of internal operations that lent themselves to incremental improvements by using computers. It was only decades later that we could see the pattern and recognize what they had done—the automation of many links in the national supply chain. I will have more to say later about the implications of computing for management, but the obvious point here is that managers in many industries learned through experience that computers do reduce costs and labor content in work within their supply chains. We can expect them to continue this action in the foreseeable future because new tools, different levels of cost justification, and as yet not fully optimized supply chains still exist.

Business school professors were admonishing managers to think beyond the confines of their industries as early as the mid-1960s,[6] but it was not until the 1980s that digital technology was finally making it possible to move effectively from visionary theory to practical realities. Even then, however, managers had to be reminded of the economic benefits of extending their supply chains,[7] although nobody recognized that that was what they were doing. Managers remained focused on making incremental changes within the confines of specific internal processes and tasks, such as automating the way in which cars were painted or blueprints were created. Not until these tasks had been automated would someone think, for example, to transmit digitized blueprints to a supplier to to use in designing parts online or to collaborate with engineers in multiple firms. Not until grocers and retailers in general had mountains of data on customers' buying patterns could they even think of linking to their suppliers to drive down unit costs and improve replenishment processes.

Second, there is the digital's effect on management's ability to centralize the control of continuous processes. We saw the most dramatic example of this possibility in the Petroleum Industry: companies that had thousands of employees running a continuous pipeline, moving crude oil to a finished product, downsized to smaller numbers that worked in remote control centers, using computers to manage the flow of products and events. We saw examples elsewhere, too, such as in purchasing activities in the Retail Industry, national trucking scheduling processes, and the coordination of the flow of components to multiple factories. Thus, for example, GM could build components in one factory to gain economies of scale (e.g., transmissions) and yet be able to deliver them to multiple assembly plants, which put together a variety of cars and trucks. Computers made that possible. So, whereas managers, on the one hand, could distribute decision making to skilled workers and to computer modeling programs, on the other hand, they could simultaneously increase their control over operations across a vast landmass, over a collection of factories and stores, and even over suppliers who were captive to them. In short, managers could both centralize and decentralize planning and control activities with greater ease at the end of the century than they could right after World War II.

This ability to centralize either the activity itself (e.g., phone centers versus local brick-and-mortar offices scattered across the landscape) or the management of it made it possible to extend the national supply chain. Managers were quicker to understand the possibility of digitally enhanced control over processes and the economics of the centralization of continuous processes than the implications of the extended supply chain. But the fact remains that management was able to extend its historic role of controlling events more precisely in every industry reviewed in this book, as well as many hundreds of others, because of a combination of computing, software, and telecommunications.

Third, there is the effect on one's ability to support more complex processes and work. Perhaps the most dramatic collections of applications in this book are those that could not be done by human activity alone. The list is long: online design of frightfully complicated products, such as the modern airplane, missiles, and hard drives; or the manufacture of disks, computers, software, and the small but powerful computer chip. The ability of someone to collect and analyze vast quantities of data is an important byproduct of the digital. In some cases it involved doing ongoing work better, more reliably, always quicker, and sometimes less expensively, as in the seismic studies of the Petroleum Industry to determine where to drill a hole. In other instances, computing made it possible to do a thorough and efficient job of load balancing and scheduling, as the MRP systems that dictated what a factory would make and how much or as trucking and rail firms increasingly improved their ability to run full loads, thereby optimizing their carrying capabilities. In the case of retailers, it was the same problem, using computers to make sure that their shelves were always stocked with the goods customers wanted. If these were not complex processes, they would have been done efficiently long before the arrival of the computer, and managers only knew that they wanted to improve these kinds of operations. As we saw in case after case, it was not intuitively clear to them in the beginning that they could cost-effectively use a particular variant of the digital to improve complex work. That revelation manifested itself slowly over a long period of time and continues today.

Yet this third capability was perhaps as profoundly transformative as was the task of improving existing operations through the integration and increasingly efficient function of supply chains. Management's increasing ability to deal with ever larger amounts and degrees of complexity created vast new opportunities. There were new products at the end of the century that were not there before: PCs, integrated circuits, and new medicines. There was the opportunity to block competitors by dramatically increasing efficiencies, as did Wal-Mart. In a related manner, the ability of a large firm to dictate to its suppliers levels of quality, prices, and even the roles they would play in an expanded cross-industry supply chain process became almost routine. The Automotive Industry led the way, but so did many others, not the least of which were the Apparel and Grocery Industries. In addition to driving down costs, the capability of handling larger volumes of complexity changed the economic balance of power in some industries. Information and technology shifted the bargaining advantage away from manufacturers to retailers, while increasing the power of the single consumer in the Automotive and Retail Industries. Individual firms, such as Wal-Mart in retailing and merged large oil producers, could acquire and maintain their dominant positions in their chosen markets. We also saw that not leveraging the computer in this way could hurt an industry, such as the Steel Industry. In short, managers learned that handling complex processes and performing new functions became one of the sweet spots of computing.

Fourth, there is the effect on centralizing R&D. It is easy to argue that R&D changed profoundly because of the digital, but that would be misleading. As many scholars have noted, R&D systems in the United States were characterized by the emergence of industrial facilities and laboratories owned by corporations, as well as the proximity of universities, which made it possible for scientists to move back and forth from private industry to academia and vice versa.[8] However, the computer played an important support role. Along with government support for research, large corporations could afford to invest in massive systems, such as those offered for sale by CDC, to conduct research on the design of new products, like aircraft and automobiles. Computers were used to create new knowledge that made possible new products, as we saw in the Pharmaceutical Industry. Other industries applied them less intensively, such as in many parts of the Chemical Industry and even less in the Steel Industry. Centralization of R&D did not always mean putting all one's scientists and engineers in the same building. Computers facilitated the centralization of the managerial processes that underpinned either a corporation's R&D or the general practices in an industry. One could still keep R&D physically dispersed. The most dramatic and instructive example of that process is the Semiconductor Industry, where today R&D is spread across North America, across East Asia, and partially in Western Europe but can be, and indeed is, controlled from the national headquarters of leading firms in the industry. The process of integration and coordination of R&D activities is so well tuned in this industry that the time it takes to create new products decreased continuously all through the period, and the goods themselves acquired more function and greater reliability and became less expensive (Moore's Law at work). All of that occurred at the same time that manufacturers spread their manufacturing and R&D work across multiple countries, involving many cultures, languages, and even various forms of government.

Fifth, there is the effect on MIS managerial systems and attitudes toward computers. I have barely touched upon this issue because it is such a large topic, one hardly studied by historians and economists, and to probe too much would have taken us away from our objectives. However, what the industry case studies point out is that a whole cadre of managers and technicians, as well as managerial and technical practices, emerged in the second half of the century in support of the deployment of computing. Little "IBM Departments" of the 1940s became MIS divisions by the end of the 1980s; departments run by first- and second-line managers in the early 1950s became large enterprises led by senior executives who were reporting to CEOs. Along the way, a large collection of managerial practices emerged in response to the needs of firms to implement digital applications or those of vendors wishing to sell computers and software. Regardless of the source, in the United States knowledge rose from a few thousand people who knew anything about computers in the early 1950s to millions who were intimate with the technology and to hundreds of thousands of managers who were familiar with its capabilities and limitations. That whole development in the world of management and economic activity awaits its historian. But what we can say is that as the new IT community emerged, it sought to protect its interests, including its livelihood and influence, by promoting the use of the digital within its firms and through cross-industry standards committees and publications.

It would be difficult to imagine that digital applications could have spread so thoroughly across the American economy without the existence of this MIS constituency that was lobbying and implementing on behalf of general management computing within thousands of firms. They were the ones who had to help line managers understand the potential uses; who had to cost-justify systems; who had to unpack the boxes arriving from IBM, Burroughs, or Microsoft; who had to teach users how to navigate an application or even turn on a terminal; and who then had to support users and firms to exploit the technology on a daily basis. In short, they were the champions of the technology's benefits and managed the mundane issues that rose from its deployment.[9]

Sixth, there is the effect of e-commerce and the Internet on the daily activities of people, firms, and industries. The story told in this book is that managers approached this new technology with caution, as they had earlier ones. This is also a new technology that has had more hyperbole and publicity than just about any other digital development, even surpassing the PC's exposure. One would have to go back to the emergence of television or nuclear energy, both in the 1950s, to find any technological development that so captured the attention of the public at large and, more specifically, managers. So it is easy to assume that the Internet was widely embraced quickly and is changing everything. What the case studies show about management's reaction tells a different story. First, they did not embrace the technology until they had some conception of how to use it. Second, they did not pay adequate attention to its emergence, and thus, when they realized that it could hurt and help, they had to move quickly to exploit its capabilities or to fend off new threats to their businesses. At best, one can generalize that their response was initially late and poorly handled. But in time, managers learned that the Internet, as innovations in earlier decades, was best used first in support of existing processes, subsuming its capabilities into existing infrastructures. Then, as they learned about its capabilities and as the technology itself improved (e.g., with the arrival of better search engines and providers), they could expand its use—which is exactly what is going on today. That pattern also matches what happened with so many earlier digital technologies.

What is also remarkable is the extent of deployment. Although every industry adopted the Internet at differing rates and speeds, they all eventually embraced it, so we can now say that it is a ubiquitous technology. The pattern is already clear: integration of the Internet with existing systems, then adoption of new applications (e.g., direct contact with customers over the Internet). The Internet is following a historic pattern of deployment, demonstrating once again that the behavior of managers toward a new technology is consistent with their unchanging purpose. That pattern of behavior demonstrates that whereas the digital changed a great deal of how work was done, it did not have a profound effect on how managers functioned.

So far managers are doing what they had done before: they are using the Internet to improve incrementally their supply chains, routes to market, and competitive position. What is different is that the speed of deployment of the Internet within existing processes is actually occurring faster than with previous technologies, and that is important to note. It is possible to deploy the Internet faster because there is a base of digitized applications (and the knowledge and confidence for exploiting, it) that makes integrating the Internet, also a digital technology, possible. Both the initial response to the new telecommunications technology and the speed of its deployment suggests that in the years to come managers will have to do a better job of staying current with emerging technologies if they are to have sufficient time to integrate them into what is clearly the digital style. Speedy response in deployment is a growing feature of this new style of operation, a feature sometimes overlooked by commentators who prefer to emphasize the desegregation of industries or how e-commerce will come to dominate economic activities. Until these two things have occurred, we are faced with speculation. What is difficult, but has occurred, is managing the speed of deployment. The speed of response to new technologies has increased with every new wave of the digital. That pattern of response may be one of the most important findings about the early history of the Internet's role in American industries because it forecasts what may happen with future innovations of information technologies.

A more theoretical, generalized view of the broad patterns of the adoption of the digital in the twentieth century is also important to help others who would study its deployment. The previous several pages are addressed more to managers than to scholars because their needs are more tactical, more operational in nature. But even the issues of interest to scholars can bear fruit for managers who constantly want to know what technologies to invest in, when, and when to displace them with newer ones.

To a large extent changes brought about by the injection of the digital into work processes were similar from one industry to another. Rather than repeat the specific transformations that occurred industry by industry, it is possible to observe some trans-industry changes that helped define the style of conducting business by the end of the century. To be sure, we are so close in time to these changes that their features are at best tentatively described. So far, only the most obvious are apparent, and even these are merely the earliest to be identified.

One of the first to manifest itself was the long, slow, subtle shift of work and memory from people to machines and then to computers. Tasks that were not automated were shifted to computers. These tasks were of an enormous variety, ranging from monitoring events and altering the flow of activities (as we saw, for example, in the production processes in the Petroleum Industry) to taking action when certain conditions existed (e.g., reordering merchandise when a sale registered at a POS terminal in the Retail Industry). Collecting, collating, and reporting data became one of the first tasks done with computers, and over time the results became more sophisticated. They led, for example, to presenting information instead of raw data and then to preparing options and recommendations (the work of simulation software). Another feature of this shift was the operation of machines that physically picked up, moved, or altered things. The CAM applications in manufacturing are obvious examples, but so are robotic devices that painted vehicles or moved inventory in a warehouse. All of this was made possible, of course, by embedding intelligence into devices that were previously operated by humans. Following a multi-century practice of moving physical (muscle) work to machines, computing alleviated humans from having to lift and bend, to do many repetitive tasks, and to make some judgments about these actions.

The second feature of this trend—moving responsibility for memory to machines—is a fascinating, even profound transformation. One of the technical characteristics of a computer is its ability to store data; to recall them very precisely, fast, and frequently; and to do so quite inexpensively. As the capacity of computer memories grew over time, the opportunity to use computers to store data increased. In fact, computer scientists are now debating when computers will be as smart as humans, although responsible scientists think this development is still a half century or more away.[10] The fact that scientists and engineers with solid credentials are willing to ponder the issue is itself revealing, a faint hint of what business practices might be like late in the twenty-first century.

Managers did not have to wait for this future to seize upon the opportunity of storing data in computers. Beginning in the 1950s with traditional accounting data and expanding in the 1960s to include customer information (e.g., addresses, buying habits, and credit history) and other facts about parts and products (e.g., their identification number, physical characteristics, etc.), use of the digital neatly paralleled the expansion in computer memory. In the 1970s and 1980s, enormous advances in database management software made it possible to collect and manipulate quantities of data that at the time were considered to be vast in comparison to what was possible in the 1950s and 1960s. With that growing capability, computers were given more responsibility for tracking events, making adjustments, and reporting results. Next, knowledge of what happened and what was occurring naturally shifted to computers. By the end of the century, human experience was beginning to be extensively shared with computers, which is why the ability to access data and information in a computer had become a critical skill, necessary for work. Every major study of the skills workers needed in the late twentieth century mentioned the requirement for computer skills. Workers not only needed to know how to operate PCs and navigate within specific software applications, they also had to understand how to find and interpret data housed in a computer. The reasons were obvious: these machines were still not anthropomorphic or intuitive, despite heroic attempts by the Software Industry to develop common look-and-feel features and to implement standard navigational and architectural forms.

A related development concerned sharing information among people, departments, firms, and industries; across geographies; and around the clock. Barely 20 years into the computer revolution, whole industries had figured out, to various degrees, how to converge computing and telecommunications. The most important macrotrend in computing technology of the last two decades of the century involved the convergence of these two classes of technology. The Internet and PCs were only the most obvious components of the trend, but as demonstrated in previous chapters, they did not represent the first instance of combined computing and telecommunications. However, with the bonding of the two, one could use computers to collect data and get them to the right person in a timely manner anywhere. Although the intent of such an application was routinely to arm a worker with data with which to make decisions and perform tasks, the byproducts were dramatic as well.

First, sharing made it possible for workers around the world to coordinate activities more tightly and to focus some of the best knowledge in a firm on a problem or situation when and where needed. A problem on an oil platform off Vietnam could be discussed with experts in Houston, Texas, complete with video and data in real time, and could include other colleagues on a platform in the North Sea. The ability of an organization, therefore, to learn collectively how best to deal with specific issues had expanded.[11]

Second, sharing information made it necessary to warehouse data in one place rather than to have many copies in different parts of a company, thereby saving on the cost of multiple copies and avoiding the problems of different versions. A mail order business could have the correct address of an individual and avoid the expense of mailing multiple catalogs to the same household or to a wrong address.

In short, single-version memories that could be accessed from across the firm saved on operating costs and made it possible to leverage workers anywhere.[12]

Third, by sharing data, companies could add informational features to their products and services that otherwise would not be possible. For example, IBM computers can call the plant that manufactured them for preventive maintenance; GE added services to its products that could track repair records; Ford automotive dealers used computerized applications to diagnose problems in a car and recommend what repairs to perform.[13] Old-economy firms quietly, and often without realizing it, were transformed into information-based companies by the end of the century.

Speed, more feedback, and increased precision of execution increased all through the half century. Computer-embedded processes steadily increased the speed with which they could conduct work over the entire period, and programmers and software developers improved the ability of application software to provide feedback either to employees or to automated activities. Thus computers were able to do more and different tasks as the century wore on, creating circumstances that encouraged management to assign additional work to these systems. These added responsibilities were either new applications, working side by side with those installed earlier, or renovations of earlier software systems to make it possible for them to do more tasks. Usually, across all industries (not just those studied for this book), managers simultaneously leveraged both approaches.

How firms and industries managed inventory—often the secondmost important asset after employees—changed over time because of the use of computers. Inventory actually increased in value and variety across the nation over the years as managers optimized the right mix of goods, supplies, and quantities, and competition for sales increased, along with the number of firms operating in the ever-expanding economy. Shelf life, however, declined; that is, the amount of time a company kept inventory before using or selling it decreased, with the result that the length of time a firm tied up capital in any item on hand also dropped. That was no surprise because the digital hand helped make inventory turn over more frequently. That development made it possible either to lower costs of inventory relative to revenues or to carry a greater variety of inventory to offer to customers. We need not go through the history of inventory management one more time; it is enough to let the record show that management of inventory in the new century had changed substantially since 1950.

The other major assets leveraged by companies and industries were their work forces. Improving the productivity of employees was always a very important motivation for using computers. Industries described in this book all enjoyed increased productivity. Collectively, all American manufacturing industries improved their productivity by a third during the half century. However, whereas computers played an extraordinarily important role in that historic trend, other factors proved influential as well. The injection of significant Asian and European competition into the American economy, essentially beginning in the second half of the 1970s, remained a relentless pressure on U.S. firms to the present day. Another factor was the use of computing in other countries. Yet, managers in all industries were never fully satisfied with how computers helped drive down the costs of labor. As we saw in the Automotive Industry, computers alone could not bridge the gap between Japanese and American productivity as measured by the number of labor hours needed to build a car. Fundamental changes in how tasks were done went beyond issues of computing and its essential role in the process. In short, although helpful, indeed essential, computers were not enough.

As management implemented computer applications across their enterprises, it became increasingly possible to expand the scope of their activities, which is an elegant way of saying that they could operate larger enterprises at levels of efficiency that were both competitive and cost-effective. I believe that this enabling function made possible the surge in mergers and acquisitions (M&A), beginning in the 1970s and continuing today. Many other reasons also helped account for the M&A activity, but without the ability to do such mundane things as report financial results at the end of every month from around the world in consolidated charts of accounts, or to take parts from several geographic areas and divisions and have them in a manufacturing plant in time for inclusion in the production of a product, increasing scale and scope would have been thwarted.[14] Even industries not surveyed in this book experienced the same thing. For example, bank mergers in the 1990s could not have occurred easily if computer systems in the two merging banks were technologically incompatible. If they were, the cost of converting one to the other could be high enough to make the merger problematic.[15] International competition and issues related to global scale and scope became crucial and intense, because of the enabling capabilities of cheap computing, communications, and transportation.

In all the industries studied, companies grew larger than the dollars discounted for inflation would suggest. Whole industries experienced growth too, not just a few dominant firms. Computers simultaneously enhanced the ability of large enterprises to acquire or preserve ogolopolistic power in their industries and markets. Wal-Mart, Microsoft, General Motors, Exxon, Mobile, IBM, Boeing, and so many others would not have remained the large firms they were if they did not have technologies that made it possible to grow. To be sure, growth was often organic, made possible by computers, such as at IBM and Wal-Mart, but in other cases it arrived by way of M&As, as frequently occurred in the Petroleum Industry. Insurance, banking, stock brokerage, and publishing also lent themselves to computer-facilitated mergers.

Computerization of processes did not cause industries to fall apart. When an industry got into trouble—such as steel or consumer electronics—managers did that all by themselves, without the help of computers. They failed to change strategies or to respond in a timely and effective manner to competition. Computing and telecommunications enabled national and global competition more often than they caused the demise of industries. Computers helped industries retain their identities, although the work they did and the links they established with other industries became closer and more mutually dependent. The lesson we can derive is that computing did not destroy industries so much as either revitalized old ones or made it possible to create entirely new ones. The U.S. government's work with

NAIC and our case studies on the Software Industry and the Hard Drive Industry suggest that creation, not destruction, was more often the byproduct of computing.

However, portions or tasks of one industry did move to others, as the ability to use computers to perform work made that possible. For example, the Trucking Industry by the 1970s had assumed tasks associated with logistics, responsibilities that had historically belonged to manufacturers or wholesalers. Observers in a manufacturing industry could argue that desegregation was going on, threatening the very existence of the industry; in fact, what happened was that both truckers and manufacturers now performed the same task. Competition over the management of logistics increased, putting pressure on those who traditionally had always done it. Did that mean that manufacturers no longer managed logistics? As we saw earlier, both industries did so. Although one could argue that manufacturing firms were gutted by other firms that wanted to do portions of their work, they were doing the same thing to other industries. Adding a raft of services, such as outsourcing from other industries, was the process in reverse. All of these activities show that the tasks performed in an existing industry changed and shifted over time: some went away, and new ones became possible to implement.

My favorite example is IBM. In 1950, IBM was clearly a manufacturer of office appliances. All its revenues came from leasing equipment and selling punch cards. In 1980, over 90 percent of its revenues still came from selling hardware. In 2002, IBM generated nearly 50 percent of its revenues from consulting and other technical services, offerings that were not a significant part of the Computer Industry in, say, 1970 or 1980. In 2002, only 34 percent of its revenues came from hardware. Also IBM used a complex network of Internet-based services and business partners, and had outsourced many functions, ranging from the manufacture of some components to the operations of mailrooms and cafeterias. Yet the public and government economists still characterized IBM as a leading member of the Computer Industry, as a manufacturer. By 2002, only a few IBM managers still thought of themselves as working just for a manufacturing company. The moral of the story about industry identification is simple: we cannot generalize about an industry or its fate solely by looking at the computer. Rather, by examining specific tasks and offerings, we can see how the content of work changed significantly in an industry. Important firms either survived or merged with others if they were competitive and effective, using computers to enable these transformations.

The implications for management are profound. They may still be managing within the context of old paradigms (e.g., as manufacturers when, in reality, they are service firms), using outmoded systems (usually in accounting and finance), and dominated by the wrong groups (e.g., manufacturing-heritage executives when their firm is no longer a pure manufacturer). This was the case through most of the 1980s at AT&T, for example, where many senior executives who had grown up in Western Electric (AT&T's manufacturing arm) won considerable control over the telecommunications firm and ran it the only way they knew—as an old-line regulated telephone company with a strong manufacturing heritage—in an age of growing deregulation and increased competition.[16] Knowing what industry one was really in, therefore, became, and continuous to be, an issue senior management had to address. Selection of what processes and, consequently, what digital applications were needed had to flow from what managers thought was their role and that of their industry.

One of the great trends of the last half century concerned applications. At the risk of repeating some of the observations made in the first and second chapters, it is important to keep in mind the grand scheme of things. Always first on any manager's list of applications were those that automated existing tasks, which essentially occurred in the 1950s across many industries when they first learned about computers. To the end of the century, the functions of an enterprise that were being automated often went through that phase, including initial Intranet-based services. Only after that initiation, as managers and workers learned what computers could do and as computing technologies became more versatile, did they install applications to do work not done before or that altered the nature of existing tasks. This pattern of transforming applications became evident by the late 1960s–early 1970s. By the 1980s, it was becoming obvious to managers and users alike that computers could radically change how work was done. Redesigning processes in the 1980s and 1990s to make work flows more compatible with the capabilities of computers (as opposed to bending the technology to existing work patterns) became the next slow twist in the deployment of the digital. These trends, I believe, are far more fundamental than the more traditional, even glib, descriptions we get about how the Internet was changing the nature of work. Linking transformations in the features and functions of an application to specific technologies—such as online computing, databases, EDI, and the Internet—remains important; however, it is equally relevant to recognize that there were more basic changes yet to be fully understood. It is this second level of basic transformations, such as the change of work to make it more user-friendly to computers, that suggests future sources of productivity and competitive advantages for firms and industries.

Transitions stimulated by computing were normally never massive in any firm; rather, they occurred in piecemeal fashion. Thus some activities changed later instead of sooner or were hardly noticed; some barely changed at all. So what did not change as a result of computing? For one thing, the vast majority of old-economy industries did not go away. The United States still has an Automotive Industry, despite extensive Japanese and European competition and globalization, and a Steel Industry, even though it was unable to compete effectively, and other industries as well. This nation's ability to continue to invest in a plethora of infrastructures ensured that its capability to move products to market through national supply chains helped fuel consumer demands around the world, not just in the domestic markets. Many missions remained the same; for example, the Automotive Industry still made automobiles; the Aerospace Industry still built airplanes and spaceships; and at the firm level, IBM still produced computers, in fact in greater numbers than a half century ago, even though they generated decreasing percentages of the company's total revenues.

Another feature of industries and firms that did not change was the basic architecture of corporations. A vast literature heralds the demise of the corporation as created in the 1930s and as described by Chandler.[17] Corporations have changed in many ways, but they are still organized by division (although today's descriptor is lines of business, or LOBs). They still have CEOs, CFOs, vice presidents of manufacturing and others for marketing, accounting, and so forth. The EDP departments became DP organizations, then were renamed MIS, and so on, but centralized control over IT assets, and now networks, remains a common feature in most enterprises. Although as evidence of the speead of computing, over 60 percent of IT purchasers are now made by end user organizations. Command-and-control hierarchical managerial cultures still thrive, despite management's extensive delegation of operational responsibilities to divisions, departments, process teams, and line personnel, which occurred in the last two decades of the century, in part because of the positive performance of computerized tools. Today CEOs are still princes of the American economy, and executives serve as members of the noble class. Unions, although significantly diminutive, are still powerful forces in manufacturing and transportation industries, less so in retailing, where they always had a smaller role long before the arrival of the computer.

The extant evidence on digital applications in these industries suggests that although much has changed (and continues to do so), arguments that computers have profoundly transformed nearly everything are often overstated. Corporate and industry cultures have proven to be very resilient to transformation, resisting change almost to the point of death, as nearly occurred in the Steel Industry. Why computers have not exerted as great an influence on the nature of corporate cultures as they did on work remains an intriguing issue, which others will have to explore. Based on the limited evidence in this book but representing over 40 percent of the U.S. economy's experience, my research suggests that culture is a byproduct of an accumulation of activities and could be expected to change after digital applications had worked their influence on daily behavior over a long period of time. Since applications of computing are immediate, specific events, whereas cultures are mixtures of handed-down values and long-standing practices and rituals that transcend immediate activities or groups of processes, they survive.

That reality, however, does not necessary reflect what people have said about computing. Each constituency in the large story of digital applications had their own points of view, which they used to temper their public statements. Vendors of computing and telecommunications technologies and the press within their industries had solid economic incentives to herald the arrival of new firms, industries, practices, and the Information Age. Taking such a position facilitated selling more products, publishing novel views of issues, and motivating individuals to transform existing operations. Users were aligned with vendors and IT-centric writers because they, too, had incentives to herald the arrival of the new, the modern, the high tech. For those with a career in computing, for example, to declare the opposite was personally counterproductive. Furthermore, in fairness to them and to IT vendors, their knowledge of the technology and of their enterprises and industries often and rightfully led them to conclude that the use of the digital made good business sense. The economic evidence confirms that they were right, even though both constituencies exaggerated the benefits and effects of the digital.

Much work has yet to be done by historians to document the effects of computerized applications in these industries, particularly on their cultures, although economists have done a great deal of analysis of the digital. We should understand their current findings because ultimately the reason for using computers in these industries was to improve the economic performance of companies.

What Were the Economic Implications?

At the dawn of the new millennium, economists had been engaged for a decade in a debate about whether the U.S. economy was "old" or "new," what constituted the differences between one and the other, and how best to measure the transformation. They had not yet reached a consensus.[18] Three reasons account for their lack of resolution. First, there were no clear statistics that demonstrated what differences existed between current and previous economic behavior and hence the reason for all the many changes currently being implemented in the counting activities of the United States by both public and private economists. Second, Americans only really began experiencing the accumulated effects of computing and telecommunications after the introduction of the Internet into mainstream economic affairs. As demonstrated in many chapters, the use of the Internet was a very new activity, so its effects are only just now being felt. Third, much of the discussion has been held at the macrolevel, exploring national economic trends with generalized accounts of economic sectors, a few narrow case studies, and very limited analysis at the industry level. To put it in less prosaic terms, until we have a street-level appreciation of what is going on "now" as compared to some prior "then," it will be difficult to make a determination of what constituted "old" or "new" economies. I have attempted to partially bridge the gap between national statistics and generalized comments about economic conditions in America and the more micro discussions about what has been happening at the firm and process levels. This study is thus a small contribution toward additional clarity in the issue of old versus new economies.

But why should we care about this issue? The answer is that American firms have invested so much in computers and so much work is now being done with this technology that we really have no choice but to understand far better than we do the economic and managerial implications. Using traditional measures of economic productivity, we know that IT had a profound, yet positive impact on the American economy. Economists did not know this in the late 1980s or even in the early 1990s. Enough research by economists has demonstrated that investments in IT contributed to the productivity of both output and labor, that the results varied by industry—one of my findings in this book—and that how managers operated their firms did make a difference. For example, it is becoming increasingly, evident that decentralized organizations do outperform highly centralized ones, although such a move requires more technically competent workers, who are more difficult to recruit in sufficient numbers. Their financial results are not always so obvious as economists would like.[19] Economists are generally pleased with the results IT investments delivered for the American economy, however, and there is growing consensus that the benefits began accruing as early as the 1970s across all sectors of the national economy. This consensus includes a recognition that IT did more than simply improve labor productivity; it also enabled firms to move into newer (or larger) markets, bringing out new products and services that had extensive IT content.[20]

One of the reasons the industries in this book were chosen is because there had been discussions among economists about the impact of IT in manufacturing, leading to the grudging conclusion that it had been beneficial; this book describes how IT was used to make it a positive experience.[21] For economists, the reasons why benefits accrue at different levels from one industry to another remain unclear.

My study of over a dozen industries suggests avenues for further investigation to resolve the issue. Timing is one: the earlier an industry embraced computing, the more time it had to learn how to use it effectively; conversely, the later one came to the game, the more difficult it proved to be because other industries could encroach or other members of the industry in other countries could make it more difficult to catch up technologically. Autos and steel demonstrated that. On the other hand, the grocers illustrated how collective action could rapidly improve productivity almost before a technology was ready or was perceived to be needed. Yet even in this instance, a compelling case had been built for doing something different, and leadership and sound industry-wide project management led the way. Related to this development was a phenomenon already recognized by economists, namely, the accumulated effects of long-term investments in IT. We saw that not all industries committed to IT as the same time or with the same level of intensity. That finding alone may be one of the most significant contributions we can make toward clarifying the issue: timing, level of commitment, and nature of applications deployed.

Another observation is that IT offered different functions from one industry to another. Not all computers were used in the same way because not all industries did the same things. Leaving aside accounting applications, which were relatively universal across all industries but which made only a one-time contribution to productivity—when companies automated accounting—line applications on the shop floor, inventory control, store management, and so forth offered long-term cumulative benefits to their firm. Accounting applications provided a one-time injection of productivity gains because when all major firms and industries adopted them, the benefits basically cancelled themselves out. Benefits accrue when productivity is gained in a way that rivals may not now have or is applied differently.[22] Sources of competitive advantage can come from the use of computers when there is some form of differentiation from rivals, such as in the timing of an adoption, function, efficiency of use, scale, or scope of deployment. Business models and firm- and industry-level core competences varied extensively enough to make a difference. As argued in this book, industries varied, and they had personalities that caused their behavior to differ. Those differences should be explored in more detail to answer the question about varying productivity results.

The same logic applies to firms within an industry. Why does one auto manufacturer perform better or worse than another? This kind of question has long fascinated economists, and also business school professors. Analyzing individual firms compared to others, as I did for industries in manufacturing, transportation, and retailing, can generate similar types of useful insights.

Finally, we are left with the issue of accumulated benefits and momentum in the use of IT. Today, economists recognize that some phenomenon of this type occurred in the U.S. economy, and I have provided evidence about how IT affected industries. Only by going through the tedious work of looking at the way the digital was used from one period to another, industry by industry, can we move from many of today's generalized observations to others more specifically grounded in a larger body of empirical evidence. What the industries I studied indicate—and recall that they account for about 40+ percent of the GDP over the half century—is that there was an accumulation of economic benefits. Table 12.1 is a brief list of some of these benefits for the last decade of the twentieth century. There was a clear correlation between investments in IT and macroeconomic trends, a link now acknowledged by economists.

By collecting these various indicators, we can enrich our understanding at the macrolevel of the effects of the digital on the United States. At industry levels, of course, one could look at a variety of data that suggested the relative contribution of one industry or another to the overall economy. As pointed out in the first several chapters of this book, the industries studied maintained their relative position as a

Table 12.1

Information Technology Investments and Related Economic Trends in the United States, 1990–2001 (as Percentages in Compound Growth Rates)

	1990–1995	1995–2000	2001
IT spending/GDP	2.5	5.1	6.0
IT spending/total capital spending	38.0	49.0	55.5
Average GDP growth rate	2.4	4.1	2.0
IT contribution to growth rate	0.3	0.9	0.3*
IT contribution to growth	13.0	22.0	n/a
Business productivity growth	1.5	2.6	1.1*
Profit share of national income	9.8	11.0	2.7*
Profit	10.4	5.5	1.1
Average labor cost per unit			
Compensation increase per hour	3.3	4.4	1.6
Less business productivity growth	1.8	1.8	2.8
Equals unit labor cost growth	1.8	1.8	2.7
Consumer Price Index (CPI) Inflation	3.1	2.5	3.1
Core CPI inflation	3.5	2.4	2.4

*Estimated.

Source: Prepared by the Office of the Economist, IBM Corp.

Table 12.2
Gross Domestic Product by Sector as a Percentage of GDP, 1995–2000

	1996	1997	1998	1999	2000
Manufacturing	16.8	16.6	16.3	16.1	15.9
Transportation	3.1	3.1	3.3	3.3	3.2
Wholesale	6.8	6.8	6.9	6.9	6.8
Retail	8.8	8.9	9.1	9.2	9.1

Source: Table 2, in Sherlene K. S. Lum and Brian C. Moyer, "Gross Domestic Product by Industry for 1997–99," *Survey of Current Business* (December 2000): 29.

percentage of the GDP for the entire period. Table 12.2 provides a snapshot of that phenomenon for the last few years of the decade, a period, economists now acknowledge, in which previous investments in IT profoundly influenced results. The pattern also held true for finance, insurance, real estate, services, and government. The adoption of computers by these industries is the subject of sequels to this book, but research in preparation for the next volume is leading me to similar conclusions about the relative rates of adoption and benefits enjoyed by the industries covered in the current study. The relative positions of industries hardly changed; even retail, which had the greatest movement, only shifted by small degrees. Had the movements been greater, we probably would have to draw different conclusions about the effects of computing.

In a very general sense, we can say that growth and productivity were enjoyed across the economy at relatively the same pace. This observation is approximately true because the economy as a whole embraced common techniques for improving productivity, and as suggested in this book, one of those common collections of techniques was the use of computing. The investments made in this technology were large enough to make a sufficient difference.

What Were the Implications for Management?

The companies in the industries reviewed in this book varied enormously in role, size, effectiveness, and management. Various communities in a firm and industry influenced the nature of the use of computing, ranging from systems men in the 1950s to IT professionals in the 1970s, from engineers in factories in the 1960s to process teams in the 1980s. Industry experts and many writers in trade journals also influenced the course of events and the rate of adoptions of computing. But the common decision makers in each decade were managers, of course, because they ultimately controlled the assets of any corporation, from money with which to invest in computing to authority to lead their companies in directions they wanted. Were there common patterns of behavior among the managerial class? The evidence suggests that the answer is yes.

First, the most obvious behavior was an early and sustained interest in exploiting technologies of many types across the entire period. However, this was not blind support for the unknown; managers were cautious, wanted to understand the financial impact of using computers, and wanted to quantify their immediate short-term costs. Middle managers often took longer to implement applications than the procomputer constituencies wished. Over the course of the half century, managers understood the fundamental benefits and costs of computing. They hardly wavered from the basic mission of their firms or industries. That they performed their roles well or poorly is less of an issue for us in this book. What is clear is that whole communities of managers did better or worse from one industry to another for a variety of reasons that were often larger in scope than their individual spheres of influence. These included such macroeconomic influences as government trade policies, Cold War politics, rate of globalized competition, availability of capital, rising and falling standards of living, and so forth. By the end of the century, it was also becoming clear that the digital was affecting these kinds of macroconditions and that managers were beginning to realize that fact. Large American firms did not hesitate to expand their global capabilities, exploiting computing and telecommunications to extend their reach into and control of many national economies.

In 1950, hardly any managers had been exposed to the computer, let alone understood its potential uses in a business context; to them, computers were complex instruments for scientific, military, or government uses. By 1970, that lack of understanding still existed among senior management, although by then most large enterprises had IT infrastructures led by first- and second-line managers comfortable with the technology. Specialized technical communities were also familiar with computers, such as engineers in product design and manufacturing. By the middle of the 1980s, middle management and junior executives had frequently become involved with computers, often by implementing major applications in their functional areas of responsibility. By the end of decade, some managers, informally and often as a hobby, had learned about computing by using PCs. By the mid-1990s, the majority of senior managers in most corporations understood the strengths and limitations of computers and how the technology worked in both their firms and industries. Of course, knowledge of computing varied from one industry to the next. The most knowledgeable worked in high-tech industries, such as the Software Industry or Aerospace Industry and less so in the Steel and Grocery Industries.

Second, with the wide diffusion of knowledge about computers and specific applications relevant to a firm's success, achieved by the late 1980s or early 1990s among all levels of management, one could see a shift in emphasis. Grand strategy began to include computing more frequently. One example of this trend was M&A activity, which was more frequently used in the Banking Industry than in some others but nonetheless was evident across the economy. Another involved linking suppliers to manufacturers, as occurred in both the Automotive and Aerospace Industries through their initiatives to outsource the manufacture and delivery of components, beginning in the late 1970s but a way of life by the end of the 1980s. In the 1990s managers had to learn about the Internet, but once they did, they took less time embracing this technology than earlier waves of IT applications, machines, or software.

Managers' comfort level with technology was an important, often overlooked, factor in explaining why investments in IT actually increased over time, both in volume and in rate of adoption. It was no surprise that economists were able to document higher percentages of capital investments in IT toward the end of the century than in earlier years, despite the fact that the cost of computing had dropped continuously over the half century, which made technology economically more attractive. One would expect these findings if managers had come to learn with ever more precision what the costs and benefits of IT should be. Indeed, American managers had reached the point where IT was so woven into the fabric of their businesses that to think of doing work without computing was no longer an option. The new *style* had totally supplanted Fordism.

Third, it is an interesting and telling indicator of that growing knowledge about computing and confidence in its effective deployment that senior and middle managers in American corporations hardly participated in the debate over the productivity paradox. It was almost exclusively an economist's game, with a few outsiders occasionally weighing in, typically some retired CIO. The business press tried to excite their readers about the subject but never got far. Why was this so? Managers had figured out when and where to implement the digital for economic benefit. All during the period from the late 1970s to the mid-1990s, when the debate on the productivity paradox took place, management kept investing in IT—adding new applications, upgrading old ones, and extending the technology into more corners of their enterprises. Had the business community taken seriously the concerns of the economists, we should have seen a pause in the adoption or an outright retreat, but that never happened in the 1980s and 1990s. Managers judged the value of computing according to how it would affect work in their companies. Grocers, factory managers, pipeline executives, and their peers in other industries did not hesitate to ask tough questions about the benefits of an application before investing in them. But once satisfied with the answers, they spent the sums necessary. In the end, they had learned, perhaps before the economists and the historians, where it made sense to use computing, and they committed resources to the task. In this case, leadership matured first in the business community, not among the commentators or scholars.[23]

Computing for management, however, did raise all kinds of operational issues, study of which is outside the scope of this book. However, an initial start in linking computing to managerial responsibilities can be helped along by going back to a model of issues proposed by Nobel Laureate Herbert A. Simon early in the history of computers. Simon was a fascinating individual. He started his professional career by developing heuristic programs in the 1950s, became involved in what eventually was called artificial intelligence (AI), and made contributions to our understanding of economics and business management. In short, he was one of the earliest experts on computing who also had knowledge of managerial issues. In a little book of essays published in 1965, he included one originally written in 1960, in which he explored the implications of science and managerial decision making and, by both inference and reference, technologies like computing.

He pointed out the obvious advantages of using operations research and mathematical modeling, as well as programmed decision making. Put in more modern terms, he referred to simulation through computers, arguing that this would ultimately become an important application of the digital. He suggested that after automating routine work and installing applications for simulating possible options for decisions, a third tier of applications would become possible. Simon recognized that computers would be used to reinforce the hierarchical nature of organizations, structures that would continue to change, but in an evolutionary manner. He did not believe that computers would dismantle the hierarchical form of organization but, as a consequence, would conform to it. In fact, in the 1950s, simulation programs functioned as hierarchical collections of activities. On software tools for decision making he observed that "the over-all program is always subdivided into subprograms. In programs of any great complexity, the subprograms are further subdivided, and so on."[24] Enterprises would operate in the same way as biological organisms: "The organizations of the future, then, will be hierarchies, no matter what the exact division of labor between men and computers."[25] Computing, along with the inherent organic nature of organizations, would function in three layers:

> An underlying system of physical production and distribution processes, a layer of programmed (and probably largely automated) decision processes for governing the routine day-to-day operation of the physical system, and a layer of non-programmed decision processes (carried out in a man-machine system) for monitoring the first-level processes, redesigning them, and changing parameter values.[26]

This is exactly what happened in the 40 years following Simon's prediction. In fact, one can track the waves of adoption of computers and their uses across many industries by using his three-tier model. In addition to providing a template with which to monitor and catalog the evolution of computer-based applications, Simon's observations can help historians to document the actual decisions made by management to implement specific applications of the digital. What ultimately is the most important implication for management is the fact that computing and the practice of management evolved into a close-knit symbiotic relationship, one in support of the other. Does this mean that computer applications acquired anthropomorphic features? I think ever so slightly yes, particularly as applications increasingly acquired responsibility for remembering, making judgments, and taking actions on behalf of employees because they could do it cheaper, faster, and more reliably. What that role means for business applications in the early twenty-first century has yet to be determined, but what Simon's thoughts imply is extended use of the digital hand in many industries, transforming more work, and in the process unknowingly affecting corporate cultures.

But as we move from such broad possibilities to a more tactical set affecting management, we can create an equally short list of critical implications for management drawn from historical experiences.

Management should pay attention to supply chains, which are important as sources of revenue and, since more controllable, as sources of cost savings and increased productivity. Managers tend to tinker with their supply chains in incremental fashion, but continuously, rather than to seek out the grand gesture. The latter is rife with risk; historical experience suggests that managers are not willing to take it on. Does that mean they should not? Bold moves have been made, but usually as a collaborative, industry-wide initiative. The most significant of the past half century was the deployment of the bar code, but almost every industry has examples. A related pattern is the adoption of industry-wide standards, such as what bankers did with checks and what various manufacturing and retailing industries did with EDI; many industries are now doing the same with interconnections and transactions through the Internet. Most important, however, is that managers can find economic value by continuously enhancing and changing their supply chains. The tendency over the past quarter century has been to expand them backward, toward suppliers with activities, responsibilities, and dependencies, and equally forward through various routes to markets and channels of distribution.

Managers' constant focus on optimizing supply chains has at its heart the deployment of new technologies or existing ones in novel ways. That has always required management teams to do three things, steps that will probably continue into the foreseeable future. First, they must pay attention to the evolution of digital and telecommunications technologies because if they do not seize upon them in a timely fashion, a competitor will. Second, since technical lockouts are made possible by IT, managers have increasingly learned that they have to be active players in their industry's debates and actions concerning IT standards. Again, as with emerging technologies, the implication for management is clear: they must pay attention to these changes and build into their managerial practices ways to do so. Most large firms in most industries have been doing this routinely for decades, usually through their MIS and technical communities; smaller firms have done less, but they can keep up through conferences and working with their largest customers.

Third, with the Internet far less expensive to use than private networks and EDI in general, competition can come from many new quarters, such as small bookstores around the world that are taking market share away from large-city book dealers. This is happening in many industries, particularly in the services sector, but manufacturing, transportation, and retailing are not immune. Thus if a small firm can negotiate arrangements for the manufacture, warehousing, and distribution of products, it can become global or cut across traditional market lines very quickly and easily. So managers are paying more attention to these threats and opportunities than a decade ago. And they know that the threat is global because the Internet and most of their competitors operate around the world. If there is one change we can say was influenced profoundly by the digital, it is the kinds of globalization of economic activity seen over the past two decades.

Technological risks were a problem in 1950, and they are still with us today. Choose the wrong standards, and we face the Beta-VHS phenomenon, with real winners and losers created directly by technology. Embracing a technology before it was ready or when it was too expensive has long haunted executives. Technical staffs tend to embrace technologies too soon (e.g., database software in the late 1960s), whereas end user managers often do so later than they should. Timing the adoption has always been a problem, although successful adoptions often involved the deployment of experimental systems first, as pilots, and then expansion. That is what occurred, for example, in the extremely cautious Grocery Industry with scanners; the risk of financial disaster was too great in an industry characterized by very narrow profit margins, and the original costs of scanning were too high. But with technology a major element in the style of how things are now done, managers are hardly left with any choice but to lead and follow simultaneously as they determine when to adopt a technology and how fast to deploy it. However, from when an industry starts deployment to when it is finished, it is not uncommon to see a period of time often less than 15 years, with 5 to 10 years fairly normal before one can call deployment widespread and influential on the economic behavior of a firm.

Our case studies have demonstrated that the sources of knowledge about the digital and its applications have consistently come from three sources. First, one's own industry always had and still has member firms that are ahead of others and share knowledge about their experiences through visits, publications, and conferences. Second, one can count on vendors of digital products to bring to the attention of managers the potential benefits and applications of their wares. In fact, more than "hawking boxes," these conversations tend to be consultative and sophisticated because the financial commitments and consequences are too great for both customers and vendors to trivialize. Third, technologies arrive in industries at different speeds. Because a particular technology is not used in one industry today does not mean that it is not alive and well in some other part of the economy. Given the fact that over the past half century the borders of an industry were porous, and because of the Internet are even more so today, it has been and continues to be imperative that managers look over the fence at what is going on elsewhere. When a dry goods retailer like Wal-Mart announced in the late 1990s that it would begin to sell groceries, many in the Grocery Industry were caught off guard. That phenomenon is now more widespread than ever in the past half century, often driven by the kinds of digital applications in evidence at Wal-Mart, Dell Computers, American Airlines, and Schneider Trucking. It is easier to watch developments in one's own industry, more difficult to monitor those of a dozen or more others. But over time, management has come to learn the value of paying increasing amounts of attention to developments elsewhere. And as the Japanese Automotive Industry demonstrated to the American industry in the 1970s and 1980s, it is important to observe managerial and operational transformations too, not just digital ones, because they can provide competitive advantages or become dangers. This was the important lesson that the three American car manufacturers learned as they lost nearly 40 percent of the American market.

What are the implications for oligopolistic market structures? In many of the manufacturing industries studied for this book, we saw that a half dozen or so firms tended to dominate old-line industries. This was the case with the petroleum, automotive, aerospace, pharmaceutical, and the steel industries, for instance. Technology did not single-handedly change that pattern; rather, it reinforced it, along with other circumstances. Pharmaceutical firms dominated because they knew how to bring products to market and had the financial wherewithal to do so. Capital-intensive industries tend to be controlled by a few firms that have access to capital in the quantities needed to dominate, and only those who had continuously had such access could expect to sustain themselves; computers played a supporting role but were not the stars of the show. There were exceptions, steel, for instance, but all the others survived. However, in each industry, all the major firms were aggressive users of IT, with the result that fewer than 100 to 150 American firms essentially created the post-Fordist period we are in today.[27]

Globalization is a necessary topic of discussion whenever management implications are reviewed. However, since it has been the topic of much discussion throughout this book, we can dispatch it quickly. The digital made it possible for firms to expand their scale and scope in economically attractive ways around the world over time. This first became possible when computers and telecommunications were merged cheaply and effectively, beginning in the late 1960s. That process gained momentum in the 1970s and 1980s with the deployment of EDI and, by the end of the 1980s, with worldwide declines in communications costs beginning to occur. The availability of the Internet in the second half of the 1990s simply accelerated the process. With cheap communications and a continuously improving transportation infrastructure around the world, the use of digital tools to enhance supply chains directly globalized economic activity beyond what might have been dreamed of in 1950. In 2000 a manager could think and act globally far more so than even three decades earlier. Many did so because going global meant reaching new markets. Despite tariffs, various government policies, wars, and so forth, the economy of the world became more global in the past 50 years than in the previous 100, largely driven by a wide array of technologies, not the least of which were computing and telecommunications. In short, whereas globalized economic activity had always existed, it picked up momentum and speed. One dollar today turns over faster in the U.S. economy than it did in 1950 and moves easily through the world economy at 100 times the speed it did in 1860. In some industries, there is no national product; products are made with components designed and built all over the world, such as automobiles and all kinds of computer hardware. The implication is clear: all firms and industries are global whether they like it or not. Staying global has meant tending to one's supply chain as a core competence. Doing so triggers partnerships, alliances, e-commerce, e-business, lobbying with regulators, market strategies, tactical plans, and so forth.

The final area of implications for managers that always was, and continuous to be, on management's mind is the role of labor. Central to any substantive discussion about why to use computers in the twentieth century were issues concerning labor: cost; productivity; skills; reliability; and requirement to train, replace, and manage. The historic trend across all industries presented in this book, and many hundreds for which they were emblematic, was to reduce the amount of human labor required to perform work. If that could not be accomplished, many firms exported labor-intensive work to other countries with lower costs. There are no signs that this pattern is changing or that it might take new turns. But all labor will not disappear, no matter how much automation is implemented. In fact, most prognostications about the future of labor in America call for a shortage of enough skilled workers as various calamities befall American industry: retirement of the Baby Boomers, aging population, wars and diseases, global warming, and so forth. One group of economists described the trends management experienced in the late 1990s and would continue to feel in the early 2000s. There will be

> sharp moves toward downsizing and growth of a contingent workforce; rede-sign of tasks and work systems that both make greater demands on employees and allow them opportunities for more meaningful work; and training arrange-ments that distribute opportunities for learning skills in an unbalanced man-ner, contributing to unequal outcomes in the labor market.[28]

The authors note changes in labor relations between employees and managers and the entrance of large numbers of women and minorities in an ever-increasing variety of jobs,[29] but the most fundamental trend, supported by computing, is the gradual delegation of routine operational decision making to nonmanagerial em-ployees and lower level management at the same time as other decisions of an even more mundane nature are transferred to ever more sophisticated digital systems. That process of delegation has become relatively obvious in management circles and seems to be working. However, computerization means that over time man-agement either loses authorities it once had or must learn how best to shift respon-sibilities. As the work force at large becomes better trained (i.e., can use computer systems and have more technical knowledge of a process than their supervisor), management teams will have to consider being as good at training and delegating as they have been in understanding when and how to use the digital. The other possibility, of course, and the one that began to appear in both the Semiconductor and Hard Drive Industries late in the century, involves transferring work to tech-nically competent workers outside the United States who can be paid lower salaries than their American counterparts.[30]

The converse applies to workers. Many lost their jobs in the second half of the century when productivity gains were achieved (e.g., in manufacturing and petro-leum), when management was unable to address global competition (e.g., in steel) and when different skills were required (e.g., pharmaceuticals, software, and aer-ospace). Computers have made workers more productive and have helped provide healthier and safer environments, frequently for higher salaries. But the digital is double-edged: unrelenting pressures to extrude human content from work has always existed. When workers go on strike for higher salaries, I worry about the long-term effects. The naked truth is that if a worker's salary increase is too large, colleagues in other countries become attractive substitutes or the impulse to auto-mate further becomes increasingly cost-justifiable. This was true, and continues to be so, in every industry studied. Labor has a history of not dealing well with this reality. Poor leadership on this issue by unions (with the possible exception of those in most parts of the Automotive Industry in the last two decades of the century) and a narrow focus on salaries, benefits, and working conditions have contributed to this situation. There is no evidence to suggest any change. Workers will become more technically savvy, will have more formal education, and will acquire greater responsibilities. Their worth will increasingly be measured by the currency and relevance of their skills, and many of those skills will be defined by the digital. That is a feature of the post-Fordist world that cannot be ignored by management, non-managerial labor, and public officials.

What Were the International Political Implications?

Economists have long acknowledged that what happens in the American economy ripples across other economies, and this circumstance has certainly been true for the entire period following World War II. To rehash that story here would be to retell old news. But let us acknowledge that the way in which the American economy operated and what it invested in had a profound influence on economic events and business practices in other nations. However, what economists say about the influence of the United States on other nations is less important than what political scientists believe and tell American policymakers. The latter implement policies, practices, and laws that directly affect business behavior and economic results. So what is this community saying about technology? We have an excellent example of a global advisor on political matters in Henry Kissinger, who is known around the world as a consummate diplomat, who has served as U.S. secretary of state in the Nixon Administration, who is the acknowledged architect of the opening of relations between the United States and Communist China, and who negotiated an end to the Vietnam War. In a book published in 2001, intended to influence the course of American foreign policy in the early years of the new century, Kissinger touched on the politics of globalization. He acknowledged, in the process of renewed globalization, the influence of many technologies on the role the United States has played:

> The United States has been the driving force behind the dynamics of globalization; it has also been the prime beneficiary of the forces it has unleashed. During the last decade of the twentieth century, American productivity became the engine of global economic growth; American capital underwrote a staggering array of new technologies and promoted their broad distribution around the world.[31]

He emphasized the benefits of a free market that accrued to the Americans, from which vendors of IT benefited enormously as well.

However, as we also saw in earlier chapters, free trade was a double-edged sword. Just as the Americans could export a great many products, free trade made it possible for rivals to enter the U.S. economy to challenge the dominance of American industries in, for example, automobiles, consumer electronics, and steel. As time passes and other nations adopt the digital in ways that make sense to their industries, the competitive edge of Americans, as a result of being early users of computers, should shrink—even though in all probability many American industries will also be able to develop additional, novel uses of technology that will offer yet additional competitive advantages. Concerning the exuberance of so many commentators on the future of America's information economy, we can turn to one of the most highly regarded experts on the economics and politics of globalization, Robert Gilpin who recently reminded us that "while these theories provide some interesting insights, the long-term consequences of the computer and the information economy will be unclear for many decades to come."[32] It is a reasonable statement. His studies of global politics and economics indicate that there has been a growing increase in the rate of technological innovations of all kinds, not just of computers and telecommunications; that there is a broadening of the applications being discovered; and that shorter process and product life cycles increasingly affect a wide array of industries around the world.[33] My study of American manufacturing, transportation, and retail industries indicates that each of these global economic features was profoundly affected by the extensive use of computers. Global uses of computing is quickly increasing, with implications not necessarily yet captured in the international trade statistics of either government agencies or the IT industry itself.

The historical record of IT adoptions indicates that it did not occur in isolation of existing political realities. Paul N. Edwards noted that the Cold War provided political incentives to use computing in ways consistent with the worldview of America's political and military leaders. Kenneth Flamm, in two important studies, made the case that Cold War politics gave public officials a purpose for investing in the development of computing, not relinquishing that leadership role until commercial uses of the digital were obvious, proven, and productive.[34] That pattern has continued to the present and could be seen playing out in how IT was used in U.S. ordnance in the second Gulf War of 2003.

There is still another political perspective, that of historian John Lewis Gaddis, one of the most prolific commentators on the Cold War. He called the entire second half of the century the period of the "Long Peace."[35] Although the world was divided essentially into two camps—the free world, aligned with the United States, and the Communist world, linked to the Soviet Union and Communist China—and faced possible nuclear war, the fact remains that World War III never happened. Despite the Korean and Vietnam wars and many surrogate regional conflagrations, the United States did not experience the kind of devastation suffered by Europe twice in the twentieth century and once by Japan. Capitalism thrives in times of peace, when property is secure, trade occurs in regular and predictable ways, and business prospects can be anticipated. All these conditions existed in the United States through the period. Had they not, the story of American industries and the way in which they deployed computers would have been a very different one.

The only recent analogy is the American experience during World War II, when government controls over all aspects of the economy were so comprehensive that one almost could not acquire a typewriter without going through some approval process; even food and clothing required ration coupons. During that war a great effort was made to develop computers to crack enemy communications codes, to help in the design of the atomic bomb, and to create artillery firing tables. Very little innovative uses of precomputer technology in a strictly business sense occurred. The prewar applications in use in manufacturing, transportation, and retailing remained the same during World War II.[36] What little we do know about wartime commercial uses of information technologies in Europe confirms the same pattern.[37] Can we extrapolate from this that had the United States experienced military destruction or extensive government controls that the economy and computing might have turned out differently? It cannot be proven, but one can answer the question with reasonable confidence—yes.

One of the most obvious patterns of behavior in all these industries for the entire period is that decisions about the acquisition of computers and how best to apply them were always made within the context of business and economic realities. With exceptions here and there, as a general rule businesses and whole industries adopted the computer for economic advantage, with minimal governmental or political constraints on the use of their machines. The one major exception, and it only affected the vendors of computer technology, were export controls on selling advanced technologies to countries considered a threat to the United States, such as the Soviet Union, China, and Libya. Yet that constraint did little to slow the expansion of American IT industries around the world because the vast majority of users of computers operated in highly advanced, industrialized, capitalist nations.

What Was the American Experience?

For nearly 170 years, historians and others commenting on American society have felt the urge to quote Alexis de Tocqueville, author of *Democracy in America*, because he described this nation in ways that seemed to ring true across time. What that means is that this nation has developed a set of behaviors and handed-down values that have transcended generations. Tocqueville observed that the primary activity of this nation was business: "In the United States the greatest industrial undertakings are executed without trouble because the whole population is engaged in industry and because the poorest man as well as the most opulent gladly joins forces therein."[38] Americans did not hesitate to invest in every form of information technology that came along over the past three centuries. I have argued increasingly in recent years that the use of information and its technologies was as salient a feature of American society as any Tocqueville had identified.[39] The hunt for profits and economic opportunities remained as fervent an initiative in the past half century as in any other period in American history. At first, markets kept growing because the nation expanded across the North American continent, requiring businesses to constantly find new ways to make, deliver, and sell across a vast landmass. In the process, the private sector made profits and tried to ward off competition. In the twentieth century, American exports around the world expanded dramatically, especially in the half century after World War II. So again, American corporations had to hunt for ways to improve productivity, scale, and scope.

By and large, most industries attempted to step up to the challenge, some better than others, but ultimately they all sought ways to preserve existing market shares, fight competition, and leverage their core competencies, employees, and physical assets. A great deal of space in this book has been devoted to discussing labor productivity and inventory control because these were two assets managers could most leverage to improve sales and increase profits. My fundamental finding bears repeating: clearly one of the most important tools used by management in that half century was the computer, as well as the digital in many forms. The past two generations of managers were at least as creative in using IT as any previous ones; indeed, because of the snowballing effect, one could as easily conclude that they exploited IT better than their forebears. Some were clear thinking and bold, others cautious and slow, but in aggregate, managers so embraced computing that they fundamentally changed the way in which work was done in the American economy. Fordism was an earlier case study of that level of change, and that, too, was an American original. At the risk of appearing jingoistic, we can conclude that the implementation of so many applications of the digital in this economy was consistently an American experience.

The evidence presented here also suggests that the history of computing technology cannot continue to be seen as primarily a technical or scientific issue. Its history is less the story of technology and more a history of business. Although technical history has its place, we miss the bigger story about computing if we do not see it also as a major component of the business affairs of the nation. The economists have figured this out; now we need business historians to do the same. Only then will scholars and managers alike understand the significance of this technology in this nation's history, and only then will they draw out the implications for future managerial activities.

The process of deployment is still underway, as new infrastructures and IT applications, most notably the Internet, sweep across the economy and as more devices used in daily life are either connected to the Internet or are configured with computer chips to provide more decision-making authority and responsibility. This is not science fiction; it is happening on a continuous basis, moving out from manufacturing plants and stores into the products used by Americans at home and at work. Informationalized appliances are already flooding the market, providing yet another example and a new generation of the digital across the economy. For better or for worse, a digital hand is being used by many industries to do the daily tasks of business, and it is reaching new areas of the economy. The process reaffirms two lifetimes of research on technology, economics, and business by Joseph A. Schumpeter and Alfred D. Chandler, Jr. Adam Smith would also understand.

APPENDIX A

How to Study the Role
of Computing by Industry

Increasingly during the twentieth century, economists and professors of business management have come to the conclusion that an effective way to look at either economic activity or the management of firms is to analyze industries. Joseph A. Schumpeter in the 1930s and 1940s was an early proponent of this approach, although not the only one. He was one of the first to link the study of technological change in an economy to analysis of industries. Several decades later, in a series of books, Michael E. Porter demonstrated both the practical importance of viewing economic activities by industries and also how to do it.[1] If one wanted to start with this approach, Porter's book, *Competitive Strategy*, describes techniques for analyzing the structure (organization) of industries and explains how to document the rivalries and competitive forces at work. In each of the case studies, in my book, I began by explaining how an industry was configured over time, such as major groups of firms; named the key corporations; and so forth.

Another approach, which can be used to great effect in tandem with Porter's, is the collection of ideas of business historian Alfred D. Chandler, Jr. He has demonstrated that companies, and by extension industries, were controlled and shaped by the attitudes, policies, and practices of managers in large corporations. He has argued that success came to those who simultaneously made sufficient investments in production, marketing, sales, and distribution to reach levels of scale and scope that made them cost-effective and competitive.[2] Through numerous case studies he demonstrated the process at work. Based on his approach, two generations of business historians and economists have filled in many details.[3]

These approaches provide some broad economic and industrial context in which to situate any discussion about the implementation of technologies of any kind. What is important to keep in mind is that no industry adopts one technology but rather a confluence of various types that over time become integrated to one degree or another. The interaction of various types of technology occurs on two dimensions. The first is vertical; that is, a body of technology is expanded or changed from time to time, such as computers or specific software tools, one replacing the other. Upgrading to large mainframes or installing a new release of a software packages are two examples. But, second, this is also a horizontal process in which different types of technology are constantly introduced, changed, upgraded, or eliminated—new machinery (not just computers), new techniques for manufacturing and selling, or novel components and materials (e.g., carbon composites instead of steel or plastic). A technology's introduction, transformation, and exit from any particular industry is complicated by the fact that these transitions spill over onto each other. For example, a papermaking machine of the 1930s is a fairly manual affair with primitive instrumentation. By the end of the 1970s, microprocessor-based sensors and instrumentation are built right into the machine. Therefore, any appreciation of the role of technology in an industry must also take into account this spillover effect.

The fundamental questions concerning the role of technology in an industry are fairly straightforward:

- What are the business issues that compel management to deploy a particular technology? The answer often changes in degree or substance over time.
- What practices are proven to be effective or ineffective in an industry? To what extent is there crossover of technology from one industry to another, and why?
- How does technology of various types come into and exit an industry, and when?
- What effect do they have on the activities and results of a particular industry? Why?
- What effect do particular technologies have on the structure and organization of firms and industries? In this book I also ask, What effects did computers, therefore, have on the work of the American economy as a whole?

There are many other questions that are specific either to an individual technology or to a business. However, the design point I recommend begins from an economic or business perspective. Understand the context, and then move to the analysis of specific technologies, processes, and so forth. Historians of technology often begin by looking at technical issues first—the supply side of the story—then move to the context in which these are deployed.[4] However, since I have long argued that the extent of deployment and the nature of its use are better indicators of how technology arrives, changes, is deployed, and declines, I led with a business and economic approach.[5]

The heart of this approach calls for one to look at the deployment of technology on an industry-by-industry basis—and ideally, a group of industries within a sector, such as a cluster of manufacturing or financial industries—because they have common patterns of adoption and issues, which influence one another over time. One can look at the whole subject by using a four-step approach. First, understand how an industry is structured (and changes over time), the key events in its history (a half century perspective is sufficient, less than a decade is not), and the current business issues it faces. Next, analyse the major tasks the industry performs (e.g., drills for oil or sells merchandise out of a store). These usually do not change from one decade to another, only how they are done. Third, identify what technologies are deployed within each of the groups of tasks, documenting what applications are implemented with what technologies, when, by whom, and how. At this stage one can document three sets of data: specific examples by company, trends in deployment across an industry (or industries), and extent of deployment. At this last phase, it is important to understand all the major technologies being introduced, not just the one at the center of the study, (in our case, the digital). Finally, one has to assess the effects of deployment on the operations of the firm and then of the industry. Often at this stage, understanding why a technology was adopted, the problems faced in implementation, and the benefits and costs achieved are determined. This four-step approach allows one to develop creditable answers to the questions posed above.

For this book, I first identified the industries that needed to be studied and why. My intent was to look at the fewest number of industries necessary to get a comprehensive enough view of how computing affected the work of one nation's economy. To do so, I had to examine 16 industries across 4 major sectors of the economy. Their total activity accounted for roughly half the work and revenue of the American economy. They were also trendsetters for other industries: major players in each of these industries caused smaller firms (usually their suppliers) to adopt specific technologies. Clustering industries by sector allows one to identify common patterns of behavior that transcend specific industries; thus, all the chapters on manufacturing industries, for example, are together in this book.

There are two major sources for this kind of information. For each major industry there is a body of articles and books that provides one of three factors: history of the industry, how it works today, or biographies of specific companies. Every major industry has at least one, and often many, journals of record that are read by its members and thus reflect their issues. Often these publications have been produced for many decades, allowing one to develop a historical perspective. Examples can be found in all the notes to this book. Then there are anthologies of industry-centric studies. The first place to begin is with the 10 editions published (so far) over the past half century by Walter Adams, *The Structure of American Industry*. New editions come out about every 5 to 10 years; have chapters on specific industries, written by economists; and cover structure, major players, key events, sales volumes, business issues, and bibliography. These are really excellent. One should look at various editions for any particular industry because the issues and emphases change over time, as do the authors of specific industry studies. Then start to read industry-specific articles and books. Other anthologies of chapter-length reviews of industries, even of their use of technologies, can be consulted. For example, in my discussion of the Chemical Industry in chapter 6, I rely on a great deal of this kind of material. Many people also wrote chapter-length surveys of the Computer Industry, and a careful check of U.S. government web sites (e.g., Department of Commerce and Department of Labor and, for Europe, the Organization for Economic Cooperation and Development [OECD]) normally yields a tremendous amount of similar material.

The next body of evidence I found particularly useful for this book was produced by the U.S. Bureau of Labor Statistics. Some 40-odd studies of dozens of industries were conducted over most of the second half of the century and were presented in a standard format.[6] Economists at the BLS interviewed members of an industry and used secondary literature to look at its structure, types of technology being adopted and extent of deployment, effects of technological innovation on the number of workers, changes in their skills, and requirements for future work forces. Most of the studies contain a traditional analysis of productivity gains; I say "traditional" because BLS measures productivity as output per worker. I cannot overstate the importance of this body of material. Criticisms can be made, such as the choice of one industry over another, but in aggregate it is a vast resource on the role of technology in America. In addition to these data, economists at the BLS have published articles and white papers on related methodological and industry issues. For every industry I looked at, I relied on BLS material, which is cited generously in my notes. The BLS stopped performing these studies in the 1990s, but the U.S. Department of Commerce began to produce annual reports on the extent of deployment of the new communications technology, all of which are available on its web site.[7] These reports deal with the kinds of issues addressed by the BLS.

Such a study as this one needs to be informed about specific examples of how a particular application or technology was used. There are four sources that are useful in providing this level of detail. First, the major journals and magazines in an industry periodically reported on the use of technology of one type or another, often based on extensive surveys and interviews. For the most part, these are excellent and rich in detail about the rationale for adoption and extent of deployment. Frequently, they provide case studies of specific companies and at least a superficial analysis of consequences.

The second source is made up of publications (usually magazines and journals) in the industry that carry articles about the deployment of that industry's products. For computing in the United States, *Computerworld* and *Datamation* are the two major publications for most of the period, and for the 1990s, *Beyond Computing* and *InformationWeek*.

A third source is made up of presentations by industry associations and articles written by end users in a myriad of journals, both industry-centric or tied to specific professions. Trade associations and newsletters routinely publish bibliographies of these materials. These individual case studies are normally presented by those who implemented a particular technology, explaining why, how, and what, and they end with lessons learned or future plans. They are surprisingly candid, although they all also try to put a positive spin on their stories. But they are specific and real and can be judged within the context of both the industry and the trade press.

A fourth body of material is made up of application briefs published by vendors of technologies. For example, in the world of computers, IBM and Burroughs published several thousand case studies of how specific companies used specific products. They were intended to be references in support of selling initiatives, but for the historian they are valuable case studies. They exist for every major industry and were published on an ongoing basis in every decade. When such a vendor has a corporate archive, one can count on the existence of some of this material. The corporate archive of IBM has thousands of pages. The biggest problem is gaining access to an archive; corporations are not always equipped to help scholars. The Burroughs Papers are full of this kind of material and are housed at the Charles Babbage Institute at the University of Minnesota, Minneapolis. It is useful to look at this kind of material from multiple vendors since no supplier necessarily offered a full range of products, not even fully integrated vendors like IBM, Burroughs, Honeywell, or Sperry. For this book, I looked at similar material in the CDC records at the Babbage Institute because this firm sold high-end computers for simulation applications. Also, different firms had varying points of emphasis in their studies. Burroughs had a high presence in the financial industries, IBM in manufacturing and the public sector, and CDC in defense and aerospace. But as a whole, these materials are the single largest untapped source of information on the use of technologies in industry, a collection rarely consulted by economists, business management professors, or historians.

There is a fifth source, much smaller but just as useful for the study of applications, namely, management or how-to books about a particular technology. In the area of computing, hundreds of DP management primers have been published, often containing case studies of specific installations similar to the application briefs prepared or reprinted by vendors. In the case of computing, these primers supplemented application briefs from other sources with commentary on management-related issues, such as how a particular technology was cost-justified and why it was managed in one part of an organization or another. Fewer in number are the application-specific articles and books describing, for example, office automation, published in the 1950s and 1960s, or guides to CAD/CAM in the 1970s and 1980s. Less frequently, they will identify in which industries the applications were installed.[8]

It turns out that the amount of material that can be examined is quite substantial, particularly industry-specific economic data and news stories about individual events. The challenge is to identify structural features, identify patterns of issues and practices, remember to include political and economic influences, and then to examine the technology at hand. Despite all this information, there are gaps in our knowledge. The biggest is any precise accounting of the extent of deployment of a technology. The evidence, at best, is often sporadic or anecdotal. Drawing general conclusions from that kind of evidence presents some obvious problems. It can help to go to the supply side, to look at the form of the technology in question. In the case of computers, there is a great deal of data on how many of one kind of computer versus another was sold by year. Often, however, these data are not broken down by industry but rather are presented by the type of machine or software. We have yet to develop a methodology for extrapolating from the data how many items of one type of technology went into specific industries. As studies are conducted on the deployment of specific technologies on an industry-by-industry basis, we should be able to overcome the problem of identifying dispersal in specific industries.

In the case of computing, there is a partial solution in that major suppliers of digital technologies from time to time commissioned consulting firms to perform market surveys and projections. On occasion these surveys involved an industry and not simply a type of product over time. The Charles Babbage Institute has a collection of such market surveys on computing by Automation Consultants, Frost & Sullivan, and Auerbach for the 1950s to the early 1970s. Whereas IBM's records of this type are quite limited, those in the Burroughs Papers are excellent. The Burroughs Papers also contain surveys of deployment of precomputer technologies, which suggest to a historian what industries to look at more closely because of their predisposition to use IT earlier (e.g., banks, insurance, and government agencies).

What this methodology does not address is the whole question of how well these technologies were managed and by whom. The case studies at the firm level have a wealth of material on this topic, along with some of the how-to management books, particularly those published in the 1950s–1970s. What our approach does not do, however, is flush out in detail management issues related to the exploitation and control of technologies. For that, either IT industry managerial literature has to be examined or one has to hunt through corporate archives of user firms. The paucity of such archival materials is a major gap in the collections being built by various archives in the United States. In short, we do not have enough material to write a substantial history of the management of IT that is built on hard evidence of an archival nature. Ultimately, we will need these kinds of studies to round out any discussion about the effectiveness of deployment of a technology. Open questions are obvious: what did it mean for IT to report to one department versus another? What were the effects on types of adoption that were caused by which kind of functional manager making the decision? To what extent did end users fundamentally influence the configuration of a new form of an existing or emerging technology? Even basic questions about the role of standards and conversions remain unexamined to any useful degree.

APPENDIX B

The Universal Product Code (UPC),

Optical Character Recognition (OCR),

and Point-of-Sale (POS)

The UPC (see figure 10.1 or B.1)—also called bar code—is widely used to give a specific item a unique identity that can then be read either by a handheld optical scanner or by a fixed scanner attached, for example, to a point-of-sale terminal system. The label is normally read as a product is passed over a glass plate on a checkout counter. The scanner uses a laser beam to read the label.

There are various types of UPC labels; however, they are all essentially designed in the same way. The stripes are called guide bars. The first five on the far left of the UPC identifies the manufacturer of the product. This unique identifier is assigned to a vendor by the Uniform Code Council. The five guide bars on the far right are numbers assigned by the manufacturer to describe individual items, for example, green miniskirt. The middle bars hold numbers (code symbols) that identify products, for instance, grocery. Each bar has numbers that are translated into digital form by POS software.

Prices are not encoded on the UPC. Rather, they are kept in a table within a computer to which a scanner is attached. When a price is assigned by the retailer to a product, it is loaded into the table that uses the product number (on the far right of the UPC) as the identifier associated with that price. A clerk scans a product; the POS system identifies a specific item as having just been scanned, goes to the table and finds the price for that product number, and then reports that information back to the POS terminal, usually by displaying the data on a screen.[1]

Other terms are often used when discussing UPC. The most frequently related term is *optical character recognition* (OCR), which is the process of converting images of machine-readable letters, symbols, and so forth into digital form. This technology

Figure B.1
*Barcode for Alfred D. Chandler, Jr.
and James W. Cortada (eds.), A*
Nation Transformed by
Information (*New York: Oxford
University Press, 2000*).

is used to recognize, for example, letters on a check, zip codes on mail, or UPC labels. A normal OCR system consists of a scanner, software and hardware, and access to a computer in which it stores the images it has read. Some systems are general in purpose; most, however, are specialized for precise applications, for example, reading zip codes in post offices, check clearing in banks, and POS in retail. The most widely used read addresses, forms, checks, bills, airline tickets, and passports.[2]

Related technologies involve point-of-sale (POS) terminals, sometimes also called POS systems. A POS system consists of a cash register (with printing capability), a credit card recording system, and a processor (usually within the terminal) to collect UPC data. The combination of these components are connected to an in-store or company-wide computer to look up a price, record the sale, and reduce the number of units of a product in stock. At the point of sale, the terminal (often with a small TV-like screen to display a price) is mounted on a platform waist high, and either to the right or left is a flat, tablelike surface upon which the customer places the goods to be purchased. Part of that surface is a square glass plate, under which is a laser gun that beams a laser at the UPC label above it that is attached to the product being purchased, transmitting its findings to the computer. Such data can also be collected with a handheld scanner that is feeding information to the computer or the processor in the cash register. The clerk can also send data to the processor or in-store computer by keypunching the inventory number printed at the top of the UPC label, along with the price stamped on the product. That price is often put on the product daily, either at the warehouse (usually by a wholesaler) or by the manufacturer.[3] The same in-store processor that contains the price table is also normally used to print the shelf labels that are mounted on the shelves in the store to inform consumers of the price for a specific product. The combined use of shelf labels and UPC eliminates the labor-intensive task of hand pricing every can and box with a paper label.

NOTES

Preface

1. In particular, I was influenced by Michael E. Porter, *Competitive Strategy: Techniques for Analyzing Industries and Competitors* (New York: Free Press, 1980).

Chapter 1

1. For recent examples, see Donald A. Norman, *The Invisible Computer: Why Good Products Can Fail, The Personal Computer Is So Complex, and Information Appliances Are the Solution* (Cambridge, Mass.: MIT Press, 1998); Michael Dertouzos, *What Will Be: How the New World of Information Will Change Our Lives* (New York: HarperEdge, 1997); Don Tapscott, *Growing Up Digital: The Rise of the Net Generation* (New York: McGraw-Hill, 1998); Thomas L. Landauer, *The Trouble with Computers: Usefulness, Usability, and Productivity* (Cambridge, Mass.: MIT Press, 1995).

2. David B. Yoffie (ed.), *Computing in the Age of Digital Convergence* (Boston: Harvard Business School Press, 1997), has over a dozen examples of this process at work. See also Robert E. Litan and Alice M. Rivlin, "The Economy and the Internet: What Lies Ahead?" in Robert E. Litain and Alice M. Rivlin (eds.), *The Economic Payoff from the Internet Revolution* (Washington, D.C.: Brookings Institution Press, 2001): 1–28.

3. The word *digital* pertains to data in the form of digits. Digits are characters that represent letters and numbers and are often expressed as a series of 0s and 1s, negative and positive electrical impulses. The key idea is that something digital is a specific fact, like a number or letter. So a digital computer produces specific pieces of data, such as the fact that the time is 11:45 P.M. The other fundamental type of computer is analog, which represents data in some continuous form. A watch that has hands is continuously representing the time as about 11:45.

4. The standard reference work on the analog computer for many years, and still the best source of information on this class of technology, is G. A. Korn and T. M. Korn, *Electronic Analog and Hybrid Computers*, 2nd ed. (New York: McGraw-Hill, 1972), because it summarizes most of what was known about the analog at the height of its popularity.

5. James S. Small, "General-Purpose Electronic Analog Computing: 1945–1955," *Annals of the History of Computing* 15, no. 2 (1993): 8–18; see also his article "Engineering Technology and Design: The Post-Second World War Development of Electronic Analogue Computers," *History of Technology* 11, no. 1 (1994): 33–48; and his book, *The Analogue Alternative: The Electronic Analogue Computer in Britain and the USA, 1930–1975* (London: Routledge, 2001).

6. Hans Queisser, *The Conquest of the Microchip* (Cambridge, Mass.: Harvard University Press, 1988): 67–68; Michael Riordan and Lillian Hoddeson, *Crystal Fire: The Birth of the Information Age* (New York: Norton, 1997): 211–213, 216–218.

7. Paul Ceruzzi, *A History of Modern Computing* (Cambridge, Mass.: MIT Press, 1998): 182–191.

8. Experts on the subject anticipate continued compression, more capacity, and more speed.

9. Manuel Castells, *The Informational City* (Oxford: Blackwell, 1989): 108.

10. James W. Cortada, "Progenitors of the Information Age: The Development of Chips and Computers," in Alfred D. Chandler, Jr., and James W. Cortada (eds.), *A Nation Transformed by Information: How Information Has Shaped the United States from Colonial Times to the Present* (New York: Oxford University Press, 2000): 177–186. The percentages reflect the circumstances in 1995.

11. James W. Cortada, *The Computer in the United States: From Laboratory to Market, 1930 to 1960* (Armonk, N.Y.: M. E. Sharpe, 1993): 54–63; Kenneth Flamm, *Targeting the Computer: Government Support and International Competition* (Washington, D.C.: Brookings Institution, 1987): 46–47, 55.

12. Charles J. Bashe, Lyle R. Johnson, John H Palmer, and Emerson W. Pugh, *IBM's Early Computers* (Cambridge, Mass.: MIT Press, 1986): 101, 165–172, 185–186, 470–471.

13. Cortada, *Computer in the United States,* 102–123.

14. The best current technical history of the subject, which summarizes the thinking of many historians, is by Ceruzzi, *History of Modern Computing*; see especially 47–108. For an equally useful study by two major historians of the subject, see Martin Campbell-Kelly and William Aspray, *Computer: A History of the Information Machine* (New York: Basic Books, 1996): 157–205.

15. Alfred D. Chandler, Jr., "The Computer Industry: The First Half-Century," in Yoffie, *Computing in the Age of Digital Convergence,* 52–53; see also Alfred D. Chandler, Jr., *Inventing the Electronic Century: The Epic Story of the Consumer Electronics and Computer Industries* (New York: Free Press, 2001): 83–131.

16. Data in James W. Cortada, *Historical Dictionary of Data Processing: Organizations* (Westport, Conn.: Greenwood Press, 1987): 18.

17. Ceruzzi, *History of Modern Computing,* 143–173; Emerson W. Pugh, *Building IBM: Shaping an Industry and Its Technology* (Cambridge, Mass.: MIT Press, 1995): 263–277.

18. The data are a summary of my more extensive description of the size and economics of the computer industry: *Information Technology as Business History: Issues in the History and Management of Computing* (Westport, Conn.: Greenwood Press, 1996): 51–74.

19. J. M. Harker et al., "A Quarter Century of Disk File Innovation," *IBM Journal of Research and Development* 25, no. 5 (September 1981): 677–689; Franklin M. Fisher, James W. McKie, and Richard B. Mancke, *IBM and the U.S. Data Processing Industry: An Economic History* (New York: Praeger, 1983): 55–56; Pugh, *Building IBM,* 224–228.

20. The majority of new products coming from the computer industry consisted of peripherals. Both IBM and Burroughs, for example, had to publish weekly and monthly reports addressed to their sales personnel just to let them keep up with new developments. The IBM Archives and the Charles Babbage Institute's archives contain thousands of pages of such material. In the case of Burroughs, for example, beginning in the 1950s monthly reports would go out to the sales force, all preserved at the Babbage, "Market Reports," Burroughs Papers, Box 70.

21. Janet Abbate, *Inventing the Internet* (Cambridge, Mass.: MIT Press, 1999): 36–39, 44–81; Arthur L. Norberg and Judy E. O'Neill, *Transforming Computer Technology: Information Processing for the Pentagon, 1962–1986* (Baltimore, Md.: Johns Hopkins University Press, 1996): 153–196.

22. Ceruzzi, *History of Modern Computing,* 124–141.

23. Ibid., 124.

24. Paul Freiberger and Michael Swaine, *Fire in the Valley: The Making of the Personal Computer* (New York: McGraw-Hill, 2000), 33–210.

25. Ulric Weil, *Information Systems in the 80s: Products, Markets, and Vendors* (Englewood Cliffs, N.J.: Prentice-Hall, 1982), 214.

26. Ceruzzi, *History of Modern Computing,* 263–290; Cortada, *Information Technology as Business History*, 81–89.

27. On the types and rates of change in IT, see Michael J. Albrecht, Jr., and James W. Cortada, "Optimizing Investments in Information Technology," *National Productivity Review* (Summer 1998): 53–60; Cortada, "A Framework for Understanding Technological Change: Lessons from Information Technology, 1868–1997," *Entrepreneurship and Economic Growth in the American Economy* 12 (2000): 47–92.

28. Ceruzzi, *History of Modern Computing,* 300–304; Jim Clark with Owen Edwards, *Netscape Time: The Making of the Billion-Dollar Start-Up That Took on Microsoft* (New York: St. Martin, 1999): 19–130; Tim Berners-Lee with Mark Fischetti, *Weaving the Web: The Original Design and Ultimate Destiny of the World Wide Web by Its Inventor* (San Francisco: HarperSanFrancisco, 1999): 107, 199–209.

29. The literature describing this process is vast. For an overview, see Cortada, *21st Century Business*; Larry Downes and Chunka Mui, *Unleashing the Killer App: Digital Strategies for Market Dominance* (Boston: Harvard Business School Press, 1998); and a collection of essays by different observers: Don Tapscott (ed.), *Creating Value in the Network Economy* (Boston: Harvard Business School Press, 1999).

30. For examples of articles describing these kinds of applications, see John A. Woods (ed.), *The Purchasing and Supply Yearbook* (New York: McGraw-Hill, 2000): 245–305; and Peter Fingar, Harsha Kumar, and Tarun Sharma, *Enterprise E-Commerce: The Software Component Breakthrough for Business-to-Business Commerce* (Tampa, Fla.: Meghan-Kiffer Press, 2000): 45–72, 77–220.

31. Thomas J. Watson, Jr., and Peter Petre, *Father, Son & Co.: My Life at IBM and Beyond* (New York: Bantam, 1990): 241.

32. Cortada, *Information Technology as Business History*, 221–246.

33. Who did what "first" is as popular a game in the history of computing as in other branches of history. Paul Ceruzzi contends that the term appeared first at Ford Motor Company in 1947 and that Diebold popularized it in 1952: Ceruzzi, *History of Modern Computing,* 32.

34. The computer thus joined a variety of new technologies that emerged in the nineteenth and twentieth centuries and caused the displacement of workers with skills no longer relevant in the economy, thus stimulating further discussion about whether or not technology cost or created new jobs. The debate over this issue has been passionate and long-standing. See Amy Sue Bix, *Inventing Ourselves Out of Jobs? America's Debate Over Technological Unemployment, 1929–1981* (Baltimore, Md.: Johns Hopkins University Press, 2000): 236–312, quote on 312.

35. D. J. Axsmith, a consultant, demonstrated how to cost-justify equipment, also arguing that it was poorly done: "Achieving Computer Profits Through Project Evaluation, Control and Costing," *Data Processing Proceedings 1965* (Philadelphia: Data Processing Management Association, 1965): 340–352; Ned Chapin was one of the earliest management consultants in the field of computing, and his ideas were influential: "Justifying The Use of an Automatic Computer," *Journal of Machine Accounting, Systems and Management* 6, no. 8 (September 1955): 9–10, 14; the most quoted, possibly the most read, article on why to install computers that was published in the 1950s was written by Harold J. Leavitt and Thomas J. Whisler, "Management in the 1980's," *Harvard Business Review* 36, no. 6 (November–December 1958):

41–48; for a survey of 27 large users on what economic benefits they gained, see Douglas J. Axsmith, "Economic Aspects of Data Processing," *Data Processing Proceedings 1963* (Detroit: DPMA, 1963): 70–91; 40 percent of 2,000 U.S. corporations did not achieve significant benefits, according to a study by T. K. Bikson and B. Gutek, *Implementation of Office Automation* (Santa Monica, Calif.: RAND Corp., 1984); for a contemporary article on how to cost-justify computers, see Rudolph E. Hirsch, "The Value of Information," *Journal of Accountancy* 125 (June 1968): 41–45; and Carol Schaller, "Survey of Computer Cost Allocation Techniques," *Journal of Accountancy* 137 (June 1974): 41–46.

36. Neil Rackham, *SPIN Selling* (New York: McGraw-Hill, 1988): 10–11.

37. For example, Ned Chapin, *An Introduction to Automatic Computers* (Princeton, N.J.: Van Nostrand, 1955, 1957, 1963): 470; James D. Fahnestock, *Computers and How They Work* (New York: Ziff-Davis, 1959): 7–8; Robert H. Gregory and Richard L. Van Horn, *Business Data Processing and Programming* (Belmont, Cal.: Wadsworth, 1963): 181–182, 368; Charles J. Sippl, *Computer Dictionary and Handbook* (Indianapolis: Bobbs-Merrill, 1966): 17–18; Harold Chestnut, *Systems Engineering Methods* (New York: Wiley, 1967): 129–130; Valerie Illingworth, Edward L. Glaser, and I. C. Pyle, *Dictionary of Computing* (New York: Oxford University Press, 1983): 14–15; IBM, *Dictionary of Computing* (Poughkeepsie, N.Y.: IBM Corp., 1987): 17–18. For a historical overview of the subject, see Cortada, *Information Technology as Business History,* 141–190.

38. For an example of the interrelationships between architecture and standards, using information technology as the case study, see Paul Ceruzzi, "Nothin New Since von Neumann: A Historical Look at Computer Architecture, 1945–1995," in Raul Rojas and Ulf Hashagen (eds.), *The First Computers: History and Architectures* (Cambridge: Cambridge University Press, 2000): 195–217.

39. For example, three well-known business management professors defined systems to mean "proceduralized reports and routinize processes such as meeting formats": James I. Cash, Jr., F. Warren McFarlan, and James L. McKenney, *Corporate Information Systems Management: The Issues Facing Senior Executives* (Homewood, Ill.: Dow Jones-Irwin, 1988): 77. For a more technical perspective, see IBM, *Dictionary of Computing*, 421: "In data processing, a collection of people, machines, and methods organized to accomplish a set of specific functions": Oxford's *Dictionary of Computing*, 356, states that "the term may be broadened to include the basic software such as operating systems and compilers."

40. On the concept of process, see James W. Cortada and John Woods, *McGraw-Hill Encyclopedia of Quality Terms and Concepts* (New York: McGraw-Hill, 1995): 264–278. H. James Harrington, a leading authority on how to manage business through the use of processes, who spent most of his career at IBM and thus was very familiar with computer systems, defined a process as "any activity or group of activities that takes an input, adds value to it, and provides an output to an internal or external customer. Processes use an organization's resources to provide definite results": *Business Process Improvement* (New York: McGraw-Hill, 1991): 9. Linking processes to computer applications and systems is best described by Thomas H. Davenport, *Process Innovation: Reengineering Work Through Information Technology* (Boston: Harvard Business School Press, 1993), a book that became an instant Bible for many in business, renovating computer-based applications in the 1990s. His theme was that achieving major improvements in the performance of a process "means redesigning them from beginning to end, employing whatever innovative technologies and organizational resources" available for the task (p. 1).

41. For a few examples out of many, see Steven L. Goldman, Rogert N. Nagel, and Kenneth Preiss, *Agile Competitors and Virtual Organizations* (New York: Van Nostrand Reinhold, 1995); Carl Shapiro and Hal R. Varian, *Information Rules: A Strategic Guide to the Network Economy* (Boston: Harvard Business School Press, 1999), which focuses on post-Internet activities; F. M. Scherer, *New Perspectives on Economic Growth and Technological Innovation* (Washington,

D.C.: Brookings Institution Press, 1999). On the effects of IT on knowledge and competencies, see Dale Neef, *A Little Knowledge Is a Dangerous Thing: Understanding Our Global Knowledge Economy* (Boston: Butterworth-Heinemann, 1999): 73–81.

42. Davenport, *Process Innovation*, was a highly visible example in the 1990s. For a more influential study of how that was actually being done, see Don Tapscott and Art Caston, *Paradigm Shift: The New Promise of Information Technology* (New York: McGraw-Hill, 1993). An example of the group of economists critical of the pro-productivity argument is Daniel E. Sichel, *The Computer Revolution: An Economic Perspective* (Washington, D.C.: Brookings Institution Press, 1997), 4–5, who argues that "despite rapid computerization, productivity growth has not broken out from the sluggish trend that has persisted since the early 1970s." However, in a far more comprehensive study of that issue, two economists, Sanjeev Dewan and Kenneth L. Kraemer, made the opposite case, arguing that the greatest bumps in productivity occurred in the United States, out of the 35 nations they studied: "Information Technology and Productivity: Evidence from Country-Level Data," *Management Science* 46, no. 4 (April 2000): 548–562.

43. Richard K. Lester, *The Productive Edge: How U.S. Industries Are Pointing the Way to a New Era of Economic Growth* (New York: Norton, 1998), first quote 164, second quote 321. How that strategy is applied was the subject of a study sponsored by IBM: James W. Cortada and Thomas S. Hargraves (eds.), *Into the Networked Age: How IBM and Other Firms Are Getting There Now* (New York: Oxford University Press, 1999). I have also documented the areas of change currently underway in James W. Cortada, *21st Century Business: Managing and Working in the New Digital Economy* (Upper Saddle River, N.J.: Prentice-Hall/Financial Times, 2001).

44. Ceruzzi, *History of Modern Computing,* 70.

45. Batch processing was originally "a method of organizing work for a computer system, designed to reduce overheads by grouping together similar jobs": *Dictionary of Computing* (New York: Oxford Univesity Press, 1983): 31. Online processing refers "to the operation of a functional unit when under the direct control of a computer," usually with a user interacting instantaneously with a computer, as opposed to batch, in which one waits for answers to come back hours or days later. Online systems refers to the situation "in which the input data enters the computer directly from the point of origin or in which output data is transmitted directly to where it is used." See IBM, *Dictionary of Computing* 301, for both online definitions.

46. Brilliantly documented by Philip Evans and Thomas S. Wurster, *Blown to Bits: How the New Economics of Information Transforms Strategy* (Boston: Harvard Business School Press, 2000): 39–97. This book documents the desegregation of industries and firms underway, for example, in the late 1990s and early 2000s.

47. The issue has been flagged as a problem by Europeans for some time, predating the Internet: Paul Gannon, *Trojan Horses and National Champions: The Crisis in Europe's Computing and Telecommunications Industry* (London: Apt-Amatic Books, 1997). For a series of country studies, see Benn Steil, David G. Victor, and Richard R. Nelson (eds.), *Technological Innovation and Economic Performance* (Princeton, N.J.: Princeton University Press, 2002): 47–226.

48. Martin C. Libicki, "Standards: The Rough Road to the Common Byte," in Brian Kahin and Janet Abbate (eds.), *Standards Policy for Information Infrastructure* (Cambridge, Mass.: MIT Press, 1995): 35.

49. Ibid., 36.

50. Examples include standards for images; technical drawings; and CAD/CAM, Fortran, COBOL, BASIC, and various telecommunications protocols, including, most recently, how things on the Internet (e.g., *.com*, *.gov*, and *.org*,) are used.

51. Gerd Meissner, *SAP: Inside the Second Software Power* (New York: McGraw-Hill, 1997): 76–107.

52. Howard Bromberg, "COBOL: Some History, Language Structure, Committees, and Current Status," *Data Processing Proceedings 1964* (New Orleans: DPMA, 1964): 281–292.

53. Kahin and Abbate, *Standards Policy for Information Infrastructure*, 51–53.

54. For a useful, early review, see Robert S. Alsom et al., *Automation in Banking* (New Brunswick, N.J.: Rutgers University Press, 1962); American Bankers Association, *Automation of Bank Operating Procedures* (New York: American Bankers Association, 1955); and on the standardization of checks, the association's *Magnetic Ink Character Recognition* (New York: American Bankers Association, 1956); see also Walter Dietrich, "Optical Handling of Checks," *Datamation* 10, no. 9 (September 1964): 39–46. Recently the role of banking in the use of credit cards was studied by David Evans and Richard Schmalensee, who found extensive use of standards: *Paying with Plastic: The Digital Revolution in Buying and Borrowing* (Cambridge, Mass.: MIT Press, 1999).

55. An important new work on standards is Agatha C. Hughes and Thomas P. Hughes (eds.), *Systems, Experts, and Computers: The Systems Approach in Management and Engineering, World War II and After* (Cambridge, Mass.: MIT Press, 2000). On early attempts to standardize and catalog knowledge and information, see Daniel R. Headrick, *When Information Came of Age: Technologies of Knowledge in the Age of Reason and Revolution, 1700–1850* (New York: Oxford University Press, 2000).

56. Hughes and Hughes, *Systems, Experts, and Computers*.

57. Sichel, *Computer Revolution*, 2–13.

58. James L. McKenney, *Waves of Change: Business Evolution Through Information Technology* (Boston: Harvard Business School Press, 1995).

59. Christina Ford Haylock and Len Muscarella, in *Net Success* (Holbrook, Mass.: Adams Media Corp., 1999): 209–303, review activities in banking, brokerage services, publishing, health care, and travel.

60. The editor of the journal of record for the history of computing, Tim Bergin, at the *IEEE Annals of the History of Computing*—which has always emphasized the role of technology—has made the point that historians have to look at more than widgets: "We need to encourage people outside the strict confines of computing per se, to become contributors. . . . I personally believe that the history of computing is on the verge of a breakthrough in the academy and elsewhere," the reason for asking for articles dealing with applications, organizations, economics, politics, sociology, and public policy, not just mainframes. For Bergin's comments, see *IEEE Annals of the History of Computing* 22, no. 3 (July–September 2000): 3.

61. David F. Noble, *Forces of Production: A Social History of Industrial Automation* (New York: Oxford University Press, 1986): 84–85, 183, 213–214, 219–222, 329–330.

62. This reinforces the well-known phenomenon of S curves in innovations; see Richard N. Foster, *Innovation: The Attacker's Advantage* (New York: Simon & Schuster, 1986): 87–111.

63. Alfred D. Chandler, Jr., *The Visible Hand: The Managerial Revolution in American Business* (Cambridge, Mass.: Harvard University Press, 1977): 490–500; Carroll Pursell, *The Machine in America: A Social History of Technology* (Baltimore, Md.: Johns Hopkins University Press, 1995): 299–319; Richard D. Brown, *Knowledge Is Power: The Diffusion of Information in Early America, 1700–1865* (New York: Oxford University Press, 1989): 270–286.

64. Campbell-Kelly and Aspray, *Computer*, 253–258; James Chposky and Ted Leonsis, *Blue Magic: The People, Power and Politics Behind the IBM Personal Computer* (New York: Facts on File, 1988): 117, 217–219; Paul Freiberger and Michael Swaine, *Fire in the Valley: The Making of the Personal Computer* (New York: McGraw-Hill, 2000): 345–354.

65. Many historians have reached a similar conclusion. I have commented extensively on the transition to the computer in *Computer in the United States*, 12–124.

66. Roddy F. Osborn, "GE and UNIVAC: Harnessing the High-Speed Computer," *Harvard Business Review* 32, no. 4 (July–August 1954): 99–107.

67. I have explored these themes elsewhere: "Framework for Understanding Technological Change," 47–92, and *Computer in the United States,* 125–139.

68. N. L. Mudd to Regional Managers, Branch Managers and Zone Sales Managers in U.S. and Canada, March 15, 1956, Burroughs Papers 90, Box 1, Folder 23.H.3.G, Charles Babbage Institute Archives. These applications briefs are a valuable resource for the study of applications and, like those from IBM, were produced in the same way. In this letter, Mudd describes the process: "Preparation of an installation story involves cooperation between the user, the representative who handles the account or who made the installation, and a writer from the Marketing Publicity Department of the Advertising Division." Also, "most installation stories are written under the by-line of an appropriate official of the company being featured. Every story is intended to nationally publicize the effectiveness of the concerned product, to stimulate inquiries from readers of the magazine." An IBM salesman in the 1970s, I had two accounts written about in exactly the same manner as, Mudd said, occurred at Burroughs in the 1950s.

69. I have looked at this issue in some detail: "Using Textual Demographics to Understand What Computers Were Used For: Insights from US Literature on Computer Applications, 1950–1990," *IEEE Annals of the History of Computing* 23, no. 1 (January–March 2001): 34–56; and "Framework for Understanding Technological Change," 47–92.

70. General Electric, the company that first used digital computing in a commercial setting in the United States, also published a lengthy book for internal use only, cautioning management about computers; at the same time it explained what these machines were capable of doing: *The Next Step in Management: An Appraisal of Cybernetics* (n.p.: GE, December 1952); Paul A. Strassmann, *The Business Value of Computers: An Executive's Guide* (New Canaan, Conn.: Information Economics Press, 1990): 73–96.

71. The best of the application studies, based on the use of computers in several organizations in Europe, is Dirk De Wit, *The Shaping of Automation: A Historical Analysis of the Interaction Between Technology and Organization, 1950–1985* (Verloren: Hilversum, 1994); for British experiences, see David Caminer, John Aris, Peter Hermon, and Frank Land, *LEO: The Incredible Story of the World's First Business Computer* (New York: McGraw-Hill, 1998). Another useful study on European practices is by Margaret Sharp (ed.), *Europe and the New Technologies: Six Case Studies in Innovation and Adjustment* (Ithaca, N.Y.: Cornell University Press, 1986). Studies on Asian practices are fewer. However, there is insight and a bibliography in Robert E. Cole, *Managing Quality Fads: How American Business Learned to Play the Quality Game* (New York: Oxford University Press, 1999). See also Lester, *Productive Edge*, for many comparisons of Asians to Americans, especially Japanese practices.

72. Historians recognize that business and industry practices vary around the world. A clear demonstration of the variations can be gleaned from Alfred D. Chandler, Jr., *Scale and Scope: The Dynamics of Industrial Capitalism* (Cambridge, Mass.: Harvard University Press, 1990), in which he described the role of companies and industries in the United States, Great Britain, and Germany over the past century. Closer to the topic of my book, Professor Lars Heide, of the Centre for Business History, Copenhagen Business School, is studying the use of punched-card systems in Great Britain, France, Germany, and the United States from 1880 to 1945.

Chapter 2

1. David C. Mowery and Nathan Rosenberg, *Paths of Innovation: Technological Change in 20th-Century America* (Cambridge: Cambridge University Press, 1998): 2.

2. Ibid., 3.

3. Ibid., 146.

4. U.S. Department of Commerce, *National Income and Product Accounts of the United States, 1929–1982* (Washington, D.C.: U.S. Government Printing Office, 1986): 254–255.

5. Sherlene K. S. Lum and Brian C. Moyer, "Gross Domestic Product by Industry for 1998–2000," *Current Business* (November 2001): 17–33.

6. For a fuller treatment of the economic conditions essential to the development and exploitation of computing technology in the United States, see James W. Cortada, "Economic Preconditions That Made Possible Application of Commercial Computing in the United States," *Annals of the History of Computing* 19, no. 3 (1997): 27–40.

7. Robert Sobel, *The Great Boom: How a Generation of Americans Created the World's Most Prosperous Society* (New York: St. Martin, 2000): 254–255.

8. For an excellent introduction to labor productivity and how to calculate it, with data on national labor productivity rates during the entire half century under study, see Norman Frumkin, *Tracking America's Economy*, 3rd ed. (Armonk, N.Y.: M. E. Sharpe, 1998): 222–238.

9. For comparative data on productivity in a number of industrialized nations, see ibid., 233–234.

10. William J. Baumol, Sue Anne Blackman, and Edward N. Wolff, *Productivity and American Leadership: The Long View* (Cambridge, Mass.: MIT Press, 1989); see especially ch. 13.

11. Lun and Moyer, "Gross Domestic Product by Industry," 20.

12. Cortada, "Economic Preconditions," 27–40.

13. International Data Corporation, *EDP Industry Report* (Waltham, Mass.: IDC, August 1974): 2.

14. Ulric Weil, *Information Systems in the '80s: Products, Markets, and Vendors* (Upper Saddle River, N.J.: Prentice Hall, 1982): 214.

15. The home PC story is told by Lee S. Sproull, "Computers in U.S. Households Since 1977," in Alfred D. Chandler, Jr., and James W. Cortada (eds.), *A Nation Transformed by Information: How Information Has Shaped the United States from Colonial Times to the Present* (New York: Oxford University Press, 2000): 257–280. It was not until after 2000 that access to the Internet through means other than PCs became possible or attractive.

16. Amy Sue Bix, *Inventing Ourselves Out of Jobs? America's Debate Over Technological Unemployment, 1929–1981* (Baltimore, Md.: Johns Hopkins University Press, 2000): 236–279.

17. Ibid., quotes on 280 and 304.

18. Ibid., 312.

19. Baumol, Blackman, and Wolff, *Productivity and American Leadership*, 29–64. For an equally learned criticism of the computer's contribution to productivity, see Daniel E. Sichel, *The Computer Revolution: An Economic Perspective* (Washington, D.C.: Brookings Institution Press, 1997), especially 77–79.

20. For a nontechnical discussion of the paradox, although critical of computer benefits, see Thomas K. Landauer, *The Trouble with Computers: Usefulness, Usability, and Productivity* (Cambrige, Mass.: MIT Press, 1995): 9–45. The case for American productivity is made by Baumol, Blackman, and Wolff, *Productivity and American Leadership*, especially 9–28.

21. Availability of data also influenced economic studies. Economists always had good and plentiful data on manufacturing productivity but far less for service industries, largely because of measurement problems. These imbalances in the availability of data affected the ability of economists to study, for example, the effects of IT on the economy. For a discussion of the problem, see John Haltiwanger and Ron S. Jarmin, "Measuring the Digital Economy," in Erik Brynjolfsson and Brian Kahin (eds.), *Understanding the Digital Economy: Data, Tools, and Research* (Cambridge, Mass.: MIT Press, 2000): 13–33. This book has several other chapters of related interest, especially 34–95.

22. The data and material for the next paragraph are drawn from Michael van Biema and Bruce Greenwald, "Managing Our Way to Higher Service-Sector Productivity," *Harvard Business Review* 75, no. 4 (July/August 1997): 87–95.

23. The most vociferous critic in recent years was an ex-Xerox executive and experienced CIO, Paul A. Strassmann, who argues that "there is no relationship between expenses for computers and business profitability"; the costs of computers and the people needed to run them are not tied to management performance, let alone to the profitability of the firm: *The Business Value of Computers: An Executive's Guide* (New Canaan, Conn.: Information Economics Press, 1990): xvii.

24. Ibid.

25. Sanjeev Dewan and Chung-ki Min, "The Substitution of Information Technology for Other Factors of Production: A Firm Level Analysis," *Management Science* 43, no. 12 (December 1997): 1660–1675.

26. For an introduction to these studies, see U.S. Bureau of Labor Statistics, *BLS Publications on Productivity and Technology*, Report No. 741 (Washington, D.C.: U.S. Government Printing Office, 1987 and subsequent editions).

27. Frost & Sullivan, Inc., "The Factory Automation Systems Market," March 1972; Market Research, CBI 55, Box 3, Folder 35, Charles Babbage Institute Archives, University of Minnesota.

28. See note 17 for an example.

29. Sanjeev Dewan and Kenneth L. Kraemer, "Information Technology and Productivity: Evidence from Country-Level Data," *Management Science*, 46, no. 4 (April 2000): 548–562; quotes on 550 and 560. They include an excellent bibliography of the productivity paradox in the economic literature. In addition, Michael D. Smith, Joseph Bailey, and Eric Brynjolfsson, "Understanding Digital Markets: Review and Assessment," in Brynjolfsson and Kahin, *Understanding the Digital Economy*, 99–136.

30. Thomas H. Davenport, *Process Innovation: Reengineering Work Through Information Technology* (Boston: Harvard Business School Press, 1993): 46.

31. On the manufacturing industry, see ibid., 41–42; on the insurance industry, see Roslyn L. Feldberg and Evelyn Nakano Glenn, "Technology and the Transformation of Clerical Work," in Robert E. Kraut (ed.), *Technology and the Transformation of White-Collar Work* (Hillsdale, N.J.: Lawrence Erlbaum, 1987): 77–97.

32. JoAnne Yates, *Control Through Communication: The Rise of System in American Management* (Baltimore, Md.: Johns Hopkins University Press, 1989).

33. Davenport, *Process Innovation*, 50–66.

34. Thomas Haigh, "Inventing Information Systems: The Systems Men and the Computer, 1950–1968," *Business History Review* 75, no. 1 (Spring 2001): 15–61.

35. Bix, *Inventing Ourselves Out of Jobs?* 236–279.

36. Coverage by the national press included, for example, *Newsweek* (February 18, 1946): 76; *Scientific American* (June 1946): 248; *Time* (February 25, 1946): 90; *Business Week*, (February 16, 1946): 50.

37. William Aspray and Donald deB. Beaver, "Marketing the Monster: Advertising Computer Technology," *Annals of the History of Computing* 8, no. 2 (April 1986): 127–143.

38. Cortada, "Using Textual Demographics," 34–36.

39. I have collected citations on some 10,000 titles in three bibliographies: James W. Cortada, *A Bibliographic Guide to the History of Computing, Computers, and the Information Processing Industry* (Westport, Conn.: Greenwood Press, 1990); *Second Bibliographic Guide to the History of Computing, Computers, and the Information Processing Industry* (Westport, Conn.: Greenwood Press, 1996); *A Bibliographic Guide to the History of Computer Applications, 1950–1990* (Westport, Conn.: Greenwood Press, 1996).

40. Cortada, "Using Textual Demographics."

41. Conversation with Rachel McCloud of Barnes and Noble, March 31, 1998.

42. During the Clinton administration, government agencies began a variety of initiatives to measure the amount of activity related to the Internet in the American economy. Many of their reports can be found on their web sites. Particularly fruitful are the many studies conducted by the Bureau of the Census, Bureau of Labor Statistics, Department of Commerce, and Department of Labor. Private foundations did the same, such as the Pew, which launched a major study program called the Pew Internet and American Life Project.

43. Sharon M. McKinnon and William J. Burns, Jr., *The Information Mosaic: How Managers Get the Information They Really Need* (Boston: Harvard Business School Press, 1992): 161–191.

44. Walter Mossberg at the *Wall Street Journal* is a good example but clearly not the only one; there are dozens in the United States, mainly with West Coast newspapers.

45. Cortada, *Computer in the United States*, 122.

46. Paul N. Edwards, *The Closed World: Computers and the Politics of Discourse in Cold War America* (Cambridge, Mass.: MIT Press, 1996): 303–351. The Charles Babbage Institute's web site has an important list of movies related to computers, organized by theme.

47. General Electric was a good example before it attempted to participate in the computer business: Homer R. Oldfield, *King of the Seven Dwarfs: General Electric's Ambiguous Challenge to the Computer Industry* (Los Alamitos, Calif.: IEEE Computer Society Press, 1996): 9–19; William J. Jones, "MGIPS and DSDPS—Two Stages of an Early Operating System," *Annals of the History of Computing* 11, no. 2 (1989): 99–108.

48. This is the key finding of Richard Nolan in his study of the influence of computing on business practices, presented by Nolan in Chandler and Cortada, *A Nation Transformed*, 217–256.

49. Haigh, "Inventing Information Systems," 15–61.

50. In fact, they had their own journal to describe this role on a continuous basis, subscribed to by over 130,000 individuals: *Beyond Computing: The Magazine for Business and Technology Executives* (1991–2000).

51. Richard F. Neuschel, *Streamlining Business Procedures* (New York: McGraw-Hill, 1950), 53.

52. There is a history of this important organization: Snja Lee Anderson, "The Data Processing Management Association: A Vital Force in the Development of Data Processing Management and Professionalism," Ph.D. dissertation, Claremont Graduate University, Claremont, Calif., 1987.

53. For an early description of the concept, see Alan D. Meacham and Van B. Thompson (eds.), *Total Systems* (Detroit: American Data Processing, 1962).

54. How things were sold awaits its historian, but their arguments have been documented. I was an IBM salesperson in the 1970s and during that period wrote a book that, in hindsight, reflects many of the arguments used by sales personnel in the 1960s–1980s: *EDP Costs and Charges: Finance, Budgets, and Cost Control in Data Processing* (Englewood Cliffs, N.J.: Prentice-Hall, 1980), especially 257–268. I continued this discussion in *Managing DP Hardware: Capacity Planning, Cost Justification, Availability, and Energy Management* (Englewood Cliffs, N.J.: Prentice-Hall, 1983).

55. This process has not been properly described. For a hint of how some of this worked, see Jonathan Littman, *Once Upon a Time in ComputerLand: The Amazing, Billion Dollar Tale of Bill Millard* (Tuscon, Ariz.: Knight-Rider Press, 1987), which gives insight into activities from the 1980s.

56. Ibid.

57. Charles H. Fergusson and Charles R. Morris, *Computer Wars: How the West Can Win in a Post-IBM World* (New York: Times Books, 1995): 115–126, 159–169.

58. John Micklethwait and Adrian Wooldridge, *The Witch Doctors: Making Sense of the Management Gurus* (New York: Times Books, 1996): 44–45, 52, 115, 210; James O'Shea and Charles Madigan, *Dangerous Company: The Consulting Powerhouses and the Businesses They Save and Ruin* (New York: Times Books, 1997): 73–108. In the early 1990s, IBM created a consulting organization called the IBM Consulting Group and, over the next several years, during the mid-1990s, consolidated all its services organizations and offerings into a larger entity called IBM Global Services. By the end of 2001, this arm of IBM was generating 50 percent of the company's revenues.

59. IBM, *Annual Report, 1999* (Armonk, N.Y.: IBM Corp., 2000); *Annual Report, 2000* (Armonk, N.Y.: IBM Corp., 2001).

60. That is why every major provider of information technology created a consulting arm, such as Hewlett-Packard, IBM, Sun, Lotus, and Microsoft, to mention only a few but obvious examples, especially by the mid-1990s. See note 78 for two books on the general consulting environment of the 1970s–1990s.

61. Edward Steinmueller, "The U.S. Software Industry: An Analysis and Interpretive History," in David C. Mowery (ed.), *The International Computer Software Industry: A Comparative Study of Industry Evolution and Structure* (New York: Oxford University Press, 1996): 15–52.

62. Michael A. Cusumano and Richard W. Selby, *Microsoft Secrets: How the World's Most Powerful Software Company Creates Technology, Shapes Markets, and Manages People* (New York: Free Press, 1995) 135–136; Stan J. Liebowitz and Stephen E. Margolis, *Winners, Losers and Microsoft: Competition and Antitrust in High Technology* (Oakland, Calif.: The Independent Institute, 1999): 180–192.

63. Chandler and Cortada, *A Nation Transformed,* 177–280.

64. This was frequently an issue with early commercial computers in the 1950s when vendors had yet to figure out how best to communicate information about them, what markets to reach, and how best to sell to them.

65. A bad product will get a great deal of negative publicity fast. That is what happened, for example, in the early 1980s to IBM's PC Jr., a machine that was not compatible with other PCs and had a tiny keyboard (called the Chiclet keyboard by one reviewer). In 2000, Windows 2000 received enough negative reviews to keep its introduction a minor event when compared to the introduction and acceptance of either Windows 95 or Windows 98. On the famous case of the PC Jr., see Ferguson and Morris, *Computer Wars,* 53–54. Since market share for Windows played a role in the U.S. government's antitrust suit against Microsoft in the late 1990s, reports from the trial document the role of marketing and communications well, see Joel Brinkley and Steve Lohr, *U.S. v. Microsoft* (New York: McGraw-Hill, 2000). The book is a compilation of their newspaper reports published in the *New York Times* between October 1998 and June 2000.

66. The literature is vast. Some recent examples include Detlev J. Hoch, Cyriac R. Roeding, Gert Purkert, and Sandro L. Lindner, *Secrets of Software Success: Management Insights from 100 Software Firms Around the World* (Boston: Harvard Business School Press, 2000); David Giber, Louis Carter, and Marshall Goldsmith (eds.), *Best Practices in Leadership Development Handbook: Case Studies, Instruments, Training* (San Francisco: Jossey-Bass, 2000); James W. Cortada, *Best Practices in Information Technology: How Corporations Get the Most Value from Exploiting Their Digital Investments* (Upper Saddle River, N.J.: Prentice Hall, 1998); James M. Utterback, *Mastering the Dynamics of Innovation: How Companies Can Seize Opportunities in the Face of Technological Change* (Boston, Mass.: Harvard Business School Press, 1994); David C. Mowery and Richard R. Nelson (eds.), *Sources of Industrial Leadership: Studies of Seven Industries* (Cambridge: Cambridge University Press, 1999).

67. Robert W. Seidel. "Crunching Numbers: Computers in the AEC Laboratories," *History and Technology* 15 (1998): 36–68; "Secret Scientific Communities: Classification and Scientific

Communication in the DOE and DoD," in Mary Ellen Bowden, Trudi Bellardo Hahn, and Robert V. Williams (eds.), Proceedings of the Second Conference on the History and Heritage of Scientific Information Systems (Medford, N.J.: Information Today, Inc., 1999).

68. The central theme of H. Thomas Johnson and Robert S. Kaplan, *Relevance Lost: The Rise and Fall of Management Accounting* (Boston: Harvard Business School Press, 1987): 1.

69. Thomas G. Gunn, *Computer Applications in Manufacturing* (New York: Industrial Press, 1981): vii.

70. J. C. Herz, *Joystick Nation: How Videogames Ate Our Quarters, Won Our Hearts, and Rewired Our Minds* (Boston: Little, Brown, 1997): 13–31. See also Van Burnham, *Supercade: A Visual History of the Videogame Age, 1971–1984* (Cambridge, Mass.: MIT Press, 2001).

71. Fred Moody, *The Visionary Position: The Inside Story of the Digital Dreamers Who Are Making Virtual Reality a Reality* (New York: Times Business, 1999), has a collection of case studies; Steven Poole, *Trigger Happy: Videogames and the Entertainment Revolution* (New York: Arcade Publishing, 2000).

72. H. Schantz, *The History of OCR* (Manchester Center, Vt.: Recognition Technologies Users Association, 1982), looks at applications through the technology and functionality of OCR.

73. For a collection of articles about illustrative applications viewed through the technology and functionality of imaging, see M. M. Trivedi (ed.), *Selected Reprints on Digital Image Processing* (Bellingham, Wash.: Optical Engineering Press, 1990).

74. Two excellent histories, both recent, are emblematic of this trend: Ceruzzi, *History of Modern Computing*, and William Aspray and Martin Campbell-Kelly, *Computer: A History of the Information Machine* (New York: Basic Books, 1996).

75. A finding from an earlier study: James W. Cortada, "Commercial Applications of the Digital Computer in American Corporations, 1945–1995," *Annals of the History of Computing* 18, no. 2 (1996): 18–29.

76. I have recently begun to look at the role of computers in the private lives of Americans by examining how they used computers for such activities as religious and political practices, learning, and vacationing: *Making of the Information Society: Experience, Consequences, and Possibilities* (Upper Saddle River, N.J.: Prentice Hall/Financial Times, 2002).

77. The literature that measures how many is vast. I have collected thousands of titles related to the topic in *A Bibliographic Guide to the History of Computing, Computers, and the Information Processing Industry* (Westport, Conn.: Greenwood Press, 1990), and *A Second Guide to the History of Computing, Computers, and the Information Processing Industry* (Westport, Conn.: Greenwood Press, 1996). The largest collection of materials useful for the study of "how many" is at the Charles Babbage Institute at the University of Minnesota in Minneapolis.

78. The data for this and the next paragraph are drawn from Sichel, *Computer Revolution*, scattered across the entire short book. His data are drawn from various U.S. government studies and data series, the same information sources other economists routinely use.

79. Ibid., 44–46.

80. Ibid., 47.

81. Ibid., 51.

82. The data in this paragraph and the basis for my discussion about deployment is Chandler and Cortada, *Nation Transformed*, 209–213.

83. Ibid., 68.

84. U.S. Department of Commerce, *Digital Economy 2000* (Washington, D.C.: U.S. Government Pritning Office, June 2000), is one of the more recent reports; however, see also U.S. Department of Commerce, *The Emerging Digital Economy II* (Washington, D.C.: U.S. Government Printing Office, June 1999).

85. Lars Nabseth and George F. Ray (eds.), *The Diffusion of New Industrial Processes: An International Study* (Cambridge: Cambridge University Press, 1974): 8.

86. Ibid., 9–10.

87. Recent examples include William F. Sharpe, *The Economics of Computers* (New York: Columbia University Press, 1969); Gerald W. Brock, *The U.S. Computer Industry: A Study of Market Power* (Cambridge, Mass.: Ballinger, 1975); Franklin M. Fisher, James W. McKie, and Richard B. Mancke, *IBM and the U.S. Data Processing Industry: An Economic History* (New York: Praeger, 1983); Paulo Bastos Tigre, *Technology and Competition in the Brazilian Computer Industry* (New York: St. Martin, 1983); Franco Malerba, *The Semiconductor Business: The Economics of Rapid Growth and Decline* (Madison: University of Wisconsin Press, 1985); Robert T. Fertig, *The Software Revolution: Trends, Players, Market Dynamics in Personal Computer Software* (New York: North-Holland, 1985); Stephen E. Siwek and Harold W. Furchtgott-Roth, *International Trade in Computer Software* (Westport, Conn.: Quorum Books, 1993); Jeff X. Zhang and Yan Wang, *The Emerging Market of China's Computer Industry* (Westport, Conn.: Quorum Books, 1993); David C. Mowery (ed.), *The International Computer Software Industry: A Comparative Study of Industry Evolution and Structure* (New York: Oxford University Press, 1996); and Jason Dedrick and Kenneth L. Kraemer, *Asia's Computer Challenge: Threat or Opportunity for the United States and the World?* (New York: Oxford University Press, 1998).

88. Landauer, *Trouble with Computers*, 1–77; Donald A. Norman, *The Invisible Computer: Why Good Products Can Fail, the Personal Computer Is So Complex, and Information Appliances Are the Solution* (Cambridge, Mass.: MIT Press, 1998): 69–87.

89. Scherer, *New Perspectives on Economic Growth*, 89–118, 120.

90. Peter Freeman and William Aspray, *The Supply of Information Technology Workers in the United States* (Washington, D.C.: Computing Research Association, 1999): 130, 137.

91. A few examples are Lester, *Productive Edge*, 213–243, 284–307; Shapiro, *Control Revolution*, 13–33; Michael Dertouzos, *What Will Be: How the New World of Information Will Change Our Lives* (New York: HarperEdge, 1997): 207–209, passim; Peter J. Denning and Robert Metcalfe (eds.), *Beyond Calculation: The Next Fifty Years of Computing* (New York: Copernicus, 1997); Peter F. Drucker, *Management Challenges for the 21st Century* (New York: HarperBusiness, 1999): 123–132, 149–154; Michael Useem, "Corporate Education and Training," in Carl Kaysen (ed.), *The American Corporation Today: Examining the Questions of Power and Efficiency at the Century's End* (New York: Oxford University Press, 1996): 292–326; Peter Cappelli et al, *Change at Work* (New York: Oxford University Press, 1997): 122–172.

92. Lawrence F. Katz, "Technological Change, Computerization, and the Wage Structure," in Brynjolfsson and Kahin, *Understanding the Digital Economy*, 218–244.

93. Rates of adoption can be measured by how fast a percentage of an industry (number of firms) acquires a technology when compared either to what was occurring simultaneously in other industries or to the number of adoptions in different decades or years within a particular industry.

94. A number of other factors will cause users to hesitate in acquiring new applications and software. The lack of software compatibility is perhaps the most obvious, the one that most influenced, for example, IBM's design of the S/360 family of computers in the early 1960s. Fear that there might not be sufficient technical support for a particular product or application has the same effect. A third consideration is the risk of failure. The bigger the project, the greater the risk of ruining one's career. It is one thing to have purchased the wrong $10,000's worth PCs, quite another to have mismanaged the implementation of a $10 million ERP project.

95. Michael E. Porter, *Competitive Strategy: Techniques for Analyzing Industries and Competitors* (New York: Free Press, 1980): 3–33; *Competitive Advantage: Creating and Sustaining Superior Performance* (New York: Free Press, 1985): 4–10.

96. Michael E. Porter, *The Competitive Advantage of Nations* (New York: Free Press, 1990); see also James F. Moore, *The Death of Competition: Leadership and Strategy in the Age of Business*

Ecosystems (New York: HarperBusiness, 1996); Alfred D. Chandler, Jr., *Scale and Scope: The Dynamics of Industrial Capitalism* (Cambridge, Mass.: Harvard University Press, 1990): 14–46.

97. An early statement of the issue came from James Brian Quinn, *Intelligent Enterprise: A Knowledge and Service Based Paradigm for Industry* (New York: Free Press, 1992); for a knowledgeable management perspective, the most influential study was done by Thomas H. Davenport and Laurence Prusak, *Working Knowledge* (Boston: Harvard Business School Press, 1998).

Chapter 3

1. The debate is nicely summarized by Frank Webster, *Theories of the Information Society* (London: Routledge, 1995): 6–29, but see also Daniel Bell, *The Coming of Post-Industrial Society: A Venture in Social Forecasting* (New York: Basic Books, 1973).

2. Jiemin Guo and Mark A. Planting, "Using Input-Output Analysis to Measure U.S. Economic Structural Changes Over a 24-Year Period," paper presented at the 13th International Conference on Input-Output Techniques, August 21–25, 2000. The paper covers 1972–1996 and is available from the U.S. Department of Commerce and its web site.

3. For an analysis of Anthony Giddens, see ibid, 52–73. The key work by Giddens is *Social Theory and Modern Sociology* (Cambridge: Polity, 1987); but see also his book *The Consequences of Modernity* (Cambridge: Polity, 1990).

4. Specifically, Manuel Castells, *The Informational City* (Oxford: Blackwell, 1989), and his three-volume work, *The Information Age: Economy, Society and Culture* (Oxford: Blackwell, 1996–1998); see also his book *The Internet Galaxy: Reflections on the Internet, Business, and Society* (Oxford: Oxford University Press, 2001).

5. Vincent DePaul Goubeau, "Toward a Unified Industrial Process," in *Toward the Factory of the Future* (New York: American Management Association, 1957): 77; epigraph or this chapter on 78.

6. Steven L. Goldman, Rogerr N. Nagel, and Kenneth Preiss, *Agile Competitors and Virtual Organizations: Strategies for Enriching the Customer* (New York: Van Nostrand Reinhold, 1995): 3.

7. Goubeau, "Toward a Unified Industrial Process," 77.

8. The U.S. government recently revised its statistics on software sales for the United States: 1982, $15.4 billion; 1987, $31.4 billion; 1992, $60.8 billion; 1996, $95.1 billion; 1997, $106.6 billion; 1998, $123.4 billion. Eugene P. Seskin, "Improved Estimates of the National Income and Product Accounts for 1959–98: Results of the Comprehensive Revision," *Survey of Current Business* (December 1999): 15–29, 21.

9. The data for this and the next several paragraphs are drawn from Carl Kaysen, "Introduction and Overview," in Carl Kaysen (ed.), *The American Corporation Today* (New York: Oxford University Press, 1996): 3–27; Guo and Planting, "Using Input-Output Analysis," 5–6, 11–14.

10. Anthony Sampson, *Company Man: The Rise and Fall of Corporate Life* (New York: Times Books, 1995): 137–167.

11. Ibid., 25–26.

12. Conveniently summarized by Peter Cappelli et al, *Change at Work*, especially 15–65.

13. Michael E. Porter, *Competitive Strategy: Techniques for Analyzing Industries and Competitors* (New York: Free Press, 1980): 217; and on how industries evolve, 156–190 where he argues the case for viewing industries through structural analysis of the "driving forces that are at the root of industry change," for example, product life cycles and changes in customers.

14. This case has been well studied by Theresa F. Rogers and Nathalie S. Friedman, *Printers*

Face Automation: The Impact of Technology on Work and Retirement Among Skilled Craftsmen (Lexington, Mass.: Lexington Books, 1980).

15. Jeremy Rifkin, *The End of Work: The Decline of the Global Labor Force and the Dawn of the Post-Market Era* (New York: Putnam, 1995), 6–8, 11, in which he blames computers for the loss of jobs: "The introduction of more sophisticated technologies, with the accompanying gains in productivity, means that the global economy can produce more and more goods and services employing an ever smaller percentage of the available workforce."

16. F. M. Scherer, *New Perspectives on Economic Growth and Technological Innovation* (Washington, D.C.: Brookings Institution Press, 1999): 89–118; Peter Freeman and William Aspray, *The Supply of Information Technology Workers in the United States* (Washington, D.C.: Computing Research Association, 1999).

17. Montgomery Phister, Jr., *Data Processing Technology and Economics* (Santa Monica, Calif.: Santa Monica Publishing, 1974): 318–328.

18. Montgomery Phister, Jr., *Data Processing Technology and Economics: 1975–1978 Supplement* (Santa Monica, Calif.: Santa Monica Publishing, 1979): 536–537.

19. Freeman and Aspray, *Supply of Information Technology Workers*, 35–36.

20. James W. Cortada, *Before the Computer: IBM, NCR, Burroughs, and Remington Rand and the Industry They Created, 1865–1956* (Princeton, N.J.: Princeton University Press, 1993): 18, 130, 269–270.

21. Quality management practices, although originating in the United States in the 1940s and early 1950s, were most embraced by Japanese industry and slowly repatriated and adopted by American manufacturing firms in the 1980s: Robert E. Cole, *Managing Quality Fads: How American Business Learned to Play the Quality Game* (New York: Oxford University Press, 1999): 3–17.

22. Cappelli et al., *Change at Work*, 134–138.

23. Ibid., 142–143.

24. The basis for these comments—microstudies—is the hundreds of application briefs written by IBM and Burroughs in support of their sales efforts. Large collections of these documents have been preserved and are the basis of much of this book. The IBM materials are located at the IBM Archives in Somers, New York. The Burroughs materials are at the Charles Babbage Institute, University of Minnesota, Minneapolis. Both collections have online search guides to facilitate access.

25. Anthony P. Carnevale and Donna Desrochers, "Training in the Old Economy," *Training and Development* (December 1999); reprinted in John A. Woods and James W. Cortada (eds.), *The 2001 ASTD Training and Performance Yearbook* (New York: McGraw-Hill, 2001): 72–82.

26. BLS, "BLS Reports on the Amount of Formal and Informal Training Received by Employees," Press Release USDL 96-515 (December 1996).

27. Official Notice, U.S. Census Bureau, "New Sectors in NAICS" (undated, circa 1998): 1–6, http://www.census.gov/epcd/www/naicsect.htm/.

28. For a full explanation of technological style, and from which most of the discussion over the next several paragraphs is drawn, see Andrew Tylecote, *The Long Wave in the World Economy: The Current Crisis in Historical Perspective* (London: Routledge, 1991): 36–60.

29. Ibid., 37.

30. B. Joseph Pine II, *Mass Customization: The New Frontier in Business Competition* (Boston: Harvard Business School Press, 1993): 9–32.

31. Alfred D. Chandler, Jr., *The Visible Hand: The Managerial Revolution in American Business* (Cambridge, Mass.: Harvard University Press, 1977): 240–284, 484–497.

32. Tylecote, *Long Wave in the World Economy*, 54–56, quote on 55.

33. Well described by David A. Hounshell, *From the American System to Mass Production, 1800–1932* (Baltimore, Md.: Johns Hopkins University Press, 1984): 15–65.

34. The need for control of business operations dates back to the origination of the modern

corporation and was the original impetus for the development of a variety of information-handling devices (e.g., adding machines, calculators, and billing equipment): James R. Beniger, *The Control Revolution: Technological and Economic Origins of the Information Society* (Cambridge, Mass.: Harvard University Press, 1986): 6–27.

35. The most important account of automation in the precomputer era was written by John Diebold, *Automation: The Advent of the Automatic Factory* (New York: Van Nostrand, 1952), published before wide use of computing in manufacturing industries. It is full of examples of automations without a computer. See also the cases of noncomputerized automation collected by *Scientific American* in the 1940s and very early 1950s: *Automatic Control* (New York: Simon & Schuster, 1955).

36. IBM, *Applications and Abstracts, 1985* (White Plains, N.Y.: IBM Corp., 1985, a variation of annual editions published since 1980): 13–1.

37. For a bibliography of this literature, see James W. Cortada, *A Bibliographic Guide to the History of Computer Applications, 1950–1990* (Westport, Conn.: Greenwood Press, 1996): 27–40, 57, 68.

38. That feature remains true today. For example, in the late 1990s IBM began implementing ERP systems in its various manufacturing operations around the world. In fact it had 21 such projects underway, all started at different times and completed to various degrees.

39. *Newsletter 1977*, Oliver Wight, Inc., 1.

40. Jeffrey G. Miller and Linda G. Sprague, "Behind the Growth in Materials Requirements Planning," *Harvard Business Review* 53, no. 5 (September–October 1975): 85.

41. IBM, *Applications and Abstracts*, 13/1–13/32.

42. Thomas E. Vollmann, William L. Berry, and D. Clay Whybark, *Manufacturing Planning and Control Systems* (Homewood, Ill.: Irwin, 1988): xi.

43. Sam G. Taylor and Steven F. Bolander, "Process Flow Scheduling: Past, Present, and Future," white paper published by APICS on its web site, August 30, 2000: http://www.apics.org/sigs/articles/process.htm.

44. JoAnne Yates, *Control Through Communication: The Rise of System in American Management* (Baltimore, Md.: Johns Hopkins University Press, 1989), is the classic study, but see her more recent comments, "Business Use of Information and Technology During the Industrial Age," in Alfred D. Chandler, Jr., and James W. Cortada (eds.), *A Nation Transformed by Information: How Information Has Shaped the United States from Colonial Times to the Present* (New York: Oxford University Press, 2000): 107–135; and Cortada, *Before the Computer*, 49–52, 128–136.

45. James W. Cortada, *Making the Information Society: Experience, Consequences, and Possibilities* (Upper Saddle River, N.J.: Financial Times/Prentice Hall, 2002): 139–145, 170–174.

46. Frost & Sullivan, "The Factory Automation Systems Market" (New York: Frost & Sullivan, 1972): 23; report in "Market Research" 55, Box 3, Folder 35, Archives of the Charles Babbage Institute, University of Minnesota, Minneapolis.

47. Ibid., 29.

48. Ibid., 36.

49. The literature is vast. However, for a thoughtful, modern view, Marco Iansiti explains the nature of the choices one must make in *Technology Integration: Making Critical Choices in a Dynamic World* (Boston: Harvard Business School Press, 1998): 121–147; the classic description of how companies innovate remains Richard Foster's, *Innovation: The Attacker's Advantage* (New York; Summit Books, 1986); but the compelling case for how and when to change is best made by George Stalk, Jr., and Thomas M. Hout, *Competing Against Time: How Time-Based Competition Is Reshaping Global Markets* (New York: Free Press, 1990).

50. Neil Rackham, *SPIN Selling* (New York: McGraw-Hill, 1988): 11.

51. Ibid., 61–65. During the 1960s–1980s, a commonly stated quip, usually told in a humorous fashion, held that "nobody ever got fired for making an IBM decision," meaning that there was less risk in selecting products from this firm than from others, even those who might have had less expensive goods or better products. The quip was always about the role of risk in decision making.

52. Charles H. Kepner and Benjamin B. Tregoe, *The Rational Manager: A Systematic Approach to Problem Solving and Decision Making* (Princeton, N.J.: Kepner-Tregoe, 1965): 173–228. Both this book and Rackham's were widely read by the IT communities of the 1960s–1970s, and the latter in the 1980s–1990s.

Chapter 4

1. A Ford vice president described many of the activities undertaken by his company in automation and computing: Malcolm L. Denis, "Automation and Employment: A Management Viewpoint," *The Annals of the American Academy of Political and Social Science* 340 (March 1962): 90–99.

2. Anderson Ashburn, "Detroit Automation," *The Annals of the American Academy of Political and Social Science* 340 (March 1962): 21–28; see J. J. Childs, *Principles of Numerical Control* (New York: Industrial Press, 1965), for an overview of the situation; Herbert E. Klein, "Numerical Control: From Glass to Mass Market," *Dun's Review* 85 (August 1965): 34–35, 63–66. This last citation provides examples of cost justification of N/C applications.

3. *Proceedings of the Department of Defense/Industry Symposium*, Davenport, Iowa, October 1969 (Washington, D.C.: U.S. Government Printing Office, 1969): 234.

4. Craig Littler, "A History of 'New' Technology," in Graham Winch (ed.), *Information Technology in Manufacturing Processes: Case Studies in Technological Change* (London: Rossendale, 1983): 136.

5. Arthur C. Ansley, *Manufacturing Methods and Processes* (Philadelphia: Chilton Company, 1957): 539, quotes on 538.

6. Ibid., 540. The Ford Motor Company, for instance, used an IBM 705 system to track parts to make sure factories had what they needed on time. For details of this application see "Pre-Production Control," report attached to an R. Hunt Brown letter to subscribers, January 1958, *Office Automation Handbook*, III A19: 1–4; CBI 55, "Market Reports," Box 70, Folder 4, Charles Babbage Institute, University of Minnesota, Minneapolis.

7. In 159 cases; see Lester Bittel et al., *Practical Automation: Methods for Increasing Plan Productivity* (New York: McGraw-Hill, 1957); Ernest Paul De Garmo, *Materials and Processes in Manufacturing* (New York: Macmillan, 1957); case study by H. Ford Dickie, "Integrating Systems Planning at G.E.," in Donald G. Malcolm et al. (eds.), *Symposium on Management Information and Control Systems*, Santa Monica, Calif., 1959 (New York: Wiley, 1960): 137–156; Vincent T. Donnelly, "Electromechanical Production Control," *Journal of Accountancy* 109 (April 1960): 66–69; B. M. Gordon, "Adapting Digital Techniques for Automatic Controls," *Electrical Manufacturing* 44 (November 1954): 136ff, 322, and (December 1954): 130ff, 198ff; "Job Shops Can Schedule Production by Computers," *Business Week* (May 7, 1956): 188ff; R. J. Sisson, "Files in a Production Control System," *Journal of Industrial Engineering* 9, no. 6 (November–December 1958): 491–497; for MRP at Carrier Air Conditioning, see "Materials Requirements and Shop Scheduling," report attached to letter by W. C. Rockwell to subscribers, December 1962, *Office Automation Handbook* III A2: 1–8, Charles Babbage Institute, University of Minnesota, Minneapolis.

8. Frank K. Shallenberger, "Economics of Plant Automation," in Eugene M. Grabbe (ed.), *Automation in Business and Industry* (New York: Wiley, 1957).

9. Most of these activities were best documented in the 1960s, after manufacturing firms

had a half dozen or more years of experience with this class of applications. For bibliography on this subject, see James W. Cortada, *A Bibliographic Guide to the History of Computer Applications* (Westport, Conn.: Greenwood Press, 1996): 59–72.

10. James R. Bright, "Progress and Payoff in Industrial Automation," *Dun's Review* (January 19, 1960): 44–49.

11. Ibid., 49.

12. Companies were not shy about describing their version of inventory control. See, for example, Herbert J. Abelman, "Inventory Management at Morton's Shoes," *Data Processing Proceedings 1965* (Dallas: DPMA, 1966): 352–356; at Raytheon, see E. G. Brooks and R. E. Doherty, "Inventory Control by Positive Relief and Data Processing: A Case Study," *APICS Quarterly Bulletin* 5, no. 4 (October 1964): 91–97; at General Dynamics, see Charles H. Buse, "A Multi-Deck Punched Card System to Control Materials Inventory," *N.A.A. Bulletin* 39 (October 1957): 71–77; at Corning Glass Works, see Norman R. Markle, "The Relationship Between the Computer and Inventory Management," *APICS Quarterly Bulletin* 6, no. 2 (April 1965): 47–52; at Burroughs, see Richard McClain, "Fully Computerized Control in a Large Company," 181–201, and on Westinghouse Electric Company's application, see George H. McDonough, "Inventory Management, Top to Bottom," 13–19, both in *APICS Annual Conference: Proceedings of the 1965 National Technical Conference* (Chicago: APICS, 1965); at Honeywell's Micro Switch Division, see R. E. Ray, "Inventory Management Through an Integrated System," *Data Processing Proceedings 1965* (Dallas, Tex.: DPMA, 1966): 229–242; and for a survey of 500 American corporations who were early users of computers in inventory management, see T. M. Whitin, "Report on an Inventory Management Survey," *Production and Inventory Management* 7, no. 1 (January 1966): 27–32.

13. The example cited by many students of applications is the American Airlines passenger reservation system, called SABRE. For an excellent description and history of this application, see James L. McKenney, *Waves of Change: Business Evolution Through Information Technology* (Boston: Harvard Business School Press, 1995): 97–140. He includes a detailed bibliography on SABRE, pp. 139–140.

14. Some of the largest inventory control applications created in the twentieth century emerged out of the need of the U.S. military to manage quantities of materiel that were massive in volume and logistically complex by civilian standards. For a sense of the early work done by the U.S. military with this application, see J. C. Busby, "New Developments in Production Planning and Inventory Control," *APICS Annual Conferences: Proceedings of the 1964 National Technical Conference* (Chicago: APICS, 1965): 74–87; "Electronics to Streamline Air Force Logistics," *Aviation Week* 61 (August 16, 1954): 154ff; H. S. Middough, "Inventory Control at Naval Supply Center, Oakland," in Charles H. Johnson (ed.), *Data Processing: 1960 Proceedings* (Mt. Prospect, Ill.: National Machine Accountants Association, 1960): 84–97.

15. *The Economics of Automated Warehousing* (Lancaster, Pa.: Control Flow Systems, 1970); all the main texts of the period discussed these economic issues, for example, J. Buchan, *Scientific Inventory Management* (Englewood Cliffs, N.J.: Prentice-Hall, 1963); C. Holt, F. Modigliani, J. Muth, and Herbert Simon, *Planning Production, Inventories, and Work Force* (Englewood Cliffs, N.J.: Prentice-Hall, 1960); J. F. Magee, *Production Planning and Inventory Control* (New York: McGraw-Hill, 1958); National Industrial Conference Board, *Inventory Management in Industry*, Studies in Business Policy no. 88 (New York: National Industrial Conference Board, 1958); Thomas E. Vollmann, William L. Berry, and D. Clay Whybark, *Manufacturing Planning and Control Systems* (Homewood, Ill: Irwin, 1988), which also includes a useful bibliography, p. 747. In the 1980s and 1990s, additional improvements in cost productivity were achieved by such techniques as having suppliers hold title and possession of inventory until needed or requiring delivery as close to the time needed to build a product or satisfy a customer's order. Both approaches required reducing the time a firm kept any inventory. To a large extent, Wal-Mart (a retailer) became the example par excellence

of this strategy, which could not be implemented without using computers and telecommunications.

16. "The Training Materials Still Exist," Series V, Typical EDP Applications, Sales Training—Data Processing Group (undated, circa 1960s), Burroughs Papers CBI 90, "Salesmen's Literature," Box 2, Folder 25, Archives of the Charles Babbage Institute, University of Minnesota, Minneapolis.

17. "IBM Data Collection in the Factory," Data Processing Application (White Plains, N.Y.: IBM Corp., undated, circa 1960s); "DP Application Briefs (1959–1971)," Box B-116-3, IBM Archives, Somers, N.Y.

18. Publishers of the *Office Automation Handbook* prepared numerous reports on how manufacturing firms used computers in inventory control in the late 1950s and early 1960s. The companies reviewed include B. F. Goodrich, Queen Knitting Mills, Ford Motor Company, American Bosch Arma, and S. C. Johnson & Co.; copies in CBI 55, "Market Reports," Box 70, Folders 1, 4, 7, Charles Babbage Institute, University of Minnesota, Minneapolis.

19. This case study was reported in "Computerized Cost Control," *Production* (August 1965); reprint distributed by J. W. Hinchcliffe, IBM industry manager, in 1965; RC 24887, Box A-1244-2, IBM Archives, Somers, N.Y.

20. Justin A. Periman, "Materials Handling: New Market for Computer Control," *Datamation* 16, no. 5 (May 1970): 133–134, quote on 134.

21. John Sullivan, "Western Electric's Automated System of Supplier Contract Fulfillment," *Data Processing Annual* (Detroit: Gille Assoc., 1961): 175–179, quote on 175.

22. "The Dock to Stock Receiving System at the IBM Rochester and Raleigh Plants," Data Processing Application (White Plains, N.Y.: IBM Corp., 1966). quote on 4; DP Application Briefs, 1960s, Box 1163, IBM Archives, Somers, N.Y.

23. For a wonderful case study of the process at work, see Gordon P. Brunow, "Manufacturing: Some Case Histories," *Data Processing Proceedings 1967* (Boston: DPMA, 1967): 327–334, quote on 333.

24. W. P. Boyle, "Progress Report on Computer Used for Inventory Control," in *Data Processing Annual* (Detroit: Gille Assoc., 1961): 67; for full article, see 164–167.

25. Philip H. Thurston, "Requirements Planning for Inventory Control," *Harvard Business Review* 50, no. 3 (May–June 1972): 67–71, quote on 67.

26. G. W. Plossl and O. W. Wight, *Production and Inventory Control* (Englewood Cliffs, N.J.: Prentice-Hall, 1967): 356. This book was the standard work on inventory control practices in the United States for well over a decade.

27. For a brief but excellent description of these changes, see Anthony Sampson, *Company Man: The Rise and Fall of Corporate Life* (New York: Times Business, 1995): 159–163.

28. The Burroughs Papers, held at the Charles Babbage Institute, University of Minnesota, Minneapolis, includes an extensive collection of case studies and application briefs from the precomputer period that clearly proves the existence of a vast array of mechanical aids to calculation and data collection. The most useful files are located in Burroughs Papers, CBI 90, "Salesmen's Literature," Box 1, but see also Market Research CBI 55, Box 71.

29. Billing and order processing received considerable attention. For a small collection of application briefs on the subject (1950s–early 1960s), involving firms such as Raytheon, Delmonico Foods, Bostitch, Frost, Carborundum, Gladding, McBean, Angelica Uniforms, Pepperell Manufacturing, Rohn & Haas, and A.&M. Karagheusian, see CBI 55, "Market Reports," Box 70, Folders 1, 4, 5, 7, Charles Babbage Institute, University of Minnesota, Minneapolis.

30. For a substantial collection of application briefs featuring the use of the UNIVAC I, IBM RAMAC, and other systems of the 1950s in office (accounting) applications, see "Market Research," CBI 55, Box 71, Folder 4, Archives of the Charles Babbage Institute, University of Minnesota, Minneapolis.

31. William R. King and Mary Ellen Hanley, "Administrative Applications," in Anthony Ralston, Edwin D. Reilly, and David Hemmendinger (eds.), *Encyclopedia of Computer Science,* 4th ed. (London: Nature Publishing Group, 2000): 27.

32. Arthur A. Brown and Leslie G. Peck, "How Electronic Machines Handle Clerical Work," *Journal of Accountancy* 99 (January 1955): 31–37; A. Charnes et al., "Application of Linear Programming to Financial Budgeting and the Costing of Funds," *Journal of Business* 32, no. 1 (January 1959): 20–46; Frank S. Howell, "Using a Computer to Reconcile Inventory Counts to Books," *N.A.A. Bulletin* 37 (June 1956): 1223–1233.

33. These issues are well summarized by O. S. Nelson and R. S. Woods, *Accounting Systems and Data Processing* (Cincinnati, Oh.: South-Western Publishing, 1961).

34. Typical was Ronald E. Williams, an EDP manager discussing inventory control, sales analysis, and accounts receivable: "General Tire & Rubber's R.C.A. 501 Applications," in Charles H. Johnson (ed.), *Data Processing: 1960 Proceedings* (Mt. Prospect, Ill.: National Machine Accounting Association, 1960): 144–158.

35. Goodrich F. Cleaver, "Auditing and Electronic Data Processing," *Journal of Accountancy* 106 (November 1958): 48–54; William R. Davies, "Management Progresses in Its Use of Internal Audit Control," *The Office* (January 1958): passim; Paul E. Hamman, "The Audit of Machine Records," *Journal of Accountancy* 101 (March 1956): 56–61; Institute of Internal Auditors, *Internal Audit and Control of Payroll and Accounts Payable (Where Accounting Machines Are Utilized)* (New York: Institute of Internal Auditors, 1957), which is a 53-page call to arms; Felix Kaufman and Leo A. Schmidt, "Auditing Electronic Records," *Accounting Review* (January 1957): 34–41; Joseph Pelej, "How Will Business Electronics Affect the Auditor's Work?" *Journal of Accountancy* 98 (July 1954): 36–44; Daniel M. Shonting and Leo D. Stone, "Audit Techniques for Electronic Systems," *Journal of Accountancy* 106 (October 1958): 54–61; Arthur B. Toan, Jr., "The Auditor and EDP," *Journal of Accountancy* 109 (June 1960): 42–46.

36. C. C. Sparks, "Fitting the Audit Program to Punched Card Accounting Systems," *Journal of Accountancy* 86, no. 3 (September 1948): 196–200; Leon E. Vannais, "The Accountant's Responsibility for Making Punched-Card Installations Successful," *Journal of Accountancy* 88, no. 4 (October 1949): 282–298.

37. David F. Noble, *Forces of Production: A Social History of Industrial Automation* (New York: Oxford University Press, 1986): 1–7.

38. For an excellent overview, see Roberto Mazzoleni, "Innovation in the Machine Tool Industry: A Historical Perspective on the Dynamics of Comparative Advantage," in David C. Mowery and Richard R. Nelson (eds.), *Sources of Industrial Leadership: Studies of Seven Industries* (Cambridge: Cambridge University Press, 1999): 169–216.

39. For details of the standardization story, see Noble, *Forces of Production*, 202–209.

40. For a description of a case from the period, involving United Aircraft Corporation, see "Numerical Control," attached to W. C. Rockwell letter to subscribers, Supplement No. 47, August 1961, *Office Automation Applications*, III A18; 1–8; CBI 55, "Market Reports," Box 70, Folder 7, Charles Babbage Institute, University of Minnesota, Minneapolis.

41. J. J. Stone, "Introducing Computers for Machine Tool Control," *Tool Engineering* 36 (April 1956): 87–91.

42. "The Factory Automation Systems Market," 38–39. On a variation of NC, called adaptive control (popular term of the 1970s), which is a continuous adjustment of machinery in response to feedback from sensors detecting changing conditions, see pp. 40–43.

43. J. Rosenberg, "Types and Selections of Contouring Systems," in Frank W. Wilson (ed.), *Numerical Control in Manufacturing* (New York: McGraw-Hill, 1963): 169–180.

44. A. Gebhardt and O. Hatzold, "Numerically Controlled Machine Tools," in Lars Nabseth and George F. Ray (eds.), *The Diffusion of New Industrial Processes: An International Study* (Cambridge: Cambridge University Press, 1974): 33–34.

45. Ibid., 39–40.

46. Ibid., 42.

47. Ibid., 44.

48. Roger Nett and Stanley A. Heitzler, *An Introduction to Electronic Data Processing* (Glencoe, Ill.: Free Press, 1959): 159.

49. Ibid., 157–178.

50. Richard G. Canning, *Electronic Data Processing for Business and Industry* (New York: Wiley, 1956): 4.

51. "Factory Automation Systems Market," 126.

52. In the 1950s, when a data center wanted to install a larger computer system, it often had to rewrite its software applications so that they would operate on the new computer. By the end of the 1950s, the cost of rewriting often exceeded the expense of the new equipment and thus made it not only technologically challenging to migrate to a new system but often very expensive. The technical community desperately wanted compatible systems, that is, various-sized models of computers and peripheral equipment, which made it possible to expand existing systems without having to rewrite much or any of the existing inventory of application software. In the 1950s and 1960s, data-processing managers were very concerned with the issue. See, for instance, D. M. Baker, "Economic Considerations of Conversion," *Datamation* 12, no. 6 (June 1966): 30–48; Harold F. Craig, *Administering a Conversion to Electronic Accounting: A Case Study of a Large Office* (Boston: Division of Research, Harvard University, 1955); Floyd C. Mann and Lawrence K. Williams, "Observations on the Dynamics of a Change to Electronic Data-Processing Equipment," *Administrative Science Quarterly* 5, no. 2 (September 1960): 217–256; Douglas A. Williams, "Conversion at Lockheed Missiles and Space," *Datamation* 13, no. 1 (January 1967): 39–45.

53. Gideon Halevi, *The Role of Computers in Manufacturing Processes* (New York: Wiley, 1980): 8.

54. "Production Automation—Big Leap in '70's," *Computer Yearbook 1972* (Detroit: Computer Yearbook Co., 1972): 431. Companies the article mentions as aggressively planning increased expenditures in 1972 include General Motors, Ford Motor, Westinghouse Electric, McDonald, and smaller firms such as Sundstrand and Harris-Intertype.

55. *The Data Bases Market* (New York: Frost & Sullivan, 1977); J. P. Fry and E. H. Sibley, "Evolution of Data-Base Management Systems," *Computing Surveys* 8, no. 1 (March 1976): 7–42; M. C. McGee, "Data Base Technology," *IBM Journal of Research and Development* 25, no. 5 (September 1981): 505–519; R. F. Schubert, "Basic Concepts in Data Base Management Systems," *Datamation* 18 (1972): 42–47. For a bibliography of much of the contemporary management discussion of databases, see James W. Cortada, *Second Bibliographic Guide to the History of Computing, Computers, and the Information Processing Industry* (Westport, Conn.: Greenwood Press, 1996): 345–348.

56. R. J. Taylor and Jerome Tagg, "Integrated Management Information and Control System: A Case Study," *Data Processing Proceedings 1966* (Chicago: DPMA, 1966): 30–54, quote on 54–55.

57. The Bell Helicopter Company thought it was well on its way to having a total systems concept, to run on its IBM 650 by 1961. For a description of Bell's perspective, see W. C. Rockwell to subscribers, *OAApplications Updating Service*, June 1961, Supplement No. 45, "Total Systems Concept at Bell Helicopter," III A17: 1–10; CBI 55, "Market Reports," Box 70, Folder 7, Charles Babbage Institute, University of Minnesota, Minneapolis.

58. T. R. Hughes, "An Integrated System for Manufacturing," *Data Processing Proceedings 1967* (Boston: DPMA, 1967): 313–325, quote on 315.

59. J. Stevens Blanchard, "We Bet Our Company on Data Base Management," *Datamation* 20, no. 9 (September 1974): 61–70; Robert L. Flynn, "A Brief History of Data Base Management," *Datamation* 20, no. 8 (August 1974): 71–77; on what was available, see Ian Palmer,

Data Base Systems: A Practical Reference (Wellesley, Mass.: Q.E.D. Information Sciences, 1975); for a thoughtful trends and directions analysis and their implications for users, see Richard F. Schubert, "Directions in Data Base Management Technology," *Datamation* 20, no. 9 (September 1974): 48–56; for an excellent historical survey reviewing database management packages from the 1950s to the early 1970s, see Fry and Sibley, "Evolution of Data-Base Management Systems," 7–42.

60. Jerome P. Rickert, "On-Line Support for Manufacturing," *Datamation* 21, no. 7 (July 1975): 46–48, quotes on 47 and 48.

61. Peter L. Laubach, *Company Investigations of Automatic Data Processing* (Boston: Division of Research, Harvard Business School, 1957), especially 220–221; James D. Gallagher, "Organization of the Data-Processing Function," in Donald G. Malcolm et al. (eds.), *Symposium on Management Information and Control Systems* (New York: Wiley, 1960): 120–134; James I. Cash, Jr., et al., *Corporate Information Systems Management* (Homewood, Ill.: Dow Jones-Irwin, 1988).

62. Larry D. Woods, "Distributed Processing in Manufacturing," *Datamation* 23, no. 10 (October 1977): 60–63, quote on 60.

63. Ibid., 61–62.

64. Ibid., 63.

65. Michael S. Flynn and David E. Cole, "The U.S. Automotive Industry: Technology and Competitiveness," in Donald A. Hicks (ed.), *Is New Technology Enough?: Making and Remaking U.S. Basic Industries* (Washington, D.C.: American Enterprise Institute, 1988): 86–161; Rebecca Morales, *Flexible Production: Restructuring of the International Automobile Industry* (Cambridge: Polity, 1994): 1–15, 57–75.

66. For an excellent summary of CAD/CAM applications, see Barry Flachsbart, David Shuey, and George Peters, "Computer-Aided Design/Computer-Aided Manufacturing (CAD/CAM)," in Ralston et al., *Encyclopedia of Computer Science,* 268–274.

67. C. B. Besant, *Computer-Aided Design and Manufacture* (Chichester, Eng.: Ellis Horwood, 1983): 12.

68. Ibid., 219.

69. Ibid., 222.

70. John K. Krouse, "Automation Revolutionizes Mechanical Design," *High Technology* (March 1984): 37.

71. A. G. Erdman and G. N. Sandor, *Mechanism Design: Analysis and Synthesis*, vol. 1. (Upper Saddle River, N.J.: Prentice Hall, 1984).

72. Roy M. Salsman and Irvin Krause, "The Impact of Automation on Engineering/Manufacturing Productivity," *Impact* (March 1980): 10; "Market Research," CBI 55, Box 8, Folder 4, Archives of the Charles Babbage Institute, University of Minnesota, Minneapolis.

73. Peter M. Blau et al., "Technology and Organization in Manufacturing," *Administrative Science Quarterly* 21, no. 1 (March 1976): 20–40.

74. G. Bylinksy, "New Industrial Revolution Is on the Way," *Fortune* 104 (October 5, 1981): 106–114.

75. For instance, D. Ciampa, "The Impact of Computer Integrated Manufacturing," *Vital Speeches* 50 (June 15, 1984): 534–539; J. P. Crestin and J. F. McWaters (eds.), *Software for Discrete Manufacturing* (New Amsterdam, N.Y.: North Holland, 1986); T. G. Gunn, "The Mechanization of Design and Manufacturing," *Scientific American* 247 (September 1982): 114–130; Office of Technology Assessment, U.S. Congress, *Computerized Manufacturing Automation: Employment, Education, and the Workplace.* OTA-CIT-235 (Washington, D.C.: U.S. Government Printing Office, April 1984); Robert Oullette et al., *Automation Impacts on Industry* (Ann Arbor, Mich.: Ann Arbor Science, 1983).

76. IBM, "Data Collection at Barnes Drill Company," undated application brief, Box B-116-3, DP Application Briefs, IBM Archives, Somers, N.Y.

77. Harodl C. Plant, "New Directions in Data Processing," *Data Processing Proceedings 1963* (Detroit: DPMA, 1963): 197–212.

78. John Herkhenhoff, "Company Profits from Simple Data Processing System," *Foundry Magazine* (September 1965); reprinted by IBM, RC2500/Box A-1245-1, IBM Archives, Somers, N.Y. A number of such installations was reported by IBM, making application briefs available across a large number of American manufacturing industries. For examples, see Ben Waddington, "Computers Centralize Data Processing at Eaton," Automotive Industries (April 15, 1965), 73–75, RC 24887/Box A-1244-2; "Description of Drywall Contractor's Data Processing Equipment to Tighten Work Schedule Control," *Gypsum Drywall Industry Newsmagazine* (April/May 1965): 15–17, RC 24887/Box A-1244-2, IBM Archives, Somers, N.Y.

79. For an excellent example of the use of cards and reports produced from them, see IBM, "Control of Die-Casting Costs at Allen-Stevens Corporation," undated IBM application brief, circulated in November 1965, and IBM's "Production Control at the Formsprag Company with the IBM 357 Data Collection System," both in "DP Applications Briefs," Box B-116-3, IBM Archives, Somers, N.Y.

80. "Information Explosion in the Factory," *Dun's Review* (March 1965): 112.

81. Ibid., 112–113, 235–236, 238–245.

82. For an example of what was used in the early 1970s, complete with photographs, see IBM, "System/3 Applications at J. P. Ward Foundaries, Inc.," undated IBM application brief, circa early 1970s, DP Applications Briefs/Box B-116-3, IBM Archives, Somers, N.Y.

83. Andrew Tylecote, *The Long Wave in the World Economy* (London: Routledge, 1991): 59.

84. "Numerical Control: From Class to Mass Market," *Dun's Review* (August 1965): 34.

85. Roy A. Lindberg, *Materials and Manufacturing Technology* (Boston: Allyn & Bacon, 1968): 576.

86. Ibid., 575–589; M. Haslehurtst, *Manufacturing Technology* (London: English Universities Press, 1969): 158–183.

87. Joseph Harrington, Jr., *Computer Integrated Manufacturing* (Malabar, Fla.: Robert E. Krieger, 1973): 12.

88. D. Kochan (ed.), *CAM: Developments in Computer-Integrated Manufacturing* (New York: Springer-Verlag, 1986): 6.

89. Roberto Mazzoleni, "Innovations in the Machine Tool Industry: A Historical Perspective on the Dynamics of Comparative Advantage," in Mowery and Nelson, *Sources of Industrial Leadership*, 196.

90. In the period 1984–1987, NC equipment installed across the United States involved most metal-working activities. A study by the *American Machinist* reported that in this period new devices were put in for turning, boring, drilling, milling, grinding, and total metal cutting and forming, among other functions: Morris A. Cohen and Uday M. Apte, *Manufacturing Automation* (Chicago: Irwin, 1997): 134.

91. Ibid., 204–205.

92. The bulk of my account of the robot is taken from Frederik L. Schodt, *Inside the Robot Kingdom: Japan, Mechatronics, and the Coming Robotopia* (Tokyo: Kodansha International, 1988): 13–72.

93. "Report on Revised JIS B 0134 (Glossary of Terms for Industrial Robots)," *Robot*, no. 53 (August 1986): 4.

94. "Now Everybody Wants to Get Into Robots," *Business Week* (February 15, 1981): 52B–52J, quote on 52B.

95. J. U. Korein and J. Ish-Shalom, "Robotics," *IBM Systems Journal* 26, no. 1 (1987): 55–95; and for a major review of robotic applications in the mid-1980s, see Shimony Nof (ed.), *Handbook of Industrial Robotics* (New York: Wiley, 1985).

96. Yet industry watchers were bullish on the technology. Roy M. Salzman, of Arthur D.

Little, predicted in late 1981 that "we expect continued growth of 35–40%/year for the next two to three years," although he acknowledge that "finding appropriate applications in the factory is more difficult than might be assumed, and the significant cost of auxiliary equipment for parts handling . . . and carrying out the installation engineering . . . often makes the basic economics unattractive": "Growth in U.S. Industrial Robotics," *Impact* (November 1981): 1–2; "Market Research," CBI 55, Box 8, Folder 5, Archives of the Charles Babbage Institute, University of Minnesota, Minneapolis.

97. Winch, *Information Technology in Manufacturing Processes*, 46.

98. Ibid., 48.

99. Data reproduced in Schodt, *Inside the Robot Kingdom*, 15.

100. Yuri Kageyama, "Robots as Part of the Family," AP story (November 24, 2000); my copy is from *Wisconsin State Journal* (November 24, 2000): A10.

101. Steven L. Goldman, Rogert N. Nagel, and Kenneth Preiss, *Agile Competitors and Virtual Organizations: Strategies for Enriching the Customer* (New York: Van Nostrand Reinhold, 1995): 4.

102. B. Joseph Pine II, *Mass Customization: The New Frontier in Business Competition* (Boston: Harvard Business School Press, 1993): 49.

103. Ibid., 49–50.

104. *Parade Magazine* (November 26, 2000): entire issue; cartoon quote on 24.

105. Slava Gerovitch, "Automation," in Ralston et al.; *Encyclopedia of Computer Science*, 124.

106. The strategy had its limitations and its critics. See, for example, David M. Upton, "What Really Makes Factories Flexible?" *Harvard Business Review* (July–August 1995): 74–84.

107. Paul R. Warndorf and M. Eugene Merchant, "Development and Future Trends in Computer-Integrated Manufacturing in the USA," *International Journal of Technology Management* 1, nos. 1–2 (1986): 161–178, which provides a thorough review of CIM.

108. Ibid., 168.

109. Reported ibid., 171.

110. For an excellent analysis of the limitations evident in the 1980s, see John Bessant, "The Lessons of Failure: Learning to Manage New Manufacturing Technology," *International Journal of Technology Management* 8, nos. 6–7 (1993): 197–214.

111. Donald A. Hicks (ed.), *Is New Technology Enough? Making and Remaking U.S. Basic Industries* (Washington, D.C.: American Enterprise Institute, 1988): 1–18, quote on 2.

112. Steven L. Goldman and Roger N. Nagel, "Management, Technology and Agility: The Emergence of a New Era in Manufacturing," *International Journal of Technology Management* 8, nos. 1–2 (1993): 18–38; Robert E. Cole, *Managing Quality Fads: How American Business Learned to Play the Quality Game* (New York: Oxford University Press, 1999): 233–247.

113. Cohen and Apte, *Manufacturing Automation*, 153.

114. J. Christopher Westland and Theodore H. K. Clark, *Global Electronic Commerce: Theory and Case Studies* (Cambridge, Mass.: MIT Press, 1999): 529–531.

115. B. J. LaLonde, "Supply Chain Evolution by the Numbers," *Supply Chain Management Review* 2, no. 1 (1998): 7–8; E. Hewitt, "Supply Chain Redesign," *International Journal of Logistics Management* 5, no. 2 (1994): 1–9; M. L. Fisher, "What Is the Right Supply Chain for Your Product?" *Harvard Business Review* 75, no. 2 (March-April 1997): 105–116; D. J. Bowersox and D. J. Closs, *Logistical Management—The Integrated Supply Chain Process* (New York: McGraw-Hill, 1996).

116. Richard A. Lancioni, Michael F. Smith, and Terence A. Oliva, "The Role of the Internet in Supply Chain Management," in John A. Woods and Edward J. Marien (eds.), *The Supply Chain Management Yearbook, 2001 Edition* (New York: McGraw-Hill, 2001): 45–61.

117. Ibid., 49–51, 57.

118. For the study and the analysis of today's limitations with SCMs, see Stephen J. Cole,

"Dynamic Trading Networks," and a subsequent study by the same organization that turned up similar findings: Stacie S. McCullough, "eMarket Hype, Apps Realities," both in *Forrester Report* (Cambridge, Mass.: Forrestter Research, January 1999 and April 2000), available on its web site: www.forrester.com.

119. Hugh D. Luke, *Automation for Productivity* (New York: Wiley, 1972): 269.

120. Ibid.

121. John Duke and Lisa Usher, "Multifactor Productivity Slips in the Nonrubber Footwear Industry," *Monthly Labor Review* 112, no. 4 (April 1989): 32–37, quote on 34.

122. Study results are summarized in Cohen and Apte, *Manufacturing Automation*, 149.

123. When I was an IBM salesperson in the 1970s, I had as a customer the Distribution Division of Mack Trucks, which provided parts to all the company's sales agencies. The firm's main warehouse for parts was located in New Jersey, where the warehouse manager proudly told me that for some parts he had 70 years' worth of supply and for most items, several years' worth. In 1978, when I first toured the warehouse, I was shown a 70 years' supply of radiators for trucks built in the 1920s–1940s.

124. The literature is vast, however, about the role of technology; see David C. Mowery and Nathan Rosenberg, *Paths of Innovation: Technological Change in 20th-Century America* (Cambridge: Cambridge University Press, 1996): 167–179, and their extensive bibliography, 181–199; Mowery and Nelson, *Sources of Industrial Leadership*, 1–18, 359–382; and for a collection of case studies that reinforce my points, see Agatha C. Hughes and Thomas P. Hughes (eds.), *Systems, Experts, and Computers: The Systems Approach in Management and Engineering, World War II and After* (Cambridge, Mass.: MIT Press, 2000), especially 191–220.

125. Noel M. Tichy, *The Leadership Engine: How Winning Companies Build Leaders at Every Level* (New York: HarperBusiness, 1997): 25.

126. Philip Evans and Thomas S. Wurster, *Blown to Bits: How the New Economics of Information Transforms Strategy* (Boston: Harvard Business School Press, 2000): xi.

Chapter 5

1. Joseph A. Schumpeter, *Business Cycles: A Theoretical, Historical, and Statistical Analysis of the Capitalist Process*, vol. 1 (New York: McGraw-Hill, 1939): 102; quote on 101–102.

2. One of the most useful introductions to Schumpeter's ideas is the collection put together by Richard Swedberg (ed.), *Joseph A. Schumpeter: The Economics and Sociology of Capitalism* (Princeton, N.J.: Princeton University Press, 1991); see especially his introduction, 3–98.

3. Michael Jackman (ed.), *Business and Economic Quotations* (New York: Macmillan, 1984): 202.

4. Charles H. Fine and Daniel M. G. Raff, "Automotive Industry: Internet-Driven Innovation and Economic Performance," in Robert E. Litan and Alice M. Rivlin (eds.), *The Economic Payoff from the Internet Revolution* (Washington, D.C.: Brookings Institution Press, 2001): 63.

5. *Almanac Issue, Automotive News* 22 (1958): 55.

6. Robert F. Lanzillotti, "The Automobile Industry," in Walter Adams (ed.), *The Structure of American Industry*, 4th ed. (New York: Macmillan, 1971): 256–301.

7. Lawrence J. White, "The Automobile Industry," in Walter Adams (ed.), *The Structure of American Industry*, 5th ed. (New York: Macmillan, 1982): 136–190.

8. Martin Anderson, "Shake-out in Detroit: New Technology, New Problems," *Technology Review* (August–September 1982): 59.

9. For a case study of automated welding at the Chevrolet Motor Division at GM, see Hugh D. Luke, *Automation for Productivity* (New York: Wiley, 1972): 42–43; for the use of

tools at Ford, see 107–108. For a visual that gives a sense of the extent of technology involved in an application, see the photograph of Ford's PCP 150 Philco Communication Processor in use on 108.

10. Edith Harwith Goodman, "Payroll," *Data Processing Annual* (Detroit: Gille Assoc. 1961): 134.

11. David A. Barr, "GM's Parts Ordering System," *Datamation* 20, no. 11 (November 1974): 79.

12. Robert V. Critchlow, "Technology and Labor in Automobile Production," *Monthly Labor Review* 100, no. 10 (October 1977): 32–35, quote on 33.

13. "Chrysler's Computer Does the Talking Faster and Cheaper," *Business Week* (August 24, 1963): 52–53; "Computer Sticks Up Auto Assembly Lines," *Business Week* (May 19, 1962): 138ff; "Finding New Ways to Make Autos," *Business Week* (September 11, 1965) 190–198; press clippings in IBM Press Review Service, circa mid- to late 1960s, "DP Applications—Automobiles," A-1019-2, Box "Press Reviews 1969," IBM Archives, Somers, N.Y.

14. See random issues of *Automotive Industries* for this period. Robots, although plentiful in the industry and touted to the public as major improvements, had a long way to go to be as flexible as desired; see John McElroy, "Robots Take Detroit," *Automotive Industries* (January 1982): 28–29.

15. "Pre-Production Control," Office Automation Applications Updating Service (October 1961); III-A-19: 1–4; CBI 55, "Market Reports," Box 70, Folder 7, Archives of the Charles Babbage Institute, University of Minnesota, Minneapolis.

16. W. P. Boyle, "Computer Use Expanded: Progress Report on Computer Used for Inventory Control," in *Data Processing Annual* (Detroit: Gille Assoc. 1961): 164–167.

17. BLS, Department of Commerce, *Technological Change and Its Labor Impact in Five Industries*, Bulletin 1961 (Washington, D.C.:U.S. Government Printing Office, 1977): 23–33, quote on 23.

18. White, "Automobile Industry," 162; his idea is further developed on 171–172.

19. *The Factory Automation Systems Market* (New York: Frost & Sullivan, 1972): 131; CBI 55 "Market Reports", Folder 35, Box 3, Archives of the Charles Babbage Institute, University of Minnesota, Minneapolis.

20. One of the best descriptions of the industry in this period is provided by Rebecca Morales, *Flexible Production: Restructuring of the International Automobile Industry* (Cambridge: Polity, 1994): 57–86.

21. For a fascinating account of how American executives in all industries reacted to Japanese practices, with many specific examples drawn from the automotive industry, see Robert E. Cole, *Managing Quality Fads: How American Business Learned to Play the Quality Game* (New York: Oxford University Press, 1999).

22. Harbour and Associates, *The Harbour Report: 1999 North America* (Troy, Mich.: Harbour and Assoc. 1999): 67, 176.

23. Kurt Hoffman and Raphael Kplinsky, *Driving Force: The Global Restructuring of Technology, Labour, and Investment in the Automobile and Components Industries* (Boulder, Col.: Westview Press, 1988): 183.

24. See ibid., 129, for both statistics and quote.

25. Ibid., 78.

26. John F. Krafcik and Daniel Roos, "High Performance Manufacturing: An International Study of Auto Assembly Practice," *Automotive Systems Technology: The Future* (Dearborn, Mich., September 25–30, 1988): 28–39; John F. Krafcik, "A New Diet for U.S. Manufacturers," *Technology Review* 92, no. 1 (1989): 28–36; Harley Shaiken, *Work Transformed: Automation and Labor in the Computer Age* (New York: Holt, Rinehart & Winston, 1984).

27. Morales, *Flexible Production*, 84.

28. Ibid., 85.

29. James W. Brock, "Automobiles," in Walter Adams and James W. Brock (eds.), *The Structure of American Industry* (Upper Saddle River, N.J.: Prentice Hall, 2001): 123.

30. Hoffman and Kplinsky, *Driving Force*, 210–221, describe GM's experiences.

31. Ibid., 274.

32. Ibid., 297.

33. Drawn from table 3-6 in Walter Adams and James W. Brock, "Automobiles," in Walter Adams and James W. Brock (eds.), *The Structure of American Industry* (Englewood Cliffs, N.J.: Prentice-Hall, 1995): 84.

34. Ibid., 230.

35. In my study of mergers in the Insurance Industry, done for internal consumption in IBM in the early 1990s, I interviewed one insurance executive whose company had acquired a number of smaller firms in the Midwest. One criterion for potential acquisition was that its information-processing systems had to be IBM-compatible. That is, its operating systems and databases had to be compatible with or the same as those of the acquiring firm so that the buyer could quickly fold into its own systems the data, customers, and operations of the other firm; get rid of duplicate staff; and thereby enjoy economies of scale. Several firms were deemed unattractive acquisitions because their systems operated on either Hewlett-Packard equipment and software or on Unisys systems, neither of which was compatible with IBM's software, operating systems, and database management tools.

36. IBM Corp., *Industrial Sector Overview Document*, December 10, 2000, report prepared for IBM customer-facing personnel.

37. Ibid., 1.

38. Other vendors of capital goods enjoyed the same experience. For example, in the 1980s, IBM began offering capital leases for its computers, thereby increasing the profit of a sale by a third. Like GM, IBM established a financing subsidiary, complete with its own annual reports, in the 1980s.

39. Brock, "Automobiles," 135. For the case that traditional dealers were a thing of the past, see Weld Royal, "Death of Salesmen," in John A. Woods (ed.), *The Purchasing and Supply Yearbook, 2000 Edition* (New York: McGraw-Hill, 2000): 278–283.

40. For a detailed description of the benefits of the Internet in this industry, see Fine and Raff, "Automotive Industry," 62–86.

41. Toole quoted in IBM press release, "B2b: Extending the E-business Infrastructure" (November 13, 2000), http://w3.ibm.com/articles/2000/11/04_b2b.html.

42. Modern trading networks and supply chains are described by Stephen J. Cole, *Dynamic Trading Networks*, Forrester Report (Cambridge, Mass.: Forrester Research, 1999). Cole reports that most firms, not just in automotive, still had a great deal to do to make these networks compatible with existing applications. For a review of the industry in the mid- to late 1990s, see Charles H. Fine, John C. Lafrance, and Don Hillebrand, "The U.S. Automobile Manufacturing Industry" (Washington, D.C.: U.S. Department of Commerce, Office of Technology Policy, December 1996), http://www.ta.doc.gov/Reports.htm.

43. B. Joseph Pine II, *Mass Customization: The New Frontier in Business Competition* (Boston: Harvard Business School Press, 1993): 35–36.

44. Fine and Raff, "Automotive Industry," 85.

45. Richard J. Fruehan, Dany A. Cheu, and David M. Vislosky, "Steel," in David C. Mowery (ed.), *U.S. Industry in 2000: Studies in Competitive Performance* (Washington, D.C.: National Academy Press, 1999): 75–102.

46. Walter Adams, "The Steel Industry," in Walter Adams (ed.), *The Structure of American Industry*, 4 ed. (New York: Macmillan, 1971): 70; Walter Adams and Hans Mueller, "The Steel Industry," in *The Structure of American Industry*, 6th ed. (New York: Macmillan, 1982): 73.

47. Adams, "Steel Industry," 76.

48. Adams and Mueller, "Steel Industry," 110.

49. Ibid., 115.

50. Donald F. Barnett, "The U.S. Steel Industry: Strategic Choices in a Basic Industry," in Donald A. Hicks (ed.), *Is New Technology Enough? Making and Remaking U.S. Basic Industries* (Lanhem, Md.: American Enterprise Institute for Public Policy, 1988): 175.

51. Ibid., 185.

52. Paul A. Tiffany, *The Decline of American Steel: How Management, Labor, and Government Went Wrong* (New York: Oxford University Press, 1988).

53. For an important, optimistic analysis from the mid-1990s, see R. M. Cyert and R. J. Fruehan, "The Basic Steel Industry" (Washington, D.C.: U.S. Department of Commerce, Office of Technology Policy, December 1996), http://www.ta.doc.gov/Reports.htm.

54. Fruehan, Cheu, and Vislosky, "Steel," 75–102.

55. I (an IBM salesperson in the 1970s–early 1980s) visited a foundry owned by Worthington Pump in New Jersey in 1979, discovering a time capsule of a data center with IBM punch-card equipment from the 1930s and 1940s still in use. The ancient data-processing manager greeted me like someone marooned on a deserted island, saying that he had not seen an IBM salesperson since the 1960s. Hundreds of IBMers and other data-processing professionals from all over New Jersey came to visit this data center over the course of the next six months. Senior DP management at Worthington quickly moved to close the center and absorb the labor reporting, plant scheduling, and accounting onto an IBM 4341 system.

56. IBM, *Data Collection at the Carpenter Steel Company* (White Plains, N.Y.: IBM Corp., undated, circa 1966), DP Application Briefs, Box B-116-3, IBM Archives, Somers, N.Y. Given how methodically IBM and Burroughs both were about publishing extensively on an industry-by-industry basis at the time, the lack of applications briefs for a particularly large industry is as telling as finding what should be there for an important segment of the economy.

57. Unsigned note, dated February 1965, "Steel Melting Process Control"; T. H. Malim, "Computer Takes Melter in Hand," *The Iron Age* (December 17, 1964): unpaginated reprint, File RC 2500, Box A-1245-1, IBM Archives, Somers, N.Y.

58. "Computer Controls Valve Production All the Way," *Steel* (December 20, 1965): 41.

59. Thomas R. Schuerger and Frank Slamar, "Control in the Iron and Steel Industry," *Datamation* (February 1966): 28–32, quotes on 29.

60. BLS, U.S. Department of Labor, *Technological Change and Manpower Trends in Five Industries*, Bulletin 1856 (Washington, D.C.: U.S. Government Printing Office, 1975): 21–33.

61. All the material for this paragraph was drawn from BLS, U.S. Department of Labor, *The Impact of Technology on Labor in Four Industries*, Bulletin 2228 (Washington, D.C.: U.S. Government Printing Office, May 1985): 20–34.

62. *Wall Street Journal* (April 4, 1983): 11. For an excellent overview of events in the 1980s, see Adams, Steel," 93–118.

63. Cyert and Fruehan, "Basic Steel Industry," 11–17.

64. International Trade Commission, "Certain Flat-Rolled Carbon Steel Products," vol. 1, publication 2664 (August 1993): 309.

65. Cyert and Fruehan, "Basic Steel Industry," 39.

66. Adams, "Steel," 110.

67. All material and quotations for this paragraph are from Scott Robertson, "Key Role Seen for E-Commerce in Steel's Future," *American Metal Market in E-Commerce*, Supplement (March 22, 2000): 4Aff.

68. Philip Clark, "Steel Market Moves Online," *Business Marketing* (October 1, 1999): 3.

69. Tom Stundza, "Boom or Bust?" *Purchasing* 128, no. 10 (June 15, 2000): S93. All the material for this paragraph is drawn from the article. It is an excellent survey of all the major Internet-based initiatives by site and company underway in the steel industry as of mid-2000.

70. Ibid.

71. On expectations and possibilities, see Fine and Raff, "Automotive Industry," 62–86; and for the first study on the benefits of the Internet in this industry, see Gary Lapidus, *Gentlemen, Start Your Engines* (New York: Goldman Sachs, 2000).

72. "Seizing the Initiative," *New Steel* 16, no. 7 (July 2000): 26–27. For an analysis of world trade, see Tom Stundza, "New Decade, Same Old Story: Friction Abounds," *Purchasing* 129, no. 6 (October 5, 2000): 48B1ff. Foreign imports to the United States in 1999 hovered at 25% of domestic consumption.

73. Stundza, "New Decade, Same Old Story," 48B1ff.

74. Bridge News, "Steelmaker's Grim Message," *Wisconsin State Journal* (December 30, 2000): E1.

75. It became one of the most quoted phrases of the president, who said it in his last presidential address, delivered on January 17, 1961. The full quotation is "In the councils of government we must guard against the acquisition of unwarranted influences, whether sought or unsought, by the military-industrial complex. The potential for the disastrous rise of misplaced power exists and will persist."

76. Frederic M. Scherer, "The Aerospace Industry," in Walter Adams (ed.), *The Structure of American Industry*, 4th ed. (New York: Macmillan, 1971): 335.

77. BLS, *Technological Change and Manpower Trends in Five Industries*, Bulletin 1856 (Washington, D.C.: U.S. Government Printing Office, 1975): 34.

78. Herman O. Stekler, *The Structure and Performance of the Aerospace Industry* (Berkeley: University of California Press, 1965): 9–11.

79. H. E. Schmit, "Manufacturing," in Edith Harwith Goodman (ed.), *Data Processing Yearbook* (Detroit: American Data Processing, 1963): 208.

80. For a detailed overview of what an integrated approach looked like, see the example of the Bell Helicopter Company in W. R. Rockwell to Subsribers, OAApplications Updating Service (June 1961), III-A-17: 1–10; CBI 55, "Market Reports," Box 70, Folder 7, Archives of the Charles Babbage Institute, University of Minnesota, Minneapolis.

81. Schmit, "Manufacturing," 208.

82. Ibid., 209.

83. Ibid., 210.

84. One might well ask, "What about the European manufacturer, Airbus, which went into direct competition with American firms late in the century?" That firm was not created because technology made it possible to compete against the Americans; it was a political initiative to create in Europe a local industry that could, with European support, compete against the Americans, ensuring that Europe would not have to rely totally on the American industry for aircraft. However, in the early years of the new century, Airbus relied on American suppliers for components, using the Internet and American computer technology in support of its supply chain. For details, see "America Helps Build the 'Bus," *Time* (July 29, 2002): B14–B15.

85. Andrew McAfee, "Manufacturing: Lowering Boundaries, Improving Productivity," in Robert E. Litan and Alice M. Rivlin (eds.), *The Economic Payoff from the Internet Revolution* (Washington, D.C.: Brookings Institution Press, 2001): 41.

86. Cohen and Apte, *Manufacturing Automation*, 225.

87. McAfee, "Manufacturing," 32.

88. Ibid., 42–50.

Chapter 6

1. For descriptions of continuous flow manufacturing, see T. H. Tsai, C. S. Lin, and J. W. Lane, *Modern Control Techniques for the Processing Industries* (New York: Marcel Dekker, 1986); Brian Roffel and Patrick Chin, *Computer Control in the Process Industries* (Elkins Park, Pa.: Franklin Book Co., 1987); Albert A. Gunkler and J. W. Bernard, *Computer Control Strategies for the Fluid Process Industries* (Research Triangle Park, N.C.: Instrumentation, Systems, and Automation Society, 1990). Specific application studies include C. E. Bodington and T. E. Baker, "A History of Mathematical Programming in the Petroleum Industry," *Interfaces* 20, no. 4 (July–August 1990): 117–127; "Computer Control in the Oil Industry," *Oil and Gas Journal* (October 26, 1964): 89–119; Andrew G. Faveret, *Introduction to Digital Computer Applications* (New York: Reinhold, 1965): 161–167; James E. Brown, "Onstream Process Analyzers," *Chemical Engineering* (May 6, 1968): 164–176; James D. Schoeffler, "Process Control Software," *Datamation* 12, no. 2 (February 1966): 33–44; Thomas M. Stout, "Process Control," *Datamation* 12, no. 2 (February 1966): 28–32.

2. On papermaking, see Robert Henderson, *The Paper-making Machine, Its Invention, and Development* (New York: Pergamon, 1967); Peter W. Hart, *Fundamentals and Applications in Pulping, Papermaking, and Chemical Preparation: The 1995 Forest Products Symposium* (New York: American Institute of Chemical Engineers, 1996). Specific application studies include Knut Angstrom, "Production Planning at Paper Mills," in A. B. Frielink (ed.), *Economics of Automatic Processing* (Amsterdam: North-Holland, 1965): 362–365; E. C. Fox, "Computer Control of the Continuous Digester at Gulf States," *Paper Trade Journal* (November 4, 1963): 36–39; Peter Inserra, "Mead Takes Giant Step in Computer Control," *Pulp and Paper* (May 10, 1965): 30–32; R. T. Canup, "Process Control System Increases Digester Productivity at Mill," *Pulp and Paper* (September 1981): 159–161; Jack Gallimore, "Mill-Wide Computer Automation Key Element in Modernization Strategy," *Pulp and Paper* (September 1981): 139–143; R. A. Kronenberg, "Weyerhaeuser's Management Information System," *Datamation* 13, no. 5 (May 1967): 28–30; J. D. Maloney, Jr., "Papermaking by the Numbers," *Tappi* (October 1966): 59–61A; Phillip R. Trapp, "Millwide MIS: Is It an Idea Whose Time Has Come?" *Paper and Trade Journal* (June 15, 1984): 32–34.

3. For an excellent comparison between discrete and continuous process methods, circa 1950s–1970s, see Frost & Sullivan, *The Factory Automation Systems Market* (New York: Frost & Sullivan, 1972): 25–31; CBI 55, "Market Reports," Box 3, 35, Archives of the Charles Babbage Institute, University of Minnesota, Minneapolis.

4. Ibid, p. 25.

5. Ibid., 33.

6. For a summary of the modern history and economic realities of this industry, see Stephen Martin, "Petroleum," in Walter Adams and James W. Brock (eds.), *The Structure of American Industry*, 10th ed. (Upper Saddle River, N.J.: Prentice Hall, 2001): 28–56.

7. Ibid., 32–34.

8. Ibid., 41.

9. For a summary of how the industry functions within its four parts, see Thomas G. Moore, "The Petroleum Industry," in Walter Adams (ed.), *The Structure of American Industry* (New York: Macmillan, 1971): 117–155.

10. BLS, *Outlook for Computer Process Control: Manpower Implications in Process Industries*, Bulletin 1658 (Washington, D.C.: U.S. Government Printing Office, 1970): 1.

11. For a description of how these applications worked, see IBM, *System/7 for Computer Production Control of Oil and Gas Wells* (White Plains, N.Y.: IBM Corp., undated, circa 1971), DP Application Briefs, Box B-116-3, IBM Archives, Somers, N.Y.

12. "On-Site Instruments Help Avoid Troubles, Optimize Drilling," *Oil and Gas Journal* (September 24, 1973); W. D. Moore III, "Computer-Aided Drilling Pays Off," *Oil and Gas*

Journal (May 31, 1976): 56–60; BLS, *Technological Changes and Its Labor Impact in Five Energy Industries*, Bulletin 2005 (Washington, D.C.: U.S. Government Printing Office, 1979): 19–20.

13. Donald C. Holmes, "Computers in Oil—1967–1987," *Computer Yearbook and Directory*, 2nd ed. (Detroit: American Data Processing, 1968): 168–169.

14. T. E. McEntee, "Computers in the Petroleum Industry," in Edith Harwith Goodman (ed.), *Data Processing Yearbook* (Detroit: American Data Processing, 1965): 246–247.

15. Ibid.

16. BLS, *Outlook for Computer Process Control*, 12.

17. Ibid., 50.

18. BLS, *Technological Change and Its Labor Impact*, 26.

19. Ibid., 28. These economists described life before and after the arrival of open-loop computing: "The duties of an operator of a fluid catalytic cracking unit before computer control were to manually adjust automatic analog controllers at the control console and to monitor automatic data logging equipment. After installation, the computer controls and monitors a large part of the process and automatically logs the data, although the operator still performs manual control. In case of emergency, the operator can take control of any part or all of the process" (p. 29).

20. For its history, see David Evans and Richard Schmalensee, *Paying with Plastic: The Digital Revolution in Buying and Borrowing* (Cambridge, Mass.: MIT Press, 1999): 61–68.

21. James C. Beardsmore, Sr., "Credit Card Accounting," *Data Processing Proceedings 1964* (New Orleans: DPMA, 1964): 2–3.

22. The material for the last two paragraphs came from ibid., 1–19.

23. Robert H. Church, Ralph P. Day, William R. Schnitzler, and Elmer S. Seeley, *Optical Scanning for the Business Man* (New York: Hobbs, Dorman, 1966): 122.

24. Ibid.

25. Ibid., 122–125; includes a flowchart of the application, 123.

26. Moore, "Petroleum Industry," 135–136.

27. J. C. Ranyard, "A History of OR and Computing," *Journal of the Operational Research Society* 39, no. 12 (December 1988): 1073–1086; Albert N. Schriber (ed.), *Corporate Simulation Models* (Seattle: University of Washington, Graduate School of Business Administration, 1970); Ron Wolfe, "Evolution of Computer Applications in Science and Engineering," *Research & Development* 31, no. 3a (March 21, 1989): 14–20.

28. Holmes, "Computers in Oil," 169–170.

29. The American Petroleum Institute tracked this form of automation very closely through the half century. For data on early implementation of unmanned trunk line stations, see Hugh D. Luke, *Automation for Productivity* (New York: Wiley, 1972): 262–263.

30. Extensive, contemporary industry literature documents these initiatives; see James W. Cortada, *A Bibliographic Guide to the History of Computer Applications, 1950–1990* (Westport, Conn.: Greenwood Press, 1996): 206–207.

31. BLS, *Technological Change and Its Labor Impact*, 39.

32. Management could then increasingly rely on visual inspections done from low-flying aircraft, augmented with ground-based inspection teams of segments of the pipeline needing further examination, based on reports from pipeline management software.

33. Automation Consultants, "The 650 Used in Refinery Sales Billing," undated case study (circa 1958), quote on III-C1-8, full case study on III-C1-1–8; CBI 55, "Market Reports," Box 70, Folder 1, Archives of the Charles Babbage Institute, University of Minnesota, Minneapolis.

34. Ibid., "EDP at Standard Oil of California," III-C2-1.

35. Ibid., "Datatron in Petroleum Accounting, III-C3-6.

36. For the early history of TI in the Petroleum Industry, see Texas Instruments, *50 Years*

of Innovation: The History of Texas Instruments: A Story of People and Their Ideas (Dallas: Texas Instruments, 1980). Although a lot of published material on TI deals with its development of computer chips, its prechip history has yet to be fully explored.

37. See, for example, Dale O. Cooper, "Advances in EDP in the Petroleum Industry," *Data Processing Proceedings* 1964 (New Orleans: DPMA, 1964): 20–30; "BP, Amoco Merger Marries IT Opposites," *Computerworld* 32, no. 33 (August 17, 1998), 76; Stuart J. Johnson, "IT Fuels Speedup in Energy Industry," *Informationweek* (September 14, 1998): 139–146.

38. The Charles Babbage Institute at the University of Minnesota, Minneapolis, houses the corporate archives of CDC, which are replete with material on this subject, although there is limited historical literature on the topic; however, see J. C. Ranyard, "A History of OR and Computing," *Journal of the Operational Research Society* 39, no.12 (October 1988): 1073–1086. Hundreds of articles and dozens of "how to" books were published that include sporadic case studies of this application across many industries, including petroleum.

39. Rose N. Zeisel and Michael D. Dymmel, "Petroleum Refining," in BLS, *A BLS Reader on Productivity*, Bulletin 2171 (Washington, D.C.: U.S. Government Printing Office, June 1983): 197–206.

40. BLS, *Technological Change and Its Labor Impact in Four Industries*, Bulletin 2316 (Washington, D.C.: U.S. Government Printing Office, December 1988): 34.

41. Ibid.

42. Ibid., 35–38.

43. Ibid., 40.

44. Bob Tippee, "Electronic Data Interchange Changing Petroleum Industry's Basic Business Interactions," *Oil and Gas Journal* 96, no. 28 (July 13, 1998): 41–47.

45. See, for example, Julia King, "BP, Amoco Merger Marries IT Opposites," *Computerworld* 32, no. 33 (August 17, 1998), 1, 76.

46. Start J. Johnston, "IT Fuels Speedup in Energy Industry," *Informationweek* (September 14, 1998), 139–146.

47. John Kennedy, "In Global Energy, Information Technology Knits It All Together," *Oil and Gas Journal*, "Windows in Energy Supplement" (Spring 1999): 1.

48. "The Middle East, New Super-Majors, and More Industry Consolidation," *Offshore* 60, no. 4 (April 2000): 124ff.

49. Jeff Sweat, "Information: The Most Valuable Asset," *Informationweek* (September 11, 2000), 213–220, quote on 213.

50. Don Painter and Robert Dorsey, *E-Business: Refining the Petroleum Industry* (Somers, N.Y.: IBM Corp., 2000).

51. Ashish Arora, Ralph Landau, and Nathan Rosenberg, "Dynamics of Comparative Advantage in the Chemical Industry," in David C. Mowery and Richard R. Nelson (eds.), *Sources of Industrial Leadership: Studies of Seven Industries* (Cambridge: Cambridge University Press, 1999): 217–266; Ralph Landau, "Strategy for Economic Growth: Lessons from the Chemical Industry," in Ralph Landau, Timothy Taylor, and Gavin Wright (eds.), *The Mosaic of Economic Growth* (Stanford, Calif.: Stanford University Press, 1996): 398–420; Allen J. Lenz and John Lafrance, "The Chemical Industry" (Washington, D.C.: U.S. Department of Commerce, Office of Technology Policy, January 1996): 9, http://www.ta.doc.gov/Reports.htm.

52. William S. Comanor and Stuart O. Schweitzer, "Pharmaceuticals," in Walter Adams and James Brock (eds.), *The Structure of American Industry*, 9th ed. (Englewood Cliffs, N.J.: Prentice-Hall, 1995): 177–196.

53. Alfred D. Chandler, Jr., "The United States: Engines of Economic Growth in the Capital-Intensive and Knowledge-Intensive Industries," in Alfred D. Chandler, Jr., Franco Amatori, and Takashi Hikino (eds), *Big Business and the Wealth of Nations* (Cambridge: Cambridge University Press, 1997): 86.

54. On the role of chemical engineers, see Arora, Landau, and Rosenberg, "Dynamics of Comparative Advantage," 252–256; David C. Mowery and Nathan Rosenberg, *Paths of Innovation: Technological Change in 20th-Century America* (Cambridge: Cambridge University Press, 1998): 81–89.

55. Mowery and Rosenberg, *Paths of Innovation*, 97.

56. David A. Hounshell and John Kenly Smith, Jr., *Science and Corporate Strategy: Du Pont R&D, 1902–1980* (Cambridge: Cambridge University Press, 1988). I found it interesting that in this book of over 750 pages, there was little discussion of how R&D was conducted by individuals, let alone the role of computers. I do not intend this remark as a criticism since the author focuses on strategy, managerial considerations, and institutional history, but simply to note one more time the need for historians to take the next step of analyzing the work of companies and industries to better understand the tasks performed. At that level, one can best judge the influence of the digital.

57. Ashish Arora and Alfonso Gambardella, "Chemicals," in David W. Mowery (ed.), *U.S. Industry in 2000: Studies in Competitive Performance* (Washington, D.C.: National Academy Press, 1999): 53.

58. Ibid., 69.

59. "How Computers Did the Job at Seadrift: Union Carbide's Ethylene Plant," *Business Week* (November 9, 1963), 146ff; C. A. Levine and A. Opler, "Computer Solves Heat Flow Problems," *Chemical Engineering* 63 (January 1956): 203; Henry Cornish et al., *Computerized Process Control: A Management Decision* (New York: Hobbs, Dorman, 1968); J. M. Lombardo, "The Case for Digital Backup in Direct Digital Control Systems," *Chemical Engineering* (July 3, 1967): 79–84; Joe F. Moore and Nicholas F. Gardner, "Process Control in the 1970s," *Chemical Engineering* (June 2, 1969): 94–137.

60. BLS, *Outlook for Computer Process Control*, 12.

61. R. D. Eisenhardt and Theodore J. Williams, "Closed-loop Computer Control at Luling," *Control Engineering* (November 1960): 103–114.

62. A. L. Giusti, R. E. Otto, and Theodore J. Williams, "Direct Digital Computer Control," *Control Engineering* (June 1962): 104–108; V. S. Morello, "Digital Computer Applied to Styrene Cracking," *Oil and Gas Journal* (February 24, 1964): 90–93.

63. W. C. Rockwell, letter dated July 1961, as Supplement No. 46 to *Office Automation Applications Newsletter*, attachment entitled "Simulation Model of a Three-Process Chemical Plant," unpaginated; CBI 55, "Market Reports," Box 70, Folder 7, Archives of the Charles Babbage Institute, University of Minnesota, Minneapolis.

64. James E. Brown, "Onstream Process Analyzers," *Chemical Engineering* (May 6, 1968): 164–176; "Computer Processes Data from 40 Chromatographs," *Chemical and Engineering News* (May 15, 1967), 63–64; "Sixth Process Control Report," *Chemical Engineering* (June 7, 1965): 142–204; E. H. Steyman, "Justifying Process Computer Control," *Chemical Engineering* (February 12, 1968): 124–129; Theodore J. Williams, "Computers and Process Control," *Industrial and Engineering Chemistry* (December 1967): 53–68.

65. S. Kahne et al., "Automatic Control by Distributed Intelligence," *Scientific American* 240 (June 1979): 78–90; A. Z. Spector, "Computer Software for Process Control," *Scientific American*, 251 (September 1984): 174–178ff.

66. W. O. Backers et al., "Computers and Research," *Science* 195 (March 18, 1977): 1134–1139.

67. See, for example, D. D. Edman et al., "Computers and Chemistry," *Chemistry* 45 (January 1972): 6–9, (March 1972): 10–15, (May 1972): 10–16, (September 1972): 13–15, "Correction," *Chemistry* 45 Ibid. (December 1972): 28; S. R. Heller et al., "Computer-based Chemical Information System," *Science* 195 (January 21, 1977): 253–259; James E. Rush, "Computer Hardware and Software in Chemical Information Processing," *Journal of Chemical Information and Computer Sciences* 25 (1985): 140–149.

68. Joel M. Vardy, "Process Control Improvements via Discovery," *Chemical Engineering* 103, no. 1 (January 1996): 88–90.

69. Jeremy Rifkin, *The End of Work: The Decline of the Global Labor Force and the Dawn of the Post-Market Era* (New York: Putnam, 1995): 137.

70. Quoted ibid., 137.

71. Jennifer Ouellette, "Riding Logistics' Wave," *Chemical Marketing Reporter* 250, no. 23 (December 2, 1996): SR15ff.

72. For a snapshot of the role of IT in the industry in 2000, see the entire issue of *CMR Focus* (July 31, 2000).

73. John Hoffman, "Chemical Companies with a High Tech Wave," *Chemical Marketing Reporter* 251, no. 5 (February 3, 1997): SR4.

74. Which means it would work after January 1, 2000: "IT Integration," *Chemical Week* 159, no. 6 (February 12, 1997): 12ff.

75. "IT Drivers Are Myriad for Chemical Manufacturers," *Chemical Marketing Reporter* 251, no. 20 (May 19, 1997): 21.

76. Lisa Nadile, "Chemicals: Seeking the Right Formula," *Information Week* (September 22, 2997), 141.

77. "Supply Chain Management Efforts Lag," *Chemical Market Reporter* 255, no. 14 (April 5, 1999): 34.

78. Rick Whiting, "Information Week 500: Chemicals: IT Opens Doors for Chemical Makers," *Information Week* (September 27, 1999), 113 ff.

79. Ibid. Subsections of the industry, such as plastics producers, reported similar findings; for example, see Frank Esposito, "Plastics Industry Taps Into E-Commerce," *Plastics News* 11 (December 6, 1994): 4.

80. "Forecast 2000: IT Takes on Supply Chains," *Chemical Week* 162, no. 1 (January 5, 2000): 34. For case studies, see "Old-Line Chemical Companies Turn to E-Commerce Marketplace," *Pittsburgh Post-Gazette* (July 13, 2000), online version of Knight-Ridder/Tribune Business News; "Chemical Companies Step Up E-Commerce and Internet Use," *Chemical Market Reporter* 258, no. 13 (September 25, 2000): 29.

81. Ibid.

82. Judith N. Mottl, "Eastman's E-Business Venture," *InternetWeek* (January 8, 2001), 41.

83. J. Anderson, "Future Directions of R&D in the Process Industries," *Computerized Industrial Engineering* 34, no. 2 (November 1997): 61–72; A. A. Linninger, S. Chowdhry, V. Bahl, and H. Krendl, "A Systems Approach to Mathematical Modeling of Industrial Processes," *Computers and Chemical Engineering* 24, nos. 2–7 (July 15, 2000): 591–598.

84. William S. Comanor and Stuart O. Schweitzer, "Pharmaceuticals," in Walter Adams and James Brock (eds.), *The Structure of American Industry*, 9th ed. (Englewood Cliffs, N.J.: Prentice-Hall, 1995): 177.

85. "IT Could Save Pharmaceutical Companies Millions of Dollars in R&D," *Marketletter* (March 29, 1999); "Annual Report of Retail Pharmacy: Suppliers Confront Opportunities, Challenges," *Chain Drug Review* 21, no. 14 (August 30, 1999): RX73.

86. Gary P. Pisano, "Pharmaceutical Biotechnology," in Benn Steil, David G. Victor, and Richard R. Nelson (eds.), *Technological Innovation and Economic Performance* (Princeton, N.J.: Princeton University Press, 2002): 347.

87. Ibid., 349–352.

88. Peter Temin, *Taking Your Medicine: Drug Regulation in the United States* (Cambridge, Mass.: Harvard University Press, 1980): 87. For an early account of the industry by an economist, see Walter S. Measday, "The Pharmaceutical Industry," in Walter Adams (ed.), *The Structure of American Industry*, 6th ed. (New York: Macmillan, 1971): 156–188; Richard W. Oliver, *The Coming Biotech Age: The Business of Bio-Materials* (New York: McGraw-Hill, 2000): 5–16, 21–26.

89. The use of computers in medicine and in medical facilities represents both applications and industries that differ from pharmaceuticals. For the first major collection of historical evidence of the role of computing in medicine, see Bruce I. Blum and Karen Duncan (eds.), *A History of Medical Informatics* (New York: ACM Press, 1990).

90. For a detailed analysis of these competencies, see Office of Technology Assessment, *Pharmaceutical R&D: Costs, Risks and Rewards* (Washington, D.C.: U.S. Government Printing Office, 1993). Temin, *Taking Your Medicine*, remains the most useful account of the industry, although it is very dated because it does not cover the biotechnology revolution, which occurred after publication. For that new development, see Oliver, *Coming Biotech Age*.

91. Comanor and Schweitzer, "Pharmaceuticals," 184.

92. For a very lucid explanation of the process, see Pisano, "Pharmaceutical Biotechnology," 354–357.

93. For an analysis of the industry in late 1998, see "Annual Report: Top 50 Pharmaceutical Companies: The Golden Age," *Medical Advertising News* 17, no. 9 (September 1998): 3ff. For an analysis of the role of emerging biotech firms, see "What Next for Biotechs?" *Barron's* (March 20, 2000), http://www.barrons.com.

94. This account and material for the next paragraph are drawn from Michael D. Lemonick, "The Future of Drugs: Brave New Pharmacy," *Time* (January 15, 2001), 59–67.

95. For a discussion of how computer technology is applied and its implications for future R&D, see Michael Freemantle, "Downsizing Chemistry," *Chemical and Engineering News* 77, no. 8 (February 22, 1999): 27–36; Engel Styli, "A Time to Outsource," *R&D Directions* 5, no. 8 (September 1999): 74ff.

96. Pisano, "Pharmaceutical Biotechnology," 357.

97. Industry CIOs acknowledged their appetite for software tools that helped them manage what amounted to an extended R&D supply chain: Thomas Trainer, "Technology in the Pharmaceutical Industry: The Patient Is Waiting," *Vital Speeches of the Day* 65, no. 2 (November 1, 1998): 50–51.

98. "Focus Report: Information Technology 2000," *Chemical Market Reporter* (July 31, 2000), FR3; Cynthia Challener, "Regulatory and Technological Changes Drive LIMS Market," *Chemical Market Reporter* (August 28, 2000), NA.

99. What contributes to a reputation for being slow to adopt are these kinds of measures of relative expenditures. In the early 1990s, for example, the spending of banks and the financial sector rose from 5 percent (1993) to 12 percent (1996).

100. For a description of outsourcing and partnering, see Patricia Van Arnum, "The Incredible Shrinking Company," *Chemical Marketing Reporter* 251, no. 5 (February 3, 1997): SR8ff.

101. W. Rivera Hernandez, "A Production Information System, An Application in the Pharmaceutical Industry," *Computerized Industrial Engineering* 33, nos. 1–2 (October 1997): 15–18.

102. Cynthia Challener, "Custom Relationship Management and R&D Are Key for Pharma Applications," *Chemical Market Reporter* (October 23, 2000): 19.

103. Liz Michalski, "Technological Innovations in Data Management," *Pharmaceutical Technology* 24, no. 11 (November 2000): 88–90. Using commercially available software tools, as opposed to writing one's own, also helped: David Bachman and Kenneth Dingman, "Enterprise Historian and Production Data Management Applications," *Pharmaceutical Technology* 24, no. 11 (November 2000): 56–66.

104. George H. Loftberg, "E-commerce Bytes: Merck & Co.," *Drug Store News* 22, no. 19 (December 18, 2000): 8.

105. George Hill, "Get Ready for E-pharma," *Medical Advertising News* 18, no. 8 (August 1999): 1.

106. The study was by Binshan Lin and Fenghueih Huarng, "Internet in the Pharmaceutical

Industry: Infrastructure Issues," *American Business Review* 18, no. 1 (January 2000): 101–106. Reports of concern at the slowness of adoption include Kim Roller, "Accelerated Market Drives Pharmaceutical Boom," *Drug Store News* 22, no. 1 (January 17, 2000): 21ff; Sidnee Pinho and Nathan Dowden, "B2B Opportunities," *Pharmaceutical Executive* 20, no. 7 (July 2000): 106–114; Wayne Koberstein, "A Rolling Wave," *Pharmaceutical Executive* (August 2000): 10–11; C. P. Spiguel, "The Pharmaceutical Industry in the 21st Century: Surviving the e-business Environment," *Drug Information Journal* 34, no. 3 (July-September 2000): 709–723.

107. "New Pharma Business Model: Can You Survive It?" *Pharmaceutical Executive* 20, no. 11 (November 2000): 94.

108. Paul Bleicher, David Van Cleave, and Gilbert Benghiat, "Pharma-Physician E-Hubs," *Pharmaceutical Executive* 20, no. 10 (October 2000): 86–96.

109. All the data for this paragraph came from "New Pharma Business Model," 94–95.

110. "US Market Growth of 16.9% Driving World Pharmaceutical Sales," *Marketletter* (October 2000): unpaginated.

111. "Pharma Companies Step Up Web Sales, Marketing Efforts," *Medical Marketing and Media* 35, no. 11 (November 2000): 24; Donald E. L. Johnson, "Web Site Experimenting Can Benefit Hospitals," *Health Care Strategic Management* 18, no. 12 (December 2000): 2–3.

112. "Direct to Cybercustomer," *Medical Advertising News* 19, no. 11 (November 2000): 34ff.

113. For a description of the static nature of the industry's business model and circumstances, see Pisano, "Pharmaceutical Biotechnology," 347–366, and his broader study, *The Development Factory: Unlocking the Potential of Process Innovation* (Boston: Harvard Business School Press, 1996).

114. Robert E. Evenson, "Agricultural Biotechnology," in Steil, Victor, and Nelson, *Technological Innovation and Economic Performance*, 367–384.

Chapter 7

1. For introductions to these issues, see Frank Webster, *Theories of the Information Society* (London: Routledge, 1995); James W. Cortada (ed.), *Rise of the Knowledge Worker* (Boston: Butterworth-Heinemann, 1998); Daniel E. Sichel, *The Computer Revolution: An Economic Perspective* (Washington, D.C.: Brookings Institution Press, 1997). Daniel Bell was one of the most influential in getting people to think in terms of a post-industrial society through his book *The Coming of Post-Industrial Society: A Venture in Social Forecasting* (New York: Penguin, 1973), but for a contrary view, which says that all societies always had a high information content, see the British sociologist Anthony Gibbons, *Modernity and Self-Identity: Self and Society in the Late Modern Age* (Cambridge: Polity, 1991); and for an analysis of Bell and Gibbons, see Webster, *Theories of the Information Society*, 30–73.

2. For discussion of the changes, see J. Steven Landefeld and Barbara M. Fraumeni, "Measuring the New Economy," paper dated May 5, 2000, Bureau of Economic Analysis.

3. U.S. Census Bureau, "New Industries in NAICS," update of March 30, 1998, http://www.census.gov/epcd/www/naicsind.htm.

4. Jeffrey R. Yost, "CBI Software History Conference at Xerox PARC," *Charles Babbage Institute Newsletter* 23, no. 2 (Winter 2001): 1, 6–7.

5. See, for example, U.S. Census Bureau, "Implementing NAICS at the Census Bureau," updated press release of May 20, 1998, which includes a bibliography of other related papers, all available online at http://ww.census.gov/epcd/www/naicensus.html; Brent R. Moulton, "Improved Estimates of the National Income and Product Accounts for 1929–99: Results of

the Comprehensive Revision," *Survey of Current Business* (April 2000): 11–17; J. Landefeld and Fraumeni, "Measuring the New Economy," passim.

6. For a complete listing of the industries, number of firms, employees, and revenues for all sectors, not just manufacturing, see U.S. Census Bureau, "1997 Economic Census: Bridge Between SIC and NAICS," dated June 27, 2000, http://www.census.gov/epcd/ec97brdg/INDXSIC2.HTM.

7. For a description of how this industry disappeared in the United States, overtaken by Japanese firms, see Alfred D. Chandler, Jr., *Inventing the Electronic Century: The Epic Story of the Consumer Electronics and Computer Industries* (New York: Free Press, 2001): 50–81.

8. Richard N. Langlois and W. Edward Steinmueller, "The Evolution of Competitive Advantage in the Worldwide Semiconductor Industry, 1947–1996," in David C. Mowery and Richard R. Nelson (eds.), *Sources of Industrial Leadership: Studies of Seven Industries* (Cambridge: Cambridge University Press, 1999): 19–78, quote on 19.

9. Jeffrey T. Macher, David C. Mowery, and David A. Hodges, "Semiconductors," in David C. Mowery (ed.), *U.S. Industry in 2000: Studies in Competitive Performance* (Washington, D.C.: National Academy Press, 1999): 245–285.

10. Langlois and Steinmueller, "Evolution of Competitive Advantage," 24–33; Macher, Mowery, and Hodges, "Semiconductors," 245.

11. Langlois and Steinmueller, "Evolution of Competitive Advantage," 26–27.

12. Macher, Mowery, and Hodges, "Semiconductors," 246–247, 249–254, 263–264.

13. David C. Mowery and Nathan Rosenberg, *Paths of Innovation: Technological Change in 20th Century America* (Cambridge: Cambridge University Press, 1998): 133.

14. For a clear discussion of the issues reviewed in this paragraph, see Macher, Mowery, and Hodges, "Semiconductors," 254–268.

15. For more formal explanations of this process for the period 1960s–1970s, see Nico Hazewindus and John Tooker, *The U.S. Microelectronics Industry: Technical Change, Industry Growth and Social Impact* (New York: Pergamon, 1982): 44–58. For the 1980s–1990s, see Kenneth A. Jackson (ed.), *Processing of Semiconductors, Vol. 16, Materials Science and Technology: A Comprehensive Treatment*, eds. R. W. Cahn, P. Haasen, and E. J. Kramer (New York: Weinheim, 1996); a flowchart of a conventional fabrication process is on 595. For a relatively nontechnical overview of the production process, see P. R. Morris, *A History of the World Semiconductor Industry* (Stevenage, Eng.: Peter Peregrinus, 1990): 64–71. For a very nontechnical discussion, see Franco Malerba, *The Semiconductor Business: The Economics of Rapid Growth and Decline* (Madison: University of Wisconsin Press, 1985): 15–19.

16. William E. Harding, "Semiconductor Manufacturing in IBM, 1957 to the Present: A Perspective," *IBM Journal of Research and Development* 25, no. 5 (September 1981): 648. For details on IBM's role, particularly for manual systems of the 1950s, see Charles J. Bashe, Lyle R. Johnson, John H. Palmer, and Emerson W. Pugh, *IBM's Early Computers* (Cambridge, Mass.: MIT Press, 1986): 399–411. For an excellent flowchart, illustrating the automatic production process for circuit boards with an IBM 1410 computer system in the early 1960s, see Emerson W. Pugh, Lyle R. Johnson, and John H. Palmer, *IBM's 360 and Early 370 Systems* (Cambridge, Mass.: MIT Press, 1991): 91.

17. Daniel Holbrook, Wesley M. Cohen, David A. Hounshell, and Steven Klepper, "The Nature, Sources, and Consequences of Firm Differences in the Early History of the Semiconductor Industry," *Strategic Management Journal* 21 (2000): 1030.

18. Harding, "Semiconductor Manufacturing in IBM," 650.

19. Ibid.

20. Ibid., 652.

21. Ibid.; CPU means central processing unit, in other words, a computer. System/360 was IBM's mainframe product line in the 1960s.

22. Ibid., 657.

23. Each of these applications is described by John McGehee, John Hebley, and Jack Mahaffey, "The MMST Computer-Integrated Manufacturing System Framework," *IEEE Transactions on Semiconductor Manufacturing* 7, no. 2 (May 1994): 107–116.

24. Robert C. Leachman and David A. Hodges, "Benchmarking Semiconductor Manufacturing," *IEEE Transactions on Semiconductor Manufacturing* 9, no. 2 (May 1996): 158.

25. Holbrook et al., "Nature, Sources, and Consequences of Firm Differences," 1017–1041.

26. For these findings, see Leachman and Hodges, "Benchmarking Semiconductor Manufacturing," 158–169.

27. Holbrook et al., "Nature, Sources, and Consequences of Firm Differences," 10–30. But see also Richard N. Langlois, "Computers and Semiconductors," in Benn Steil, David G. Victor, and Richard R. Nelson (eds.), *Technological Innovation and Economic Performance* (Princeton, N.J.: Princeton University Press, 2002): 265–284.

28. Charles S. Meyer, David K. Lynn, and Douglas J. Hamilton, *Analysis and Design of Integrated Circuits* (New York: McGraw-Hill, 1968): 12–35; Peter R. Shepherd, *Integrated Circuit Design, Fabrication and Test* (New York: McGraw-Hill, 1996): 1–19.

29. The entire paragraph is based on data from Macher, Mowery, and Hodges, "Semiconductors," 268–270.

30. Undated slide presentation (circa late 2000), "IBM Burlington," in my possession.

31. Holbrook et al., "Nature, Sources, and Consequences of Firm Differences," 1031.

32. The coordinating role of management was the essential function Chandler identified in his study of modern industries: Alfred D. Chandler, Jr., *Strategy and Structure: Chapters in the History of the Industrial Enterprise* (Cambridge, Mass.: MIT Press, 1962).

33. See Macher, Mowery, and Hodges, "Semiconductors," 271–273 for a useful overview of this organization and other collaborative initiatives.

34. Ibid., 282–286.

35. Jeffrey T. Macher, David C. Mowery, and David A. Hodges, "Reversal of Fortune? The Recovery of the U.S. Semiconductor Industry," *California Management Review* 41, no. 1 (Fall 1998): 107–136.

36. Ron Bohm, "The Semiconductor Market Has Its . . . 'Ups and Downs,' " *Electronic Buyers News Semiconductor Megatrends Special Report* (November 1, 1999).

37. Material for this paragraph comes from Jennifer Baljko Shah, "Special Report: The Automotive Supply Chain: Racing for the Checkered Flag," *Electronic Buyers News* (February 14, 2000), 1ff.

38. Tom Polischuk, "Packaged Industrial Computer Solutions Are on the Move," *Instrumentation and Control Systems* 69, no. 8 (August 1996): 25–39.

39. For an explanation of disk drives, written when they had become the most widely used form of digital storage, see Nancy Stern and Robert A. Stern, *Computers in Society* (Englewood Cliffs, N.J.: Prentice-Hall, 1983): 103–107. See also David McKendrick, "Hard Disk Drives," in David C. Mowery (ed.), *U.S. Industry in 2000: Studies in Competitive Performance* (Washington, D.C.: National Academy Press, 1999): 287–328.

40. Gordon Bell and James N. Gray, "The Revolution Yet to Happen," in Peter J. Denning and Robert M. Metcalfe (eds.), *Beyond Calculation: The Next Fifty Years of Computing* (New York: Copernicus, 1997): 12–14.

41. For a major census on data, see Peter Lyman and Hal R. Varian, "How Much Information," undated (circa 2000) and available at how-much-info@sims.berkeley.edu. See Appendix B in this volume for a summary based on their findings.

42. McKendrick, "Hard Disk Drives," 293.

43. J. M. Harker et al. "A Quarter Century of Disk File Innovation," *IBM Journal of Research and Development* 25, no. 5 (September 1981): 677–689; and in the same issue, L. D. Stevens,

"The Evolution of Magnetic Storage," 663–675. Think of 1 byte as a letter, like *e*, and 10 bytes as a word, like *easy*.

44. For details, see Kanu G. Ashar, *Magnetic Disk Drive Technology: Heads, Media, Channel, Interfaces and Integration* (New York: IEEE Press, 1997); F. Mrad, "The Characterization of a Clean Room Assembly Process," *IEEE Transactions on Industrial Applications* 35, no. 2 (March–April 1999): 399–404; T. Cowburn, C. Savage, J. Hunt, and J. Putnam, "High Density Flex Assembly for Advanced High End Disc Drives," in *IPC Fourth Annual National Conference on Flexible Circuits: Meeting the Challenge of the Next Generation of Packaging, 1998* (Northbrook, Ill: Institute for Interconnecting and Packaging Electronic Circuits, 1998), vol 1: 15–21.

45. Z. Stamenkovic, N. Stojadinovic, and S. Simitrijev, "Modeling of Integrated Circuit Yield Loss Mechanisms," *IEEE Transactions on Semiconductor Manufacturing* 9, no. 2 (1996): 270–272; A. Amemoto, "Information System That Supports Production Operation of Hard Disk Drives," *Fujitsu* 50, no. 1 (1999): 43–49 (in Japanese).

46. For an excellent analysis of the role of yields in the HDD Industry, see Roger E. Bohn and Christian Terwiesch, "The Economics of Yield-Driven Processes," unpublished paper, September 1, 1998, available from the Bohn at Rbohn@ucsd.edu. For an account of simulation in one aspect of production, see Guao Lin, "Reducing the Manufacturing Costs Associated with Hard Disk Drives: A New Disturbance Rejection Control Scheme," *IEEE/ASME Transactions Mechatronics* 2, no. 2 (June 1997): 77–85.

47. McKendrick, "Hard Disk Drives," 291–292.

48. For a list of the firms that entered and exited the industry and those that survived at the end of the century, see James Porter, "Disk Drives' Evolution," paper presented at the 100th Anniversary Conference on Magnetic Recording and Information Storage, December 14, 1998, Santa Clara University, Santa Clara, Calif., available at http://www.distrend.com. In the spring of 2002, IBM announced that it was getting out of the business of manufacturing disk drives, recognizing that these devices had become commodities, with razor-thin profit margins. In earlier decades, they had been high-profit margin products for all their suppliers; now they were like PCs and terminals.

49. Dieter Ernst, "From Partial to Systemic Globalization: International Production Networks in the Electronics Industry," paper dated April 1997: 8, http://brie.berkeley.edu/-briewww/pubs/wp/wp98.html.

50. Ibid., 10.

51. Ibid., 14.

52. McKendrik, "Hard Disk Drives," passim. But see also David McKendrick, *From Silicon Valley to Singapore: Location and Competitive Advantage in the Hard Disk Drive Industry* (Stanford, Calif.: Stanford University Press, 2000).

53. Emerson W. Pugh, *Memories That Shaped an Industry: Decisions Leading to IBM System 360* (Cambridge, Mass.: MIT Press, 1984): 250–251.

54. Ernst, "From Partial to Systemic Globalization," 24–30.

55. Ibid., 28.

56. Ibid., 40.

57. McKindrick, "Hard Disk Drives," 314–322.

58. Product design is a critical element in this industry; see C. M. Christensen, F. F. Suarez, and James M. Utterbach, "Strategies for Survival in Fast-Changing Industries," *Management Science* 44, no. 12 (December 1998): 207–220.

59. McKendrick, "Hard Disk Drives," 323.

60. Ibid., 324.

61. Ibid., 326.

62. For a detailed analysis of deployment, see James W. Cortada, *Making the Information Society: Experience, Consequences, and Possibilities* (Upper Saddle River, N.J.: Prentice Hall/Financial Times, 2002): 136–189.

63. For example, Nancy Stern and Robert A Stern , *Computers in Society* (Englewood Cliffs, N.J.: Prentice-Hall, 1983): 127–139; Paul E. Ceruzzi, *A History of Modern Computing* (Cambridge, Mass.: MIT Press, 1998): 9, 80–81; see also notes below, citing overviews of the Software Industry.

64. For two bibliographic introductions to the literature, see James W. Cortada, *A Bibliographic Guide to the History of Computing, Computers, and the Information Processing Industry* (Westport, Conn.: Greenwood Press, 1990): 343–491, and my *Second Bibliographic Guide to the History of Computing, Computers, and the Information Processing Industry* (Westport, Conn.: Greenwood Press, 1996): 276–279. For a useful, short history of software, see Detlev J. Hoch, Cyriac R. Roeding, Gert Purkert, and Sandro K. Lindner, *Secrets of Software Success: Management Insights from 100 Software Firms Around the World* (Boston: Harvard Business School Press, 2000): 259–271.

65. This was a standard practice at IBM for supplying updates to mainframes in the 1980s and to its own employees, using the company's Intranet, in the 1990s.

66. Robert V. Head, "The Packaged Program," *Data Processing Digest* (April 1968): 1–12; Martin Campbell-Kelly, "Development and Structure of the International Software Industry, 1950–1990," *Business and Economic History* 24 (1995): 73–110; T. Cottrell, "Strategy and Survival in the Microcomputer Software Industry, 1981–1986," unpublished Ph.D. dissertation, Haas School of Business, University of California, Berkeley, 1995. The PC is generating a vast literature; the earliest collection, with reviews of some 400 items, (some dealing with PC marketing), is Michael Nicita and Ronald Petrusha, *The Reader's Guide to Micro Computer Books* (Brooklyn, N.Y.: Golden-Lee Books, 1983).

67. For a brief account of these shifts in definition, see Stephen E. Siwek and Harold W. Furchtgott-Roth, *International Trade in Computer Software* (Westport, Conn.: Quorum Books, 1993): 11–26.

68. Franklin M. Fisher, James W. McKie, and Richard B. Mancke, *IBM and the U.S. Data Processing Industry: An Economic History* (New York: Praeger, 1983): 176–177; Franklin M. Fisher, John J. McGowan, and Joen E. Greenwood, *Folded, Spindled, and Mutilated: Economic Analysis and U.S. v. IBM* (Cambridge, Mass.: MIT Press, 1983): 209–211.

69. W. Edward Steinmueller, "The U.S. Software Industry: An Analysis and Interpretive History," in David C. Mowery (ed.), *The International Computer Software Industry: A Comparative Study of Industry Evolution and Structure* (New York: Oxford University Press, 1996): 19.

70. Ibid., 26.

71. Daniel E. Sichel, *The Computer Revolution: An Economic Perspective* (Washington, D.C.: Brookings Institution Press, 1997): 46–47.

72. Ibid., 50–51.

73. Siwek and Furchtgott-Roth, *International Trade in Computer Software*, 4.

74. Reid Henderson, "Personnel Recruitment, Selection and Management," *Data Processing Proceedings 1969* (Montreal: DPMA, 1970): 251–257; U.S. Bureau of Labor Statistics, *Computer Manpower Outlook*, Bulletin 1826 (Washington, D.C.: U.S. Government Printing Office, 1974): 6–31; William A. Delaney, "Software Managers Speak Out," *Datamation* 23, no. 10 (October 1977): 77–78; U.S. Bureau of Labor Statistics, *Industry Wage Survey: Computer and Data Processing Services, 1987*, Bulletin 2318 (Washington, D.C.: U.S. Government Printing Office, November 1988): 3–17; Edward Yourdon, *Decline and Fall of the American Programmer* (Englewood Cliffs, N.J.: Yourdon Press, 1992): 25.

75. Peter Freeman and William Aspray, *The Supply of Information Technology Workers in the United States* (Washington, D.C.: Computing Research Association, 1999): 34–35.

76. Yourdon, *Decline and Fall of the American Programmer*, 73–131; James Martin, *Application Development Without Programmers* (Englewood Cliffs, N.J.: Prentice-Hall, 1982): 14–50.

77. For illustration of the issues involved, see "The Fourth Generation Makes Its Mark,"

Dun's Business Month (July 1985): 79–80; for a fuller bibliography, see Cortada, *Second Bibliographic Guide*, 349–372.

78. See, For example, Bernard Boar, *Application Prototyping* (Reading, Mass.: Addison-Wesley, 1984); Grace Murray Hopper, "Standardization and the Future of Computers," *Data Processing Proceedings 1969* (Montreal: DPMA, 1970): 329–335; H. D. Mills, "Software Engineering," *Science* 195 (March 18, 1977): 1199–1205. See also notes 79–81 for further references.

79. James P. Anderson, "Better Processing Through Better Architecture," *Datamation* 13, no. 8 (August 1967): 37–43; the massive survey by Barry W. Boehm, *Software Engineering Economics* (Englewood Cliffs, N.J.: Prentice-Hall, 1981); C. West Churchman, *The Systems Approach* (New York: Delacorte Press, 1968); Michael A. Cusumano, "Factory Concepts and Practices in Software Development," *IEEE Annals of the History of Computing* 13, no. 1 (1991): 3–32; the highly influential study by Tom DeMarco, *Controlling Software Projects* (Englewood Cliffs, N.J.: Yourdon Press, 1982); James R. Donaldson, "Structured Programming," *Datamation* 19, no. 12 (December 1973): 52–57; Tom Gilb, *Principles of Software Engineering Management* (Reading, Mass.: Addison-Wesley, 1989); Capers Jones, *Programming Productivity* (New York: McGraw-Hill, 1986); the encyclopedic work by James Martin, *Information Engineering*, 3 vols. (Englewood Cliffs, N.J.: Prentice-Hall, 1990); D. A. Pearson, "Multiprogramming," *Scientific American* 248 (March 1983): 50–57; Yourdon, *Decline and Fall of the American Programmer*, 92–131, which also includes substantial amounts of bibliography on these subjects.

80. Yourdon, *Decline and Fall of the American Programmer*; the entire volume is devoted to these themes.

81. On early initiatives, see Thomas R. Gildersleeve, *Data Processing Project Management* (New York: Van Nostrand Reinhold, 1974); a popular how-to book from the 1960s is Charles Leech, *The Management of Computer Programming Projects* (New York: American Management Association, 1967); a classic for many American DP managers is Philip Metzger, *Managing a Programming Project* (Englewood Cliffs, N.J.: Prentice-Hall, 1983, and earlier editions).

82. For a summary of various economic studies, see Sichel, *Computer Revolution*, 52–53, 55–58. A recent study of software prices, prepared in connection with a book on Microsoft's antitrust problems in the United States, offers considerable detail: Stan J. Liebowitz and Stephen E. Margolis, *Winners, Losers and Microsoft: Competition and Antitrust in High Technology* (Oakland, Calif.: Independent Institute, 1999): 135–233.

83. See notes 77–80 and also "Managing Systems Development [at] Montgomery Ward," *Installation Management* (November 1973), "Applications," Box A-1074-2, IBM Archives, Somers, N.Y.

84. For a description and history of CASE tools and a useful contemporary bibliography, see Yourdon, *Decline and Fall of the American Programmer*, 132–176.

85. Peter Hall, Ann Markusen, Richard Cohen, and Barbara Wachsman, "The Computer Software Industry: Prospects and Policy Issues," Working Paper No. 410, July 1983 (Berkeley: Institute of Urban and Regional Development, University of California, 1983), mimeographed copy in the University of Wisconsin Memorial Library, Madison.

86. Because these tools keep changing, major sources of information can be found in such publications as *ComputerWorld, InfoWeek, IBM Research and Development*, and *IBM Systems Journal*.

87. Hoch et al., *Secrets of Software Success*, 9.

88. The issue was recognized early in the history of IT: Richard F. Clippinger, "The Standards Outlook," *Datamation* 8, no. 1 (January 1962): 35–37; and see also Paul Ward and Stephen J. Mellor, *Structured Systems Development for Real-Time Systems*, 3 vols. (Englewood Cliffs, N.J.: Yourdon Press, 1986). I have commented elsewhere on the standards issue in more detail: James W. Cortada, "A Framework for Understanding Technological Change:

Lessons from Information Technology, 1868–1997," in Gary D. Libecap (ed.), *Entrepreneurship and Economic Growth in the American Economy* (Amsterdam: JAI, 2000): 47–92.

89. Frederick P. Brooks, Jr., *The Mythical Man-Month: Essays on Software Engineering* (Reading, Mass.: Addison-Wesley, 1982): 177.

90. "Michigan Bell Adopts Sophisticated Information Processing," *Journal of Machine Accounting* (January 1965): 10–12; Installation DP Management, RC 2500/Box A-1245-1, IBM Archives, Somers, N.Y. Alvin L. Kustanowitz, "System Life Cycle Estimation (SLICE): A New Approach to Estimating Resources for Application Program Development," Attachment to IBM, *Marketing Newsletter*, January 27, 1978 (White Plains, N.Y.: IBM Corp., 1978), MS-78-004, in my possession. The IBM Archives also has an extensive collection of these newsletters for the period 1960s–1980s.

91. For an excellent review of conventional and emerging software development practices, along with a detailed view of software development at Microsoft, see Michael A. Cusumano and Stanely A. Smith, "Beyond the Waterfall: Software Development at Microsoft," in David B. Yoffie (ed.), *Competing in the Age of Digital Convergence* (Boston: Harvard Business School Press, 1997): 371–411. *Waterfall* refers to the name of the formal software development process most companies used in the 1950s–1980s, which includes a top-down design, modular writing of code, and testing.

92. James W. Cortada, "Using Textual Demographics to Understand Computer Use: 1950–1990," *IEEE Annals of the History of Computing* 23, no. 1 (January-March 2001): 34–56. Both the Burroughs Papers at the Archives of the Charles Babbage Institute, University of Minnesota, Minneapolis, and the IBM Archives, Somers, N.Y., have massive collections of these kinds of materials. The S/360 documentation (circa 1960s) alone amounts to over 80 linear feet of bookshelves. For a bibliography on bibliographies that contain this kind of literature, see Cortada, *Bibliographic Guide to the History of Computing*, 7–15.

93. Only at the end of the century did the major software firms, such as Microsoft and Norton, begin to deliver products over the Internet.

94. This was part of the firm's knowledge management strategy and delivery tactics. For details, see Kuan-Tsae Huang, Yang W. Lee, and Richard Y. Wang, *Quality Information and Knowledge* (Upper Saddle River, N.J.: Prentice Hall, 1999): 9–32; Kuan-Tsae Huang, "Capitalizing on Intellectual Assets," *IBM Systems Journal* 37, no. 4 (1998), reprinted in James W. Cortada and John A. Woods (eds.), *The Knowledge Management Yearbook, 1999–2000* (Boston: Butterworth-Heinemann, 1999): 346–366.

95. For months in advance of the delivery of this product, for example, all the major U.S. TV channels carried multiple, about it stories. These channels included ABC, CBS, NBC, Fox, and especially CNN.

96. One reporter commented in the 1990s about Microsoft's marketing: "Windows 95 seemed to have received more press attention than the presidential campaign": Wendy Goldman Rohm, *The Microsoft File: The Secret Case Against Bill Gates* (New York: Times Business, 1998): 210; see 210–211 for a more detailed account of the marketing blitz associated with this product.

97. I have preserved all of these CD-based advertisements—which are, of course, software packages—sent to my home during the late 1990s. I have received an average of 2 to 3 of these packages per month since 1997, resulting in a collection of over 200. They came in the mail, along with free samples of soap, which had been delivered to American homes for decades.

98. Michael E. Porter pointed this out in *Competitive Strategy: Techniques for Analyzing Industries and Competitors* (New York: Free Press, 1980): 173–174, 201–211.

99. For example, see Mowery, "Computer Software Industry," 133–168.

100. Jason Dedrick and Kenneth L. Kraemer, *Asia's Computer Challenge: Threat or Opportunity for the United States and the World?* (New York: Oxford University Press, 1998) is a

good model for looking at national experiences with high-tech industries. The bibliography includes examples of process- and firm- level economic studies.

101. From Microsoft, there is Bill Gates, the firm's CEO in the 1990s, who wrote *The Road Ahead* (New York: Viking, 1995) and *Business @ The Speed of Thought: Using a Digital Nervous System* (New York: Time Warner, 1999); Jeff Papows was CEO of Lotus when he wrote *Enteprise.com: Market Leadership in the Information Age* (Reading, Mass.: Perseus Books, 1998).

102. From Apple, the most prolific manager is Guy Kawasaki, *The Macintosh Way* (Glenview, Ill.: Scott, Foresman, 1989), and *The Computer Curmudgeon* (Carmel, 2nd.: Hayden, 1991).

103. See, for instance, Andrew S. Grove, *High Output Management* (New York: Random House, 1966); *The Physics and Technology of Semiconductor Devices* (New York: Wiley, 1967); *One On One With Andy Grove* (New York: Putnam, 1987); *Only the Paranoid Survive: How to Exploit the Crisis Points That Challenge Every Company and Career* (New York: Currency Doubleday, 1996).

104. At GE, for instance, medical-imaging products at the dawn of the new century were essentially specialized computer systems.

105. Carl Shapiro and Hal R. Varian, *Information Rules: A Strategic Guide to the Network Economy* (Boston: Harvard Business Press School, 1999): 1–2.

106. Although the literature on this issue is extensive, particularly for such topics as Silicon Valley and the Semiconductor Industry, it applies across many low-tech industries and across many nations. See, for instance, on the United States Annalee Saxenian, *Regional Advantage: Culture and Competition in Silicon Valley and Route 128* (Cambridge, Mass.: Harvard University Press, 1995); on East Asia: Dedrick and Kraemer, *Asia's Computer Challenge;* on the European semiconductor business: Malerba, *Semiconductor Business;* on Brazil: Paulo Bastos Tigre, *Technology and Competition in the Brazilian Computer Industry* (New York: St. Martin, 1983); on China: Jeff X. Zhang and Yan Wang, *The Emerging Market of China's Computer Industry* (Westport, Conn.: Quorum Books, 1995); on the British: G. Ashe, P. Jowett, and J. McGee, *The Software Industry in the U.K.* (London: London Business School, 1986); and on a cross-national comparison, T. Nakahara, "The Industrial Organization and Information Structure of the Software Industry: A U.S.-Japan Comparison," unpublished MS thesis, Center for Economic Policy Research, May 1993, Stanford University, Stanford, Cal. The Japanese continue to be a source of great interest to students of the industry. See, for instance, Yasunori Baba, Shinji Takai, and Yuji Mizuta, "The User-Driven Evolution of the Japanese Software Industry: The Case of Customized Software for Mainframes," in David C. Mowery (ed.), *The International Computer Software Industry: A Comparative Study of Industry Evolution* (New York: Oxford University Press, 1996): 104–130

107. Many of these issues were at the heart of the U.S. government's antitrust case against Microsoft in the late 1990s, the first major antitrust case involving a software manufacturer. For details, see Liebowitz and Margolis, *Winners, Losers and Microsoft*, 245–268; Richard B. McKenzie, *Trust on Trial: How the Microsoft Case Is Reframing the Rules of Competition* (Cambridge, Mass.: Perseus, 2000): 27–47; Ken Auletta, *World War 3.0: Microsoft and Its Enemies* (New York: Random House, 2001): 77–107; John Heilemann, *Pride Before the Fall: The Trials of Bill Gates and the End of the Microsoft Era* (New York: HarperCollins, 2001): 11–26.

Chapter 8

1. Agatha C. Hughes and Thomas P. Hughes (eds.), *Systems, Experts, and Computers: The Systems Approach in Management and Engineering, World War II and After* (Cambridge, Mass.: MIT Press, 2000): 6–8.

2. J. Williford and A. Chang, "Modeling the FedEx IT Division: A System Dynamics Approach to Strategic IT Planning," *Journal of Systems and Software* 46, nos. 2–3 (April 1999):

203–211; John E. Frook, "FedEx Extranet Application Customizes Tracking," *InternetWeek* (June 29, 1998): 25–26; Bob Brewin and Linda Rosencrance, "UPS: Tightly Linked to Its Customers," *Computerworld* 35, no. 12 (March 19, 2001): 60; Kristin S. Krause, "The UPS Way Forward," *Traffic World* 264, no. 5 (October 30, 2000): 11–12; Douglas Bartholomew, "IT Delivers for UPS," *Industry Week* 247, no. 23 (December 21, 1998): 58–64; Don Cohen and Laurence Prusak, *In Good Company: How Social Capital Makes Organizations Work* (Boston: Harvard Business School Press, 2001): 1–3, 21–22; "UPS Company of the Year," *Forbes* (January 10, 2000): 17–30.

3. Alfred D. Chandler, Jr., *The Visible Hand: The Managerial Revolution in American Business* (Cambridge, Mass.: Harvard University Press, 1977): 80.

4. For example, he noted that "the revolution in the processes of distribution and production rested in large part on the new transportation and communication infrastructure." Ibid., 207.

5. Emma S. Woytinsky, *Profile of the U.S. Economy: A Survey of Growth and Change* (New York: Praeger, 1967): 341–345.

6. BLS, *Railroad Technology and Manpower in the 1970s*, Bulletin 1717 (Washington, D.C.: U.S. Government Printing Office, 1972): 6–7; BLS, *Technological Change and Its Labor Impact in Four Industries*, Bulletin 2316 (Washington, D.C.: Government Printing Office, December 1988): 13.

7. For an excellent description of a variety of early railroad applications and for the case study of the New York Central System, see "Railroad's Data Processing Network Spans Canada" (undated, circa 1957); "Market Reports," CBI 55, Box 71, Folder 11, Archives of the Charles Babbage Institute, University of Minnesota, Minneapolis.

8. Dean E. Richardson, "The Use of Displays in a Freight Car Movement Information System," *Data Processing Proceedings 1965* (Dallas, Tex.: DPMA, 1966): 538–544, quote on 543.

9. The term *classification yards* refers to the place where trains go to be disassembled, with individual cars then hooked together to make up new trains.

10. BLS, *Railroad Technology and Manpower*, 28–30.

11. Ibid., 29. A table in this report indicated that, by industry, the percentage of adoption of computers within the last three years was as follows: mining, 79 percent; other transportation and communications industries, 71 percent; electric utilities, 57 percent; commercial, 68 percent; other businesses, 70 percent, (p. 30).

12. It was of intense interest across the industry, as described in a variety of publications from the period. See, for example, IBM, *Data Processing at Trailer Train* (White Plains, N.Y.: IBM Corp., undated, circa mid-1960s); IBM, *Louisville and Nashville Railroad and the Operating System* (White Plains, N.Y.: IBM Corp., undated, circa mid-1960s); IBM, *Special Railroad Equipment Control Systems Louisville and Nashville Railroad Company* (White Plains, N.Y.: IBM Corp., circa late 1960s); IBM, *Total Operations Processing System for the Southern Pacific Company* (White Plains, N.Y.: IBM Corp., 1968; rev. ed., 1969), all publications from "DP Application Briefs," Box B-116-3, IBM Archives, Somers, N.Y.

13. For detailed descriptions of each application, see IBM, *Total Operations Processing System*, 27–32.

14. A. L. Davis, "Railroad Information System for Management Control," *Computer Yearbook and Directory* (Detroit: American Data Processing, 1966): 219–228.

15. IBM, *Total Operations Processing System*, 3–6.

16. Ibid., 11–12.

17. Fred Cottrell, *Technological Change and Labor in the Railroad Industry* (Lexington, Mass: Heath Lexington, 1970): 137.

18. BLS, *Technological Change and Its Labor Impact in Five Industries*, Bulletin 1961 (Washington, D.C.: U.S. Government Printing Office, 1977): 34–36.

19. For a description of each application, see IBM, *Applications and Abstracts* (White Plains, N.Y.: IBM Corp., 1985): 22–1–22–7.

20. BLS, *Technological Change and Its Labor Impact,* 15.

21. Ibid., 15–16; see also Gus Welty, "A Growth Market for CTC," *Railway Age* (February 1983): 25.

22. Caused by passenger traffic lost to airlines and some freight traffic taken over by the Trucking Industry.

23. BLS, *Technological Change and Its Labor Impact*, 18–21.

24. "Railroads on the Comeback Trail," *Rough Notes* 140, no. 8 (August 1997): 41.

25. "Railway Customers Can Link Electronically," *Automatic I.D. News* 14, no. 12 (November 1998): 1.

26. Brian Milligan, "An Industry Still in Need of Integration," *Purchasing* 128, no. 8 (May 18, 2000): 147.

27. Michael Alexander, "Railroads Lay New E-Market Tracks," *InternetWeek* (February 5, 2001): 10; "RailMarket.com," *Feedstuffs* 73, no. 12 (March 19, 2001): 27.

28. For the story of the caboose, see BLS, *Technological Change and Its Labor Impact*, 15.

29. For a detailed discussion of the economic advantages truckers had over railroads, see William J. Hudson and James A. Constantin, *Motor Transportation: Principles and Practices* (New York: Ronald Press, 1958): 162–165.

30. Sherlene K. S. Lum and Brian C. Moyer, "Gross Domestic Product by Industry for 1998–2000," *Survey of Current Business* (November 2001): 26.

31. Trucks and trains have virtually disappeared in recent years from the literature. For example, in the industry surveys I researched for this book, they are not discussed at all. These include Walter Adams and James Brock (eds.), *The Structure of American Industry*, 9th ed. (Englewood Cliffs, N.J.: Prentice-Hall, 1995; also 10th ed., 2001); David C. Mowery and Richard R. Nelson (eds.), *Sources of Industrial Leadership: Studies of Seven Industries* (Cambridge: Cambridge University Press, 1999); J. Christopher Westland and Theodore H. K. Clark, *Global Electronic Commerce: Theory and Case Studies* (Cambridge, Mass: MIT Press, 1999); Richard K. Lester, *The Productive Edge: How U.S. Industries Are Pointing the Way to a New Era of Economic Growth* (New York: W. W. Norton, 1998). One important exception, although it discusses only the Trucking Industry, is David C. Mowery (eds.), *U.S. Industry in 2000: Studies in Competitive Performance* (Washington D.C.: National Academy Press 1999). Currently, there are no significant studies of the Railroad Industry of the type done on lean retailing, banking, and manufacturing.

32. Woytinsky, *Profile of the U.S. Economy*, 338.

33. Anuradha Nagarajan, Enrique Canessa, Will Mitchell, and C. C. White III, "Trucking Industry: Challenges to Keep Pace," in Robert E. Litan and Alice M. Rivlin (eds.), *The Economic Payoff from the Internet Revolution* (Washington, D.C.: Brookings Institution Press, 2001): 130–131.

34. Bank of America data, cited in Anuradha Nagarajan, James L. Bander, and Chelsea C. White III, "Trucking," in David C. Mowery (ed.), *U.S. Industry in 2000: Studies in Competitive Performance* (Washington, D.C.: National Academy Press, 1999): 124.

35. Nagarajan et al., "Trucking Industry: 131.

36. For a short overview, circa early 1960s, see Samuel H. Brooks and Irvin R. Whiteman, "Transportation," in Alan D. Meacham (ed.), *Data Processing Yearbook* (Detroit: American Data Processing, 1962): 173–180.

37. G. L. Williams, Jr., "The Advancement of Data Processing in the Motor Freight Industry," *Data Processing Proceedings 1965* (Dallas: DPMA, 1966): 289.

38. Ibid., 291.

39. One of the most comprehensive texts on the industry, published in 1958, did not even mention the computer in its 700 pages; however, it did briefly discuss the role of

automation, which at the time meant such items as forklifts to pick up freight and electronic sensors for materials handling: Hudson and Constantin, *Motor Transportation*; for automation, see 350–352.

40. M. Peterson, "Valuable New Hand," *Michigan Motor Carrier-Folks* (June 1965): 1–2.

41. At an industry conference, held May 4–6, 1965, 18 presentations were made on various uses of computers then in operation, from discussions about total systems (then also deployed on in the Railroad Industry) to the use of computers with waybills, tariff and freight rate setting, car tracking, and so forth; see Ohio Chapter Transportation Research Forum, *Automation Breakthrough: Second National Conference on "Tariff Computerization"* (Oxford, 2nd: Transportation Research Forum, 1965). Because this was published in a very limited edition, it should be noted that the one I used is located at the University of Wisconsin, Madison, HE 5623 T7.

42. For a brief description of each of these applications, see IBM, *IBM System/360 Model 20 in the Motor Freight Industry* (White Plains, N.Y.: IBM Corp., 1967): 5–30; DP Application Briefs, Box B-116-3, IBM Archives, Somers, N.Y.

43. BLS, *The Impact of Technology on Labor in Five Industries*, Bulletin 2137 (Washington, D.C.: U.S. Government Printing Office, December 1982): 48.

44. Ibid., 50.

45. Both quotes are in John Hess, *The Mobile Society: A History of the Moving and Storage Industry* (New York: McGraw-Hill, 1973): 188.

46. Ibid., 189.

47. IBM, *Industry Applications and Abstracts* (White Plains, N.Y.: IBM Corp., 1988): 21-1–21-15.

48. American Trucking Associations, *American Trucking Trends 1989* (Alexandria, Va.: ATA, 1989): 8–9. This same report has a table the number of firms from 1945 through 1988. In 1945, there were nearly 21,000 companies; through the next 20 years that number declined to 15,500, reflecting the effects of consolidations and mergers. The number of firms actually increased in the 1970s and 1980s, to over 39,600 in 1988 (p. 13). Failure rates for firms in this industry jumped substantially in the 1980s, as those that could not compete effectively in a deregulated industry closed or were absorbed by other firms. Before deregulation, the industry experienced just under 400 failures a year; by the mid-1980s, over 1,500 annually had become the norm. See American Trucking Associations, *American Trucking Trends 1991–92 Edition* (Alexandria, Va.: ATA, 1992): 7.

49. Frederick H. Abernathy, John T. Dunlop, Janice H. Hammond, and David Weill, *A Stitch in Time: Lean Retailing and the Transformation of Manufacturing, Lessons from the Apparel and Textile Industries* (Cambridge, Mass.: Harvard University Press, 1999): 77. Most of the material for this and the previous paragraph was drawn from various sections of ibid.

50. How trucking firms approached their relations with customers affected the nature of their deployment of IT. This is the finding of the only economic study of this issue, Atreya Chakraborty and Mark Kazarosian, *Product Differentiation and the Use of Information Technology: Evidence from the Trucking Industry*, Working Paper 7222 (Cambridge, Mass.: National Bureau of Economic Research, July 1999): 1–30.

51. Nagarajan et al., "Trucking," 126. See also Federal Highway Administration (FNA), *Commercial Vehicle Fleet Management and Information Systems*, DTFH61-93-C00084 (Washington, D.C.: FHA, October 1997): 2; and yes, this document also had a bar code on it.

52. David Bovet and Yossi Sheffi, "The Brave New World of Supply Chain Management," in John A. Woods and Edward J. Marien (eds.), *The Supply Chain Yearbook 2001 Edition* (New York: McGraw-Hill, 2001): 3–16; originally published in *Supply Chain Management Review* (Spring 1998).

53. Nagarajan et al., "Trucking," 128–130.

54. Ibid., 135–138.

55. Economic evidence that onboard computing had a positive effect on the Trucking Industry is beginning to appear. The first study to present this kind of evidence is Thomas N. Hubbard, *Why Are Process Monitoring Technologies Valuable? The Use of On-Board Information Technology in the Trucking Industry*, Working Paper 6482 (Cambridge, Mass.: National Bureau of Economic Research, March 1998): 5–27.

56. Nagarajan et al., "Trucking," 139–143.

57. Ibid., 149.

58. FHA, *Commercial Vehicle Fleet Management*, 8.

59. Ibid., 19.

60. "Driving ITS Development: Technology and Market Forces," *GPS World*, 7, no. 10 (October 1996): 50ff; "Truckin' On, Wirelessly," *Wireless Week* 5, no. 44 (November 1, 1999): 34; John D. Schulz, "Wal-Mart of Trucking," *Traffic World* 248, no. 4 (October 28, 1996): 28; Daniel J. McConville, "Fragile Links in the Supply Chain," *Distribution* 96, no. 12 (November 1997): 48. McConville made the observation that "the less-than-truckload trucking industry is swept up in the throes of the biggest supply-chain revolution since deregulation overtook the transportation industry nearly two decades ago." For EDI, see "EDI Study: More Shippers and Fleets Interchange Data Electronically," *Commercial Carrier Journal* 155, no. 7 (July 1998): 42–43.

61. "How Schneider Logistics Grows by Using More Than 900 Carrier-Partners," *Commercial Carrier Journal* 155, no. 11 (November 1998): 62.

62. "Internet Service for Motor Carriers," *Traffic World* 248, no. 5 (November 4, 1996): 53; "After 10 Years, Market Is Still Hot," *Traffic World* 249, no. 11 (March 17, 1997): 28; Brad Smith, "Wireless Rules the Road," *Wireless Week* (March 27, 2000): 22; Joel Smith, "UPS Delivers with High-Tech Help," Gannett News Service (May 9, 2000), http://www.usatoday.com/life/cyber/ccarch/ccjoe020.htm; "FedEx to Help Customers Build E-Stores," Associated Press (June 12, 2000), http://www.usatoday.com/life/cyber/tech/cti084.htm; Steve Weinstein, "Trucking Into the 21st Century," *Progressive Grocer* (October 1999): 107–109,110.

63. For the various studies and surveys, see Nagarajan et al., "Trucking Industry," 129–171, especially 141.

64. Ibid., 141.

65. Ibid., 149.

66. Ibid., 152–153.

67. Ibid., 158.

68. Ibid. 164–166. See also Nagarajan et al., "E-Commerce and the Changing Terms of Competition in the Trucking Industry: A Study of Firm Level Responses to Changing Industry Structure," *Tracking a Transformation: E-Commerce and the Terms of Competition in Industries* (Washington, D.C.: Brookings Institution Press, 2001).

69. Parry Desmond, "The Top 100," *Commercial Carrier Journal* 157, no. 8 (August 2000): 39–40.

70. "Distribution: Transportation," *Business Week* (January 8, 2001): 130.

71. Every BLS study cited in this book cataloged industry-specific technologies, not all of which were pure computing. In the Railroad Industry, the diesel locomotive is an example of a nondigital technology.

72. For an excellent introduction to the issues involved, see Philip Evans and Thomas S. Wurster, *Blown to Bits: How the Economics of Information Transforms Strategy* (Boston: Harvard Business School Press, 2000).

73. Industries that depend on highly networked flows of information are developing patterns of behaviors and dependencies that economists and technologists are only just now beginning to understand. For a multi-industry historical description of these emerging patterns, see P. H. Longstaff, *Networked Industries: Patterns in Development, Operation, and Regulation* (Cambridge, Mass.: Center for Information Policy Research, Harvard University,

2000), Transportation Industry, on 33–50. This publication is available on the center's web site: http://www.pirp.harvard.edu.

74. This phenomenon appears in everyone's life at the dawn of the new century. For example, automated voice response systems, such as those deployed by telephone companies to provide telephone numbers or to communicate routine messages to customers, are now almost all universally done by computers, not people. Even phone mail systems have replaced telephone switchboard operators, reducing a significant function of secretaries in earlier decades.

75. Nagarajan et al., "Trucking Industry," 159. On the consistency of the Trucking Industry's patterns of behavior with that of other sectors of the economy, see D. Wilson, "IT Investments and Its Productivity Effects: An Organizational Sociologist's Perspective on Directions for Future Research," *Economics of Innovation and New Technology* 3 (1995): 235–251; T. C. Powell and A. Dent-Micallef, "Information Technology as Competitive Advantage: The Role of Humans, Business, and Technology Resources," *Strategic Management Journal* 15, no. 5 (1997): 375–405.

Chapter 9

1. Roger D. Blackwell, *From Mind to Market: Reinventing the Retail Supply Chain* (New York: HarperBusiness, 1997): 214–216; Kate Maddox, "E-Commerce Becoming Reality," *Advertising Age* 69, no. 43 (October 26, 1998): S-1–S-2; Susan Reda, "Groundbreaking Consumer Survey Tracks Nation's Biggest On-line Merchants," *Stores* (September 1999): 1–10, http://www.stores.org/eng/archives/sept99cover.html; U.S. Department of Commerce, *The Emerging Digital Economy* (Washington, D.C.: U.S. Government Printing Office, 1997).

2. Edwin Merton McBrier, *Woolworth's First 75 Years, 1870–1954* (New York: F.W. Woolworth, 1954): 9.

3. U.S. Department of Commerce, *Historical Statistics of the United States: Colonial Times to 1970* (Washington, D.C.: U.S. Government Printing Office, 1975), part 1: 233.

4. For an overview of modern applications, see Normand Brin, Wojeich Zagala, and Steve Schaffer, *Information Warehouse in the Retail Industry* (San Jose, Calif.: IBM Corp., 1994).

5. I have examined the role of Burroughs and NCR elsewhere: *Before the Computer: IBM, NCR, Burroughs, and Remington Rand and the Industry They Created, 1865–1956* (Princeton, N.J.: Princeton University Press, 1993): 25–43, 64–78, 105–127.

6. Brian L. Friedman, "Productivity Trends in Department Stores, 1967–86," *Monthly Labor Review* 111, no. 3 (March 1988): 17–21; Samuel B. Harvey, "Computers in Retailing," *Datamation* 12, no. 8 (August 1966): 25–27; J. Barry Mason and Morris L. Mayer, "Retail Merchandise Information Systems for the 1980's," *Journal of Retailing* 56, no. 1 (Spring 1980): 56–76; David McConaughy, "An Appraisal of Computers in Department Store Inventory Control," *Journal of Retailing* 46, no. 1 (Spring 1970): 3–19; R. Lee Paulson, *The Computer Challenge in Retailing* (New York: Chain Store Publishing, 1973); Hugh G. McKay, "What's New in Inventory Control," *Data Processing: Proceedings 1965* (Dallas: DPMA, 1966): 338–351.

7. For an excellent history of UPC, which argues that this technology is central to the use of IT in retailing, see Stephen A. Brown, *Revolution at the Checkout Counter* (Cambridge, Mass.: Harvard University Press, 1997): xiii–xvii, 1–38.

8. The literature published in this period (1950s–1960s) inside the industry or about it is replete with discussions of computing. For some of the citations, see James W. Cortada, *A Bibliographic Guide to the History of Computer Applications, 1950–1990* (Westport, Conn.: Greenwood Press, 1996): 101–102. Almost every industry trade magazine also carried articles

from time to time on the role of computing; that literature provided much of the data on which the next chapter is based.

9. Don L. James, Bruce J. Walker, and Michael J. Etzel, *Retailing Today: An Introduction* (New York: Harcourt Brace Jovanovich, 1975): 18–19.

10. Laurie Aron, "Delivering on E-Commerce," *Chain Store Age* (June 1999): 6, 130; Elizabeth Daniel and George Klimis, "The Impact of Electronic Commerce on Market Structure: An Evaluation of the Electronic Market Hypothesis," *European Management Journal* (June 1999): 326–328; Ernest & Young, *The Digital Channel Continues to Gather Steam: The Second Annual Ernest & Young Internet Shopping Survey* (Washington, D.C.: National Retail Federation, 1999); Patricia Seybold, *Customers.Com* (New York: Random House, 1998).

11. The most thorough study of the firm also includes a large deal of bibliography: Robert Spector, *Amazon.com: Get Big Fast* (New York: HarperBusiness, 2000): 237–245. See also Rebecca Saunders, *Business the Amazon.com Way: Secrets of the World's Most Astonishing Web Business* (Dover, N.H.: Capstone, 1999); Adam Cohen, *The Perfect Store: Inside eBay* (Boston: Little, Brown, 2002).

12. The seminal studies have been done by the U.S. Department of Commerce, and its most important publication on the subject is *The Emerging Digital Economy II* (Washington, D.C.: U.S. Government Printing Office 1999); see also its earlier study, *The Economic and Social Impact of Electronic Commerce* (Washington, D.C.: U.S. Government Printing Office, 1998); both include references to other government studies.

13. For examples, see David Bunnell and Richard Luecke, *The Ebay Phenomenon: Business Secrets Behind the World's Hottest Internet Company* (New York: Wiley, 2000); Peter Fingar, Harsha Kumar, and Tarun Sharma, *Enterprise E-Commerce: The Software Component Breakthrough for Business-to-Business Commerce* (Tampa, Fla.: Meghan-Kiffer, 2000): 21–48; David S. Pottruck and Terry Pearce, *Clicks and Mortar: Passion Driven Growth in an Internet Driven World* (San Francisco: Jossey-Bass, 2000): 255–264; David Siegel, *Futurize Your Enterprise: Business Strategy in the Age of the E-Customer* (New York: Wiley, 1999); and J. Christopher Westland and Theodore H. K. Clark (eds.), *Global Electronic Commerce: Theory and Case Studies* (Cambridge, Mass.: MIT Press, 1999).

14. Michael Levy and Barton A. Weitz, *Retailing Management*, 4th ed. (Burr Ridle, Ill.: McGraw-Hill Irwin, 2001): 5. The first edition, published in 1992, became the standard text during the last decade of the twentieth century in the United States.

15. Committee on Retailing, *Principles of Retailing* (New York: Pitman, 1955): 18.

16. This term is used in the IT community to refer to a terminal that has no memory, relying instead on the memory within a mainframe to which it is attached. By contrast, a PC has memory and thus can operate as a standalone computer or as a dumb terminal attached to a mainframe.

17. For an excellent example and a useful source of explanations for the value and application of computing in modern retail operations, see Frederick H. Abernathy, John T. Dunlop, Janice H. Hammond, and David Weil, *A Stitch in Time: Lean Retailing and the Transformation of Manufacturing: Lessons from the Apparel and Textile Industries* (New York: Oxford University Press, 1999): 39–54.

18. BLS, *Technological Change and Manpower Trends in Five Industries*, Bulletin 1856 (Washington, D.C.: U.S. Government Printing Office, 1975): 52.

19. For a description of the wholesale business circa mid-1950s, see Committee on Retailing, *Principles of Retailing*, 232–237.

20. BLS, *Technological Change and Manpower Trends*, 50; Kenneth B. Ackerman, R. W. Gardner, and Lee P. Thomas, *Understanding Today's Distribution Center* (Washington, D.C.: Traffic Service Corp., 1972): 52.

21. BLS, *Technological Change and Manpower Trends*, 52.

22. BLS, *Technology and Its Impact on Labor in Four Industries*, Bulletin 2263 (Washington, D.C.: U.S. Government Printing Office, November 1986): 42.

23. IBM, "Wholesale Distribution Industry" internal report (September 21, 2000), in my possession.

24. One small example illustrates the lack of focus. Levy and Weitz, in their otherwise outstanding text on retailing, *Retailing Management*, devote 2 pages out of 754 to the topic. However, there is a specialized literature on wholesaling and its use of IT. On developments in the early 1970s, see Frank A. Tully, "Build High for Storage Savings," *Automation* (March 1973): 44–47; Hale C. Bartlett (ed.), *Readings in Physical Distribution* (Danville, Ill.: Interstate Printers, 1972); James L. Heskett, "Sweeping Changes in Distribution," *Harvard Business Review* (March–April 1973): 123–132; Richard S. Lopata, "Faster Pace in Wholesaling," *Harvard Business Review* (July–August 1969): 130–143. For the 1980s, see Arthur Andersen & Co., *Future Trends in Wholesale Distribution: A Time of Opportunity*. For Distribution Research and Education Foundation of the National Association of Wholesaler-Distributors (Washington, D.C.: Arthur Andersen, 1983); John A. White, "Warehousing in a Changing World," *1983 International Conference on Automation and Warehousing Proceedings* (Washington, D.C.: Institute of Industrial Engineers, 1983): 3–6. On the early 1990s, see James A. Narus and James C. Anderson, "Rethinking Distribution: Adaptive Channels," *Harvard Business Review* 74, no. 4 (July/August 1996): 112–120.

25. BLS, *Technological Trends in Major American Industries*, 240.

26. U.S. Department of Commerce, *U.S. Industrial Outlook 1973* (Washington, D.C.: U.S. Government Printing Office, 1973): 397; James, et al., *Retailing Today*, 6.

27. Levy and Weitz, *Retailing Management*, 12.

28. *Retail Industry Indicators* (Washington, D.C.: National Retail Institute, May 1998): 7, 10.

29. Data drawn from Abernathy et al., *Stitch in Time*, 46–47.

30. For an overview of the role of malls in the United States, see Levy and Weitz, *Retailing Management*, 241–249, bibliography on 705–706.

31. U.S. Census Bureau, "1997 Economic Census: Bridge Between SIC and NAICS SIC: Menu of SIC Divisions" (November 11, 2000); http://www.census.gov/epcd/ec9brdg/INDXSIC2.HTM.

32. James, et al., *Retailing Today*, 203.

33. Robert D. Henderson, "Recent Developments in Procedure and Techniques of Modern Wholesalers," *Journal of Retailing* 27, no. 2 (Summer 1951): 94–99.

34. For the three descriptions, see BLS, *Technology and Its Impact on Labor*, 38.

35. U.S. Census Bureau, "1997 Economic Census," 3.

36. BLS, *Technological Trends in Major American Industries*, 238.

37. BLS, *Technological Change and Manpower Trends*, 48; BLS, *Technology and Its Impact on Labor*, 38.

38. Economists measure the relative performance of specific industries by examining their real GPO growth rates and their shares of GDP. These concepts, and the data used in this paragraph, are drawn from Sherlene K. S. Lum, Brian C. Moyer, and Robert E. Yuskavage, "Improved Estimates of Gross Product by Industry for 1947–98," *Survey of Current Business* (June 2000): 24–38. Recent revisions of GDP data for the U.S. economy for the half century indicate that the gross product by industry as a percentage of GDP for wholesale did not change from 1947 through 1998; annual percentages ranged roughly from 6.6–6.7 to 7. In retail, these percentages dropped from 11.6 in 1947 to 8.9 percent in 1998. As a whole, private industry in the entire period occupied about 87.5 percent of GDP (p. 29). For a critique and useful analysis of how government agencies are collecting GDP data insofar as they relate to IT expenditures, see John Haltiwanger and Ron S. Jarmin, "Measuring the Digital

Economy," in Erik Brynjolfsson and Brian Kahin (eds.), *Understanding the Digital Economy: Data, Tools, and Research* (Cambridge, Mass.: MIT Press, 2000): 13–33; and also in the same volume, Brent R. Moulton, "GDP and the Digital Economy: Keeping Up with the Changes," 34–48.

39. Although TQM came first to manufacturing, once retailers understood its customer-centric focus (which is central to retailing in any era), many embraced its practices. For collections of literature on TQM in retailing, see the annual bibliographies published in James W. Cortada and John A. Woods (eds.), *The Quality Yearbook* (New York: McGraw-Hill, 1994–2002, especially 1994–1998).

40. The bulk of this brief history of retailing is drawn from Abernathy et al, *Stitch in Time*, 23–50.

41. See note 44 for details.

42. Abernathy et al., *Stitch in Time*, 447; SKU data, on 46.

43. Alfred D. Chandler, Jr., *The Visible Hand: The Managerial Revolution in American Business* (Cambridge, Mass.: Harvard University Press, 1977): 385, 485; see also his *Scale and Scope: The Dynamics of Industrial Capitalism* (Cambridge, Mass.: Harvard University Press, 1990): 28–31, 58–62.

44. This is the main theme of Blackwell, *From Mind to Market*; dozens of examples of this process at work in the late twentieth century are scattered throughout the book; see especially pp. 139–141.

45. Geoffrey D. Austrian, *Herman Hollerith: Forgotten Genius of Information Processing* (New York: Columbia University Press, 1982): 203–205, 249.

46. The whole concept of integrating IT hardware, paper-based systems, and information flows through the enterprise in an organized, rationale manner had been advanced in the late nineteenth century and during the early decades of the twentieth. This process is described by JoAnne Yates, *Control Through Communication: The Rise of System in American Management* (Baltimore, Md.: Johns Hopkins University Press, 1989): 1–64.

47. James F. Moore, "The Death of Competition," *Fortune* (April 15, 1996) 144; see also his book, *The Death of Competition: Leadership and Strategy in the Age of Business Ecosystems* (New York: HarperBusiness, 1996): 168, 174–175; Pete Hisey, "Wal-Mart Seeks Shoppers with On-line Service," *Discount Store News* 35, no. 16 (August 1996): 1–2; Jackie Bivens, "On Line Not Yet On Target," *Discount Store News* 37, no. 11 (June 8, 1998): 122; "Wal-Mart Stores, Bentonville, AR," *Forbes ASAP Technology Supplement* (August 24, 1998): 80; James Fallon, "Data Sharing with Vendors Key to Wal-Mart's Strategy," *Supermarket News* 47, no. 14 (April 5, 1999): 17ff; Mike Troy, "Wal-Mart Expansion Will Include Internet," *Discount Store News* 38, no. 20 (October 25, 1999): 5; "Wal-Mart and Target and Kmart, Oh My!" *Forecast* 20, no. 4 (April 5, 2000): 5ff.

48. This happened so fast that most of the literature up to the end of the twentieth century did not reflect the convergence. For representations of this literature, one must go to industry trade journals, presentations at business conferences, and comments by consultants. Barnes and Noble, the U.S. bookseller with both retail and Internet channels, is one of the operative case studies of the new model, as are J.C. Penney, Sears, and others. For details on issues and trends, see Susan Reda, "Websites and Stores: Integrate or Separate?" *Stores* (March 1999): 1–5, http://www.stores.org/eng/archives/mar99cover.html; Clinton Wilder, "Information Week 500: Retail and Distribution: Retail Turns to Clicks and Mortar," *InformationWeek* (September 27, 1999): 257ff; Joseph P. Bailey, "Retail Services: Continuing the Internet Success," in Robert E. Litan and Alice M. Rivlin (eds.), *The Economic Payoff from the Internet Revolution* (Washington, D.C.: Brookings Institution Press, 2001): 172–188.

49. Levy and Weitz, *Retailing Management*, 75–126; Gerald Lohse and Peter Spiller, "Electronic Shopping," *Communications of the ACM* 41 (July 1998): 81–88; Ginger Koloszyc,

"Internet-Only Retailers Struggle to Improve Product Return Process," *Stores*, (July 1999): 54–59; George Anders, "Virtual Reality: Web Firms Go on Warehouse Building Boom," *Wall Street Journal* (September 8, 1999): B1, B9.

50. On the link between the practices of catalog retailing and those of the Internet, two experts on the industry said that: "catalog retailers are best positioned to exploit electronic retailing. They have order fulfillment systems and database management skills needed for effective electronic retailing. Also, the visual merchandising skills necessary for preparing catalogs are similar to those needed in setting up an effective website," and they cited the experience of Lands' End: Levy and Weitz, *Retailing Management*, 96.

51. Westland and Clark, *Global Electronic Commerce*, 141–155.

52. IBM, *Industry Applications and Abstracts* (White Plains, N.Y.: IBM Corp., February 1988): 4-1–4-9, 18-1–18-19.

53. IBM, *Applications and Abstracts: Industries/User Segments* (White Plains, N.Y.: IBM Corp., April 1985): 6–1.

54. For a detailed description of these applications, see ibid., 6-1–6-6, 18-1–18-21.

Chapter 10

1. Undated report in my possession.

2. For an account of precomputer uses of IT, see Benham Eppes Morris, "Department Stores' Digital Information Processing Computer Techniques," unpublished M.A. thesis, 1952, MIT, Cambridge, Mass.; and despite its title, it focuses on applications that use cash registers and accounting machines, not computers (i.e., digital central processing users).

3. "W.T. Grant Adopts Point-of-Sale Accounting," undated (circa 1958); CBI 55, "Market Reports," Box 70, Folder 4, III-F4-1, Archives of the Charles Babbage Institute, University of Minnesota, Minneapolis.

4. Lawrence R. Robinson and Eleanor G. May, *Self-Service in Variety Stores* (Cambridge, Mass.: Division of Research, Harvard Business School, July 1956): 1–2.

5. Ibid., 2–3.

6. Ibid., 4.

7. Reformatting determined how stores were laid out, for example, moving all checkout activities from scattered departments to a cluster near the entrance, moving departments from one physical spot to another, reducing the number of sales clerks on the floor to answer questions or to persuade customers to buy, and creating warehouse-style formats (e.g., as in Sam's Club). For an introduction to this important subject, see Lawrence J. Israel, *Store Planning/Design: History, Theory, Process* (New York: Wiley, 1994); for effects on customers, see the study by Paco Underhill, who used the techniques of the anthropologist, in *Why We Buy: The Science of Shopping* (New York: Simon & Schuster, 1999).

8. Walter M. Carlson, "Transforming an Industry Through Information Technology," *IEEE Annals of the History of Computing* 15, no. 1 (1993): 39.

9. Esther M. Love, *Operating Results of Limited Price Variety Chains in 1950* (Cambridge, Mass.: Division of Research, Harvard Business School, July 1951): 1.

10. Anita C. Hersum, *Operating Results of Variety Chains in 1957* (Cambridge, Mass.: Division of Research, Harvard Business School, August 1958): 1.

11. "Just the Ticket for Inventory Control and Sales Analysis," application brief for the Kobacker Stores (July 1956); CBI 55, "Market Reports," Box 70, Folder 2, III-F1-p1, Archives of the Charles Babbage Institute, University of Minnesota, Minneapolis.

12. Ibid., III-F3-4.

13. For a detailed description of the application and system involved, see "Two Applications of Kimball Tag Equipment (undated, circa 1956); CBI 55, "Market Reports," Box 70,

Folder 2, F3-1–8, Archives of the Charles Babbage Institute, University of Minnesota, Minneapolis.

14. "W.T. Grant Adopts Point-of-Sale Accounting" CBI 55, "Market Reports," Box 70, Folder 2, III-F4-1–III-F4-10, Archives of the Charles Babbage Institute, University of Minnesota, Minneapolis.

15. "Point-of-Sale Recording Used by Florida Store," attachment to OAA letter by R. Hunt Brown, June 1958, CBI 55, "Market Reports," Box 70, Folder 4, III-F5-1–F5-8, Archives of the Charles Babbage Institute, University of Minnesota, Minneapolis.

16. The application is described in detail, and with flowcharts in R. Hunt Brown, "Haggarty Stores: The UNIVAC 60 In Retailing," *Office Automation Applications Supplement* no. 14 (November 1958); CBI 55, "Market Reports," Box 70, Folder 5, III-F7-1–F7-16, Archives of the Charles Babbage Institute, University of Minnesota, Minneapolis.

17. "Order Processing and Inventory Control with Electronic Computer," OAA Updating Service (undated, circa 1959); CBI 55, "Market Reports," Box 70, Folder 5, III-F10-1–F10-8, Archives of the Charles Babbage Institute, University of Minnesota, Minneapolis.

18. "Pharmacal Firm Automates Data Processing," OAA Updating Service (undated, circa 1959); CBI 55, "Market Reports," Box 70, Folder 5, III-F13-6, Archives of the Charles Babbage Institute, University of Minnesota, Minneapolis.

19. IBM, *IBM 1401 Data Processing System with Tapes for Merchandise Control at Retail Chains* (White Plains, N.Y.: IBM Corp., 1959); DP Application Briefs, Box B-116-3, IBM Archives, Somers, N.Y.

20. "Rx for Wholesale Drug Firm," OAA Updating Service (undated, circa 1959); CBI 55, "Market Reports," Box 70, Folder 5, III-F11-1–F11-6, Archives of the Charles Babbage Institute, University of Minnesota, Minneapolis.

21. "Warehouse Order Processing and Inventory Control"; CBI 55, "Market Reports," Box 70, Folder 5, III-F12-1–F12-8, Archives of the Charles Babbage Institute, University of Minnesota, Minneapolis.

22. "UNIVAC 60 Speeds Order Processing for Wholesale Drug Firm," attachment to R. Hunt Brown's OAA Updating Service (April 1959); CBI 55, "Market Reports," Box 70, Folder 5, III-F8-6, Archives of the Charles Babbage Institute, University of Minnesota, Minneapolis.

23. "Computer Analyzes Sales," *Data Processing Annual* (Detroit: Gille Assoc., 1961): 158–160; "How Computer Guides a Mass Merchant," *Building Materials Merchandiser* (June 1965): 86–89; Howard E. Levine, "Computer Eases Service Firm's Growing Pains," *Rack Merchandising* (September 1965): 44, 46–47.

24. Burton Peck, "New Trends in Retail Industry Data Processing Methods," in Edith Harwith Goodman (ed.), *Data Processing Yearbook* (Detroit: American Data Processing, 1965): 249. For an early introduction to optical scanning, with case studies, see Ralph Dyer, James E. Hoelter, and James A. Newton, *Optical Scanning for the Business Man* (New York: Hobbs, Dorman, 1966), 120–122; P. L. Anderson, "Optical Character Recognition," *Datamation* 15, no. 7 (July 1969): 43–48.

25. Dyer et al., *Optical Scanning for the Business Man*, 169–172.

26. For example, IBM, *IBM 1401 Tape System for Accounts Receivable and Merchandise Management at Maison Blanche* (White Plains, N.Y.: IBM Corp., 1962); DP Application Briefs, Box B-116-3, IBM Archives, Somers, N.Y.

27. C. Robert McBrier, "A Concept for the Use of Electronics in Retailing," *Data Processing Proceedings 1963* (Detroit: DPMA, 1963): 166.

28. Ibid., 167.

29. Ibid., 171.

30. BLS, *Technological Trends in Major American Industries,* Bulletin 1474 (Washington, D.C.: U.S. Government Printing Office, 1966): 238–239.

31. Donald H. Sanders, "Experiences of Small Retailers with Electronic Data Processing," *Journal of Retailing* 42, no. 1 (Spring 1966): 13–17, 61–62, quote on 16.

32. Samuel B. Harvey, "Computers in Retailing: The Technical Problems," *Datamation* (August 1966): 25–27, quote on 26.

33. Malcolm K. Lee, "Stock Control at the May Company," *Datamation* (August 1966): 35–37; Byron L. Carter, "Retail Systems," *Data Processing Proceedings 1967* (Boston: DPMA, 1967): 335–339; IBM, *IBM 1440 Data Processing System for Retail Fashion Inventory Control* (White Plains, N.Y.: IBM Corp., 1968); DP Application Briefs, Box B-116-3, IBM Archives, Somers, N.Y.; David McConaughy, "An Appraisal of Computers in Department Store Inventory Control," *Journal of Retailing* 46, no. 1 (Spring 1970): 3–19; Leroy G. Olson and Richard H. Olson, "A Computerized Merchandise Budget for Use in Retailing," *Journal of Retailing* 46, no. 2 (Summer 1970): 3–17, 88; Malcolm McNair and Eleanor May, *The American Department Store, 1920–1960* (Boston: Harvard Business School Press, 1963).

34. McConaughy, "Appraisal of Computers," 17.

35. For a case study, see IBM, *Merchandise Control at Bramson's Using the IBM System 360 Model 20* (White Plains, N.Y.: IBM Corp., 1970); DP Application Briefs, Box B-116-3, IBM Archives, Somers, N.Y.

36. Spencer B. Smith, "Automated Inventory Management for Staples," *Journal of Retailing* 47, no. 1 (Spring 1971): 56.

37. For an overview of these systems, using one chain as a case study, see ibid., 55–62.

38. William D. Power, "Retail Terminals . . . A POS Survey," *Datamation* (July 15, 1971): 22.

39. Jack A. French, "EDP Technology and Retail Planning," *Datamation* (July 15, 1971): 34.

40. Power, "Retail Terminals," 24; material for this and the previous paragraph are drawn from the same article.

41. French, "EDP Technology," 32.

42. Ibid., 32–33.

43. Ibid., 34. For a clear description of POS applications of the early to mid-1970s, see BLS, *Technological Change and Its Labor Impact in Five Industries*, Bulletin 1961 (Washington, DC.: U.S. Government Printing Office, 1977): 45–46; and Jay Scher, *Department and Specialty Store and Merchandising Results of 1974* (New York: National Retail Merchants Association, 1975).

44. Scher, *Department and Specialty Store*, 38–39.

45. A discussion of what constituted a revolution is outside the scope of this book, but most researchers have relied on the descriptions of such radical changes in science and technology by Thomas S. Kuhn, in which he describes the arrival of a new paradigm: *The Structure of Scientific Revolutions*, 2nd ed. (New York: New American Library, 1986): 76–110.

46. There are as yet few reliable data on the extent of deployment of the UPC around the world, but it appears to have spread rapidly in all industrialized economies.

47. Stephen A. Brown, *Revolution at the Checkout Counter: The Explosion of the Bar Code* (Cambridge, Mass.: Harvard University Press, 1997): xi.

48. On the status of POS technology just before the arrival of the UPC, see William D. Power, "Retail Terminals: A POS Survey," *Datamation* 17 (July 15, 1971): 22–31.

49. Brown, *Revolution at the Checkout Counter*, xiv–xvii.

50. Ibid., 7–8 shows the distribution of UPC registrations by industry; most account for single-digit percentage of totals because these registrations had spread across so many sectors of the economy.

51. Ibid., 117. The entire book was the major source of information for this and the next paragraph.

52. Edward W. Wheatley and Richard Tash, "Point of Sale Retail Information Systems:

Theory to Reality," in Douglas Hawes and Robert Tamelia (eds.), *Developments in Marketing Science* (Greenville, N.Y.: Academy of Marketing Science, 1978): vol. I, 211–214.

53. Brown, *Revolution at the Checkout Counter*, 194–202.

54. John T. Dunlop and Jan W. Rivkin, "Introduction," ibid., 10.

55. The effects of computers on purchasing practices of retailers, however, did begin to appear in the technical literature in the late 1970s; see, for example, Barry Landau, "MIS and Buying Control," *Journal of Systems Management* 28 (May 1978): 24–27.

56. Brown, *Revolution at the Checkout Counter*, 203–210.

57. For the role of retail industries in EDI's development, see ibid., 163–173.

58. Ibid., 13.

59. Dunlop and Rivkin, "Introduction," 17.

60. Fresh fruits and vegetables remain problematic, although when packaged could have a UPC label.

61. B. Barry Mason and Morris L. Mayer, "Retail Merchandise Information Systems for the 1980's," *Journal of Retailing* 56, no. 1 (Spring 1980): 56–76; Michael D. Pommer, Eric N. Berkowitz, and John R. Walton, "UPC Scanning: An Assessment of Shopper Response to Technological Change," *Journal of Retailing* 56, no. 2 (Summer 1980): 25–44.

62. BLS, *Technological Change and Its Labor Impact*, 46.

63. BLS, *Technology and Labor in Three Service Industries: Utilities, Retail Trade, and Lodging*, Bulletin 2367 (Washington, D.C.: U.S. Government Printing Office, September 1990): 15.

64. Ibid., 16.

65. On the role of credit cards, see David Evans and Richard Schmalensee, *Paying with Plastic: The Digital Revolution in Buying and Borrowing* (Cambridge, Mass.: MIT Press, 1999): 86–90, 121–127. The authors report that "between 1970 and 1995, the percentage of households with at least one credit card more than quadrupled, from only 16 percent to more than 65 percent" (p. 86). For other diffusion statistics, see 86–94. The wide use of credit cards made e-commerce possible since they are the medium for making payments for online transactions.

66. John A. White and Michael A. Mullens, "Management Support Systems for Warehousing," *Annual Conference Proceedings* (n.p.: National Council of Physical Distribution Management, 1984): 561.

67. BLS, *Technology and Labor in Three Service Industries*, 19.

68. BLS, *Technological Change and Manpower Trends in Five Industries*, Bulletin 1856 (Washington, D.C.: U.S. Government Printing Office, 1975): 48–51; Kenneth B. Ackerman, R. W. Gardner, and Lee P. Thomas, *Understanding Today's Distribution Center* (Washington, D.C.: Traffic Service Corp., 1972): 52.

69. BLS, *Technology and Its Impact on Labor*, Bulletin 2263 (Washington, D.C.: U.S. Government Printing Office, November 1986): 38.

70. William L. Cron and Marion G. Sobol, "The Relationship Between Computerization and Performance: A Strategy for Maximizing the Economic Benefits of Computerization," *Information and Management* 6 (1983): 171–181, is based on a survey of 138 wholesalers.

71. BLS, *Technology and Its Impact on Labor*, 40.

72. Ibid., 40–42.

73. One of the first warehouses in the nation to operate in a partial lights-out mode was IBM's in Endicott, N.Y., where, beginning at the end of the 1970s, lights were left off in portions of the warehouse; when equipment maintenance personnel entered the area, they often wore miner's hats, with mounted lights. When I toured the facility for the first time in 1978–1979, my guide turned on the lights so that I could see a large area of high racks, yellow AGVs, and very few people.

74. Dale D. Achabal and Shelby H. McIntyre, "Information Technology Is Reshaping Retailing," *Journal of Retailing* 63, no. 4 (Winter 1987): 321.

75. Ibid., 322–324. Others were making similar points; see, for example, Margaret A. Emmelhainz, "The Impact of EDI on the Purchasing Process," unpublished Ph.D. dissertation, 1986, Ohio State University, Columbus; F. Warren McFarlan, "Information, Technology Changes the Way You Compete," *Harvard Business Review* 12 (May–June 1984): 98–103; Jagdish N. Sheth, "Emerging Trends for the Retailing Industry," *Journal of Retailing* 59 (Fall 1983): 6–18.

76. "Survey of Retail Information Technology and Trends," *Chain Store Executive* 66, no. 10, sect. 2 (October 1990): p8A, p5A, 7A, 33A, 38A.

77. "Survey of Retail Information Technology Expenses and Trends: Supermarkets," *Chain Store Age Executive* 66, no. 10, sect. 2 (October 1990): p15A–17A.

78. Roger D. Blackwell, *From Mind to Market: Reinventing the Retail Supply Chain* (New York: HarperBusiness, 1997): 188–190. For examples and analysis of the kinds of data collected, see "The Department Store Saga," WW Dinfortacts Supplement to *Women's Wear Daily* (June 1997): 4ff. For detailed descriptions of these applications and how they were being implemented, see Normand Brin, Wojeich Zagala, and Steve Schaffer, *Information Warehouse in the Retail Industry* (San Jose, Calif.: IBM Corp., 1994); and Bill Moore et al., *B2B E-commerce Using WebSphere Commerce Business Edition Patterns for E-business Series* (San Jose, Calif.: IBM Corp., 2002).

79. Christina Le Beau, "Mountains to Mine," *American Demographics* 22, no. 8 (August 2000): 40.

80. Elaine Walker, "Many Shoppers Cut In-store Time by Using the Internet to Do Research," *Miami Herald* (May 18, 1998).

81. Underhill, *Why We Buy.*

82. Susan Reda, "Customer Relationship Management," *Stores* (April 2000): 1–6, http://www.stores.org/archives/april00cover.html; Brin, et al., *Information Warehouse in the Retail Industry,* 33–46.

83. Ibid., 3.

84. Lisa Vincenti, "Wal-Mart Upgrades Information Systems," *HFN* 73, no. 33 (August 23, 1999): 1–2; "Wal-Mart Offers More Retail Link Data," *Supercenter and Club Business* 6, no. 16 (August 30, 1999): 2. At the time, Wal-Mart had 2,400 stores.

85. Kmart nearly went out of business in the early years of the new century because of its inability to compete effectively, proving once again that all the computers in the world were never a substitute for good business strategy and effectiveness in execution.

86. Patricia A. Murphy, "Technology Opens Up New World at the Point of Sale," *Stores* (March 2001): 1–5, http:www.stores, org/eng/cover.html; Ted Kemp, "Retailers Slow to Integrate Kiosks," *InternetWeek* (November 6, 2000), 12; Debbie Howell, "New 7-Eleven Kiosks Bring On-line Transactions Home," *Discount Store News* 39, no. 4 (February 21, 2000): 2.

87. Michael Levy and Dhruv Grewel, "Supply Chain Management in a Networked Economy," *Journal of Retailing* 76, no. 4 (Winter 2000): 415–429. This whole issue is devoted to modern supply chain management processes and applications.

88. James Frederick, "'Time Is Money' Drives Supply Chain Re-engineering," *Drug Store News* 19, no. 10 (June 16, 1997): 320.

89. David Siegel, *Futurize Your Enterprise: Business Strategy in the Age of the E-Customer* (New York: Wiley, 1999): 37–48; James Slevin, *The Internet and Society* (Cambridge: Polity, 2000): 40–44; Manuel Castells, *The Power of Identity* (Oxford: Blackwell, 1997). I have discussed these issues in more detail in *Making of the Information Society: Experiences, Consequences, and Possibilities* (Upper Saddle River, N.J.: Prentice Hall/Financial Times, 2002).

90. For example, U.S. Department of Commerce, *The Emerging Digital Economy II* (Washington, D.C.: U.S. Government Printing Office, 1999), and its earlier study, *The Economic and Social Impact of Electronic Commerce* (Washington, D.C.: U.S. Government Printing Office, 1998).

91. "Retailers Disappointed with Internet Shopping Venue," *Accessories* 99, no. 6 (June 1998): 21.

92. Peter Wexler, quoted in Geanne Rosenberg, "The E-tailing Phenomenon," *Investment Dealers' Digest* (May 31, 1999): 18.

93. "Drug Chains Stake Claims on Internet," *Chain Drug Review* 21, no. 13 (August 19, 1999): 4–5.

94. "Retailers Scurry to the Internet," *Chain Store Executive Retail Information Technology* (October 1999): 10.

95. Ibid.

96. Stacie S. McCullough, "E-Marketplace Hype, Apps Realities," *Forrester Report* (April 2000): unpaginated.

97. "B2B Equals Efficiency in Communications, Speed in Transactions," *NMR* 17, no. 16 (September 4, 2000): 10. There is an excellent comparison of EDI to the Internet in this article: "With Wal-Mart's success serving as a powerful example, excellence in supply chain management and logistics has increasingly emerged as a power cost-reduction tool and competitive weapon for suppliers and retailers alike. But EDI networks are costly, and their hefty price tags have barred most small companies from playing on the same field as larger firms with ample information technology budgets. The Internet is tearing down that barrier. The low cost and easy access to the Internet has ignited the latest boom in E-commerce: the B2B exchange."

98. "America's Best Technology Users," *Forbes ASAP* (August 24, 1998): 82.

99. "Consumers Spent $3.4 Billion Online in February," National Retail Federation press release (March 29, 2001), http://www.nrf.com; Timothy P. Henderson, "After Overcoming Their Apprehensions, Mall Owners Embrace E-Commerce," *Stores* (July 2000): 1–5, http://ww.stores.org/eng/archives/jul00edit.html; Susan Reda, "VeriFone and Russell Reynolds Associates Top 100 Internet Retailers," *Stores* (September 2000): 1–12, http://ww.stores.org/eng/archives/sept00edit.html.

100. For a brief overview of this development, see "Shopping for Savings," *Informationweek* (July 1, 2002): 37, 40, 42–45.

101. Internal IBM market assessments made in 1999–2001 indicated that wholesalers were distracted by Y2K concerns in 1998–1999 and were still searching for killer apps that would prevent them from being threatened by the newnetwork-centric supply chains.

102. Blackwell, *From Mind to Market*, 178.

103. David Bunnell and Richard Luecke, *The eBay Phenomenon: Business Secrets Behind the World's Hottest Internet Company* (New York: Wiley, 2000): viii.

104. Maria Halkias, "Department Stores Are Under Attack," *Wisconsin State Journal* (May 27, 2001), B1.

105. For trends, circa 2002, see Samuel Greengard, "The Evolution of Retail," *iQ* (March–April 2002): 43–51; for case studies of some firms, see Sahhon Weich, Constant Innovation," and James A. Martin, "What's in Store," both in *iQ* (March–April 2002): 52–59 and 60–67, respectively.

Chapter 11

1. The concurrent use of multiple types of IT and other informational artifacts has been a central theme of my most recent research. For summaries of my findings, see James W. Cortada, *Before the Computer: IBM, NCR, Burroughs & Remington Rand & the Industry They Created, 1865–1956* (Princeton, N.J.: Princeton University Press, 1993); *Making of the Information Age: Experience, Consequences, and Possibilities* (Upper Saddle River, N.J.: Financial Times/Prentice Hall PTR, 2002); Alfred D. Chandler, Jr., and James W. Cortada (eds.), *A*

Nation Transformed by Information: How Information Has Shaped the United States from Colonial Times to the Present (New York: Oxford University Press, 2000): 177–216.

2. Willard F. Mueller and Leon Garoian, *Changes in the Market Structure of Grocery Retailing* (Madison: University of Wisconsin Press, 1961): 3; Michael Levy and Barton A. Weitz, *Retailing Management* (New York: McGraw-Hill Irwin, 2001): 39.

3. Mueller and Garoian, *Changes in the Market Structure*, 9.

4. Rachel Bowlby, *Carried Away: The Invention of Modern Shopping* (New York: Columbia University Press, 2001): 134–151.

5. For a useful overview of the industry's history, see Ryan Mathews's series of articles in *Progressive Grocer* in the December 1996 edition, which is almost entirely devoted to a retrospective on the industry; data on p. 61.

6. Mueller and Garoian, *Changes in the Market Structure*, 12.

7. Bowlby, *Carried Away*, 140.

8. M. M. Zimmerman, "Super Market Boom," *Super Market Merchandizing* (April 1957): 131; *Grocery Distribution* (Progressive Grocer, 1959): F-8. For details on this sector of the grocery world of the 1950s, see Wilbur B. England, *Operating Results of Food Chains in 1957* (Boston,: Division of Research, Harvard Business School, 1958): 1–3.

9. Mueller and Garoian, *Changes in the Market Structure*, 116.

10. David Appel, "The Supermarket: Early Development of an Institutional Innovation," *Journal of Retailing* 48, no. 1 (Spring 1972): 49.

11. Bruce W. Marion et al., *The Food Retailing Industry: Market Structure, Profits, and Prices* (New York: Praeger, 1979): 5.

12. James L. Brock, *A Forecast for the Grocery Retailing Industry in the 1980s* (Ann Arbor: University of Michigan Research Press, 1980): 91.

13. Ibid., 13.

14. Ibid., 14.

15. For an early explanation of the economic pressures, see England, *Operating Results of Food Chains*, 3.

16. In 1981, for example, 38 cents of every dollar was spent in restaurants and bars, up from 26 cents in 1960: Mathews, *Progressive Grocer*, 80.

17. Jay Coggins and Ben Senauer, "Grocery Retailing," in David C. Mowery (ed.), *U.S. Industry in 2000: Studies in Competitive Performance* (Washington, D.C.: National Academy Press, 1999): 158.

18. Ibid., 159.

19. "Food and Beverage: Battle for Grocery Share Ensues," sect. 2 of "Global Online Retailing: An Ernst & Young Special Report," *Stores* (January 2000): unpaginated, http://www.stores.org.

20. All the data were drawn from ibid., 155–165, quote on 165. For an early, very thorough analysis of labor productivity, see John L. Carey and Phyllis Flohr Otto, "Output per Unit of Labor Input in the Retail Food Store Industry," originally published in 1977 in the *Monthly Labor Review*, covering the years 1958–1975; reprinted in BLS, *A BLS Reader on Productivity*, Bulletin 2171 (Washington, D.C.: U.S. Government Printing Office, June 1983): 112–117.

21. FMI Information Service, "57th Annual Report of the Grocery Industry" (April 1990): 8; and "67th Annual Report of the Grocery Industry" (April 2000): 20, both available at http://www.fmi.org/facts_figs/key facts/grocery.html.

22. Labor data came from various Food Marketing Institute (FMI) studies, all of which are summarized on one chart, "Sales and Expense Growth During the Last Decade," http://ww.fmi.org/facts_figs/keyfacts/decade.html.

23. FMI Information Service, "Supermarket Facts Industry Overview 2000" (March 28,

2001), http://www.fmi.org/facts_figs/superfact.html. For an overview of what constituted the industry in 2000, see Levy and Weitz, *Retailing Management*, 14–15, 44–49.

24. John S. Ewing and James Murphy, "Impact of Automation on United States Retail Food Distribution," *Journal of Retailing* 41, no. 1 (Spring 1965): 38–39.

25. IBM, *General Information Manual. The IBM 1440-1311 System for the Chain and Whole-sale Grocery* (White Plains, N.Y.: IBM Corp., undated, circa early 1960s): 6; the publication explains each major accounting application in detail; DP Application Briefs, Box B-116-3, IBM Archives, Somers, N.Y.

26. "EDP at FMC," *Institutional Distribution* (June 1965): 40, 42–43.

27. "How One Wholesaler Adjusted to Meet Changing Data Processing Requirements," *Voluntary and Cooperative Groups Magazine* (May 1965): 43–44, 54.

28. Ewing and Murphy, "Impact of Automation," 38–47.

29. Control Data Corporation, "At Allied Supermarkets, Inc. Computer Technology Streamlines Merchandising," Application Report (Minneapolis, Minn.: CDC, 1972), unpaginated, quote on third page; CDC Files, CBI 80, Box 1, Archives of the Charles Babbage Institute, University of Minnesota, Minneapolis.

30. "Scanning Hits a Snag," *Progressive Grocer* (December 1975): 47–50; "Equipment Front: Mandatory Pricing Will Slow, Not Kill, Scanning," *Progressive Grocer* (December 1975): 55; "Consumer Front: So Far, the 'Boss' Likes What She Sees," *Progressive Grocer* (December 1975): 25–26; "For Five-Store Operator 'Efficiencies Sprout Everywhere' with Scanners at Work," *Progressive Grocer* (December 1978): 49–55; Michael D. Pommer, Eric N. Berkowitz, and John R. Walton, "UPC Scanning: An Assessment of Shopper Response to Technological Change," *Journal of Retailing* 56, no. 2 (Summer 1980): 25–44.

31. BLS, *Technological Change and Its Labor Impact in Five Industries*, Bulletin 1961 (Washington, D.C.: U.S. Government Printing Office, 1977): 45–56.

32. The major book on the subject Stephen A. Brown, *Revolution at the Checkout Counter: The Explosion of the Bar Code* (Cambridge, Mass.: Harvard University Press, 1997); and for an academic study, see Louis P. Bucklin, "Technological Change and Store Operations: The Supermarket Case," *Journal of Retailing* 56, no. 1 (Spring 1980): 3–15.

33. J. Barry Mason and Morris L. Mayer, "Retail Merchandise Information Systems for the 1980's," *Journal of Retailing* 56, no. 1 (Spring 1980): 68–69.

34. Pommer et al., "UPC Scanning," 27–28; "Scanning Picks Up Converts," *Chain Store Age Executive* 54 (June 1978): 31–33; "Giant Shoots for 100% Scanning," *Chain Store Age Executive* 54 (May 1979): 91; "Year of the Scanner," *Progressive Grocer* 57 (December 1978): 49.

35. For a discussion of consumer concerns, see Pommer, et al., "UPC Scanning," 28–31.

36. For a description of the application, with examples, see Ronald Tanner, "A Friendly CAD," *Progressive Grocer* (February 1987): 63–64, 66, 68.

37. "50th Annual Report," *Progressive Grocer* (April 1983): 60.

38. "Survey of Retail Information Technology Expenses and Trends: Supermarkets," *Chain Store Age Executive* 66, no. 10, sect. 2 (October 1990): 15A–17A.

39. "50th Annual Report," *Progressive Grocer*, 60.

40. Robert E. O'Neill, "New DSD Systems: Generate More Profit, Less Hassle," *Progressive Grocer* (November 1980): 33, 36, 38–39, 44–46, 48, quote on 38; Robert E. O'Neill, "DSD Update: Chipping Away at the Problems," *Progressive Grocer* (August 1981): 117–121, 129–131.

41. Warren Thayer, "Database Marketing Demystified," *Progressive Grocer* (November 1989): 22.

42. Robert E. O'Neill, "How to Sell Your Scanning Data," *Progressive Grocer* (February 1983): 63–64, 66, 68, 72; "A New Dimension in Marketing," *Progressive Grocer* (May 1987):

133–134, 136; Warren Thayer, "How Are We Really Using Our Scanning Data?" *Progressive Grocer* (August 1990): 146–148, 150; Warren Thayer, "Database Marketing Demystified," *Progressive Grocer* (November 1989): 21–24, 26, 28.

43. Robert E. O'Neill, "What's New in EFT," *Progressive Grocer* (August 1985): 59–60, 62, 64, 66; Robert E. O'Neill, "Is This America's Most Efficient Supermarket?" *Progressive Grocer* (March 1986): 109–110, 112, 114, 116; Stephen Bennett, "Draw Your Debit Card, Pardner," *Progressive Grocer* (January 1988): 61–62, 64; Richard De Santa, "A Bold Experiment," *Progressive Grocer* (February 1988): 67, 70.

44. Steve Weinstein, "Building Loyalty," *Progressive Grocer* (June 1999): 89; on experiences in the late 1980s and early 1999s, see "The Pathway to Category Management," *Progressive Grocer* (December 1992): 50–52; Carlene A. Thissen, "Getting to Know Your Customers," *Progressive Grocer* (December 1993): 25, 28; Michael Garry, "Making Sense Out of Data," *Progressive Grocer* (June 1995): 75–77; "Taking Category Management to the Real World . . . Yours," *Progressive Grocer* (August 1997): 10–11; Len Lewis, "Private Lives," *Progressive Grocer* (February 1998): 47–48, 50.

45. Warren Thayer, "Electronic Shelf Labels: How They Stack Up," *Progressive Grocer* (January 1990): 61–64, 66; Michael Garry, "Will Supermarkets Play Electronic Tag?" *Progressive Grocer* (July 1991): 99–100, 102–104; Jerry Morton, "ESL: Up and Running," *Progressive Grocer* (December 1993): 23–24; Michael Garry, "Are ESLs Worth It?" *Progressive Grocer* (August 1994): 135–136.

46. On the benefits, see Ronald Tanner, "A Payback Measured in Months," *Progressive Grocer* (April 1987): 107–108, 110. Also on this application, see Robert E. O'Neill, "How to Coax Greater Productivity from the Front End," *Progressive Grocer* (January 1986): 89–90, 92, 94; Warren Thayer, "Computerized Payroll Pays Off," *Progressive Grocer* (June 1988): 39–40, 42.

47. Michael Garry, "Keeping an Eye on Labor," *Progressive Grocer* (April 1992): 63, 65–66; Terry Hennessy, "Scheduling That Works," *Progressive Grocer* (December 1993): 35–36.

48. Quoted in Ronald Tanner, "Computerization: The Future Is Now," *Progressive Grocer* (January 1987): 40.

49. Ibid., 40.

50. Ibid., 42.

51. Ed Martin, Save Mart Stores, quoted in Michael Garry, "Inventory Control: Moving Ahead," *Progressive Grocer* (January 1993): 63.

52. Michael Garry, "The Stepping Stone to ECR," *Progressive Grocer* (June 1994): 59; on the subjects of CAO and ECR in the 1990s, see Michael Garry, "UCS II Breaking Through?" *Progressive Grocer* (April 1993): 109–110, 112; Michael Sansolo, "ECR," *Progressive Grocer* (November 1993): 47–48, 50; Michael Garry, "Efficient Replenishment: The Key to ECR," *Progressive Grocer* (December 1993): 5–6, 8; Steve Weinstein, "To Buy or Not to Buy?" *Progressive Grocer* (June 1994): 19–20, 24.

53. Len Lewis, "Tech Trends," *Progressive Grocer* (September 1998): 115.

54. Michael Garry, "Cross–Docking: The Road to ECR," *Progressive Grocer* (August 1993): 107–108, 110–111; "Networking in the '90s," *Progressive Grocer* (March 1996): 145–146; Michael Garry, "Battle of the Networks," *Progressive Grocer* (February 1994): 69–72; Michael Garry, "Completing the Loop," *Progressive Grocer* (February 1995): 75, 78, 80; Len Lewis, "Managing Technology," *Progressive Grocer* (June 1997): 47–48; on the power shift, see "Information Is the New Currency," *Progressive Grocer* (April 1995): 18–20.

55. For quote, Michael Garry, "Linchpin of the New Fleming," *Progressive Grocer* (January 1995): 57; "High-Tech Building Blocks," *Progressive Grocer* (December 1997): 26; "A Look at Fleming's New Look," *Progressive Grocer* (January 1995): 47.

56. Barry Janoff, "Chain of Command," *Progressive Grocer* (March 2001): 7172, 74.

57. One of the first articles about the Internet published by *Progressive Grocer* was by Ryan

Mathews, "The Power of the Internet," (March 1997): 39–41, 44; he did a sequel, "Virtual Retailing: Beantown's Battle of the Boxes" (April 1997): 37–38, 40; Ryan Mathews, "Consumer-Direct: Will Stores Survive?" (April 1997): 31–34, 36, 38.

58. Carol Radice, "Nothing but Net," *Progressive Grocer* (January 1998): 67–68; Victor J. Orler and David H. Friedman, "The Consumers Behind Consumer-Direct," *Progressive Grocer* (February 1998): 39–40, 42; Barry Janoff, "Scuttling the Cyberpirates," *Progressive Grocer* (November 1999): 61–62, 64; Barry Janoff, "Click and Stick," *Progressive Grocer* (February 2000): 61–62, 64 and also his "Building the Better Intranet," *Progressive Grocer* (February 2000): 67–68, 70.

59. Food Marketing Institute, "The E-tail Experience: What Grocery Shoppers Think About Online Shopping," (Richmond, Va.: FMI, 2000), unpaginated summary.

60. Barry Janoff, "Hot Wired," *Progressive Grocer* (January 2001): 54. For further information on A&P's initiatives, see Denise Power, "IT to Play Key Role in Forging a New A&P," *Supermarket News* 48, no. 39 (September 25, 2000): 12.

61. When two e-tailers shut down—Webvan.com and HomeRuns—one reporter emphasized that their failure was due to three problems: e-supermarkets overestimated how fast customers would move from buying books and music online to groceries; these two firms spent the inventor's venture capital too fast; and their management proved too eager to please customers with, for example, one-hour delivery service, which drove up operating costs. The article was written by Chris Taylor, "E-Grocers Check Out," *Time* (July 23, 2001): 65.

62. Barry Janoff, "Boston E-party," *Progressive Grocer* (February 2001): 57–58; FMI, "On-line Grocery Shopping: Learnings from the Practioners" (undated, circa spring 2001), MyWebGrocer.com, http://www.fmi.org/e_business/webgrocer.htm; see also, at the same site, "Executive Summary" (undated, circa spring 2001); Barry Janoff, "Thick as a Brick," *Progressive Grocer* (May 2001): 87–88.

63. For examples, see Len Lewis, "Box Stores," *Progressive Grocer* (May 1998): 57–58, 60; "Self-Checkout Systems Add 'On-Line' Efficiency," *Discount Store News* 37, no. 11 (June 8, 1998): 70; Len Lewis, "DSD: Unleashing the Power," *Progressive Grocer* (November 1998): 4–11; Barry Janoff, "User-Friendly Computer-Based Training," *Progressive Grocer* (March 1999): 65–66, 68, 70; Richard Turcsik, "Front-End Fingerprints," *Progressive Grocer* (December 1999): 109–110; "Food Lion Automates Checkout," *Chain Store Age Executive* 76, no. 4 (April 2000): 90ff. "Of Time and Technology," *Supermarket News* 48, no. 29 (July 17, 2000): 23.

64. Len Lewis, "High-tech or Too Tech?" *Progressive Grocer* (June 1998): 35–36, 38.

65. Steve Weinstein, "Tackling Technology," *Progressive Grocer* (February 1999): 43–44, 46, 49, 52.

66. Susan Reda, "Grocery Stores: Leaders or Laggards on Technology/" *Stores* (February 2001): 1, http://www.stores.org/eng/archives/feb01.edit.html.

67. Ibid., 1.

68. For an excellent example, see Peter Doeringer and Audrey Watson, "Apparel," in David C. Mowery (ed.), *U.S. Industry in 2000: Studies in Competitive Performance* (Washington, D.C.: National Academy Press, 1999): 329–362; has an excellent bibliography on the industry.

69. Frederick H. Abernathy, John T. Dunlop, Janice H. Hammond, and David Weil, *A Stitch in Time: Lean Retailing and the Transformation of Manufacturing—Lessons from the Apparel and Textile Industries* (New York: Oxford University Press, 1999), provides a review of both manufacturing arms of the industry, including a discussion of their use of computers.

70. Doeringer and Watson, "Apparel," 342.

71. P. Berg, E. Applebaum, T. Bailey, and A. Kalleberg, "The Performance Effects of Modular Production in the U.S. Apparel Industry," *Industrial Relations* 35, no. 3 (July 1996): 356–373.

72. Doeringer and Watson, "Apparel," 344.

73. Ibid. 345.

74. Abernathy et al., *Stitch in Time,* 3.

75. Ibid., 50–51.

76. For a useful description of the applications and their costs for each of these building blocks, see ibid., 39–70.

77. Ibid; that discuss major sources of productivity data on 315–318.

78. These data came from various U.S. government sources but are nicely summarized in a table in Abernathy et al., *Stitch in Time,* 76.

79. Theodore Clarke and Janice H. Hammond, "Reengineering Channel Reordering Processes to Improve Total Supply Chain Performance," *Journal of Production and Operations Management* 6, no. 3 (Fall 1997): 248; Charles L. Munson, Meir J. Rosenblatt, and Zehava Rosenblatt, "The Use and Abuse of Power in Supply Chains," in John A. Woods and the National Association of Purchasing Management (eds.), *The Purchasing and Supply Yearbook: 2000 Edition* (New York: McGraw-Hill, 2000): 113–131.

80. Abernathy et al., *Stitch in Time,* 248–249.

81. Doeringer and Watson, "Apparel," 344–353.

82. Forrester Research; the same firm predicted that online sales of clothing would reach approximately 11 percent of all sales by the end of 2004.

83. Ernst & Young, "Global Online Retailing," *Stores* (January 2000), sect. 2, unpaginated, http://www.stores.org; quote in "Specialty Apparel: Fit, Feel and Brand."

84. Levy and Weitz, *Retailing Management,* 96–97.

85. The study, along with other support materials, is available at its own web site, "Measuring the Internet Economy," January 2001, http://www.internetindicators.com. The study team is continuing to report on the extent of the deployment of the Internet across the U.S. economy, producing data on a quarterly basis.

86. David Siegel, *Futurize Your Enterprise: Business Strategy in the Age of the E-customer* (New York: Wiley, 1999): xi.

87. "Measuring the Internet Economy," 1.

88. Ibid.

89. "Internet Sales Growing at Healthy Rate," *Sacramento Bee* (April 27, 2001).

90. Ibid.

91. Ibid.

92. Robert Spector, *Amazon.com: Inside the Revolutionary Business Model That Changed the World* (New York: HarperBusiness, 2000): 179–206; Rebecca Saunders, *Business the Amazon.com Way: Secrets of the World's Most Astonishing Web Business* (Dover, N.H.: Capstone, 1999): 1–24. "Originally" because by the dawn of the new century, it was investing in bricks-and-mortar warehouses to be able to buy books in bulk.

93. Carl Shapiro and Hal R. Varian, *Information Rules: A Strategic Guide to the Network Economy* (Boston: Harvard Business School Press, 1999): 2.

94. For a detailed review of the topic, see Bill Moore et al., *B2B E-commerce Using WebSphere Commerce Business Edition Patterns for E-business Series* (Research Triangle Park, N.C.: IBM Corp., 2002).

95. The literature on these tasks is now vast, the subject of several hundred books published annually and thousands of articles. For an introduction to the applications, see Peter Fingar, Harsha Kumar and Tarun Sharma, *Enterprise E-commerce* (Tampa, Fla.: Meghan-Kiffer Press, 2000); see also the excellent collection of material from J. Christopher Westland and Theodore H. K. Clark, *Global Electronic Commerce: Theory and Case Studies* (Cambridge, Mass.: MIT Press, 1999); and for a very typical, sensationalized "how to" book, see Siegel, *Future Your Enterprise.*

96. David Bunnell and Richard Luecke, *The ebay Phenomenon: Business Secrets Behind the*

World's Hottest Internet Company (New York: Wiley, 2000): 4–6, 22; Adam Cohen, *The Perfect Store: Inside e-Bay* (Boston: Little, Brown, 2002)..

97. Robert Spector, *Amazon.com: Get Big Fast* (New York: HarperCollins, 2000).

98. Susan Reda, "VeriFone and Russell Reynolds Associates Top 100 Internet Retailers," *Stores* (September 2000), unpaginated, http://www.stores.org/eng/archives/sept00cover. html; see also, Susan Reda, "Groundbreaking Consumer Survey Tracks Nation's Biggest On-line Merchants," *Stores* (September 1999).

99. "Amazon Was Busiest Holiday e-Tailer," *Warehouse Management* 8, no. 1 (January 2001): 15.

100. "Profitability Is the New Priority for E-Tailers," *Chain Store Age* (August 2000): 35A–C.

101. For an analysis of causes of failure and case studies from 1999–2001, see "A Look at IBM's Early E-business Pilot Projects," *VARBusiness* (April 2, 2001); Gregory J. Gilligan, "Past Year Has Been Unkind to Internet Retailers," *Richmond Times-Dispatch* (December 9, 2000); "Creating the Structure for an e-Commerce Hub," *International Money Marketing* (April 12, 2001), 34.

102. Material for the last two paragraphs was drawn from Jupiter Research press releases (December 27, 2000).

103. For example, "E-Bay May Forge Ties with Major Shippers," *Newsbytes News Network* (March 10, 2000); "E-Bay Gets Into Auctionflow," *InternetWeek* (October 23, 2000): 9.

104. "E-Toys to Close Up Shop," *Warehousing Management* 8, no. 3 (April 2001): 13; "Re-searchers Say Internet-Only Retailers Are Likely to Fade," *Washington Times* (April 13, 2000). See another example that received wide publicity, the case of Furtinute.com: Susan Bishop, "Requiem for a Promising E-Tailer," *Home Furnishing News* 74, no. 45 (November 13, 2000) 1ff.

105. For example, "Net Retailing Reaching 29 Bil This Year," *Newsbytes News Network* (June 27, 2000); "On-Line Sales to Soar," *MMR* 17, no. 13 (July 24, 2000): 12.

106. The IBM models are drawn from internal company materials in my possession that are used by the firm's consultants in their work with clients. For examples of the kinds of models deployed by IBM, see James W. Cortada and Thomas S. Hargraves, *Into the Networked Age: How IBM and Other Firms Are Getting There Now* (New York: Oxford University Press, 1999); Harvey Thompson, *The Customer-Centered Enterprise: How IBM and Other World-Class Companies Achieve Extraordinary Results by Putting Customers First* (New York: McGraw-Hill, 2000); and Stephan H. Haeckel, *Adaptive Enterprises: Creating and Leading Sense-and-Respond Organizations* (Boston: Harvard Business School Press, 1999). The Archives of the Charles Babbage Institute, at the University of Minnesota, Minneapolis, have many examples of these kinds of models in the papers of consulting firms and even computer companies (e.g., Bur-roughs), dating back to the 1930s; see in particular both the Burroughs Papers and the Auerbach Papers.

107. At the end of the century, the most extensive users of computing were banks (8.5 percent), financial services (nearly 15 percent), and telecommunications firms (18 percent). Data are drawn from IBM market surveys in my possession and from various U.S. Department of Commerce reports.

Chapter 12

1. John W. Kendrick, *Productivity Trends in the United States* (Princeton, N.J.: Princeton University Press, 1961), quote on 19.

2. Of course, there were exceptions: Wal-Mart began as a small firm that grew, largely because of good strategy and effective use of the digital.

3. Neil Rackam, *SPIN Selling* (New York: McGraw-Hill, 1988): 162; Buck Rodgers, *The IBM Way: Insights Into the World's Most Successful Marketing Organization* (New York: Harper & Row, 1986): 47–65, 92–94; James W. Cortada, *The Computer in the United States: From Laboratory to Market, 1930 to 1960* (Armonk, N.Y.: M.E. Sharpe, 1993): 77–89.

4. Robert A. Fischer, "Insurance Tomorrow: The Data Processing Picture," *Best's Review*, Property/Liability ed. (May 1975): 104–109; George P. Jones, "Emerging Technologies for the Insurance Industry," *Best's Review*, Property and Casualty Insurance ed. (January 1985): 58, 60, 62.

5. This point was made by the great historian of technology George Basalla, *The Evolution of Technology* (Cambridge: Cambridge University Press, 1988).

6. See, for instance, the pleas of Felix Kaufman, "Data Systems That Cross Company Boundaries," *Harvard Business Review* 46, no. 1 (January–February 1966): 141.

7. See, for example, James I. Cash, Jr., and Benn R. Konsynski, "IS Redraws Competitive Boundaries," *Harvard Business Review* 64, no. 2 (March–April 1985): 134–142.

8. David C. Mowery and Richard R. Nelson, "The U.S. Corporation and Technical Progress," in Carl Kaysen (ed.), *The American Corporation Today: Examining the Questions of Power and Efficiency at the Century's End* (New York: Oxford University Press, 1996): 187–241.

9. I have discussed briefly what this community looked like in James W. Cortada, *Information Technology as Business History: Issues in the History and Management of Computers* (Westport, Conn.: Greenwood Press, 1996): 221–246.

10. For a collection of articles by scientists and engineers on the subject, see Peter J. Denning and Robert M. Metcalfe (eds.), *Beyond Calculation: The Next Fifty Years of Computing* (New York: Copernicus, 1997).

11. Thomas H. Davenport and Laurence Prusak, *Working Knowledge: How Organizations Manage What They Know* (Boston: Harvard Business School Press, 1998): 19–24.

12. Many firms, however, also kept multiple copies of the same data on different computers for security and backup. If a computer broke down, a firm could switch to another that had what in the IT world is called a "mirror image" of what the broken system had installed.

13. The book that brought this subject to the attention of the American business community is by Stan Davis and Bill Davidson, *2020: Transform Your Business Today to Succeed in Tomorrow's Economy* (New York: Simon & Schuster, 1991): 81–110.

14. Alfred D. Chandler, Jr., *Scale and Scope: The Dynamics of Industrial Capitalism* (Cambridge, Mass.: Harvard University Press, 1990): 3–46.

15. At the end of the 1990s, when all industries in the United States were focused on Y2K, bank mergers were either impeded or went forward according to the degree to which a targeted bank had fixed its Y2K problems.

16. Peter Temin and Louis Galambos, *The Fall of the Bell System* (Cambridge: Cambridge University Press, 1987): 28–69; Steve Coll, *The Deal of the Century: The Breakup of AT&T* (New York: Atheneum, 1986): 375–380.

17. For works that touch on this theme, see Erik Brynjolfsson and Brian Kahin (eds.), *Understanding the Digital Economy: Data, Tools, and Research* (Cambridge, Mass.: MIT Press, 2000); Dale Neef, *A Little Knowledge Is a Dangerous Thing: Understanding Our Global Knowledge Economy* (Boston: Butterworth-Heinemann, 1999).

18. For a summary of the issues involved and an excellent bibliography on the topic, see J. Steven Landefeld and Barbara M. Fraument, "Measuring the New Economy," *Survey of Current Business* (March 2001): 23–40.

19. John McMillan, *Reinventing the Bazaar: A Natural History of Markets* (New York: Norton, 2002): 148–153, 167–168, 170.

20. The points made in this paragraph grew out of a major study of IT economic performance sponsored by IBM and the National Science Foundation: Jason Dedrick, Vijay Gur-

baxani, and Kenneth L. Kraemer, "Information Technology and Economic Performance: Firm and Country Evidence," unpublished paper, July 2001. This paper also includes an outstanding and complete bibliography on the subject.

21. Peter Weill, "The Relationship Between Information Technology and Firm Performance: A Study of the Valve Manufacturing Sector," *Information Systems Research* 3, no. 4 (1992): 307–333; Gary W. Loveman, "An Assessment of the Productivity Impact of Information Technologies," in Thomas J. Allen and Michael S. Scott Morton (eds.), *Information Technology and the Corporation of the 1990s: Research Studies* (New York: Oxford University Press, 1994): 84–110; Anitesh Barau, Charles H. Kriebel, and Tridas Mukhopadhyay, "Information Technologies and Business Value: An Analytical and Empirical Investigation," *Information Systems Research* 6, no. 1(1995): 3–23.

22. Alfred D. Chandler, Jr., reached this conclusion as one of his major findings in his new book, *Inventing the Electronic Century: The Epic Story of the Consumer Electronics and Computer Industries* (New York: Free Press, 2001): 7–11.

23. This statement, although generally true, minimizes the small number of academics who have maintained influential links with specific industries, usually through industry-centric institutes at their universities. Institutes of these types exist in the United States for Automotive, Retail, Manufacturing, Banking, and Insurance Industries, to mention a few. They typically conduct studies and surveys of issues within an industry and provide training to management or consulting services. Their role has yet to be studied properly.

24. Herbert A. Simon, *The Shape of Automation for Men and Management* (New York: Harper Torchbooks, 1965): 101.

25. Ibid., 102.

26. Ibid., 110.

27. This statement applies only to the firms in the physical economy (manufacturing, trucking, wholesaling, and retailing).

28. Peter Cappelli et al., *Change at Work* (New York: Oxford University Press, 1997): 208.

29. Ibid., 208–209.

30. The example most obvious in the American IT community was the practice in the 1990s of sending programming work to India, where software programmers were paid far less than their American counterparts but were seen as productive and qualified. For a description of the Indian situation, see Edward Yourdon, *Decline and Fall of the American Programmer* (Englewood Cliffs, N.J.: Yourdon Press/PTR Prentice-Hall, 1992): 279–312.

31. Henry Kissinger, *Does America Need a Foreign Policy? Toward a Diplomacy for the 21st Century* (New York: Simon & Schuster, 2001): 211.

32. Robert Gilpin, *The Challenge of Global Capitalism: The World Economy in the 21st Century* (Princeton, N.J.: Princeton University Press, 2000): 30.

33. Ibid., 29–34.

34. Pail N. Edwards, *The Closed World: Computers and the Politics of Discourse in Cold War America* (Cambridge, Mass.: MIT Press, 1996): 43–73; Kenneth Flamm, *Targeting the Computer: Government Support and International Competition* (Washington, D.C.: Brookings Institution, 1987): 42–124, and *Creating the Computer: Government, Industry, and High Technology* (Washington, D.C.: Brookings Institution, 1988): 29–79.

35. John Lewis Gaddis, *The Long Peace* (New York: Oxford University Press, 1987).

36. James W. Cortada, *Before the Computer: IBM, NCR, Burroughs, and Remington Rand and the Industry They Created, 1865–1956* (Princeton, N.J.: Princeton University Press, 1993): 187–205.

37. Lars Heide, "From Invention to Production: The Development of Punched-Card Machines by R. R. Bull and K. A. Knulsen, 1918–1930," *IEEE Annals of the History of Computing* 13, no. 3 (1991): 261–272; Edwin Black, *IBM and the Holocaust* (New York: Crown Publishing, 2001); Jan Van den Ende, "The Number Factory: Punched-card Machines at the Dutch

Central Bureau of Statistics," *IEEE Annals of the History of Computing* 16, no. 3 (1994): 15–24; and his, *The Turn of the Tide: Computerization in Dutch Society, 1900–1965* (Delft, The Netherlands: Delft University Press, 1994).

38. Alexis de Tocqueville, *Democracy in America*, George Lawrence (Trans.) J. P. Mayer (ed.) (New York: HarperPerennial, 1966): 553–554.

39. A team of scholars described that pattern in Alfred D. Chandler, Jr., and James W. Cortada (eds.), *A Nation Transformed by Information: How Information Has Shaped the United States from Colonial Times to the Present* (New York: Oxford University Press, 2000), and I did the same, focusing primarily on contemporary circumstances, in *Making of the Information Society: Experience, Consequences, and Possibilities* (Upper Saddle River, N.J.: Financial Times/Prentice Hall, 2002).

Appendix A

1. Michael E. Porter, *Competitive Strategy: Techniques for Analyzing Industries and Competitors* (New York: Free Press, 1980); *Competitive Advantage: Creating and Sustaining Superior Performance* (New York: Free Press, 1985); *The Competitive Advantage of Nations* (New York: Free Press, 1990).

2. Alfred D. Chandler, Jr., *The Visible Hand: The Managerial Revolution in American Business* (Cambridge, Mass.: Harvard University Press, 1977); *Scale and Scope: The Dynamics of Industrial Capitalism* (Cambridge, Mass.: Harvard University Press, 1990); with Franco Amatori and Takashi Hikino (eds.), *Big Business and the Wealth of Nations* (Cambridge: Cambridge University Press, 1997), especially 24–57; and with James W. Cortada (eds.), *A Nation Transformed by Information: How Information Has Shaped the United States from Colonial Times to the Present* (New York: Oxford University Press, 2000). See also Alfred D. Chandler, Jr., *Inventing the Electric Century: The Epic Story of the Consumer Electronics and Computer Industries* (New York: Free Press, 2001).

3. For examples, see James M. Utterback, *Mastering the Dynamics of Innovation: How Companies Can Seize Opportunities in the Face of Technological Change* (Boston: Harvard Business School Press, 1994); David B. Yoffie (ed.), *Competing in the Age of Digital Convergence* (Boston: Harvard Business School Press, 1997).

4. A recently well-researched and written technical history illustrates this approach: Paul E. Ceruzzi, *A History of Modern Computing* (Cambridge, Mass.: MIT Press, 1998): 5–12.

5. Most recently in James W. Cortada, "Progenitors of the Information Age: The Development of Chips and Computers," in Chandler and Cortada, *Nation Transformed by Information*, 177–216.

6. BLS, *BLS Publications on Productivity and Technology*, Report 741 (Washington, D.C.: U.S. Government Printing Office, August 1987): 16–17.

7. See http://www.ecommerce.gov. The first of these major reports was *Digital Economy 2000* (Washington, D.C.: U.S. Government Printing Office, June 2000), a report updated each year.

8. For a detailed listing of these kinds of publications, see James W. Cortada, *A Bibliographic Guide to the History of Computer Applications, 1950–1990* (Westport, Conn.: Greenwood Press, 1996); and James W. Cortada, "Researching the History of Software from the 1960s," *IEEE Annals of the History of Computing* 24, no. 1 (January–March 2002): 72–79.

Appendix B

1. For a detailed explanation of this technology, see Edwin D. Reilly, "Universal Product Code," in Anthony Ralston, Edwin D. Reilly, and David Hemmendinger (eds.), *Encyclopedia of Computer Science*, 4th ed. (London: Nature Publishing Group, 2000): 1814–1816.

2. For an explanation of the technology, see Sargur N. Srihari, Ajay Shekhawat, and Stephen W. Lam, "Optical Character Recognition (OCR)," in *Encyclopedia of Computer Science*, 4th ed. (London: Nature Publishing Group, 2000), 1326–1333.

3. For a technical description of a POS system, with illustrations, circa late 1970s, see Marilyn Bohl, *Information Processing* (Chicago: Science Research Associates, 1980): 129–132.

BIBLIOGRAPHIC ESSAY

This brief bibliographic essay discusses some of the most obvious and useful sources for those interested in exploring in more detail the subject of this book. Citations in the endnotes point to sources and to additional materials used in highly specific ways, for example, Internet addresses. Those are not repeated below. I emphasize books rather than articles because the former cover broader subjects more suitable for the purposes of this essay.

Archival Sources

The two primary archival collections used for this book are the IBM Corporate Archives and the Archives of the Charles Babbage Institute at the University of Minnesota. IBM's archives are normally not open to researchers, since they are organized to support internal needs. They are, however, very similar to over 50 corporate archives in the United States, many of which also contain files related to the use of computing by their firms. Another important archive is the Hagley Museum and Library, located in Wilmington, Delaware. It houses part of the corporate records for Remington-Rand and includes some materials on applications used on computers in the 1950s. For additional archival information, a community of business archivists, The Business Archives Section of the Society of American Archivists, can be reached through www.archivists.org.

For those wanting to look at primary materials on applications of computing, the mother lode is housed at the Charles Babbage Institute (CBI). This facility is home to the corporate archives of several major computer vendors, including Burroughs and CDC, without which I could not have reconstructed the use of computing in the 1950s and 1960s. Equally important, it contains the archives of leading consulting firms working in the industry, early software companies, product brochures, private papers of hundreds of participants in the industry, and has an impressive collection of IT conference proceedings from the past half-century. Its oral interviews, collection of photographs, and historical publications are second to none. CBI also sponsors major historical research projects, including supporting graduate students writing dissertations on the history of computing through its Tomash Fellowship program, and hosts various international conferences and publications. This center maintains online catalogues and finding aids, which can be reached through its Web site at www.cbi.umn.edu.

The industries studied for this book do not have industry-wide archives, such as the IT Industry through CBI. Therefore, after using the collections cited above, one should contact the largest companies within an industry and inquire about any corporate archives that might contain the appropriate materials. When dealing with corporate archives, the most successful lines of research involve looking at files containing materials on product design and engineering, as well as organizational records for large plant sites, accounting departments, and data processing organizations. The library at the Harvard Business School and the U.S. Library of Congress each have large collections of contemporary industry magazines and newspapers, all of which are excellent sources of material on how computers were used. These kinds of publications are essential to document industry-wide issues, establish timing of key events, and for survey data on the extent of deployment of specific technologies, software products, and applications. As a rule, industry associations do not have extensive historical collections, although some did occasionally publish on the subject. Those published references can be found in the endnotes.

Computing, Applications, and Economics

The two best general histories of computing are by Paul E. Ceruzzi, *A History of Modern Computing* (Cambridge, Mass.: MIT Press, 1998), and Martin Campbell-Kelly and William Aspray, *Computer: A History of the Information Machine* (New York: Basic Books, 1996). For the PC and its related effects there is the highly useful book by Paul Freiberger and Michael Swaine, *Fire in the Valley: The Making of the Personal Computer* (New York: McGraw-Hill, 2000). For an understanding of the broader role of information and its technologies within American business and society at large, there is, primarily for the supply side of the story, Alfred D. Chandler, Jr. and James W. Cortada (eds.), *A Nation Transformed by Information: How Information Has Shaped the United States From Colonial Times to the Present* (New York: Oxford University Press, 2000). On the demand side of the story, see James W. Cortada, *Making of the Information Society: Experience, Consequences, and Possibilities* (Upper Saddle River, N.J.: Financial Times/Prentice Hall, 2002). There are many good histories of the Internet, but the acknowledged best is by Janet Abbate, *Inventing the Internet* (Cambridge, Mass.: MIT Press, 1999). Because IT infrastructures are so important to this story, see Raul Rojas and Ulf Hashagen (eds.), *The First Computers: History and Architectures* (Cambridge: Cambridge University Press, 2000).

There is a paucity of material on the history of digital applications, which is why I wrote this book. The one existing work is by James L. McKenney with Duncan C. Copeland and Richard O. Mason, *Waves of Change: Business Evolution through Information Technology* (Boston: Harvard Business School Press, 1995), which provides case studies drawn primarily from the banking and airline industries. Although not a history book, Thomas H. Davenport's *Process Innovation: Reengineering*

Work through Information Technology (Boston: Harvard Business School Press, 1993) uses many examples to demonstrate the linkage between how processes work and the use of computers in support of these. Also not a history, but with an historical sense to it, is the important book on the role of the Internet in business written by Carl Shapiro and Hal R. Varian, *Information Rules: A Strategic Guide to the Network Economy* (Boston: Harvard Business School Press, 1999). For a bibliography of over 1,600 citations on the use of applications and computing, see James W. Cortada, *A Bibliographic Guide to the History of Computer Applications, 1950–1990* (Westport, Conn.: Greenwood Press, 1996).

A series of books on general business history provide context and perspective in which to set much of what happened with computing, primarily within corporations, but also industries. The basic works are by Alfred D. Chandler, Jr. *The Visible Hand: The Managerial Revolution in American Business* (Cambridge, Mass.: Harvard University Press, 1977), which describes the emergence of the corporation and the managerial class in the United States between the 1840s and the end of the 1920s, and its sequel, *Scale and Scope: The Dynamics of Industrial Capitalism* (Cambridge, Mass.: Harvard University Press, 1990), which describes the kinds of investments firms and industries made to develop globally competitive industries, and compares patterns evident in the United States, Great Britain, and Germany. For us to link his work to day-to-day issues evident in industries and companies, several books by Michael E. Porter are essential reading. From his many books, begin with *Competitive Strategy: Techniques for Analyzing Industries and Competitors* (New York: Free Press, 1980), which shows how to define an industry and what goes on within it. For an example of that approach applied to an industry, see James W. Cortada, *Before the Computer: IBM, NCR, Burroughs, and Remington Rand and the Industry They Created, 1965–1956* (Princeton, N.J.: Princeton University Press, 1993). The second book to read by Porter is *Competitive Advantage: Creating and Sustaining Superior Performance* (New York: Free Press, 1985), which builds on the first while discussing the issue of how companies and industries compete by leveraging skills and capabilities. For a global comparison, and a nice companion to Chandler's *Scale and Scope*, see Porter's *The Competitive Advantage of Nations* (New York: Free Press, 1990), in which he also includes case studies of specific industries.

A variety of anthologies of industry overviews address not only economic issues concerning structure, productivity, and innovation, but also business strategies and the role of technologies. Walter Adams, and a variety of coeditors, put together the most useful collections for the latter half of the twentieth century. Between the start of the 1950s and the end of the century, he published ten editions with various publishers, but all with the same title, *The Structure of American Industry*, with the latest edition in 2001. Specific editions are cited in the endnotes. These chapter-length surveys of individual industries include bibliographies of all the major works dealing with the contemporary state of an industry and normally include citations of major works of history. These surveys routinely mention the role of various types of technologies, although they provide no account of computer-based applications. For a more specific set of publications dealing with the types of technologies deployed in industries, see the large collection written by economists at the U.S.

Bureau of Labor Statistics (BLS) discussed in detail in Appendix A and cited in endnotes in almost every chapter of this book. I cannot overemphasize their value. Each contains a 10- to 30-page report on the structure of an industry, the types of technologies it was installing (including computing), extent of deployment, anticipated uses, productivity of labor, and effects of technology on productivity and employment within an industry. These publications began appearing in the 1960s and were published until the early 1990s. There exists no other consistent source of material on specific industries and their adoptions of technology that covers so many years. When used alongside the documentation found at both IBM and at CBI, I was able to reconstruct what applications existed and how extensively they were deployed across the 1950s through the late 1980s, all with a high degree of reliability. Both sets of sources—BLS and the archives—are not as useful for the 1990s, however. For a bibliography of most of these BLS publications, see U.S. Bureau of Labor Statistics, *BLS Publications on Productivity and Technology*, Report No. 741 (Washington, D.C.: Government Printing Office, 1987, and subsequent editions).

The valuable economic literature on the history of technology in modern industries is quite extensive and, while less useful for describing what applications were used by whom, is effective in assessing a particular technology's effect on labor productivity, the financial performance of corporations, and the economic impact of investments in high-tech tools. Because so much was changing within industries that affected the American economy, conducting an analysis of the role of any technology in any industry for the last five to six decades without taking into account economic considerations makes little sense. Analyzing these changes as they relate to the economy does. A variety of publications are helpful in providing linkages among applications, corporate and industry dynamics, and the role of information technologies. F.M. Scherer's *New Perspectives on Economic Growth and Technological Innovation* (Washington, D.C.: Brookings Institution Press, 1999) is one of the latest publications to discuss the economic role of technology. There is also Daniel E. Sichel, *The Computer Revolution: An Economic Perspective* (Washington, D.C.: Brookings Institution Press, 1997), which, although dated, demonstrates how economists go about determining the economic value of computing. Dale Neef provides a useful introduction to the information economy in the highly readable *A Little Knowledge Is a Dangerous Thing: Understanding Our Global Knowledge Economy* (Boston: Butterworth-Heinemann, 1999). I would add Richard K. Lester, *The Productive Edge: How U.S. Industries Are Pointing the Way to a New Era of Economic Growth* (New York: W.W. Norton, 1998), which also looks at various industries and how they changed during the last two decades of the century. For routine statistical data on the economy, a useful book is Norman Frumkin, *Tracking America's Economy* (Armonk, N.Y.: M.E. Sharpe, 1998, and earlier editions).

Fortunately, we have available a variety of industry-specific economic studies that focus extensively on the role of technology, innovations, and the use of digital technology. David C. Mowery and Nathan Rosenberg, *Paths of Innovation: Technological Change in 20th Century America* (Cambridge: Cambridge University Press, 1998), is an excellent starting point. For a series of industry case studies, there is

David C. Mowery and Richard R. Nelson (eds.), *Sources of Industrial Leadership: Studies of Seven Industries* (Cambridge: Cambridge University Press, 1999). A useful anthology of papers on the role of technology within the context of specific industries is David C. Mowery (ed.), *U.S. Industry in 2000: Studies in Competitive Performance* (Washington, D.C.: National Academy Press, 1999). An earlier work that does a thorough job in discussing the whole question of productivity across the entire economy and has become a minor classic is William J. Baumol, Sue Ann Blackman, and Edward N. Wolff, *Productivity and American Leadership: The Long View* (Cambridge, Mass.: MIT Press, 1989). One of first useful studies on diffusion of technology relevant to my book was by Lars Nabseth and George F. Ray (eds.), *The Diffusion of New Industrial Processes: An International Study* (Cambridge: Cambridge University Press, 1974). For a discussion of unemployment caused by technology, an excellent introduction to the issues and its literature, see Amy Sue Bix, *Inventing Ourselves Out of Jobs? America's Debate over Technological Unemployment, 1929–1981* (Baltimore, Md.: Johns Hopkins University Press, 2000).

Two other sources on economic issues are relevant to the general theme of this book. Joseph A. Schumpeter was concerned about the role of technology in industries and was the originator of much current thinking on these issues. Reading his publications from the 1930s can be a daunting exercise because they are long and complex. For a thorough introduction to the man and his work see Richard Swedberg (ed.), *Joseph A. Schumpeter: The Economics and Sociology of Capitalism* (Princeton, N.J.: Princeton University Press, 1991). I have also relied extensively on the thinking about styles offered by Andrew Tylecote, *The Long Wave in the World Economy: The Current Crisis in Historical Perspective* (London: Routledge, 1991). I recommend his book as a useful introduction to the issues of styles in business and for an understanding of the notion of historical waves.

Manufacturing Industries

The early state of numerical control can be understood with J. J. Childs, *Principles of Numerical Control* (New York: The Industrial Press, 1965), whereas early uses of technology of all types can be appreciated by reading Arthur C. Ansley, *Manufacturing Methods and Processes* (Philadelphia, Pa.: Chilton Company, 1957). In addition, there is a useful collection of essays on the same theme by Eugene M. Grabbe (ed.), *Automation in Business and Industry* (New York: John Wiley and Sons, 1957). An important introduction to the whole issue of inventory management was written by J. Buchan, *Scientific Inventory Management* (Englewood Cliffs, N.J.: Prentice-Hall, 1963). For a more modern overview of this issue, and others related to production processes, see Thomas E. Vollmann, William L. Berry, and D. Clay Whybark, *Manufacturing Planning and Control Systems* (Homewood, Ill.: Irwin, 1988). The major historical work, and one that concentrates largely on numerical control applications and their social implications, is by historian David F. Noble, *Forces of Production: A Social History of Industrial Automation* (New York: Oxford University Press, 1986).

For a nonhistorical review of applications from the 1970s, see Gideon Halevi, *The Role of Computers in Manufacturing Processes* (New York: John Wiley & Sons, 1980).

The revitalization of American industry in the 1980s has been the subject of many studies. A good place to begin is Donald A. Hicks (ed.), *Is New Technology Enough?: Making and Remaking U.S. Basic Industries* (Washington, D.C.: American Enterprise Institute, 1988). For an introduction to state-of-the-art American manufacturing strategies of the late 1980s and early 1990s, there is the excellent survey by Steven L. Goldman, Roger N. Nagel, and Kenneth Preiss, *Agile Competitors and Virtual Organizations* (New York: VNR, 1995). Rebecca Morales studied the emergence of new forms of manufacturing in *Flexible Production: Restructuring the International Automobile Industry* (Cambridge: Polity Press, 1994), whereas for IT tools in support of this new trend there is J. P. Crestin and J. F. McWaters (eds.), *Software for Discrete Manufacturing* (New Amsterdam, N.Y.: North Holland, 1986). The one major study of use to historians on the subject, covering the period just prior to flexible manufacturing, is by Joseph Harrington, Jr., *Computer Integrated Manufacturing* (Malabar, Fla.: Robert E. Krieger, 1973), but also consult D. Kochan (ed.), *CAM: Developments in Computer-Integrated Manufacturing* (New York: Springer-Verlag, 1986).

As we move into the 1990s, the classic work on mass customization, the work to explain fully the business rationale for this form of production with examples, is by B. Joseph Pine II, *Mass Customization: The New Frontier in Business Competition* (Boston: Harvard Business School Press, 1993). For a good introduction to supply chain issues, see D. J. Bowersox and D. J. Closs, *Logistical Management—The Integrated Supply Chain Process* (New York: McGraw-Hill, 1996).

On the Automotive Industry, each of Walter Adams's volumes on *The Structure of American Industry* discusses this important topic. There are no formal histories of computing in this industry, although various BLS studies are a good source of data. Do not forget to read Rebecca Morales's *Flexible Production*, cited above. Published several years before her study is another by Kurt Hoffman and Raphael Kplinsky, *Driving Force: The Global Restructuring of Technology, Labour, and Investment in the Automobile and Components Industries* (Boulder, Colo.: Westview Press, 1988). One of the most recent studies of the industry to include technological issues was written by Charles H. Fine, John C. Lafrance, and Dan Hillebrand, "The U.S. Automobile Manufacturing Industry" (Washington, D.C.: U.S. Department of Commerce, December 1996). Their white paper can be found at http://www.ta.doc.gov/Reports.htm. Finally, we have a massive new history of the Ford Motor Company that comments extensively on the industry by Douglas Brinkley, *Wheels for the World: Henry Ford, His Company, and a Century of Progress, 1903–2003* (New York: Viking Press, 2003).

On the Steel Industry, begin by reading Paul A. Tiffany, *The Decline of American Steel: How Management, Labor, and Government Went Wrong* (New York: Oxford University Press, 1988). The Adams volumes and BLS studies are also useful for this industry. There is, sadly, no history of the use of technology by this industry for the last half of the 1900s. Most of the literature on this industry either concerns its poor economic performance or debates the political consequences to the nation, with minimal discussion of computing applications.

On the Aerospace Industry, see the Adams volume published in 1971, as well as the BLS. The most important of the early studies on this industry was written by Herman O. Stekler, *The Structure and Performance of the Aerospace Industry* (Berkeley, Calif.: University of California Press, 1965). As with the other industries already discussed, we do not yet have a book-length history of the role of technology in this industry.

Process Industry applications have their own literature. The key concept to understand is *continuous flow manufacturing*. For that consult T. H. Tsai, C. S. Lin, and J. W. Lane, *Modern Control Techniques for the Processing Industries* (New York: Marcel Dekker, 1986). On the role of computers, there are two useful surveys: Patrick Chin, *Computer Control in Process Industries* (Elkins Park, Pa.: Franklin Book Co., 1987), and Albert A. Gunkler and J. W. Bernard, *Computer Control Strategies for the Fluid Process Industries* (Research Triangle Park, N.C.: Instrumentation, Systems and Automation Society [ISA], 1990). Both are technical studies.

The Petroleum Industry's primary industry periodical, *The Oil and Gas Journal*, routinely published articles on the role of computing throughout the last five decades of the twentieth century. Various editions of Adams and the BLS studies serve as good beginning points on this industry. However, there is a detailed and comprehensive U.S. government publication on all process industries worth pointing out: U.S. Bureau of Labor Statistics, *Outlook for Computer Process Control: Manpower Implications in Process Industries*, Bulletin 1658 (Washington, D.C.: U.S. GPO, 1970).

On the Chemical Industry, begin with Mowery and Nelson, *Sources of Industrial Leadership*, then consult Ralph Landau, Timothy Tayler, and Gavin Wright (eds.), *The Mosaic of Economic Growth* (Stanford, Calif.: Stanford University Press, 1996). For the most recent survey of the industry, see a white paper by Allen J. Lenz and John Lafrance, "The Chemical Industry" (Washington, D.C.: U.S. Department of Commerce, January 1996) and available at http://www.ta.doc.gov/Reports.htm. For a discussion closer to technical issues, see Mowery and Rosenberg, *Paths of Innovation*, and Mowery, *U.S. Industry in 2000*. The only large study dealing with any aspect of technology in this industry, including some commentary on computing, is by David A. Hounshell and John Kenly Smith, Jr., *Science and Corporate Strategy: Du Pont R&D, 1902–1980* (Cambridge: Cambridge University Press, 1988). An industry trade publication, *Chemical Engineering*, frequently published articles on various computer applications over the years and is a reliable contemporary source on the topic. For more recent years also consult the *Journal of Chemical Information and Computer Sciences*.

On the Pharmaceutical Industry, begin with Peter Temin's excellent study, *Taking Your Medicine: Drug Regulation in the United States* (Cambridge, Mass.: Harvard University Press, 1980), then go to Adams, *The Structure of American Industry*, 1971 and 1995 editions, and then examine Stuart O. Schweitzer, *Pharmaceutical Economics and Policy* (New York: Oxford University Press, 1997). These three sources provide excellent economic background. For more discussion about the role of technology and innovation, turn to Mowery, *U.S. Industry in 2000*, which includes a chapter on the industry. The only major study that includes historical commentary on computer applications in this industry is by Bruce I. Blum and Karen Duncan (eds.), *A History of Medical Informatics* (New York: ACM Press, 1990). Also useful is the Office of Technology Assessment, *Pharmaceutical R&D: Costs, Risks and Rewards* (Washington, D.C.: U.S. GPO, 1993). Over the years, the journals *Chemical and Engineering* and *Pharmaceutical Technology* have published some material dealing with computing in this industry as well.

On the Semiconductor Industry there is a large body of literature on the history of the computer chip, far less on the industry, and a paucity of material on computer applications within it. That said, however, Mowery and Nelson, *Sources of Industrial Leadership*, has an excellent introduction to the industry; for very recent developments, see Mowery, *U.S. Industry in 2000*. An early study that provides some insight into the nuts and bolts of how the industry operated is Nico Hazewindus and John Tooker, *The U.S. Microelectronics Industry: Technical Change, Industry Growth and Social Impact* (New York: Pergamon Press, 1982). For a brief discussion of how chips were made, see P. R. Morris, *A History of the World Semiconductor Industry* (Stevenage, U.K.: Peter Peregrinus, 1990). On the actual manufacturing processes, but of a more technical nature and covering an earlier period, there is Charles S. Meyer, David K. Lynn, and Douglas L. Hamilton, *Analysis and Design of Integrated Circuits* (New York: McGraw-Hill, 1968); for a contemporary description, see Peter R. Shepherd, *Integrated Circuit Design, Fabrication and Test* (New York: McGraw-Hill, 1996). Both books are aimed, however, at a technical audience, but the topic is essential to understand in order to appreciate the processes involved in manufacturing integrated circuits (chips), along with the effects of these processes on the industry's strategies, such as on outsourcing production to Asia.

On hard disk drives, a useful technical discussion is by Kanu G. Ashar, *Disk Drive Technology: Heads, Media, Channel, Interfaces and Integration* (New York: IEEE Press, 1997). The only study available on the industry itself is by David McKendrik, *From Silicon Valley to Singapore: Location and Competitive Advantage in the Hard Disk Drive Industry* (Stanford, Calif.: Standord University Press, 2000).

On the Software Industry, begin with Detlev J. Hoch, Cyriac R. Roeding, Gert Purkert, and Sandro K. Lindner, *Secrets of Software Success: Management Insights from 100 Software Firms Around the World* (Boston: Harvard Business School Press, 2000), then move to a doctoral dissertation: T. Cottrell, "Strategy and Survival in the Microcomputer Software Industry, 1981–1986" (Unpublished Ph.D. dissertation, Haas School of Business, University of California, Berkeley, 1995), and the most thorough study of the industry itself, Martin Campbell-Kelly, *From Airline Reservations to Sonic the Hedgehog: A History of the Software Industry* (Cambridge, Mass.: MIT Press, 2003). To put the industry's work into international perspective there is Stephen E. Siwek and Harold W. Furchtgott-Roth, *International Trade in Computer Software* (Westport, Conn.: Quorum Books, 1993). Finally, do not overlook the collection of articles in David C. Mowery (ed.), *The International Computer Software Industry: A Comparative Study of Industry Evolution and Structure* (New York: Oxford University Press, 1996). There is a vast literature on the design and writing of software, much of it devoted to application development by end-user departments, as opposed to the kind of development that goes on within software companies. Begin with Edward Yourdon, *Decline and Fall of the American Programmer* (Englewood Cliffs, N.J.: Yourdon Press, 1992), because he includes a substantial bibliography on earlier works. Do not be confused by his message—that programming was declining in the U.S. because his forecast was wrong—and focus instead on his considerable knowledge about how software is developed and, of course, use his bibliography to get to other materials. A minor classic on the subject of software development, and as useful today as it was when first published, is Frederick P. Brooks, Jr., *The Mythical Man-Month: Essays on Software Engineering* (Reading, Mass.: Addison-Wesley, 1982). Do not be misled by the title; it reads very well and makes sense to nontechnical audiences. On Microsoft's product development, see David B. Yoffie (ed.), *Competing in the Age of Digital Convergence* (Boston, Mass.: Harvard Business School Press, 1997).

Transportation Industries

On the Railroad Industry, see U.S. Bureau of Labor Statistics, *Railroad Technology and Manpower in the 1970s*, Bulletin 1717 (Washington, D.C.: U.S. GPO, December 1988). A useful overview of the industry during the 1950s and 1960s is Fred Cottrell, *Technological Change and Labor in the Railroad Industry* (Lexington, Mass.: Heath Lexington Books, 1970). See also the BLS industry studies as they provide data on the 1970s and 1980s. Currently, there are no studies on this industry comparable to what we have for some manufacturing and retailing industries.

On the Trucking Industry, see Mowery, *U.S. Industry in 2000*, one of the very few business and economic overviews of the industry to include discussion of technological issues.

Wholesale and Retailing Industries

On the Retail Industry in general, see Michael Levy and Barton A. Weitz, *Retailing Management* (Burr Ridge, Ill.: McGraw-Hill Irwin, 2001, and various earlier editions; the first is 1992). This outstanding textbook includes comments on wholesaling, a bibliography, extensive discussion of the role of information technologies, provides historical perspective, and is specific in its examples. An excellent study on the impact of computing on industry strategies in the 1990s is by Roger D. Blackwell, *From Mind to Market: Reinventing the Retail Supply Chain* (New York: HarperBusiness, 1997). Various BLS studies also discuss retail and wholesale developments for most of the last half of the 1900s. Because of the important role of credit cards in retailing, see David Evans and Richard Schmalensee, *Paying With Plastic: The Digital Revolution in Buying and Borrowing* (Cambridge, Mass.: MIT Press, 1999). Because of Wal-Mart's importance and extensive use of IT, see Robert Slater, *The Wal-Mart Decade:*

How A New Generation of Leaders Turned Sam Walton's Legacy into the World's #1 Company (New York: Portfolio, 2003).

On the Grocery Industry, the central issue is, of course, scanning and bar codes. For a very informative history of the technology's development, see Stephen A. Brown, *Revolution at the Checkout Counter* (Cambridge, Mass.: Harvard University Press, 1997), which can also serve as a good example of how to write a history of a technology's emergence, adoption, and effects on an industry.

On the Apparel Industry, the key study is by Frederick H. Abernathy, John T. Dunlop, Janice H. Hammond, and David Weill, *A Stitch in Time: Lean Retailing and the Transformation of Manufacturing, Lessons from the Apparel and Textile Industries* (Cambridge, Mass.: Harvard University Press, 1999). It is, in my opinion, the model that should be used by historians to study the role of technology and computers in any industry.

Since e-tailing is a relatively new phenomenon, books with some historical perspective are scarce. However, for Amazon there is Robert Spector, *Amazon.com: Get Big Fast* (New York: HarperBusiness, 2000), and Rebecca Saunders, *Business the Amazon.com Way: Secrets of the World's Most Astonishing Web Business* (Dover, N.H.: Capstone, 1999). On eBay, see David Bunnell and Richard Luecke, *The ebay Phenomenon: Business Secrets Behind the World's Hottest Internet Company* (New York: John Wiley & Sons, 2000), and Adam Cohen, *The Perfect Store: Inside EBay* (Boston: Little, Brown, 2002). Two seminal studies by the American government are U.S. Department of Commerce, *The Economic and Social Impact of Electronic Commerce* (Washington, D.C.: U.S. GPO, 1998) and *The Emerging Digital Economy II* (Washington, D.C.: U.S. GPO, 1999). My endnotes for chapters 10 and 11 include bibliographies on the business of e-commerce.

Index

Accounting applications, 47, 49
  Automotive Industry, 147
  Chemical Industry, 181, 191
  Petroleum Industry, 174–176
  Retail Industry, 276, 280, 290, 291,
    306, 350
  Steel Industry, 147
  transformation of manufacturing
    industries and, 97–98
  Wholesale Industry, 290, 291, 303
Achabal, Dale D., 304
Adams, Walter, 145, 391
Aerospace Industry, 131
  case study of application adoption by,
    152–160
    deployment, 154–158
    effects of deployment, 158–160
  computer-aided engineering (CAE) in,
    107
  diffusion of applications in, 1960s–
    1980s, 122, 124
  numerical control (NC) in, 91, 99, 101,
    157
  outsourcing in, 378
Agents, 268
Agriculture Industry, 70
Airline Industry, 94
Air transport, 229
Allen-Bradley Company, 104–105, 111
Allied Supermarkets, Inc., 326
Aluminum Industry, 123
Amazon.com, 261, 277, 287, 311, 316,
    345, 348
American Airlines, 254, 382

American Management Association (AMA),
    68
American Motors Corporation, 133
American National Standards Institute
    (ANSI), 299, 300
American Oil Company, 170–171
American Production and Inventory
    Control Society (APICS), 52, 83
American Trucking Association (ATA),
    251
Ampex Corporation, 213
Analog devices, 6–7
Anderson, Martin, 134
Ansley, Arthur C., 92
Apparel Industry, 263, 271, 314
  ability to deal with complexity, 364
  case study of application adoption by,
    318, 321, 336–343
    deployment, 338–341
    recent trends, 341–343
  losses in 1985, 274
  as percentage of total manufacturing
    sector, 1950–2000, 77
  stockkeeping units (SKUs) in, 294, 338,
    339
  universal product code (UPC) in, 299–
    300, 339–341
Apple Computer, Inc., 14
Apple Computers, 224
Applications, 16–27
  acceptance of, 25
  approach to study of, 23–27
  arrival of commercial software, 47–
    48

Applications (*continued*)
  basic pattern of adoption and use, 62–64
  defined, 16–18
  diffusion of, 27, 49, 52, 58–59, 87, 225–226, 255–256, 350, 382
  effect on business behavior, 18–20, 372, 378–385
  manufacturing, adoption of. *See* Manufacturing applications, adoption of
  sources of knowledge about, 382
  standards and, 20–22
  timing of adoption of, 381–382
  transfer of experience and, 25
  transportation industries, adoption of. *See* Transportation applications, adoption of
  types introduced in to American economy, 49–52
A&P Supermarkets, 334
Apte, Uday M., 159
Areal density, 209–210
Arthur Andersen LLP, 47
Ashland Oil and Refining Company, 175
Ashton-Tate Corporation, 218
Asian manufacturing:
  competition from, 369
  Hard Disk Drive Industry, 212–215
  Steel Industry, 151
  See also East Asia; Japanese firms
Aspen Technology, Inc., 183
Assembly line manufacturing, 77
Associated Merchandising Corporation, 289
ATR Media Integration and Communications Research Laboratories, 113
AT&T, 7, 371
AuctionWeb, 347
Auditing practices, 98
Automatic Car Identification System (ACI), 233, 234
Automatic guided vehicles (AGVs), 304
Automatic teller machines (ATMs), 21, 23, 38, 57, 330
Automatic vehicle location (AVL) systems, 249

Automation, 16, 17, 72–73, 79–80, 85
  dawn of, 1940s–early 1960s, 90–102
  islands of, 135, 162
  See also Applications; Technological innovation
Automotive Industry, 67, 79, 93
  ability to deal with complexity, 364
  case study of application adoption by, 131–143, 158–160
    deployment, 134–139
    effects of deployment, 158–160
    recent trends, 139–142
    21st-century challenges, 142–143
  computer-aided engineering (CAE) in, 107
  diffusion of applications in, 1960s–1980s, 122, 123
  global competition and, 105, 114, 133, 370, 372
  Internet and, 139–143, 150–151, 190–191
  inventory control applications in, 97, 125, 136, 137
  Japanese competition and, 114, 133, 136–139, 141
  numerical control (NC) applications in, 101, 134, 137
  outsourcing in, 378
  product development and packaging in, 188
  robotics in, 113, 135, 137
  semiconductors in, 207
  Steel Industry and, 150–151
AutoNation, 140

Banking Industry, 21, 23, 33, 297, 370, 378
  automatic teller machines (ATMs), 21, 23, 38, 57, 330
  installation of Burroughs 205 systems, 1955–1960, 55
  investment in technology, 53
Bar code. *See* Universal product code (UPC)
Barnes Drill Company, 109
Barnes & Noble, Inc., 42, 277, 348
Barnett, Donald F., 146
Batch processing, 19–20
Batch production, 79, 144

Baumol, William, 31
Beardsmore, James C., 172
Bell, Daniel, 66–67
Bell Labs, 7
Bergen Drug Company, 290–291
Besant, C. B., 107
Bessant, John, 116
Best Buy Company, Inc., 348
Best practices, 49, 87
Bethlehem Steel Company, 144
Beyond Computing, 392
Bioinformatics, 187–188
Biotechnology firms, 75, 76
Bix, Amy Sue, 17, 34, 35
Blackman, Sue Ann, 31
Blackwell, Roger D., 314
Bloomingdale's, Inc., 289
Boeing Airplane Company, 157, 370
Boo.com, 349
Book publishers, 42
Braverman, Harry, 182
Brock, James L., 320
Brokers, 268
Brooks, Frederick P., Jr., 221
Brown, R. Hunt, 157
Brown, Stephen A., 297–298
Bunnell, David, 314
Burdine's Department Store, 289
Burroughs Corporation, 40, 152, 153,
    156, 158, 168, 175, 196, 265,
    276, 325
  archives of surveys by, 392–393
  case studies published by, 392–393
  sales force of, 45–46
  205 systems:
    installation by industry or function,
      1955–1960, 55
    sample application runs on, 1954–
      1957, 56
Business applications, 49–50, 93, 97–98
  See also Applications
Business behavior, effect of applications
    on, 18–20, 372, 378–385
Business press, 41
Business Week, 113

Cabooses, demise of, 238–239
Campbell-Kelly, Martin, 195
Canning, Richard G., 101

Carlson, Walter M., 287
CarMax, 140
Carnavele, Anthony P., 75
Carpenter Steel Company, 147
Cash registers, 261, 270, 275, 295, 314,
    325, 328
Castells, Manuel, 67
Category killers, 271–272, 274
Cathode ray tube (CRT) displays, 106,
    109, 233, 295
CBS News, 43
CDs, 222–224
Cells, 115, 116
Centralization:
  of continuous processes, 363
  of research and development (R&D),
    364–365
Centralized computing vs. decentralized
    computing, 105
Centralized traffic control (CTC), 233,
    234, 236, 237
Ceruzzi, Paul E., 13, 19
Chains, retail, 276–277, 304–305, 315–
    316
  Apparel Industry, 337, 339
  Grocery Industry, 273, 286, 319–
    321, 323, 324, 325, 328, 330,
    335
  inventory control applications, 290, 293–
    294
  predigital point-of-sale (POS) terminal
    initiatives, 289
Chandler, Alfred D., Jr., 11, 179, 230,
    275, 323, 373, 388, 389
Charge accounts, 290
Charles Babbage Institute, 393, 394
Charpie, Glen P., 289
Checkout clerks, 331
Check scanning, 50, 51
CheMatch, 184
ChemConnect, 184
Chemde, 184
Chemical engineers, 163–164, 179–180
Chemical Industry, 80, 364
  case study of application adoption by,
    161–166, 178–185
  deployment, 180–182
  effects of deployment, 190–192
  recent trends, 182–185

Chemical Industry (*continued*)
　distribution of computer systems in,
　　1959–1974, 120, 121
　installation of Burroughs 205 systems,
　　1955–1960, 55
　labor and, 144, 182
　number of firms, 196
　as percentage of total manufacturing
　　sector, 1950–2000, 77
Chemical Week, 184
Chrysler Corporation, 96, 133, 135, 137,
　138
Circuit design, 107, 108
Clark, John Maurice, 89
Closed-loop systems, 163
COBOL, 21
Coggins, Jay, 322
Cohen, Morris A., 159
Cold War, 152–154, 198, 249, 378, 386
Commercial vehicle fleet management
　decisions, 1990s, 251
Commission merchants, 268
Communications industries, 55
Competition:
　global, 23, 67, 105, 113–114, 117, 369
　　Apparel Industry, 337
　　Automotive Industry, 105, 114, 133,
　　　136–139, 370, 372
　　Chemical Industry, 179
　　computing's effect on, 370
　　Internet and, 381
　　Steel Industry, 144
　Grocery Industry, 321–322, 334
　Internet, 334, 381
　Retail Industry, 315–316
Competitive Strategy (Porter), 389
Complexity, ability to deal with, 363–364
Computer-aided design (CAD), 50, 79,
　90, 91, 106, 107
　in Automotive Industry, 134, 137
　diffusion in manufacturing industries,
　　122, 123
　in Grocery Industry, 328
　in Hard Disk Drive Industry, 214
Computer-aided design/computer-aided
　　manufacturing (CAD/CAM), 21,
　　37, 38, 91–94, 103–109, 114
　in Aerospace Industry, 155
　in Apparel Industry, 337

　in Automotive Industry, 136
　diffusion in manufacturing industries,
　　122–124
　in Semiconductor Industry, 203
Computer-aided dispatching (CAD), 237
Computer-aided engineering (CAE), 107,
　108
Computer-aided manufacturing (CAM),
　50, 91, 106
Computer-aided order (CAO) systems,
　333
Computer chips, 67
　as basic building block, 5–6
　birth of, 7–9
　coordination and, 79
　manufacture of, 200–207
　See also Semiconductor Industry
　value of, 52
Computer compatible systems, 11
Computer Industry, 196, 212–213
Computer-integrated manufacturing
　　(CIM), 20, 115, 116
　in Automotive Industry, 137, 139
　in Semiconductor Industry, 203–204
Computer languages, 10, 20
Computer memory, 213, 367, 368
Computers, 5
　birth of, 9–14
　efficiency and, 16
　work flow impact of, 17
　workplace culture and task impact of,
　　17
　See also Applications; Technological
　　innovation
Computer Sciences Corporation (CSC),
　183, 218
Computer skills, 60–62, 73–75
Computerworld, 392
Computing. *See* Technological innovation
Computing Research Association (CRA),
　62
Conferences, presentations at, 40
Consumer Electronics Industry, 122, 143,
　197
Consumer Price Index (CPI) inflation,
　1990–2001, 376
Consumer Reports, 138
Continuous manufacturing, 84, 85, 162,
　164

Continuous processes, centralization of, 363

Control data Corporation (CDC), 155, 364

Conveyer systems, microprocessor-controlled, 302–304

Coordination, 79

Corporate architecture, 372–373

Credit cards, 297
  Petroleum Industry, 172–173
  Retail Industry, 172, 276, 284

Credit checking, 294–295, 302, 330

Critchlow, Robert V., 135

Cross-docking, 333, 339

Cross-industry adoptions, 27, 49, 52, 58–59, 87, 225–226, 255–256, 350, 382

Customer care applications, 347

Customer relations management (CRM), 306, 308, 309

Cypress Group LLC, 334

DaimlerChrysler, 140, 142, 151

Danjczk, Tom, 150

Databases, 104

Data collection, shop floor, 109–110

Data entry:
  evolution of, 12
  online, 104

Data entry clerks, 73–74

Datamation, 42, 294, 295, 392

Data-mining tools, 307–308

Data Processing (DP) Department or Center, 15

Data Processing Management Association (DPMA), 45, 172

Data warehouses, 307–309

Data warehousing, 308–309

Davenport, Thomas H., 39, 40

Dayton Hudson Corporation, 272

Decentralized vs. centralized computing, 105

Decision making, delegation to nonmanagerial employees, 384

De facto standards, 21–22

Dell, Inc., 382

Delphi Automotive, 143

Democracy in America (Tocqueville), 387

Dennison Print-Punch System, 287–288

Denrich, Stuart, 331

Department stores, 274–276, 286, 315–316, 319

Deregulation of transportation industries, 245

Desk Set (film), 43

Desktop computers, 79

Desrochers, Donna, 75

Devol, George, 112

Dewan, Sanjeev, 38–39

Diebold, John, 3, 16, 26, 45

Digital Equipment Corporation (DEC), 13

Digital style, 80–86

Dillard's, Inc., 338–339

Direct marketing firms, 271

Direct store delivery (DSD), 329, 333

Discrete manufacturing, 84–86, 162–164

Disk drives, 11, 12, 19
  See also Hard Disk Drive Industry

Diskettes, 222, 223

Dispatching applications, 237, 244, 248

Distributed computing, 103–105, 181

Distribution, mechanization of, 93

Distribution industries:
  installation of Burroughs 205 systems, 1955–1960, 55
  number of UNIVAC 60 and 120 systems installed, circa 1958, 54

DNA-based products, 187, 188, 190–192

Douglas Aircraft Company, 157

Dow Chemical Company, 183

Downsizing, 126

Drafting tools, automated, 155

Drilling operation applications, 169–170

Dun's Review, 109, 110

DuPont de Nemours, E. I., and Company, 183, 184

Durable goods, sale of, 268–269

Dynamic trading networks, 119–120

East Asia:
  Hard Disk Drive Industry and, 212–214
  programmer population, 221

eBay, 277, 314, 345, 347

E-business. *See* E-commerce

e-Chemicals, 184

Eckert, J. Presper, 40

E-commerce, 71, 158, 277
  Apparel Industry, 341–343

E-commerce (*continued*)
  Automotive Industry, 140–143, 150–151
  case study of adoption of, 318, 343–354
  Chemical Industry, 184, 190
  dynamic trading networks and, 120
  early patterns, 310–313
  Grocery Industry, 322, 333–335
  literature on, 261–262
  management's reaction to, 365–367
  merger of in-store retailing with, 316
  Pharmaceuticals Industry, 189–190
  Software Industry, 223
  Wholesale Industry, 270
  See also Internet
Economy, American:
  manufacturing industries and, 66–88
    activities. *See* Manufacturing styles
    Automotive Industry, 133
    labor and automation, 72–73
    relative position, 69–71
    stages, patterns, and practices in
      adoption of computer applications,
      86–88
    technology industries, 194–195
    training, 73–75
  Retail Industry and, 258–263
    e-commerce, 343–344
    Grocery Industry, 323–324
    information flows, 278–282
    makeup, 270–274
    role, 265–267
    size, 267
    technical styles and changes, 274–277
  technological innovation and, 28–65,
    355–388
    American behaviors and values and,
      387–388
    basic pattern of adoption and use, 62–64
    changing makeup of the economy, 32
    economic growth and, 30
    economic implications, 374–377
    effects on management, 362–367
    extent of deployment, 52–59, 358–362
    human capital, 60–62
      international political implications,
        385–387
      investment in technology, 33–34, 36–40, 53, 57–58
      labor and, 30–32, 34, 36–40, 62, 383–385
      link between, 29–30
      managerial implications, 377–385
      patterns of adoption behavior, 59–60
      productivity paradox, 35–40
      sources of exposure to computers, 40–48
      theoretical, generalized view of, 367–374
      types of applications introduced, 49–52
  Trucking Industry and, 252
  Wholesale Industry and, 260
    makeup, 267–270
    role, 263–265
    size, 267
    technical styles and changes, 274–275
Economy, global. *See* Global economy
Eddie Bauer, 341–342
Education, formal, 75
Edwards, Paul N., 386
Efficient consumer response (ECR), 333
Eisenhower, Dwight D., 152
Electrical Machinery Industry:
  distribution of computer systems in,
    1959–1974, 120
  as percentage of total manufacturing
    sector, 1950–2000, 77
Electronic data interchange (EDI), 21,
  118, 119
  in Apparel Industry, 338–341
  in Automotive Industry, 139
  in Chemical Industry, 182
  in e-commerce, 346
  in Grocery Industry, 322, 332, 333
  in Hard Disk Drive Industry, 214
  in Railroad Industry, 237
  in Retail Industry, 264, 266, 272, 276,
    277, 282, 300–301, 304, 305,
    314, 316
  in Trucking Industry, 248, 249
Electronic Data Processing (EDP), 15, 98,
  325

Electronic funds transfer (EFT), 297, 330
E-mail, 15, 23
Embedded processors. *See* Computer chips
Employment. *See* Labor
End user skills, 60–62
Engelberger, Joseph, 112
Engineering applications category, 50
Engineering functions affected by computer-aided engineering (CAE) applications, 108
Engineers, 44, 45, 61, 163–164, 179–180
Enterprise resource-planning (ERP), 47, 48, 60, 183–184, 306
Entertainment applications category, 50
Ernst, Dieter, 212–213
Ernst & Young LLP, 342, 343
e-Steel, 150
E-tailers. *See* E-commerce
eToys, 348, 349
Etzel, Michael J., 263
European firms:
  investment in technology, 57
  manufacturing, 71, 72, 111
    Automotive Industry, 138
    Chemical Industry, 179
    competition from, 369
    flexible manufacturing system (FMS) in, 112
    robotics in, 113
    Steel Industry, 144, 151
Evans, Philip, 126–127
Expert systems, 211
Exxon Corporation, 178, 370

Fabless companies, 205
Fairchild Semiconductor, 8
Federal Accounting Standards Board (FASB), 22
Federated Department Stores, Inc., 272, 339
FedEx Corporation, 252, 347
Feedback control, 93
Feedback from production operations, 82–83
Fiat Auto, 143
Finance Industry:
  distribution of computer systems in, 1959–1978, 55

number of UNIVAC 60 and 120 systems installed, circa 1958, 54
  as percent of American economy, 1947–1998, 32
Fingar, Peter, 347
Finite element analysis (FEA), 107, 108
Flamm, Kenneth, 386
Fleet management, Trucking Industry:
  decisions, 1990s, 251
  technologies, circa 1997, 250
Fleming Companies, Inc., 333
Flexible manufacturing systems (FMS), 105, 110–111, 115–117
  in Automotive Industry, 137, 139
  diffusion in manufacturing industries, 122, 124
Florida Retail Owned Grocers, 325
Folding Paperboard Box Industry, 123
Food goods or perishables, sale of, 268
Food Industry:
  as percentage of total manufacturing sector, 1950–2000, 77
  universal product code (UPC) in, 298
Food Lion, 333, 334
Food Marketing Corporation, 325
Food Marketing Institute, 330
Food retail firms, 271
Food services firms, 271
Forbes ASAP, 312
Ford, Henry, 77
Fordist style, 78–80, 131, 136, 137, 274
Ford Motor Company, 16, 133, 135, 140, 142, 143, 151
  Automation Department, 90–92
  internal computer service bureau, 134
Forecasting, 118
Forrester Research, 119, 344–345
Fortune 500, 70
Forward integration, 167
Foster Wheeler Corporation, 95
Foundries, 205
Freight bill applications, 242
Freightquote.com, 252
Freight tracking applications, 246, 249
Frequent shopper programs, 330
Furniture Industry, 263

Gaddis, John Lewis, 386
Game applications, 50

Gap, 336
Gap, Inc., 312, 351
Gas credit cards, 172–173
Gates, Bill, 193, 322
General Electric Company, 25, 110
General food stores, family-owned, 319
General merchandise firms, 271, 340
General Motors Acceptance Corporation (GMAC), 140
General Motors Corporation, 126, 133, 134, 136–140, 142, 143, 150, 256, 318, 370
General Petroleum Corporation, 175
Geological and geophysical mapping applications, 169
Geophysical Service, 176
Giant Food Stores, 328, 333, 334
Giant Target Company, 291
Giddens, Anthony, 67
Gilpin, Robert, 386
Gimbels Department Store, 275, 276
Glass, David, 283
Global economy:
    Automotive Industry and, 141–142
        alliances, 136, 139, 140
        competition, 105, 114, 133, 136–139, 370, 372
    Chemical Industry and, 179
    competition. *See* Competition: global
    Hard Disk Drive Industry and, 211–213, 215
    investment in technology, 33
    labor productivity and, 31
    managerial implications of computing's affect on, 383
    Petroleum Industry and, 178, 191–192
    Pharmaceuticals Industry and, 190
    politics of, 385–387
    relative position of U.S. manufacturing industries in, 71–72
    Semiconductor Industry and, 197–198
    Steel Industry and, 144, 151
Gordons Transport Company, 243
Goubeau, Vincent Paul, 66, 68
Government:
    distribution of computer systems in, 1959–1978, 55
    installation of Burroughs 205 systems, 1955–1960, 55
    number of UNIVAC 60 and 120 systems installed, circa 1958, 54
    percent of U.S. economy, 1947–1998, 70
GPS technology, 249
Grant Distributape system, 289
Greenspan, Alan, 30
Grocery Industry, 263, 266, 267, 272, 273, 286, 296, 314, 382
    ability to deal with complexity, 364
    case study of application adoption by, 318–336, 350–354
        deployment, 324–333
        recent trends, 333–336
    point-of-sale (POS) terminals in, 266, 301, 326–330, 333
    universal product code (UPC) and, 296, 298–300, 302, 320, 326–327, 333
GroceryWorks.com, 335
Gross domestic product (GDP), 39, 57, 71, 376, 377
Grove, Andy, 224
Gulf Oil Company, 172–173

Haas School, University of California at Berkeley, 49
Halevi, Gideon, 102
Hall-Mark Electronics, 91
Hand-held terminals, 67, 328–329
Hannaford brothers supermarket chain, 334
Hard Disk Drive Industry case study of application adoption, 193–194, 208–216, 224–226, 371
    basic product, 208–210
    deployment, 211–214
    effects of deployment, 224–226
    recent trends, 215–216
Harvard Business Review, 82, 96
Harvard Business School, 49
Harvey, Samuel B., 292
Hemmendinger, David, 108
Henry B. Gilpin Company, 291
Hepburn, Katharine, 43
Herzog, Bertram, 108
Hewlett-Packard Company, 13, 47, 155, 213
Hicks, Donald A., 117

High-tech industries. *See* Technology industries
High throughput screening (HYS), 189
Highway system, national, 246, 264
Hollander, Richard A., 244–245
Home Depot, The, 272, 312
HomeRuns.com, 334
Honda, 138
Honda Motor Company, 71, 133
Honeywell Micro Switch Division, 104
Hosiery Industry, 123
Hounshell, David A., 180
Houston Technical Laboratories, 176
How-to books, 393
Hughes, Thomas P., 228
Human capital, 60–62, 73
Hunt Logistics, 248

IBM Corporation, 10–11, 14, 20, 22, 370
  Aerospace Industry applications, 155–157
  availability of applications by industrial sector manufacturing/process, 81–82
  case studies published by, 392–393
  Chemical Industry applications, 165
  data collection applications, 109, 147
  Data Processing Division, 46
  disk drives, 209, 210, 212, 213, 215, 216
  1140 Data Processing System, 325
  evolution from manufacturing firm to primarily service firm, 371
  information flows in a department store, circa 1960, 278
  inventory control equipment, 95, 96, 290
  manufacturing applications portfolio, circa 1960, 84
  Microelectronics Division, 205
  optical scanners, 291
  personal computer (PC), 25
  Petroleum Industry applications, 163, 169, 172, 175
  point-of-sale (POS) terminals, 281, 282, 285, 288
  Railroad Industry applications, 232, 235
  Retail Industry applications, 279–282
  sales force, 45–47
  S/36 computer system, 331
  software, 218, 223
  solid logic technology (SLT), 202–203
  Steel Industry and, 147
  transistors, 200, 202
  Trucking Industry and, 251
  view of manufacturing integrated systems, circa 1985, 80, 81
Image processing, 50
Incremental process improvements:
  Automotive Industry, 134, 135
  Steel Industry, 148–149
Industrial Machinery Industry, 77
Industrial robots (IRs), 112–113
Industry identification, 371–372
Information, 67–69
Information flows in Retail Industry, 278–282
InfoWeek, 392
Instruments Industry, 77
Insurance Industry, 32, 33
  installation of Burroughs 205 systems, 1955–1960, 55
  investment in technology, 53
  number of UNIVAC 60 and 120 systems installed, circa 1958, 54
Integrated applications, 102–112, 117–119, 331–332
Integrated circuits. *See* Computer chips; Semiconductor Industry
Integrated control room, 181
Intel Corporation, 8, 9
Intermodal transportation, 238
Internal experts, exposure to computers and, 40, 44–45
Internet, 20, 23, 24, 30, 64, 67, 68, 71, 72, 216, 368
  Aerospace Industry and, 155, 157–158
  Apparel Industry and, 341–343
  Automotive Industry and, 139–143, 150–151, 190–191
  birth of, 14–15
  Chemical Industry and, 184, 190
  competition and, 334, 381
  coverage of computing and information handling, 41, 42, 48
  dynamic trading networks and, 119–120
  global implications of, 383

Internet (*continued*)
  Grocery Industry and, 322, 333–335
  Hard Disk Drive Industry and, 214, 216
  management's reaction to, 365–367,
    378–379
  Petroleum Industry and, 178
  Pharmaceuticals Industry and, 188–191
  Railroad Industry and, 237, 238
  Retail Industry and, 261–262, 277, 305–
    314
  Software Industry and, 223
  Steel Industry and, 149–150
  strategies and, 126–127
  supply chain management (SMC) and,
    118, 119
  Trucking Industry and, 191, 249, 251–
    253
  Wholesale Industry and, 270
Intranets, 223, 372
Inventory control applications, 82, 92–97,
    369
  Apparel Industry, 338, 340
  Automotive Industry, 136–139, 141
  Grocery Industry, 326, 328, 329, 340
  just-in-time (JIT) practices, 118, 119,
    125, 136–139, 141
  Retail Industry, 273–275, 280, 282,
    283, 287–289, 291, 293–294, 300,
    316
  Steel Industry, 147–148
  Wholesale Industry, 291, 292, 303
Investment in technology, 33–34, 36–40,
    53, 57–58, 376
Ioli, Nick, Jr., 334
Islands of automation, 135, 162
IT deployment. *See* Applications

James, Don L., 263
Japanese firms:
  investment in technology, 57
  manufacturing, 71, 72, 111, 117
    Automotive Industry, 114, 125, 133,
      136–139, 370
    Chemical Industry, 179
    Consumer Electronics Industry, 143
    flexible manufacturing system (FMS)
      in, 112
    inventory control practices in, 97,
      125

robotics in, 113
  Semiconductor Industry, 198–199,
    205
  Steel Industry, 144, 145
J.B. Hunt Transport, Inc., 248
J.C. Penney Company, Inc., 247, 258,
    271, 272, 281, 286, 312, 315,
    336, 338, 344, 348, 351
J.J. Haggarty Stores, 289–290
Job displacements, 73
Jobs, Steve, 14, 223
Johnson, Lyndon Baines, 32
Journal of Retailing, 304
Journals, computer industry, 42
Just-in-time (JIT) practices, 118, 119, 125
  Apparel Industry, 338
  Automotive Industry, 136–139, 141
  Retail Industry, 314
  Trucking Industry, 239, 247, 255
  Wholesale Industry, 303

Kaplinsky, R., 80
Karchner, J. Clarence, 176
Kendrick, John W., 355
Kidall, Gary, 14
"Killer apps," 282
Kiosks, 309
Kissinger, Henry, 385
Kmart, 271–273, 272, 299, 345
  kiosks, 309
  supply chain refurbishment by, 309
Kraemer, Kenneth L., 38–39
Kroger Company, 271, 272, 331, 335
Kumar, Harsha, 347

Labor:
  automation and role and composition
    of, 72–73
  average labor cost per unit, 1990–2001,
    376
  computing's affect on, 30–32, 34, 62,
    383–385
  human capital, 60–62
  manufacturing industries and, 159–160,
    369
    Automotive Industry, 132–133, 135
    Chemical Industry, 144, 182
    Petroleum Industry, 177
    process industries, 166

Steel Industry and, 133, 144–146, 149, 151
Retail Industry and, 266, 283
Grocery Industry, 286
Grocery Industry and, 322, 323, 331
size of labor force, 266
technological innovation and growth of, 30–32
transportation industries and, 232
Railroad Industry, 236
Trucking Industry and, 243
unions, 31, 74, 144, 182, 239, 243, 326, 373, 384
Wholesale Industry and, 304
Laboratory information management systems (LIMS), 188
Land's End, Inc., 341, 343
Langlois, Richard N., 197, 198
Lapham, Lewis H., 130
Leadership, 126
Lecht, Charles P., 28, 52
Lester, Richard K., 19, 23
Levy, Michael, 262, 264, 272, 312
Libicki, Martin C., 20
Life Office Management Association (LOMA), 52
Lindberg, Roy A., 110
Line staffs, exposure to computers and, 44
L.L. Bean, Inc., 341
Load planning applications, 244
Local area networks (LANs), 115, 116
Lofberg, George H., 189
Logistics, 118–119, 248
Lotus, 218, 222
Lowe, Deborah, 322
LTV Corporation, 151
Luecke, Richard, 314
Luke, Hugh D., 121
Lukens Steel Company, 147
Luling Company, 181
Lunkenheimer Company, 147–148

Machinery Industry, 120
Machine Tool Industry, 91–94, 99–102
MacKrell, John, 108
Macy's Deaprtment Store, 289
Magnetic tape, 222
Mainframe computers, 79
Management books, 393

Management Information Systems (MIS), 15, 45, 47, 365
Managers:
computing's effect on
changes, 362–367
implications, 377–385
exposure to computers and, 44
Managing by objectives (MBO), 270
Manifold, George O., 161
Manufacturers' sales branches and offices, 268
Manufacturing applications, adoption of, 33
Aerospace Industry case study, 152–160
deployment, 154–158
effects of deployment, 158–160
Automotive Industry case study, 131–143
deployment, 134–139
effects of deployment, 158–160
recent trends, 139–142
21st-century challenges, 142–143
Chemical Industry case study, 178–185
deployment, 180–182
effects of deployment, 190–192
recent trends, 182–185
evolution of, 89–127
extent of deployment, 120–124
first period: Late Fordism and the dawn of automation, 1940s–early 1960s, 90–102
second period: start of integrated computer-aided manufacturing, 1960s–1980s, 102–113
Third Period: mass production to flexible manufacturing, 1980s–1990s, 113–120
Hard Disk Drive Industry case study, 193–194, 208–216
basic product, 208–210
deployment, 211–214
effects of deployment, 193–194
recent trends, 215–216
Petroleum Industry case study, 161–178
deployment, 168–176
effect of software on productivity, 177–178
effects of deployment, 190–192

Manufacturing applications (*continued*)
  Pharmaceuticals Industry case study,
       185–192
    deployment, 186–189
    effects of deployment, 190–192
    recent trends, 189–190
  portfolio, circa 1960, 84
  Semiconductor Industry case study, 193–
       195, 197–207, 224–226
    deployment, 202–205
    effects of deployment, 224–226
    recent trends, 205–207
  Software Industry case study, 193–194,
       216–226
    deployment, 219–221
    effects of deployment, 224–226
    recent developments, 221–224
  stages, patterns, and practices in, 86–88
  Steel Industry case study, 143–151
    deployment, 146–149
    effects of deployment, 158–160
    recent trends, 149–151
  type of manufacturing and, 84–86
Manufacturing functions, circa 1950s-
       1970s, 83–84
Manufacturing industries:
  adoption of applications by. *See*
       Manufacturing applications,
       adoption of
  American economy and, 66–88
    activities. *See* Manufacturing styles
    labor and automation, 72–73
    makeup of sector, 75–77
    relative position, 69–71
    training, 73–75
  defined, 69
  distribution of computer systems in,
       1959–1978, 55
  global economy and, 71–72
  gross domestic product (GDP), 1995–
       2000, 377
  integration between distribution
       industries and, 227–229
  investment in technology, 33, 53
  number of UNIVAC 60 and 120
       systems installed, circa 1958, 54
  as percent of American economy, 1947–
       1998, 32
  Retail Industry and, 264, 301

  Trucking Industry and, 240, 246–247,
       253–256
  unions and, 31
Manufacturing information systems
       applications, 105–106, 110–112
Manufacturing machines, mechanization
       of feed to and from, 92
Manufacturing styles, 76–86
  adoption of, 77
  digital, 80–86
  Fordist, 78–80, 131, 136, 137
  steel and electricity, 78
  water, 78
Marcus, Stanley, 315
Marketing applications, 188, 347
Marshall Fields, 275, 276
Mason, J. Barry, 327
Massachusetts Institute of Technology
       (MIT), 49, 179–180
Mass customization, 114–115
Master production planning (MRP), 81–
       83, 364
Mastrian, James, 310
Materials handling applications. *See*
       Inventory control applications
Mauchly, John, 40
Mayer, Morris L., 327
Mazzoleni, Roberto, 111
McBrier, C. Robert, 291–292
McBrier, Edwin Merton, 258, 259
McConaughy, David, 293
McDermott, Eugene, 176
McGraw-Hill Companies, 149
McIntyre, Shelby H., 304
McKendrick, David, 215
McKenney, James L., 23–24
McKenzie, Sally, 342
Mechanism analysis, 107, 108
Mercata.com, 349
Merchant, M. Eugene, 117
Merchant wholesalers, 267–268
Mergers and acquisitions (M&A), 64
  Chemical Industry, 183
  computing's effect on, 370, 378
  Petroleum Industry, 168, 178
  Railroad Industry, 238
Metals Industry:
  numerical control (NC) applications in,
       100, 110

as percentage of total manufacturing sector, 1950–2000, 77
MetalSite, 150
Michigan Bell Telephone Company, 221
Microelectronics, 79
Microprocessors, 14, 102, 111, 116, 135, 181
Microsoft Corporation, 20, 22, 47, 63, 218, 222, 370
Microsoft Word, 48, 83
Military applications, 49, 91, 99, 101, 152, 155
Military-industrial complex, 152
Minicomputers, 12–13, 79, 102, 148, 155, 169, 174, 244
Minimills, 145, 148, 149, 159
Minor, W. K., 175
Mobile communications, onboard, 251
MobShop.com, 349
Modeling applications:
   Chemical Industry, 181–185
   Petroleum Industry, 175, 176
Monitoring software, 175–177
Monroe Calculating Machine Company, 289
Monsanto Company, 182
Montgomery Ward, 286, 290
Morales, Rebecca, 137–138
Mosaic, 15
Motorola, Inc., 213
Motor Vehicles Industry, 77
Movies, exposure to computers and, 43
Mowery, David C., 29
Mudd, N. L., 26

Nasbeth, Lars, 58
National Aeronautics and Space Administration (NASA), 152
National Association of Food Chains (NAFC), 298
National Cash Register (NCR), 281, 299, 325, 331
National Machine Accountants Association, 45
National Semiconductor Corporation, 213
National Steel Corporation, 144
Netscape, 15
Neuschel, Richard, 45
Newsletters, 392

New York Central Railroad, 232
Niche firms, retail, 315, 319, 323
Nissan, 138
Nissan Motor Company, Ltd., 71, 133
Noble, David E., 99, 102
Nondurable goods, sale of, 268, 269
Nonrubber Footwear Manufacturing Industry, 122, 124
North American Aviation, 157
North American Industry Classification System (NAICS), 195, 225, 267, 371
Norwich Pharmaceutical Company, 290
Numerical control (NC), 59, 110
   in Aerospace Industry, 157
   in Automotive Industry, 101, 134, 137
   diffusion in manufacturing industries, 122, 124
   early, 91–94, 99–102
   flexible manufacturing systems (FMS) and, 110–112, 116
   integration with CAD/CAM, 106, 107, 114
   robotics and, 110, 112

Oil and Gas Journal, 178
Oil embargo of 1973, 244
Oligopolistic power, 370, 382–383
Omidyar, Pierre, 347
O'Neill, Robert E., 332
Online processing, 10
Open-loop systems, 171
"Open standards" movement, 22
Operations, integration of, 102–110
Optical character recognition (OCR), 50, 51, 395–396
Optical scanners, 173, 291
Oracle Corporation, 21
Order replenishment, automatic, 332–333, 340
Organization for Economic Cooperation and Development (OECD), 52, 391–392
Organization of Petroleum Exporting Countries (OPEC), 168
Outsourcing, 371
   Aerospace Industry, 378
   Automotive Industry, 378
   Chemical Industry, 182–183

Outsourcing (*continued*)
  Pharmaceuticals Industry, 188
  Trucking Industry, 248

Packaged industrial computers, 207
Package tracking applications, 249, 252
Packaging, mechanization of, 93
Paper & Allied Industry, 77
Parade Magazine, 114–115
Pareto, Vilfredo, 229
Parker, Robert, 219
Peapod.Inc, 322, 334, 335, 347
People's Republic of China, 386, 387
Periman, Justin A., 95
Peripheral equipment, 11
Personal computers (PCs), 9, 25–26, 31,
    46, 52, 67, 79, 81, 368
  birth of, 14
  evolution of sales of, 33
  Software Industry and, 218–219, 223
  software packages, 48
  software sales and, 56–57
Petopia, 349
Petrochemical Industry, 167, 179, 181
Petroleum Industry, 284, 285, 363, 367
  automation and, 80
  case study of application adoption by,
      161–178
    deployment, 168–176
    effect of software on productivity,
        177–178
    effects of deployment, 190–192
  distribution of computer systems in,
      1959–1974, 120, 121
  installation of Burroughs 205 systems,
      1955–1960, 55
  labor and, 144
  number of firms, 196
Pharmaceuticals Industry, 64, 383
  case study of application adoption by,
      161–166, 185–192
    deployment, 186–189
    effects of deployment, 190–192
    recent trends, 189–190
    research and development (R&D) in,
        185–188, 364
Phister, Montgomery, Jr., 55, 73, 120
Pilferage, 325–326
Pine, B. Joseph, II, 114

Pipelines, oil, 173–174, 177
Piping design, 107, 108
Pisano, Gary P., 186
Plant operations planning, 82
Plossl, George P., 97
Point-of-sale (POS) terminals, 22, 38, 259,
    261, 262, 264, 269, 272, 276,
    284, 285, 301, 317
  in Apparel Industry, 321, 339, 340
  before the birth of digital cash registers,
      294–296
  defined, 396
  in Grocery Industry, 266, 301, 326–
      330, 333
  IBM, 281, 282, 285, 288
  importance to Retail Industry, 304–305
  patterns of adoption, 302
  predigital initiatives, 289–290
  web-enabled, 309
Politics of global economy, 385–387
Polymer science, 180
Porter, Michael E., 64, 72–73, 355, 389
Price label applications, 330–331
Priceline.com, 322, 334, 347–348
Print Industry, 77
Processes, defined, 18
Process flow scheduling (PFS), 83
Process manufacturing:
  case studies of, 161–192
  See also Chemical Industry;
      Pharmaceuticals Industry;
      Petroleum Industry
  vs. discrete manufacturing, 162–164
Production process, mechanization of, 92–
    93
Productivity, 355
  Apparel Industry, 339–340
  Automotive Industry, 135, 138
  computing's effect on, 31–32, 369–370,
      374–377, 384
  Grocery Industry, 323
  growth of, 31–32, 125, 126
  manufacturing sector, 36
  Petroleum Industry, 177–178
  productivity paradox, 35–40
  Retail Industry, 286–287, 302
  Steel Industry, 146
  Wholesale Industry, 264, 269–270
Productivity paradox, 35–40

Profit trends, 1990–2001, 376
Programmable controllers (PLCs), 116
Programmers, 60, 219–221
Programming languages, 219, 220
Progressive Grocer, 326, 330, 331, 334,
    335
Publications, coverage of computing and
    information handling by, 41
Public policy, 67
Publishing Industry, 76, 77
Punch cards, 98, 222, 231, 232, 242, 243,
    276, 290
Pure-play retailers, 311, 322, 346, 349,
    350

Quaker Oats, 296
Qualcomm, Inc., 251

Rackham, Neil, 88
Radio and television manufacturing, 92
Radio Corporation of America (RCA), 68,
    109
Radio exposure, 43
Railmarketplace.com, 238
Railroad Industry case study of application
    adoption, 228–239, 254–257
    deployment, 231–237, 240
    effects of deployment, 254–257
    recent trends, 237–239
Ralston, Anthony, 108
Rapid prototyping, 107, 108
Ray, George F., 58
Real Estate Industry:
    investment in technology, 53
    as percent of American economy, 1947–
        1998, 32
Reda, Susan, 336
Refining operations, 167, 170–171
Refrigeration facilities, 320
Regional distribution centers, 276–277
Reilly, Edwin D., 108
Republic Steel, 144
Research and development (R&D):
    in Chemical Industry, 179–182, 184–
        185, 191
    computing's affect on, 364–365
    in Hard Disk Drive Industry, 213, 215,
        216
    in Petroleum Industry, 165–166, 191

in Pharmaceuticals Industry, 185–188,
    364
in Semiconductor Industry, 365
Retail Industry, 33
    American economy and, 258–263
        e-commerce, 343–344
        Grocery Industry, 323–324
        information flows, 278–282
        makeup, 270–274
        role of, 265–267
        size, 267
        technical styles and changes, 274–
            277
    case studies of application adoption by,
        317–354
    See also Apparel Industry; E-commerce;
        Grocery Industry
    credit cards, 172, 276, 284
    distribution of computer systems in,
        1959–1978, 55
    evolution of application adoption by,
        283–316
        first period: arrival of digital to stores,
            1950s–mid-1970s, 286–296
        second period: age of growth and
            UPC revolution, mid-1970s–
            1980s, 296–302, 304–305
        third period: the networked age:
            arrival of the Internet, 1990s and
            beyond, 305–313
    gross domestic product (GDP), 1995–
        2000, 377
    information flows, 278–282
    makeup, 270–274
    manufacturing industries and, 264, 301
    as percent of American economy, 1947–
        1998, 32
    Petroleum Industry and, 167, 172–173
    segments served by Wholesale Industry,
        1973, 268
    technical styles and changes, 274–277
    Trucking Industry and, 240, 246–247,
        253–256
    typical functions:
        circa 1950s–1970s, 263
        circa 1980s–2000s, 264
Returns on investment, 38–39
Reusable code, 221
Revco, 309, 310

Ridout, Robert, 183, 184
Robotics applications, 110, 112–113, 367
   in Automotive Industry, 113, 135, 137
   in Pharmaceuticals Industry, 186, 188
Rosenberg, Nathan, 29
Route scheduling, 303
Royal Ahold, 335
Royal Dutch/Shell Group, 178
Rubber/Plastics Industry, 77
Rucker, Pamela, 345

Safeway, Inc., 272, 335
Sanders, Donald H., 292
SAP AG, 47, 48, 60, 63, 183, 184
Scanning. *See* Optical character
      recognition (OCR); Universal
      product code (UPC)
Scheduling applications:
   Grocery Industry, 331
   Petroleum Industry, 174
   Railroad Industry, 233
   Trucking Industry, 233, 248–249
Scherer, Frederic M., 62, 152–153
Schneider Logistics, Inc., 248, 250–251
Schneider National, Inc., 248, 251, 382
School-of-fish phenomenon, 87
Schumpeter, Joseph A., 58, 128–130, 388,
      389
Scientific applications, 49
Seagate Technology, Inc., 212–214
Sears, Roebuck and Company, 247, 271–
      273, 275, 281, 286, 299, 336,
      345
SEMATECH, 206
Semiconductor Industry:
   case study of application adoption, 193–
      195, 197–207, 224–226
   deployment, 202–205
   effects of deployment, 224–226
   recent trends, 205–207
   research and development (R&D) in,
      365
Semicontinuous manufacturing, 85, 162–
      164
Senauer, Ben, 322
Sensing devices, 110
Service sector, 31, 33, 67, 69–70, 195
   distribution of computer systems in,
      1959–1978, 55

installation of Burroughs 205 systems,
      1955–1960, 55
investment in technology, 53
as percent of American economy, 1947–
      1998, 32
productivity, 36, 37
Servomechanism Laboratory, MIT, 99
Shapiro, Carl, 225, 345
Sharing information, 368–369
Sharma, Tarum, 347
Shop floor data collection, 109–110
ShopLine.com, 334
Shopping malls, 266
Siegel, David, 344
Simon, Herbert A., 379–380
Simulation applications, 154, 155, 380
   Chemical Industry, 183, 190
   Hard Disk Drive Industry, 211
   Petroleum Industry, 170, 174, 177
   Pharmaceuticals Industry, 186
Singapore, Hard Disk Drive Industry in,
      213
Single store style, 275
Sloan School, Massachusetts Institute of
      Technology (MIT), 49
Smith, Adam, 388
Smith, John Kenly, Jr., 180
Software:
   commercial, arrival of, 47–48
   packages, 48, 56, 57
   sales, 54, 56–57
Software Industry, 76
   case study of application adoption by,
      193–194, 216–226, 371
   deployment, 219–221
   effects of deployment, 224–226
   recent developments, 221–224
Solid logic technology (SLT), 202–203
Sony Aibo, 113
Southern Pacific Company, 234–235, 256
Soviet Union, 153, 386, 387
Specialization, in Semiconductor Industry,
      205
Specialty retail firms, 271
Sperry Univac Company, 45–46
Standard Industrial Classification (SIC)
      codes, 194
Standard Oil Company, 175
Standard Oil of California, 170

Standards, 11, 18, 178, 256, 381
  in Apparel Industry, 339
  role of, 20–22
  Uniform Code Council (UCCnet), 313
  Uniform Communication Standard
    (UCS), 331
  universal product code (UPC), 299, 300
Stanford University, 49
Statistical process control (SPS), 204
Steel and electricity style, 78
Steel Industry, 67, 79, 125, 131, 314, 364
  batch production, 79, 144
  case study of application adoption by,
    143–151
    deployment, 146–149
    effects of deployment, 158–160
    recent trends, 149–151
  diffusion of applications in, 1960s–
    1980s, 124
Stefflre, Greg, 238
Steinmueller, W. Edward, 197, 198
Stockkeeping units (SKUs), 273, 276, 294,
  338, 339
Streamline.com Inc., 334, 349
Streamlining Business Procedures
  (Neuschel), 45
Structure of American Industry, The
  (Adams), 391
Supermarkets. *See* Grocery Industry
Super Valu Stores, 291
Supply chain management (SCM), 356, 381
  Chemical Industry, 183–184
  computing's affect on, 362–363
  e-commerce, 347
  emerging role of, 118–120
  Grocery Industry, 322
  Hard Disk Drive Industry, 212–213
  Retail Industry, 306, 309–310, 314
  Trucking Industry, 249–250
  Wholesale Industry, 313
Surface-mount technologies (SMT), 214
Systems, defined, 18
Systems analysts, 221
Systems applications products (SAPs), 21
Systems men, 44–45

Tags, merchandise, 317
Tandem Computers, Inc., 213
Tanker ships, 173

Tanner, Ronald, 331
Teamsters Union, 239, 243
Technical staffs, exposure to computers
  and, 44
Technical standards. *See* Standards
Technical styles:
  in manufacturing, 76–86
    adoption of, 77
    digital, 80–86
    Fordist, 78–80, 131, 136, 137, 274
    steel and electricity, 78
    water, 78
  in wholesaling, 274–275
Technological innovation, 3–27
  American economy and, 28–65, 355–
    388
    effects on management, 362–367
    American behaviors and values and,
      387–388
    basic pattern of adoption and use, 62–
      64
    changing makeup of the economy, 32
    economic growth and, 30
    economic implications, 374–377
    extent of deployment, 52–59, 358–
      362
    human capital, 60–62
    international political implications,
      385–387
    investment in technology, 33–34, 36–
      40, 53, 57–58
    labor and, 30–32, 36–40, 62, 383–
      385
    link between, 29–30
    managerial implications, 377–385
    patterns of adoption behavior, 59–60
    productivity paradox, 35–40
    sources of exposure to computers, 40–
      48
    theoretical, generalized view of, 367–
      374
    types of applications introduced, 49–
      52
  applications. *See* Applications
  long-term evolution of, 7–15
    computer chips, 7–9
    computers, 9–14
    Internet, 14–15
    personal computers (PCs), 14

Technological risks, 381–382
Technology industries:
  case studies of application adoption by,
    193–226
  See also Hard Disk Drive Industry;
    Semiconductor Industry; Software
    Industry
  identification of, 194–195
Telecommunications, 67, 116, 119, 149,
    155, 177, 178
  Chemical Industry and, 182–183
  convergence of computing with, 368
  Grocery Industry and, 335
  Hard Disk Drive Industry and, 214, 216
  Internet. *See* Internet
  Pharmaceuticals Industry and, 188
  transportation industries and:
    Railroad Industry, 231
    Trucking Industry, 244, 248, 249,
      251–252
Television exposure, 43
Testing, mechanization of, 93
Texas Instruments, Inc., 8, 13, 176
Textile Industry:
  diffusion of applications in, 1960s–
    1980s, 124
  as percentage of total manufacturing
    sector, 1950–2000, 77
Tichy, Noel M., 126
Tiffany, Paul A., 146
Time, 185
Tire Industry, 123
Tocqueville, Alexis de, 387
Tool Engineering, 100
Total Operations Processing System
    (TOPS), 234–235
Total Quality Management (TQM), 118,
    204, 270
Total Systems, 80, 234
Toyota Motor Sales, 97, 133, 137, 138
Toys 'R Us, 348, 349
Tracy, Spencer, 43
Trade associations, 392
Trade industries. *See* Retail Industry;
    Wholesale Industry
Trade publications, 41
Training, 60–62, 73–75
Trane Company, 93
Transistors, 7, 8, 200–204

Transplace.com, 252
Transportation applications, adoption of,
    227–257
  Railroad Industry case study, 228–239
    deployment, 231–237, 240
    effects of deployment, 254–257
    recent trends, 237–239
  Trucking Industry case study, 228, 229,
    239–257
    deployment, 242–247
    effects of deployment, 254–257
    recent trends, 247–254
Transportation Equipment Industry, 120
Transportation industries:
  application adoption by. *See*
    Transportation applications,
    adoption of
  distribution of computer systems in,
    1959–1978, 55
  employment in, 1970–1996, 232
  gross domestic product (GDP), 1995–
    2000, 377
  installation of Burroughs 205 systems,
    1955–1960, 55
  number of UNIVAC 60 and 120
    systems installed, circa 1958, 54
  Petroleum Industry, 167, 173–174,
    177
  relative size, 1970–1996, 231
Trip-recording applications, 249
Trucking Industry, 238, 371
  case study of application adoption by,
    228, 229, 239–257
    deployment, 242–247
    effects of deployment, 254–257
    recent trends, 247–254
  employment in, 1970–1996, 232
  Internet and, 191, 249, 251–253
Truman, Harry S, 145
2001: A Space Odyssey (film), 43
Tylecote, Andrew, 78, 79, 274–276

Uniform Code Council (UCCnet), 313
Uniform Communication Standard (UCS),
    331
Unimate, 112
Unions, 31, 74, 144, 182, 239, 243, 326,
    373, 384
United Airlines, 254

UNIVAC:
  1 system, 10, 25, 40, 43
  60 and 120 systems, number installed
    by industry, circa 1958, 54
Universal Grocery Product Identification
    Code, Ad Hoc Committee on, 298–
    299
Universal product code (UPC), 261, 262,
    264, 266, 272, 276, 284, 296–302
  in Apparel Industry, 299–300, 339–341
  defined, 395–396
  extent of adoption of, 57, 297
  in Grocery Industry, 296, 298–300,
    302, 320, 324, 326–327, 333
  origins of initiative, 297–301
  in Wholesale Industry, 303
University of Texas, 343–344
UPS, Inc., 252
U.S. Air Force, 91, 99, 101, 152
U.S. Bureau of Economic Analysis, 194–
    195, 219
U.S. Bureau of Labor Statistics (BLS), 58,
    75, 121–124, 148–149, 153, 171,
    177, 181, 195, 236, 244, 302–
    303, 392
U.S. Bureau of Transportation Statistics,
    231, 232
U.S. Census Bureau (CB), 76, 194–195
U.S. Department of Commerce, 194, 391,
    392
U.S. Department of Defense, 21, 37, 121,
    299
U.S. Department of Labor, 391
U.S. Federal Highway Administration, 251
U.S. Food and Drug Administration
    (FDA), 188, 190
U.S. Postal Service, 240, 248, 275, 347
U.S. Steel Corporation, 144, 148
Utilities:
  distribution of computer systems in,
    1959–1978, 55
  installation of Burroughs 205 systems,
    1955–1960, 55
  number of UNIVAC 60 and 120
    systems installed, circa 1958, 54

Vacuum tubes, 7
Varian, Hal R., 225, 345
Vauxhall, 143

Vehicle load planning, 303
Vending machines, 325
Vendor-managed inventory (VMI), 340
Vendor management applications, 347
Vendors, as sources of knowledge about
    technology, 40, 45–47, 382
Very large-scale integration (VLSI), 203,
    204
Video merchandising, 302

W. T. Grant Company, 289
Walker, Bruce J., 263
Wal-Mart, 125, 226, 240, 247, 258, 271–
    277, 272, 281, 282, 299, 315,
    351, 352, 370
  ability to deal with complexity, 364
  apparel business, 338
  data mining and data warehousing by,
    308–309
  e-commerce, 345, 348
  "everday low-price" (EDLP) approach,
    322
  food business, 322, 334, 382
  supply chain refurbishment, 309
  as user of IT, 312
Walton, Sam, 273
Warehousing:
  Apparel Industry, 339
  e-commerce, 316
  Grocery Industry, 324, 331–333
  Wholesale Industry, 290–292, 302–
    305, 313
Warndorf, Paul R., 117
Water style, 78
Watson, Thomas, Jr., 15
Wecker, Dan, 207
Weingarten, Joe, 317, 320
Weinstein, Steve, 330
Weitz, Barton A., 262, 264, 272, 312
Western Digital, 215
Western Electric, 95–96
White, Lawrence J., 135–136
Wholesale Industry:
  American economy and, 260
    makeup, 267–270
    role, 263–265
    size, 267
    technical styles and changes, 274–
    275

Wholesale Industry (*continued*)
distribution of computer systems in, 1959–1978, 55
evolution of application adoption by, 283–285, 314–315
first period: 1950s–mid-1970s, 290–292
second period: mid-1970s–1980s, 302–304
third period: 1990s and beyond, 305–313
gross domestic product (GDP), 1995–2000, 377
investment in technology, 53
Petroleum Industry, 167, 172
technical styles and changes, 274–275
Wight, Oliver W., 82, 97
Windows 95, 223

Wireless communications, 20, 251–252
Wireless communications firms, 75, 76
Withington, Dennet, 332
Wolf, Eric, 163
Wolff, Edward, 31
Woods, Larry D., 105
Woolworth, Frank W., 259
Word 2000, 222
WordPerfect, 48
Work flows, 17–19
Work force. *See* Labor
Work styles. *See* Technical styles
World War II, 386–387
World Wide Web, 15
Wozniak, Steve, 14
Wurster, Thomas S., 126–127

Yates, JoAnne, 39–40